D1287410

LANGUAGES OF POWER

LANGUAGES OF POWER

*A Sourcebook of Early American
Constitutional History*

Jefferson Powell

CAROLINA ACADEMIC PRESS
DURHAM, NORTH CAROLINA

For Mom and in memory of Dad, with love

Copyright © 1991 Jefferson Powell
All Rights Reserved
ISBN: 0-89089-379-9 (cloth)
ISBN: 0-89089-380-2 (paper)
Library of Congress Catalog
Card Number: 90-85342

Printed in the United States of America

Carolina Academic Press
700 Kent Street
Durham, NC 27701
(919) 489-7486

Contents

Preface

Soon after the Philadelphia framers went home, a friend attempted to pay one of them—Gouverneur Morris—a compliment: "You have given us a good Constitution." Morris was not so sure. "That depends," he replied, "on how it is construed."[1] Subsequent history has confirmed what he implicitly asserted: the meaning of American constitutionalism, and specifically of the federal Constitution of 1787, is not a simple given to be found in the events of 1787 and 1788 (or 1866–70 or any other "founding" era). From the beginning, American constitutional history has been a story of intellectual and political struggle over the distribution and limits of power in this country. At the federal level, the ratification of the 1787 Constitution and its initial implementation by the First Congress (which included the framing and transmittal to the states of the Bill of Rights) initiated as many debates as they resolved. By the time the third session of that Congress met, people who had labored together to shape the Constitution and to secure its adoption found themselves in deep disagreement over how it ought to be construed, and similar disagreements have continued to the present day.

For a variety of historical and institutional reasons, the decisions of the United States Supreme Court are at the center of contemporary constitutional debate, and as a consequence constitutional lawyers tend to concern themselves with what one scholar has labeled "the Constitution in the Supreme Court,"[2] when they look beyond the actual "founding" itself. Such a focus is understandable and, for many purposes, appropriate. To do so too exclusively, however, is to risk overlooking the rich discursive culture of constitutional argument that developed prior to the series of great decisions of the Marshall Court which began late in the nineteenth century's second decade. The thirty years between the opening of the First Congress and the Court's decision in *M'Culloch v. Maryland* was not, as some constitutional law casebooks seem to suggest, a period of constitutional inactivity briefly punctuated by the Supreme Court's articulation of its powers to review the constitutionality of federal statutes and state court decisions. Still less, as I have already suggested, was it a time of constitutional consensus.

The period was, instead, characterized by intellectual and political ferment, during which many of the terms and concepts of later discussion were formulated. But the Supreme Court was not, in the 1791–1818 era, the primary forum for constitutional argument, and the (relatively few) Supreme Court opinions on constitutional matters during the era present only an incomplete portrait of the range of issues and ideas debated. For a more adequate picture—and thus for a more rounded understanding of subsequent constitutional history, including the history of Supreme Court case law—one must

turn to state and lower federal court decisions, legislative debates and resolutions, newspaper editorials and political pamphlets, private letters and public lectures (see Additional Sources). This source book is a collection of such
materials that displays the major themes and trends in American constitutionalism from 1791 (the year that the debate over congressional power irrev-
ocably shattered the coalition that had secured the Constitution's ratification)
to 1818 (the year before the Supreme Court's great decision in *M'Culloch*).

Four major criteria were employed for including documents and speeches.
I strove, first, to include those that contemporaries would have considered of
major importance. The Kentucky Resolutions of 1798 and 1799 and the 1808
federal circuit court decision in *Gilchrist v. Collector of Charleston* are examples
of expressions of constitutional views that were immediately perceived as
significant. As a subset of this category, a few documents have been included
that became important with relative speed. One example is the excerpt from
St. George Tucker's appendix to his edition of Blackstone's *Commentaries*,
which became one of the most widely read discussions of the federal Constitution in the early nineteenth century.

Secondly, this source book includes some materials that I believe were
representative of or influential in important constitutional discussions though
they were not themselves well known then or now. The speeches in the House
of Representatives in 1817 and 1818 over the constitutionality of a federal
internal-improvement bill are, for example, indispensable background reading
for a full historical understanding of John Marshall's opinion in *M'Culloch*.

Thirdly, some documents have been reproduced precisely because they
point to matters that (most) constitutionalists of the 1791–1818 period did *not*
regard as of constitutional interest. The Massachusetts high court's decision
in *Martin v. Commonwealth*, for example, exemplifies the unwillingness or
inability of most (white, male) articulate and powerful Americans of the era
to see anything of constitutional or high political significance in the legal
system's treatment of women.

Finally, some materials of minor intrinsic interest are present solely in order
to provide a richer context for other documents.

Both the application of these criteria and the criteria themselves clearly are
somewhat subjective, and during the years I have taught constitutional history
I have used a variety of documents of interest and importance that are not
present in this book. In particular, my primary concern here with federal
constitutional history has compelled me to reduce the number of state constitutional materials.

It is my belief, however, that this source book presents a fair picture of the
development of constitutional argument over the period between 1791 and
M'Culloch. The sources have been edited primarily for the sake of readability
and focus: legal citations and footnotes in judicial opinions, for example,
usually have been silently excised, and for the most part portions of letters
and speeches that seemed irrelevant to constitutional matters were dropped.
My editorial notes are brief and of two types: introductions that provide
historical context for the reader; and "Comments" (so labeled) that provide
my own views of the documents' meaning and significance.

This source book is arranged into eleven chapters, preceded by an introductory essay that analyzes some of the most important and persistent themes in the materials. Chapters 1–3 cover the period from 1791 to 1798, during which nationalists such as Alexander Hamilton strove to carry out their vision of a strong central government and to legitimate that vision under the federal Constitution. In reaction, opposition leaders such as James Madison and Thomas Jefferson insisted on a narrower and more closely text-bound interpretation of the Constitution. At the same time, both state and federal courts were struggling to identify the role of the judiciary in a legal system with written constitutions. Chapter 4 deals with the constitutional crisis sparked by Congress's passage of the Alien and Sedition acts of 1798. The opposition Republicans' victory in the federal elections of 1800 was treated by them subsequently as a referendum on the proper interpretation of the United States Constitution, and as a decisive endorsement of their own constitutional views (the "principles of '98").

Chapters 5–11 trace developments during the administrations of Jefferson and Madison, a period the latter characterized as the time of the "Republican Ascendancy."[3] During Jefferson's years in office, the crucial constitutional debate revolved around the conflicting claims of the president and the federal courts to finality in the interpretation of the law and of the Constitution. During Madison's presidency, and especially after the War of 1812, the focus of constitutional argument shifted back to dispute over the extent of federal legislative power, with Republican leaders (including the president) struggling to reconcile their desire for a more active federal government with the legacy of 1798. *M'Culloch v. Maryland* was a vindication by the Supreme Court of this new "Republican nationalism," though one that occurred as political support for a powerful federal government was waning.

It will be clear to the reader, I hope, that there are no heroes or villains in this source book. I do not view either nationalistic Federalists or states' rights Republicans, Hamilton or Madison, John Marshall or Spencer Roane, as "wrong" in any straightforward sense. Nor do I think it useful or appropriate to understand either the triumph of the Jeffersonian Republicans after 1800 or the revival of nationalist constitutional thought after the War of 1812 as a victory for those "faithful" (or "unfaithful") to the Constitution's original meaning. My interest in these documents, in this source book, has been simply to understand how and why American constitutional discourse evolved as it did, though obviously my interest (like that of everyone else interested in constitutional history) is fueled in part by concern for the contemporary legal, political and moral significance of constitutionalism in this country.

Many people have contributed, personally or through their writings, to my work on constitutional history and to this source book; to all of these individuals I am grateful. Among them, I want especially to thank Linda Kerber and Lawrence Baxter, both of whom played a crucial role in encouraging me as well as by commenting on this book. I appreciate greatly Laura Underkuffler's generous sharing of her notes on lectures I gave at Yale in 1986, Carolyn Tappan's careful conversion of a mass of photocopied documents of all shapes and sizes into a usable and revisable set of course materials, and Judy Williamson's cheerful willingness to undertake the mammoth task of converting the course materials into that modern equivalent of parchment, the computer disk. Keith Sipe's enthusiasm (and his patience!) make him an ideal publisher; my debt to him and to the other folks at the Carolina Academic Press is great. Finally, I thank the students in my constitutional history classes at the University of Iowa, Yale, and Duke. Teaching is itself a great teacher, and I have learned much from them.

LANGUAGES OF POWER

Some Themes in Early Constitutional Interpretation: An Introductory Essay

During the two centuries since the federal Constitution was drafted and ratified, American lawyers, judges, politicians, and scholars have evolved a variety of categories, doctrines, and metaphors with which to organize and analyze constitutional issues. These familiar headings—judicial review, federalism, the commerce clause, separation of power, due process, and so on—are appropriate tools for considering and analyzing the early constitutional debates reproduced in this source book; and the reader may wish to employ them for those purposes.

The use of modern terms and categories, however, carries with it a price: in attempting to fit the founding generation into our constitutional world, we may ignore or misconstrue the issues and responses they emphasized. The editorial comments on the documents reproduced in this volume stress, for the most part, the factors that seem to have been of the most interest and significance to the speakers or writers and their contemporaries. In the same vein, this introductory essay integrates some of the most important contemporaneous themes reflected by the documents.

The Sources of Constitutional Argument

A fundamental question often raised in early constitutional argument—as it has been again today—concerned the sources of such argument. In discussing the scope of legislative or executive authority, or the validity of an asserted individual right, were the terms of the discussion bound by the letter of the relevant constitution, or was it legitimate to resort to extratextual principles of justice and reason? How literally should the interpreter of a constitution read the text, and with what presuppositions or interpretive biases? What weight should precedent be given? Each of these questions was, from time to time, hotly debated, and for the most part respectable constitutionalists were on each side of every disputed issue.

There was one clear exception to this last statement: Americans in the 1791–1818 period of every political persuasion and constitutional school of thought agreed that a fundamental feature of American constitutionalism[4] was the existence of written constitutional instruments. Judge St. George Tucker spoke for many Americans when he stated in 1794 that, before the American Revolution, the world had not truly understood the notion of a constitution: "What the *constitution* of any country *was* or rather *was supposed to be*, could only be collected from what the *government had at any time done*; what had been *acquiesced* in by the people, or other component parts of the government; or what had been *resisted* by either of them. Whatever the government or any branch of it had *once done*, it was inferred they had a *right* to do *again*" (p. 84). But Americans, Tucker went on to say, had changed all that by writing down their fundamental laws. "[W]ith us, the constitution is not an 'ideal thing,' but a real existence: it can be produced in a visible form: its principles can be ascertained from the living letter, not from obscure reasoning or deductions only" (p. 84). The federal Constitution, Representative Peter Porter reminded the House in 1811, was a document, "a *printed Constitution* . . . drawn up with the greatest care and deliberation; with the utmost attention to perspicuity and precision" (p. 261).

From this basic premise of the textuality of American constitutions, almost everyone in the 1791–1818 period drew the corollary that an American constitution is "the first law of the land" (p. 84). Unlike, for example, the English Bill of Rights of 1689, which put legal constraints only on the Crown and not on Parliament, an American constitution "is to the *governors*, or rather to the departments of government, what a law is to individuals—nay, it is not only a *rule* of *action* to the branches of government, but it is that from which their existence flows, and by which the powers . . . which may have been committed to them, are prescribed—It is their commission—nay, it is their *creator*" (p. 74). John Marshall said nothing controversial in deciding *Marbury v. Madison* when he asserted that the status of "fundamental and paramount law" is "essentially attached to a written constitution" (p. 179). Again and again, throughout the period, constitutionalists affirmed the connection between the American constitutions' written nature, their supreme legal authority, and their capacity to render definite and fixed the forms and limits of governmental power, though an undercurrent of worry can sometimes be detected over the ambiguity of constitutional texts.

The centrality of constitutional documents in American political life repeatedly formed the basis for asserting or accepting the legitimacy of some form of judicial review. In 1808 Judge John Davis held that the judicial power to declare statutes "void" "exists, only, in cases of contravention, opposition or repugnancy, to some *express* restrictions or provisions contained in the constitution" (p. 243; emphasis supplied). Davis rejected the argument that a federal court could hold unconstitutional an exercise of congressional authority solely on the basis of the claim that Congress had exceeded the scope of a textually delegated power as "extremely difficult, if not impracticable, in execution." On the other hand, "[a]ffirmative provisions and express restrictions, contained in the constitution, are sufficiently definite to render decisions, probably in all cases, satisfactory" (p. 244). By creating written constitutions, Americans had rendered constitutional debate susceptible to legal resolution: as James Kent explained to his law students in 1794, "the interpretation or construction of the Constitution is as much as a JUDICIAL act, and requires the exercise of the same LEGAL DISCRETION, as the interpretation or construction of a Law" (p. 92). Almost a quarter-century later, James Madison explained his veto of an internal-improvement bill as a defense of the United States Constitution's written nature and thus of the federal courts' power of judicial review. If Congress were not limited to the powers textually delegated to it but were free to legislate on all issues involving the common defense and general welfare, "the effect" would be to "exclud[e] the judicial authority of the United States from its participation in guarding the boundary between the legislative powers of the General and the State Governments, inasmuch as questions relating to the general welfare, being questions of policy and expediency, are unsusceptible of judicial cognizance and decision" (p. 313).

Opponents of expansive views of congressional power seized upon the federal Constitution's textuality from the beginning as a major component of their argument against Alexander Hamilton's nationalist political program. Madison's great speech attacking Hamilton's bank bill began with what was virtually a mini-treatise on interpreting a written constitution; particular emphasis was laid on the assertion that the bill could be justified only by a reading of the text that would "render nugatory the enumeration of particular powers" (p. 38). Madison did not deny that Congress legitimately might exercise "accessory or subaltern" powers, not enumerated in the text, that were "necessary and proper for executing the enumerated powers." He maintained, however, that it was illegitimate for Congress to wield a nontextual "great and important power" simply because that power was "necessary and proper for the Government or Union" (p. 39). In his 1791 bank-bill opinion, Thomas Jefferson was, if possible, even more insistent that Congress be confined by the text ("[i]t was intended to lace them up straitly," he wrote) to its "enumerated powers, and those without which, as means, these powers could not be carried into effect" (p. 43). For an implied power to fit within the confines of Jefferson's "necessary and proper" clause, in other words, it had to be one "without which [a textual] grant of power would be nugatory" (p. 43).[5]

Supporters of an expansive view of federal power responded not by denying the Constitution's textual nature but by criticizing the interpretive practices of their opponents. Representative Fisher Ames attacked Madison's claim of unique loyalty to the Constitution's textual limits on power as false. Do "the opposers of the bank," he asked, "mark out the limits of power which they will leave to us with more certainty than is done by the advocates of the bank? Their rules of interpretation . . . will be found as obscure, and of course as formidable as that which they condemn" (p. 40). Ames flatly refused to concede that Madison and his allies had the constitutional text on their side: "[T]hey only set up one construction against another" (p. 40). Hamilton crafted an elaborate argument in support of the bank bill in his cabinet opinion. Jefferson's strict interpretation of "necessary" in the "necessary and proper" clause was required neither by "the grammatical, nor popular sense of the term" (p. 46), whereas the "whole turn of the clause containing it, indicates, that it was the intent of the convention, by that clause to give a liberal latitude to the exercise of the specified powers" (p. 46). Jefferson's apparent hostility to congressional power rested not on the requirements of the text but on the busy activity of the "[i]magination" (p. 45), Hamilton insisted. A true respect for the written Constitution required instead the application of the "sound maxim of construction" that governmental powers "ought to be construed liberally in advancement of the public good" (pp. 46–47).

Throughout the 1791–1818 period, nationalists and their opponents battled over who could lay proper claim to the text in support of their constitutional views. Representative Alexander Smyth confidently assumed in 1818 that faithfulness to the text required a narrow reading of federal authority—he described "liberal construction" as "that is, a stretch of the Constitution" and a "usurpation" of power (p. 319). But Justice Joseph Story had been equally confident, two years before, that "a reasonable construction, according to the import of [the Constitution's] terms" supported his own nationalist views (p. 303).

The interminable debate over how to read constitutional language produced a variety of formulaic expressions of interpretive approach. In the 1790s nationalistic Federalists tended to emphasize the purposive nature of the text, its orientation toward authorizing certain ends and achieving certain purposes. Ames was representative: "Congress may do what is necessary to the end for which the Constitution was adopted, provided it is not repugnant to the natural rights of man or to those which they have expressly reserved to themselves or to the powers which are assigned to the States" (p. 41). Opposition constitutionalists, unsurprisingly, focused on the Constitution's limiting functions; in 1803 Tucker wrote that "[a]s federal it is to be construed strictly, in all cases where the antecedent rights of *states* may be drawn in question; as a social compact it ought likewise to receive the same strict construction, wherever the right of personal liberty, or personal security, or of private property may become the subject of dispute" (p. 155).[6]

The emergence of Republican nationalism in the wake of the War of 1812 brought with it new and creative efforts to explicate standards for constitutional interpretation. As Henry Clay insisted in 1818, these new nationalists regarded themselves as faithful heirs of the "principles of '98": Clay cited Madison's Report of 1800 and then explained that "from that paper, and from others of analogous principles, he had imbibed those constitutional principles which had influenced his political course" (p. 320). But Clay, like most of the other Republican leadership in Washington, had come to fear federal weakness more than federal oppression. As a consequence, his formulation of the proper approach to construing the Constitution was an attempt to reconcile nationalist goods with Republican principles. "In expounding the instrument, he [Clay] said, constructions unfavorable to personal freedom, or those which might lead to great abuse, ought to be carefully avoided. But if, on the contrary, the construction insisted upon was, in all its effects and consequences, beneficent; if it were free from the danger of abuse; if it promoted and advanced all the great objects which led to the confederacy; if it materially tended to effect the greatest of all those objects—the cementing of the Union, the construction was recommended by the most favorable considerations" (p. 320).

The Republican Clay's standard of interpretation, and indeed his application of it, scarcely differed from that enunciated a year later by Federalist Chief Justice John Marshall.[7]

On occasion, arguments about the meaning of a constitutional text were couched in terms of a narrow literalism. Delivering his opinion in *Chisholm v. Georgia* on the question of whether article three of the Constitution[8] authorized a suit against an unwilling state by the citizen of another state, Justice John Blair asserted that "[t]he constitution of the United States is the only fountain from which I shall draw; the only authority to which I shall appeal" (p. 59). For him, *Chisholm*, therefore, was easy. "A dispute between A. and B. is surely a dispute between B. and A." (p. 59). By contrast, Judge William Nelson was unwilling to draw any certain conclusions from the verbal structure of a sentence in the Virginia constitution's provision regarding the state judiciary.[9] "[P]erhaps it would be unjustifiable to rest such an opinion on so critical a construction" (p. 75). The rejection of literalism sometimes, indeed, went even further. A literal interpretation of the ex post facto clause, Justice Samuel Chase concluded in *Calder v. Bull*, was simply impossible; he was "under a necessity to give a construction, or explanation of the words '*ex post facto* laws,' because they have not any certain meaning attached to them" (p. 97). Justice William Johnson held a similar opinion of the contracts clause, expressing regret that "words of less equivocal signification had not been adopted in that article of the Constitution" (p. 278). He was confident that the Constitution was not meant to prohibit a great variety of beneficial legislative adjustments of contract law, but professed himself (almost) at a loss about "where to draw the line, or how to define or limit the words, 'obligation of contracts' " (p. 278).

Constitutional arguments in the 1791–1818 period often rested on the claim that (some of) the terms used in a constitution had fixed or technical meanings prior to their use there, and that these meanings were carried over into the constitution itself. Despite their dislike for the restrospective state legislative action at issue in *Calder v. Bull*, the justices of the United States Supreme Court refused to invalidate it as a violation of the ex post facto clause. As Justice Chase pointed out, the term "ex post facto law," according to Blackstone, Woodeson (Blackstone's successor as Vinerian Professor), the *Federalist*, and the constitutions of Massachusetts, Maryland, and North Carolina, referred only to laws creating or increasing criminal liability (p. 96). Because *Calder v. Bull* did not involve the criminal law, the Court held the ex post facto clause inapplicable. The justices believed, as Justice William Paterson explained, that the words of the clause "must be taken in their technical, which is also their common and general acceptation, and are not to be understood in their literal sense" (p. 98).

The debate over the constitutionality of the Sedition Act of 1798 produced a variety of arguments over how to employ the pre-adoption history of language used in the United States Constitution in the interpretation of that instrument. Defending the act, Representative Harrison Gray Otis used the same form of argument accepted by the justices in *Calder v. Bull*. Otis cited

Blackstone as well as pre-1789 state law to support his claim that, when the
First Amendment guaranteed "the freedom of speech, [and] of the press,"
it had used terminology with "a certain [that is, fixed] and technical meaning." So understood, "the liberty of the press is merely an exemption from
all previous restraints," which restraints, of course, the Sedition Act made
no attempt to create (p. 127). Critics of the act responded that the profound
political differences between "the British government and the American constitutions" (p. 143) rendered this crabbed Blackstonian understanding of freedom of the press inapplicable to an American constitutional provision. Madison's 1798 Virginia Resolutions and his Report of 1800 added a second
argument. The Virginia state convention that ratified the federal Constitution
had submitted with its instrument of ratification a resolution explaining that
it approved the Constitution with the understanding that "the liberty of
conscience and the press cannot be cancelled, abridged, restrained, or modified, by any authority of the United States" (p. 144) *as well as* a proposed
amendment (also suggested by other state conventions, Madison added) safeguarding those freedoms (pp. 144–145). This history, Madison argued, reen-
forced his claim that, according to the "plain sense and intention" (p. 140)
of the First Amendment, the Sedition Act was unconstitutional.

The language of "intent(ion)," invoked by Jefferson and Madison in their
respective 1798 resolutions, played a varying role in constitutional debate in
the 1791–1818 period. At times, as in the anonymous 1799 Kentucky Resolutions' reference to the Constitution's "obvious and real intention" (p. 138),
these terms seem to be little more than synonyms for "meaning," and to be
compatible with various forms of strictly textual argument. On certain, relatively rare occasions, the suggestion was made that the meaning of constitutional language could be established by consulting the history of its creation;
such suggestions seldom if ever went unchallenged on the ground of interpretive impropriety. Madison, for example, criticized President Washington's reference, in a 1796 message to the House of Representatives, to the
actions of the Philadelphia framers as misguided because it was the state
ratifying conventions that turned the framers' "draft of a plan, nothing but
a dead letter" into a living fundamental law (p. 111). Madison recalled that
his own incidental reference to the framers in a 1791 speech against the
national bank bill "was animadverted on by several" other congressmen,
including Madison's fellow-framer Elbridge Gerry, who "protest[ed], in strong
terms, against arguments drawn from that source"; indeed, Madison asserted
that he "did not believe a single instance could be cited in which the sense
of the Convention had been required or admitted as material in any Constitutional question" (p. 110).[10] The usual attitude of most constitutionalists in
the 1791–1818 period was expressed by Judge Spencer Roane, interpreting
the Virginia Declaration of Rights in an 1804 case. "I have . . . examined the
journals of the convention [which drafted and adopted the Declaration] touching the present subject," Roane explained, and he was satisfied that there
was "in them nothing varying the construction, arising from the instrument
itself." But he had done so solely "as a matter of curiosity" for he "deem[ed]

it right to reject all extraneous information in forming my conclusion upon the constitution" (p. 199). Roane was no textual literalist, but neither he nor anyone else at that time regarded the records of a constitution's origins as the sole determinants of its meaning.

American constitutional discourse in the 1791–1818 period was not conducted solely in terms of arguments from, or about the meaning of, the texts of the federal and state constitutions. Indeed, a striking feature of early constitutional debate was the invocation of a veritable host of extratextual authorities: "the spirit of the Constitution"; the "fundamental principles" of the constitution, of free government, or of republicanism; "natural justice"; and so on. Such phrases often are difficult to interpret with confidence,[11] though certain general tendencies in their use do seem to be identifiable.

Apparent references to extratextual sources of constitutional argument often were nothing more than rhetorical modes of rejecting a narrow literalism. Attorney General Edmund Randolph told the Supreme Court in a 1793 argument that, having shown that he had "the advantage of the letter [of article three] on our side," he would then "advert to the spirit of the constitution, or rather its genuine and necessary interpretation" (p. 56). His subsequent remarks primarily discuss other clauses of the Constitution as well as its overall nature. His "spirit of the constitution" seems essentially identical to Justice James Wilson's "general texture of the constitution" in Wilson's opinion in the same case (p. 64). The point of such rhetoric was to insist on the legitimacy of treating the constitutional text as a coherent whole with an overall structure rather than as a collection of isolated and disparate rules. Hamilton's discussion of "resulting powers" in his bank opinion is in large part the same sort of argument: the Congress legitimately possesses not only the discrete powers explicitly enumerated in the text, and the (again discrete) implied powers accompanying the former, but also those powers that "result from the whole mass of the powers of the government" contained in the Constitution (p. 45). Hamilton went on, however, to refer to a second ground of the "resulting powers"—"the nature of political society"—which is an example of a second form of argument in extratextual terms.

References to "fundamental principles" and so on frequently seem to refer to those political values, theories, and goals that the speaker or writer believed were the background to a constitutional text, and were therefore somehow embodied in it. This form of argument clearly went beyond textual exegesis without thereby asserting the direct or unmediated constitutional significance of extratextual principle. In 1793 Judge John Tyler defined the Virginia constitution in successive sentences as "the great contract of the people" and as "[a] system of fundamental principles" (p. 80). It was a "fundamental principle" of the Virginia constitution, Judge Tucker asserted in 1804, "that private property shall be sacred and inviolable" (p. 194), and legislative acts protecting property rights "may be considered as pursuing the injunctions of moral justice" (p. 194). But this great moral principle did not need to be ascertained through philosophical inquiry, for it was "to be found in our bill of rights."[12]

The previous year, Chief Justice Marshall had stated as a general proposition that "[t]he very essence of civil liberty certainly consists in the right of every individual to claim the protection of the laws, whenever he receives an injury" (p. 214), but Marshall's affirmative assertion that the plaintiff before him (William Marbury) possessed such a right rested on the text of article three defining "the judicial power of the United States." "This power is expressly extended to all cases arising under the laws of the United States; and consequently, in some form, may be exercised over the present case; because the right claimed is given by a law of the United States" (p. 178).[13]

A decade later, North Carolina Chief Justice John Louis Taylor described a state law permitting debtors to obtain stays on the execution of adverse judgments as a violation of "the first principles of justice" (p. 280), but he plainly did not rest his opinion invalidating the law on that basis. Instead, he described the federal Constitution as designed to embody the "master principles and comprehensive truths" of political morality and thereby "to give them practical effect" (p. 279). The North Carolina statute could not be enforced because it was "clearly irreconcilable" (p. 281) with "the plain and natural import of the words of the Constitution of the United States" (p. 279).

Perhaps the most interesting set of extratextual arguments is that which, arguably, indicated a judicial willingness to invalidate legislative acts directly on the basis of extratextual principle.[14] Unfortunately, most seemingly clear examples of judicial review on extratextual grounds turn out on examination to be ambiguous. The *locus classicus* is Justice Samuel Chase's opinion in *Calder v. Bull*. Chase rather flamboyantly announced that "[t]here were certain vital principles in our free Republican governments, which will determine and overrule an apparent and flagrant abuse of legislative power; as to authorize manifest injustice by positive law"; "[t]he genius, the nature, and the spirit of our state governments, amount to a prohibition of such acts of legislation; and the general principles of law and reason forbid them" (pp. 94–95). Chase's language at first seems unequivocally to endorse direct judicial use of these principles regardless of their embodiment in a constitutional text: "To maintain that our federal, or state, Legislature possesses such powers, if they had not been expressly restrained, would, in my opinion, be a political heresy, altogether inadmissible in our free republican governments" (p. 95). Chase's actual behavior, however, sets this interpretation of his meaning in question. He resolved the case on the basis of a strictly textual argument, and later in his opinion apparently denied the federal Supreme Court's power to invalidate a state statute except "in a very clear case" of conflict with the United States Constitution (p. 97).

Other well-known instances of extratextual judicial review present similar ambiguities. In *Fletcher v. Peck*, Marshall followed Hamilton's much earlier example (p. 273) of combining textual and extratextual bases for his decision: "[T]he state of Georgia was restrained, either by general principles which are common to our free institutions, or by the particular provisions of the constitution of the United States" (p. 277). Only Justice William Johnson, in a concurring opinion, relied unequivocally and exclusively on what he termed "a general principle, on the reason and nature of things" (p. 277). Justice Joseph Story's opinion five years later in *Terrett v. Taylor* again yoked the textual and extratextual: "[W]e think ourselves standing upon the principles of natural justice, upon the fundamental laws of every free government, upon the spirit and letter of the constitution of the United States, and upon the decisions of the most respectable judicial tribunals" (p. 284). (Story, to be sure, did not explain on *which* part of the "letter of the constitution" he had found his footing.)

Argument—even ambiguous argument—from extratextual sources of authority sometimes provoked criticism. Justice James Iredell responded to Chase's opinion in *Calder v. Bull* by denying that the Supreme Court possessed any power to invalidate a statute "merely" because it was "contrary to the principles of natural justice" in the judges' opinion. Iredell sharply distinguished the "ideas of natural justice [which] are regulated by no fixed standard [and upon which] the ablest and purest men have differed" from the "fundamental law" established by written constitutions that "define with precision the objects of the legislature power, and . . . restraining its exercise within marked and settled boundaries" (p. 99). Only such a written constitution, in Iredell's view, could provide a legitimate basis for judicial review. Judges less skeptical than he about the possibility of identifying the "dictates of moral justice" (p. 194) shared his unwillingness to rest the power of judicial review on that basis: Tucker wrote in *Turpin v. Locket* that "a court of justice can only pronounce the act [of the legislative] void so far as it contains anything, which the constitution of the commonwealth prohibits" (p. 195).

The proper role of legislative and judicial precedent in constitutional argument was ambiguous in the 1791–1818 period. Americans often contrasted their written fundamental laws with the English "constitution," made up of what Representative Peter Porter called in 1811 "immemorial usage or prescription" (p. 260). The latter was, in its essence, nothing but a collection of precedents: "Whatever the government, or any branch of it had *once done*, it was inferred they had a *right* to do *again*" (p. 84). The very point of a "printed Constitution" thus might seem the rejection of reliance on precedent, and such an argument was made on a number of important occasions. When the national bank act came up for renewal in 1811, its supporters relied in part on the argument that the "constitutional question" about its legitimacy "must be considered as settled, adjudicated, and at rest" (p. 260)—the First Congress had debated fully the original act's constitutionality and President Washington had approved it after careful consideration of the issue; and later Congresses, presidents, and the federal courts had assumed and acted upon the act's validity. Representative Porter attacked this argument as a "doctrine of prescriptive Constitutional rights," and explained subsequent acquiescence in the original bank act as based on respect for the private rights it created. Senator Henry Clay denounced reliance on legislative precedent as "fraught with the most mischievous consequences." "[O]nce substitute practice for principle, the expositions of the Constitution for the text of the Constitution, and in vain shall we look for the instrument in the instrument itself. It will be as diffused and intangible as the pretended Constitution of England; and it must be sought for in the statute book, in the fugitive journals of Congress, and in reports of the Secretary of the Treasury" (p. 263).[15] As members of Congress, Porter told the House, he and his colleagues were "solemnly bound, by our oaths, to obey" the Constitution's "injunctions . . . as we in our best judgments shall understand them and not as they shall be interpreted to us by others" (p. 261).

Despite the theoretical cogency of Porter's and Clay's position, most politicians and lawyers in the 1791–1818 period rejected it in favor of some recognition of the legitimate role of legislative precedent in deciding constitutional questions. Justifying an 1817 internal-improvement bill on the basis of earlier exercises of Congress's spending power, Representative John C. Calhoun (at this point in his career a strong supporter of federal power) denied that his reliance on a "uniform course of legislation" replaced a Constitution of "positive and written principles" with one "founded on precedents": he "introduced these instances to prove the uniform sense of Congress and the country (for they had not been objected to) as to our powers; and surely, said he [Calhoun], they furnished better evidence of the true interpretation of the Constitution than the most refined and subtle arguments" (p. 312). Madison defended the apparent inconsistency in his attitude toward a national bank— constitutional opposition in 1791 followed by presidential approval in 1816— as a simple consequence of his acceptance of "the respect due to deliberate and reiterated precedents" (p. 294). For Madison it was "a constitutional rule of interpreting a Constitution" that "abstract and individual opinions" of the text's meaning had to yield to "a course of precedents amounting to the requisite evidence of the national judgment and intention" (p. 294). Unless "practice" and "uniform acquiescence" could "serve as . . . landmarks for subsequent legislatures," Henry St. George Tucker[16] argued to the House of Representatives in 1818 (p. 321), debatable constitutional issues could never be settled. "Do gentlemen suppose that if, which Heaven permit! this confederation of states shall last for a century, we shall, throughout that period, be continually mooting Constitutional points; holding nothing as decided; admitting no construction to have been agreed upon; and instead of going on with the business of the nation, continually occupied with fighting, over and over again, battles a thousand times won" (p. 321)? Writing of legislative interpretations of the Virginia Declaration of Rights, Judges Peter Lyons and Paul Carrington summarized this widely held view: "[W]ritten constitutions are, like other instruments, subject to construction; and, when expounded, the exposition, after long acquiescence, becomes, as it were, part of the instrument and can, no more, be departed from, than that" (p. 201).

Those who accepted the power of legislative precedent or "practice" to fix constitutional meaning did not, of course, mean to suggest that any and every legislative action, by itself and immediately, become "part of the [constitutional] instrument" (p. 201). Arguments from legislative precedent almost invariably relied on the existence of "a course of practice" approved deliberately and repeatedly over time by the responsible organs of government (p. 294) and approved by "the uniform acquiescence of the nation" (p. 321). Madison's explanation of his 1816 approval of the second bank bill and his 1817 veto of an internal-improvement bill was that the former was supported by twenty-five years of acceptance of the legitimacy of national banks (p. 294)[17] which the latter did not enjoy. The argument from practice could not, in other words, be based on "insufficient precedents" (p. 314), ones ill-thought-through, short-lived, or intermittent.[18]

There were, supporters of the authority of legislative precedent admitted, other grounds for denying precedential status to legislative acts. Roane refused to recognize Virginia legislation on the subject of church lands as an authoritative interpretation of the religious freedom provision of the state bill of rights because of the legislation's "errors and inconsistency." The statute, he wrote, not only was "in direct hostility . . . with the spirit of the bill of rights" but even contradicted its own preamble (pp. 197–98). Roane's insistence that "an act . . . marked with a want of knowledge of our constitution" (p. 198) was not a precedent was echoed later by Henry St. George Tucker's concession that legislation "against the clear meaning of the Constitution" was of no authority (p. 321), and Marshall's suggestion in *M'Culloch v. Maryland* that even long acquiescence could not sanctify "a bold and daring usurpation" or an act infringing "the great principles of liberty."[19]

Even the critics of legislative practice tended to treat judicial precedent with more respect. Although denouncing any attempt to bind the Eleventh Congress to the constitutional judgments of its predecessors, Senator Clay freely conceded the "utility of uniformity of decision" in "courts of justice" as a check on judicial waywardness (p. 263); and his ally Representative Porter admitted the authority of the courts "to explain . . . the practical operation of each particular law," including the immediate question of its constitutionality. Porter denied only the power of judicial precedent to restrict subsequent legislative choice: "[T]he commentaries of courts are not to furnish the principles upon which I am afterwards to legislate" (p. 261). Others do not seem to have admitted even this restriction. In his Report of 1800—no paean to judicial power—Madison seems to have agreed with his opponents that, "in all questions submitted to it by the forms of the Constitution," the federal judiciary was the constitutional interpreter "in the resort . . . in relation to the authorities of the other departments of the government" (p. 141).[20] Unlike state legislative resolutions, a judicial decision on "the constitutionality of measures of the federal government is an authoritative legal declaration: it "enforces the general will, whilst that will and that opinion continue unchanged" (p. 145).

Courts in this period regularly followed both formal and informal constitutional precedents. When the repeal of the "Midnight Judges Act" of 1801 once again compelled the justices of the federal Supreme Court to ride circuit, the renewed imposition of that duty was challenged as unconstitutional. Although several of the justices privately believed that the challenge was valid as an original matter, Justice William Paterson for the Court rejected it as coming too late: the Court's acceptance of the requirement "for a period of several years, commencing with the organization of the judicial system ... has indeed fixed the construction" (p. 171). Writing of the Virginia constitution, Judge Tucker explained that "the duty of expounding [the law, including the constitution] must be exclusively vested in the judiciary" (p. 84) and that as a consequence "the decisions of the supreme court of this commonwealth, upon any question [concerning] the operation or construction ... of the constitution of this commonwealth, are to be resorted to by all other courts, as expounding, in their truest sense, the laws of the land" (p. 87).

As with legislative precedents, the authority of judicial precedent was not without its limits. Few constitutionalists would have disagreed with Roane's general comment in 1815 that a precedent that "has never received the solemn and deliberate discussion and decision" of a court would be of little independent value (p. 301). Reviewing and rejecting Roane's substantive conclusion, Justice Story was careful to rest his judgment "upon a foundation of authority" consisting not only of "judicial decisions of the Supreme Court through so long a period" but also of the "contemporaneous exposition" of the First Congress that vested the jurisdiction in the Court, and of the "acquiescence of enlightened state courts" (p. 307). Perhaps because of the relatively small volume of court decisions on constitutional matters in the 1791–1818 period, criticism of the authority of judicial precedent tended to be focused not on its validity in arguments before courts, but on attempts to impose judicial interpretations on other constitutional actors. Thus, the question of the sources of constitutional argument blended into a second important theme: the authority of the interpreter.

The Authority of the Interpreter

During his struggle to impose a royalist vision of the English legal order on the common-law courts, King James I angrily rejected the judicial claim to exclusive authority to "interpret" the laws of the realm. "If the Judges interpret the lawes themselves and suffer none else to interprete," the king remarked, "then they may easily make of the lawes shipmens hose."[21] The remark reflected his awareness of a characteristic not only of early Stuart England but also of all Western legal orders: interpretive authority is a potent source of political power, and the final or exclusive possession of that authority identifies a major center of power in the legal order. Americans of the 1791–1818 era were well aware of James's insight, and a major theme in early constitutional debate concerned rival claims of interpretive authority. Various people during the era claimed major roles in constitutional interpretation for Congress, the president, the federal courts, the state legislatures, the state courts, and state conventions; the two primary disputes were over the finality of judicial interpretation and the identity of ultimate interpretive authority in the federal Union.

Americans generally agreed that both federal and state legislatures enjoyed the power, and were subject to the obligation, to interpret the constitutions under which they were acting. Occasionally, particularly in the First Congress, legislators expressed doubts about their ability or authority to interpret constitutional language. During the 1789 debate over whether to grant the president sole authority to remove officers appointed with the advice and consent of the Senate, Representative Alexander White observed that "it seems a difficult point to determine whether he has or has not this power by the Constitution." Under such circumstances, he preferred "to leave the construction to himself [the president] . . . I will venture to say, the occasion for the exercise of it will be a better comment on the Constitution than any we can give."[22] Other congressmen insisted that interpretation was an exclusively judicial task. As Madison phrased this position, it was the claim "that the legislature itself has no right to expound the Constitution; that wherever its meaning is doubtful, you must leave it to take its course until the Judiciary is called upon to declare its meaning." Madison was not hostile to the courts' interpretive authority: "I acknowledge, in the ordinary course of Government, that the exposition of the laws and Constitution devolves upon the Judiciary." But, he insisted, the courts' ordinary or primary role in interpretation was not an exclusive one. "It is incontrovertibly of as much importance to this branch of government as to any other," he reminded the House, "that the Constitution should be preserved entire"; and he saw no reason, in principle or in constitutional text, why "it will be less safe that the exposition should issue from the Legislative authority than any other."[23]

The debate over the legitimacy of legislative interpretation was in fact artificial. Fisher Ames told the House of Representatives in 1791 that legislative interpretation was unavoidable because the formulation of legislation under a constitution defining legislative power almost always involved decisions as to the constitution's meaning: "[W]e have scarcely made a law in which we have not exercised our discretion with regard to the true intent of the Constitution" (p. 40). State legislatures, most of which were not expressly limited to a set of enumerated powers, found occasion to construe the procedural provisions of their constitutions as well as their state bills of rights (the statute at issue in *Turpin v. Locket* and *Terrett v. Taylor* was an expression of the state legislature's interpretation of the Virginia Declaration of Rights). Constitutionally controversial legislation usually provoked intense debate over the proper construction of the fundamental law: the debates in Congress over national bank bills in 1791 and 1811 and over internal-improvement bills in 1817 and 1818 excerpted in this source book are examples of the seriousness with which legislators took their interpretive task.

For Congress at least, the legislative role in proposing constitutional amendments was often seen as a special subset of the general legislative duty to interpret the Constitution. James Madison, for example, regularly insisted that the amendments in the federal Bill of Rights were only "explanatory"

(p. 40), meant to declare authoritatively the meaning of the 1787 constitution (p. 145); Thomas M'Kean similarly referred to the Eleventh Amendment as a "legislative declaration of the meaning of the constitution" (p. 123). Jefferson welcomed both the passage of the 1817 improvements bill and Madison's veto of it because he believed (mistakenly) that this would lead to a constitutional amendment granting Congress the requisite power and "setl[ling] forever the meaning" of the words "provide for the general welfare and the common defense" in article one, section eight (p. 314). Henry St. George Tucker, on the other hand, rejected the call for an internal-improvement amendment precisely because he understood the "general welfare" language differently than did Jefferson and thus believed Congress already possessed the power to fund internal improvements. Such an "unnecessary" amendment "only serves to narrow and circumscribe the instrument, and whilst it gives one power, furnishes a weapon by which ten more may be wrested from us" (p. 318).

From the beginning, the presidents also regarded themselves as obliged and entitled to interpret the federal Constitution. George Washington, for example, withdrew his original nomination of William Paterson to be a justice of the Supreme Court when it was pointed out to Washington that Paterson's uncompleted term in office as a United States senator encompassed the period in which Congress had created the position of associate justice. Because article one, section six, forbade the appointment of any member of Congress "during the time for which he was elected . . . to any civil office under the authority of the United States, which shall have been created . . . during such time," Washington withdrew the nomination, informing the Senate that "I think it my duty, therefore, to declare that I deem the nomination to have been null by the Constitution."[24] Washington also explained one of his two vetoes on constitutional grounds.[25] Most famous, of course, was his concern over whether to sign the national bank bill, concern that led him to request written opinions as to the bill's constitutionality from three members of his cabinet. In responding, they all assumed that the president legitimately might employ the veto to give effect to his constitutional views, and Jefferson described the very purpose of the veto power as "the shield provided by the Constitution to protect against the invasions of the legislature" into the rights of the executive, judiciary, and the states (p. 43), a view shared by James Kent (p. 92). Neither John Adams nor Jefferson exercised the veto, but Madison's seven vetoes included several based on constitutional objections to legislation (pp. 255–56, 313–14).

The most dramatic confrontation during the 1791–1818 period between the Congress and the president over claims to interpretive authority occurred in 1796, when Washington requested that the Congress implement the Jay Treaty with Britain by appropriate legislation. When the House of Representatives requested Washington to transmit to it certain secret documentation concerning the treaty so as to fulfill its constitutional duty of deliberation with regard to the proposed legislation, he refused. He justified his refusal to acquiesce in the House's constitutionally based demand as based on "a just regard to the Constitution," which he interpreted differently than had the House (p. 109). In turn, the House majority restated its own views of the constitutional issue, though no further attempt was made to obtain the documents. The dispute highlighted the consequences of having no final interpreter: Washington's views prevailed in the practical sense that the House found no way to compel him to adopt its opinion as well as release the documents and, finally, enacted the implementing legislation. But the interpretive questions themselves were not resolved.

The potential problem of legislative-executive conflict over the Constitution's meaning was raised by the Jay Treaty affair, but for the most part such conflict was not a major element of the constitutional history of the period. Although the specter of governmental paralysis in the case of severe and unresolved constitutional disagreement occasionally was raised (p. 107), it did not in fact occur. In contrast, debate over who possessed interpretive authority in the federal system and over questions of federal power and state autonomy was one of the most hotly canvassed issues of the era.

Nationalists consistently maintained that both reason and text supported their ascription to the federal government, and specifically to the federal courts, of final interpretive authority on questions of federalism. Despite having denied in the Federalist No. 81 that the Constitution would subject states to suit in federal court (p. 56), Hamilton described opposition to the Supreme Court's contrary decision simply as "opposition to the Constitution."[26] In 1799 the Massachusetts Senate observed that federal powers were "entrusted" to the national authorities "by the people" and that successful state interference with federal legislation—what the Senate described as a state opposing "her force and will to those of the nation"—would reduce the Constitution itself "to a mere cipher, to the form and pageantry of authority without the energy of power" (p. 135). Legal questions involving the proper construction of the Constitution, the Senate stated, "are exclusively vested by the people in the judicial courts of the United States" (p. 135). As Story asserted years later, the nationalist position saw as inextricably intertwined the supremacy of the Constitution and "the paramount authority of the United States" (p. 306). To make the former a reality, the latter had to be granted as well. "States as States," Clay told the Senate in 1818, "have no right to oppose the execution of the powers which the General Government asserts" (p. 322); the constitutionally appropriate interpretive authority to judge and limit the assertion of these powers was itself "General"—the federal judiciary.

The exercise during the late 1790s of federal power in accord with a nationalist interpretation of the Constitution provoked in its turn a vigorous assertion of the states' role in constitutional interpretation. Thomas M'Kean's 1798 opinion in *Respublica v. Cobbett* denied the existence of any final interpretive authority on disputed issues of federalism and national power short of the people: "If a state should differ with the United States about the construction of [the Constitution], there is no common umpire but the people, who should adjust the affair by making amendments in the constitutional way, or suffer from the defect" (p. 122). The Kentucky and Virginia resolutions of 1798 arguably appeared to reject both the nationalist view and M'Kean's "no-umpire" theory by locating final interpretive authority in "each party [that is, state]" (p. 130) or in "the states" (p. 134). The nullifiers of the late 1820s and 1830s were to seize upon this language as locating ultimate constitutional authority in the individual state convention (subject to article five's amendment process), but the original meaning of the two sets of resolutions was in fact much more ambiguous. Jefferson (the drafter of the 1798 Kentucky Resolutions) may have meant to suggest that each individual state was, equally and independently, the final constitutional interpreter within its jurisdiction:[27] in his draft, though not in the final version adopted by the state legislature, he stated that each state had "a natural right in cases not within the compact . . . to nullify of their own authority all assumptions of power by others within their limits."[28] In the anonymously drafted Kentucky Resolutions of 1799, the legislature, despite its use of the term "nullification," fudged the issue by speaking of state action in the plural, by stating that "this commonwealth as a party to the federal compact, will bow to the laws of the Union," and by implying that "its solemn protest" was the opposition "in a constitutional manner" that it stated it was carrying out (p. 138).

In the Report of 1800, Madison so downplayed the Virginia Resolutions' assertion of state interpretive authority that nationalist critic Alexander Addison regarded the report's theoretical position in the matter as indistinguishable from the nationalist view.[29] The "states" that possess final interpretive power, the report explained, were "the people composing those political societies, in their highest sovereign capacity" rather than the state governments or even the states as "societies organized into those particular governments" (p. 140). The power of "interposition" Madison mentioned in the report was, it seems, simply a restatement of "the fundamental principle on which our independence itself was declared" that "the people" are sovereign "over constitutions" (p. 142), a position no nationalist would have denied. Nationalist James Bayard, for example, asked rhetorically in Congress in 1802 "if the power to decide upon the validity of our laws resides with the people? Gentlemen cannot deny this right to the people. I admit that they possess it" (p. 165).

The exercise of interpretive authority by state legislatures in the 1791–1818 era was confined to two closely related modes: the enunciation of respectable opinion intended to sway the views of others; and the attempt to deny precedential status to disputed federal actions. Madison described the Virginia Resolutions as "expressions of opinion, unaccompanied with any other effect than what they may produce on opinion, by exciting reflection" and thus perhaps producing "a change in [Congress's or the judiciary's] expression of the general will" (p. 145); the Kentucky legislature described its "solemn protest" as intended to prevent future interpreters from drawing any conclusions from "a supposed acquiescence on the part of this commonwealth in the Constitutionality" of the Alien and Sedition acts (p. 138). Similarly, the Pennsylvania Resolutions of 1811 against a renewal of the national bank bill were directed to the state's delegation in Congress, instructing its senators and requesting its representatives "to use every exertion in their power" to defeat renewal (p. 259).

Despite the sometimes heated rhetoric found in state legislative discussions of federal behavior, those discussions seldom if ever went beyond the expression of opinion or a call for amendments to the Constitution. The primary function in this period of recognizing state interpretive authority was negative: the denial of finality to federal interpretations. This was perhaps clearest in *Hunter v. Martin*, where the Virginia Court of Appeals relied on its own interpretation of the United States Constitution in denying the federal Supreme Court's jurisdiction to review state judgments. Judge William Cabell described the state court's position as nothing more than a refusal to equate obedience to the Constitution with "a subjection to the Federal Courts" (p. 298). Neither Cabell nor any of his colleagues claimed that the federal judges were bound to accept the state court's constructions of the Constitution; they simply asserted their own independent judgment in constitutional interpretation, while leaving to "the impartial investigation" of the people the final decision as to "the constitutionality of Federal adjudications" (p. 299).

Notwithstanding the widespread respect accorded legislative interpretations and the peculiarly nationalist and states' rights predilections for, respectively, presidential and "state" constructions of the federal Constitution, there was general agreement, over a broad range of political and constitutional opinion, about the special responsibility of the judiciary in constitutional interpretation. Upholding the power of judicial review, the great state sovereignty judge Spencer Roane stated that it was "the province of the judiciary to expound the laws" and in doing so to expound "that law which is of the highest authority of any" (p. 76). The eminent nationalist judge and scholar James Kent, writing almost simultaneously, agreed: "[T]he interpretation or construction of the Constitution is as much a JUDICIAL act, and requires the exercise of the same LEGAL DISCRETION, as the interpretation or construction of a Law" (p. 92). "I consider," he concluded, "the Courts of Justice, as the proper and intended Guardians of our limited Constitutions, against the factions and encroachments of the Legislative Body" (p. 93). Respect for the interpretive authority of the courts was often put in the strongest terms. St. George Tucker asserted that the task of "expound[ing] *what the law* is" was "the duty and office of the judiciary" and that "the duty of expounding must be exclusively vested in the judiciary" (p. 84). Writing more generally of the judicial power to interpret all laws, Justice William Johnson stated that "[o]f these laws the courts are the constitutional expositors; and every department of government must submit to their exposition; for laws have no legal meaning but what is given them by the courts to whose exposition they are submitted" (p. 237). The same was true, John Marshall wrote, of the great unwritten constitutional principle of respect for vested rights: "The question whether a right has vested or not, is, in its nature, judicial, and must be tried by the judicial authority" (p. 215). The "decision of all cases" involving the construction of the federal Constitution and laws, the Massachusetts General Court stated in 1799, "was exclusively vested by the people in the courts of the United States" (p. 135).

The authoritativeness of judicial interpretation was sometimes based on the intrinsic "nature" of such questions, as in the quotations from Kent and Marshall. At other times, the courts' interpretive powers were based on the need to give reality to the American constitutions' attempt to limit governmental power. "If you mean to have a constitution," Congressman James Bayard told his colleagues, "you must discover a power to which the acknowledged right is attached of pronouncing the invalidity of the acts of the legislature which contravene the instrument" (p. 164). "To maintain, therefore, the Constitution, the judges are a check upon the legislature" (p. 164). The Federalist Bayard agreed with the Republican Roane that, in the latter's words, the judiciary is "not only the proper, but a perfectly disinterested tribunal" whenever a claim is raised that the constitution has been violated (p. 76). As Kent explained, "the efficacy" of constitutional limitations "would be totally lost" "if the Legislature was left the ultimate Judge of the nature and extent of the [constitutional] barriers" (p. 92). The dangers of factional struggle and of "considerations of temporary expediency" rendered the legislature incapable of policing its own constitutional limitations. "The Courts of Justice which are organized with peculiar advantages to exempt them from the baneful influence of Faction" were, in Kent's view, "the most proper power in the Government . . . to maintain the Authority of the Constitution" (p. 92). Roane framed a similar point in the language of separation of powers rather than that of checks and balances: "[E]very legislative exposition," he wrote, "contravenes that principle requiring a separation of the legislative and judicial departments" by uniting "the powers of passing and executing laws in the same persons [which is] no contemptible definition of despotism" (p. 199). As a consequence, "a legislative construction of the law and constitution . . . however respectable . . . must yield to that of the judiciary"(p. 198). Similarly, Story wrote that "[w]hatever weight" a legislative interpretation "might properly have as the opinion of wise and learned men, as a declaration of what the law has been or is, it can have no decisive authority" (p. 283).

James Madison's view of the authority of judicial interpretation is particularly instructive because he firmly believed in an active interpretive role for both the executive and the legislative branches, and (in the federal context) in some final, if ambiguous, place for "state" interpretation. When the Massachusetts legislature accused its Virginia counterpart of usurping the interpretive authority of the federal courts, Madison's Report of 1800 at first responded by pointing out that not all "instances of usurped power" could eventuate in justiciable cases, and then defined the Virginia legislature's assertion of "state" interpretive power as concerned with "those great and extraordinary cases in which all the forms of the Constitution may prove ineffectual against infractions" (p. 141). Somewhat equivocally, Madison concluded his response to the Massachusetts resolutions by writing that the finality of federal judicial interpretation "must necessarily be deemed last in relation to the authorities of the other departments of the [federal] government; not in relation to the rights of the parties to the constitutional compact"

(p. 141) without expressly stating the authority of the federal courts' interpretations for state legislatures and courts. However, much later in the report, Madison returned to the subject. There, he carefully differentiated the "declarations" of citizens or legislatures as "expressions of opinion" from the enforceable "expositions of the judiciary": the latter, he stated, "enforce[d] the general will" in accordance with the judiciary's opinion of that will as embodied in the Constitution (p. 145).[30] As president, Madison took a similar position. Responding to the Pennsylvania governor's call for assistance in resisting what both the governor and the state legislature saw as an unconstitutional invasion of state autonomy by the Supreme Court, Madison refused even to discuss the merits of the constitutional question. Instead, he stressed his duty as president "to carry into effect any such decree," and strongly implied the existence of a duty on the state's part to accept the Court's decision (p. 254).

The widely held view that judicial interpretation was, short of the direct action of the people, of primary or even final authority on constitutional questions was not without its critics. The 1802 struggle in Congress over the bill to repeal the "Midnight Judges Act" provoked a direct denial of the power of judicial review, and consequently of judicial interpretive power, from a few radical Republicans—somewhat to the surprise of the Republican leadership, which accepted the legitimacy of some form of judicial review while disliking the contemporaneous Federalist judiciary.[31] As Jefferson wrote to Abigail Adams two years later, he did not question the courts' "right to decide what laws are constitutional and what not" but only the claim that they could do so "not only for themselves in their own sphere of action but for the legislature and executive also in their own spheres" (p. 159). Jefferson's view was that every branch was "equally independent in the sphere of action assigned to them." As a consequence, he accepted as legitimate, for example, both the federal judges' enforcement of the Sedition Act, because they believed it constitutional, and his own pardon of those convicted under the act, because he thought it unconstitutional (p. 159). Jefferson's theory of coordinate interpretive authorities was echoed on occasion later in the 1791–1818 period, as for example in Peter Porter's 1811 speech in Congress accepting the interpretations of the executive and judiciary in "the practical operation of each particular law" while rejecting "the commentaries of courts" as a guide for future legislation (p. 261). Most of Jefferson's fellow Republicans, however, seem to have accepted Madison's less conflict-ridden vision of interpretive authority, in which legislative and executive opinion played appropriate roles without challenging the primacy of judicial construction in the ordinary course of government.

The Locus of Sovereignty

When Alexander Hamilton ridiculed the notion that the United States might "furnish the singular spectacle of a political society without *sovereignty"* (p. 44), he was expressing a widely held sense that "sovereignty" was an unavoidable concept in political thought. And yet, when Justice James Wilson asked: "Who, or what, is a sovereignty? What is his or its sovereignty? On this subject, the errors and the mazes are endless and inexplicable" (p. 62), he too captured a central feature of the 1791–1818 era's talk about "sovereignty." Although not all of his contemporaries shared his dislike for the terms, few of them can have doubted that "sovereign" and "sovereignty" were concepts as contested and confusing as they were common in American political debate. The language itself was an inheritance from the British colonial past. In the English Tory tradition, "the sovereign" primarily referred to the "supreme lord" (in Dr. Johnson's definition),[32] that is, in the British context, to the king. The term "sovereignty" denoted the king's "attribute of . . . preeminence."[33] From the monarch's personal sovereignty, English lawyers derived such characteristics as his immunity from compulsive suit and the legal impossibility of ascribing to him any wrong.[34] Using the term in a broader sense, Blackstone and many others defined "sovereign power" as "the making of laws," possession of which obliges "all others [to] conform to, and be directed by it."[35] In this sense of ultimate legislative power, "the sovereignty of the British constitution," post-1688 lawyers agreed, was "lodged" in the composite body of Parliament, consisting of King, Lords, and Commons.[36]

English "Country" thinkers and pre-Revolutionary American Whigs[37] tended to use the language of sovereignty in a different manner: to designate the ultimate location of political authority in the people rather than in their royal or parliamentary agents. James Otis's 1764 pamphlet, "The Rights of British Colonies Asserted and Proved," for example, conceded the necessity of sovereign power in every polity: "an original supreme Sovereign, absolute and uncontrollable, *earthly* power *must* exist in and preside over every society." But, for Otis, sovereignty in this proper sense could only rest *"originally* and *ultimately* in the people,"* who for convenience's sake then delegate their authority, in trust, to the actual executive and legislative powers of the state.[38]

American political discussion after independence was influenced both by the legal definitions of sovereignty and by Whig notions about the popular foundations of legitimate government, and a central issue in this early period was the identification of the role these various ideas should play in the new American constitutional order. People across the range of political opinion shared Whig language about "the people": ultra-nationalist John Jay wrote that "the people" are "the sovereigns of the country" (p. 66) at almost the same time anti-Federalist Spencer Roane was defining "the people of this country" as "the only sovereign power" (p. 76). Americans of disparate views also shared the Blackstonian use of "sovereign(ty)" in connection with the organs of government. Federalist John Marshall, for example, could refer to the legislature of Georgia as "the supreme sovereign power of a state" (p. 274) as easily as states' rights jurist Robert White would speak of the "rights, Sovereignty and Independence of the respective State Governments" (p. 295). But rhetorical agreement masked and sometimes confused profound constitutional disagreement. By "the people," a nationalist like Jay meant Americans as a whole; Roane was referring to Virginians as a distinct political community. Marshall's ascription of "sovereignty" to a state legislature merely echoed Blackstone's near-equation of "sovereign" and "legislative," but White meant to invoke strong notions of the states' judicial and legislative autonomy from federal interference. There was, in fact, no agreed-upon definition of sovereignty and no uncontroversial identification of its location in the American constitutional order.[39]

The varying meanings of "sovereignty" in the period 1791–1818 may be grouped into four categories: the rhetoric of divided sovereignty, the use of "sovereign" to identify the possessor(s) of governmental discretion, the designation of the nation as sovereign, and the contrary identification of the states as sovereignties. The earliest, and most persistent, was the language of divided sovereignty. Despite the view widespread in 1787–88 that sovereignty was necessarily indivisible and thus that either the states *or* the nation had to be sovereign, soon after 1789 it became common to assert, as Hamilton wrote in 1791, that "the powers of sovereignty are in this country divided between the National and State Governments" (p. 44). Constitutional arguments often referred in parallel fashion to "the sovereignty of the nation" and "the residuary sovereignty of each state" (p. 66), or to "the divided sovereignty" (p. 297) of the Union.

The language of divided sovereignty often seems simply to have been a means of recognizing verbally the existence of separate and complete governmental structures and deliberative and legislative powers in the several states and on the federal level: when Henry Clay described the United States as a combination of "twenty local sovereignties" with parochial and "municipal" concerns and "one great sovereignty" entrusted with external and commercial responsibilities (p. 320), the use of "sovereignty" rather than "government" or "legislature" was little more than a rhetorical flourish. In the 1805 case of *Hepburn v. Ellzey*, E. J. Lee's argument for the plaintiff involved a denial that the states were radically distinct legally from other subnatural polities such as the District of Columbia; and Charles Lee's opposing position insisted on the unique constitutional role of the states. The former therefore stressed that the states lacked "certain rights of sovereignty" (p. 184), and the latter stressed their "peculiar" role in the Union. For neither attorney, however, was some concrete concept of "sovereignty" crucial to his argument; and both would have subscribed to Charles Lee's remark that "[t]he states are not absolutely sovereigns, but (if I may use the expression) they are demi-sovereigns" (p. 185).

The use of divided sovereignty talk was not always this nearly empty; and, when it was not, it usually served as a means for designating the existence of decisional autonomy and discretion, what E. J. Lee described in 1805 as "the free exercise of all the rights of sovereignty, uncontrolled by any other power" (p. 184). Hamilton's bank opinion accepted the sovereignty of both state and federal governments as to their respective spheres of activity in order to claim for Congress the power to exercise discretion in its choice of means to pursue its constitutional ends (p. 44). Congress's decisions about means thus shared in the supremacy over conflicting claims of the Constitution's designation of its ends (p. 45). Judge William Cabell's rejection of federal Supreme Court jurisdiction over state court decisions used similar logic to reach a politically contrary result. Given the "residuary sovereignty of the states," neither Congress nor the Supreme Court could compel state courts to conform their interpretations of the United States Constitution to the Court's. To admit such a power would be to deny the state judges' inherent obligation and ability to apply law "according to their own judgments" (p. 298). Lower courts within a single sovereignty, Cabell admitted, were required to follow the decisions of the sovereignty's highest court; the very point of calling the states sovereign was to deny that state and federal courts were instruments of the same sovereignty (p. 298). Cabell's fellow states' rights Virginian Robert White used divided sovereignty language in an effort to demonstrate that Congress could not confer jurisdiction over a federal offense on a state court: Congress's attempt to do so was unconstitutional both because it invaded the state's sovereign autonomy and because it improperly derogated from the Union's own sovereignty, "an important part" of which was "a right to expound its laws" in its own courts (p. 295). "Sovereignty," as Hamilton, Cabell, White, and others sometimes used it, was thus a concept intimately connected with the question of discretion, which will be discussed in the next section of this essay.

The best-known use of the language of sovereignty had to do with identifying the fundamental nature of the political and constitutional order. On at least two important occasions in the 1790s, an attempt was made to capture the language of sovereignty as a means to express a particular vision of the United States Constitution. Although the earlier, nationalist effort was politically unsuccessful, the Republicans' political victory in the 1800 elections—the so-called "Revolution of 1800"—was regarded by the now-majority party as a decisive vindication of its state-sovereignty constitutionalism (the "principles of '98"). Constitutional argument between 1801 and 1819 took place against a theoretical and political backdrop partially shaped by the Republicans' identification of the Union as a confederacy or compact among sovereign states.

The U.S. Supreme Court's first great case, *Chisholm v. Georgia*, almost unavoidably posed for the Court the question of the locus of sovereignty. Georgia's obvious justification for its refusal to recognize the Court's jurisdiction—a justification articulated only after the fact because the state declined even to argue the point before the Court (p. 69)—rested on the legal rule found in Blackstone and elsewhere that the sovereign could not be sued without his (or its) consent. The rule's viability in a federal court system had been discussed during the ratification campaign of 1787–88; and Hamilton among other supporters of the Constitution had insisted that the states would retain, "as one of the attributes of sovereignty," their immunity from suit under the proposed Constitution (p. 55). Georgia's implied position thus enjoyed significant support from the history of the Constitution's origins. On the other hand, as Attorney General Edmund Randolph (the plaintiff's counsel), told the Court, a variety of considerations supported the claim that an unconsenting state was subject to compulsory federal jurisdiction. His primary argument was strictly textual: article three extended federal jurisdiction to controversies "between a state and citizens of another state." No one would doubt, Randolph observed, that under such language Georgia constitutionally could sue Chisholm (a South Carolinian) in federal court; both logic and the grammar of the clauses in the article strongly implied that the reverse was true as well (p. 56). The states' sovereign status, which Randolph admitted (p. 57), did not contradict this textual argument. Precisely as sovereigns, "with the free will, arising from absolute independence" (p. 57), the states had formed a federal union that limited their powers and independence both by the delegation of authority to the federal government and by implicit prohibitions on state action. Such undenied "diminutions of sovereignty" proved, in Randolph's opinion, that "there is nothing in the nature of sovereignties, combined as those of America are, to prevent the words of the constitution [apparently subjecting states to suit] . . . from receiving an easy and usual construction" (p. 57).

Randolph's argument attempted to combine the usual rhetorical position of locating "sovereignty" partially in the states while insisting that, on the issue of amenability to suit, among others, state sovereignty had been abridged by the states' own action in adopting the Constitution. As Justice James Iredell intimated, this position was not without its problems. By recognizing a state's right to sue as *plaintiff* in federal court, "every word in the Constitution" could be given effect without the necessity of admitting that a state might also be compelled to be a *defendant* (p. 59). Randolph had no clear answer to the assertion that the words of article three could only be read properly against the background of legal history and political assumptions shared by Americans in 1787–88. Nor did he satisfy nationalists who rejected as "common-place rant"[40] the very ascription of sovereignty to the states upon which he based argument.

The members of the Supreme Court in the majority attempted to remedy the weaknesses of Randolph's reasoning in their opinions upholding his client's right to sue Georgia. Justice James Wilson launched a frontal assault on the very use of sovereignty language at all in American political discussion. No intellectual or rhetorical confusion had done "mischief so extensive or so practically pernicious . . . in politics and jurisprudence," in Wilson's view, as the words "states" and "sovereigns" (p. 60). He pointed out that the terminology of "sovereignty" was wholly absent from the Constitution's text, and unsurprisingly so, because only the people of the nation as a whole could properly assume the title of "sovereign" in a government of freedom and equal rights (p. 61). Talk of a "sovereign" was simply inapposite and misleading in America, where there were no "subjects." In particular, a state such as Georgia had no claim to be called or treated as "sovereign." It was not "sovereign" in the sense of the law of nations because under the Constitution it did not govern itself "without any dependence on another power"

(p. 62); nor was it "sovereign" in terms of republican theory, for the "citizens of Georgia, as a part of the 'People of the United States' " had not surrendered "the supreme or sovereign power to that state; but, as to the purposes of the union, retained it to themselves" (p. 62). Having disposed of the entire notion of state sovereignty, Wilson had no need to deal with the argument that the Constitution presumed or preserved state-sovereign immunity.

Chief Justice John Jay reached Wilson's (and Randolph's) conclusion by yet another, in Jay's case historical, route. During the colonial period, he wrote, the Crown had been the sovereign and the American colonists were fellow-subjects of one another and of the inhabitants of Great Britain. When the colonies as a united group declared themselves independent, "the sovereignty of the country passed to the people of it," the American people as a whole. The vicissitudes of war and political confusion along with "local convenience and considerations" misled Americans into reconceiving the nation as a "confederation" of "thirteen sovereignties." The failure of the Articles of Confederation, however, reawakened the American people to "their collective and national capacity," and in that capacity they "executed their own rights, and their own proper sovereignty" to establish the Constitution. Thus, the language of state sovereignty was a historical error,[41] subsequently corrected, and compulsory federal jurisdiction over state-defendants "brings into action, and enforces this great and glorious principle, that the people are the sovereign of this country" (pp. 66, 68).

On a political level, Wilson's and Jay's attempt to claim "sovereignty" for the nation, or to banish the term altogether, ran afoul of the clamor aroused by the possibility of federal judgments being enforced against debt-ridden states. The Eleventh Amendment swiftly overturned the specific holding of *Chisholm v. Georgia*, and the Revolution of 1800 rendered ultra-nationalist views politically unacceptable. On the other hand, Wilson and Jay had identified correctly the importance of debate over sovereignty and over the proper recounting of constitutional history in American constitutional argument. Their outright rejection of state sovereignty, and Jay's historical picture of a national "people" that preceded the post-independence state polities, were minority views (especially after 1800), but in more subtle forms their positions influenced the jurisprudence of the Marshall Court and the Republican nationalism of the late 1810s.

The states' status as sovereigns, contested by Wilson and Jay but generally admitted rhetorically by both nationalists and their opponents in the 1790s, became a central constitutional concept in the theory (or theories) propounded by Republican leaders during the 1798–1800 crisis. In a series of widely publicized public papers—Pennsylvania Chief Justice M'Kean's opinion in *Respublica v. Cobbett*, the Kentucky Resolutions of 1798 and 1799, the Virginia Resolutions of 1798, and the Virginia Report of 1800—the Republicans sketched an anti-nationalist constitutional vision that regarded state sovereignty as the fundamental political datum in the constitutional order. The electoral Revolution of 1800, which permanently ousted the Federalists from national political power, and the dissemination of the "principles of '98" through such influential channels as St. George Tucker's 1803 edition of Blackstone, ensured that federal constitutional argument before *M'Culloch*[42] would have, as explicit subject or implicit backdrop, a complex of concepts and questions surrounding the notion of the states as sovereigns.[43]

The second and third articles of the Articles of Confederation defined the fundamental nature of the confederacy the document was establishing, and enunciated a fundamental interpretive principle flowing from that nature. The second stated that "[e]ach State retains its sovereignty, freedom and independence," and the third that the "states hereby enter into a firm league of friendship." The second article concluded that—as a consequence—each state "retains . . . every power, jurisdiction, and right, which is not by this confederation expressly delegated to the United States, in Congress assembled." The heart of the "principles of '98" was the claim that these concepts—the states as original sovereigns; the Union as a league or compact created by a written, quasi-contractual agreement; the interpretive obligation of reading the compact's delegation of authority to the federal government narrowly, in strict accord with the compact's text and the states' intent—were applicable as well to the 1787 Constitution and should govern its interpretation.

The Republicans of 1798 shared a common account of the Union's origin. As M'Kean wrote, before the Constitution's adoption, "the several states had absolute and unlimited sovereignty within their respective boundaries." When these sovereigns replaced the Articles' "league of friendship," Jefferson wrote, they did so "by compact," "constitut[ing] a general government for special purposes, delegat[ing] to that government certain definite powers, reserving, each state to itself, the residuary mass of right to their own self-government" (p. 130). As a consequence, Madison asserted, unlike the state governments, the federal government's power "result[ed] from the compact" and was "limited by the plain sense and intention of the instrument constituting that compact . . . no further valid than they are authorized by the grants enumerated in that compact" (p. 134). As was suggested earlier, Jefferson and Madison may not have been wholly in agreement. Jefferson's 1798 Kentucky Resolutions conceived of the constitutional compact as an agreement between "each state . . . as a state and . . . an integral party, its co-states forming as to itself, the other party." The resulting image of a (series of?) two-party compacts is conceptually confusing but yielded a conclusion Jefferson apparently welcomed: that each individual state had "an equal right to judge for itself, as well of infractions as of the mode and measure of redress" (p. 130). Madison, in contrast, consistently referred to "the states" in the plural as the "sovereign parties to the constitutional compact" (p. 140), and does not seem to have anticipated unilateral state action except in the expression of opinion.

A second ambiguity concerned the mode in which the state could act as a "party" to the compact. The 1798 resolutions' vigorous denunciations of the Alien and Sedition acts unsurprisingly were read as legislative exercises of Kentucky's and Virginia's asserted sovereign right to "judge . . . of infractions" (p. 130) and to "interpose for arresting the progress of the evil" (p.

134); the Massachusetts legislature, for example, described the Virginia Resolutions as "the assumption of the right to declare the acts of the national
government unconstitutional" (p. 135). In their subsequent statements, both
state legislatures denied this interpretation of their resolutions. Despite the
use of the inflammatory word "nullification," the Kentucky legislature expressly labeled its 1799 resolutions a "solemn protest" with no legal effect
(p. 138), and Madison's Report of 1800 expressly defined the "states" that
are constitutional parties and sovereigns as "the people composing those
political societies, in their highest sovereign capacity" rather than as any
ordinary state organ (p. 140).

This vision of the Constitution as a compact among sovereigns—the Pennsylvania legislature in 1811 described it as "to all intents and purposes a treaty
between sovereign states" (p. 258)—played an intermittent, if important and
sometimes tragic, role in future constitutional history as the justification for
state defiance of federal authority, state interference with federal activity, and
for secession and civil war. In the 1791–1818 period, its primary function was
to provide a conceptual basis on which to rest a narrow construction of the
Constitution's grants of power to the federal government. As a matter of
political and international law, St. George Tucker wrote in 1803, "several
sovereign and independent states may unite themselves together by a perpetual confederacy, without each ceasing to be a perfect state" (p. 153); such
"a federal compact, or alliance between . . . states" customarily was reduced
to writing (p. 156), which in turn was "to be construed strictly, in all cases
where the antecedent rights of *states* may be drawn in question" (p. 155).[44]

The state-compact and strict-construction themes of the "principles of '98"
were a constant feature of constitutional discourse between 1800 and 1819.
Obviously and inevitably they provided the language for constitutional opposition, invoked by New England Federalists against President Jefferson's
embargo and President Madison's war as readily as by Pennsylvania Republicans against the bank-bill renewal and by Virginia Republicans against Supreme Court jurisdiction. But these concepts were not without influence on
those supporting expansive readings of federal power. After 1800 these individuals almost invariably couched their constitutional views in terms of
close textual exegesis rather than of grand pronouncements about the federal
government's undefined "resulting powers" or sovereignty of choice. Story's
opinion in *Martin v. Hunter's Lessee*, which squarely rejected the 1798 "principle" that the states as sovereignties established the Constitution in favor of
the ultra-nationalist ascription of the Constitution's creation to "the people
of the United States" (p. 303),[45] upheld a statutory grant of jurisdiction to the
Supreme Court by a rigorous parsing of article three's text.

Republican nationalist justifications of the internal improvement bills of
1817 and 1818 were similar blends of '98 "principle" and Hamiltonian substance. In 1817, for example, Calhoun accepted "the position" that "our Constitution was founded on positive and written principles" (p. 312), and he
defended the bill by a careful examination of the language of article one,
section eight. Clay began an 1818 speech with the statement that he "had

imbibed those constitutional opinions which had influenced his political course" from the Report of 1800 and other documents "of analogous principle" (p. 320); he went on to assert the legitimacy "in all that relates essentially to the preservation of this Union" of giving federal powers "a liberal construction" (p. 320). As Jefferson wrote Albert Gallatin in 1817, "almost the only landmark which now divides the federalists [among whom Jefferson classed many Republican nationalists] from the republicans" was the debate over how to read—indeed almost over how to punctuate (p. 314)—the beginning of article one, section eight. The great 1790s debate over the locus of sovereignty had as its most immediate result the reenforcement of textual argument as the primary vehicle of constitutional discourse.

The Problem of Discretion

In his great *Dictionary*, published in 1755, Dr. Samuel Johnson identified two distinct sets of meanings for the word "discretion." In the first group of definitions, he listed "Prudence; knowledge to govern or direct one's self; skill; wise management." Among the examples of usage he gave were two that linked "wisdom and discretion," and one, a quotation from Pope's *Essay on Criticism*, that used "discretion" to refer to care or skill in the writing of poetry. Johnson's second set of definitions was unaccompanied by examples from literature, so he provided not only the definitions but a sample of the word used accordingly: "Liberty of acting at pleasure uncontrolled, and unconditional power; as, he surrenders at discretion; that is without stipulation."[46] "Discretion" was an important and extremely controversial concept in early American constitutional discourse, and much of its controversiality stemmed from the fact that for Americans of the late eighteenth and early nineteenth centuries the word retained both of the sets of meanings Johnson had recognized. Many, perhaps most, of the major constitutional disputes of the period involved a claim by someone to the legitimate exercise of discretion in the sense of wisdom, skill, or knowledge, and a rejoinder by others that this was in fact a claim to the unconstitutional and oppressive possession of uncontrolled power. Debate over the role and legitimacy of "discretion" in the American constitutional order played a significant part in discussions of the extent of congressional power, the scope of judicial review, the relationship between the executive and the judiciary, and the sanctity of vested rights; all three branches of government under the American constitutions defined themselves in part on the basis of what form of discretion they legitimately could exercise.[47]

Central to constitutionalism in the eyes of most American leaders in the 1791–1818 period was the search for a means of empowering government and yet controlling it in the interests of the people's welfare and liberty. Without some means of control, Americans would be no safer from their own governments than they had been from king and Parliament. An excess of control, on the other hand, would "paralyze the powers of the Constitution" (p. 115) and thus render the American experiment in republican government self-defeating. Everyone agreed with Hamilton that "no government has a right to do *merely what it pleases*" (p. 46), but in one way or another almost everyone also agreed with his cynical observation that "in politics, power and right are equivalent" (p. 209), at least as a statement of the tendency of power to claim legitimacy. The very point of written constitutions was to deny the automatic equation of power with right and thereby to put a check on power's tendency toward oppression. "[I]t is jealousy, and not confidence, which prescribes limited constitutions to bind down those whom we are obliged to trust with power," Jefferson stated in 1798, adding that "our Constitution has accordingly fixed the limits to which, and no further, our confidence [in our governors] may go" (p. 133). Hamilton wrote that to recognize "unlimited discretion" in Congress would be to "destroy the very idea of a Constitution limiting its discretion. The Constitution would at once vanish!" (p. 106). Boundless executive discretion was, if possible, even less acceptable: Justice William Johnson claimed that "[t]he officers of our government, from the highest to the lowest, are equally subjected to legal restraint" (p. 231).

The most important and controversial questions about "discretion" concerned its exercise by legislatures, and especially by Congress. The activity of legislation clearly involved "discretion" in Dr. Johnson's first sense of "prudence" or "wise management." The Constitution gave powers to Congress, Madison told the House of Representatives in 1796, on the presumption that "the legislature would exercise its authority with discretion, allowing due weight" to considerations of policy, expediency, and circumstance (p. 105); the power to engage in a degree of "deliberation and discretion" was "essential to the nature of Legislative power" (p. 106). The "political discretion" of Congress, Judge John Davis wrote in 1808, "embraces, combines and considers, all circumstances, events and projects, foreign or domestick, that can affect the national interests" (p. 244).

Legislators engaged in making choices about the exercise of "the authority delegated to them," according to Justice James Iredell, "exercise the discretion vested in them by the people" (p. 99). As Fisher Ames had reminded the House in 1791, few pieces of legislation literally tracked the language of article one, which grants Congress power; as a consequence, in virtually all its lawmaking, Congress was obliged to exercise "our discretion with regard to the true intent of the Constitution" (p. 40). The needs of the nation "are of such infinite variety, extent and complexity," Hamilton wrote, that Congress must enjoy "of necessity . . . great latitude of discretion in the selection and application of [the] means" of meeting those needs (p. 47). Hamilton conceded the possibility of "controversy and difference of opinion" over the constitutionality of legislation intended to address national concerns, and he argued that "a reasonable latitude and judgment" on the constitutional question "must be allowed" to Congress (p. 47). On this nationalist view, the Constitution was to be regarded as what Henry St. George Tucker called "a rule of conduct for the legislative body" rather than a list of exactly what Congress could and could not do (p. 317); Ames explained that "[t]he Constitution contains the principles which are to govern in making laws," but that, in applying these constitutional principles to specific legislative concerns, the Congress was "to exercise our judgments, and on every occasion to decide according to an honest conviction of its true meaning" (p. 40).

According Congress discretion in the interpretation and application of the Constitution, nationalists argued, did not entail permitting it to "govern by its own arbitrary discretion" (p. 40): the discretion they were endorsing was Dr. Johnson's "prudence" ("wisdom applied to practice" as he defined it) rather than his "uncontrolled power." Congress itself was capable of determining what means of carrying out its tasks were appropriately related to the Constitution's ends and appropriately respectful of the rights of individuals and states. The nationalists admitted that "there must always be great difference of opinion, as to the 'direct relationship,' and 'real necessity' of the accessory powers" selected (p. 321), but insisted that this fact did not mean that Congress's choices were arbitrary. "No, sir," Tucker told his congressional colleagues, "it is not a mathematical, it is a moral certainty, that we are to expect in these great questions of political right." "Constitutional powers, which admit not of precise definition," were, he added, "to be referred to practical good sense and sound discretion" (p. 321). Nationalists stressed this "internal" check of rational argument on congressional arbitrariness; they also invoked "representative responsibility" (p. 316) and judicial review (p. 161) as "external" checks on legislative waywardness.

The early opponents of expansive readings of federal power are often viewed as motivated primarily by a general fear of centralized power. Although that concern undeniably fueled the development of opposition thought and its crystallization in the "principles of '98," the fear of discretion was at least as important a factor. Opposition constitutionalists of the 1790s, by and large, doubted that the activity of prudential reasoning could be distinguished from the exercise of arbitrary choice; as a consequence, they did not believe that an "internal" check on Congress's powers could exist once the legislature abandoned a strict observance of its "chartered authorities" (p. 39). "To take a single step beyond the boundaries thus specially drawn around the powers of Congress is to take possession of a boundless field of power, no longer susceptible of any definition" (p. 42). The nationalists' claim that Congress was constrained by its obligation to pursue the Constitution's designated ends, and especially "the general welfare" named in article one, section eight, was, Jefferson wrote, empty. It amounted to a reduction of "the whole instrument to a single phrase, that of instituting a Congress with power to do whatever would be for the good of the United States; and, as they would be the sole judges of the good or evil, it would be also a power to do whatever evil they please" (p. 42). "The Constitution of the United States is not . . . a mere general designation of the ends or objects for which the Federal Government was established," Peter Porter told the House of Representatives in 1811, "leaving to Congress a discretion as to the means or powers by which these ends shall be brought about." The Constitution was equally "a specification of the powers or means themselves" by which its ends were to be achieved. "The powers of the Constitution, carried into execution according to the strict terms and import of them, are the appropriate means and the only means within the reach of this Government for the attainment of its ends" (p. 259).

The intellectual struggle between advocates and opponents of congressional discretion in applying the Constitution was waged in large part over the proper reading of two clauses of article one, section eight: the ambiguous language about the "general welfare" at the beginning of the section,[48] and the "necessary and proper" clause at its conclusion.[49] The "general welfare" language was susceptible to at least three different interpretations. The most nationalist and least popular was to construe the clause to grant Congress three separate and distinct powers: to collect taxes, to pay debts, and to "provide for the common defense and general welfare of the United States." Alexander Addison's critique of the Report of 1800 adopted this position. The Constitution, according to him, "gives to Congress power over the means, and imposes the duty of providing for the general welfare in all cases whatever, to which in its discretion the means ought to be applied."[50]

Critics of this view, such as Jefferson, regarded this as "a claim of universal power" by Congress based on "a mere grammatical quibble" (p. 314); and most nationalists also rejected it as inconsistent with the apparent effort in the rest of section eight to enumerate Congress's powers.[51] These nationalists, and their state-sovereignty opponents, agreed that the phrase "provide for the common defense and general welfare" modified Congress's power to raise money and spend it. The debate then became one over whether Congress could spend the revenues it raised on any object that seemed to it to benefit the nation's defense or welfare, or rather was restricted to expenditures connected with the powers subsequently enumerated in the section. Hamiltonian Federalists in the 1790s and many Republican nationalists in the period following the War of 1812 maintained the former position. As Calhoun explained in 1817, "[f]irst the power is given to lay taxes; next, the objects are enumerated to which the money accruing from the exercise of this power may be applied; to pay the debts, provide for the common defense, and promote the general welfare" (p. 311). He rejected a limitation of the spending power to the other powers listed in the section as inconsistent with the constitutional text. "If the framers had intended to limit the use of the money to the powers afterwards enumerated and defined, nothing could be more easy than to have expressed it plainly" (p. 311). The scope of Congress's spending power thus involved not a question of constitutional interpretation but of political policy. So long as Congress did not attempt to appropriate money for a "purpose merely or purely local," Hamilton wrote, the question of "how far it will really promote or not the welfare of the union, must be a matter of conscientious discretion" and not of "constitutional right" (p. 49).

Critics of this position argued that its pragmatic effect would be identical to that of the ultra-nationalist claim that there was a substantive "general welfare" power. The latter gave Congress "a general power of legislation instead of the defined and limited one hitherto understood to belong to them," Madison wrote in 1817. "A restriction of the power 'to provide for the common defense and general welfare' to cases which are to be provided for by the expenditure of money" was no better; it "would still leave within the legislative power of Congress all the great and most important measures of Government, money being the ordinary and necessary means of carrying them into execution" (pp. 314–14). Madison and those who shared his view of the "general welfare" phrase rejected such a result as textually unacceptable because it "would render negatory the enumeration of particular powers" (p. 38). Equally unacceptable was the vast expansion of federal governmental discretion that would result. A Congress empowered to spend money in all matters involving the general welfare, the Report of 1800 argued, would be too busy to give careful attention to all "the objects of legislative care," as well as unable to adapt its legislation properly to "the diversity of particular situations." "One consequence must be, to enlarge the sphere of discretion allowed to the executive magistrate" (p. 142), thus raising the specter of a president wielding quasi-royal "prerogative and patronage" (p. 143). Madison's message vetoing the 1817 Bonus Bill added to this an argument from judicial review, which he asserted would be unavailable to restrain congressional misuses of a "general welfare" power or an enlarged spending power "inasmuch as questions relating to the general welfare, being questions of policy and expediency, are unsusceptible of judicial cognizance and decision" (p. 313). To avoid such unacceptable results, Alexander Smythe told the House the following year, the phrase had to be construed to limit Congress to "expending the money raised in the execution of the other powers expressly granted" (p. 319).

In their attack on the original bank bill, Madison and Jefferson crafted what became the standard non-nationalist interpretation of the "necessary and proper" clause. The clause authorized Congress to exercise a power not expressly given, according to Madison, only if it was "evidently and necessarily involved in an express power" (p. 39). Any other argument would construe the clause to give Congress "an unlimited discretion," a conclusion that would undercut "the essential characteristic of the Government": its limited nature (p. 38). Jefferson was even more emphatic, writing that the Constitution legitimized only "those means without which the grant of power would be nugatory" (p. 43). This stringent reading of the clause reappeared in the 1811 bank-renewal debate when Peter Porter, for example, insisted that the clause "gives no latitude of discretion on the selection of means or powers" (p. 259). "If you undertake to justify a law" as necessary and proper to executing an enumerated power, he continued, "you must show the incidentality and applicability of the law to the power itself, and not merely its relation to any supposed end which is to be accomplished by its execution"; "the plain, direct, ostensible, obvious, primary object and tendency of your law [must be] to execute the [enumerated] power" (p. 260).

Nationalists attacked the strict reading of the "necessary and proper" clause as implausible. According to Hamilton, "neither the grammatical, nor popular sense of the term requires that construction. According to both, *necessary* often means no more than *needful, requisite, incidental, useful*, or *conducive to"* (p. 46). The "whole turn of the clause"—with its references to *"all laws,"* *"all* other powers," *"any* department or officer," and so on—indicated, Hamilton argued, that "it was the intent of the convention, by that clause to give a liberal latitude to the exercise of the specified powers" (p. 46). The "necessary and proper" clause in fact was an explicit authorization of Congress's "great latitude of discretion in the selection and application of those means" (p. 47). Later nationalists reiterated Hamilton's analysis. Marshall's 1805 opinion in *United States v. Fisher*, for example, rejected a Jeffersonian strict necessity construction as an interpretive nightmare because it would always be possible to argue that any given means could be replaced by a different one. Instead, "Congress must possess the choice of means, and must be empowered to use any means which are in fact conclusive to the exercise of a power granted by the constitution" (p. 188).

The problem of discretion was not confined to the legislative sphere. Indeed, the most persistent constitutional issue during Jefferson's presidency was probably the struggle between the administration and the federal courts over the nature and limits of executive discretion. Even though one of the Republicans' complaints about the Alien Act was its sweeping grant of discretionary authority to the president, Jefferson was a staunch defender of the discretion of the executive to interpret the Constitution and to act on his interpretation (p. 159); to govern his conduct by his own view of the law notwithstanding contrary judicial opinion (p. 217); to make independent judgments about issues of special executive concern such as foreign affairs and national security (p. 228); and to resist judicial attempts to "direct the use to be made" of executive power (p. 234).

The response of the federal courts was to recognize the existence of presidential "political powers, in the exercise of which he is to use his own discretion," but to insist that the courts, not the president, were the final judges of the limits of those powers. Marshall's opinion in *Marbury* conceded that "in cases in which the executive possesses a constitutional or legal discretion, nothing can be more perfectly clear, than that their acts are only politically examinable" (pp. 214–15). But, where the law assigned a duty to the executive, or there was a question of constitutional right, the president's actions were subject to judicial examination. The president "cannot, in his discretion, sport away the vested rights of others," Marshall wrote, adding that a claim of vested right "must be tried by the judicial authority" (pp. 214–15). Presidential invasion of such a right would entitle the injured party to a remedy even if that entailed subjecting a high executive officer to a peremptory judicial writ. Nor did the president enjoy discretion about whether to enforce the laws. "If he could," Justice William Paterson observed, "it would render the execution of the laws dependent on his will and pleasure; which is a doctrine that has not been set up, and will not meet with any supporters in our government" (p. 222).

Jefferson's claim to independent interpretive authority was flatly denied by the courts. Marshall's famous statement that "[i]t is emphatically, the province and duty of the judiciary department, to say what the law is" (p. 180) was directed against the pretensions of the legislature, but he and his colleagues were equally ready to apply it to the executive. Justice William Johnson put their position forcefully in his newspaper defense of his decision in *Gilchrist v. Collector*: "Of these laws [the "laws of the United States"] the courts are the constitutional expositors; and every department of government must submit to their exposition; for laws have no legal meaning but what is given them by the courts to whose exposition they are submitted" (p. 237).

The replacement of Jefferson by Madison in the presidency eased relations between the executive and the judiciary, in large part because Madison quickly receded from Jefferson's more militant positions. Although Madison did not hesitate on a number of occasions to veto a bill because he disagreed with Congress about its constitutionality, from early on in his administration he denied that any "legal discretion lies with the Executive of the U[nited] States" to interfere with judicial decisions or interpretations of law (p. 254).

Courts, too, frequently were said to have discretion, but here the usage clearly belonged in Dr. Johnson's first set of definitions, such as prudence, skill, and knowledge. In exercising its proper form of discretion, a court was not to choose arbitrarily but in accordance with the rules of law. When United States Attorney George Hay argued to the circuit court in the *Burr* case that it could *choose* not to grant Burr's motion for a subpoena *duces tecum* to the president, Chief Justice Marshall replied that Hay had misunderstood judicial discretion. "This is said to be a motion to the discretion of the court. This is true, but a motion to its discretion is a motion, not to its inclination, but to its judgment; and its judgment is to be guided by sound legal principles" (p. 225). The court's discretion was to be exercised in determining the legal relevance of the documents sought by the subpoena, and the legal cogency of any claim by the executive that the national interests required the document's exclusion from evidence, but "the court has no right to refuse its aid to motions for papers to which the accused may be entitled" by legal principle (p. 226). "Discretion" in the judicial context thus had little to do with choice; it was, rather, the court's skillful exercise of judgment in discussing and applying correctly the rules of law. "Courts are the mere instruments of the law, and can will nothing," Marshall wrote in 1824. "Where they are said to exercise a discretion, it is a mere legal discretion, a discretion to be exercised in discerning the course presented by law."[52] Legal discretion, the process of determining the correct application of given principles to specific cases, thus had little in common with the political discretion of a legislature or an executive magistrate, even when the term was ascribed to either in a positive sense. As Judge John Davis explained, "[l]egal discretion is limited. It is thus defined by Lord Coke, 'Discretion is to discern, by means of law, what is just.' Political discretion has a far wider range. It embraces, combines and considers, all circumstances, events and projects, foreign or domestick, that can affect the national interests" (p. 244).[53] Judicial discretion could only play a role in questions where the applicable principles of decision permitted "precision and certainty" (p. 244), but it is of the very essence of political discretion that it is exercised in conditions of uncertainty and with regard to considerations of expediency and necessity.

Despite the obvious fact that not all judicial decisions, and particularly those involving constitutional matters, were uncontroversial, legal discretion and politics were usually differentiated sharply. The Constitution, Marshall insisted in 1800, "had never been understood, to confer on [the judiciary] any political power whatever" but only the authority to resolve specific questions that could take "a legal form" and thus be decided by legal rules (p. 174). Judicial discretion thus involved "the exercise of a rational Judgment," in James Kent's words, rather than "arbitrary will" (p. 93). Judicial interpretation of a constitution, with all its political ramifications, was no less "legal" in nature than statutory construction or common-law reasoning. Constitutional interpretation, like all legal interpretation, rested on demonstrable principles, which St. George Tucker asserted "can be ascertained from the living letter, not from obscure reasoning or deductions only" (p. 84). Although there certainly were critics of specific constitutional decisions throughout the 1791–1818 period, their complaints seldom if ever were directed against the assertion that courts must wield (legal) discretion in determining and applying the law. The intense warfare waged against the Federalist judges in the first years of Jefferson's presidency did not involve, for the most part, any rejection of judicial power, only of its unworthy possessors. There was no paradox in the fact that the most prominent Jeffersonian jurist of the 1810s, Spencer Roane, held a very high view of judicial authority. When he attacked the federal Supreme Court's claim of jurisdiction to review state court decisions, his criticism was that the Court had abused its discretion by applying the wrong legal principles, not that judicial discretion was itself illegitimate or indistinguishable from political choice.

One

Setting up "One Construction against Another": The Dispute over the National Bank Bill

On December 14, 1790, Secretary of the Treasury Alexander Hamilton submitted to the First Congress a proposal that it create a national bank by federal corporate charter. The purposes of the bank, according to this report, were to facilitate the fiscal operations of the government and to benefit the national economy by providing an adequate circulating medium and some degree of central control over state-chartered banks. The emerging congressional opposition to Hamilton's programs coalesced around an attack on the bank bill as unconstitutional, an attack led by his erstwhile ally James Madison.

James Madison
Speech in the U.S. House of Representatives
(February 2, 1791)[54]

. . . Is the power of establishing an incorporated Bank among the powers vested by the Constitution in the Legislature of the United States? This is the question to be examined.

After some general remarks on the limitations of all political power, he [Madison] took notice of the peculiar manner in which the Federal Government is limited. It is not a general grant out of which particular powers are excepted; it is a grant of particular powers only, leaving the general mass in other hands. So it had been understood by its friends and its foes, and so it was to be interpreted.

As preliminaries to a right interpretation, he laid down the following rules:

An interpretation that destroys the very characteristic of the Government cannot be just.

Where a meaning is clear, the consequences, whatever they may be, are to be admitted—where doubtful, it is fairly triable by its consequences.

In controverted cases, the meaning of the parties to the instrument, if to be collected by reasonable evidence, is a proper guide.

Contemporary and concurrent expositions are a reasonable evidence of the meaning of the parties.

In admitting or rejecting a constructive authority, not only the degree of its incidentality to an express authority is to [be] regarded, but the degree of its importance also; since on this will depend the probability or improbability of its being left to construction.

Reviewing the Constitution with an eye to these positions, it was not possible to discover in it the power to incorporate a Bank. The only clauses under which such a power could be pretended are either:

1. The power to lay and collect taxes to pay the debts, and provide for the common defence and general welfare; or,
2. The power to borrow money on the credit of the United States; or,
3. The power to pass all laws necessary and proper to carry into execution those powers.

The bill did not come within the first power. It laid no tax to pay the debts, or provide for the general welfare. It laid no tax whatever. It was altogether foreign to the subject.

No argument could be drawn from the terms "common defence and general welfare." The power as to these general purposes was limited to acts laying taxes for them; and the general purposes themselves were limited and explained by the particular enumeration subjoined. To understand these terms in any sense that would justify the power in question, would give to Congress an unlimited power; would render nugatory the enumeration of particular powers; would supersede all the powers reserved to the State Governments. These terms are copied from the Articles of Confederation; had it ever been pretended that they were to be understood otherwise than as here explained? . . .

The second clause to be examined is that which empowers Congress to borrow money.

Is this a bill to borrow money? It does not borrow a shilling. Is there any fair construction by which the bill can be deemed an exercise of the power to borrow money? The obvious meaning of the power to borrow money is that of accepting it from and stipulating payment to those who are able and willing to lend.

To say that the power to borrow involves a power of creating the ability, where there may be the will, to lend, is not only establishing a dangerous principle, as will be immediately shown, but is as forced a construction as to say that it involves the power of compelling the will where there may be the ability to lend.

The third clause is that which gives the power to pass all laws necessary and proper to execute the specified powers.

Whatever meaning this clause may have, none can be admitted that would give an unlimited discretion to Congress.

Its meaning must, according to the natural and obvious force of the terms and the context, be limited to means necessary to the end and incident to the nature of the specified powers.

The clause is in fact merely declaratory of what would have resulted by unavoidable implication, as the appropriate and, as it were, technical means of executing those powers. In this sense it has been explained by the friends of the Constitution, and ratified by the State Conventions.

The essential characteristic of the Government as composed of limited and enumerated powers would be destroyed, if instead of direct and incidental means, any means could be used which, in the language of the preamble to the bill, "might be conceived to be conducive to the successful conducting of the finances, or might be conceived to tend to give facility to the obtaining of loans." He [Madison] urged an attention to the diffuse and ductile terms which had been found requisite to cover the stretch of power contained in the bill. He compared them with the terms necessary and proper, used in the Constitution, and asked whether it was possible to view the two descriptions as synonymous, or the one as a fair and safe commentary on the other.

If, proceeded he, Congress, by virtue of the power to borrow, can create the means of lending and in pursuance of these means can incorporate a Bank, they may do any thing whatever creative of like means . . .

If, again, Congress by virtue of the power to borrow money can create the ability to lend, they may by virtue of the power to levy money create the ability to pay it. The ability to pay taxes depends on the general wealth of the society, and this on the general prosperity of agriculture, manufactures, and commerce. Congress then may give bounties and make regulations on all of these objects.

The States have, it is allowed on all hands, a concurrent right to lay and collect taxes. This power is secured to them, not by its being expressly reserved, but by its not being ceded by the Constitution. The reasons for the bill cannot be admitted because they would invalidate that right; why may it not be conceived by Congress that a uniform and exclusive imposition of taxes would not less than the proposed Banks "be conducive to the successful conducting of the national finances, and tend to give facility to the obtaining of revenue, for the use of the Government"?

The doctrine of implication is always a tender one. The danger of it has been felt in other Governments. The delicacy was felt in the adoption of our own; the danger may also be felt, if we do not keep close to our chartered authorities.

Mark the reasoning on which the validity of the bill depends! To borrow money is made the end, and the accumulation of capitals implied as the means. The accumulation of capitals is then the end, and a Bank implied as the means. The Bank is then the end, and a charter of incorporation, a monopoly, capital punishments, &c., implied as the means.

If implications, thus remote and thus multiplied, can be linked together, a chain may be formed that will reach every object of legislation, every object within the whole compass of political economy.

The latitude of interpretation required by the bill is condemned by the rule furnished by the Constitution itself.

Congress have power "to regulate the value of money"; yet it is expressly added, not left to be implied, that counterfeiters may be punished.

They have the power "to declare war," to which armies are more incident than incorporated banks to borrowing; yet the power "to raise and support armies" is expressly added; and to this again, the express power "to make rules and regulations for the government of armies"; a like remark is applicable to the powers as to the navy.

The regulation and calling out of the militia are more appertinent to war than the proposed Bank to borrowing; yet the former is not left to construction.

The very power to borrow money is a less remote implication from the power of war than an incorporated monopoly Bank from the power of borrowing; yet, the power to borrow is not left to implication.

It is not pretended that every insertion or omission in the Constitution is the effect of systematic attention. This is not the character of any human work, particularly the work of a body of men. The examples cited, with others that might be added, sufficiently inculcate, nevertheless, a rule of interpretation very different from that on which the bill rests. They condemn the exercise of any power, particularly a great and important power, which is not evidently and necessarily involved in an express power.

. . . [T]he power of incorporation exercised in the bill could never be deemed an accessory or subaltern power, to be deduced by implication, as a means of executing another power; it was in its nature a distinct, an independent and substantive prerogative, which not being enumerated in the Constitution, could never have been meant to be included in it, and not being included, could never be rightfully exercised.

He [Madison] here adverted to a distinction, which he said had not been sufficiently kept in view, between a power necessary and proper for the Government or Union and a power necessary and proper for executing the enumerated powers. In the latter case, the powers included in the enumerated powers were not expressed, but to be drawn from the nature of each. In the former, the powers composing the Government were expressly enumerated. This constituted the peculiar nature of the Government; no power, therefore, not enumerated could be inferred from the general nature of Government. Had the power of making treaties, for example, been omitted, however necessary it might have been, the defect could only have been lamented, or supplied by an amendment of the Constitution . . .

It appeared on the whole, he [Madison] concluded, that the power exercised by the bill was condemned by the silence of the Constitution; was condemned by the rule of interpretation arising out of the Constitution; was condemned by its tendency to destroy the main characteristic of the Constitution; was condemned by the expositions of the friends of the Constitution, whilst depending before the public; was condemned by the apparent intention of the parties which ratified the Constitution; was condemned by the explanatory amendments proposed by Congress themselves to the Constitution; and he hoped it would receive its final condemnation by the vote of this House.

Fisher Ames
Speech in the U.S. House of Representatives
(February 3, 1791)[55]

...In making this reply I am to perform a task for which my own mind has not admonished me to prepare. I never suspected that the objections I have heard stated had existence; I consider them as discoveries; and had not the acute penetration of that gentleman brought them to light, I am sure that my own understanding would never have suggested them...

Two questions occur; may Congress exercise any powers which are not expressly given in the Constitution, but may be deduced by a reasonable construction of that instrument? And, secondly, will such a construction warrant the establishment of the bank?

The doctrine that powers may be implied which are not expressly vested in Congress has long been a bugbear to a great many worthy persons. They apprehend that Congress, by putting constructions upon the Constitution, will govern by its own arbitrary discretion; and therefore that it ought to be bound to exercise the powers expressly given, and those only.

If Congress may not make laws conformably to the powers plainly implied, though not expressed in the frame of Government, it is rather late in the day to adopt it as a principle of conduct. A great part of our two years labor is lost, and worse than lost to the public, for we have scarcely made a law in which we have not exercised our discretion with regard to the true intent of the Constitution. Any words but those used in that instrument will be liable to a different interpretation. We may regulate trade; therefore we have taxed ships, erected lighthouses, made laws to govern seamen, &c., because we say that they are the incidents to that power. The most familiar and undisputed acts of Legislation will show that we have adopted it as a safe rule of action to legislate beyond the letter of the Constitution.

He [Ames] proceeded to enforce this idea by several considerations, and illustrated it by various examples. He said that the ingenuity of man was unequal to providing, especially beforehand, for all the contingencies that would happen. The Constitution contains the principles which are to govern in making laws; but every law requires an application of the rule to the case in question. We may err in applying it; but we are to exercise our judgments, and on every occasion to decide according to an honest conviction of its true meaning.

The danger of implied power does not arise from its assuming a new principle; we have not only practised it often, but we can scarcely proceed without it; nor does the danger proceed so much from the extent of the power as from its uncertainty. While the opposers of the bank exclaim against the exercise of this power by Congress, do they mark out the limits of the power which they will leave to us with more certainty than is done by the advocates of the bank? Their rules of interpretation by contemporaneous testimony, the debates of Conventions and the doctrine of substantive and auxiliary powers, will be found as obscure, and of course as formidable as that which they condemn; they only set up one construction against another.

The powers of Congress are disputed. We are obliged to decide the question according to truth. The negative, if false, is less safe than the affirmative, if true. Why, then, shall we be told that the negative is the safe side? Not exercising the powers we have may be as pernicious as usurping those we have not. If the power to raise armies had not been expressed in the enumeration of the powers of Congress, it would be implied from other parts of the Constitution. Suppose, however, that it were omitted and our country invaded, would a decision in Congress against raising armies be safer than the affirmative? The blood of our citizens would be shed and shed unavenged. He [Ames] thought, therefore, that there was too much prepossession with some against the Bank and that the debate ought to be considered more impartially, as the negative was neither more safe, certain, nor conformable to our duty than the other side of the question. After all, the proof of the affirmative imposed a sufficient burden, as it is easier to raise objections than to remove them. Would any one doubt that Congress may lend money, that they may buy their debt in the market, or redeem their captives from Algiers? Yet no such power is expressly given, though it is irresistibly implied. . .

Congress may do what is necessary to the end for which the Constitution was adopted, provided it is not repugnant to the natural rights of man or to those which they have expressly reserved to themselves or to the powers which are assigned to the States. This rule of interpretation seems to be safe, and not a very uncertain one, independently of the Constitution itself. By that instrument certain powers are specially delegated, together with all powers necessary or proper to carry them into execution. That construction may be maintained to be a safe one which promotes the good of the society, and the ends for which the Government was adopted, without impairing the rights of any man, or the power of any State . . .

Despite Madison's efforts, Congress passed the bank bill and sent it to President George Washington. Washington formally requested the opinions of Hamilton, Secretary of State Thomas Jefferson, and Attorney General Edmund Randolph on the bank's constitutionality. Jefferson's and Hamilton's opinions subsequently were regarded as classic expositions of, respectively, the narrow and broad interpretations of congressional power. (Randolph's opinion, not reproduced in this volume, basically agreed with Jefferson's.)

Thomas Jefferson
Opinion on the Constitutionality
of the Bill for Establishing a National Bank
(February 15, 1791)[56]

The bill for establishing a national bank undertakes, among other things:

1. To form the subscribers into a corporation.

2. To enable them in their corporate capacities to receive grants of land; and so far is against the laws of mortmain.

3. To make alien subscribers capable of holding lands; and so far is against the laws of alienage.

4. To transmit these lands, on the death of a proprietor, to a certain line of successors; and so far changes the course of descents.

5. To put the lands out of the reach of forfeiture or escheat; and so far is against the laws of forfeiture and escheat.

6. To transmit personal chattels to successors in a certain line; and so far is against the laws of distribution.

7. To give them [the bank's stockholders and managers] the sole and exclusive right of banking under the national authority; and so far is against the laws of monopoly.

8. To communicate to them a power to make laws paramount to the laws of the states; for so they must be construed, to protect the institution from the control of the state legislature; and so, probably, they will be construed.

I consider the foundation of the Constitution as laid on this ground: That "all powers not delegated to the United States, by the Constitution, nor prohibited by it to the states, are reserved to the states or to the people." To take a single step beyond the boundaries thus specially drawn around the powers of Congress is to take possession of a boundless field of power, no longer susceptible of any definition.

The incorporation of a bank, and the powers assumed by this bill, have not, in my opinion, been delegated to the United States by the Constitution.

1. They are not among the powers specially enumerated; for these are:

First, a power to lay taxes for the purpose of paying the debts of the United States; but no debt is paid by this bill, nor any tax laid. Were it a bill to raise money, its origination in the Senate would condemn it by the Constitution.

Second, "to borrow money." But this bill neither borrows money nor insures the borrowing it. The proprietors of the bank will be just as free as any other moneyholders to lend or not to lend their money to the public. The operation proposed in the bill, first, to lend them $2,000,000, and then to borrow them back again, cannot change the nature of the latter act, which will still be a payment and not a loan, call it by what name you please.

Third, to "regulate commerce with foreign nations, and among the states, and with the Indian tribes." To erect a bank and to regulate commerce are very different acts. He who erects a bank creates a subject of commerce in its bills; so does he who makes a bushel of wheat or digs a dollar out of the mines; yet neither of these persons regulates commerce thereby. To make a thing which may be bought and sold is not to prescribe regulations for buying and selling. Besides, if this was an exercise of the power of regulating commerce, it would be void, as extending as much to the internal commerce of every state as to its external.

For the power given to Congress by the Constitution does not extend to the internal regulation of the commerce of a state (that is to say of the commerce between citizen and citizen), which remain exclusively with its own legislature; but to its external commerce only, that is to say, its commerce with another state, or with foreign nations, or with the Indian tribes. Accordingly the bill does not propose the measure as a regulation of trade, but as "productive of considerable advantages to trade." Still less are these powers covered by any other of the special enumerations.

2. Nor are they within either of the general phrases, which are the two following:

First, to lay taxes to provide for the general welfare of the United States, that is to say, "to lay taxes for *the purpose* of providing for the general welfare." For the laying of taxes is the *power*, and the general welfare the *purpose* for which the power is to be exercised. They are not to lay taxes *ad libitum* [at pleasure] *for any purpose they please but only to pay the debts or provide for the welfare of the Union*. In like manner, they are not *to do anything they please* to provide for the general welfare but only to *lay taxes* for that purpose. To consider the latter phrase, not as describing the purpose of the first but as giving a distinct and independent power to do any act they please which might be for the good of the Union, would render all the preceding and subsequent enumerations of power completely useless.

It would reduce the whole instrument to a single phrase, that of instituting a Congress with power to do whatever would be for the good of the United States; and, as they would be the sole judges of the good or evil, it would be also a power to do whatever evil they please.

It is an established rule of construction where a phrase will bear either of two meanings to give it that which will allow some meaning to the other parts of the instrument and not that which would render all the others useless. Certainly no such universal power was meant to be given them. It was intended to lace them up straitly within the enumerated powers, and those without which, as means, these powers could not be carried into effect. It is known that the very power now proposed *as a means* was rejected *as an end* by the Convention which formed the Constitution. A proposition was made to them to authorize Congress to open canals, and an amendatory one to empower them to incorporate. But the whole was rejected, and one of the reasons for rejection urged in debate was that then they would have a power to erect a bank, which would render the great cities, where there were prejudices and jealousies on the subject, adverse to the reception of the Constitution.

Second. The second general phrase is "to make all laws necessary and proper for carrying into execution the enumerated powers." But they can all be carried into execution without a bank. A bank therefore is not necessary and consequently not authorized by this phrase.

It has been urged that a bank will give great facility or convenience in the collection of taxes. Suppose this were true; yet the Constitution allows only the means which are "necessary," not those which are merely "convenient" for effecting the enumerated powers. If such a latitude of construction be allowed to this phrase as to give any nonenumerated power, it will go to every one, for there is not one which ingenuity may not torture into a convenience in some instance or other, to some one of so long a list of enumerated powers. It would swallow up all the delegated powers and reduce the whole to one power, as before observed. Therefore it was that the Constitution restrained them to the necessary means, that is to say, to those means without which the grant of power would be nugatory . . .

Can it be thought that the Constitution intended that for a shade or two of *convenience*, more or less, Congress should be authorized to break down the most ancient and fundamental laws of the several states; such as those against mortmain, the laws of alienage, the rules of descent, the acts of distribution, the laws of escheat and forfeiture, the laws of monopoly? Nothing but a necessity invincible by any other means can justify such a prostitution of laws, which constitute the pillars of our whole system of jurisprudence. Will Congress be too straitlaced to carry the Constitution into honest effect, unless they may pass over the foundation laws of the state government for the slightest convenience of theirs?

The negative of the President is the shield provided by the Constitution to protect against the invasions of the legislature: (1) the right of the executive; (2) of the judiciary; (3) of the states and state legislatures. The present is the case of a right remaining exclusively with the states, and consequently one of those intended by the Constitution to be placed under its protection.

It must be added, however, that unless the President's mind on a view of everything which is urged for and against this bill is tolerably clear that it is unauthorized by the Constitution; if the pro and con hang so even as to balance his judgment, a just respect for the wisdom of the legislature would naturally decide the balance in favor of their opinion. It is chiefly for cases where they are clearly misled by error, ambition, or interest that the Constitution has placed a check in the negative of the President.

Alexander Hamilton
Opinion on the Constitutionality of an Act to Establish a Bank (February 23, 1791)[57]

. . . [My] chief solicitude arises from a firm persuasion, that principles of construction like those espoused by the Secretary of State and the Attorney General would be fatal to the just & indispensable authority of the United States.

In entering upon the argument it ought to be premised, that the objections of the Secretary of State and Attorney General are founded on a general denial of the authority of the United States to erect corporations. The latter indeed expressly admits, that if there be any thing in the bill which is not warranted by the constitution, it is the clause of incorporation.

Now it appears to the Secretary of the Treasury, that this *general principle is inherent* in the very *definition* of *Government* and *essential* to every step of the progress to be made by that of the United States; namely—that every power vested in a Government is in its nature *sovereign*, and includes by *force* of the *term*, a right to employ all the *means* requisite, and fairly *applicable* to the attainment of the *ends* of such power; and which are not precluded by restrictions & exceptions specified in the constitution; or not immoral, or not contrary to the essential ends of political society.

This principle in its application to Government in general would be admitted as an axiom. And it will be incumbent upon those, who may incline to deny it, to *prove* a distinction; and to shew that a rule which in the general system of things is essential to the preservation of the social order is inapplicable to the United States.

The circumstances that the powers of sovereignty are in this country divided between the National and State Governments, does not afford the distinction required. It does not follow from this, that each of the *portions* of powers delegated to the one or to the other is not sovereign *with regard to its proper objects*. It will only *follow* from it, that each has sovereign power as to *certain things*, and not as to *other things*. To deny that the Government of the United States has sovereign power as to its declared purpose & trusts, because its power does not extend to all cases, would be equally to deny, that the State Governments have sovereign power in any case; because their power does not extend to every case. The tenth section of the first article of the constitution exhibits a long list of very important things which they may not do. And thus the United States would furnish the singular spectacle of a *political society* without *sovereignty*, or of a people *governed* without *government*.

If it would be necessary to bring proof to a proposition so clear as that which affirms that the powers of the federal government, *as to its objects*, are sovereign, there is a clause of its constitution which would be decisive. It is that which declares, that the constitution and the laws of the United States made in pursuance of it, and all treaties made or which shall be made under their authority shall be the supreme law of the land. The power which can create the *Supreme law* of the land, in any case, is doubtless sovereign *as to such case*.

This general & indisputable principle puts at once an end to the *abstract* question— Whether the United States have power to *erect a corporation?* that is to say, to give a *legal or artificial capacity* to one or more persons, distinct from the natural. For it is unquestionably incident to *sovereign power* to erect corporations, and consequently to *that* of the United States, in *relation to the objects* intrusted to the management of the government. The difference is this—where the authority of the government is general, it can create corporations in *all cases*; where it is confined to certain branches of legislation, it can create corporations only in those cases.

Here then as far as concerns the reasonings of the Secretary of State & the Attorney General, the affirmative of the constitutionality of the bill might be permitted to rest. It will occur to the President that the principle here advanced has been untouched by either of them.

For a more complete elucidation of the point nevertheless, the arguments which they have used against the power of the government to erect corporations, however foreign they are to the great & fundamental rule which has been stated, shall be particularly examined. And after shewing that they do not tend to impair its force, it shall also be shewn, that the power of incorporation incident to the government in certain cases, does fairly extend to the particular case which is the object of the bill.

The first of these arguments is, that the foundation of the constitution is laid on this ground "that all powers not delegated to the United States by the Constitution nor prohibited to it by the States are reserved to the States or to the people," whence it is meant to be inferred, that congress can in no case exercise any power not included in those enumerated in the constitution. And it is affirmed that the power of erecting a corporation is not included in any of the enumerated powers.

The main proposition here laid down, in its true signification, is not to be questioned. It is nothing more than a consequence of this republican maxim, that all government is a delegation of power. But how much is delegated in each case, is a question of fact to be made out by fair reasoning & construction upon the particular provisions of the constitution—taking as guides the general principles & general ends of government.

It is not denied, that there are *implied*, as well as *express* powers, and that the former are as effectually delegated as the latter. And for the sake of accuracy it shall be mentioned, that there is another class of powers, which may be properly denominated *resulting* powers. It will not be doubted that if the United States should make a conquest of any of the territories of its neighbours, they would possess sovereign jurisdiction over the conquered territory. This would rather be a result from the whole mass of the powers of the government & from the nature of political society, than a consequence of either of the powers specially enumerated.

But be this as it may, it furnishes a striking illustration of the general doctrine contended for. It shews an extensive case, in which a power of erecting corporations is either implied in, or would result from some or all of the powers, vested in the National Government. The jurisdiction acquired over such conquered territory would certainly be competent to every species of legislation.

To return—It is conceded, that implied powers are to be considered as delegated equally with express ones.

Then it follows, that as a power of erecting a corporation may as well be *implied* as any other thing; it may as well be employed as an *instrument* or *mean* of carrying into execution any of the specified powers, as any other instrument or mean whatever. The only question must be, in this as in every other case, whether the mean to be employed, or in this instance the corporation to be erected, has a natural relation to any of the acknowledged objects or lawful ends of the government. Thus a corporation may not be erected by congress, for superintending the police of the city of Philadelphia because they are not authorised to *regulate* the *police* of that city; but one may be erected in relation to the collection of the taxes, or to the trade with foreign countries, or to the trade between the States, or with the Indian Tribes, because it is the province of the federal government to regulate those objects & because it is incident to a general *sovereign* or *legislative power* to *regulate* a thing, to employ all the means which relate to its regulation to the *best & greatest advantage*.

A strange fallacy seems to have crept into the manner of thinking & reasoning upon the subject. Imagination appears to have been unusually busy concerning it. An incorporation seems to have been regarded as some great, independent, substantive thing— as a political end of peculiar magnitude & moment; whereas it is truly to be considered as a *quality, capacity*, or *mean* to an end. Thus a mercantile company is formed with a certain capital for the purpose of carrying on a particular branch of business. Here the business to be prosecuted is the *end*; the association in order to form the requisite capital is the primary mean. Suppose that an incorporation were added to this; it would only be to add a new *quality* to that association; to give it an artificial capacity by which it would be enabled to prosecute the business with more safety & convenience . . .

To this mode of reasoning respecting the right of employing all the means requisite to the execution of the specified powers of the Government, it is objected that none but *necessary* & proper means are to be employed, & the Secretary of State maintains, that no means are to be considered as *necessary*, but those without which the grant of the power would be *nugatory*. Nay so far does he go in his restrictive interpretation of the word, as even to make the case of *necessity* which shall warrant the constitutional exercise of the power to depend on *casual & temporary* circumstances, an idea which alone refutes the construction. The *expediency* of exercising a particular power, at a particular time, must indeed depend on *circumstances*; but the constitutional right of exercising it must be uniform & invariable—the same today, as tomorrow . . .

It is essential to the being of the National government, that so erroneous a conception of the meaning of the word *necessary*, should be exploded.

It is certain, that neither the grammatical, nor popular sense of the term requires that construction. According to both, *necessary* often means no more than *needful, requisite, incidental, useful,* or *conducive to*. It is a common mode of expression to say, that it is *necessary* for a government or a person to do this or that thing, when nothing more is intended or understood, than that the interests of the government or person require, or will be promoted, by the doing of this or that thing. The imagination can be at no loss for exemplifications of the use of the word in this sense.

And it is the true one in which it is to be understood as used in the constitution. The whole turn of the clause containing it, indicates, that it was the intent of the convention, by that clause to give a liberal latitude to the exercise of the specified powers. The expressions have peculiar comprehensiveness. They are—"to make *all laws*, necessary & proper for *carrying into execution* the foregoing powers & all *other powers* vested by the constitution in the *government* of the United States, or in any *department* or *officer* thereof." To understand the word as the Secretary of State does, would be to depart from its obvious & popular sense, and to give it a *restrictive* operation; an idea never before entertained. It would be to give it the same force as if the word *absolutely* or *indispensibly* had been prefixed to it.

Such a construction would beget endless uncertainty & embarrassment. The cases must be palpable & extreme in which it could be pronounced with certainty, that a measure was absolutely necessary, or one without which the exercise of a given power would be nugatory. There are few measures of any government, which would stand so severe a test. To insist upon it, would be to make the criterion of the exercise of any implied power a *case of extreme necessity*; which is rather a rule to justify the over-leaping of the bounds of constitutional authority, than to govern the ordinary exercise of it.

It may be truly said of every government, as well as of that of the United States, that it has only a right, to pass such laws as are necessary & proper to accomplish the objects intrusted to it. For no government has a right to do *merely what it pleases*. Hence by a process of reasoning similar to that of the Secretary of State, it might be proved, that neither of the State governments has a right to incorporate a bank. It might be shewn, that all the public business of the State, could be performed without a bank, and inferring thence that it was unnecessary it might be argued that it could not be done, because it is against the rule which has been just mentioned. A like mode of reasoning would prove, that there was no power to incorporate the Inhabitants of a town, with a view to a more perfect police: For it is certain, that an incorporation may be dispensed with, though it is better to have one. It is to be remembered, that there is no *express* power in any State constitution to erect corporations.

The *degree* in which a measure is necessary, can never be a test of the *legal* right to adopt it. That must ever be a matter of opinion; and can only be a test of expediency. The *relation* between the *measure* and the *end*, between the *nature* of *the mean* employed towards the execution of a power and the object of that power, must be the criterion of constitutionality not the more or less of *necessity* or *utility*.

The practice of the government is against the rule of construction advocated by the Secretary of State. Of this the act concerning light houses, beacons, buoys & public piers, is a decisive example. This doubtless must be referred to the power of regulating trade, and is fairly relative to it. But it cannot be affirmed, that the exercise of that power, in this instance, was strictly necessary; or that the power itself would be *nugatory* without that of regulating establishments of this nature.

This restrictive interpretation of the word *necessary* is also contrary to this sound maxim of construction namely, that the powers contained in a constitution of government, especially those which concern the general administration of the affairs of a country, its finances, trade, defence &c ought to be construed liberally, in advancement of the public good. This rule does not depend on the particular form of a government or on the particular demarkation of the boundaries of its powers, but on the nature and objects of government itself. The means by which national exigencies are to be provided for, national inconveniencies obviated, national prosperity promoted, are of such infinite variety, extent and complexity, that there must, of necessity, be great latitude of discretion in the selection & application of those means. Hence consequently, the necessity & propriety of exercising the authorities intrusted to a government on principles of liberal construction . . .

The truth is that difficulties on this point are inherent in the nature of the federal constitution. They result inevitably from a division of the legislative power. The consequence of this division is, that there will be cases clearly within the power of the National Government; others clearly without its power; and a third class, which will leave room for controversy & difference of opinion, & concerning which a reasonable latitude of judgment must be allowed.

But the doctrine which is contended for is not chargeable with the consequence imputed to it. It does not affirm that the National government is sovereign in all respects, but that it is sovereign to a certain extent: that is, to the extent of the objects of its specified powers.

It leaves therefore a criterion of what is constitutional, and of what is not so. This criterion is the *end* to which the measure relates as a *mean*. If the end be clearly comprehended within any of the specified powers, & if the measure have an obvious relation to that end, and is not forbidden by any particular provision of the constitution—it may safely be deemed to come within the compass of the national authority. There is also this further criterion which may materially assist the decision. Does the proposed measure abridge a preexisting right of any State, or of any individual? If it does not, there is a strong presumption in favour of its constitutionality; & slighter relations to any declared object of the constitution may be permitted to turn the scale.

The general objections which are to be inferred from the reasonings of the Secretary of State and of the Attorney General to the doctrine which has been advanced, have been stated and it is hoped satisfactorily answered. Those of a more particular nature shall now be examined.

The Secretary of State introduces his opinion with an observation, that the proposed incorporation undertakes to create certain capacities, properties, or attributes which are *against* the laws of *alienage, descents, escheat* and *forfeiture, distribution* and *monopoly,* and to confer a power to make laws paramount to those of the States. And nothing says he, in another place, but a *necessity invincible by other means* can justify such a *prostration of laws* which constitute the pillars of our whole system of jurisprudence, and are the foundation laws of the State Governments.

If these are truly the foundation laws of the several states, then most of them have subverted their own foundations. For there is scarcely one of them which has not, since the establishment of its particular constitution, made material alternations in some of those branches of its jurisprudence especially the law of descents. But it is not conceived how any thing can be called the fundamental law of a State Government which is not established in its constitution unalterable by the ordinary legislature. And with regard to the question of necessity it has been shewn, that this can only constitute a question of expediency, not of right.

To erect a corporation is to substitute a *legal* or *artificial* to a *natural* person, and where a number are concerned to give them *individuality.* To that legal or artificial person once created, the common law of every state of itself *annexes* all those incidents and attributes, which are represented as a prostration of the main pillars of their jurisprudence. It is certainly not accurate to say, that the erection of a corporation is *against* those different *heads* of the State laws; because it is rather to create a kind of person or entity, to which *they* are inapplicable, and to which the general rule of those laws assign a different regimen. The laws of alienage cannot apply to an artificial person, because it can have no country. Those of descent cannot apply to it, because it can have no heirs. Those of escheat are foreign from it for the same reason. Those of forfeiture, because it cannot commit a crime.

Those of distribution, because, though it may be dissolved, it cannot die. As truly might it be said, that the exercise of the power of prescribing the rule by which foreigners shall be naturalised, is *against* the law of alienage; while it is in fact only to put them in a situation to cease to be the subject of that law. To do a thing which is *against* a law, is to do something which it forbids or which is a violation of it.

But if it were even to be admitted that the erection of a corporation is a direct alteration of the State laws in the enumerated particulars; it would do nothing towards proving that the measure was unconstitutional. If the government of the United States can do no act, which amounts to an alteration of a State law, all its powers are nugatory. For almost every new law is an alteration, in some way or other of an old *law*, either *common*, or *statute*.

There are laws concerning bankruptcy in some states—some states have laws regulating the values of foreign coins. Congress are empowered to establish uniform laws concerning bankruptcy throughout the United States, and to regulate the values of foreign coins. The exercise of either of these powers by Congress necessarily involves an alteration of the laws of those states.

Again: Every person by the common law of each state may export his property to foreign countries, at pleasure. But Congress, in pursuance of the power of regulating trade, may prohibit the exportation of commodities: in doing which, they would alter the common law of each state in abridgement of individual rights.

It can therefore never be good reasoning to say—this or that act is unconstitutional, because it alters this or that law of a State. It must be shewn, that the act which makes the alteration is unconstitutional on other accounts, not *because* it makes the alteration . . .

Another argument made use of by the Secretary of State, is, the rejection of a proposition by the convention to empower Congress to make corporations, either generally, or for some special purpose.

What was the precise nature or extent of this proposition, or what the reasons for refusing it, is not ascertained by any authentic document, or even by accurate recollection. As far as any such document exists, it specifies only canals. If this was the amount of it, it would at most only prove, that it was thought inexpedient to give a power to incorporate for the purpose of opening canals, for which purpose a special power would have been necessary; except with regard to the Western Territory, there being nothing in any part of the constitution respecting the regulation of canals. It must be confessed however, that very different accounts are given of the import of the proposition and of the motives for rejecting it. Some affirm that it was confined to the opening of canals and obstructions in rivers; others, that it embraced banks; and others, that it extended to the power of incorporating generally. Some again alledge, that it was disagreed to, because it was thought improper to vest in Congress a power of erecting corporations—others, because it was thought unnecessary to *specify* the power, and inexpedient to furnish an additional topic of objection to the constitution. In this state of the matter, no inference whatever can be drawn from it.

But whatever may have been the nature of the proposition or the reasons for rejecting it concludes nothing in respect to the real merits of the question. The Secretary of State will not deny, that whatever may have been the intention of the framers of a constitution, or of a law, that intention is to be sought for in the instrument itself, according to the usual & established rules of construction. Nothing is more common than for laws to *express* and *effect*, more or less than was intended. If then a power to erect a corporation, in any case, be deducible by fair inference from the whole or any part of the numerous provisions of the constitution of the United States, arguments drawn from extrinsic circumstances, regarding the intention of the convention, must be rejected . . .

There is an observation of the secretary of state to this effect, which may require notice in this place. Congress, says he, are not to lay taxes *ad libitum for any purpose they please*, but only to pay the debts, or provide for the *welfare* of the Union. Certainly no inference can be drawn from this against the power of applying their money for the institution of a bank. It is true, that they cannot without breach of trust, lay taxes for any other purpose than the general welfare but so neither can any other government. The welfare of the community is the only legitimate end for which money can be raised on the community. Congress can be considered as under only one restriction, which does not apply to other governments—They cannot rightfully apply the money they raise to any purpose *merely* or purely local. But with this exception they have as large a discretion in relation to the *application* of money as any legislature whatever. The constitutional *test* of a right application must always be whether it be for a purpose of *general* or *local* nature. If the former, there can be no want of constitutional power. The quality of the object, as how far it will really promote or not the welfare of the union, must be matter of conscientious discretion. And the arguments for or against a measure in this light, must be arguments concerning expediency or inexpediency, not constitutional right. Whatever relates to the general order of the finances, to the general interests of trade & being general objects are constitutional ones for *the application* of *money*.

A Bank then whose bills are to circulate in all the revenues of the country, is *evidently* a general object, and for that very reason a constitutional one as far as regards the appropriation of money to it. Whether it will really be a beneficial one, or not, is worthy of careful examination, but is no more a constitutional point, in the particular referred to than the question whether the western lands shall be sold for twenty or thirty cents per acre.

A hope is entertained, that it has by this time been made to appear, to the satisfaction of the President, that a bank has a natural relation to the power of collecting taxes; to that of borrowing money; to that of regulating trade; to that of providing for the common defence; and that as the bill under consideration contemplates the government in the light of a joint proprietor of the stock of the bank, it brings the case within the provision of the clause of the constitution which immediately respects the property of the United States.

Under a conviction that such a relation subsists, the Secretary of the Treasury, with all deference conceives, that it will result as a necessary consequence from the position, that all the specified powers of the government are sovereign as to the proper objects; that the incorporation of a bank is a constitutional measure, and that the objections taken to the bill, in this respect, are ill founded . . .

It is remarkable, that the State Conventions who have proposed amendments in relation to this point [on the power to regulate commerce], have most, if not all of them, expressed themselves nearly thus—"Congress shall not grant monopolies, nor *erect any company* with exclusive advantage of commerce;" thus at the same time expressing their sense, that the power to erect trading companies or corporations, was inherent in Congress, & objecting to it no further, than as to the grant of *exclusive* privileges.

The Secretary entertains all the doubts which prevail concerning the utility of such companies; but he cannot fashion to his own mind a reason to induce a doubt, that there is a constitutional authority in the United States to establish them. If such a reason were demanded, none could be given unless it were this—that congress cannot erect a corporation; which would be no better than to say they cannot do it, because they cannot do it: first presuming an inability, without reason, & then assigning that *inability* as the cause of itself.

Illustrations of this kind might be multiplied without end. They shall however be pursued no further.

There is a sort of evidence on this point, arising from an aggregate view of the constitution, which is of no inconsiderable weight. The very general power of laying & collecting taxes & appropriating their proceeds—that of borrowing money indefinitely—that of coining money & regulating foreign coins—that of making all needful rules and regulations respecting the property of the United States—these powers combined, as well as the reason & nature of the thing speak strongly this language: That it is the manifest design and scope of the constitution to vest in congress all the powers requisite to the effectual administration of the finances of the United States. As far as concerns this object, there appears to be no parsimony of power.

To suppose then, that the government is precluded from the employment of so usual as well as so important an instrument for the administration of its finances as that of a bank, is to suppose, what does not coincide with the general tenor & complexion of the constitution, and what is not agreeable to impressions that any mere spectator would entertain concerning it. Little less than a prohibitory clause can destroy the strong presumptions which result from the general aspect of the government. Nothing but demonstration should exclude the idea, that the power exists.

In all questions of this nature the practice of mankind ought to have great weight against the theories of Individuals.

The fact, for instance, that all the principal commercial nations have made use of trading corporations or companies for the purposes of *external commerce*, is a satisfactory proof, that the Establishment of them is an incident to the regulation of that commerce.

This other fact, that banks are an usual engine in the administration of national finances, & an ordinary & the most effectual instrument of loans & one which in this country has been found essential, pleads strongly against the supposition, that a government clothed with most of the most important prerogatives of sovereignty in relation to the revenues, its debts, its credit, its defence, its trade, its intercourse with foreign nations—is forbidden to make use of that instrument as an appendage to its own authority.

It has been stated as an auxiliary test of constitutional authority, to try, whether it abridges any preexisting right of any state, or any Individual. The proposed incorporation will stand the most severe examination on this point. Each state may still erect as many banks as it pleases; every individual may still carry on the banking business to any extent he pleases.

Another criterion may be this, whether the institution or thing has a more direct relation as to its uses, to the objects of the reserved powers of the State Governments, than to those of the powers delegated by the United States. This rule indeed is less precise than the former, but it may still serve as some guide. Surely a bank has more reference to the objects entrusted to the national government, than to those, left to the care of the State Governments. The common defence is decisive in this comparison.

Comments

Less than three years after the Constitution's ratification, the debate over the national bank bill revealed the existence of fundamental disagreement over the nature of American constitutionalism. In their attack on the bill, Madison and Jefferson relied on a central theme of Revolutionary-era political thought: the unceasing struggle between power and liberty. The precious but fragile possession of liberty could only be preserved by exercise of a careful awareness of the "delicacy" and "danger" involved in acknowledging the legitimacy of power. The very point of a written Constitution was to confine the restless urges of those with authority, "to lace them up straitly" within the enumerated powers. Much of the political influence of anti-federalist politicians in the 1790s stemmed from their success in evoking these old fears of unbounded power.

Despite their common allegiance to the Whig equation of liberty with restraint on government power, Madison and Jefferson took significantly different approaches to attacking the bank bill. For Madison, the "essential," defining characteristic of the Constitution was that it created a federal government of limited and enumerated powers. The government's limited nature was its "peculiar" characteristic: it rightfully could exercise only "particular powers" that had been carved out of a "general mass" that remained under state authority. This image of a great body of government power from which the Constitution extracted a limited set of competences to delegate to the federal government was to play an important role in later constitutional discourse.

The enumerated nature of federal power rested on its intrinsic link to the text of the Constitution. The most fundamental virtue of constitutional morality, Madison believed, was to "keep close to our chartered authorities." In part, this was a clear allusion to the colonial American struggle to confine governors and the Crown within the authority recognized by the provincial charters (as interpreted by Americans!). For Madison, however, more was involved. American constitutionalism, he insisted in 1791 and consistently thereafter, is at its heart a discourse of textual interpretation, proceeding by close attention to the details of the text and by the use of traditional legal methods of documentary interpretation.

In this view, it was essential that interpretation preserve, and not destroy, "the very characteristic of the Government"; in other words, the interpreter must maintain the limits on federal power and respect the textual definition of that power. Unlike some later textualists, Madison recognized and expressly acknowledged what may be called the doctrine of "the omitted case." A written Constitution that grants limited powers may have denied the government it created powers that the polity needs for its own well-being. But no matter how "necessary and proper for the Government or Union" a power might be, unless justified by proper exegesis of the constitutional text it could not be rightfully exercised. Federal power should not be inferred from "the general nature of Government." Indeed, the more important a nonenumerated power, the stronger the presumption against its existence.

Jefferson, in contrast, located the central theme of the Constitution in a presumption against federal power. Quoting the Tenth Amendment as "the foundation of the Constitution," he reasoned that the fact federal power was delegated meant that it was to be strictly limited. Congress could not legislate in the absence of express authorization, and implied powers were to be limited to "those means without which the [express] power would be nugatory."

Jefferson's essentially negative constitutionalism stemmed from two rather different sources. The first was his opposition to a centralizing view of the federal government. His opinion began and ended with a careful recitation of the state laws that, he argued, the bank bill would abridge. Because the state laws Jefferson claimed the bank bill would affect were concerned for the most part with real estate, they were well calculated to alarm a wealthy landowner such as Washington. Jefferson's implication was that the bank bill as well as Hamilton's program in general were a threat to the landed gentry's control of its primary resource and basis of power. Jefferson, it should be noted, was not a conservative defender of traditional land law, but rather a vigorous critic of legal rules such as primogeniture and the fee tail. His objection to interference with those rules was not based on a quixotic jurisprudential opposition to change, as Hamilton slyly suggested at one point, but rather to the transfer of authority from the states to an aggressive central government.

Jefferson's second basic concern was a deep suspicion of governmental discretion: "To take a single step beyond the boundaries thus specially drawn around the powers of Congress is to take possession of a boundless field of power, no longer susceptible of any definition." *Either* federal power was strictly defined by the text *or* it was limited only by the good faith and wisdom of Congress: there was no middle ground. To accord the federal government a general power "to do whatever would be for the good of the United States" would permit and require it to act at its discretion ("do any act they please"). For Jefferson, as for earlier Whigs, such governmental discretion was a key part of the very definition of tyranny: "as they would be the sole judges of the good or evil, it would also be a power to do whatever evil they please." The bank bill itself illustrated the results, in that by it Congress had determined "to break down . . . the pillars of our whole system of jurisprudence" for "the slightest convenience of theirs."

The approach Ames and Hamilton took to the Constitution was the polar opposite of Jefferson's, and distant from Madison's. For Jefferson, discretion in the exercise of legislative power meant the oppressive ability to act lawlessly, as the legislators wished; for Ames and Hamilton, discretion was the power to select the appropriate means to achieve lawful ends. Ames dismissed the charge that a generous construction of congressional power meant that Congress "will govern by its own arbitrary discretion" as "a bugbear," resting on a fundamental misunderstanding of the Constitution's nature. The impossibility of determining at any one point in time the future needs of the nation meant that the Constitution could not be an exhaustive list of federal powers; it was, rather, the set of "principles which are to govern in making laws." Because general principles do not decide specific cases, Ames concluded, legislative discretion in constitutional interpretation was simply unavoidable, and Congress in fact had acted on this premise from the beginning.

Ames flatly rejected any claim that accepting congressional discretion in the exercise of its powers opened the door to arbitrary government. The exercise of an implied power, he asserted, must first survive the test of congressional debate, where its proponents would bear the burden of proving its legitimacy—and in any event would be unconstitutional if it violated express constitutional restrictions or "the natural rights of man." (Ames did not explain who would define or enforce these restrictions.) The possibility of disagreement over the constitutionality of a given legislative proposal was the necessary consequence of the necessary exercise of discretion, and Madison's elaborate interpretive canons could not eliminate it: Madison, he said, "only set[s] up one construction against another."

Ames directly attacked two key themes of Madison's speech. Madison's underlying presumption that power was inimical to freedom, and thus suspect, was false. It could be "as pernicious" not to exercise legitimate authority as to usurp power. Rejecting a presumption against implied powers, Ames argued that the "safe" rule of interpretation was to recognize congressional authority to do whatever "promotes the good of the society, and the ends for which the Government was adopted" so long as reserved personal rights and state powers were not impaired. Ames also repudiated the notion of the "omitted case": if the constitutional text omitted a power necessary to the national welfare, the existence of that power could and should be exercised anyway as "irresistably implied."

Hamilton's defense of the bank bill and of legislative discretion in the exercise of unenumerated powers took a rhetorically different tack. The cornerstone of Jefferson's opinion—his derivation of a presumption against the legitimacy of implied powers from the principle of delegated federal authority—was false according to Hamilton. The principle, to be sure, was true, but was simply a specific instance of the "republican maxim, that *all* government is a delegation of power." No inference as to the (non) existence of a given power could be drawn from such an abstract political truth. The proper starting point in analyzing a question of implied power was instead the recognition that all governmental powers are by definition sovereign, and that sovereignty invariably carries with it discretion in the exercise of power. The American division of authority between states and nation did not affect the federal government's sovereignty, but merely limited its proper objects to those entrusted to it. Congress's choice of a particular means of accomplishing its legitimate goals, incorporating a bank for example, could raise only issues of expediency, and thus of political opinion and judgment, not questions of constitutional authority. Jefferson's attack on legislative discretion was thus an attack on government itself.

Hamilton treated similarly Jefferson's attempt to limit strictly the objects of federal concern. Rather than viewing congressional power as a threat to freedom, Hamilton saw it as the servant of national needs. The Constitution's delegations of power therefore should be "construed liberally in advancement of the public good." Unless expressly prohibited or politically "immoral," any implied power could be exercised that possessed an "obvious" or "natural" relationship to the government's enumerated ends. Those ends, furthermore, were not a collection of individual goals to be defined in isolation from one another. They formed, instead, a connected whole, from which the interpreter should infer not only discretion in their implementation, but also the existence of further legitimate ends, which Hamilton called "resulting powers" because they were implied by "the whole mass of the powers of the government [and by] the nature of political society." There were no "omitted cases" in matters of national concern and importance. As his opponents realized, Hamilton's insistence that the federal government was limited in its ends (though not in its choice of means) was significantly undercut by his willingness to take "an aggregate view of the constitution" and of the responsibilities of the federal government.

Hamilton also identified and attacked the anti-centralizing theme in Jefferson's opinion. While he denied that the bank bill interfered with the states' laws, he insisted that, even if it did, this fact would raise no constitutional problem. The exercise of federal power frequently and legitimately would displace state law. Although Congress could not address legitimately issues *"merely* or purely local" (Hamilton gave as an example the maintenance of law and order on the municipal level), even that question "must be a matter of conscientious discretion."

The debate over the bank bill foreshadowed much of the later course of constitutional discussion. Jefferson's constitutionalism, and to a lesser degree Madison's, derived from the English "Country" tradition and the colonial past a general suspicion of power as well as a specific fear of centralizing government. The proper response to these concerns, in the view of Jefferson and Madison, was to insist on a stringent and lawyerly parsing of the constitutional text and to defend the autonomy of state power within its own sphere. Jefferson in particular suggested that legitimate federal power could be sharply distinguished from those powers retained by the states.

All these themes—textualism, localism, the division of power into rigid categories, and the implicit equation of constitutional discourse with legal argument—are characteristic of one pole in later debate.

Ames and Hamilton, in contrast, were united by a vision of national government as the vehicle of public safety and prosperity. Although Hamilton in particular was careful to address Jefferson's interpretive arguments, neither he nor Ames understood constitutionalism fundamentally as a matter of construing a text. It was for them instead a mode of organizing and facilitating the beneficent activities of government. To the opposition's constitutional law of suspicion, the centralizers posed a constitutional philosophy of energetic government. The difference between these visions of the Constitution is perhaps most striking in their contrasting understanding of time. Madison and Jefferson applied to the 1787 text one of the central themes of English political rhetoric: the notion of "the ancient Constitution" threatened by the innovations of the power-hungry. Ames and Hamilton stressed the Constitution's orientation to an unpredictable future and ridiculed invocations of ratification-era discussions as "obscure" (Ames on Madison) or flatly contrary to "the usual & established rules of construction" (Hamilton on Jefferson's reference to events at the Philadelphia convention).

Two

The Place of the Judiciary in American Constitutionalism

Section A: *The Suability of the States*

Section two of article three of the Constitution states that "The judicial power shall extend . . . to controversies . . . between a State and citizens of another State," and section three provides that in "all cases . . . in which a State shall be a party, the Supreme Court shall have original jurisdiction." The two provisions, read together, suggested that a citizen of one state could sue another state without its consent in the Supreme Court, though the Constitution's supporters during the ratification struggle sometimes had denied this to be the case. Subjection of the states to federal judicial process was controversial in the 1790s both on theoretical grounds—if the Constitution abolished the states' traditional sovereign immunity, had it abolished their sovereignty entirely?—and for the extremely practical reason that many states were heavily endebted. Federal jurisdiction over debt actions against them could have a radical impact on their finances. It is unsurprising, therefore, that the federal Supreme Court's first great case involved its jurisdiction over a debt action against an unwilling state.

Alexander Hamilton
The Federalist No. 81
(May 28, 1788)

. . . Though it may rather be a digression from the immediate subject of this paper. I shall take occasion to mention here a supposition which has excited some alarm upon very mistaken grounds. It has been suggested that an assignment of the public securities of one State to the citizens of another would enable them to prosecute that State in the federal courts for the amount of those securities; a suggestion which the following considerations prove to be without foundation.

It is inherent in the nature of sovereignty not to be amenable to the suit of an individual without its consent. This is the general sense and the general practice of mankind: and the exemption, as one of the attributes of sovereignty, is now enjoyed by the government of every State in the Union. Unless, therefore, there is a surrender of this immunity in the plan of the convention, it will remain with the States, and the danger intimated must be merely ideal. The circumstances which are necessary to produce an alienation of State sovereignty were discussed in considering the article ot taxation, and need not be repeated here. A recurrence to the principles there established will satisfy us that there is no colour to pretend that the State governments would by the adoption of that plan, be divested of the privilege of paying their own debts in their own way, free from every constraint but that which flows from the obligations of good faith. The contracts between a nation and individuals are only binding on the conscience of the sovereign and have no pretensions to a compulsive force. They confer no right of action independent of the sovereign will. To what purpose would it be to authorize suits against States for the debts they owe? How could recoveries be enforced? It is evident it could not be done without waging war against the contracting State; and to ascribe to the federal courts, by mere implication, and in destruction of a pre-existing right of the State governments, a power which would involve such a consequence, would be altogether forced and unwarrantable . . .

Chisholm v. Georgia
2 U.S. (2 Dall.) 419 (Feb. 18, 1793)

Chisholm v. Georgia **was brought by the South Carolina executors of a person who had supplied the state of Georgia with cloth during the Revolution and who had not been paid. The state's officials ignored the U.S. Supreme Court's process and refused even to enter an appearance by counsel. Attorney General Edmund Randolph, acting in his private capacity as the executors' attorney, argued the case alone.**

Randolph, for the Plaintiff:
. . . The Constitution vests a jurisdiction in the Supreme Court over a state, as a defendant, at the suit of a private citizen of another state. Consult the letter of the constitution, or rather the influential words of the clause in question. The judicial power is extended to controversies between a state and citizens of another state. I pass over the word, "between," as in no respect indicating who is to be plaintiff or who defendant. In the succeeding paragraph, we read a comment on these words, when it is said that in cases, in which a state shall be a party, the Supreme Court shall have original jurisdiction. Is not a defendant a party as well as a plaintiff? . . . The order in this instance, works no difference. In common language too, it would not violate the substantial idea, if a controversy, said to be between A.B. and C.D. should appear to be between C.D. and A.B. Nay the opportunity fairly occurs in two pages of the judicial article, to confine suits to states, as plaintiffs; but they are both neglected, notwithstanding the consciousness which the convention must have possessed, that the words unqualified, strongly tended at least to subject states as defendants.

With the advantage of the letter on our side let us now advert to the spirit of the constitution, or rather its genuine and necessary interpretation. I am aware of the danger of going into a wide history of the constitution, as a guide of construction; and of the still greater danger of laying any important stress upon the preamble as explanatory of its powers. I resort therefore, to the body of it; which shows that there may be various actions of states which are to be annulled. If, for example, a state shall suspend the privilege of a writ of *habeas corpus*, unless when in cases of rebellion or invasion the public safety may require it; should pass a bill of *attainder* or *ex post facto* law; should enter into any treaty, alliance, or confederation; should grant letters of marque and reprisal; should coin money; should emit bills of credit; should make anything but gold and silver coin tender in payment of debts; should pass a law impairing the obligation of contracts; should without the consent of congress lay imposts or duties on imports or exports, with certain exceptions; should, without the consent of congress, lay any duty on tonnage, or keep troops or ships of war in time of peace; these are expressly prohibited by the constitution; and thus is announced to the world the probability, but certainly the apprehension, that states may injure individuals in their property, their liberty, and their lives; may oppress sister states; and may act in derogation of the general sovereignty.

Are states then to enjoy the high privilege of acting thus eminently wrong, without control; or does a remedy exist? The love of morality would lead us to wish that some check should be found; if the evil, which flows from it, be not too great for the good contemplated. The common law has established a principle, that no prohibitory act shall be without its vindicatory quality; or, in other words, that the infraction of a prohibitory law, although an express penalty be omitted, is still punishable. Government itself would be useless, if a pleasure to obey or transgress with impunity should be substituted in the place of a sanction to its laws. This was a just cause of complaint against the deceased confederation. In our solicitude for a remedy, we meet with no difficulty, where the conduct of a state can be animadverted on through the medium of an individual. For instance, without suing a state, a person arrested may be liberated by *habeas corpus*; a person attainted and a convict under an *ex post facto* law, may be saved; those, who offend against improper treaties, may be protected, or who execute them may be punished; the actors under letters of marque and reprisal may be mulcted; coinage, bills of credit, unwarranted tenders, and the impairing of contracts between individuals, may be annihilated. But this redress goes only half way; as some of the preceding unconstitutional actions must pass without censure unless states can be made defendants. What is to be done, if in consequence of a bill of attainder, or an *ex post facto* law, the estate of a citizen shall be confiscated, and deposited in the treasure of a state? What, if a state should adulterate or coin money below the constitutional standard, emit bills of credit, or enact unconstitutional tenders, for the purpose of extinguishing its own debts? What if a state should impair her own contracts? These evils, and others which might be enumerated like them, cannot be corrected without a suit against the state. It is not denied, that one state may be sued by another, and the reason would seem to be the same, why an individual who is aggrieved should sue the state aggrieving. A distinction between the cases is supportable only on a supposed comparative inferiority of the plaintiff. But, the framers of the constitution could never have thought thus. They must have viewed human rights in their essence, not in their mere form. They had heard, seen—I will say felt; that Legislators were not so far sublimed above other men, as to soar beyond the region of passion. Unfledged as America was in the vices of old governments, she had some incident to her own new situation; individuals had been victims to the oppression of states . . .

I acknowledge and shall always contend, that the states are sovereignties. But with the free will, arising from absolute independence, they might combine in government for their own happiness. Hence sprang the confederation; under which indeed the states retained their exemption from the forensic jurisdiction of each other, and except under a peculiar modification, of the United States themselves. Nor could this be otherwise; since such a jurisdiction was nowhere (according to the language of that instrument) expressly delegated. This government of supplication cried aloud for its own reform; and the public mind of America decided, that it must perish of itself, and that the union would be thrown into jeopardy, unless the energy of the general system should be increased. Then it was the present constitution produced a new order of things. It derives its origin immediately from the people; and the people individually are, under certain limitations, subject to the legislative, executive, and judicial authorities thereby established. The states are in fact assemblages of these individuals who are liable to process. The limitations, which the Federal government is admitted to impose upon their powers are diminutions of sovereignty, at least equal to the making of them defendants. It is not pretended, however, to deduce from these arguments alone, the amenability of states to judicial cognizance; but the result is, that there is nothing in the nature of sovereignties, combined as those of America are, to prevent the words of the constitution, if they naturally mean, what I have asserted, from receiving an easy and usual construction. But pursue the idea a step farther; and trace one, out of a multitude of examples, in which the general government may be convulsed to its centre with[out] this judicial power. If a state shall injure an individual of another state, the latter must protect him by a remonstrance. What if this be ineffectual? To stop there would cancel his allegiance, one state cannot sue another for such a cause;

acquiescence is not to be believed. The crest of war is next raised; the Federal head cannot remain unmoved amidst these shocks to the public harmony. Ought then a necessity to be created for drawing out the general force on an occasion so replete with horror? Is not an adjustment by a judicial form far preferable? Are not peace and concord among the states two of the great ends of the constitution? . . .

I hold it, therefore, to be no degradation of sovereignty, in the states, to submit to the supreme judiciary of the United States. At the same time, by way of anticipating an objection, I assert, that it will not follow from these premises, that the United States themselves may be sued. For the head of a confederacy is not within the reach of the judicial authorities of its inferior members. It is exempted by its peculiar preeminences . . .

Still we may be pressed with the final question: "What if the state is resolved to oppose the execution?" This would be an awful question indeed! He, to whose lot it should fall to solve it, would be impelled to invoke the god of wisdom to illuminate his decision. I will not believe that he would recall the tremendous examples of vengeance, which in past days have been inflicted by those who claim, against those who violate, authority. I will not believe that in the wide and gloomy theatre, over which his eye should roll, he might perchance catch a distant glimpse of the federal arm uplifted. Scenes like these are too full of horror, not to agitate, not to rack, the imagination. But at last we must settle on this result: there are many duties, precisely defined, which the states must perform. Let the remedy which is to be administered, if these should be disobeyed, be the remedy on the occasion, which we contemplate. The argument requires no more to be said; it surely does not require us to dwell on such painful possibilities. Rather, let me hope and pray, that not a single star in the American constellation will ever suffer its lustre to be diminished by hostility against the sentence of a court which itself has adopted . . .

With this discussion, though purely legal, it will be impossible to prevent the world from blending political considerations. Some may call this an attempt to consolidate. But before such an imputation shall be pronounced, let them examine well, if the fair interpretation of the constitution does not vindicate my opinions. Above all, let me personally assure them, that the prostration of state rights is not an object with me; but that I remain in perfect confidence, that with the power, which the people and the legislatures of the states indirectly hold over almost every movement of the national government, the states need not fear an assault from bold ambition, or any approaches of covered stratagem.

IREDELL, *Justice*: [Iredell argued that the Court could not act in the absence of congressional legislation granting it jurisdiction and establishing its process, and that the only relevant statute, section 14 of the Judiciary Act of 1789, simply directed the Court to issue writs "agreeable to the principles and usages of law." In a lengthy historical discussion, Iredell endeavored to prove that according to those "principles and usages of law" a sovereign could not be sued without its consent].

. . . I have now, I think, established the following particulars,—1st. That the constitution so far as it respects the judicial authority, can only be carried into effect by acts of the legislature appointing courts, and prescribing their methods of proceeding. 2d. That Congress has provided no new law in regard to this case, but expressly referred us to the old. 3d. That there are no principles of the old law, to which we must have recourse, that in any manner authorize the present suit, either by precedent or by analogy. The consequence of which, in my opinion, clearly is, that the suit in question cannot be maintained, nor, of course, the motion made upon it be complied with.

From the manner in which I have viewed this subject, so different from that in which it has been contemplated by the attorney general, it is evident that I have not had occasion to notice many arguments offered by the attorney general, which certainly were very proper, as to his extended view of the case, but do not affect mine. No part of the law of nations can apply to this case, as I apprehend, but that part which is termed "The Conventional Law of Nations;" nor can this any otherwise apply than as furnishing rules of interpretation, since unquestionably the people of the United States had a right to form what kind of union, and upon what terms they pleased, without reference to any former examples. If upon a fair construction of the Constitution of the United States, the power contended for really exists, it undoubtedly may be exercised, though it be a power of the first impression. If it does not exist, upon that authority, ten thousand examples of similar powers would not warrant its assumption. So far as this great question affects the constitution itself, if the present afforded, consistently with the particular grounds of my opinion, a proper occasion for a decision upon it, I would not shrink from its discussion. But it is of extreme moment that no judge should rashly commit himself upon important questions, which it is unnecessary for him to decide. My opinion being, that even if the constitution would admit of the exercise of such a power, a new law is necessary for the purpose, since no part of the existing law applies, this alone is sufficient to justify my determination in the present case. So much however, has been said on the constitution, that it may not be improper to intimate that my present opinion is strongly against any construction of it, which will admit, under any circumstances, a compulsive suit against a state for the recovery of money. I think every word in the constitution may have its full effect without involving this consequence, and that nothing but express words, or an insurmountable implication (neither of which I consider, can be found in this case) would authorize the deduction of so high a power. This opinion I hold, however, with all the reserve proper for one, which, according to my sentiments in this case, may be deemed in some measure extra-judicial. With regard to the policy of maintaining such suits, that is not for this court to consider, unless the point in all other respects was very doubtful. Policy might then be argued from with a view to preponderate the judgment. Upon the question before us, I have no doubt. I have therefore nothing to do with the policy. But I confess, if I was at liberty to speak on that subject, my opinion on the policy of the case, would also differ from that of the attorney general. It is however, a delicate topic. I pray to God, that if the attorney general's doctrine, as to the law, be established by the judgment of this court, all the good he predicts from it may take place, and none of the evils with which, I have the concern to say, it appears to me to be pregnant.

BLAIR, *Justice:* In considering this important case, I have thought it best to pass over all the strictures which have been made on the various European confederations; because, as on the one hand, their likeness to our own is not sufficiently close to justify any analogical application; so, on the other, they are utterly destitute of any binding authority here. The constitution of the United States is the only fountain from which I shall draw; the only authority to which I shall appeal. Whatever be the true language of that, it is obligatory upon every member of the union; for, no state could have become member, but by an adoption of it by the people of that state. What then do we find there requiring the submission of individual states to the judicial authority of the United States? This is expressly extended, among other things, to controversies between a state and citizens of another state. Is then the case before us one of that description? Undoubtedly it is unless it may be a sufficient denial to say, that it is a controversy between a citizen of one state and another state. Can this change of order be an essential change in the thing intended? And is this alone a sufficient ground from which to conclude that the jurisdiction of this court reaches the case where a state is plaintiff, but not where it is defendant? In this latter case, should any man be asked, whether it was not a controversy between a state and citizen of another state, must not the answer be in the affirmative? A dispute between A. and B. is surely a dispute between B. and A. Both cases, I have no doubt, were intended; and probably the state was first named, in respect to the dignity of a state. But that very dignity seems to have been thought a sufficient reason for confining the sense to the case where a state is plaintiff. It is, however, a sufficient answer to say, that our constitution most certainly contemplates, in another branch of the cases enumerated, the maintaining a jurisdiction against a state, as defendant; this is unequivocally asserted when the judicial power of the United States is extended to controversies between two or more states; for there, a state must, of necessity, be a defendant. It is extended also, to controversies between a state and foreign states; and if the argument taken from the order of designation were good, it would be meant here, that this court might have cognizance of a suit, where a state is plaintiff, and some foreign state a defendant, but not where a foreign state brings a suit against a state. This however, not to mention that the instances may rarely occur, when a state may have an opportunity of suing in the American courts a foreign state, seems to lose sight of the policy which, no doubt, suggested this provision, viz. That no state in the union should, by withholding justice, have it in its power to embroil the whole confederacy in disputes of another nature. But if a foreign state, though last named, may nevertheless, be a plaintiff against an individual state, how can it be said that a controversy between a state and a citizen of another state means, from the mere force of the order of the words, only such cases where a state is plaintiff? . . .

WILSON, *Justice*: This is a case of uncommon magnitude. One of the parties to it is a state; certainly respectable, claiming to be sovereign. The question to be determined, is whether this state, so respectable, and whose claim soars so high, is amenable to the jurisdiction of the supreme court of the United States? This question, important in itself, will depend on others, more important still; and may, perhaps, be ultimately resolved into one, no less radical than this—"do the people of the United States form a nation?"

A cause so conspicuous and interesting should be carefully and accurately viewed from every possible point of sight. I shall examine it, 1st. By the principles of general jurisprudence. 2d. By the laws and practice of particular states and kingdoms. From the law of nations little or no illustration of this subject can be expected. By that law the several states and governments spread over our globe, are considered as forming a society, not a nation. It has only been by a very few comprehensive minds, such as those of Elizabeth and the fourth Henry, that this last great idea has been even contemplated. 3dly. and chiefly, I shall examine the important question before us, by the Constitution of the United States, and the legitimate result of that valuable instrument.

I. I am, first, to examine this question by the principles of general jurisprudence. What I shall say upon this head, I introduce by the observation of an original and profound writer, who, in the philosophy of mind, and all the sciences attendant on this prime one, has formed an era not less remarkable, and far more illustrious, than that formed by the justly celebrated Bacon, in another science, not prosecuted with less ability, but less dignified as to its object: I mean the philosophy of matter. Dr. Reid, in his excellent enquiry into the human mind, on the principles of common sense, speaking of the sceptical and illiberal philosophy, which under bold, but false pretensions to liberality, prevailed in many parts of Europe before he wrote, makes the following judicious remark: "The language of philosophers, with regard to the original faculties of the mind, is so adapted to the prevailing system, that it cannot fit any other; like a coat that fits the man for whom it was made, and shows him to advantage, which yet will fit very awkward upon one of a different make, although as handsome and wellproportioned. It is hardly possible to make any innovation in our philosophy concerning the mind and its operations, without using new words and phrases, or giving a different meaning to those that are received." With equal propriety may this solid remark be applied to the great subject on the principles of which the decision of this court is to be founded. The perverted use of genus and species in logic, and of impressions and ideas in metaphysics, have never done mischief so extensive or so practically pernicious, as has been done by states and sovereigns, in politics and jurisprudence; in the politics and jurisprudence even of those who wished and meant to be free. In the place of those expressions I intend not to substitute new ones, but the expressions themselves I shall certainly use for purposes different from those, for which hitherto they have been frequently used; and one of them I shall apply to an object still more different from that to which it has hitherto been more frequently, I may say almost universally applied. In these purposes and in this application, I shall be justified by example the most splendid, and by authority the most binding; the example of the most refined as well as the most free nation known to antiquity; and the authority of one of the best constitutions known to modern times. With regard to one of the terms—state—this authority is declared: With regard to the other—sovereign—the authority is implied only:

But it is equally strong: For, in an instrument well drawn as in a poem well composed, silence is sometimes most expressive.

To the Constitution of the United States the term sovereign is totally unknown. There is but one place where it could have been used with propriety. But, even in that place it would not, perhaps, have comported with the delicacy of those, who ordained and established that constitution. They might have announced themselves "sovereign" people of the United States: But serenely conscious of the fact, they avoided the ostentatious declaration.

Having thus avowed my disapprobation of the purpose, for which the terms, state and sovereign, are frequently used, and of the object to which the application of the last of them is almost universally made; it is now proper that I should disclose the meaning which I assign to both and the application which I make of the latter. In doing this, I shall have occasion incidently [sic] to evince, how true it is that states and governments were made for man; and at the same time how true it is that his creatures and servants have first deceived, next vilified, and at last, oppressed their master and maker.

Man, fearfully and wonderfully made, is the workmanship of his all perfect Creator: A state, useful and valuable as the contrivance is, is the inferior contrivance of man; and from his native dignity derives all its acquired importance. When I speak of a state as an inferior contrivance, I mean that is it a contrivance inferior only to that, which is divine: Of all human contrivances, it is certainly most transcendantly [sic] excellent. It is concerning this contrivance that Cicero says so sublimely, "Nothing which is exhibited upon our globe, is more acceptable to that divinity, which governs the whole universe, than those communities and assemblages of men, which, lawfully associated, are denominated states."

Let a state be considered as subordinate to the people: But let everything else be subordinate to the state. The latter part of this position is equally necessary with the former. For in the practice and even at length, in the science of politics there has very frequently been a strong current against the natural order of things, and an inconsiderate or an interested disposition to sacrifice the end to the means. As the state has claimed precedence of the people; so in the same inverted course of things, the government has often claimed precedence of the state; and to this perversion in the second degree, many of the volumes of confusion concerning sovereignty owe their existence. The ministers, dignified very properly by the appellation of the magistrates, have wished, and have succeeded in their wish, to be considered as the sovereigns of the state. This second degree of perversion is confined to the old world, and begins to diminish even there; but the first degree is still too prevalent even in the several states of which our union is composed. By a state I mean, a complete body of free persons united together for their common benefit, to enjoy peaceably what is their own, and to do justice to others. It is an artificial person. It has its affairs and its interests: It has its rules: It has its rights: And it has its obligations. It may acquire property distinct from that of its members. It may incur debts to be discharged out of the public stock, not out of the private fortunes of individuals. It may be bound by contracts; and for damages arising from the breach of those contracts. In all our contemplations, however, concerning this feigned and artificial person, we should never forget, that, in truth and nature, those who think and speak and act, are men.

Is the foregoing description of a state a true description? It will not be questioned, but it is. Is there any part of this description, which intimates in the remotest manner, that a state, any more than the men who compose it, ought not to do justice and fulfil engagements? It will not be pretended that there is. If justice is not done; if engagements are not fulfilled; is it upon general principles of right, less proper, in the case of a great number than in the case of an individual, to secure, by compulsion, that which will not be voluntarily performed? Less proper it surely cannot be. The only reason, I believe why a free man is bound by human laws, is that he binds himself. Upon the same principles, upon which he becomes bound by the laws, he becomes amenable to the courts of justice, which are formed and authorized by those laws. If one free man, an original sovereign, may do all this, why may not an aggregate of free men, a collection of original sovereigns do this likewise? If the dignity of each singly is undiminished, the dignity of all jointly must be unimpaired. A state, like a merchant, makes a contract: A dishonest state, like a dishonest merchant, wilfully refuses to discharge it: The latter is amenable to a court of justice: Upon general principles of right shall the former when summoned to answer the fair demands of its creditor, be permitted, proteus-like, to assume a new appearance, and to insult him and justice, by declaring, I am a sovereign state? Surely not. Before a claim, so contrary, in its first appearance, to the general principles of right and equality, be sustained by a just and impartial tribunal, the person, natural or artificial, entitled to make such claim, should certainly be well known and authenticated. Who, or what, is a sovereignty? What is his or its sovereignty? On this subject, the errors and the mazes are endless and inexplicable. To enumerate all, therefore, will not be expected: To take notice of some will be necessary to the full illustration of the present important cause. In one sense, the term sovereign, has for its correlative, subject. In this sense, the term can receive no application; for it has no object in the Constitution of the United States. Under that constitution there are citizens, but no subjects. "Citizens of the United States." "Citizens of another state," "Citizens of different states." "A state or citizen thereof." The term, subject, occurs, indeed, once in the instrument; but to mark the contrast strongly, the epithet "foreign" is prefixed. In this sense, I presume the state of Georgia has no claim upon her own citizens: In this sense, I am certain, she can have no claim upon the citizens of another state.

In another sense, according to some writers, every state, which governs itself without any dependence on another power is a sovereign state. Whether, with regard to her own citizens, this is the case of the state of Georgia; whether, those citizens have done, as the individuals of England are said, by their late instructors, to have done, surrendered the supreme power to the state or government, and reserved nothing to themselves; or whether like the people of other states and of the United States, the citizens of Georgia have reserved the supreme power in their own hands; and on that supreme power have made the state dependent, instead of being sovereign: these are questions, to which as a judge in this cause, I can neither know nor suggest the proper answer; though, as a citizen of the union, I know and am interested to know, that the most satisfactory answers can be given. As a citizen, I know the government of that state to be republican; and my short definition of such a government is,—one constructed on this principle, that the supreme power resides in the body of the people. As a judge of this court, I know, and can decide upon the knowledge, that the citizens of Georgia, when they acted upon the large scale of the union, as a part of the "People of the United States," did not surrender the supreme or sovereign power to that state; but, as to the purposes of the union, retained it to themselves. As to the purposes of the union, therefore, Georgia is not a sovereign state. If the judicial decision of this case forms one of those purposes; the allegation, that Georgia is a sovereign state, is unsupported by the fact. Whether the judicial decision of this cause is, or is not, one of those purposes, is a question which will be examined particularly in a subsequent part of my argument . . .

I have now fixed, the scale of things, the grade of a state; and have described its composure: I have considered the nature of sovereignty; and pointed its application to the proper object. I have examined the question before us, by the principles of general jurisprudence. In those principles, I find nothing, which tends to evince an exemption of the state of Georgia from the jurisdiction of the court. I find everything to have a contrary tendency.

[In the second section of his opinion, Wilson discussed various historical examples of states or monarchs submitting to suit.]

III. I am thirdly, and chiefly, to examine the important question now before us, by the Constitution of the United States, and the legitimate result of that valuable instrument. Under this view, the question is naturally subdivided into two others. 1. Could the Constitution of the United States vest a jurisdiction over the state of Georgia? 2. Has that constitution vested such jurisdiction in this court? I have already remarked, that in the practice, and even in the science of politics, there has been frequently a strong current against the natural order of things; and an inconsiderate or an interested disposition to sacrifice the end to the means. This remark deserves a more particular illustration. Even in almost every nation, which has been denominated free, the state has assumed a supercilious pre-eminence above the people who have formed it: Hence the haughty notions of state independence, state sovereignty, and state supremacy. In despotic governments, the Government has usurped, in a similar manner, both upon the state and the people: Hence all arbitrary doctrines and pretensions concerning the supreme, absolute, and incontrollable, power of government. In each, man is degraded from the prime rank, which he ought to hold in human affairs: In the latter, the state as well as the man is degraded. Of both degradations, striking instances occur in history, in politics, and in common life . . .

In the United States, and in the several states which compose the union, we go not so far [as England, where, Wilson has just observed, Parliament rather than the people is said to be "the great body politic"] but still we go one step farther than we ought to go in this unnatural and inverted order of things. The states, rather than the people, for whose sakes the states exist, are frequently the objects which attract and arrest our principal attention. This, I believe, has produced much of the confusion and perplexity, which have appeared in several proceedings and several publications on state politics, and on the politics too, of the United States. Sentiments and expressions of this inaccurate kind prevail in our common, even in our convivial, language. Is a toast asked? "The United States" instead of the "People of the United States," is the toast given. This is not politically correct. The toast is meant to present to view the first great object in the union: It presents only the second: It presents only the artificial person, instead of the natural persons, who spoke it into existence. A state I cheerfully admit, is the noblest work of man: But man himself, free and honest, is, I speak as to this world, the noblest work of God . . .

With the strictest propriety, therefore, classical and political, our national scene opens with the most magnificent object which the nation could present. "The people of the United States" are the first personages introduced. Who were those people? They were the citizens of thirteen states, each of which had a separate constitution and government, and all of which were connected together by articles of confederation. To the purposes of public strength and felicity, that confederacy was totally inadequate. A requisition on the several states terminated its legislative authority: Executive or judicial authority it had none. In order, therefore, to form a more perfect union, to establish justice, to ensure domestic tranquillity, to provide for common defense, and to secure the blessings of liberty, those people among whom were the people of Georgia, ordained and established the present constitution. By that constitution legislative power is vested, executive power is vested, judicial power is vested.

The question now opens fairly to our view; could the people of those states, among whom were those of Georgia, bind those states, and Georgia among the others, by the legislative, executive, and judicial power so vested? If the principles, on which I have founded myself, are just and true, this question must unavoidably receive an affirmative answer. If those states were the work of those people; those people, and that I may apply the case closely, the people of Georgia, in particular, could alter, as they pleased, their former work: To any given degree, they could diminish as well as enlarge it. Any or all of the former state powers they could extinguish or transfer. The inference, which necessarily results, is, that the constitution ordained and established by those people; and, still closely to apply the case, in particular by the people of Georgia, could vest jurisdiction or judicial power over these states and over the state of Georgia in particular.

The next question under this head, is.—Has the constitution done so? Did those people mean to exercise this, their undoubted power? These questions may be resolved, either by fair and conclusive deductions, or by direct and explicit declarations. In order, ultimately, to discover, whether the people of the United States intended to bind those states by the judicial power vested by the national constitution, a previous enquiry will naturally be:

Did those people intend to bind those states by the legislative power vested by that constitution? The articles of confederation, it is well known, did not operate upon individual citizens; but operated only upon states. This defect was remedied by the national constitution, which as all allow, has an operation on individual citizens. But if an opinion, which some seem to entertain, be just; the defect remedied, on one side, was balanced by a defect introduced on the other. For they seem to think that the present constitution operates only on individual citizens, and not on states. This opinion, however, appears to be altogether unfounded. When certain laws of the states are declared to be "subject to the revision and control of the Congress," it cannot surely, be contended that the legislative power of the national government was meant to have no operation on the several states. The fact, uncontrovertibly established in one instance, proves the principle in all other instances, to which the facts will be found to apply. We may then infer, that the people of the United States intended to bind the several states, by the legislative power of the national government.

In order to make the discovery, at which we ultimately aim, a second previous enquiry will naturally be—Did the people of the United States intend to bind the several states by the executive power of the national government? The affirmative answer to the former question directs, unavoidably, an affirmative answer to this. Ever since the time of Bracton, his maxim, I believe has been deemed a good one—. . . "It would be superfluous to make laws, unless those laws, when made, were to be enforced." When the laws are plain and the application of them is uncontroverted, they are enforced immediately by the executive authority of government. When the application of them is doubtful or intricate, the interposition of the judicial authority becomes necessary. The same principle, therefore, which directed us from the first to the second step will direct us from the second to the third and last step of our deduction. Fair and conclusive deduction, then, evinces that the people of the United States did vest this court with jurisdiction over the state of Georgia. The same truth may be deduced from the declared objects, and the general texture of the constitution of the United States. One of its declared objects is, to form a union more perfect than before that time, had been formed. Before that time, the union possessed legislative, but uninforced [sic] legislative power over the states. Nothing could be more natural than to intend that this legislative power should be enforced by powers executive and judicial. Another declared object is "to establish justice." This points, in a particular manner, to the judicial authority. And when we view this object in conjunction with the declaration, "that no state shall pass a law impairing the obligation of contracts;" we shall probably think, that this object points, in a particular manner, to the jurisdiction of the court over the several states. What good purpose could this constitutional provision secure, if a state might pass a law impairing the obligation of its own contracts; and be amenable, for such a violation of right, to no controlling judiciary power? We have seen, that on the principles of general jurisprudence, a state, for the breach of a contract, may be liable for damages. A third declared object is—"to ensure domestic tranquillity." This tranquillity is most likely to be disturbed by controversies between states. These consequences will be most peaceably and effectually decided by the establishment and by the exercise of a superintending judicial authority. By such exercise and establishment, the law of nations; the rule between contending states; will be enforced among the several states, in the same manner as municipal law.

Whoever considers, in a combined and comprehensive view, the general texture of the constitution, will be satisfied, that the people of the United States intended to form themselves into a nation for national purposes. They instituted for such purposes, a national government, complete in all its parts, with powers legislative, executive, and judiciary; and in all those powers extending over the whole nation. Is it congruous, that, with regard to such purposes, any man or body of men, any person, natural or artificial, should be permitted to claim successfully an entire exemption from the jurisdiction of the national government? Would not such claims, crowned with success, be repugnant to our very existence as a nation? When so many trains of deduction coming from different quarters, converge and unite, at last, in the same point; we may safely conclude, as the legitimate result of this constitution, that the state of Georgia is amenable to the jurisdiction of this court.

But, in my opinion, this doctrine rests not upon the legitimate result of fair and conclusive deduction from the constitution: It is confirmed beyond all doubt, by the direct and explicit declaration of the constitution itself. "The judicial power of the United States shall extend, to controversies between two states." Two states are supposed to have a controversy between them: This controversy is supposed to be brought before those vested with the judicial power of the United States. Can the most consummate degree of professional ingenuity devise a mode by which this "controversy between two states" can be brought before a court of law; and yet neither of those states be a defendant? "The judicial power of the United States shall extend to controversies, between a state and citizens of another state." Could the strictest legal language; could even that language, which is peculiarly appropriated to an art, deemed by a great master, to be one of the most honorable, laudible, and profitable things in our law; could this strict and appropriated language, describe, with more precise accuracy, the cause now depending before the tribunal? Causes and not parties to causes, are weighed by justice on her equal scales: On the former solely, her attention is fixed: To the latter, she is as she is painted, blind.

I have now tried this question by all the touchstones, to which I proposed to apply it. I have examined it by the principles of general jurisprudence; by the laws and practice of states and kingdoms; and by the constitution of the United States. From all, the combined inference is, that the action lies.

CUSHING, *Justice*: . . . Further; if a state is entitled to justice in the federal court, against a citizen of another state, why not such citizen against the state, when the same language equally comprehends both? The rights of individuals and the justice due to them, are as dear and precious as those of states. Indeed the latter are founded upon the former; and the great end and object of them must be to secure and support the rights of individuals, or else vain is government.

But still it may be insisted, that this will reduce states to mere corporations, and take away all sovereignty. As to the corporations, all states whatever, are corporations or bodies politic. The only question is, what are their powers? As to individual states and the United States the constitution marks the boundary of powers. Whatever power is deposited with the union by the people for their own necessary security, is so far a curtailing of the power and prerogatives of states. This is, as it were, a self-evident proposition; at least it cannot be contested . . .

JAY, *Chief Justice*:—The question we are now to decide has been accurately stated, viz., Is a state suable by individual citizens of another state?

It is said, that Georgia refuses to appear and answer to the plaintiff in this action, because she is a sovereign state, and therefore not liable to such actions. In order to ascertain the merits of this objection, let us enquire, 1st. In what sense Georgia is a sovereign state. 2d. Whether suability is incompatible with such sovereignty. 3d. Whether the constitution (to which Georgia is a party) authorizes such an action against her.

Suability and suable are words not in common use, but they concisely, correctly convey the idea annexed to them.

1st. In determining the sense in which Georgia is a sovereign state, it may be useful to turn our attention to the political situation we were in, prior to the revolution, and to the political rights which emerged from the revolution: All the country now possessed by the United States was then a part of the dominions appertaining to the crown of Great Britain. Every acre of land in this country was then held mediately or immediately by grants from that crown. All the people of this country were then, subjects of the king of Great Britain, and owed allegiance to him: and all the civil authority then existing or exercised here, flowed from the head of the British Empire. They were in strict sense, fellow subjects, and in a variety of respects, one people. When the revolution commenced, the patriots did not assert that only the same affinity and social connection subsisted between the people, of the colonies, which subsisted between the people of Gaul, Britain and Spain, while Roman provinces, viz., only that affinity and social connection which result from the mere circumstances of being governed by the same prince; different ideas prevailed, and gave occasion to the Congress of 1774 and 1775.

The revolution or rather the Declaration of Independence, found the people already united for general purposes, and at the same time providing for their more domestic concerns by state conventions, and other temporary arrangements. From the crown of Great Britain, the sovereignty of their country passed to the people of it; and it was then not an uncommon opinion, that the unappropriated lands, which belonged to that crown, passed not to the people of the colony or states within whose limits they were situated, but to the whole people; on whatever principles this opinion rested, it [gave] way to the other, and thirteen sovereignties were considered as emerged from the principles of the revolution, combined with local convenience and considerations; the people nevertheless continued to consider themselves, in a national point of view, as one people; and they continued without interruption to manage their national concerns accordingly; afterwards, in the hurry of the war, and in the warmth of mutual confidence, they made a confederation of the states, the basis of a general government. Experience disappointed the expectations they had formed from it; and then the people, in their collective and national capacity, established the present constitution. It is remarkable that in establishing it, the people exercised their own rights, and their own proper sovereignty, and conscious of the plentitude of it, they declared with becoming dignity, "We the people of the United States," "do ordain and establish this constitution." Here we see the people acting as sovereigns of the whole country; and in the language of sovereignty, establishing a constitution by which it was their will, that the state governments should be bound, and to which the state constitutions should be made to conform. Every state constitution is a compact made by and between the citizens of a state to govern themselves in a certain manner; and the constitution of the United States is likewise a compact made by the people of the United States to govern themselves as to general objects, in a certain manner. By this great compact however, many prerogatives were transferred to the national government, such as those of making war and peace, contracting alliances, coining money, etc. etc.

If then it be true, that the sovereignty of the nation is [in] the people of the nation, and the residuary sovereignty of each state, in the people of each state, it may be useful to compare these sovereignties, with those in Europe, that we may thence be enabled to judge, whether all the prerogatives which are allowed to the latter, are so essential to the former. There is reason to suspect that some of the difficulties which embarrass the present question, arise fron inattention to differences which subsist between them.

It will be sufficient to observe briefly, that the sovereignties in Europe, and particularly in England, exist on feudal principles. That system considers the prince as the sovereign and the people as his subjects; it regards his person as the object of allegiance; and excludes the idea of his being on an equal footing with a subject, either in a court of justice or elsewhere. That system contemplates him as being the fountain of honor and authority; and from his grace and grant derive all franchises, immunities and privileges; it is easy to perceive that such a sovereign could not be amenable to a court of justice, or subjected to judicial control and actual constraint. It was of necessity, therefore, that suability, became incompatible with such sovereignty. Besides, the prince having all the executive powers, the judgment of the courts would, in fact, be only monitory, not mandatory to him, and a capacity to be advised, is a distinct thing from a capacity to be sued. The same feudal ideas run through all their jurisprudence, and constantly remind us of the distinction between the prince and the subject. No such ideas obtain here; at the revolution, the sovereignty developed on the people; and they are truly the sovereigns of the country, but they are sovereigns without subjects (unless the African slaves among us may be so called) and have none to govern but themselves; the citizens of America are equal as fellow citizens, and as joint tenants in the sovereignty.

From the differences existing between feudal sovereignties and governments founded on compacts, it necessarily follows that their respective prerogatives must differ. Sovereignty is the right to govern; a nation or state-sovereign in the person or persons in whom that resides. In Europe the sovereignty is generally ascribed to the prince; here it rests with the people; there, the sovereign actually administers the government; here, never in a single instance; our governors are the agents of the people, and at most stand in the same relation to their sovereign, in which regents in Europe stand to their sovereigns. Their princes have personal powers, dignities, and pre-eminences, our rulers have none but official; nor do they partake in the sovereignty otherwise, or in any other capacity, than as private citizens.

2d. The second object of enquiry now presents itself, viz., whether suability is compatible with state sovereignty:

Suability, by whom? Not a subject, for in this country there are none; not an inferior, for all the citizens being as to civil rights perfectly equal, there is not, in that respect, one citizen inferior to another. It is agreed, that one free citizen may sue another; the obvious dictates of justice, and the purposes of society demanding it. It is agreed that one free citizen may sue any number on whom process can be conveniently executed; nay, in certain cases one citizen may sue forty thousand; for where a corporation is sued all the members of it are actually sued, though not personally sued. In this city [Philadelphia] there are forty odd thousand free citizens, all of whom may be collectively sued by any individual citizen. In the state of Delaware, there are fifty odd thousand free citizens, and what reason can be assigned why a free citizen who has demands against them should not prosecute them? Can the difference between forty odd thousand, and fifty odd thousand make any distinction as to right? Is it not as easy, and as convenient to the public and parties, to serve a summons on the governor and attorney general of Delaware, as on the mayor or other officers of the corporation of Philadelphia? Will it be said, that the fifty odd thousand citizens in Delaware being associated under a state government, stand in a rank so superior to the forty odd thousand of Philadelphia, associated under their charter, that although it may become the latter to meet an individual as an equal footing in a court of justice yet that such a procedure would not comport with the dignity of the former? In this land of equal liberty, shall forty odd thousand in one place be compellable to do justice, and yet fifty odd thousand in another place be privileged to do justice only as they may think proper? Such objections would not correspond with the equal rights we claim; with the equality we profess to admire and maintain, and with that popular sovereignty in which every citizen partakes. Grant that the governor of Delaware holds an office of superior rank to the mayor of Philadelphia, they are both nevertheless the officers of the people and however more exalted the one may be than the other, yet in the opinion of those who dislike aristocracy, that circumstance cannot be a good reason for impeding the course of justice.

If there be any such incompatibility as is pretended, whence does it arise? In what does it consist? There is at least one strong undeniable fact against this incompatibility, and that is this, any one state in the union may sue another state, in this court, that is, all the people of one state may sue all the people of another state. It is plain then, that a state may be sued, and hence it plainly follows, that suability and state sovereignty are not incompatible. As one state may sue another state in this court, it is plain that no degradation to a state is thought to accompany her appearance in this court. It is not therefore to an appearance in this court that the objection points. To what does it point? It points to an appearance at the suit of one or more citizens. But why it should be more incompatible, that all the people of a state should be sued by one citizen, then by one hundred thousand, I cannot perceive, the process in both cases being alike; and the consequences of a judgment alike. Nor can I observe any greater inconveniences in the one case than in the other, except what may arise from the feelings of those who may regard a lesser number in an inferior light . . .

I perceive, and therefore candor urges me to mention, a circumstance, which seems to favor the opposite side of the question. It is this: the same section of the constitution which extends the judicial power to controversies "between a state and the citizens of another state," does also extend that power to controversies to which the United States are a party. Now, it may be said, that if the word, party, comprehends both plaintiff and defendant, it follows, that the United States may be sued by any citizen, between whom and them there may be a controversy. This appears to me to be fair reasoning; but the same principles of candor which urge me to mention this objection, also urge me to suggest an important difference between the two cases. It is this: in all cases of actions against states or individual citizens, the national courts are supported in all their legal and con- stitutional proceedings and judgments, by the arm of the executive power of the United States; but in cases of actions against the United States, there is no power which the courts can call to their aid. From this distinction important conclusions are deducible, and they place the case of a state and the case of the United States, in very different points of view.

I wish the state of society was so far improved, and the science of government advanced to such a degree of perfection, as that the whole nation could in the peaceable course of law, be compelled to do justice, and be sued by individual citizens. Whether that is, or is not, now the case, ought not to be thus collaterally and incidentally decided: I leave it a question.

As this opinion, though deliberately formed, has been hastily reduced to writing be- tween the intervals of the daily adjournments, and while my mind was occupied and wearied by the business of the day, I fear it is less concise and connected than it might otherwise have been. I have made no references to cases, because I know of none that are not distinguishable from this case; nor does it appear to me necessary to show that the sentiments of the best writers on government and the rights of men, harmonize with the principles which direct my judgment on the present question. The acts of the former Congresses, and the acts of many of the state conventions are replete with similar ideas; and to the honor of the United States, it may be observed, that in no other country are subjects of this kind better, if so well, understood. The attention and attachment of the Constitution to the equal rights of the people are discernable in almost every sentence of it; and it is to be regretted that the provision in it which we have been considering, has not in every instance received the approbation and acquiescence which it merits. Georgia has in language advocated the cause of republican equality; and there is reason to hope that the people of that state will yet perceive that it would not have been consistent with that equality, to have exempted the body of her citizens from that suability which they are at this moment exercising against citizens of another state.

For my own part, I am convinced that the sense in which I understand and have explained the words "controversies between states and citizens of another state," is the true sense. The extension of the judiciary power of the United States to such controversies, appears to me to be wise, because it is honest, and because it is useful. It is honest, because it provides for doing justice without respect of persons, and by securing individual citizens as well as states, in their respective rights, performs the promise which every free gov- ernment makes to every free citizen, of equal justice and protection. It is useful, because it is honest, because it leaves not even the most obscure an[d] friendless citizen without means of obtaining justice from a neighboring state; because it obviates occasions of quarrels between states on account of the claims of their respective citizens; because it recognizes and strongly rests on this great moral truth, that justice is the same whether due from one man or a million, or from a million to one man; because it teaches and greatly appreciates the value of our free republican national government, which places all our citizens on an equal footing, and enables each and every one of them to obtain justice without any danger of being overborne by the weight and number of their opponents; and, because it brings into action, and enforces this great and glorious principle, that the people are the sovereign of this country, and consequently that fellow citizens and joint sovereigns cannot be degraded by appearing with each other in their own courts to have their controversies determined. The people have reason to prize and rejoice in such valuable privileges; and they ought not to forget, that nothing but the free course of constitutional law and government can insure the continuance and enjoyment of them . . .

Governor Edward Telfair
Message to the Georgia Legislature
(November 4, 1793)[58]

. . . Notwithstanding certain amendments have taken place in the Federal Constitution, it still rests with the State Legislatures to act thereon as circumstances may dictate. A process from the Supreme Court of the United States, at the instance of Chisholm, Executor of Farquhar, has been served on me and the Attorney General. I declined entering any appearance, as this would have introduced a precedent replete with danger to the Republic, and would have involved this state in complicated difficulties abstracted from the infractions it would have made on her retained sovereignty. The singular predicament to which she has been reduced by savage inroads has caused emission of paper upwards of one hundred and fifty thousand pounds since the close of the late war, a considerable part of which is yet outstanding, and which in good faith and upon constitutional principles is the debt of the United States. I say were [an] action [against the state] admissible under such grievous circumstances, an annihilation of her political existence must follow. To guard against civil discord as well as the impending danger, permit me most ardently to request your most serious attention to the measure of recommending to the Legislatures of the several States that they effect a remedy in the premises by an amendment to the constitution; and that to give further weight to this matter the delegation of this state in Congress be required to urge that body to propose such an amendment to the said several Legislatures . . .

An Act Declaratory of Certain Parts of the
Retained Sovereignty of the State of Georgia
(passed by the State House of Representatives,
November 21, 1793)[59]

. . . *And it be further enacted,* That any Federal Marshal, or any other person or persons levying, or attempting to levy, on the territory of this State, or any part thereof, or on the Treasury, or any other property belonging to the said State, or on the property of the Governor or Attorney General, or any of the people thereof, under or by virtue of any execution or other compulsory process issuing out of or by authority of the Supreme Court of the United States, or any other Court having jurisdiction under their authority, or which may at any period hereafter under the constitution of the said United States, as it now stands, be constituted, for, or in behalf of the before mentioned Alexander Chisholm, Executor of Robert Farquhar, or for, or in behalf of, any other person or persons whatsoever, for the payment or recovery of any debt, or pretended debt, or claim, against the said State of Georgia, shall be, and he or they attempting to levy as aforesaid are hereby declared to be guilty of felony, and shall suffer death, without the benefit of clergy, by being hanged.

The state senate declined to concur in this violent response to *Chisholm*.

The Eleventh Amendment
(proposed by Congress to the states on September
5, 1794; declared ratified on January 8, 1798)

The Judicial power of the United States shall not be construed to extend to any suit in law or equity, commenced or prosecuted against one of the United States by Citizens of another State, or by Citizens or Subjects of any Foreign State.

Comment

The Supreme Court's decision in *Chisholm* was remarkable in several ways. In his oral argument, Attorney General Edmund J. Randolph acknowledged that his maintenance of federal jurisdiction over an unconsenting state would be viewed as a political rather than a legal conclusion and "an attempt to consolidate." Several of the justices echoed this concern. Iredell noted the delicacy of the issue, Blair its importance, and Jay stressed the deliberation with which he approached the case. Wilson even claimed that the case presented the question of whether the United States was a real nation. With the exception of Iredell, nonetheless, the attorney general and the justices agreed that the Court could assert compulsory power over the state of Georgia; follow its own interpretation of the federal Constitution in the teeth of the Georgia public law of sovereign immunity (what would later be called the "judicial review" of the state law); supplement the 1789 Judiciary Act in order to devise a mode of process against the state; and upset expectations created by ratification-era assurances, such as Hamilton's, that the states would retain their sovereign immunity.

The Court's institutional self-confidence was matched by a remarkable intellectual boldness. Randolph and the Court's members (including the dissenting Iredell) rejected any suggestion that the question of state-sovereign immunity in federal court should be analyzed by analogy to European public or international law—which was precisely what Hamilton had implied would be done in Federalist No. 81. Blair denied the relevance of European experience with the assertion that "their likeness to our own [confederation] is not sufficiently close to justify any analogical application"; and Iredell conceded that the constitutional question could only be answered by "a fair construction of the Constitution" itself because the people were free to grant federal powers "upon what terms they pleased, without reference to any former example." Randolph, Blair, and Cushing therefore concluded that article three was to be read literally, to encompass suits against a state, and buttressed this textual argument by observing that federal jurisdiction in such cases was good constitutional policy because it provided a peaceful means of resolving potentially disruptive controversies. They also concurred in viewing *Chisholm* as an issue of "human rights" (Randolph) or "the rights of individuals" (Cushing).

Iredell's disagreement with his colleagues was based primarily on his concern that the Court proceed only in ways authorized by Congress, and not on any acceptance of a theory of state sovereignty, though he did express concern over the practical implications of Randolph's argument.

Wilson and Jay delivered more ambitious and more significant opinions. Wilson's statement that *Chisholm* put into question what he viewed as the Constitution's fundamental accomplishment—the perfection of American nationhood—was matched by an equally dramatic description of the proper answer: in order to decide the right of Robert Farquhar's estate to collect the debt allegedly owed it, the Supreme Court was obligated to rectify centuries of linguistic and conceptual confusion. Most of the difficulties in *Chisholm*, Wilson believed, arose from misunderstanding of the terms "state" and "sovereign." Political philosophers and ordinary Americans alike understood an organized polity, or even less accurately its government, as the "state," the fundamental entity in a given society. "Sovereignty," at the same time, was the label attached to those persons wielding political authority, or to any state that was politically independent of others. Wilson assailed both definitions as wrong or inapplicable. The "state," in fact, was the personification of the actual human beings who constituted it, and therefore should lay claim to no moral pretensions (immunity from judicial process, for example) that its makers did not assert. Language about state "sovereignty" was equally mistaken. Because Americans recognized the primacy of the people over the state-as-polity, the notion that Georgia (a subpolity within the federal state) was exempt from the claims of justice or the national polity was simply confused, and any assertion of independence was plainly untrue. The Constitution, Wilson noted, never used the term, and could have done so only in one place, in announcing its authorship by the sovereign American people.

Having redefined two crucial terms in late eighteenth-century political thought, Wilson then could view *Chisholm* as an exceedingly important but quite easy case. The Constitution explicitly submitted the states to federal legislative authority. It therefore, of necessity, bound the states to obey the federal executive power to enforce national law as well as the federal judicial power to interpret that law. (Despite his criticism of contemporaneous political science, Wilson here made passing use of the axiom that the judicial should be co-extensive with the legislative power.) There was no reason, therefore, to reject the "direct and explicit" language of article three.

Jay reached Wilson's position by a different, though equally bold, line of reasoning. As a historical matter, the chief justice insisted, Americans had been, "in a variety of respects, one people," even before the Revolution, and in throwing off the king's sovereignty they had asserted their own as a single national body. When Congress under the Articles of Confederation proved inefficient as a national government, the people of America adopted a new compact of government among themselves as individuals and "joint tenants in the sovereignty" of the nation. Thus, there was no magic in the fact that any particular group of individuals within the nation were labeled a "state" and enjoyed certain specified roles in the national political system. Philadelphia's forty thousand citizens and Delaware's fifty thousand were equally subject to the national government's authority to do justice.

Defenders of state autonomy correctly perceived the Court's decision in *Chisholm*, and the opinions of Wilson and Jay in particular were considered to be direct attacks on the legal and political bases for that "retained sovereignty" (Governor Telfair), as well as a serious threat to the states' fiscal stability (what Telfair labeled "complicated difficulties"). The *National Gazette*, a journal opposed to the incumbent administration, charged that the Court had abolished the federal system; the decision, it editorialized, "fritters the States away to corporations"—an accusation that Justice Cushing had expressly acknowledged. Another anti-nationalist writer noted that the Constitution's proponents had "denied peremptorily" federal jurisdiction over states "as an absurdity in terms. But it is now said that the profound and eloquent reasoning of the Chief Justice has made that to be right which was, at first, doubtful and improper."

Although much of the opposition to *Chisholm* was genuinely constitutional, the overwhelming majorities by which Congress proposed an amendment to revoke the decision (23–2 in the Senate and 81–9 in the House) support the conjecture that the Eleventh Amendment's success was due in large part to a nonideological concern with the decision's potential to create "complicated difficulties."

Section B: *The Emergence of Judicial Review*

The practice of judicial review—the power of courts of law to disregard or set aside statutes that conflict with the polity's fundamental law—gradually emerged in the decade or so following 1785. The practice did not exist, of course, in the British system, though late colonial Americans resisting royal authority often quoted an ambiguous statement by Lord Coke in *Dr. Bonham's Case* (Court of Common Pleas 1610) that "when an act of Parliament is against common right or reason . . . the common law will controul it, and adjudge such act to be void." In 1761 the Massachusetts Superior Court was asked (unavailingly) to invalidate the practice of issuing "writs of assistance" (roughly, a general search warrant) to royal customs officials; in the course of doing so, James Otis, Jr., argued that "an Act against the Constitution is void . . . and if [such] an Act of Parliament should be made . . . the Executive Courts must pass such Acts into disuse." Of Otis's argument, John Adams later wrote that "then and there the child Independence was born."

The debates in the 1787 Philadelphia convention, and subsequently over the Constitution's adoption, did not pay close attention to the question of judicial review, for the most part, but it seems fair to assert that supporters and opponents alike assumed that some form of it would exist.

One of the earliest judicial confrontations with the problem of the unconstitutional statute occurred in Virginia in 1788, when the state legislature enacted a law requiring the judges of the chancery, admiralty and general courts to take on extensive new duties as common-law trial judges. The statute did not increase salaries or reduce previous duties, and meeting in conference the judges collectively determined that it therefore violated the state constitution's guarantees of the tenure and salary of the judiciary. The judges therefore sent a "Respectful Remonstrance" to the legislature explaining their reasoning, and asking that "the present infraction of the constitution may be remedied by the legislature themselves." If not, the judges concluded, "they see no other alternative for a decision between the legislature and judiciary than an appeal to the people." What the latter statement meant became clear when the legislature declined to modify the statute: the judges all resigned. The legislature then amended the legislation, and the judges accepted new appointments.

This 1788 affair did not arise out of litigation; and, though the judges clearly accepted the idea that statutes could violate the state constitution, they did not address the question of whether, in a proper case, they could exercise the power to ignore or annul unconstitutional legislation that courts in several other states had recently asserted. The latter issue squarely confronted the Virginia General Court a few years later.

Kamper v. Hawkins
1 Va. Cas. 20 (Gen. Ct. Nov. 16, 1793)

The adjournment of this case originated in novelty and difficulty, touching the constitutionality, or judicial propriety of the judges of the District Court, carrying the following clause of an act of the General Assembly into execution, which was conceived to be opposed to, or in direct violation of the Constitution of the Commonwealth of Virginia.

The title and clause of the said act are thus: An act reducing into one, the several acts concerning the establishment, jurisdiction, and powers of District "Courts." (Passed December 12, 1792.)

Sect. XI. Each of the said district courts in term time, or any judge thereof in vacation, shall, and may have and exercise the same power of granting injunctions to stay proceedings on any judgment obtained in any of the said district courts, as is now had and exercised by the Judge of the high court of chancery in similar cases, and said district courts may proceed to the dissolution or final hearing of all suits commencing by injunction, under the same rules and regulations as are now prescribed by law for conducting similar suits in the high court of chancery.

The Record, Arguments, and Decision, here follow.

At a District Court, held in Dumfries, the twenty-third day of May, one thousand seven hundred and ninety-three—Present, the Honorable Spencer Roane, Esq.

Peter Kamper, vs. Mary Hawkins.

Upon a motion for an injunction to stay the proceedings on a judgment obtained at the last term held for this district, by Mary Hawkins, against the said Peter Kamper, under an act of assembly, entitled, "an act reducing into one, the several acts concerning the establishment, jurisdiction, and power of district courts."

The court is of opinion, that the said question should be adjourned to the General Court for novelty and difficulty, as to the constitutionality of the said law in this behalf . . .

At a General Court held at the capitol in the city of Richmond [on] Saturday November 16, 1793—Present, Saint George Tucker, John Tyler, James Henry, Spencer Roane, and William Nelson, jun., esquires, judges.

The honorable the judges, delivered their respective opinions touching the case aforesaid, in the following manner:

JUDGE NELSON. . . . I shall consider the question under two points.

First. Whether, if this clause be contrary to the constitution of this commonwealth, it can be executed.

And, *Secondly,* Whether it be contrary to the constitution.

I. As to the first point, although it has been decided by the judges of the court of appeals, (whether judicially or not is another question,) that a law contrary to the constitution is void—I beg leave to make a few observations on general principles.

The difference between a free and an arbitrary government I take to be—that in the former limits are assigned to those to whom the administration is committed; but the latter depends on the will of the departments or some of them. Hence the utility of a written constitution.

A *Constitution* is that by which the powers of government are limited.

It is to the *governors,* or rather to the departments of government, what a *law* is to individuals—nay, it is not only a *rule* of *action* to the branches of government, but it is that from which their existence flows, and by which the powers, (or portions of the right to govern,) which may have been committed to them, are prescribed—It is their commission—nay, it is their *creator.*

The calling this instrument the *constitution* or *form* of government, shews that the framers intended it to have this effect . . .

I ask then, whether the legislature do not sit under the constitution?

The answer in the affirmative to me is inevitable . . .

And can the legislature impugn that charter under which they claim, and to which by their acts they themselves have acknowledged an obligation?—I apprehend not, nor can any argument against this position be drawn from an acquiescence in some acts which may be unconstitutional.

1st, Because we may presume, that if there be any such, their unconstitutionality has not yet been discovered by the legislature, which, if it had been done, . . . we have reason to think, would have produced a . . . declaration [of unconstitutionality] from that body.—And

2ndly, Because no individual may have yet felt the operation of them, and consequently they have not been brought to investigation.

But the greatest objection still remains, that the judiciary, by declaring an act of the legislature to be no law, assumes legislative authority, or claims a superiority over the legislature.

In answer to this,—I do not consider the judiciary as the champions of the people, or of the Constitution, bound to sound the alarm, and to excite an opposition to the legislature.—But, when the cases of individuals are brought before them judicially, they are bound to decide.

And, if one man claim under an act contrary to the Constitution, that is, under what is *no* law, (if my former position, that the legislature cannot impugn the Constitution, and consequently that an act against it is void—be just,) must not a court give judgment against him?

Nor is it a novelty for the judiciary to declare, whether an act of the legislature *be in force* or *not in force,* or in other words, whether it be a *law* or *not.*

In many instances one statute is virtually repealed by another, and the judiciary must decide which is the law, or whether both can exist together.

The only difference is, that in one instance that which was once in existence is carried out of existence, by a subsequent act virtually contrary to it, and in the other the prior *fundamental law* has prevented its *coming into existence* as *a law.*

With respect to the idea that for the judiciary to declare an act of the legislature void, is to claim a superiority to the legislature,—if the legislative authority is derived from the constitution, and such a decision be a judicial act (as I have endeavoured to prove) this objection seems to be refuted.

For the reasons I have given, I am of opinion that the fundamental act of government controls the legislature, who owe their existence and powers to it;—this concludes the first point—

That if the clause under consideration be unconstitutional, it is *void*.

II. The second point—whether it be unconstitutional, is next to be considered.

By the fourteenth section of the Constitution, "the two houses of assembly shall, by joint ballot, appoint judges of the supreme court of appeals, and general court, *judges* in chancery, judges of admiralty, &c."

I was at first inclined to think that the insertion of the word *judges* between the *general court* and *chancery*, evinced an intention that the judges of the general court and those in chancery should be distinct persons; but perhaps it would be unjustifiable to rest such an opinion on so critical a construction.

However, this opinion is supported by the sixteenth and seventeenth sections.

By the sixteenth, the governor and others offending against the state, by maladministration, corruption, &c. are impeachable before the general court. And,

By the seventeenth, the judges of the general court are to be impeached before the court of appeals. This might prove then that a judge of the general court could not, according to the Constitution, be a judge of the supreme court of appeals, because all officers (except the judges of the general court,) are to be tried before the general court; but judges of the general court, are to be tried before the court of appeals—and the Constitution intended to prevent a man being tried in that court of which he is a member; because in causes which might give rise to an impeachment, the judges of a court might act jointly, and the influence of partiality, or an *esprit de corps*, was to be guarded against.

However, to decide whether a judge of the general court could be a judge of the court of appeals, would be extrajudicial, as that question is not before the court; but this research enables me to decide the question that is before the court—that is, whether the same person can, under the Constitution, be a judge in chancery, and a judge of the general court. I think that he cannot, for these reasons—

A judge in chancery is to be tried before the general court.—A judge of the general court cannot be a judge in chancery, because a judge in chancery must be tried before the general court; but if a judge of the general court be a judge in chancery, then he (a judge of the general court) will be tried in the general court, which is against the seventeenth article, which declares that a judge of the general court shall be impeached before the court of appeals.

My inference is, that a judge in chancery, and a judge of the general court, were intended under the Constitution to be distinct individuals.

This is one reason against the law; but there are others also of force. Whoever is appointed a judge in chancery under the Constitution, must be elected by joint ballot, and commissioned by the governor; neither of which requisitions have been complied with.

On the whole, I am for certifying to the court below, that the motion for an injunction be overruled, the clause under which it is prayed being unconstitutional.

JUDGE ROANE. This great question was adjourned by me from the district court of Dumfries. I thought it necessary to obtain the opinion of this court, for the government of the several district courts, who might otherwise have differed in their construction of the clause in question, and the administration of the law in this instance been consequently partial.

My opinion then was, upon a short consideration, that the district courts ought to execute this law; for I doubted how far the judiciary were authorized to refuse to execute a law, on the ground of its being against the spirit of the Constitution.

My opinion, on more mature consideration, is changed in this respect, and I now think that the judiciary may and ought not only to refuse to execute a law expressly repugnant to the Constitution; but also one which is, by a plain and natural construction, in opposition to the fundamental principles thereof.

I consider the people of this country as the only sovereign power.—I consider the legislature as not sovereign but subordinate; they are subordinate to the great constitutional charter, which the people have established as a fundamental law, and which alone has given existence and authority to the legislature. I consider that at the time of the adoption of our present Constitution, the British government was at an end in Virginia: it was at an end, because among many other weighty reasons very emphatically expressed in the first section of our Constitution, "George the Third, heretofore entrusted with the exercise of the kingly office in this colony, had abandoned the helm of government, and declared us out of his allegiance and protection."

The people were therefore at that period, they were at the period of the election of the Convention, which formed the Constitution, absolved from the former kingly government, and free, as in a state of nature, to establish a government for themselves. But admitting for a moment that the old government was not then at an end, I assert that the people have a right by a convention, or otherwise, to change the existing government, whilst such existing government is in actual operation, for the ordinary purposes thereof. The example of all America in the adoption of the federal government, and that of several states in changing their state constitutions in this temperate and peaceable manner, undeniably proves my position. The people of Virginia, therefore, if the old government should not be considered as then at an end, permitted it to proceed, and by a convention chosen by themselves, with full powers, for they were not restrained, established then a Constitution.

This convention was not chosen under the sanction of the former government; it was not limited in its powers by it, if indeed it existed, but may be considered as a spontaneous assemblage of the people of Virginia, under a recommendation of a former convention, to consult for the good of themselves, and their posterity. They established a bill of rights, purporting to appertain to their posterity, and a constitution evidently designed to be permanent. This constitution is sanctioned by the consent and acquiescence of the people for seventeen years; and it is admitted by the almost universal opinion of the people, by the repeated adjudications of the courts of this commonwealth, and by very many declarations of the legislature itself, to be of superior authority to any opposing act of the legislature. The celebrated Vattel in a passage of his, which I will not fatigue this audience by quoting, denies to the ordinary legislature the power of changing the fundamental laws, "for, (says he,) it is necessary that the Constitution of the state be fixed."

But if the legislature may infringe this Constitution, it is no longer fixed; it is not this year what it was the last; and the liberties of the people are wholly at the mercy of the legislature.

A very important question now occurs, viz. whose province it is to decide in such cases. It is the province of the judiciary to expound the laws, and to adjudge cases which may be brought before them—the judiciary may clearly say, that a subsequent statute has not changed a former for want of sufficient words, though it was perhaps intended it should do so. It may say too, that an act of assembly has not changed the Constitution, though its words are expressly to that effect; because a legislature must have both the power and the will (as evidenced by words) to change the law, and it is conceived, for the reasons above mentioned, that the legislature have not power to change the fundamental laws. In expounding laws, the judiciary considers *every* law which relates to the subject: would you have them to shut their eyes against that law which is of the highest authority of any, or against a part of that law, which either by its words or by its spirit, denies to any but the people the power to change it? In cases where the controversy before the court does not involve the private interest, or relate to the powers of the judiciary, they are not only the proper, but a perfectly disinterested tribunal;—e.g. if the legislature should deprive a man of the trial by jury—there the controversy is between the legislature on one hand,

and the whole people of Virginia (through the medium of one individual) on the other, which people have declared that the trial by jury shall be held sacred.

In other cases where the private interest of judges may be affected, or where their constitutional powers are encroached upon, their situation is indeed delicate, and let them be ever so virtuous, they will be censured by the ill-disposed part of their fellow-citizens: but in these cases, as well as others, they are bound to decide, and they do actually decide on behalf of the people; for example, though a judge is interested privately in preserving his independence, yet it is the right of the people which should govern him, who in their sovereign character have provided that the judges should be independent; so that it is in fact a controversy between the legislature and the people, though perhaps the judges may be privately interested. The only effect on the judges in such case should be, to distrust their own judgment if the matter is doubtful, or in other words to require clear evidence before they decide in cases where interest may possibly warp the judgment.

From the above premises I conclude that the judiciary may and ought to adjudge a law unconstitutional and void, if it be plainly repugnant to the letter of the Constitution, or the fundamental principles thereof. By fundamental principles I understand, those great principles growing out of the Constitution, by the aid of which, in dubious cases, the Constitution may be explained and preserved inviolate; those land-marks, which it may be necessary to resort to, on account of the impossibility to foresee or provide for cases within the spirit, but without the letter of the Constitution.

To come now more immediately to the question before the court; can those who are appointed judges in chancery, by an act of assembly, without ballot, and without commission during good behavior, constitutionally exercise that office?... If those may be judges who are not appointed by joint ballot, but by an act of assembly, the senate have in that instance more power than the Constitution intended; for they control the other branch, by their negative upon the law, whereas if they mixed with that branch in a joint ballot, a plurality of votes of senators and delegates would decide.

If there can be judges in chancery who have no commission during good behavior, their tenure of office is absolutely at the will of the legislature, and they consequently are not independent. The people of Virginia intended that the judiciary should be independent of the other departments: they are to judge where the legislature is a party, and therefore should be independent of it, otherwise they might judge corruptly, in order to please the legislature and be consequently continued in office. It is an acknowledged principle in all countries, that no man shall be judge in his own cause; but it is nearly the same thing, where the tribunal of justice is under the influence of a party. If the legislature can transfer from constitutional to legislative courts, all judicial powers, these dependent tribunals being the creatures of the legislature itself, will not dare to oppose an unconstitutional law, and the principle I set out upon, viz. that such laws ought to be opposed, would become a dead letter, or in other words, this would pave the way to an uncontrolled power in the legislature. The constitution requires the concurrence of the legislature to appoint, and the executive to commission a judge:—but an appointment by act of assembly, will invest with this high power one who has not the sanction of the executive; and will throw a new office upon a man, without the liberty of declining such appointment, if he thinks proper. For these reasons, and others which it would be tedious to enumerate, I am of opinion, that the clause in question, is repugnant to the fundamental principles of the Constitution, in as much as the judges of the general court have not been balloted for and commissioned as judges in chancery, pursuant to the fourteenth article of the Constitution.

MR. ROANE then said, Although it is not in my opinion now necessary to decide, whether the offices of a judge in chancery and of the general court, may be united in the same person or not, supposing a constitutional appointment to have been made of the same person to each—yet in as much as this question is in some measure involved in the one just discussed, I will give my present impressions upon it, leaving myself free to decide hereafter the one way or the other, should it come judicially before me.

The constitution has declared that the three departments of government should be separate and distinct.—There are great political evils which would arise from their union;—for example, if according to Montesquieu, the members of the legislature were also members of the judiciary, the same man would as a legislator make a tyrannical law, and then as a judge would enforce it tyrannically. This union, it is evident, would produce a complete despotism.

It is therefore a fundamental principle not only of our constitution, but acknowledged by all intelligent writers, to be essential to liberty, that such an union should not take place.

But is there any great political evil resulting from the same person being a judge in chancery, and of the general court?

Is there any constitutional impediment? It would be wise in the legislature to keep the offices separate; for an union of several functions in one person, will put it out of his power to be perfect in either, and the commonwealth will be better served by dividing than by accumulating the public duties.

But it has been said, and I confess with great force, that in as much as the judges in chancery are to be tried, on impeachment, before the general court, if the judges of the general court are also judges in chancery, they in their latter character must be tried before themselves in their former, and consequently there will be a defect of an impartial tribunal. I can only answer this objection by saying, that the former court of appeals was composed of the judges of the general court, court in chancery, and admiralty.—The legislature might have so organized the said courts as to have had nine-tenths of the court of appeals members of the general court.

The judges of the general court are by the constitution to be tried before the court of appeals, i.e. under that organization, before themselves; and the judges of appeals before the general court, which would produce the same dilemma.

This case then is precisely similar to the case before us. And yet the judges of the court of appeals did in the remonstrance of May, one thousand seven hundred and eighty-eight, declare "that the forming the court of appeals, so as to consist of all the judges, is no violation of the constitution;" thereby over-ruling the objection which must have occurred in that case as well as in this.

Upon the whole I must say, that however inconvenient and unwise it might be to unite these distinct offices in the same person;—however in the case that has been supposed, there might be a defect of an impartial tribunal to try an offending chancellor upon an impeachment;—still not seeing any express provision in, or fundamental principle of, the constitution, restricting the power of the legislature in this respect; and grounding myself upon the above recited opinion of the former court of appeals as to the constitutionality of the union of offices which then existed in that body;—my present impressions are, that there is no constitutional impediment, plainly apparent, against uniting the two offices in the same person.

JUDGE HENRY. . . . There is a proposition which I take to be universally true in our constitution, which to gentlemen whose ideas of parliament, and parliamentary powers, were formed under the former government, may not be always obvious; it is this—We were taught that Parliament was omnipotent, and their powers beyond control; now this proposition, in our constitution, is limited, and certain rights are reserved . . . —if this were always kept in mind, it might free the mind from a good deal of embarrassment in discussing several questions where the duty, and the power of the legislature is considered . . .

It is alleged by some of my brethren, that the legislature are not warranted in appointing the same men to be judges both at common law and in chancery. The words of the plan of government are, "they shall appoint judges of the high court of appeals and general court, judges in chancery, &c." These words, *judges in chancery*, are supposed to design different persons from the judges of the general court, and an argument to enforce this opinion is drawn from sect. 16 and 17, where it is provided, that any judge of the general court, offending against the state, may be prosecuted in the high court of appeals; but a chancery judge offending must be prosecuted in the general court; therefore it is alleged, a common law judge cannot be a chancery, nor a chancery a common law judge in our government.

This question has heretofore been alleged as one of the reasons of the high court of appeals for declining to execute a very important law of the land;—without saying anything about the propriety or impropriety of that business, it is sufficient for my present purpose to observe, that the question did not then come before the court in a judicial manner,—it was taken up as a general proposition, and when published, contained an appeal to the people; this looked like a dissolution of the government,—therefore I cannot view it as an adjudged case, to be considered as a binding precedent.

It is much to be wished that the question had been then decided, by calling a convention of the people. But unfortunately the legislature neither yielded the point nor insisted, but adopted an expedient. They new-modelled the courts.—The question then went to sleep, but the legislature preserved the principle; they appointed judges of the high court of appeals, with unlimited jurisdiction, both in law and equity; they appointed judges of the general court, and a judge in chancery.

If the common law and chancery jurisdiction ought not to be united in the same persons in the first instance, I do not see how it can be justified in the appellate jurisdiction. If the form of government has provided that justice at common law ought to be administered by one set of men, and in chancery by another, it seems to me to follow as a necessary inference, that the appellate, as well as the original jurisdiction, ought to be separate and distinct, and that those gentlemen who now exercise the appellate jurisdiction have admitted the legislative construction of the form of government formerly objected to.

But I do not rest the question on this ground. Where I am not bound by regular adjudications of the superior court, I cannot rest on other men's opinions. I must and will think for myself.

Our government is declared to be founded on the authority of the people. The people, in convention, have ordered that a legislature shall be chosen, a governor and council shall be chosen, judges all be appointed.—All these different characters are servants of the people, have different duties, and are amenable to them. When the legislature were intrusted with the appointment of judges, I can find no particular characters, or any description of men, declared to be ineligible, but those holding legislative or executive authority, who are forbidden to interfere. To the discretion of the legislature is committed the choice of the judges, who shall fill all the superior courts, and therefore, if they have chosen, or shall hereafter choose to appoint the same set of men to administer justice to the people, both at common law and in chancery, I cannot find anything in the form of government to restrain them. They are to appoint judges in chancery, at their discretion; and for me to say I cannot act as a chancery judge in any case, because if I should offend, I am to be prosecuted for such an offense before my brethren in the general court, seems to be a strange reason for me to assign for declining the office.

I am therefore very clear and decided in my opinion, that the legislature were fully authorized by the form of government, to appoint the district judges to exercise a chancery jurisdiction in the case before us, and I do cheerfully embrace this public opportunity of declaring my hearty approbation of the measure, and my willingness to act when the appointment is regularly made.

This brings me to the second point in the case. Have the legislature made the appointment in the manner prescribed by the form of government?

I wish most seriously I could have given an affirmative answer to this question. It is provided by the form of government, so often alluded to, that judges in chancery shall be chosen by joint ballot of both houses, shall be commissioned by the governor, shall hold their office during good behavior, and to secure their independence and remove them from all temptations to corruption, their salaries shall be adequate and fixed.—If a chancellor in any case must be chosen by ballot, be commissioned and hold his office during good behavior, surely it is proper, it is necessary in all cases, that every judge shall be so chosen, shall be so commissioned, and hold his office so long as he behaves well. The business of hearing causes originating in that court by injunction, is of a permanent nature. To exercise this duty without the appointment and commission prescribed by the constitution, would be an exercise of a power according to the will of the legislature, who are servants of the people, not only without, but expressly against the will of the people. This would be a solecism in government,—establishing the will of the legislature, servants of the people, to control the will of their masters, if the word may be permitted. Till the appointment is made agreeable to the directions of the constitution, I cannot think myself duly authorized to take upon me the office . . .

[Henry went on to defend his previous conduct in sitting on a special court of appeals for which he had not been duly commissioned.] I freely acknowledge, that I consider this special court, with respect to me, who have been neither appointed nor commissioned since the passing of that law, as unconstitutional; but it is temporary. The case cannot often happen; it is exceedingly disagreeable to be faulting the legislature; and, perhaps, one particular mischief had better be submitted to, than a public inconvenience. These were my reasons for sitting in this special court.

It is most devoutly to be wished, that the present subject, now become the topic of public discussion, may be fully and generally understood, by the legislature, by the judiciary, and by the public at large, that there be no more of these unhappy differences of opinion between any of the different departments of government.

It remains only for me to add, that where I have been appointed and commissioned, I obey with alacrity,—when a new appointment shall be made, and a commission be directed, authorizing me to exercise the office of a judge in chancery, in any case whatever, I shall then have it in my power to exercise the right of every other free man,—to accept or refuse,—though I have no difficulty in declaring, were the appointment perfect, that I might hold during good behavior, I should have no objection to enter upon the discharge of those new duties;—but until that is done, in justice to the public, whose rights are concerned, and to myself as an individual, I must decline the duty prescribed by the law in question, not being as yet such a judge in chancery as the people have said shall exercise that kind of jurisdiction.

Of course, my opinion is that the district court of Dumfries be advised to over-rule the motion for an injunction in this cause.

JUDGE TYLER. . . . Before I proceed to say anything on the adjourned case now under contemplation, I will beg leave to make a few observations on the opinion that some gentlemen have taken up, of the impropriety of the judiciary in deciding against a law which is in contradiction to the Constitution.

A little time and trouble bestowed on this subject, I am sure, would enable any person, endowed with common understanding, to see the fallacy of such sentiments.

What is the Constitution but the great contract of the people, every individual whereof having sworn allegiance to it?—A system of fundamental principles, the violation of which must be considered as a crime of the highest magnitude. That this great and paramount law should be faithfully and rightfully executed, it is divided into three departments, to wit: the legislative, the executive, and judiciary, with an express restraint upon all, so that neither shall encroach on the rights of the other. In the Bill of Rights many things are laid down, which are reserved to the people—trial by jury, on life and death, liberty of conscience, &c. Can the legislature rightfully pass a law taking away these rights from the people? Can the judiciary pass sentence without a conviction of a citizen by twelve of his peers? Can the executive do anything forbidden by this bill of rights, or the constitution? In short, can one branch of the government call upon another to aid in the violation of this sacred letter? The answer to these questions must be in the negative.

But who is to judge of this matter? the legislature only? I hope not.—The object of all governments is and ought to be, the faithful administration of justice.—It cannot, I hope, be less the object of our government, which has been founded on principles very different from any we read of in the world, as it has ingrafted in it a better knowledge of the rights of human nature, and the means of better securing those rights . . . Hence it may reasonably be inferred, that if the commonwealth itself is subordinate to this department of government at times, so therefore will necessarily be the acts of the legislature, when they shall be found to violate first principles, notwithstanding the supposed *"omnipotence of parliament,"* which is an abominable insult upon the honour and good sense of our country, as nothing is omnipotent as it relates to us, either religious or political but the *God of Heaven* and our constitution!

I will not in an extra-judicial manner assume the right to negative a law, for this would be as dangerous as the example before us; but if by any legal means I have jurisdiction of a cause, in which it is made a question how far the law be a violation of the constitution, and therefore of no obligation, I shall not shrink from a comparison of the two, and pronounce sentence as my mind may receive conviction. To be made an agent, therefore, for the purpose of violating the constitution, I cannot consent to. As a citizen I should complain of it; as a public servant, filling an office in one of the great departments of government, I should be a traitor to my country to do it. But the violations must be plain and clear, or there might be danger of the judiciary preventing the operation of laws which might be productive of much public good. These premises being admitted, as I think they must, I will now draw a comparison of the law before us with the constitution. The constitution declares there shall be judges in chancery, judges of the general court, &c; and the first question that occurs in this—Can the office of a judge in chancery and common law be rightfully vested in the same persons, provided the appointment be regular—To which I answer, I see no incompatibility, in the exercise of these offices, by the same persons—for although they be distinct offices, possessing distinct powers, they do not necessarily blend and run together, because they are placed in the same hands. The judge who knows the powers and duties of both, will well know how to keep them apart—like the rays of the sun, they radiate from one common centre, and may run parallel forever, without an interference. But to this, an ingenious and subtile argument is offered, and taken from the 17th article of the constitution, wherein it is directed, that when the judges of the general court are impeached, the court of appeals shall set in judgment—but all other officers of government, shall be impeached before the general court. Therefore, the constitution meant to keep the offices distinct, in distinct hands, because it is possible that they may try one another, and perhaps form a combination, in favour of the fraternity. This is too nice a deduction, and is a better argument in favour of an amendment of the constitution, than of the question under consideration. We cannot supply defects; nor can we reconcile absurdities, if any there be; this must be done by the people; and were we about the business of amendments duly authorized, it might be well to consider this point. But I cannot see why a judge in chancery, if he be a judge also of the general court, may not be tried by the court of appeals; for if he be convicted of such a crime, as he ought to be displaced from office in either capacity, he would hardly be allowed to hold the other; nor do I see why the judges of the general court, cannot try their brothers in chancery . . .

The next inquiry we are to make, brings us pointedly to the comparison of the law now under contemplation, and the constitution; and how does it stand? The constitution says that judges in chancery shall be appointed by joint ballot of both houses of assembly, and commissioned by the governor during good behaviour—and for the most valuable purposes; to secure the independence of the judiciary. Contrary to this express direction, which admits of no doubt, implication or nice construction, that bane to political freedom, the legislature has made the appointment by an act mandatory, to the judges, leaving them not at liberty to accept or refuse the office conferred, which is a right every citizen enjoys in every other case—a right too sacred to be yielded to any power on earth. But, were I willing to do it as it relates to myself, as a judge I ought not; because it would frustrate that most important object before-mentioned—intended by the constitution to be kept sacred, for the wisest and best of purposes—to wit, that justice and the law be done to all manner of persons without fear or reward.

For how would the rights of individuals stand when brought in contest with the public, or even an influential character, if the judges may be removed from office by the same power who appointed them, to wit, by a statute appointment as in this case, and by a statute disappointment as was the case in court of appeals. Might not danger be apprehended from this source when future times shall be more corrupt and yet, thank Heaven, the time has not arrived, when any judge has thus degraded his office, or dignity as a man, by a decision governed by fear or any other base motive; and I hope a long time will yet elapse before this will be the case. But our constitution was made, not only for the present day, but for ages to come, subject only to such alterations as the people may please to make. Let me now compare the law and the constitution in the other point; that of the want of a commission during good behaviour, and the reasons will fully or forcibly apply— when I receive the commission, I see the ground on which I stand. I see that my own integrity is that ground, and no opinions, but such as are derived from base motives, can be sufficient to remove me from office—in which case whensoever an appeal is made to me by an injured citizen, I will do him justice, as far as my mental powers will enable me to discover it, without any apprehensions of an unjust attack—that if the proudest sovereign on earth was in contest with the lowest peasant, that creeps through this vale of sorrow, yet should the arm of justice be extended to him also.

To conclude, I do declare that I will not hold an office, which I believe to be unconstitutional; that I will not be made a fit agent, to assist the legislature in a violation of this sacred letter; that I form this opinion from the conviction I feel that I am free to think, speak, and act, as other men do upon so great a question; that as I never did sacrifice my own opinions for the sake of popularity in the various departments I have had the honour to fill, however desirable popular favour may be, when obtained upon honorable principles; so now that I am grown old I cannot depart from those motives which I have both in public and private life made my standard—I concur therefore most heartily with my brothers, who have gone before me, in the last two points, that the law is unconstitutional and ought not to be executed; the injunction therefore must be over ruled—and this opinion I form not from a view of the memorials, nor from writers who know not the blessings of free government, but as they were seen and felt through the prospect of future times, but from honest reason, common sense, and the great letter of a *Free Constitution*!

JUDGE TUCKER. . . . The question which it is now incumbent on this court to decide, seems to me to be shortly this—whether a *judge of the general court* of this commonwealth, can constitutionally exercise the functions of a judge in chancery? This calls upon us for recurrence to fundamental principles, a duty which our bill of rights expressly imposes upon all the servants of the commonwealth. And this renders it necessary not only to investigate the *principles* upon which our government is founded, but the *authority* by which it was established; inasmuch as there are doubts in the breasts of many, whether our *constitution* itself is any more than an act of the ordinary legislature, revocable, or subject to alteration by them, in any manner, and at any time.

In considering this question, I shall first state my own impressions, arising from the text of the constitution, and the spirit of our government, only unsupported by any former judicial opinions on the subject and, secondly, as founded on the authority and decisions of the court of appeals.

I. In stating my own impressions, I shall consider:

1st, Whether the constitution, or form of government of this commonwealth, be an act of the ordinary legislature, and, consequently revocable, or subject to alteration by the same authority; or something paramount thereto?

2dly, Whether, according to that constitution, the functions of a *judge of the general court*, and a *judge in chancery*, were intended to be distinct; or might be blended in the same person?

1st, Whether the constitution be an act of the ordinary legislature; or something paramount thereto? [Tucker, like his colleagues, rejected the suggestion made by Jefferson among others that the Virginia Constitution was defective in authority because the convention that adopted it also enacted ordinary legislation.]

It seems to me an observation of great importance, that the *declaration of independence* by *this state* [on June 29, 1776] was *first made* in that instrument which *establishes our constitution*. The instant that the declaration of independence took effect, had the convention proceeded no farther, the government, as formerly exercised by the crown of Great Britain, being thereby totally dissolved, there would never have been an ordinary legislature, nor any other organized body, or authority in Virginia. Every man would have been utterly absolved from every social tie, and remitted to a perfect state of nature. But a power to demolish the existing fabric of government, which no one will, I presume, at this day, deny to that convention, without authority to erect a new one, could never be presumed. A new organization of the fabric, and a new arrangement of the powers of government, must instantly take place, to prevent those evils which the absence of government must infallibly produce in any case; but more especially under circumstances so awful, and prospects so threatening, as those which surrounded the people of America, at that alarming period. It would therefore have been absurdity in the extreme, in the people of Virginia, to authorize the convention to absolve them from the bonds of one government, without the power to unite them under any other, at a time when the utmost exertions of government were required to preserve both their liberties and their lives; but since they are *both* in *form* and *effect*, only *different clauses of the same act*, and necessary consequences of each other, to question the validity of the one, is to deny the effect of the other. The *declaration of independence*, and the *constitution*, as the ACTS OF THE PEOPLE, must therefore stand, or fall together . . .

From what I have said, I am inclined to hope, that it will appear that our constitution was not the act of the ordinary legislature: a few words concerning its operation, authority, and effect, as the act of the people, may not be improper . . .

Vattel, in treating of the fundamental laws of a state, observes, "that a nation may entrust the exercise of the legislative power to the prince, or to an assembly, or to that assembly and the prince, jointly; who have then a right of making new, and of abrogating old laws. It is here demanded, whether if their power extends as far as the fundamental laws, they may change the constitution of the state? To this he answers, we may decide with certainty, that the authority of these legislators does not extend so far, and that they ought to consider the fundamental laws as sacred, if the nation has not in *express terms given them power to change them*. For the constitution of the state ought to be fixed; and since that was first established by the nation, which afterwards trusted certain persons with the legislative powers, the fundamental laws are excepted from their commission. In short, these legislators derive their power from the constitution: how then can they change it, without destroying the foundation of their authority?"

That the legislature of this commonwealth have regarded our Constitution in this light, will appear from more than one authority. I shall select the preamble of an act passed in May session, 1783, . . . entitled an act to amend an act, . . . concerning the appointment of sheriffs, which recites "that the former act was contrary to the Constitution, or form of government," for which reason it was repealed . . . Other instances doubtless may be found in our laws, where the legislature have either expressly, or tacitly, recognized the Constitution as paramount to their own legislative acts; so that reasoning, in this instance, is confirmed by precedent.

But here an objection will no doubt be drawn from the authority of those writers who affirm, that the constitution of a state is a rule to the legislature only, and not to the judiciary, or the executive: the legislature being bound not to transgress it; but that neither the executive nor judiciary can resort to it to enquire whether they do transgress it, or not.

This sophism could never have obtained a moment's credit with the world, had such a thing as a written Constitution existed before the American revolution. "All the governments that now exist in the world, (says a late writer [Tucker cited Sir James Mackintosh's 1791 *Vindiciae Gallicae*]) except the United States of America, have been fortuitously formed. They are the produce of chance, not the work of art. They have been altered, impaired, improved, and destroyed, by accidental circumstances, beyond the foresight or control of wisdom; their parts, thrown up against present emergencies, formed no systematic whole." What the *constitution* of any country *was* or rather *was supposed to be*, could only be collected from what the *government had at any time done*; what had been *acquiesced* in by the people, or other component parts of the government; or what had been *resisted* by either of them. Whatever the government, or any branch of it had *once done*, it was inferred they had a *right* to do *again*. The union of the legislative and executive powers in the same men, or body of men, ensured the success of their usurpations; and the judiciary, having no *written constitution* to refer to, were obliged to *receive* whatever *exposition* of it the legislature might think proper to make. But, with us, the constitution is not an "ideal thing, but a real existence: it can be produced in a visible form" [quoting Thomas Paine's *The Rights of Man*]: its principles can be ascertained from the living letter, not from obscure reasoning or deductions only. The government, therefore, and all its branches must be governed by the constitution. Hence it becomes the first law of the land, and as such must be resorted to on every occasion, where it becomes necessary to expound *what the law is*. This exposition it is the duty and office of the judiciary to make; our constitution expressly declaring that the legislative, executive, and judiciary, shall be separate and distinct, so that neither exercise the powers properly belong[ing] to the other. Now since it is the province of the legislature to make, and of the executive to enforce obedience to the laws, the duty of expounding must be exclusively vested in the judiciary. But how can any just exposition be made, *if that which is the supreme law of the land be withheld from their view*? Suppose a question had arisen on either of the acts before cited, which the legislature have discovered to be unconstitutional, would the judiciary have been bound by the act, or by the constitution?

But that the constitution is a rule to all the departments of the government, to the judiciary as well as to the legislature, may, I think, be proved by reference to a few parts of it.

The bill of rights, art. 8 provides, that in all capital and criminal prosecutions, the party accused shall be tried by a *jury of the vicinage*, and cannot be found guilty without their *unanimous* consent.

Suppose any future act of the legislature should abridge either of these privileges, what would be said of a court that should act in conformity to such an act? . . .

Art. 10. declares that general warrants are illegal and oppressive, and ought not to be granted. Is this . . . a dead letter, because we have no act of the legislature to enforce the obligation?

Art. 16. secures the free exercise of our religious duties, according to the dictates of every man's own conscience. Should the legislature, at any future period, establish any particular mode of worship, and enact penal laws to support it, will the courts of this commonwealth be bound to enforce those penalties?

Art. 15 of the constitution, declares that the clerks of courts shall hold their offices during good behaviour, to be judged of and determined in the general court. Can any legislative act give any other court cognizance of such a case? Or can any impeachment be tried in any court of this commonwealth, except this court, and the court of appeals, even should an act of the legislature (as was once contemplated) erect a court for that especial purpose?

From all these instances it appears to me that this deduction clearly follows, viz. that the *judiciary* are *bound* to take notice of the constitution, *as the first law of the land*; and that whatsoever is contradictory thereto, is not the law of the land . . . [Tucker went on to quote at length from Federalist No. 78, in which Hamilton asserted the legitimacy of judicial review.]

Such is the reasoning of one of the most profound politicians in America. It is so full, so apposite, and so conclusive, that I think it unnecessary to add anything farther on the subject, and shall now proceed to the second point, viz.

2. Whether, according to the constitution of this commonwealth, a judge of the general court can exercise the functions of a judge in chancery?

There again I must recur to one of the fundamental principles of our government, a principle essentially and indispensably necessary to its existence as a free government, exercised by the immediate authority of the people, delegated to the servants of their own choice, viz. the separation of the legislative, executive, and judiciary departments.

These departments, as I have before observed, our constitution declares shall be for ever [sic] separate and distinct. To be so, they must be independent one of another, so that neither can control, or annihilate the other.

The independence of the judiciary results from the tenure of their office, which constitution declares shall be *during good behaviour*. The offices which they are to fill must therefore in their nature be permanent as the constitution itself, and not liable to be discontinued or annihilated by any other branch of the government. Hence the constitution has provided that the judiciary department should be arranged in such a manner as not to be subject to legislative control. The court of appeals, court of chancery, and general court, are tribunals expressly required by it; and in these courts the judiciary power is either immediately, or ultimately vested.

These courts can neither be annihilated nor discontinued by any legislative act; nor can the judges of them be removed from their offices for any cause, except a breach of their good behavior.

But if the legislature might at any time discontinue or annihilate either of these courts, it is plain that their tenure of office might be changed, since a judge, without any breach of good behaviour, might in effect be removed from office, by annihilating or discontinuing the office itself.

This has been proved in the case of the former court of appeals. The moment it was discovered that that court was not constituted according to the directions of the constitution, the legislature, without any charge of a breach of good behavior by any one of that court, *removed a majority* of the judges from their office, as judges of that court, *by new modelling the court altogether*.

I am far from considering this act of the legislature as unconstitutional, for reasons that I shall hereafter mention.

But it proves that the judiciary can never be independent, so long as the existence of the office depends upon the will of the ordinary legislature, and not upon a constitutional foundation.

The district courts considered as independent of the *general court*, and not a modification of it, are merely *legislative* courts; and consequently may be discontinued, or annihilated, whenever the legislature may think proper to abolish them. And if the judges of those courts held their offices only as judges of the district courts, they might be virtually, and in fact, removed from office, as the judges of the former court of appeals were, by a legislative act, discontinuing the courts, and transferring their jurisdiction to other tribunals, *without any breach of good behaviour*.

Hence arises a most important distinction between *constitutional* and *legislative* courts. The judges of the former hold an office co-existent with the government itself, and which they can only forfeit by a breach of good behaviour. The judges of the latter, although their commissions should import upon the face of them, to be during good behaviour, may be at any time discontinued from their office, by abolishing the courts. In other words, constitutional judges may be an independent branch of the government, legislative judges must ever be dependent on that body at whose will their offices exist.

If the principles of our government have established the judiciary as a barrier against the possible usurpation, or abuse of power in the other departments, how easily may that principle be evaded by converting our courts into legislative, instead of constitutional tribunals?

To preserve this principle in its full vigour, it is necessary that the constitutional courts should all be restrained within those limits which the constitution itself seems to have assigned to them respectively.

What those limits are, may be collected from the 14th article, which provides for the appointment of "*judges* of the supreme court of *appeals*, and *general court*, *judges* in *chancery*, *judges* of *admiralty*," &c. This specification of judges of *several tribunals* would lead us of itself to conclude, that the tribunals themselves were meant to be separate and distinct. This conclusion seems to be warranted by two circumstances, the one extrinsic, the other arising out of the constitution itself. Those who recollect the situation of our jurisprudence, at the time of the revolution, will remember that civil and criminal, common law, and equity jurisdiction, all in the general court, was one of the worst defects of the system. In truth, nothing can be more dangerous to the citizen, than the union of criminal courts, and courts of equity. On the European continent, wheresoever the civil law has been adopted, criminal and civil proceedings have been conducted upon the like principles: the defendant in *civil* cases might be examined upon oath by interrogatories, to which if he gave not satisfactory answers he might be committed until he did: this principle being extended to *criminal* cases, was denominated by the moderate term of putting the person accused to the *question*: but inasmuch as the forcing a criminal to accuse himself on oath, might prove a *snare to his conscience*, the obligation to answer to the question was *inforced by torture*. To separate for ever [*sic*], courts, whose principles and proceedings are so diametrically opposite as those of the common and civil law, was, I should presume, one of the fundamental principles which the framers of our constitution had an eye to. They, therefore, distributed the powers of the *then existing general court* into three distinct branches, viz. the court of appeals, the court of chancery, and the court of general juris-diction, at common law. The repetition of the term, judges, shows that it was in contem-plation that both the tribunals, and the judges should be distinct and separate. This is further confirmed by art. 16 and 17: the former of which provides that impeachments in general shall be prosecuted in this court, the latter that impeachments against the judges of this court, shall be prosecuted in the court of appeals. Nothing, then, can be clearer than that the constitution intended they should be distinct judges of distinct courts. And hence I am satisfied, that the former court of appeals was unconstitutionally organized. This reasoning, I apprehend, will apply no less forcibly to the separation of the general court from the court of chancery. A judge of the general court, if impeached, can be prosecuted in the *court of appeals only*; a judge in chancery *only* in the *general court*: if these offices be united in the same person, it must be by separate commissions; a judgment on impeachment in the general court cannot vacate the commission of a judge of that court, because the constitution has assigned another tribunal, where a judge of that court shall be tried; a judgment in the court of appeals cannot vacate the commission of a judge in chancery, because he must be tried, as such, in the general court. Hence it seems to me we are driven to conclude that the constitution meant that the two offices shall be separate and distinct. This construction removes every difficulty; the contrary, I apprehend, creates a multitude, and those insurmountable. In pursuance of this direction, contained in the constitution, the legislature, when it set about organizing the courts, distributed them as above-mentioned. The criminal and common law court, was separated from the court of equity; and both from the court of appeals, in form, though not in reality, until the legislature, by the act of 1788, corrected its former error. And thus distinct have they remained, until the act of the last session, which hath not indeed united the constitutional courts, but hath blended them in effect, by assigning the functions of a judge in chancery to the judges of this court; and if carried into effect may lead to the total annihilation of all the courts which the constitution had in contemplation to establish.

I have said before that the district courts considered as independent of the general court, and not a modification of it, are mere legislative, and not constitutional courts. If they are a modification only of the general court, it flows from what I have already said, that the constitution prohibits the exercise of chancery jurisdiction therein. If they be mere leg-islative courts, it cannot be the duty of any judge of a constitutional court, merely as such, to exercise the functions of a judge of these courts: and it is, I conceive, expressly contrary to the duty of a constitutional judge of one court, to exercise the functions of a constitutional judge of another distinct constitutional court.

It appears then immaterial, whether, on the present question, the district courts are to be considered as branches of the general court, or not: yet it would be easy to show, that as they are at present modified and organized, they are nothing more than branches of that court; and not distinct, independent, legislative courts; unless the operation of the act in question should be construed to affect and change their whole system and constitution.

But, if they are mere legislative courts, they may at any time, be organized at the will of the legislature: legislative judges may be appointed, the tenor of whose commission may import that their office shall be during good behaviour, and yet that office be discontinued whenever the legislature may think fit. If the jurisdiction of the court of chancery can be constitutionally transferred to them, so may that of the general court, and of the court of appeals. In fine these legislative courts may absorb all the jurisdictions, powers and functions of the constitutional courts. These last then must either be suppressed as useless, which the constitution forbids; or the judges of them will hold *sinecures* instead of *offices*, which is expressly contrary to the bill of rights, art. 4. Add to this that such an arrangement must ever render the judiciary the mere creature of the legislative department, which both the constitution, and the bill of rights most pointedly appear to have guarded against.

[II.] I shall now proceed to take a short view of the subject, as founded upon a solemn decision of the court of appeals, on a similar occasion.

It will not, I presume, be denied that the decisions of the supreme court of appeals in this commonwealth, upon any question, whether arising upon the general principles of law, the operation or construction of any statute or act of assembly, or of the constitution of this commonwealth, are to be resorted to by all other courts, as expounding, in their truest sense, the laws of the land; and where any decision of that court applies to a case depending before any other tribunal, that tribunal is bound to regulate its decision conformably to those of the court of appeals. This postulatum I conceive to be too obviously founded upon the principles of our government to require an attempt to demonstrate it. Proceeding upon this ground, I shall take up the question upon the authority of a previous decision of that court, on a similar question.

In the year 1787, the first act establishing district courts was passed. This act "declared it to be the duty of the judges of the high court of appeals to attend the said courts, allotting among themselves the district, any two of whom should constitute a court."

It should be remembered, that at that time the court of appeals was composed of the judges of the high court of chancery, judges of the general court, and judges of the court of admiralty. The office of the judge of the court of appeals was, at that time, as it were, incidentally annexed to their appointment to a seat on either of the other tribunals.

A part of the duty assigned to the court of appeals by that act was the appointment of clerks to the district courts, which the act required should be done at the next succeeding session of the court of appeals.

On the 12th of May following, the court made the following entry upon their records. "On consideration of a late act of assembly, entitled an act establishing district courts, after several conferences, and upon mature deliberation, the court do *adjudge* that clerks of the said courts ought not now to be appointed, for reasons contained in a remonstrance to the general assembly"—which remonstrance is likewise entered on record, and contains, among other things, the following important passages.

"1. That in discussing the act establishing district courts, the court found it unavoidable to consider, whether the principles of that act do not violate those of the constitution, or form of government, which the people, in 1776, when the former bands of their society were dissolved, established as the foundation of that government which they judged necessary for the preservation of their persons and property; and if such violation were apparent, whether they had power, and it was their duty to declare that the act must yield to the constitution?

2. That they found themselves obliged to decide, whatever temporary inconveniences might arise, and in that decision to declare, that the constitution and the acts were in opposition, and could not exist together, and that the former must control the latter.

3. That the propriety and necessity of the independence of the judges is evident in reason, and the nature of their office, since they are to decide between government and the people, as well as between contending citizens; and if they be dependent on either, corrupt influence may be apprehended.

4. That this applies more forcibly to exclude a dependence on the legislature, a branch of whom, in cases of impeachment, is itself a party.

5. To obviate a possible objection that the court while they are maintaining the independence of the judiciary, are countenancing encroachments of that branch upon the departments of others, and assuming a right to control the legislature, it may be observed, that when they decide between an act of the people, and an act of the legislature, they are within the line of their duty, declaring what the law is, and not making a new law.

6. That although the duties of their office were not ascertained at the time of establishing the constitution, yet in respect thereto, the constitution gives a principle, namely, that no future regulation should blend the duties of the judges of the general court, court of chancery, and court of admiralty, which the constitution seems to require to be exercised by distinct persons . . . "

These declarations, according to my weak apprehensions, comprehend the present question in the fullest extent. I should therefore be of opinion, upon the ground of this authority, as well as upon the conviction of my own mind, independent thereof, which, unless so fortified, I might have mistrusted, that we ought to certify to the district court of Dumfries "That in the opinion of this court, a judge of the general court cannot constitutionally exercise the functions of a judge in chancery." But the judges who have already delivered their opinions, although some of them appear to dissent from me upon this point, having unanimously concurred in another, viz. That the functions of a judge in chancery can only be exercised by those who may be constituted judges in chancery, in the manner prescribed by the constitution; I shall concur in their unanimous judgment, without offering any reasons on a subject which has been so fully and satisfactorily discussed by them.

Comment

Kamper v. Hawkins, like most early cases involving the possibility of judicial review, arose out of a legislative intervention into the organization and jurisdiction of the judiciary itself; and it provoked the most elaborate discussion of the legitimacy of judicial review prior to *Marbury v. Madison*.

Perhaps the most striking feature of *Kamper* was the unanimity with which judges who sharply disagreed over the rationale and methodology of judicial review agreed on the propriety of some form of it. None of the judges disputed Judge Nelson's pronouncement that the state constitution was "a rule of action to the branches of government" limiting the legitimate authority of legislature, executive, and courts alike, or that any public servant who knowingly acted contrary to the Constitution would be, in Tyler's strong language, "a traitor to [his] country." The court, however, was divided over the proper means of fulfilling its obligation to the constitution.

Judge Henry offered the narrowest description of judicial review, as a sheerly defensive tool by which the judges could decline to exercise jurisdiction "according to the will of the legislature, who are servants of the people . . . but expressly against the will of the people." Henry clearly regarded even this limited power as extraordinary in character. He denied, for example, that the Judges' Remonstrance of 1788 was of any constitutional authority, and expressed his wish that such a clash of constitutional opinion within the government had been resolved by a convention of the people. Henry went on to justify his own earlier failure to decline an unconstitutional grant of jurisdiction in terms indicating his extreme reluctance to disobey a statutory command: "[I]t is exceedingly disagreeable to be faulting the legislature; and, perhaps, one particular mischief had better be submitted to, than a public inconvenience."

Judge Tyler provided a slightly more aggressive interpretation of judicial review. Although he insisted that a decision "to negative a law" should only be taken in an actual case (a critical allusion to the 1788 Remonstrance), where judges did have the duty to decide a controversy, they were obligated to refuse "to aid in the violation of this sacred letter." Tyler agreed with Henry's assumption that "the case cannot often happen" that a court would be justified in holding a statute unconstitutional; as Tyler put the test, "the violation must be plain and clear." His desire to limit the judicial power he was recognizing did not rest solely on respect for legislative prerogatives, but also picked up on the fear of judicial discretion common to Enlightenment thought and certain aspects of the English Whig tradition. In what was probably a comment on Roane's enthusiastic endorsement of judicial interpretation of the Constitution, Tyler attacked "nice construction" as "that bane to political freedom" and renounced any power to "supply defects" or "reconcile absurdities" in the Constitution as written.

At the opposite pole from Henry and Tyler, who acknowledged only a passive judicial ability to avoid involvement in constitutional usurpation, Judges Roane and Tucker argued that judicial review was the key element in making American constitutionalism function. A case in which an individual invoked a constitutional right against a statute was, in fact, in Roane's words, a "controversy between the legislature on one hand, and the whole people of Virginia . . . on the other." Rather than being the *only* situations in which courts might ignore statutes, as Henry and Tyler implied, cases involving the judges' own jurisdiction were the *least* suitable for judicial review.

The power of judicial review, according to Roane and Tucker, was inherent in the notion of a written Constitution. Such an instrument entailed the existence of some means to prevent legislative modification of its terms, and its provisions and "fundamental principles" afforded judges standards by which to measure the legitimacy of legislative acts. A written Constitution was law, and, because it was the exclusive power of the judges to say "what the law is," judicial interpretations of the Constitution necessarily took precedence over legislative ones. For this reason, both Roane and Tucker, unlike their colleagues, regarded the 1788 Judges' Remonstrance as binding constitutional authority, though they disagreed over its application in *Kamper*.

The centrality of judicial review in Roane's and Tucker's constitutionalism was accompanied by a confidence in judicial interpretation that stemmed from the common-law approach to statutory construction. Roane asserted that courts should invalidate not only a law "expressly repugnant to the Constitution; but also one which is, by a plain and natural construction, in opposition to the fundamental principles thereof"; and Tucker invoked as parallel authorities the constitutional text, "the spirit of our government," and the "decisions of the court of appeals." Because the meaning of all law was authoritatively fixed by a jurisdiction's highest court, decisions of the state court of appeals necessarily "expound, in their truest sense," the constitution as well.

Judge Nelson provided a rationale for judicial review that lay between the passive and activist arguments of his colleagues. He dismissed the assumption (implicit in the opinions of Roane and Tucker) that the courts were "the champions of the people, or of the Constitution," but he rejected with equal vigor any limitation of judicial review to situations involving unconstitutional grants of jurisdiction. The power to declare a statute void, he insisted, was a necessary incident of the judges' power to decide any cases whatever. All lawyers conceded that a court confronted by two contradictory statutes had no option but to declare which was in force; in like manner, where both a constitutional provision and a statute applied to a case yet commanded contrary results, a court could not legitimately avoid deciding which should govern. The decision against the statute that must follow did not involve any assertion of judicial supremacy, for it was no more than an ordinary exercise of the power to decide cases—in Nelson's language, "a judicial act."

On the merits, the *Kamper* judges agreed that the 1792 district court act was invalid because it appointed them to judicial office without observing the requirements of process and tenure ordained by the state constitution. The judges, however, disagreed on the reasoning behind this conclusion. Roane, for example, regarded the constitution's procedures as designed to safeguard the exercise of judicial review itself, but Henry, at the other extreme, simply expressed his unwillingness to exercise chancery powers until "duly authorized." Nelson and Tucker also endorsed a second ground for the decision: the act's combination of common law and equity powers in individual judges. In doing so, Tucker drew a distinction, important in later federal constitutional law, between constitutional courts, which were independent of the legislature, and legislative courts, subject to plenary legislative control. In *Kamper*, however, none of the other judges endorsed Tucker's approach.

Kamper is important for subsequent United States constitutional history for several reasons. Roane and Tucker both were to play significant roles in that history, and *Kamper* was the fullest exposition either man ever gave of his aggressive concept of judicial review. More indirectly, Nelson's "process" justification of judicial review may have influenced the views of Virginia lawyers such as John Marshall.

James Kent
"Introductory Lecture to a Course of Law Lectures"
(November 17, 1794)[60]

Most, if not all, of the Virginia judges in *Kamper v. Hawkins* supported the Republican position in federal politics. James Kent, of New York, was a political supporter of the

Federalist party, and on most issues a staunch nationalist. In 1794 he began a series of law lectures at Columbia. Although he was an unsuccessful teacher, three years later he began a career on the New York bench that eventually led to almost universal contemporaneous recognition as one of America's greatest judges and legal scholars.

... The first Congress, which assembled in the year 1774, discovered a familiar acquaintance with the sound principles of Government, and just notions of the social Rights of Mankind. They declared and asserted these Rights with a perspicuity, force, manliness and firmness, which threw much lustre on the American Character. The late Earl of Chatham said he could discover no Nation or Council that surpassed them, notwithstanding he had read Thucydides, and had studied and admired the master-states of antiquity.

By thus comparing the excellent Principles of our Civil Policy, with their effects upon the progress of our Government, and the spirit of our People, we are insensibly and properly led to feel for them an uncommon share of reverence and attachment. I cannot but be of opinion, that the Rudiments of a Law and Senatorial Education in this country, ought accordingly to be drawn from our own History and Constitutions. We shall by this means imbibe the principles of Republican Government from pure fountains: and prevent any improper impressions being received from the artificial distinctions, the oppressive establishments, or the wild innovations which at present distinguish the Trans-Atlantic World.

The British Constitution and Code of Laws, to the knowledge of which our Lawyers are so early and deeply introduced by the prevailing course of their professional inquiries, abounds, it is true, with invaluable Principles of Equity, of Policy, and of Social Order: Principles which cannot be too generally known, studied and received. It must however be observed at the same time, that many of the fundamental doctrines of their Government, and Axioms of their Jurisprudence, are utterly subversive of an Equality of Rights, and totally incompatible with the liberal spirit of our American Establishments. The Student of our Laws should be carefully taught to distinguish between the Principles of the one Government, and the Genius which presides in the other. He ought to have a correct acquaintance with genuine Republican Maxims, and be thereby induced to cultivate a superior regard for our own, and I trust more perfect systems of Liberty and Justice. In the words of a discerning writer in this country [Nathaniel Chipman], who has very ably unfolded the doctrine of Representative Republics, "the Student should be led thro' a System of Laws applicable to our Governments, and a train of reasoning congenial to their Principles."

But there is one consideration, which places in a strong point of view, the importance of a knowledge of our constitutional principles, as a part of the education of an American Lawyer; and this arises from the uncommon efficacy of our Courts of Justice, in being authorized to bring the validity of a law to the test of the Constitution. As this is however a subject of a very interesting tendency, and has in many cases inspired doubts and difficulties, I will take the liberty of devoting a few reflections to it, even in this Introductory Discourse.

The doctrine I have suggested, is peculiar to the United States. In the European World, no idea has ever been entertained (or at least until lately) of placing constitutional limits to the exercise of the Legislative Power. In England, where the Constitution has separated and designated the Departments of Government with precision and notoriety, the Parliament is still considered as transcendently absolute; and altho some Judges have had the freedom to observe, that a Statute made against natural equity was void, yet it is generally laid down as a necessary principle in their Law, that no Act of Parliament can be questioned or disputed. But in this country we have found it expedient to establish certain rights, to be deemed paramount to the power of the ordinary Legislature, and this precaution is considered in general as essential to perfect security, and to guard against the occasional violence and momentary triumphs of party. Without some express provisions of this kind clearly settled in the original compact, and constantly protected by the firmness and moderation of the Judicial department, the equal rights of a minor faction, would perhaps very often be disregarded in the animated competitions for power, and fall a sacrifice to the passions of a fierce and vindictive majority.

No question can be made with us, but that the Acts of the Legislative body, contrary to the true intent and meaning of the Constitution, ought to be absolutely null and void. The only inquiry which can arise on the subject is, whether the Legislature is not of itself the competent Judge of its own constitutional limits, and its acts of course to be presumed always conformable to the commission under which it proceeds; or whether the business of determining in this instance, is not rather the fit and exclusive province of the Courts of Justice. It is easy to see, that if the Legislature was left the ultimate Judge of the nature and extent of the barriers which have been placed against the abuses of its discretion, the efficacy of the check would be totally lost. The Legislature would be inclined to narrow or explain away the Constitution, from the force of the same propensities or considerations of temporary expediency, which would lead it to overturn private rights. Its will would be the supreme law, as much with, as without these constitutional safeguards. Nor is it probable, that the force of public opinion, the only restraint that could in that case exist, would be felt, or if felt, would be greatly regarded. If public opinion was in every case to be presumed correct and competent to be trusted, it is evident, there would have been no need of original and fundamental limitations. But sad experience has sufficiently taught mankind, that opinion is not an infallible standard of safety. When powerful rivalries prevail in the Community, and Parties become highly disciplined and hostile, every measure of the major part of the Legislature is sure to receive the sanction of that Party among their Constituents to which they belong. Every Step of the minor Party, it is equally certain will be approved by their immediate adherents, as well as indiscriminately misrepresented or condemned by the prevailing voice. The Courts of Justice which are organized with peculiar advantages to exempt them from the baneful influence of Faction, and to secure at the same time, a steady, firm and impartial interpretation of the Law, are therefore the most proper power in the Government to keep the Legislature within the limits of its duty and to maintain the Authority of the Constitution.

It is regarded also as an undisputed principle in American Politics, that the different departments of Government should be kept as far as possible separate and distinct. The Legislative body ought not to exercise the Powers of the Executive and Judicial, or either of them, except in certain precise and clearly specified cases. An innovation upon this natural distribution of power, has a tendency to overturn the balance of the Government, and to introduce Tyranny into the Administration. But the interpretation or construction of the Constitution is as much a JUDICIAL act, and requires the exercise of the same LEGAL DISCRETION, as the interpretation or construction of a Law. The Courts are indeed bound to regard the Constitution [as] what it truly is, a Law of the highest nature, to which every inferior or derivative regulation must conform. It comes from the People themselves in their original character, when defining the permanent conditions of the social alliance. And to contend that the Courts must adhere implicitly to the Acts of the Legislature, without regarding the Constitution, and even when those Acts are in opposition to it, is to contend that the power of the Agent is greater than that of his Principal, and that the will of only one concurrent and co-ordinate department of the subordinate authority, ought to controul the fundamental Laws of the People.

This power in the Judicial, of determining the constitutionality of Laws, is necessary to preserve the equilibrium of the government, and prevent usurpations of one part upon another; and of all the parts of government, the Legislative body is by far the most impetuous and powerful. A mere designation on paper, of the limits of the several departments, is altogether insufficient, and for this reason in limited Constitutions, the executive is armed with a negative, either qualified or complete upon the making of Laws. But the Judicial Power is the weakest of all, and as it is equally necessary to be preserved entire, it ought not in sound theory to be left naked without any constitutional means of defence. This is one reason why the Judges in this State are associated with the Governor to form the Council of Revision, and this association renders some of these observations less applicable to our own particular Constitution, than to any other. The right of expounding the Constitution as well as Laws, will however be found in general to be the most fit, if not only effectual weapon, by which the Courts of Justice are enabled to repel assaults, and to guard against encroachments on their Chartered Authorities.

Nor can any danger be apprehended, lest this principle should exalt the Judicial above the Legislature. They are co-ordinate powers, and equally bound by the instrument under which they act, and if the former should at any time be prevailed upon to substitute arbitrary will, to the exercise of a rational Judgment, as it is possible it may do even in the ordinary course of judicial proceeding, it is not left like the latter, to the mere controul of public opinion. The Judges may be brought before the tribunal of the Legislature, and tried, condemned, and removed from office.

I consider then the Courts of Justice, as the proper and intended Guardians of our limited Constitutions, against the factions and encroachments of the Legislative Body. This affords an additional and weighty reason, for making a complete knowledge of those Constitutions to form the Rudiments of a public, and especially of a law Education. Nor are the accomplishments of Academical learning any ways repugnant to a rapid improvement in the Law. On the contrary, the course of instruction which is taught within these walls, will greatly assist the researches of the Student into the nature and history of all Governments,—will give him a just sense of the force of moral and political obligation, and will especially crown the career of his active life, with increasing honour and success. A Lawyer in a free country, should have all the requisites of Quintilian's orator. He should be a person of irreproachable virtue and goodness. He should be well read in the whole circle of the Arts and Sciences. He should be fit for the administration of public affairs, and to govern the commonwealth by his councils, establish it by his Laws, and correct it by his Example. In short, he should resemble Tully, whose fruitful mind, as this distinguished Teacher of oratory observes, was not bounded by the walls of the Forum, but by those of nature. Nor do I recollect any material part of the attractive chain of classical studies, but which may be useful as well as ornamental in our legal pursuits.

Comment

Kent's remarks on the power of judicial review closely paralleled the views expressed by Roane and Tucker in *Kamper*, an indication of how rapidly the idea was taking hold in differing regions and across political divisions. Like Tucker, Kent saw judicial review as a uniquely American solution to the problem of governmental oppression, one that imposed the rule of law on the highest governmental functions and officials. Implicit in Kent's discussion (as in Roane's and Tucker's opinions) was an assumption that the exercise of "legal discretion" in judicial interpretation of a constitution could be guided by "rational Judgment" rather than merely by the judges' "arbitrary will." Later constitutional debate often revolved around the legitimacy of this assumption.

Section C: *The Exercise of Judicial Review*

Calder v. Bull
3 U.S. (3 Dall.) 386 (Aug. 8, 1798)

The United States Supreme Court's first significant interpretation of a federal constitutional restraint on state legislation arose out of a dispute between two Connecticut families

over who should inherit the estate of a Dr. Morrison. The Bulls claimed under the will of Dr. Morrison's grandson; the Calders claimed under the law of intestate succession. A state probate court set aside the grandson's will, but the Bulls successfully petitioned the Connecticut legislature for legislation granting them a new hearing. Taking the legislators' hint, the probate court approved the will, and its decision was upheld by the state appellate courts. The Calders then obtained a writ of error from the federal Supreme Court.

CHASE, *Justice*:—The decision of one question determines (in my opinion) the present dispute . . .

The counsel for the [Calders], contend, that the said resolution or law of the Legislature of Connecticut, granting a new hearing, in the above case, is an *ex post facto* law, prohibited by the Constitution of the United States; that any law of the federal government, or of any of the state governments, contrary to the constitution of the United States, is void; and that this court possesses the power to declare such law void.

It appears to me a self-evident proposition, that the several state legislatures retain all the powers of legislation, delegated to them by the state constitutions; which are not expressly taken away by the constitution of the United States. The establishing courts of justice, the appointment of judges, and the making regulations for the administration of justice, within each state, according to its laws, on all subjects not entrusted to the federal government, appears to me to be the peculiar and exclusive province, and duty of the state Legislatures. All the powers delegated by the people of the United States to the Federal government are defined, and no constructive powers can be exercised by it, and all the powers that remain in the state governments are indefinite; except only in the constitution of Massachusetts.

The effect of the resolution or law of Connecticut, above stated, is to revise a decision of one of its inferior courts, called the court of probate for Hartford, and to direct a new hearing of the case by the same court of probate, that passed the decree against the will of Normand Morrison. By the existing law of Connecticut a right to recover certain property had vested in Calder and wife (the appellants) in consequence of a decision of a court of justice, but, in virtue of a subsequent resolution or law, and the new hearing thereof, and the decision in consequence, this right to recover certain property was divested, and the right to the property declared to be in Bull and wife, the appellees. The sole enquiry is, whether this resolution or law of Connecticut, having such operation, is an *ex post facto* law, within the prohibition of the federal constitution?

Whether the Legislature of any of the states can revise and correct by law, a decision of any of its courts of justice, although not prohibited by the constitution of the state, is a question of very great importance, and not necessary now to be determined; because the resolution or law in question does not go so far. I cannot subscribe to the omnipotence of a state Legislature, or that it is absolute and without control, although its authority should not be expressly restrained by the constitution, or fundamental law, of the state. The people of the United States erected their constitutions, or forms of government, to establish justice, to promote the general welfare, to secure the blessings of liberty, and to protect their persons and property from violence. The purposes for which men enter into society will determine the nature and terms of the social compact; and as they are the foundation of the legislative power, they will decide what are the proper objects of it: The nature, and ends of legislative power will limit the exercise of it. This fundamental principle flows from the very nature of our free Republican governments, that no man should be compelled to do what the laws do not require; nor to refrain from acts which the laws permit. There are acts which the federal, or state, Legislature cannot do, without exceeding their authority. There are certain vital principles in our free Republican governments, which will determine and overrule an apparent and flagrant abuse of legislative power; as to authorize manifest injustice by positive law; or to take away that security for personal liberty, or private property, for the protection whereof the government was established. An act of the Legislature (for I cannot call it a law) contrary to the great first principles of the social compact, cannot be considered a rightful exercise of legislative authority. The obligation of a law in governments established on express compact, and on republican principles, must be determined by the nature of the power, on which it is founded. A few instances will suffice to explain what I mean. A law that punished a citizen for an innocent action, or, in other words, for an act, which, when done, was in violation of no existing law; a law that destroys, or impairs, the lawful private contracts of citizens; a law that makes a man a judge in his own cause; or a law that takes property from A, and gives it to B. It is against all reason and justice, for a people to entrust a Legislature with such powers; and, therefore, it cannot be presumed that they have done it. The genius, the nature, and the spirit, of our state governments, amount to a prohibition of such acts of legislation; and the general principles of law and reason forbid them. The Legislature may enjoin, permit, forbid, and punish; they may declare new crimes; and establish rules of conduct for all its citizens in future cases; they may command what is right, and prohibit what is wrong; but they cannot change innocence into guilt; or punish innocence as a crime; or violate the right of an antecedent lawful private contract; or the right of private property. To maintain that our federal, or state, Legislature possesses such powers, if they had not been expressly restrained, would, in my opinion, be a political heresy, altogether inadmissible in our free republican governments.

All the restrictions contained in the constitution of the United States on the power of the state Legislatures, were provided in favor of the authority of the federal government. The prohibition against their making any *ex post facto* laws was introduced for greater caution, and very probably arose from the knowledge, that the Parliament of Great Britain claimed and exercised a power to pass such laws, under the denomination of bills of attainder, or bills of pains and penalties; the first indicting capital, and the other less, punishment. These acts were legislative judgments; and an exercise of judicial power . . . With very few exceptions, the advocates of such laws were stimulated by ambition, or personal resentment, and vindictive malice. To prevent such, and similar, acts of violence and injustice, I believe, the Federal and State Legislatures, were prohibited from passing any bill of attainder; or any *ex post facto* law.

The constitution of the United States, article 1, section 9 prohibits the legislature of the United States from passing any *ex post facto* law; and, in section 10, lays several restrictions on the authority of the Legislatures of the several states; and, among them, "that no state shall pass any *ex post facto* law" . . .

I shall endeavor to show what law is to be considered an *ex post facto* law, within the words and meaning of the prohibition in the Federal constitution. The prohibition, "that no state shall pass any *ex post facto* law," necessarily requires some explanation; for, naked and without explanation, it is unintelligible, and means nothing. Literally, it is only that a law shall not be passed concerning, and after the fact, or thing done, or action committed. I would ask, what fact: of what nature, or kind; and by whom done? That Charles 1st, king of England, was beheaded; that Oliver Cromwell was Protector of England; that Louis 16th, late king of France, was guillotined; are all facts, that have happened; but it would be nonsense to suppose, that the states were prohibited from making any law after either of these events, and with reference thereto. The prohibition, in the letter, is not to pass any law concerning and after the fact; but the plain and obvious meaning and intention of the prohibition is this; that the Legislatures of the several states shall not pass laws, after a fact done by a subject or citizen, which shall have relation to such fact, and shall punish him for having done it. The prohibition considered in this light, is an additional bulwark in favor of the personal security of the subject, to protect his person from punishment by legislative acts, having a retrospective operation. I do not think it was inserted to secure the citizen in his private rights, of either property, or contracts. The prohibition not to make anything but gold and silver coin a tender in payment of debts, and not to pass any law impairing the obligation of contracts, were inserted to secure private rights; but the restriction not to pass any *ex post facto* law, was to secure the person of the subject from injury, or punishment, in consequence of such law. If the prohibition against making *ex post facto* laws was intended to secure personal rights from being affected, or injured, by such laws, and the prohibition is sufficiently extensive for that object, the other restraints, I have enumerated, were unnecessary, and therefore improper; for both of them are retrospective.

I will state what laws I consider *ex post facto* laws, within the words and the intent of the prohibition. 1st. Every law that makes an action done before the passing of the law; and which was innocent when done, criminal; and punishes such action. 2d. Every law that aggravates a crime, or makes it greater than it was, when committed. 3d. Every law that changes the punishment, and inflicts a greater punishment, than the law annexed to the crime, when committed. 4th. Every law that alters the legal rules of evidence, and receives less, or different, testimony, than the law required at the time of the commission of the offense, in order to convict the offender. All these, and similar laws, are manifestly unjust and oppressive. In my opinion, the true distinction is between *ex post facto* laws, and retrospective laws. Every *ex post facto* law must necessarily be retrospective; but every retrospective law is not an *ex post facto* law: The former, only, are prohibited. Every law that takes away, or impairs, rights vested, agreeably to existing laws, is retrospective, and is generally unjust, and may be oppressive; and it is a good general rule, that a law should have no retrospect; but there are cases in which laws may justly, and for the benefit of the community, and also of individuals, relate to a time antecedent to their commencement; as statutes of oblivion, or of pardon. They are certainly retrospective, and literally both concerning, and after, the facts committed. But I do not consider any law *ex post facto*, within the prohibition, that mollifies the rigor of the criminal law; but only those that create, or aggravate, the crime; or increase the punishment, or change the rules of evidence, for the purpose of conviction. Every law that is to have an operation before the making thereof, as to commence at an antecedent time; or to save time from the statute of limitations; or to excuse acts which were unlawful, and before committed, and the like; is retrospective. But such laws may be proper or necessary, as the case may be. There is a great and apparent difference between making an unlawful act lawful; and the making an innocent action criminal, and punishing it as a crime. The expressions "*ex post facto* laws," are technical, they had been in use long before the Revolution, and had acquired an appropriate meaning, by legislators, lawyers, and authors. The celebrated and judicious Sir William Blackstone in his commentaries, considers an *ex post facto* law precisely in the same light I have done. His opinion is confirmed by his successor, Mr. Wooddeson; and by the author of the Federalist, who I esteem superior to both, for his extensive and accurate knowledge of the true principles of government.

I also rely greatly on the definition, or explanation of *ex post facto* laws, as given by the conventions of Massachusetts, Maryland, and North Carolina; in their several constitutions, or forms of government . . .

In the present case, there is no fact done by [Calder] and wife, plaintiffs in error, that is in any manner affected by the law or resolution of Connecticut: It does not concern, or relate to, any act done by them. The decree of the court of probate of Hartford (on the 21st, March) in consequence of which Calder and wife claim a right to the property in question, was given before the said law or resolution, and in that sense, was affected and set aside by it; and in consequence of the law allowing a hearing and the decision in favor of the will, they have lost, what they would have been entitled to, if the law or resolution, and the decision in consequence thereof, had not been made. The decree of the court of probate is the only fact, on which the law or resolution operates. In my judgment the case of the plaintiffs in error, is not within the letter of the prohibition; and for the reasons assigned, I am clearly of opinion, that it is not within the intention of the prohibition; and if within the intention, but out of the letter, I should not, therefore, consider myself justified to continue it within the prohibition, and therefore that the whole was void.

It was ordered by the counsel for the plaintiffs in error, that the Legislature of Connecticut had no constitutional power to make the resolution (or law) in question, granting a new hearing, etc.

Without giving an opinion, at this time, whether this court has jurisdiction to decide that any law made by Congress, contrary to the constitution of the United States, is void,

I am fully satisfied that this court has no jurisdiction to determine that any law of any state Legislature, contrary to the constitution of such state, is void. Further, if this court had such jurisdiction, yet it does not appear to me, that the resolution (or law) in question, is contrary to the charter of Connecticut, or its constitution, which is said by counsel to be composed of its charter, acts of assembly, and usages, and custom. I should think, that the courts of Connecticut are the proper tribunals to decide, whether laws, contrary to the constitution thereof, are void. In the present case they have, both in the inferior and superior courts, determined that the resolution (or law) in question was not contrary to either their state, or the federal, constitution . . .

It was further urged, that if the provision does not extend to prohibit the making any law after a fact, then all choses in action; all lands by devise; all personal property by bequest, or distribution, by elegit; by execution; by judgments, particularly on torts; will be unprotected from the legislative power of the states; rights vested may be divested at the will and pleasure of the state legislatures; and, therefore, that the true construction and meaning of the prohibition is, that the states pass no law to deprive a citizen of any right vested in him by existing laws.

It is not to be presumed, that the federal or state legislatures will pass laws to deprive citizens of rights vested in them by existing laws: unless for the benefit of the whole community; and on making full satisfaction. The restraint against making any *ex post facto* laws was not considered, by the framers of the constitution, as extending to prohibit the depriving a citizen even of a vested right to property; or the provision, "that private property should not be taken for public use, without just compensation," was unnecessary.

It seems to me, that the right of property, in its origin, could only arise from compact express or implied, and I think it the better opinion, that the right as well as the mode, or manner, of acquiring property, and of alienating or transferring, inheriting, or transmitting it, is conferred by society; it is regulated by civil institution, and is always subject to the rules prescribed by positive law. When I say that a right is vested in a citizen, I mean, that he has the power to do certain actions; or to possess certain things, according to the law of the land.

If any one has a right to property such right is a perfect and exclusive right; but no one can have such right before he has acquired a better right to the property, than any other person in the world; a right, therefore only to recover property cannot be called a perfect and exclusive right. I cannot agree, that a right to property vested in Calder and wife, in consequence of the decree (of the 21st of March, 1783) disapproving of the will of Morrison, the grandson. If the will was valid, Mrs. Calder could have no right, as heiress of Morrison, the physician; but if the will was set aside, she had an undoubted title.

The resolution (or law) alone had no manner of effect on any right whatever vested in Calder and wife. The resolution (or law) combined with the new hearing, and the decision, in virtue of it, took away their right to recover the property in question. But when combined they took away no right of property vested in Calder and wife; because the decree against the will (21st March, 1783) did not vest in or transfer any property to them.

I am under a necessity to give a construction, or explanation of the words "*ex post facto* laws," because they have not any certain meaning attached to them. But I will not go farther than I feel myself bound to; and if I ever exercise the jurisdiction I will not decide any law to be void, but in a very clear case.

I am of opinion, that the decree of the supreme court of errors of Connecticut be affirmed, with costs.

PATERSON, *Justice*:—The constitution of Connecticut is made up of usages, and it appears that its legislature have, from the beginning, exercised the power of granting new trials. This has been uniformly the case till the year 1762, when this power was, by a legislative act, imparted to the superior and county courts. But the act does not remove or annihilate the prexisting [*sic*] power of the legislature, in this particular; it only communicates to other authorities a concurrence of jurisdiction, as to awarding of new trials. And the fact is, that the legislature have, in two instances, exercised this power since the passing of the law in 1762. They acted in a double capacity, as a house of legislation, with undefined authority, and also as a court of judicature in certain exigencies. Whether the latter arose from the indefinite nature of their legislative powers, or in some other way, it is not necessary to discuss. From the best information, however, which I have been able to collect on this subject, it appears, that the legislature, or general court of Connecticut, originally possessed, and exercised all legislative, executive, and judicial authority; and that, from time to time, they distributed the two latter in such manner as they thought proper; but without parting with the general superintending power, of the right of exercising the same, whenever they should judge it expedient. But be this as it may, it is sufficient for the present to observe, that they have on certain occasions exercised judicial authority from the commencement of their civil polity. This usage makes up part of the constitution of Connecticut, and we are bound to consider it as such, unless it be [in]consistent with the constitution of the United States. True it is, that the awarding of new trials falls properly within the province of the judiciary; but if the legislature of Connecticut have been in the uninterrupted exercise of this authority, in certain cases, we must, in such cases, respect their decisions as flowing from a competent jurisdiction, or constitutional organ. And therefore we may, in the present instance, consider the legislature of the state, as having acted in their customary judicial capacity. If so, there is an end of the question. For if the power, thus exercised, comes more properly within the description of a judicial than of a legislative power; and if by usage or the constitution, which, in Connecticut, are synonymous terms, the legislature of that state acted in both capacities; then in the case now before us, it would be fair to consider the awarding of a new trial, as an act emanating from the judiciary side of the department. But as this view of the subject militates against the plaintiffs in error, their counsel has contended for a reversal of the judgment, on the ground, that the awarding of a new trial, was the effect of a legislative act, and that it is unconstitutional, because an *ex post facto* law. For the sake of ascertaining the meaning of these terms, I will consider the resolution of the general court of Connecticut, as the exercise of a legislative and not a judicial authority. The question then which arises on the pleadings in this cause, is, whether the resolution of the legislature of Connecticut, be an *ex post facto* law, within the meaning of the constitution of the United States? I am of opinion, that it is not. The words, *ex post facto*, when applied to a law, have a technical meaning, and, in legal phraseology, refer to crimes, pains and penalties . . .

Again, the words of the Constitution of the United States are, "That no state shall pass any "bill of attainder, *ex post facto* law, or law impairing the obligation of contracts."

Where is the necessity or use of the latter words, if a law impairing the obligation of contracts, be comprehended within the terms *ex post facto* law? It is obvious from the specification of contracts in the last member of the clause, that the framers of the Constitution, did not understand or use the words in the sense contended for on the part of the plaintiffs in error. They understood and used the words in their known and appropriate signification, as referring to crimes, pains, and penalties, and no further. The arrangement of the distinct members of this section, necessarily points to this meaning.

I had an ardent desire to have extended the provision in the Constitution to retrospective laws in general. There is neither policy nor safety in such laws; and, therefore, I have always had a strong aversion against them. It may, in general, be truly observed of retrospective laws of every description, that they neither accord with sound legislation, nor the fundamental principles of the social compact. But on full consideration, I am convinced, that *ex post facto* laws must be limited in the manner already expressed; they must be taken in their technical, which is also their common and general acceptation, and are not to be understood in their literal sense.

IREDELL, *Justice*:—Though I concur in the general result of the opinions, which have been delivered, I cannot entirely adopt the reasons that are assigned upon the occasion . . .

But, let us, for a moment, suppose, that the resolution granting a new trial, was a legislative act, it will by no means follow, that it is an act affected by the constitutional prohibition, that "no state shall pass any *ex post facto* law." I will endeavor to state the general principles, which influence me, on this point, succinctly and clearly, though I have not had an opportunity to reduce my opinion to writing.

If, then, a government, composed of legislative, executive and judicial departments, were established, by a Constitution, which imposed no limits on the legislative power, the consequence would inevitably be, that whatever the legislative power chose to enact, would be lawfully enacted, and the judicial power, could never interpose to pronounce it void. It is true, that some speculative jurists have held, that a legislative act against natural justice must, in itself, be void; but I cannot think that, under such a government, any court of justice would possess a power to declare it so. Sir William Blackstone, having put the strong case of an act of parliament, which should authorize a man to try his own cause, explicitly adds, that even in that case, "there is no court that has power to defeat the intent of the legislature, when couched in such evident and express words as leave no doubt whether it was the intent of the legislature, or no."

In order, therefore, to guard against so great an evil, it has been the policy of all the American states, which have, individually, framed their state constitutions since the revolution, and of the people of the United States, when they framed the federal constitution, to define with precision the objects of the legislative power, and to restrain its exercise within marked and settled boundaries. If any act of Congress, or of the legislature of a state, violates those constitutional provisions, it is unquestionably void; though, I admit, that as the authority to declare it void is of a delicate and awful nature, the court will never resort to that authority, but in a clear and urgent case. If on the other hand, the legislature of the union, or the legislature of any member of the union, shall pass a law, within the general scope of their constitutional power, the court cannot pronounce it to be void, merely because it is, in their judgment, contrary to the principles of natural justice. The ideas of natural justice are regulated by no fixed standard; the ablest and the purest men have differed upon the subject; and all that the court could properly say, in such an event, would be, that the legislature (possessed of an equal right of opinion) had passed an act which, in the opinion of the judges, was inconsistent with the abstract principles of natural justice. There are then but two lights, in which the subject can be viewed. 1st. If the legislature pursue the authority delegated to them, their acts are valid. 2d. If they transgress the boundaries of that authority, their acts are invalid. In the former case, they exercise the discretion vested in them by the people, to whom alone they are responsible for the faithful discharge of their trust; but in the latter case, they violate a fundamental law, which must be our guide, whenever we are called upon as judges to determine the validity of a legislative act.

Still, however, in the present instance, the act or resolution of the legislature of Connecticut, cannot be regarded as an *ex post facto* law; for, the true construction of the prohibition extends to criminal, not to civil, cases . . .

The policy, the reason and humanity of the prohibition, do not, I repeat, extend to civil cases, to cases that merely affect the private property of citizens. Some of the most necessary and important acts of legislation are, on the contrary, founded upon the principle, that private rights must yield to public exigences [*sic*]. Highways are run through private grounds. Fortifications, light-houses, and other public edifices, are necessarily sometimes built upon the soil owned by individuals. In such, and similar cases, if the owners should refuse voluntarily to accommodate the public, they must be constrained, as far as the public necessities require; and justice is done, by allowing them a reasonable equivalent. Without the possession of this power the operations of government would often be obstructed, and society itself would be endangered. It is not sufficient to urge, that the power may be abused, for, such is the nature of all power,—such is the tendency of every human institution; and, it might as fairly be said, that the power of taxation, which is only circumscribed by the discretion of the body, in which it is vested, ought not to be granted, because the legislature, disregarding its true objects, might, for visionary and useless projects, impose a tax to the amount of nineteen shillings in the pound. We must be content to limit power where we can, and where we cannot, consistently with its use, we must be content to repose a salutary confidence. It is our consolation that there never existed a government, in ancient or modern times, more free from danger in this respect, than the governments of America.

Upon the whole, though there cannot be a case, in which an *ex post facto* law in criminal matters is requisite, or justifiable (for providence never can intend to promote the prosperity of any country by bad means) yet, in the present instance the objection does not arise. Because, 1st, if the act of the legislature of Connecticut was a judicial act, it is not within the words of the constitution; and 2d, even if it was a legislative act, it is not within the meaning of the prohibition.

CUSHING, *Justice*:—The case appears to me to be clear of all difficulty, taken either way. If the act is a judicial act, it is not touched by the federal constitution; and, if it is a legislative act, it is maintained and justified by the ancient and uniform practice of the state of Connecticut.

JUDGMENT *Affirmed*.

Comment

The Calders presented three distinct arguments. They contended, first, that the legislature's action violated Connecticut's state constitution. The justices, however, unanimously held that the legislature's previous exercise of the power to award new trials validated its action in *Calder* under the state's constitution "of usages." (Connecticut did not adopt a written constitution until 1818, and governed itself before that time under its colonial charter and traditional political customs.)

The Calders' second argument was that the state had violated the ban on ex post facto laws in article one. The justices agreed that the constitutional expression "ex post facto" was to be construed in accordance with its meaning in English law, and, therefore, restricted to criminal matters. Chase and Paterson also suggested that extending the prohibition to noncriminal retrospective laws would make other parts of section ten redundant, and therefore was improper under the ordinary legal rules of construction.

The Calders' most potent argument was their contention that the state had deprived them retrospectively of a property right that had already vested in them. Late eighteenth-century Americans regarded legislative respect for vested rights as one of the main purposes and primary duties of government, and at least one justice—Chase—agreed with the Calders that American constitutional principles forbade interference with vested rights regardless of the existence of a constitutional text to that effect. (Chase did not think the Calders' right to Dr. Morrison's estate had ever vested.) In response, Iredell rejected the power to review legislation on the basis of extratextual "principles of natural justice."

Calder was an important decision for several reasons. The justices assumed, without much discussion and with only Chase expressing reservations, that they could "determine the validity of a legislative act." The Court's construction of "ex post facto," on the other hand, limited the potential area within which to exercise judicial review by disavowing the most obvious textual basis for federal constitutional protection of vested rights. As the debate between

Chase and Iredell indicated, however, the question was not settled. Iredell's opinion, finally, expressed the attitude of nationalist constitutionalists to judicial review of *congressional* acts: as long as the statute was "within the general scope of [Congress's] constitutional power," it was an exercise of legislative discretion with which the judges should not tamper. Constitutionalism, for Iredell as for Alexander Hamilton, could not be based on an inordinate suspicion of government.

Woodson v. Randolph
1 Va. Cas. 128 (Gen. Ct. Nov. 14, 1800)

In 1800 the Virginia General Court numbered among its members such stalwart supporters of state-sovereignty constitutionalism as St. George Tucker. As *Woodson* reveals, adherence to a state-sovereignty vision of the Union did not lead automatically to hostility toward particular exercises of federal power.

The plaintiff instituted an action of debt in the District Court of Prince Edward, in September, 1798, against the defendant on a bond conditioned for the payment of £30. The bond bore [the] date the 18th July, 1798, and was not on stamped paper. The defendant objected to the bond going in evidence to the jury, on the ground that it was not duly stamped, pursuant to the act of congress in such case made and provided: by consent a juror was withdrawn, and the point was adjourned to the general court for novelty and difficulty.

The general court decided, that the bond in the said record mentioned, ought not to be permitted to go in evidence to the jury on the trial of the cause, because the said bond is not stamped agreeably to the act of congress intituled, "an act of laying duties on stamped vellum, parchment, and paper."

Note [by the reporters]. The question in this case was, whether the act of congress was constitutional or not. Some persons had supposed, that congress had no power to change the rules of evidence in the state courts: the general court, however, were of opinion that, as congress had power to lay and collect taxes, duties, imposts and excises, and to make all laws necessary and proper for carrying into execution the specified powers, the aforesaid act was within the limits of their chartered authority.

Three

Congress, the President, and Foreign Affairs

George Mason
Letter to James Monroe
(January 30, 1792)[61]

Mason was the primary author of the Virginia Bill of Rights, and one of the few delegates to the Philadelphia convention who declined to sign the Constitution. In this letter to Monroe, at the time a United States senator, Mason addressed one of the most difficult constitutional issues of the 1790s: the relative parts the president and the two houses of Congress should play in the development of a foreign policy.

...I see by a late Paper, that [Gouverneur] Morris is appointed our Minister, to the Court of France; so that, I suppose, the Opposition in the Senate has been outvoted.

I don't think a more injudicious Appointment could have been made. In the present Situation of France, to appoint a Man of his known monarchical Principles has rather the Appearance of Insult, than of Compliment, or Congratulation. And altho' Mr. Morris's Political Creed may not be known generally in France, it must be well known to Mr. de la Fayette, the most influential Character in the Nation. What a Man seems to value himself upon, and glory in, can't long remain a Secret, in a public Character. "Coercion by G-d" is his favorite Maxim in government. And in his place, as a Member of the federal Convention in Philadelphia, I heard him express the following sentiment. "We must have a Monarch sooner or later" (tho' I think his word was a *Despot*) "and the sooner we take him, while we are able to make a Bargain with him, the better." Is this a Man to represent the United States of America, in a Country, which has just reformed an arbitrary Monarchy into a free government? Such a Character, perhaps, wou'd not have been displeasing at the Court of Petersburg, or Berlin; but is surely very ill suited to that of Paris.

The Question lately agitated in the Senate is a most important one. I am decidedly of opinion, that the Words of the Constitution "He shall nominate, and by & with the Advice and Consent of the Senate, appoint Ambassadors" &c. give the Senate the Power of interfering in every part of the Subject, except the Right of nominating. There is some thing remarkable in the Arrangement of the Words "He shall nominate." This gives to the President *alone* the Right of *Nomination*. And if the Senate were to refuse their Approbation of the person nominated (which the subsequent Part of the Clause puts in their Power) they wou'd have no Right to nominate another Person; the Right of Nomination being complete in the President. "And by and with the Advice & Consent of the Senate appoint Ambassadors" &c. The Word *"Advice"* here clearly relates in the Judgment of the Senate on the Expediency or Inexpediency of the Measure, or Appointment; and the Word *"Consent"* to their Approbation or Disapprobation of the Person nominated; otherwise the word *Advice* has no Meaning at all—and it is a well known Rule of Construction, that no Clause or Expression shall be deemed superfluous, or nugatory, which is capable of a fair and rational Meaning. The Nomination, of Course, brings the Subject fully under the Consideration of the Senate; who have then a Right to decide upon its Propriety or Impropriety.

The peculiar Character or Predicament of the Senate in the Constitution of the General Government, is a strong Confirmation of this Construction.

The Senate are not the immediate Representatives of the people at large, nor elected by them. They are elected by the Legislatures of the different States, and they represent respectively, the Sovereignty of the separate States, in the general Union. Upon no other Principle can the Equality of Representation, in the larger and smaller States be justified. The Senate act in a diplomatic, as well as a legislative Character; and it is in the former Capacity that they give advice to the President; and partake of some Executive Powers. The Constitution therefore wisely & Properly directs, that Ambassadors &c. shall not be appointed, but with the Advice & Approbation of the States, which form the Union, thro' their Organ, or Representative, the Senate. I wish this important Subject to be fairly discussed, upon its merits, and decided upon, in the Infancy of the new Government, and in the presidency of General Washington; who, I am sure, is strongly attach'd to the Rights & Liberty of our country; but we are not sure, that this will be the Case with his Successors.

Comment

The First Congress, after extensive debate, provided by statute that most executive officials would hold office at the president's pleasure (and thus could be dismissed by him), though senatorial confirmation was required for their appointment. When President Washington nominated the colorful and controversial Morris to be minister to France, the president's congressional supporters met opposition to the appointment with the claim that the Senate had no part to play in judging the political views of nominees to offices held "at pleasure."

Mason's rebuttal to this assertion rested in part on a lawyerly parsing of the appointments clause of article two, and in part on a view of the Senate derived from the theory of separation of powers. Americans such as Mason who held strong versions of that theory usually found the Senate perplexing or even disturbing. Viewed as a part of the legislature, the Senate violated the separation principle by possessing executive and judicial powers—respectively, its role in treaties and appointments and its designation as the federal court of impeachment. Mason and others resolved this theoretical problem (in part) by interpreting the Senate, for some purposes, as a diplomatic assembly of state ambassadors. This view of the Senate was politically most significant in discussion of the relationship between senators and the state legislatures that appointed them. Many of the latter asserted the right to issue binding instructions to their "ambassadors."

The Jay Treaty

In the summer and autumn of 1794, Chief Justice John Jay negotiated a treaty of "Amity and Commerce" with Great Britain. (He had accepted a presidential appointment as envoy without resigning his judgeship, provoking sharp criticism on separation-of-powers grounds by opposition politicians.) The Jay Treaty, which became public only when it was leaked to the press on the eve of Senate ratification, was bitterly criticized as a poor bargain and as proof of the Washington administration's pro-British and anti-French biases.

The Senate, dominated by supporters of the administration, ratified the treaty, but only after rejecting an especially obnoxious provision surrendering American shippers' right to carry British West Indies goods to any but American ports. The treaty faced an even more difficult course in the House, where its supporters believed the opposition might be able to defeat legislation needed to carry the treaty into effect. Washington delayed proposing the legislation, and on March 2, 1796, Representative Edward Livingston presented a resolution to the House requesting the president to transmit to the House his instructions to Jay "together with the correspondence and other documents relative to the said Treaty." Supporters of the president saw the Livingston resolution as an unwarrantable intrusion into the diplomatic and treaty-making prerogatives of the president and Senate; opposition spokesmen asserted the House's right and duty to exercise its powers of legislation independently. The House eventually adopted a modified form of Livingston's motion, and Washington flatly refused to comply. In response, the House adopted additional resolutions declaring the House's authority "to deliberate on the expediency or inexpediency of carrying . . . into effect" treaties requiring supplemental legislation. Following still more impassioned oratory and closed-door politicking, the committee of the whole of the House voted to implement the treaty by the casting vote of its chairman.

James Madison
Speech in the U.S. House of Representatives
(March 10, 1796)[62]

. . . The Constitution of the United States is a constitution of limitations and checks. The powers given up by the people for the purposes of Government, had been divided into two great classes. One of these formed the State Governments; the other, the Federal Government. The powers of the Government had been further divided into three great departments; and the Legislative department again subdivided into two independent branches. Around each of these portions of power were seen also exceptions and qualifications, as additional guards against the abuses to which power is liable. With a view to this policy of the Constitution, it could not be unreasonable, if the clauses [of Livingston's motion] under discussion were thought doubtful, to lean towards a construction that would limit and control the Treaty-making power, rather than towards one that would make it omnipotent.

He came next to the [opinion] which left with the President and Senate the power of making Treaties, but required at the same time the Legislative sanction and co-operation, in those cases where the Constitution had given express and specific powers to the Legislature. It was to be presumed, that in all such cases the Legislature would exercise its authority with discretion, allowing due weight to the reasons which led to the Treaty, and to the circumstances of the existence of the Treaty. Still, however, this House, in its Legislative capacity, must exercise its reason; it must deliberate; for deliberation is implied in legislation. If it must carry all Treaties into effect, it would no longer exercise a Legislative power; it would be the mere instrument of the will of another department, and would have no will of its own. Where the Constitution contains a specific and peremptory injunction on Congress to do a particular act, Congress must, of course, do the act, because the Constitution, which is paramount over all the departments, has expressly taken away the Legislative discretion of Congress. The case is essentially different where the act of one department of Government interferes with a power expressly vested in another, and no where expressly taken away: here the latter power must be exercised according to its nature; and if it be a Legislative power, it must be exercised with that deliberation and discretion which is essential to the nature of Legislative power . . .

Alexander Hamilton
Letter to William Loughton Smith
(March 10, 1796)[63]

. . . I observe Madison brings the power of the House of Representatives in the case of the Treaty to this Question. Is the Agency of the House of Representatives on this subject *deliberative* or *Executive*? On the sophism that this Legislature and each Branch of it is *essentially deliberative* & consequently must have discretion will he, I presume, maintain the freedom of the House to concur or not.

But this sophism is easily refuted. The legislature & each branch of it is *deliberative* but with *various* restrictions not with *unlimited discretion*. All the injunctions & restrictions in the constitution for instance abridge its *deliberative* faculty & leave it *quoad hoc* merely *executive*. Thus the Constitution enjoins that there shall be a fixed allowance for the Judges which shall not be diminished. The Legislature cannot therefore deliberate whether they will make a permanent provision & when the allowance is fixed they cannot deliberate whether they will appropriate & pay the money. So far their deliberative faculty is abridged. The *mode* of raising & appropriating the money only remains matter of deliberation.

So likewise the Constitution says that the President & Senate shall make Treaties & that these Treaties shall be supreme laws. It is a contradiction to call a thing a law which is not binding. It follows that by constitutional injunction the House of Representatives *quoad* the stipulation of Treaties, as in the case cited respecting the Judges are not deliberative, but merely executive *except* as to the *means of executing*.

Any other doctrine would vest the Legislature & each House with *unlimited discretion* & destroy the very idea of a Constitution limiting its discretion. The Constitution would at once vanish!

Besides the *legal* power to refuse the execution of a law is a *power to repeal* it. Thus the House of Representatives must as to Treaties concenter in itself the whole legislative power & undertake without the Senate to repeal a law. For the law is *complete* by the action of the President & Senate.

Again a Treaty which is a contract between nation & nation abridges even the legislative discretion of the whole legislature by the moral obligation of keeping its faith; *a fortiori* that of one branch. In theory there is no method by which the obligations of a Treaty can be annulled but by mutual consent of the contracting parties—by ill faith in one of them or by a revolution of Government which is of a nature so to change the condition of parties as to render the Treaty inapplicable . . .

William Vans Murray
Speech in the U.S. House of Representatives
(March 23, 1796)[64]

Murray, an opponent of the Livingston resolution, attacked opposition arguments that the House of Representatives, like the British House of Commons, was peculiarly the representative and defender of the people.

... In America, he [Murray] saw in the collective capacity of the nation the sovereign, and [in] Government, its established mode of action. The Commons in England grant supplies to the King. Here we grant supplies to fulfill the views and obligations of the people. Here an appropriation is less a grant of money than an act of duty to which the Constitution, that is the will of the nation, obliges us. There, supplies and grievances have been for centuries a measure of compromise and the mode by which the Commons have accumulated powers and checks against a throne. There, we see the powers of the Commons growing by absorption from the prerogative of the Crown. Here, we see in the powers of this House, not the spoils of contest, not the trophies of repeated victory over the other branches of the Government, but a specific quantum of trust placed in our hands to be exercised for the people agreeably to the Constitution. We ascend for our derivation of authority and strength to the fountain of all political power; they gain theirs by cutting away that royal reservoir that has been sucking in for ages by dark and now unexplorable channels, the authorities and powers of the nation. The Commons are called by the King, and may not be called by him more than once in three years. Their very existence depends upon their instrumentality in furnishing supplies to the King. The Lords are of his creation. The Commons, if refractory, can be dissolved, and an appeal thus be made to the nation. The Senate here is created by the people, and elected for only six years. Here the PRESIDENT cannot dissolve Congress, even if they chose to adopt a right of stopping the wheels of Government. Theirs is a system in which jealousy must hold the balance between branches, some of which have at best but a precarious existence, and another branch, which is the only great substantive figure in their form of Government. In fact, the two Constitutions differ essentially. The branches here are elected for short periods by the people. The PRESIDENT is one organ constituted and elected by the people. The Senate are constituted and elected by the people. This House is elected by the people, not to struggle with each other, but to give action to the Constitution; and no right can be assumed by any one branch that gives a power of making the Constitution inactive or inefficient to its great ends. To overturn this Constitution is not merely to oppose it by violence. To refuse to act, to withhold an active discharge of the duties it enjoins upon the different branches, would as effectually prostrate it as open violence could do.

George Washington
Message to the U.S. House of Representatives
(March 30, 1796)[65]

Gentlemen of the House of Representatives: With the utmost attention I have considered your resolution of the 24th. instant, requesting me to lay before your House, a copy of the instructions to the Minister of the United States who negotiated the Treaty with the King of Great Britain, together with the correspondence and other documents relative to that Treaty, excepting such of the said papers as any existing negotiation may render improper to be disclosed.

In deliberating upon this subject, it was impossible for me to lose sight of the principle which some have avowed in its discussion; or to avoid extending my views to the consequences which must flow from the admission of that principle.

I trust that no part of my conduct has ever indicated a disposition to withhold any information which the Constitution has enjoined upon the President as a duty to give, or which could be required of him by either House of Congress as a right; and with truth I affirm, that it has been, as it will continue to be, while I have the honor to preside in the Government, my constant endeavour to harmonize with the other branches thereof; so far as the trust delegated to me by the People of the United States, and my sense of the obligation it imposes to "preserve, protect and defend the Constitution" will permit.

The nature of foreign negotiations requires caution; and their success must often depend on secrecy: and even when brought to a conclusion, a full disclosure of all the measures, demands, or eventual concessions, which may have been proposed or contemplated, would be extremely impolitic: for this might have a pernicious influence on future negotiations; or produce immediate inconveniences, perhaps danger and mischief, in relation to other powers. The necessity of such caution and secrecy was one cogent reason for vesting the power of making Treaties in the President, with the advice and consent of the Senate, the principle on which that body was formed confining it to a small number of Members.

To admit then a right in the House of Representatives to demand, and to have as a matter of course, all the Papers respecting a negotiation with a foreign power, would be to establish a dangerous precedent.

It does not occur that the inspection of the papers asked for, can be relative to any purpose under the cognizance of the House of Representatives, except that of an impeachment, which the resolution has not expressed. I repeat, that I have no disposition to withhold any information which the duty of my station will permit, or the public good shall require to be disclosed: and in fact, all the Papers affecting the negotiation with Great Britain were laid before the Senate, when the Treaty itself was communicated for their consideration and advice.

The course which the debate has taken, on the resolution of the House, leads to some observations on the mode of making treaties under the Constitution of the United States.

Having been a member of the General Convention, and knowing the principles on which the Constitution was formed, I have ever entertained but one opinion on this subject; and from the first establishment of the Government to this moment, my conduct has exemplified that opinion, that the power of making treaties is exclusively vested in the President, by and with the advice and consent of the Senate, provided two thirds of the Senators present concur, and that every treaty so made, and promulgated, thenceforward became the Law of the land. It is thus that the treaty making power has been understood by foreign Nations: and in all the treaties made with them, *we* have declared, and *they* have believed, that when ratified by the President with the advice and consent of the Senate, they became obligatory. In this construction of the Constitution every House of Representatives has heretofore acquiesced; and until the present time, not a doubt or suspicion has appeared to my knowledge that this construction was not the true one. Nay, they have more than acquiesced: for till now, without controverting the obligation of such treaties, they have made all the requisite provisions for carrying them into effect.

There is also reason to believe that this construction agrees with the opinions entertained by the State Conventions; when they were deliberating on the Constitution; especially by those who objected to it, because there was not required, in *commercial treaties*, the consent of two thirds of the whole number of the members of the Senate, instead of two thirds of the Senators present; and because in treaties respecting territorial and certain other rights and claims, the concurrence of three fourths of the whole number of the members of both houses respectively, was not made necessary.

It is a fact declared by the General Convention and universally understood that the constitution of the United States was the result of a spirit of amity and mutual concessior and it is well known that under this influence the smaller States were admitted to equal representation in the Senate with the larger States, and that this branch of the Government was invested with great powers, for on the equal participation of those powers the sovereignty and political safety of the smaller States were deemed essentially to depend.

If other proofs than these and the plain letter of the Constitution itself be necessary to ascertain the point under consideration, they may be found in the journals of the General Convention, which I have deposited in the office of the Department of State. In those journals it will appear that a proposition was made "that no treaty should be binding on the United States which was not ratified by a law," and that the proposition was explicitly rejected.

As, therefore, it is perfectly clear to my understanding that the assent of the House of Representatives is not necessary to the validity of a treaty; as the treaty with Great Britain exhibits in itself all the objects requiring legislative provision, and on these the papers called for can throw no light, and as it is essential to the due administration of the Government that the boundaries fixed by the Constitution between the different departments should be preserved, a just regard to the Constitution and to the duty of my office, under all the circumstances of this case, forbids a compliance with your request.

James Madison
Speech in the U.S. House of Representatives
(April 6, 1796)[66]

... If there were any question which could make a serious appeal to the dispassionate judgment, it must be one which respected the meaning of the Constitution; and if any Constitutional question could make the appeal with peculiar solemnity, it must be in a case like the present, where two of the constituted authorities interpreted differently the extent of their respective powers.

It was a consolation, however, of which every member would be sensible, to reflect on the happy difference of our situation, on such occurrences, from that of Governments in which the constituent members possessed independent and hereditary prerogatives. In such Governments, the parties having a personal interest in their public stations, and not being amenable to the national will, disputes concerning the limits of their respective authorities might be productive of the most fatal consequences. With us, on the contrary, although disputes of that kind are always to be regretted, there were three most precious resources against the evil tendency of them. In the first place, the responsibility which every department feels to the public will, under the forms of the Constitution, may be expected to prevent the excesses incident to conflicts between rival and irresponsible authorities. In the next place, if the difference cannot be adjusted by friendly conference and mutual concession, the sense of the constituent body, brought into the Government through the ordinary elective channels, may supply a remedy. And if this resource should fail, there remains, in the third and last place, that provident article in the Constitution itself, by which an avenue is always open to the sovereignty of the people, for explanations or amendments, as they might be found indispensable.

If, in the present instance, it was to be particularly regretted that the existing difference of opinion had arisen, every motive to the regret was a motive to calmness, to candor, and the most respectful delicacy towards the other constituted authority. On the other hand, the duty which the House of Representatives must feel to themselves and to their constituents required that they should examine the subject with accuracy, as well as with candor, and decide on it with firmness, as well as with moderation.

In this temper, he [Madison] should proceed to make some observations on the Message before the Committee, and on the reasons contained in it...

One of the reasons was, that it did not occur to the Executive that the papers could be relative to any purpose under the cognizance, and in the contemplation of the House. The other was, that the purpose for which they were wanted was not expressed in the resolution of the House.

With respect to the first, it implied that the Executive was not only to judge of the proper objects and functions of the Executive department, but, also, of the objects and functions of the House. He was not only to decide how far the Executive trust would permit a disclosure of information, but how far the Legislative trust could derive advantage from it. It belonged, he said, to each department to judge for itself. If the Executive conceived that, in relation to his own department, papers could not be safely communicated, he might, on that ground, refuse them, because he was the competent though a responsible judge within his own department. If the papers could be communicated without injury to the objects of his department, he ought not to refuse them as irrelative to the objects of the House of Representatives; because the House was, in such cases, the only proper judge of its own objects . . .

He [Madison] proceeded to review the several topics on which the Message relied. First. The intention of the body which framed the Constitution. Secondly. The opinions of the State Conventions who adopted it. Thirdly. The peculiar rights and interests of the smaller States. Fourthly. The manner in which the Constitution had been understood by the Executive and the foreign nations, with which Treaties had been formed. Fifthly. The acquiescence and acts of the House on former occasions.

1. When the members on the floor, who were members of the General Convention, particularly a member from Georgia and himself, were called on in a former debate for the sense of that body on the Constitutional question, it was a matter of some surprise, which was much increased by the peculiar stress laid on the information expected. He acknowledged his surprise, also, at seeing the Message of the Executive appealing to the same proceedings in the General Convention, as a clue to the meaning of the Constitution.

. . . He [Madison] should have reminded them that this was the ninth year since the convention executed their trust, and that he had not a single note in this place to assist his memory. He should have remarked, that neither himself nor the other members who had belonged to the Federal Convention, could be under any particular obligation to rise in answer to a few gentlemen, with information, not merely of their own ideas at that period, but of the intention of the whole body; many members of which, too, had probably never entered into the discussions of the subject. He might have further remarked, that there would not be much delicacy in the undertaking, as it appeared that a sense had been put on the Constitution by some who were members of the Convention, different from that which must have been entertained by others, who had concurred in ratifying the Treaty . . .

It would have been proper for him, also, to have recollected what had, on a former occasion, happened to himself during a debate in the House of Representatives. When the bill for establishing a National Bank was under consideration, he had opposed it, as not warranted by the Constitution, and incidentally remarked, that his impression might be stronger, as he remembered that, in the Convention, a motion was made and negatived, for giving Congress a power to grant charters of incorporation. This slight reference to the Convention, he said, was animadverted on by several, in the course of the debate, and particularly by a gentleman from Massachusetts [Elbridge Gerry], who had himself been a member of the Convention, and whose remarks were not unworthy the attention of the Committee. Here Mr. M. read a paragraph from Mr. Gerry's speech, from the Gazette of the United States, page 814, protesting, in strong terms, against arguments drawn from that source.

Mr. M. said, he did not believe a single instance could be cited in which the sense of the Convention had been required or admitted as material in any Constitutional question. In the case of the Bank, the Committee had seen how a glance at that authority had been treated in this House. When the question on the suability of the States was pending in the Supreme Court, he asked, whether it had ever been understood that the members of the Bench, who had been members of the Convention, were called on for the meaning of the Convention on that very important point, although no Constitutional question would be presumed more susceptible of elucidation from that source.

He then adverted to that part of the Message which contained an extract from the Journal of the Convention, showing that a proposition "that no Treaty should be binding on the United States, which was not ratified by law," was explicitly rejected. He allowed this to be much more precise than any evidence drawn from the debates in the Convention, or resting on the memory of individuals. But, admitting the case to be as stated, of which he had no doubt, although he had no recollection of it, and admitting the record of the Convention to be the oracle that ought to decide the true meaning of the Constitution, what did this abstract vote amount to? Did it condemn the doctrine of the majority? So far from it, that, as he understood their doctrine, they must have voted as the Convention did; for they do not contend that no Treaty shall be operative without a law to sanction it; on the contrary, they admit that some Treaties will operate without this sanction; and that it is no further applicable in any case than where Legislative objects are embraced by Treaties. The term "ratify" also deserved some attention; for, although of loose signification in general, it had a technical meaning different from the agency claimed by the House on the subject of Treaties.

But, after all, whatever veneration might be entertained for the body of men who formed our Constitution, the sense of that body could never be regarded as the oracular guide in expounding the Constitution. As the instrument came from them it was nothing more than the draft of a plan, nothing but a dead letter, until life and validity were breathed into it by the voice of the people, speaking through the several State Conventions. If we were to look, therefore, for the meaning of the instrument beyond the face of the instrument, we must look for it, not in the General Convention, which proposed, but in the State Conventions, which accepted and ratified the Constitution. To these also the Message had referred, and it would be proper to follow it.

2. The debates of the Conventions in three States (Pennsylvania, Virginia, and North Carolina) had been before introduced into the discussion of this subject, and were believed the only publications of the sort which contained any lights with respect to it. He would not fatigue the Committee with a repetition of the passages then read to them. He would only appeal to the Committee to decide whether it did not appear, from a candid and collected view of the debates in those Conventions, and particularly in that of Virginia, that the Treaty-making power was a limited power; and that the powers in our Constitution, on this subject bore an analogy to the powers on the same subject in the Government of Great Britain. He wished, as little as any member could to extend the analogies between the two Governments; but it was clear that the constituent parts of two Governments might be perfectly heterogeneous, and yet the powers be similar.

At once to illustrate his meaning, and give a brief reply to some arguments on the other side, which had heretofore been urged with ingenuity and learning, he would mention, as an example, the power of pardoning offences. This power was vested in the President; it was a prerogative also of the British King. And, in order to ascertain the extent of the technical term "pardon," in our Constitution, it would not be irregular to search into the meaning and exercise of the power in Great Britain. Yet, where is the general analogy between an hereditary Sovereign, not accountable for his conduct, and a Magistrate like the President of the United States, elected for four years, with limited powers, and liable to impeachment for the abuse of them?

In referring to the debates of the State Conventions as published, he wished not to be understood as putting entire confidence in the accuracy of them. Even those of Virginia, which had been probably taken down by the most skillful hand, (whose merit he wished by no means to disparage,) contained internal evidence in abundance of chasms and misconceptions of what was said.

The amendments proposed by the several Conventions were better authority, and would be found, on a general view, to favor the sense of the Constitution which had prevailed in this House. But even here it would not be reasonable to expect precision and system in all their votes and proceedings. The agitations of the public mind on that occasion, with the hurry and compromise which generally prevailed in settling the amendments to be proposed, would at once explain and apologize for the several apparent inconsistencies which might be discovered . . .

Comment

Republican supporters of Livingston's motion made two major constitutional points. The first rested on the ultimately ancient notion of a mixed government in which all classes—the one, the few, and the many—were represented. As the organ of the people ("the many"), the House of Representatives was analogous to the British Commons, and like that body was entitled to participate freely in all questions involving the people's liberty or property. Nationalist spokesmen denied that American society was divisible into classes, which produced the ironic spectacle of radically inegalitarian politicians such as Fisher Ames vehemently insisting that Americans "almost universally, possess some property and some pretensions of learning." They then, logically, rejected the mixed-government analysis of the federal Constitution, and any analogy between the American House and the British Commons.

The opposition's second constitutional argument was an insistence that within its sphere of competence each department of the government was entitled to act autonomously. In the hands of a systematic thinker like Madison, this line of reasoning became almost syllogistic: the exercise of legislative power by definition requires deliberation; the House's powers are legislative; therefore the exercise of its powers requires the House to deliberate and to obtain all information necessary to do so. Madison conceded that under a "peremptory injunction" of the constitutional text the House might be obliged to act, but in all other cases he maintained the representatives' right and duty to act according to their own judgment. The nationalist response, as exemplified in Hamilton's letter to William L. Smith, accused the opposition of a rigid and inappropriate compartmentalizing of the government. The very notion of a limited Constitution, Hamilton pointed out, contradicted Madison's assumption of unlimited deliberative discretion. Wherever the Constitution entrusted a power to decide to organs other than the House, the latter's only legislative function was to decide how to execute the decision, reached elsewhere.

At first glance, Madison and Hamilton appear simply to have exchanged positions on the validity of legislative discretion since their earlier clash over the bank, and some degree of opportunism in their arguments cannot be ruled out. There is, nonetheless, an underlying logic to both men's views betwen 1791 and 1796. Hamilton was consistently concerned to preserve the capacity to act of the federal government *as a whole*. In 1791 and 1792, this involved asserting the Congress's discretion to interpret its powers broadly, but in 1796 Hamilton found himself opposing an assertion by members of the House that they could effectively annul a treaty adopted by the designated

federal actors. As Hamilton's ally Murray told the House, Livingston's resolution laid claim to a "right" to "mak[e] the Constitution inactive or inefficient
to its great ends." To preserve the federal government's overall discretion,
nationalists had to oppose the House's discretion as to treaties.

Madison's consistency was subtler, but real. Both in 1791–92 and in 1796,
his constitutionalism rested in large part on suspicion of power, and so in
the later debate he argued against views that in his opinion would render
the executive/senatorial treaty power "omnipotent" or deny that it was "a
limited power." To preserve the circumscribed nature of governmental authority in 1791 and 1792, Madison insisted on drawing sharp textual lines
between Congress and the states; in 1796 he strove to police the boundary
between the presidential power to negotiate and the congressional power to
legislate.

Washington's invocation of the Philadelphia framers' rejection of an express
requirement that treaties receive statutory ratification provoked an important
subsidiary debate over one of Madison's particular interests, the theory of
constitutional interpretation. The role of the framers' discussions in constitutional debate had been introduced earlier when Representative Murray had
called on Madison to instruct the House on the relevant events in the 1787
convention, probably in order to embarrass the Republican leader. Responding
to Washington's apparent claim to privileged constitutional knowledge as "a
member of the General Convention," Madison denounced both Murray's
request and Washington's assertion as surprising, and he proceeded to list
the objections to reliance on the framers' debates. Madison noted that descriptions of the convention's intent were conflicting and that his own "incidental" reference to the convention's deliberations in the bank bill debate
had been roundly criticized by opponents. Even the records of the convention
journal, which were not subject to the vagaries of memory, were still subject
to differing interpretations.

But Madison's primary objection to Washington's use of the Philadelphia
debates was theoretical rather than evidentiary. Such information was deemed
irrelevant in legal interpretation of the instrument because, Madison implied,
the framers were mere draftsmen. The authorities who had made the Constitution a text with legal significance were the state conventions acting on
the people's behalf. However, even those conventions' debates, being fragmentary and inaccurate, were unreliable guides to constitutional meaning,
and Madison treated them as more or less equivalent to the evidence derived
from the British precedents. In a striking anticipation of the position he would
take during the crisis of 1798–1800, he ascribed the highest authority to "a
general view" of the amendments proposed by some of the state conventions,
"[i]f we were to look . . . for the meaning of the instrument beyond the face
of the instrument."

James A. Bayard
Speech in the U.S. House of Representatives
(February 27, 1798)[67]

Debate over the role of the House (and of Congress generally) in foreign affairs did not end with the Jay Treaty's implementation. Two years later, opposition Republicans were again seeking to embarrass administration policy. Federalist Congressman Bayard made the following speech against a bill that would have required a reduction in the size of the government's diplomatic establishment.

. . . The case of checks to be derived from the Constitution, I apprehend, may be classed under three heads:

1. Where an express power is given to one branch to control the operations of another.
2. Where a branch of the Government exceeds its powers, and
3. Where a general power is given to one branch and a substantive power, included within the terms of it, given to another.

Thus, in the first case, in the Legislature the Senate is a check upon this House and this House upon the Senate and the President upon both; in the Executive, the Senate on the President, as to treaties and appointments; and, in the Judiciary, one Court upon another.

Upon the second head, a case . . . much relied on, furnishes a striking example. Even the Judges, [it is] said, are a check upon the Legislature. This arises from the nature of the Legislature, the powers of which are limited. If the Legislature transgress the bounds of their authority, their acts are void, and neither the people nor the Judges are bound by them. So if the President should commission [an officer], after an appointment non-concurred in by the Senate, the commission would be void. And in all cases where an act is done without power, a check may be found wherever we please to look for it.

The third case which has been mentioned is, where the general power of one branch is controlled by a particular power given to another branch. To this head may be assigned another case much relied on . . . The case I refer to is that of a treaty made by the President having war for its object. Now, as the exclusive power to declare war is vested in Congress, I have no hesitation in saying the President has not the power to make a treaty of offensive and defensive alliance. For though such a power may be embraced in the general terms giving the power to make treaties, yet as the right to declare war is distinctly given to Congress, it must operate as an exception to the general treaty-making power.

These are the cases of legitimate checks which occur to me. But as to the wild doctrine which has been contended for that, wherever one branch of the Government possesses any degree of power, a discretion necessarily accompanies the exercise of it, nothing, I conceive, can be more dangerous, or have a more direct tendency to disorganization. If the principle were asserted by each branch, the operations of the Government must cease. The President might say he was not bound blindly to execute laws which he conceived to be absurd or impolitic. We create offices, he refuses to fill them; we appropriate money, he refuses to apply it; we declare war, he refuses to carry it on, because, consulting his own judgment, he conceived our measures to be unwise and that it would be better for the country to check us by refusing the aid of his Constitutional power to carry our schemes into effect. I beg leave to put a case which comes up to the strongest point of the argument on the other side.

Suppose Congress declare war? This can be done by a majority of both Houses. The President participates [in] the power of appropriating money [by the veto power]. Now, suppose war actually declared by a power competent and expressly allowed to judge of its expediency, and the President, afterwards conceiving the war to be unjust or the declaration premature, refuses to concur in an appropriation to support it? In such case, we should be Constitutionally at war, and Constitutionally restrained from carrying it on.

Such are the absurdities which flow from the imported doctrine of checks. Consequences which tend to paralyze the powers of the Constitution, and effectually to stop the wheels of Government . . .

Comment

Nationalists did not reject blanketly or blindly the notion of checks and balances, but they insisted that limits on governmental action "be derived from the Constitution" and not from any "imported doctrine of checks." A given branch of government was entitled to impede another if the former had a specific power to do so, or if the active branch had transgressed a clear limit to its authority. A mere difference of opinion would not justify "stop[ping] the wheels of Government," a view often echoed in later years by those insisting that the president enforce congressional statutes or execute judicial decrees. What Bayard left unclear, as did most nationalists in the 1790s, was the proper course to take when the responsive branch was genuinely convinced that the active branch was violating the Constitution.

Four

The Crisis of 1798 and the Formulation of Republican Constitutionalism

Section A: *Judicial Foreshadowings*

United States v. Worrall
28 Fed. Cas. 774 (C.C.D. Pa. April 1798)

The defendant was charged with an attempt to bribe Tench Coxe, the commissioner of the revenue; and the indictment containing two counts, set forth the case as follows:

The grand inquest of the United States of America, for the Pennsylvania district, upon their respective oaths and affirmations do present . . . [O]n the 28th day of September, 1797, at the district aforesaid, Tench Cox, Esq. (he the said Tench Coxe, then and there being commissioner of the revenue, in the department of the secretary of the treasury,) then and there was appointed and instructed by the Secretary of the Treasury, by and with the authority of the president of the said United States, to receive proposals for building the light house aforesaid, and beacon aforesaid [at Cape Hatteras, North Carolina]. Robert Worrall, late of the same district, yeoman, being an ill-disposed person, and wickedly contriving and contending to bribe and seduce the said Tench Coxe, so being commissioner of the revenue, from the performance of the trust and duty so in him reposed, on the said 28th day of September, 1797, at the district aforesaid, and within the jurisdiction of this court, wickedly, advisedly and corruptly, did compose, write, utter, and publish, and cause to be delivered to the said Tench Coxe a letter, addressed to him the said Tench Coxe[:]

"Dear Sir . . . [I] should be happy in serving you in the executing this job, and always content with a reasonable profit; therefore every reasonable person would say that 1,400 [profit] was not unreasonable, in the two jobs. If I should be so happy in your recommendation of this work, I should think myself very ungrateful, if I did not offer you one half of the profits as above stated, and would deposit in your hand at receiving the first payment 350, and the other 350 at the last payment, when the work is finished and completed.

Robert Worrall"

. . . To the evil example of others in the like case offending, and against the peace and dignity of the said United States.

And the grand inquest . . . do further present, that Robert Worrall . . . wickedly, advisedly, and corruptly did solicit, urge and endeavor to procure Tench Coxe . . . to receive proposals for [the contracts] and in order to prevail upon him the said Tench Coxe, to agree to give him, the said Robert Worrall, the preference in, and the benefit of, such contract, he, the said Robert Worrall, then and there did . . . offer to give the said Tench Coxe . . . a large sum of money, to wit—the sum of seven hundred pounds . . . in contempt of the laws and constitution of the said United States . . .

[The evidence indicated that Worrall had written the September 28 letter while Coxe was considering the bids, including Worrall's, on the Cape Hatteras contracts, and that on receiving the letter Coxe, on the advice of governmental counsel, invited Worrall to a personal conference at which Worrall repeated the offer of the £700 kickback, and finally that Worrall again repeated his offer at a subsequent meeting with Coxe.]

Verdict—Guilty on both counts of the indictment.

Dallas, (who had declined speaking on the facts before the jury) now moved in arrest of judgment, alleging that the circuit court could not take cognizance of the crime charged in the indictment . . .

It will be admitted, that all the judicial authority of the federal courts, must be derived, either from the constitution of the United States, or from the acts of congress made in pursuance of the constitution. It is therefore, incumbent upon the prosecution to show, that an offer to bribe the commissioner of the revenue, is a violation of some constitutional, or legislative, prohibition. The constitution contains express provisions in certain cases, which are designated by a definition of the crimes: by a reference to the characters of the parties offending; or by the exclusive jurisdiction of the place where the offenses were perpetrated: but the crime of attempting to bribe, the character of a Federal officer, and the place where the present offense was committed, do not form any part of the constitutional express provisions, for the exercise of judicial authority in the courts of the union. The judicial power, however, extends, not only to all cases, in law and equity, arising under the constitution; but, likewise, to all such as shall arise under the laws of the United States, and besides the authority, specially vested in Congress to pass laws for enumerated purposes, there is a general authority given "to make all laws which shall be necessary and proper for carrying into execution all the powers vested by the constitution in the government of the United States, or any department or office thereof." Whenever, then, Congress think any provision necessary to effectuate the constitutional power of the government, they may establish it by law; and whenever it is so established, a violation of its sanctions will come within the jurisdiction of this court, under the 11th section of the judicial act, which declares, that the circuit court "shall have exclusive cognizance of all crimes and offenses cognizable under the authority of the United States, etc." Thus, Congress have provided by law for the punishment of treason, misprision of treason, piracy, counterfeiting any public certificate, stealing or falsifying records, etc.; for the punishment of various crimes, when committed within the limits of the exclusive jurisdiction of the United States; and for the punishment of bribery itself in the case of a judge, an officer of the customs, or an officer of the excise. But in the case of the commissioner of the revenue, the act constituting the office does not create or declare the offense; it is not recognized in the act under which proposals for building the lighthouse were invited; and there is no other act that has the slightest relation to the subject.

. . . But another ground may, perhaps, be taken to vindicate the present claim of jurisdiction: it may be urged, that though the offense is not specified in the constitution, nor defined in any act of Congress; yet, that it is an offense at common law, and that the common law is the law of the United States, in cases that arise under their authority. The nature of our Federal compact, will not, however, tolerate this doctrine. The 12th article of the amendment, stipulates, that "the powers not delegated to the United States by the constitution, nor prohibited by it to the States, are reserved to the states respectively, or to the people." In relation to crimes and punishments, the objects of the delegated power of the United States are enumerated and fixed. Congress may provide for the punishment of counterfeiting the securities and current coin of the United States; and may define and punish piracies and felonies committed on the high seas and offenses against the law of nations. And, so, likewise Congress may make all laws which shall be necessary and proper for carrying into execution the powers of the general government. But here is no reference to a common law authority: Every power is matter of definite and positive grant; and the very powers that are granted cannot take effect until they are exercised through the medium of a law. Congress had undoubtedly a power to make a law, which should render it criminal to offer a bribe to the commissioner of the revenue; but not having made the law, the crime is not recognized by the federal code, constitutional or legislative; and, consequently, it is not a subject on which the judicial authority of the union can operate . . .

Rawle (the attorney of the district) observed, that [Dallas's argument], taken in support of the motion in arrest of judgment, struck at the root of the whole system of the national government; for, if opposition to the pure, regular, and efficient administration of its affairs could thus be made by fraud, the experiment of force might next be applied; and doubtless with equal impunity and success. He concluded, however, that it was unnecessary to reason from the inconveniency and mischief of the [argument]; for, the offense was strictly within the very terms of the constitution, arising under the laws of the United States. If no such office had been created by the laws of the United States, no attempt to corrupt such an officer could have been made; and it is unreasonable to insist, that merely because law has not prescribed an express and appropriate punishment for the offense, that, therefore, the offense, when committed, shall not be punished by the circuit court, upon the principles of common law punishment. The effect, indeed, of the position is still more injurious; for, unless this offense is punishable in the Federal courts, it certainly is not cognizable before any state tribunal. . . .

CHASE, *Justice.*—Do you mean, Mr. Attorney, to support this indictment solely at common law? If you do, I have no difficulty upon the subject: The indictment cannot be maintained in this court.

Rawle, answering in the affirmative, CHASE, *Justice*, stopped Mr. Levy, who was about to reply, in support of the motion in arrest of judgment; and delivered an opinion to the following effect.

CHASE, *Justice.*—This is an indictment for an offense highly injurious to morals, and deserving the severest punishment; but, as it is an indictment at common law, I dismiss, at once everything that has been said about the constitution and laws of the United States.

In this country, every man sustains a two-fold political capacity; one in relation to the state, and another in relation to the United States: In relation to the state, he is subject to various municipal regulations, founded upon the state constitution and policy, which do not affect him in his relation to the United States: For, the constitution of the Union, is the source of all the jurisdiction of the national government; so that the departments of the government can never assume any power, that is not expressly granted by that instrument, nor exercise a power in any other manner than is there prescribed. Besides the particular cases, which the 8th section of the 1st article designates, there is a power granted to Congress to create, define, and punish crimes and offenses, whenever they shall deem it necessary and proper by law to do so, for effectuating the objects of the government; and although bribery is not among the crimes and offenses specifically mentioned, it is certainly included in this general provision. The question, however, does not arise about the power; but about the exercise of the power:—Whether the courts of the United States can punish a man for any act, before it is declared by a law of the United States to be criminal? Now, it appears to my mind, to be as essential, that Congress should define the offenses to be tried, and apportion the punishments to be inflicted, as that they should erect courts to try the criminal, or to pronounce a sentence on conviction.

It is attempted, however, to supply the silence of the constitution and statutes of the union, by resorting to the common law, for a definition and punishment of the offense which has been committed: But, in my opinion, the United States, as a Federal government, have no common law; and, consequently no indictment can be maintained in their courts, for offenses merely at the common law. If, indeed, the United States can be supposed, for a moment, to have a common law, it must, I presume, be that of England; and, yet, it is impossible to trace when, or how, the system was adopted, or introduced. With respect to the individual states, the difficulty does not occur. When the American colonies were first settled by our ancestors, it was held, as well by the settlers, as by the judges and lawyers of England, that they brought hither, as a birth-right and inheritance, so much of the common law, as was applicable to their local situation, and change of circumstances. But each colony judged for itself, what parts of the common law were applicable to its new condition; and in various modes, by Legislative acts, by judicial decisions, or by constant usage, adopted some parts, and rejected others. Hence, he who shall travel through the different states, will soon discover, that the whole of the common law of England has been no where introduced; that some states have rejected what others have adopted; and that there is, in short, a great and essential diversity; in the subjects to which the common law is applied, as well as in the extent of its application. The common law, therefore, of one state, is not the common law of another; but the common law of England, is the law of each state, so far as each state has adopted it; and it results from the position, connected with the judicial act, that the common law will always apply to suits between citizen and citizen, whether they are instituted in a Federal, or State court.

But the question recurs, when and how, have the courts of the United States acquired a common law jurisdiction, in criminal cases? The United States must possess the common law themselves, before they can communicate it to their judicial agents. Now, the United States did not bring it with them from England; the constitution does not create it; and no act of Congress has assumed it. Besides, what is the common law to which we are referred? Is it the common law entire, as it exists in England; or modified as it exists in some of the states; and of the various modifications, which are we to select, the system of Georgia or New Hampshire, of Pennsylvania or Connecticut?

Upon the whole, it may be defect in our political institutions, it may be inconvenience in the administration of justice, that the common law authority, relating crimes and punishments, has not been conferred upon the government of the United States, which is a government in other respects also of a limited jurisdiction; but judges cannot remedy political imperfections, nor supply any Legislative omission. I will not say whether the offense is at this time cognizable in a state court. But, certainly, Congress might have provided for other cases, of a similar nature; and yet if Congress had ever declared and defined the offense without prescribing a punishment, I should still have thought it improper to exercise a discretion upon that part of the subject.

Peters [District Judge],—Whenever a government has been established, I have always supposed, that a power to preserve itself, was a necessary, and an inseparable, concomitant. But the existence of the Federal government would be precarious, it could no longer be called an independent government, if, for the punishment of offenses of this nature, tending to obstruct and pervert the administration of its affairs, an appeal must be made to the state tribunals, or the offenders must escape with absolute impunity.

The power to punish misdemeanors, is originally and strictly a common law power; of which, I think, the United States are constitutionally possessed. It might have been exercised by Congress in the form of a Legislative act; but, it may, also, in my opinion be enforced in a course of judicial proceeding. Whenever an offense aims at the subversion of any Federal institution, or at the corruption of its public officers, it is an offense against the well-being of the United States: from its very nature, it is cognizable under their authority; and, consequently, it is within the jurisdiction of this court, by virtue of the 11th section of the judicial act.

The court being divided in opinion, it became a doubt, whether sentence could be pronounced upon the defendant; and a wish was expressed by the judges and the attorney of the district, that the case might be put into such a form, as would admit of obtaining the ultimate decision of the supreme court, upon the important principle of the discussion. But the counsel for the prisoner did not think themselves authorized to enter into a compromise of that nature. The court, after a short consultation, and declaring that the sentence was mitigated in consideration of the defendant's circumstances, proceeded to adjudge,

That the defendant be imprisoned for three months; that he pay a fine of 200 dollars; and that he stand committed, 'til this sentence be complied with, and the costs of prosecution paid.

Comment

For nationalist thinkers of the 1790s, it was self-evident that federal courts could exercise jurisdiction over prosecutions brought for offenses "against the well-being of the United States" (Peters) regardless of the existence of a federal statute defining the crime or its punishment. To suggest otherwise would be to concede that the federal government lacked (or possessed only imperfectly) the power of self-preservation from "fraud [or] force" (Rawle); because such a power "was a necessary, and an inseparable concomitant" to the existence of any government, it followed that *this* government possessed it.

Opposition constitutionalists, of course, were comfortable with the notion of the "omitted case," and Alexander Dallas relied in his argument in *Worrall* on the absence from the constitutional text of any general grant of "common law authority." (Somewhat bizarrely, Justice Samuel Chase agreed with Dallas, but then agreed to join in sentencing the defendant.)

The debate over the existence of a federal common law of crimes was to remain of great constitutional importance for the next fifteen years. In the immediate aftermath of *Worrall*, defenders of the 1798 Sedition Act insisted that the act could not be an infringement of preexisting rights of free speech and press because (1) without the act, the United States could punish seditious libel at common law; and (2) the act was less harsh than this federal common law (which they presumed to be identical to Blackstone's views on libel and liberty of the press).

The claim that the federal courts enjoyed a common-law jurisdiction seemed to Republican thinkers to put in jeopardy the limited and text-bound nature of the Constitution's delegation of power to the federal government. If federal courts could punish crimes as defined by "the common law," with its amorphous body of precedents (potentially from each state as well as from England), the criminal law power of the United States would no longer be limited to "enumerated and fixed" objects.

Respublica v. Cobbett
3 Dallas 467 (Pa. Dec. 1798)

William Cobbett was the most notorious Federalist propagandist of the 1790s. Through his Philadelphia newspaper, *Porcupine's Gazette*, and a series of scurrilous pamphlets published under the pseudonym "Peter Porcupine," he assailed the Republicans as Jacobin terrorists, atheists, and stooges of Revolutionary France. Eventually, the Republican state authorities charged Cobbett with being a "common libeller," and compelled him entered into a recognizance (a bond) guaranteeing his "good behavior." When he continued his publishing career with unchanged rhetoric, the state brought an action to recover on his allegedly violated recognizance. An English subject, he petitioned to remove the case to the federal circuit court pursuant to a provision of the 1789 Judiciary Act granting aliens that right. The petition came before staunchly Republican Chief Justice Thomas M'Kean.

M'KEAN, *Chief Justice:*—This action is brought on a recognizance to the commonwealth of Pennsylvania, for the good behavior entered into by the defendant before me. The defendant has appeared to the action, and exhibited his petition to the court, praying that the jurisdiction thereof be transferred to the circuit court of the United States, as he is an alien, and a subject of the king of Great Britain. His right to this claim of jurisdiction is said to be grounded on the 12th section of the act of Congress, entitled "an act to establish the judicial courts of the United States," passed the 24th of September, 1789, in the first clause [of] which section it is enacted, that if a suit be commenced in any state court against an alien, etc., and the matter in dispute exceeds the sum of value of five hundred dollars, exclusive of costs, on a petition of the defendant, and a tender of bail to appear in the circuit court, etc., it shall be the duty of the state court to accept the surety, and proceed no further in the case, etc.

Previous to the delivery of my opinion in a cause of such importance, as to the consequences of the decision, I will make a few preliminary observations on the constitution and laws of the United States of America.

Our system of government seems to me to differ, in form and spirit, from all other governments, that have heretofore existed in the world. It is as to some particulars national, in others federal, and in all the residue territorial, or in districts called states.

The divisions of power between the national, federal, and state government, (all derived from the same source, the authority of the people) must be collected from the constitution of the United States. Before it was adopted, the several states had absolute and unlimited sovereignty within their respective boundaries; all the powers, legislative, executive, and judicial, excepting those granted to Congress under the old constitution: They now enjoy them all, excepting such as are granted to the government of the United States by the present instrument and the adopted amendments, which are for particular purposes only. The government of the United States forms a part of the government of each state; its jurisdiction extends to the providing for the common defense against exterior injuries and violence, the regulation of commerce, and other matters specially enumerated in the constitution; all other powers remain in the individual states, comprehending the interior and other concerns; these combined, form one complete government. Should there be any defect in the form of government, or any collision occur, it cannot be remedied by the sole act of the Congress, or of a state; the people must be resorted to, for enlargement or modification. If a state should differ with the United States about the construction of them, there is no common umpire but the people, who should adjust the affair by making amendments in the constitutional way, or suffer from the defect. In such a case the constitution of the United States is federal, it is a league or treaty made by the individual states, as one party, and all the states, as another party. When two nations differ about the meaning of any clause, sentence, or word in a treaty, neither has an exclusive right to decide it; they endeavor to adjust the matter by negotiation, but if it cannot be thus accomplished, each has a right to retain its own interpretation, until a reference be had to the mediation of other nations, an arbitration, or the fate of war. There is no provision in the constitution, that in such a case the judges of the supreme court of the United States shall control and be conclusive: neither can the congress by a law confer that power. There appears to be a defect in this matter, it is a *casus omissus*, which ought in some way to be remedied. Perhaps the vice-president and senate of the United States; or commissioners appointed, say one by each state, would be a more proper tribunal than the supreme court. Be that as it may, I rather think the remedy must be found in an amendment of the constitution.

I shall now consider the case before us. It is an action brought in the name of the commonwealth of Pennsylvania, against an alien, a British subject. By the express words of the second sentence of the second section of the 3d article of the constitution of the United States, in such an action the supreme court shall have original jurisdiction; whereas it is now prayed by the defendant, that original jurisdiction be given to the circuit court. From this, it would reasonably be concluded, that the congress, in the 12th section of the judicial law, did not contemplate an action wherein a state was plaintiff, though an alien was defendant, for it is there said, "that if a suit be commenced in any state court against an alien, etc." as it does not mention by a state, the presumption and construction must be, that it meant by a citizen. This will appear pretty plain from a perusal of the 11th section of the same act, where it is enacted, that the circuit courts shall have original cognizance; concurrent with the courts of the several states, of all suits of a civil nature; of a certain value, where the United States are plaintiffs or petitioners, or where alien is a party. This confines the original cognizance of the circuit courts, concurrent with the courts of the several states, to civil actions commenced by the United States, or citizens against aliens, or where an alien is a party, etc., and does not extend to actions brought against aliens by a state, for of such the supreme court had, by the constitution, original jurisdiction. I would further remark, that the jurisdiction of the circuit courts is confined to actions of a civil nature against aliens, and does not extend to those of a criminal nature; for although the word "suit" is used generally in the 12th section, without expressing the words "of a civil nature," yet the slightest consideration of what follows, manifestly shows that no other suit was meant; for the matter in dispute must exceed five hundred dollars in value, special bail must be given, etc., terms applicable to actions of a civil nature only.

Let us now consider, whether this suit against William Cobbett is of a civil or criminal nature. It is grounded on a recognizance for the good behavior entered into before the chief justice of this state. This recognizance, it must be conceded, was taken to prevent criminal actions by the defendant, in violation of the peace, order, and tranquility of the society; it was to prevent crimes, or public wrongs, and misdemeanors, and for no other purpose. It is evidently of a criminal nature and cannot be supported unless he shall be convicted of having committed some crime, which would incur its breach since its date, and before the day on which the process issued against him. Besides, a recognizance is a matter or record, it is in the nature of a judgment, and the process upon it, whether a *scire facias* or summons, is for the purpose of carrying it into execution, and is rather judicial than original; it is no farther to be reckoned an original suit, than that the defendant has a right to plead to it; it is founded upon the recognizance, and must be considered as flowing from it, and partaking of its nature; and when final judgment shall be given the whole is to be taken as one record. It has been well observed by the attorney general, that by the last amendment, or legislative declaration of the meaning of the constitution, respecting the jurisdiction of the courts of the United States over the causes of states, it is strongly implied, that states shall not be drawn against their will directly or indirectly before them, and that if the present application should prevail this would be the case. The words of the declaration are: "The judicial power of the United States shall not be construed to extend to any suit in law or equity commenced or prosecuted against one of the United States, by citizens of another state, or by citizens or subjects of any foreign state." When the judicial law was passed, the opinion prevailed that states might be sued, which by this amendment is settled otherwise.

The argument *ab inconvenienti* is also applicable to the construction of this section of the act of Congress. Can the Legislature of the United States be supposed to have intended (granting it was within their constitutional powers) that an alien, residing three or four hundred miles from where the circuit court is held, who has, from his turbulent and infamous conduct in his neighborhood, been bound to the good behavior by a magistrate of a state, should, after a breach of his recognizance and a prosecution for it commenced, be enabled to remove the prosecution before a court at such a distance, and held but twice in a year, to be tried by a jury, who know neither the persons, nor characters, of the witnesses, and consequently are unqualified to try their credit; and to oblige the prosecutor and witnesses to incur such an expense of time and money, in order to prove that he had committed an assault, or any other offense that would amount to a violation of it? If so, such a recognizance, though it would operate as a security to the public against a citizen, would be of little avail against an alien. It cannot be conceived, that they intended to put an alien in a more favorable situation than a citizen in such a case, and by difficulties thrown in the way to discourage and weaken, if not defeat the use of, a restraint, found often to be very salutary in preserving the peace and quiet of the people. Many other inconveniences have been mentioned by the counsel, which I shall not repeat. If, therefore, any other construction can be made it ought to prevail.

Upon the whole, our opinion is, that where a state has a controversy with an alien about a contract, or other matter of a civil nature, the supreme court of the United States has original jurisdiction of it, and the circuit or district courts have nothing to do with such a case. The reason seems to be founded in a respect for the dignity of a state, that the action may be brought in the first instance before the highest tribunal, and also that this tribunal would be most likely to guard against the power and influence of a state over a foreigner. But that neither the constitution nor the Congress ever contemplated, that any court under the United States should take cognizance of any thing favoring of criminality against a state: That the action before the court is of a criminal nature and for the punishment of a crime against the state: That yielding to the prayer of the petitioner would be highly inconvenient in itself and injurious in the precedent: And that cognizance of it would not be accepted by the circuit court, if sent to them; for even consent cannot confer jurisdiction. For the reasons, and others, omitted for the sake of brevity, I conclude, the prayer of William Cobbett cannot be granted.

Comment

M'Kean's opinion anticipated many of the themes other Republicans were shortly to use in attacking the constitutionality of the Sedition Act. He identified as constitutionally important a particular account of American history in which originally sovereign and independent states delegated part of their authority to the federal government. The legal consequence of this account was that the Constitution was, on at least some issues, a "league" or treaty rather than the organic law of a national polity. M'Kean's understanding of the constitutional compact at first seems peculiar: each state is one party and all the other states are the other. As a matter of political metaphor, the resulting image of a series of treaties (New Hampshire and the other states, Massachusetts and the other states, etc.) is confusing, but its practical and intended consequence was in accord with Republican solicitude for state autonomy: because the Constitution is a (series of) *bilateral* agreement(s) there could be no question of majority rule in a dispute over the boundary between federal and state power. Later Republicans viewed *Cobbett* as a seminal expression of the correct understanding of the Constitution.

Section B: *The Alien and Sedition Acts*

Many Americans in 1798 believed that the Republic was threatened by a frightening array of enemies. Externally, Franco-American relations had worsened steadily, and conflict on the high seas had become an undeclared naval war. In March 1798 negotiations broke down altogether, and the next month President John Adams released information about the XYZ Affair, in which agents of the French foreign minister threatened and sought a bribe from the American peace commission in Paris, which included John Marshall. In May, Congress authorized Adams to order the United States Navy to seize French vessels interfering with American shipping, and to raise a large volunteer army.

The international crisis was mirrored, many supporters of the government believed, in domestic affairs. Federalists often perceived the Republicans as unwitting or even voluntary agents of the French. Immigrants, who provided significant electoral support for the Republicans in the cities, were regarded as especially suspect. Ideologically, the Republican combination of democratic rhetoric and opposition to a strong national government seemed tailored to pave the way for a French-style revolution.

In this crisis atmosphere, the Federalist majority in Congress enacted, and President Adams signed, a set of statutes intended to strengthen the federal government's ability to defend itself, the Constitution, and the nation. The Naturalization Act (June 18) lengthened the residency required for citizenship from five to fourteen years, and the Enemy Aliens Act (July 6) authorized the apprehension and banishment during wartime of subjects of hostile powers. Although Republicans objected to these acts as oppressive and partisan, they reserved their primary and constitutional criticisms for the Alien Act (June 25) and the Sedition Act (July 14). The Alien Act was designed to enable the president to control the activities during peacetime of foreign residents deemed a threat to national security. The Sedition Act was intended to place the federal government's ability to prosecute seditious libel on a statutory basis and therefore circumvent the controversy over the existence of a federal common law of crimes. The Alien Act was to expire in two years, but the Sedition Act was to remain in effect until March 3, 1801—in other words throughout the upcoming presidential election campaign.

William Blackstone
Commentaries on the Laws of England
Volume 4 (1769)[68]

Blackstone represented the conservative, restrictive common-law interpretation of freedom of the press. Many Americans, including such Republican stalwarts as Chief Justice M'Kean, of Pennsylvania, interpreted state guarantees of press freedom as constitutionalizations of Blackstone. Supporters of the Sedition Act were therefore able to use Blackstone to portray the act, which included several reforms long sought by opponents of the common-law rules, as an amelioration of the common law, and as a libertarian rather than a repressive measure.

. . . Of a nature very similar to challenges are *libels, libelli famosi*, which, taken in their largest and most extensive sense, signify any writings, pictures, or the like, of an immoral or illegal tendency; but, in the sense under which we are now to consider them, are malicious defamations of any person, and especially a magistrate, made public by either printing, writing, signs, or pictures, in order to provoke him to wrath, or expose him to public hatred, contempt, and ridicule. The direct tendency of these libels is the breach of the public peace, by stirring up the objects of them to revenge, and perhaps to bloodshed. The communication of a libel to any one person is a publication in the eye of the law: and therefore the sending an abusive private letter to a man is as much a libel as if it were openly printed, for it equally tends to a breach of the peace. For the same reason it is immaterial with respect to the essence of a libel, whether the matters of it be true or false; since the provocation, and not the falsity, is the thing to be punished criminally: though, doubtless, the falsehood of it may aggravate its guilt, and enhance its punishment . . .

In this, and the other instances which we have lately considered, where blasphemous, immoral, treasonable, schismatical, seditious, or scandalous libels are punished by the English law, some with a greater, others with a less degree of severity; the *liberty of the press*, properly understood, is by no means infringed or violated. The liberty of the press is indeed essential to the nature of a free state: but this consists in laying no *previous* restraints upon publications, and not in freedom from censure for criminal matter when published. Every freeman has an undoubted right to lay what sentiments he pleases before the public: to forbid this, is to destroy the freedom of the press: but if he publishes what is improper, mischievous, or illegal, he must take the consequence of his own temerity. To subject the press to the restrictive power of a licenser, as was formerly done, both before and since the revolution, is to subject all freedom of sentiment to the prejudices of one man and make him the arbitrary and infallible judge of all controverted points in learning, religion, and government. But to punish (as the law does at present) any dangerous or offensive writings, which, when published, shall on a fair and impartial trial be adjudged of a pernicious tendency, is necessary for the preservation of peace and good order, of government and religion, the only solid foundations of civil liberty. Thus the will of individuals is still left free; the abuse only of that free will is the object of legal punishment . . . So true will it be found, that to censure the licentiousness, is to maintain the liberty, of the press.

Harrison Gray Otis
Speech in the U.S. House of Representatives
(July 10, 1798)[69]

In Congress the Sedition bill was attacked as an exercise of power not delegated to the federal government as well as an unconstitutional restriction on freedom of speech. Federalist representative Otis was one of the bill's chief defenders.

Mr. Otis said the professions of attachment to the Constitution, made by the gentleman from Virginia [John Nicholas, a Republican critic of the Sedition bill] are certainly honorable to him; and he could not believe that an attachment so deeply engrafted as he states his to be would be shaken by this bill. The gentleman had caught an alarm on the first suggestion of a sedition bill which had not yet subsided; and though the present bill is perfectly harmless, and contains no provision which is not practised upon under the laws of the several States in which gentlemen had been educated, and from which they had drawn most of their ideas of jurisprudence, yet the gentleman continues to be dissatisfied with it.

The objections of the gentleman from Virginia, he believed, might be reduced to two inquiries. In the first place, had the Constitution given Congress cognizance over the offences described in this bill prior to the adoption of the amendments to the Constitution? and, if Congress had that cognizance before that time, have those amendments taken it away? With respect to the first question, it must be allowed that every independent Government has a right to preserve and defend itself against injuries and outrages which endanger its existence; for unless it has this power, it is unworthy the name of a free Government and must either fall or be subordinate to some other protection. Now some of the offences delineated in the bill are of this description. Unlawful combinations to oppose the measures of Government, to intimidate its officers, and to excite insurrections are acts which tend directly to the destruction of the Constitution, and there could be no doubt that the guardians of that Constitution are bound to provide against them. And if gentlemen would agree that these were acts of a criminal nature, it follows that all means calculated to produce these effects whether by speaking, writing, or printing, were also criminal . . .

It was . . . most evident to his mind that the Constitution of the United States, prior to the amendments that have been added to it, secured to the National Government that cognizance of all the crimes enumerated in the bill, and it only remained to be considered whether those amendments divested it of this power. The amendment quoted by the gentleman from Virginia is in these words: "Congress shall make no law abridging the freedom of speech and of the press." The terms "freedom of speech and of the press," he supposed, were a phraseology perfectly familiar in the jurisprudence of every State, and of a certain and technical meaning. It was a mode of expression which we had borrowed from the only country in which it had been tolerated, and he pledged himself to prove that the construction which he should give to those terms should be consonant not only to the laws of that country, but to the laws and judicial decisions of many of the States composing the Union. This freedom, said Mr. O., is nothing more than the liberty of writing, publishing, and speaking one's thoughts, under the condition of being answerable to the injured party, whether it be the Government or an individual, for false, malicious, and seditious expressions, whether spoken or written; and the liberty of the press is merely an exemption from all previous restraints.

In support of this doctrine, he quoted *Blackstone's Commentaries*, under the head of libels, and read an extract to prove that in England, formerly, the press was subject to a licenser; and that this restraint was afterward removed, by which means the freedom of the press was established. He would not, however, dwell upon the law of England, the authority of which it might suit the convenience of gentlemen to question; but he would demonstrate that although in several of the State constitutions the liberty of speech and of the press were guarded by the most express and unequivocal language the Legislatures and Judicial departments of those States had adopted the definitions of the English law and provided for the punishment of defamatory and seditious libels . . .

The Alien Act
Ch. 58, 1 Stat. 570 (June 25, 1798)

Section 1. *Be it enacted by the Senate and House of Representatives of the United States of America, in Congress assembled,* that it shall be lawful for the President of the United States at any time during the continuance of this Act to order all such aliens as he shall judge dangerous to the peace and safety of the United States, or shall have reasonable grounds to suspect are concerned in any treasonable or secret machinations against the government thereof, to depart out of the territory of the United States within such time as shall be expressed in such order, which order shall be served on such alien by delivering him a copy thereof or leaving the same at his usual abode, and returned to the office of the secretary of state by the marshal or other person to whom the same shall be directed. And in case any alien so ordered to depart shall be found at large within the United States after the time limited in such order for his departure, and not having obtained a license from the President to reside therein, or having obtained such license shall not have conformed thereto, every such alien shall, on conviction thereof, be imprisoned for a term not exceeding three years, and shall never after be admitted to become a citizen of the United States.

Provided always, and be it further enacted, that if any alien so ordered to depart shall prove to the satisfaction of the President, by evidence to be taken before such person or persons as the President shall direct, who are for that purpose hereby authorized to administer oaths, that no injury or danger to the United States will arise from suffering such alien to reside therein, the President may grant a license to such alien to remain within the United States for such time as he shall judge proper, and at such place as he may designate. And the President may also require of such alien to enter into a bond to the United States, in such penal sum as he may direct, with one or more sufficient sureties to the satisfaction of the person authorized by the President to take the same, conditioned for the good behavior of such alien during his residence in the United States, and not violating his license, which license the President may revoke whenever he shall think proper.

Section 2. And be it further enacted, that it shall be lawful for the President of the United States, whenever he may deem it necessary for the public safety, to order to be removed out of the territory thereof any alien who may or shall be in prison in pursuance of this Act: and to cause to be arrested and sent out of the United States such of those aliens as shall have been ordered to depart therefrom and shall not have obtained a license as aforesaid, in all cases where, in the opinion of the President, the public safety requires a speedy removal. And if any alien so removed or sent out of the United States by the President shall voluntarily return thereto, unless by permission of the President of the United States, such alien on conviction thereof shall be imprisoned so long as, in the opinion of the President, the public safety may require . . .

Section 4. *And be it further enacted*, that the Circuit and District courts of the United States shall respectively have cognizance of all crimes and offenses against this Act. And all marshals and other officers of the United States are required to execute all precepts and orders of the President of the United States issued in pursuance or by virtue of this Act.

Section 5. *And be it further enacted*, that it shall be lawful for any alien who may be ordered to be removed from the United States, by virtue of this Act, to take with him such part of his goods, chattels, or other property as he may find convenient; and all property left in the United States by any alien who may be removed, as aforesaid, shall be and remain subject to his order and disposal, in the same manner as if this Act had not been passed.

Section 6. *And be it further enacted*, that this Act shall continue and be in force for and during the term of two years from the passing thereof.

The Sedition Act
Ch. 74, 1 Stat. 596 (July 14, 1798)

Section 1. *Be it enacted by the Senate and House of Representatives of the United States of America, in Congress assembled*, that if any persons shall unlawfully combine or conspire together with intent to oppose any measure or measures of the government of the United States which are or shall be directed by proper authority, or to impede the operation of any law of the United States, or to intimidate or prevent any person holding a place or office in or under the government of the United States from undertaking, performing, or executing his trust or duty; and if any person or persons, with intent as aforesaid, shall counsel, advise, or attempt to procure any insurrection, riot, unlawful assembly, or combination, whether such conspiracy, threatening, counsel, advice, or attempt shall have the proposed effect or not, he or they shall be deemed guilty of a high misdemeanor, and on conviction before any court of the United States having jurisdiction thereof shall be punished by a fine not exceeding $5,000 and by imprisonment during a term not less than six months nor exceeding five years; and further, at the discretion of the court, may be held to find sureties for his good behavior in such sum and for such time as the said court may direct.

Section 2. *And be it further enacted*, that if any person shall write, print, utter, or publish, or shall cause or procure to be written, printed, uttered, or published, or shall knowingly and willingly assist or aid in writing, printing, uttering, or publishing any false, scandalous, and malicious writing or writings against the government of the United States, or either house of the Congress of the United States, or the President of the United States with intent to defame the said government, or either house of the said Congress, or the said President, or to bring them, or either of them, into contempt or disrepute; or, to excite against them, or either or any of them, the hatred of the good people of the United States, or to stir up sedition within the United States, or to excite any unlawful combinations therein, for opposing or resisting any law of the United States, or any act of the President of the United States, done in pursuance of any such law, or of the powers in him vested by the Constitution of the United States, or to resist, oppose, or defeat any such law or act, or to aid, encourage or abet any hostile designs of any foreign nation against the United States, their people, or government, then such person being thereof convicted before any court of the United States having jurisdiction thereof shall be punished by a fine not exceeding $2,000 and by imprisonment not exceeding two years.

Section 3. *And be it further enacted and declared*, that if any person shall be prosecuted under this Act, for the writing or publishing any libel aforesaid, it shall be lawful for the defendant, upon the trial of the cause, to give evidence in his defense, the truth of the matter contained in the publication charged as a libel. And the jury who shall try the case shall have a right to determine the law and the fact, under the direction of the court, as in other cases.

Section 4. *And be it further enacted*, that this Act shall continue and be in force until the third day of March, 1801, and no longer: *provided*, that the expiration of the Act shall not prevent or defeat a prosecution and punishment of any offense against the law during the time it shall be in force.

Comment

The Alien Act was objectionable to Republicans both on practical and ideological grounds. Its practical effect, if it had ever been invoked, would have been to give a Federalist administration extensive power over a group of residents who tended to be pro-Republican. Ideologically, the Alien Act excited deeply held fears of executive discretion. The government never invoked the act, however, and probably could not have used the act effectively if it had attempted to do so: enforcement of the provisions would have required a much larger bureaucracy than even the most ardent nationalist of the 1790s was willing to create.

The Sedition Act was portrayed by its supporters, not unreasonably, as an amelioration of the common law. The act made the truth of the alleged libel a defense against prosecution under the act and guaranteed to the jury the power to decide the meaning of the law and the facts of the case—on both matters adopting reforms of seditious libel law sought by English free-speech activists for decades. Republicans, nevertheless, saw the act as an assault on liberty and as a naked effort to stifle criticism of the Adams administration and of the federalist majority. It was no accident, critics of the act insisted, that it did not criminalize seditious libel of the vice-president, Republican Thomas Jefferson. The Sedition Act was used by the Adams administration and with some results: about fifteen indictments were secured, and several major Republican newspapers were closed down.

Section C: *The "Doctrines of '98"*

In response to the passage of the Alien and Sedition acts, the southern Republican leadership turned to the state governments. Jefferson drafted a set of resolutions originally planned for the North Carolina legislature, but they were eventually presented to the Kentucky assembly by John Breckenridge without any indication that they came from the vice-president's pen. The Kentucky legislators adopted the resolutions, though after Jefferson's original reference to state "nullification" of federal law was omitted. Madison's draft was presented to the Virginia legislature by John Taylor, again without acknowledgment of the author, and adopted over the opposition of a Federalist minority led by John Marshall.

Jefferson and Madison hoped that the Kentucky and Virginia resolutions would stimulate other state legislatures to join in assailing the acts as well as the policies of the Washington and Adams administrations generally. In the short term, this strategy failed: no other state endorsed the resolutions, and seven mid-Atlantic and northeastern legislatures officially rejected them. This negative response led the Kentucky legislature to adopt in late 1799 an additional set of resolves that included the inflammatory word "nullification."

Kentucky Resolutions of 1798
(adopted on November 16, 1798)[70]

1. *Resolved*, that the several states composing the United States of America are not united on the principle of unlimited submission to their general government; but that, by compact, under the style and title of a Constitution for the United States, and of amendments thereto, they constituted a general government for special purposes, delegated to that government certain definite powers, reserving, each state to itself, the residuary mass of right to their own self-government. And that whensoever the general government assumes undelegated powers, its acts are unauthoritative, void, and of no force: that to this compact each state acceded as a state and is an integral party, its co-states forming, as to itself, the other party; that this government, created by this compact, was not made the exclusive or final judge of the extent of the powers delegated to itself, since that would have made its discretion, and not the Constitution, the measure of its powers; but that, as in all other cases of compact among parties having no common judge, each party has an equal right to judge for itself, as well of infractions as of the mode and measure of redress.

2. *Resolved*, that the Constitution of the United States having delegated to Congress a power to punish treason, counterfeiting the securities and current coin of the United States, piracies and felonies committed on the high seas, and offenses against the laws of nations, and no other crimes whatever; and it being true, as a general principle, and one of the amendments to the Constitution having also declared "that the powers not delegated to the United States by the Constitution, nor prohibited by it to the states, are reserved to the states respectively, or to the people"; therefore, also, the same act of Congress, passed on the 14th day of July, 1798, and entitled "An Act in Addition to the Act Entitled 'An Act for the Punishment of Certain Crimes Against the United States,' " as also the act passed by them on the 27th day of June, 1798, entitled "An Act to Punish Frauds Committed on the Bank of the United States" (and all other of their acts which assume to create, define, or punish crimes other than those enumerated in the Constitution), are altogether void and of no force; and that the power to create, define, and punish, such other crimes is reserved, and of right appertains, solely and exclusively, to the respective states, each within its own territory.

3. *Resolved*, that it is true, as a general principle, and is also expressly declared by one of the amendments to the Constitution, that "the powers not delegated to the United

States by the Constitution, nor prohibited by it to the states, are reserved to the states respectively, or to the people;" and that no power over the freedom of religion, freedom of speech, or freedom of the press, being delegated to the United States by the Constitution, nor prohibited by it to the states, all lawful powers respecting the same did of right remain, and were reserved to the states, or to the people; that thus was manifested their determination to retain to themselves the right of judging how far the licentiousness of speech, and of the press, may be abridged without lessening their useful freedom, and how far those abuses, which cannot be separated from their use, should be tolerated rather than the use be destroyed. And thus also they guarded against all abridgment, by the United States, of the freedom of religous principles and exercises, and retained to themselves the right of protecting the same, as this, State, by a law passed on the general demand of its citizens, had already protected them from all human restraint or interference [the Virginia Statute for Religious Freedom, drafted by Jefferson and enacted in 1786] and that, in addition to this general principle and express declaration, another and more special provision has been made by one of the amendments to the Constitution, which expressly declares that "Congress shall make no laws respecting an establishment of religion, or prohibiting the free exercise thereof, or abridging the freedom of speech, or of the press," thereby guarding, in the same sentence, and under the same words, the freedom of religion, of speech, and of the press, insomuch that whatever violates either throws down the sanctuary which covers the others; and that libels, falsehood, and defamation, equally with heresy and false religion, are withheld from the cognizance of federal tribunals. That, therefore, the act of the Congress of the United States, passed on the 14th of July, 1798, entitled "An Act in Addition to the Act Entitled 'An Act for the Punishment of Certain Crimes Against the United States,' " which does abridge the freedom of the press, is not law, but is altogether void and of no force.

4. *Resolved*, that alien friends are under the jurisdiction and protection of the laws of the state wherein they are; that no power over them has been delegated to the United States, nor prohibited to the individual states, distinct from their power over citizens; and it being true, as a general principle, and one of the amendments to the Constitution having also declared, that "the powers not delegated to the United States by the Constitution, nor prohibited to the states, are reserved to the states, respectively, or to the people," the act of the Congress of the United States, passed the 22nd day of June, 1798, entitled "An Act Concerning Aliens," which assumes power over alien friends not delegated by the Constitution, is not law, but is altogether void and of no force.

5. *Resolved*, that, in addition to the general principle, as well as the express declaration, that powers not delegated are reserved, another and more special provision inserted in the Constitution from abundant caution has declared, "that the migration or importation of such persons as any of the states now existing shall think proper to admit shall not be prohibited by the Congress prior to the year 1808." That this commonwealth does admit the migration of alien friends described as the subject of the said act concerning aliens; that a provision against prohibiting their migration is a provision against all acts equivalent thereto, or it would be nugatory; that to remove them, when migrated, is equivalent to a prohibition of their migration, and is, therefore, contrary to the said provision of the Constitution, and void.

6. *Resolved*, that the imprisonment of a person under the protection of the laws of this commonwealth, on his failure to obey the simple order of the president to depart out of the United States, as is undertaken by the said act, entitled, "An Act Concerning Aliens," is contrary to the Constitution, one amendment in which has provided, that "no person shall be deprived of liberty without due process of law;" and that another having provided, "that, in all criminal prosecutions, the accused shall enjoy the right of a public trial by an impartial jury, to be informed as to the nature and cause of the accusation, to be confronted with the witnesses against him, to have compulsory process for obtaining witnesses in his favor, and to have assistance of counsel for his defense," the same act undertaking to authorize the president to remove a person out of the United States who is under the

protection of the law, on his own suspicion, without jury, without public trial, without confrontation of the witnesses against him, without having witnesses in his favor, without defense, without counsel, contrary to these provisions also of the Constitution, is therefore not law, but utterly void and of no force.

That transferring the power of judging any person who is under the protection of the laws from the courts to the President of the United States, as is undertaken by the same act concerning aliens, is against the article of the Constitution which provides, that "the judicial power of the United States shall be vested in the courts, the judges of which shall hold their office during good behavior," and that the said act is void for that reason also. And it is further to be noted that this transfer of judiciary power is to that magistrate of the general government who already possesses all the executive, and a qualified negative in all the legislative powers.

7. *Resolved*, that the construction applied by the general government (as is evident by sundry of their proceedings) to those parts of the Constitution of the United States which delegate to Congress power to lay and collect taxes, duties, imposts, excises; to pay the debts, and provide for the common defense and general welfare of the United States, and to make all laws which shall be necessary and proper for carrying into execution the powers vested by the Constitution in the government of the United States, or any department thereof, goes to the destruction of all the limits prescribed to their power by the Constitution; that words meant by that instrument to be subsidiary only to the execution of the limited powers, ought not to be so construed as themselves to give unlimited powers, nor a part so to be taken as to destroy the whole residue of the instrument; that the proceedings of the general government, under color of those articles, will be a fit and necessary subject for revisal and correction at a time of greater tranquility, while those specified in the preceding resolutions call for immediate redress.

8. *Resolved*, that the preceding resolutions be transmitted to the senators and representatives in Congress from this commonwealth, who are enjoined to present the same to their respective houses and to use their best endeavors to procure, at the next session of Congress, a repeal of the aforesaid unconstitutional and obnoxious acts.

9. *Resolved*, lastly, that the governor of this commonwealth be, and is, authorized and requested to communicate the preceding resolutions to the legislatures of the several states, to assure them that this commonwealth considers union for special national purposes, and particularly for those specified in their late federal compact, to be friendly to the peace, happiness, and prosperity, of all the states; that, faithful to that compact, according to the plain intent and meaning in which it was understood and acceded to by the several parties, it is sincerely anxious for its preservation.

That it does also believe, that, to take from the states all the powers of selfgovernment and transfer them to a general and consolidated government, without regard to the special government, and reservations solemnly agreed to in that compact, is not for the peace, happiness, or prosperity of these states; and that, therefore, this commonwealth is determined, as it doubts not its co-states are, to submit to undelegated and consequently unlimited powers in no man, or body of men, on earth; that, if the acts before specified should stand, these conclusions would flow from them.

That the general government may place any act they think proper on the list of crimes, and punish it themselves, whether enumerated or not enumerated by the Constitution as cognizable by them; that they may transfer its cognizance to the President, or any other person, who may himself be the accuser, counsel, judge, and jury, whose suspicions may be the evidence, his order the sentence, his officer the executioner, and his breast the sole record of the transaction; that a very numerous and valuable description of the inhabitants of these states, being, by this precedent, reduced, as outlaws, to absolute dominion of one man, and the barriers of the Constitution thus swept from us all, no rampart now remains against the passions and the power of a majority of Congress, to protect from a like exportation, or other grievous punishment, the minority of the same body, the legislatures, judges, governors, and counselors of the states, nor their other peaceable inhabitants, who may venture to reclaim the constitutional rights and liberties of the states and people, or who, for other causes, good or bad, may be obnoxious to the view, or marked by the suspicions, of the President, or be thought dangerous to his or their elections, or other interests, public or personal.

That the friendless alien has been selected as the safest subject of a first experiment; but the citizen will soon follow, or rather has already followed; for already has a Sedition Act marked him as a prey. That these and successive acts of the same character, unless arrested on the threshold, may tend to drive these states into revolution and blood, and will furnish new calumnies against republican governments, and new pretexts for those who wish it to be believed that man cannot be governed but by a rod of iron; that it would be a dangerous delusion were a confidence in the men of our choice to silence our fears for the safety of our rights; that confidence is everywhere the parent of despotism; free government is founded in jealousy, and not in confidence; it is jealousy, and not confidence, which prescribes limited constitutions to bind down those whom we are obliged to trust with power; that our Constitution has accordingly fixed the limits to which, and no further, our confidence may go; and let the honest advocate of confidence read the Alien and Sedition Acts, and say if the Constitution has not been wise in fixing limits to the government it created, and whether we should be wise in destroying those limits. Let him say what the government is, if it be not a tyranny, which the men of our choice have conferred on the President, and the President of our choice has assented to and accepted, over the friendly strangers to whom the mild spirit of our country and its laws had pledged hospitality and protection; that the men of our choice have more respected the bare suspicions of the President than the solid rights of innocence, the claims of justification, the sacred force of truth, and the forms and substance of law and justice.

In questions of power, then, let no more be said of confidence in man, but bind him down from mischief by the chains of the Constitution. That this commonwealth does therefore call on its co-states for an expression of their sentiments on the acts concerning aliens, and for the punishment of certain crimes herein before specified, plainly declaring whether these acts are or are not authorized by the federal compact. And it doubts not that their sense will be so announced as to prove their attachment to limited government, whether general or particular, and that the rights and liberties of their co-states will be exposed to no dangers by remaining embarked on a common bottom with their own; but they will concur with this commonwealth in considering the said acts as so palpably against the Constitution as to amount to an undisguised declaration, that the compact is not meant to be the measure of the powers of the general government, but that it will proceed in the exercise over these states of all powers whatsoever. That they will view this as seizing the rights of the states, and consolidating them in the hands of the general government with a power assumed to bind the states, not merely in cases made federal but in all cases whatsoever, by laws made, not with their consent but by others against their consent. That this would be to surrender the form of government we have chosen, and live under one deriving its powers from its own will, and not from our authority; and that the co-states, recurring to their natural rights not made federal, will concur in declaring these void and of no force, and will each unite with this commonwealth in requesting their repeal at the next session of Congress.

Virginia Resolutions of 1798
(adopted on December 24, 1798)[71]

Resolved, that the General Assembly of Virginia does unequivocally express a firm resolution to maintain and defend the Constitution of the United States, and the constitution of this state against every aggression, either foreign or domestic, and that they will support the government of the United States in all measures warranted by the former.

That this Assembly most solemnly declares a warm attachment to the union of the states, to maintain which it pledges its powers; and that, for this end, it is their duty to watch over and oppose every infraction of those principles which constitute the only basis of that union, because a faithful observance of them can alone secure its existence and the public happiness.

That this Assembly does explicitly and peremptorily declare that it views the powers of the federal government as resulting from the compact to which the states are parties, as limited by the plain sense and intention of the instrument constituting that compact, as no further valid than they are authorized by the grants enumerated in that compact; and that, in case of a deliberate, palpable, and dangerous exercise of other powers, not granted by the said compact, the states who are parties thereto, have the right, and are in duty bound to interpose for arresting the progress of the evil, and for maintaining, within their respective limits, the authorities, rights, and liberties, appertaining to them.

That the General Assembly does also express its deep regret that a spirit has, in sundry instances, been manifested by the federal government to enlarge its powers by forced constructions of the constitutional charter which defines them; and that indications have appeared of a design to expound certain general phrases (which, having been copied from the very limited grant of powers in the former Articles of Confederation, were the less liable to be misconstrued) so as to destroy the meaning and effect of the particular enumeration which necessarily explains and limits the general phrases, and so as to consolidate the states, by degrees, into one sovereignty, the obvious tendency and inevitable result of which would be to transform the present republican system of the United States into an absolute or, at best, a mixed monarchy.

That the General Assembly does particularly protest against the palpable and alarming infractions of the Constitution in the two late cases of the Alien and Sedition Acts, passed at the last session of Congress; the first of which exercises a power nowhere delegated to the federal government, and which, by uniting legislative and judicial powers to those of executive, subverts the general principles of free government, as well as the particular organization and positive provisions of the federal Constitution; and the other of which acts exercises, in like manner, a power not delegated by the Constitution, but, on the contrary, expressly and positively forbidden by one of the amendments thereto, a power which, more than any other, ought to produce universal alarm, because it is leveled against the right of freely examining public characters and measures, and of free communication among the people thereon, which has ever been justly deemed the only effectual guardian of every other right.

That this state having, by its Convention, which ratified the federal Constitution, expressly declared that, among other essential rights, "the liberty of conscience and the press cannot be canceled, abridged, restrained, or modified, by any authority of the United States," and from its extreme anxiety to guard these rights from every possible attack of sophistry and ambition, having, with other states, recommended an amendment for that purpose, which amendment was, in due time, annexed to the Constitution, it would mark a reproachful inconsistency and criminal degeneracy if an indifference were now shown to the most palpable violation of one of the rights thus declared and secured, and to the establishment of a precedent which may be fatal to the other.

That the good people of this commonwealth, having ever felt, and continuing to feel, the most sincere affection for their brethren of the other states; the truest anxiety for establishing and perpetuating the union of all; and the most scrupulous fidelity to that Constitution, which is the pledge of mutual friendship and the instrument of mutual happiness; the General Assembly does solemnly appeal to the like dispositions in the other states, in confidence that they will concur with this commonwealth in declaring, as it does hereby declare, that the acts aforesaid are unconstitutional; and that the necessary and proper measures will be taken *by each* for cooperating with this state, in maintaining unimpaired the authorities, rights, and liberties, reserved to the states respectively, or to the people.

That the governor be desired to transmit a copy of the foregoing resolutions to the executive authority of each of the other states, with a request that the same may be communicated to the legislature thereof and that a copy be furnished to each of the senators and representatives representing this state in the Congress of the United States.

Massachusetts Resolutions in Reply to Virginia (adopted on February 13, 1799)[72]

The Legislature of Massachusetts, having taken into serious consideration the resolutions of the state of Virginia, passed the 21st day of December last, and communicated by his excellency the governor, relative to certain supposed infractions of the Constitution of the United States by the government thereof; and being convinced that the federal Constitution is calculated to promote the happiness, prosperity, and safety of the people of these United States, and to maintain that union of the several states so essential to the welfare of the whole; and being bound by solemn oath to support and defend that Constitution, feel it unnecessary to make any professions of their attachment to it or of their firm determination to support it against every aggression, foreign or domestic.

But they deem it their duty solemnly to declare that, while they hold sacred the principle that consent of the people is the only pure source of just and legitimate power, they cannot admit the right of the state legislatures to denounce the administration of that government to which the people themselves, by a solemn compact, have exclusively committed their national concerns.

That, although a liberal and enlightened vigilance among the people is always to be cherished, yet an unreasonable jealousy of the men of their choice and a recurrence to measures of extremity upon groundless or trivial pretexts have a strong tendency to destroy all rational liberty at home and to deprive the United States of the most essential advantages in relations abroad.

That this legislature are persuaded that the decision of all cases in law and equity arising under the Constitution of the United States, and the construction of all laws made it [in] pursuance thereof, are exclusively vested by the people in the judicial courts of the United States.

That the people, in that solemn compact which is declared to be the supreme law of the land, have not constituted the state legislatures the judges of the acts or measures of the federal government but have confided to them the power of proposing such amendments of the Constitution as shall appear to them necessary to the interests, or conformable to the wishes, of the people whom they represent.

That, by this construction of the Constitution, an amicable and dispassionate remedy is pointed out for any evil which experience may prove to exist, and the peace and prosperity of the United States may be preserved without interruption.

But, should the respectable state of Virginia persist in the assumption of the right to declare the acts of the national government unconstitutional, and should she oppose successfully her force and will to those of the nation, the Constitution would be reduced to a mere cipher, to the form and pageantry of authority without the energy of power. Every act of the federal government which thwarted the views or checked the ambitious projects of a particular state, or of its leading and influential members, would be the object of opposition and of remonstrance, while the people, convulsed and confused by the conflict between two hostile jurisdictions, enjoying the protection of neither, would be wearied into a submission to some bold leader who would establish himself on the ruins of both.

The legislature of Massachusetts, although they do not themselves claim the right nor admit the authority of any of the state governments to decide upon the constitutionality of the acts of the federal government, still—lest their silence should be construed into disapprobation or at best into a doubt as to the constitutionality of the acts referred to by the state of Virginia, and as the General Assembly of Virginia has called for an expression of their sentiments—do explicitly declare that they consider the acts of Congress, commonly called the Alien and Sedition Acts, not only constitutional but expedient and necessary.

That the former act respects a description of persons whose rights were not particularly contemplated in the Constitution of the United States, who are entitled only to a temporary protection while they yield a temporary allegiance, a protection which ought to be withdrawn whenever they become "dangerous to the public safety" or are found guilty of "treasonable machination" against the government.

That Congress, having been especially entrusted by the people with the general defense of the nation, had not only the right but were bound to protect it against internal as well as external foes.

That the United States, at the time of passing the Act Concerning Aliens, were threatened with actual invasion; had been driven by the unjust and ambitious conduct of the French government into warlike preparations, expensive and burdensome; and had then, within the bosom of the country, thousands of aliens, who, we doubt not, were ready to cooperate in any external attack.

It cannot be seriously believed that the United States should have waited till the poniard had in fact been plunged. The removal of aliens is the usual preliminary of hostility and is justified by the invariable usages of nations. Actual hostility had unhappily long been experienced, and a formal declaration of it the government had reason daily to expect. The law, therefore, was just and salutary; and no officer could with so much propriety be entrusted with the execution of it as the one in whom the Constitution has reposed the executive power of the United States.

The Sedition Act, so-called, is, in the opinion of this legislature, equally defensible. The General Assembly of Virginia, in their resolve under consideration, observe that when that state by its convention ratified the federal Constitution, it expressly declared, "that, among other essential rights, the liberty of conscience and of the press cannot be canceled, abridged, restrained, or modified by an authority of the United States," and, from its extreme anxiety to guard these rights from every possible attack of sophistry or ambition, with other states, recommended an amendment for that purpose, which amendment was, in due time, annexed to the Constitution; but they did not surely expect that the proceedings of their state convention were to explain the amendment adopted by the Union. The words of that amendment on this subject are, "Congress shall make no law abridging the freedom of speech or of the press."

The act complained of is no abridgment of the freedom of either. The genuine liberty of speech and the press is the liberty to utter and publish the truth; but the constitutional right of the citizen to utter and publish the truth is not to be confounded with the licentiousness, in speaking and writing, that is only employed in propagating falsehood and slander. This freedom of the press has been explicitly secured by most if not all the state constitutions; and of this provision there has been generally but one construction among enlightened men—that it is a security for the rational use and not the abuse of the press—of which the courts of law, the juries, and people will judge; this right is not infringed but confirmed and established by the late act of Congress.

By the Constitution, the legislative, executive, and judicial departments of government are ordained and established, and general enumerated powers vested in them respectively, including those which are prohibited to the several states. Certain powers are granted in general terms, by the people, to their general government for the purposes of their safety and protection. The government is not only empowered but it is made their duty to repel invasions and suppress insurrections; to guarantee to the several states a republican form of government; to protect each state against invasion and, when applied to, against domestic violence; to hear and decide all cases in law and equity arising under the Constitution and under any treaty or law made in pursuance thereof, and all cases of admiralty and maritime jurisdiction, and relating to the law of nations. Whenever, therefore, it becomes necessary to effect any of the objects designated, it is perfectly consonant to all just rules of construction to infer that the usual means and powers necessary to the attainment of that object are also granted. But the constitution has left no occasion to resort to implication for these powers; it has made an express grant of them, in Section 8 of Article I, which ordains,

> that Congress shall have power to make all laws which shall be necessary and proper for carrying into execution the foregoing powers, and all other powers vested by this Constitution in the government of the United States, or in any department or officer thereof.

This Constitution has established a Supreme Court of the United States, but has made no provision for its protection, even against such improper conduct in its presence as might disturb its proceedings, unless expressed in the section before recited. But as no statute has been passed on this subject, this protection is, and has been for nine years past, uniformly found in the application of the principles and usages of the common law. The same protection may unquestionably be afforded by a statute passed in virtue of the before-mentioned section, as necessary and proper for carrying into execution the powers vested in that department. A construction of the different parts of the Constitution, perfectly just and fair, will, on analogous principles, extend protection and security against the offenses in question to the other departments of government in discharge of their respective trusts.

The President of the United States is bound by his oath "to preserve, protect, and defend the Constitution"; and it is expressly made his duty "to take care that the laws be faithfully executed." But this would be impracticable by any created being if there could be no legal restraint of those scandalous misrepresentations of his measures and motives which directly tend to rob him of the public confidence; and equally impotent would be every other public officer, if thus left to the mercy of the seditious.

It is held to be a truth most clear that the important trusts before enumerated cannot be discharged by the government to which they are committed without the power to restrain seditious practices and unlawful combinations against itself, and to protect the officers thereof from abusive misrepresentations. Had the Constitution withheld this power, it would have made the government responsible for the effects, without any control over the causes which naturally produce them, and would have essentially failed of answering the great ends for which the people of the United States declare, in the first clause of that instrument, that they establish the same; viz.,

> to form a more perfect union, establish justice, insure domestic tranquillity, provide for the common defense, promote the general welfare, and secure the blessings of liberty to ourselves and our posterity.

Seditious practices and unlawful combinations against the federal government or any officer thereof in the performance of his duty, as well as licentiousness of speech and of the press, were punishable on the principles of common law in the courts of the United States before the act in question was passed. This act, then, is an amelioration of that law in favor of the party accused, as it mitigates the punishment which that authorizes and admits of any investigation of public men and measures which is regulated by truth. It is not intended to protect men in office, only as they are agents of the people. Its object is to afford legal security to public offices and trusts created for the safety and happiness of the people, and therefore the security derived from it is for the benefit of the people and is their right.

This construction of the Constitution, and of the existing law of the land, as well as the act complained of, the legislature of Massachusetts most deliberately and firmly believe results from a just and full view of the several parts of the Constitution; and they consider that act to be wise and necessary as an audacious and unprincipled spirit of falsehood and abuse had been too long unremittingly exerted for the purpose of perverting public opinion, and threatened to undermine and destroy the whole fabric of government.

The legislature further declare that in the foregoing sentiments they have expressed the general opinion of their constituents, who have not acquiesced without complaint in those particular measures of the federal government but have given their explicit approbation by reelecting those men who voted for the adoption of them. Nor is it apprehended that the citizens of this state will be accused of supineness or of an indifference to their constitutional rights; for while, on the one hand, they regard with due vigilance the conduct of the government; on the other, their freedom, safety, and happiness require that they should defend that government and its constitutional measures against the open or insidious attacks of any foe, whether foreign or domestic.

And, lastly, that the legislature of Massachusetts feel a strong conviction that the several United States are connected by a common interest, which ought to render their union indissoluble; and that this state will always cooperate with its confederate states in rendering that union productive of mutual security, freedom, and happiness.

Kentucky Resolutions of 1799
(adopted on November 22, 1799)[73]

Resolved, that this commonwealth considers the federal Union, upon the terms and for the purposes specified in the late compact, conducive to the liberty and happiness of the several states. That it does now unequivocally declare its attachment to the Union and to that compact, agreeably to its obvious and real intention, and will be among the last to seek its dissolution. That if those who administer the general government be permitted to transgress the limits fixed by that compact, by a total disregard to the special delegations of power therein contained, an annihilation of the state governments and the creation, upon their ruins, of a general consolidated government will be the inevitable consequence.

That the principle and construction contended for by sundry of the state legislatures that the general government is the exclusive judge of the extent of the powers delegated to it, stop not short of despotism, since the discretion of those who administer the government and not the Constitution would be the measure of their powers. That the several states who formed that instrument, being sovereign and independent, have the unquestionable right to judge of the infraction; and, that a nullification by those sovereignties, of all unauthorized acts done under color of that instrument, is the rightful remedy.

That this commonwealth does, under the most deliberate reconsideration, declare that the said Alien and Sedition laws are, in their opinion, palpable violations of the said Constitution; and however cheerfully it may be disposed to surrender its opinion to a majority of its sister states in matters of ordinary or doubtful policy, yet, in momentous regulations like the present, which so vitally wound the best rights of the citizen, it would consider a silent acquiescence as highly criminal.

That although this commonwealth, as a party to the federal compact, will bow to the laws of the Union, yet it does, at the same time, declare that it will not now or ever hereafter cease to oppose, in a constitutional manner, every attempt, at what quarter soever offered, to violate that compact.

And finally, in order that no pretext or arguments may be drawn from a supposed acquiescence on the part of this commonwealth in the constitutionality of those laws, and be thereby used as precedents for similar future violations of the federal compact, this commonwealth does now enter against them its solemn protest.

James Madison
"Report of 1800"
(approved on January 8, 1800)[74]

Federalist opposition to the Kentucky and Virginia resolutions in Virginia, though a minority viewpoint in the state, was sufficiently strong that Jefferson and other Republicans prevailed on Madison to enter the state legislature in order to defend his handiwork. Madison was promptly appointed to chair a committee to which the Federalist state resolutions criticizing the "doctrines of '98" were referred. On behalf of the committee, he drafted a careful exegesis and defense of the General Assembly's 1798 Resolutions. This "Report of 1800" (sometimes called the "Report of 1799") soon became widely acknowledged as a standard by which Republican constitutional orthodoxy might be measured.

Whatever room might be found in the proceedings of some of the states, who have disapproved of the resolutions of the General Assembly of this commonwealth, passed on the 21st day of December, 1798, for painful remarks on the spirit and manner of those proceedings, it appears to the committee most consistent with the duty, as well as dignity, of the General Assembly, to hasten an oblivion of every circumstance which might be construed into a diminution of mutual respect, confidence, and affection, among the members of the Union.

The committee have deemed it a more useful task to revise, with a critical eye, the resolutions which have met with their disapprobation; to examine fully the several objections and arguments which have appeared against them; and to inquire whether there can be any errors of fact, of principle, or of reasoning, which the candor of the General Assembly ought to acknowledge and correct . . .

The *third* resolution is in the words following:—[The report quoted the 1798 resolution defining the Constitution as a compact and asserting the duty of state interposition.]

On this resolution the committee have bestowed all the attention which its importance merits. They have *scanned* it not merely with a strict, but with a severe eye; and they feel confidence in pronouncing that, in its just and fair construction, it is unexceptionably true in its several positions, as well as constitutional and conclusive in its inferences.

The resolution declares, *first*, that "it views the powers of the federal government as resulting from the compact to which the states are parties;" in other words, that the federal powers are derived from the Constitution; and that the Constitution is a compact to which the states are parties.

Clear as the position must seem, that the federal powers are derived from the Constitution, and from that alone, the committee are not unapprized of a late doctrine which opens another source of federal powers, not less extensive and important than it is new and unexpected. The examination of this doctrine will be most conveniently connected with a review of a succeeding resolution. The committee satisfy themselves here with briefly remarking that, in all the contemporary discussions and comments which the Constitution underwent, it was constantly justified and recommended on the ground that the powers not given to the government were withheld from it; and that, if any doubt could have existed on this subject, under the original text of the Constitution, it is removed, as far as words could remove it, by the 12th amendment, now a part of the Constitution, which expressly declares, "that the powers not delegated to the United States by the Constitution, nor prohibited by it to the states, are reserved to the states respectively, or to the people."

The other position involved in this branch of the resolution, namely, "that the states are parties to the Constitution," or compact, is, in the judgment of the committee, equally free from objection. It is indeed true that the term "states" is sometimes used in a vague sense, and sometimes in different senses, according to the subject to which it is applied.

Thus it sometimes means the separate sections of territory occupied by the political societies within each; sometimes the particular governments established by those societies; sometimes those societies as organized into those particular governments; and lastly, it means the people composing those political societies, in their highest sovereign capacity. Although it might be wished that the perfection of language admitted less diversity in the signification of the same words, yet little inconvenience is produced by it, where the true sense can be collected with certainty from the different applications. In the present instance, whatever different construction of the term "states," in the resolution, may have been entertained, all will at least concur in that last mentioned; because in that sense the Constitution was submitted to the "states;" in that sense the "states" ratified it; and in that sense of the term "states," they are consequently parties to the compact from which the powers of the federal government result.

The next position is, that the General Assembly views the powers of the federal government "as limited by the plain sense and intention of the instrument constituting that compact," and "as no further valid than they are authorized by the grants therein enumerated." It does not seem possible that any just objection can lie against either of these clauses. The first amounts merely to a declaration that the compact ought to have the interpretation plainly intended by the parties to it; the other, to a declaration that it ought to have the execution and effect intended by them. If the powers granted be valid, it is solely because they are granted; and if the granted powers are valid because granted, all other powers not granted must not be valid.

The resolution, having taken this view of the federal compact, proceeds, to infer, "That, in case of a deliberate, palpable, and dangerous exercise of other powers, not granted by the said compact, the states, who are parties thereto, have the right, and are in duty bound, to interpose for arresting the progress of the evil, and for maintaining, within their respective limits, the authorities, rights, and liberties, appertaining to them."

It appears to your committee to be a plain principle, founded in common sense, illustrated by common practice, and essential to the nature of compacts, that, where resort can be had to no tribunal superior to the authority of the parties, the parties themselves must be the rightful judges, in the last resort, whether the bargain made has been pursued or violated. The Constitution of the United States was formed by the sanction of the states, given by each in its sovereign capacity. It adds to the stability and dignity, as well as to the authority, of the Constitution, that it rests on this legitimate and solid foundation. The states, then, being the parties to the constitutional compact, and in their sovereign capacity, it follows of necessity that there can be no tribunal, above their authority, to decide, in the last resort, whether the compact made by them be violated; and consequently, that, as the parties to it, they must themselves decide, in the last resort, such questions as may be of sufficient magnitude to require their interposition.

It does not follow, however, because the states, as sovereign parties to their constitutional compact, must ultimately decide whether it has been violated, that such a decision ought to be interposed either in a hasty manner or on doubtful and inferior occasions. Even in the case of ordinary conventions between different nations, where, by the strict rule of interpretation, a breach of a part may be deemed a breach of the whole,—every part being deemed a condition of every other part, and of the whole,—it is always laid down that the breach must be both wilful [sic] and material, to justify an application of the rule. But in the case of an intimate and constitutional union, like that of the United States, it is evident that the interposition of the parties, in their sovereign capacity, can be called for by occasions only deeply and essentially affecting the vital principles of their political system.

The resolution has, accordingly, guarded against any misapprehension of its object, by expressly requiring, for such an interposition, "the case of a deliberate, palpable, and dangerous breach of the Constitution, by the exercise of powers not granted by it." It must be a case not of a light and transient nature, but of a nature dangerous to the great purposes for which the Constitution was established. It must be a case, moreover, not obscure or doubtful in its construction, but plain and palpable. Lastly, it must be a case not resulting from a partial consideration or hasty determination, but a case stamped with a final consideration and deliberate adherence. It is not necessary, because the resolution does not require, that the question should be discussed, how far the exercise of any particular power, ungranted by the Constitution, would justify the interposition of the parties to it. As cases might easily be stated, which none would contend ought to fall within that description,—cases, on the other hand, might, with equal ease, be stated, so flagrant and so fatal as to unite every opinion in placing them within the description.

But the resolution has done more than guard against misconstruction, by expressly referring to cases of a deliberate, palpable, and dangerous nature. It specifies the object of the interposition, which it contemplates to be solely that of arresting the progress of the evil of usurpation, and of maintaining the authorities, rights, and liberties, appertaining to the states as parties to the Constitution.

From this view of the resolution, it would seem inconceivable that it can incur any just disapprobation from those who, laying aside all momentary impressions, and recollecting the genuine source and object of the Federal Constitution, shall candidly and accurately interpret the meaning of the General Assembly. If the deliberate exercise of dangerous powers, palpably withheld by the Constitution, could not justify the parties to it in interposing even so far as to arrest the progress of the evil, and thereby to preserve the Constitution itself, as well as to provide for the safety of the parties to it, there would be an end to all relief from usurped power, and a direct subversion of the rights specified or recognized under all the state constitutions, as well as a plain denial of the fundamental principle on which our independence itself was declared.

But it is objected, that the judicial authority is to be regarded as the sole expositor of the Constitution in the last resort; and it may be asked for what reason the declaration by the General Assembly, supposing it to be theoretically true, could be required at the present day and in so solemn a manner.

On this objection it might be observed, first, that there may be instances of usurped power, which the forms of the Constitution would never draw within the control of the judicial department; secondly, that, if the decision of the judiciary be raised above the authority of the sovereign parties to the Constitution, the decision of the other departments, not carried by the forms of the Constitution before the judiciary, must be equally authoritative and final with the decisions of that department. But the proper answer to the objection is, that the resolution of the General Assembly relates to those great and extraordinary cases, in which all the forms of the Constitution may prove ineffectual against infractions dangerous to the essential rights of the parties to it. The resolution supposes that dangerous powers, not delegated, may not only be usurped and executed by the other departments, but that the judicial department, also, may exercise or sanction dangerous powers beyond the grant of the Constitution; and, consequently, that the ultimate right of the parties to the Constitution, to judge whether the compact has been dangerously violated, must extend to violations by one delegated authority as well as by another—by the judiciary as well as by the executive, or the legislature.

However true, therefore, it may be, that the judicial department is, in all questions submitted to it by the forms of the Constitution, to decide in the last resort, this resort must necessarily be deemed the last in relation to the authorities of the other departments of the government; not in relation to the rights of the parties to the constitutional compact, from which the judicial, as well as the other departments, hold their delegated trusts. On any other hypothesis, the delegation of judicial power would annul the authority delegating it; and the concurrence of this department with the others in usurped powers, might subvert forever, and beyond the possible reach of any rightful remedy, the very Constitution which all were instituted to preserve.

The truth declared in the resolution being established, the expediency of making the declaration at the present day may safely be left to the temperate consideration and candid judgment of the American public. It will be remembered, that a frequent recurrence to fundamental principles is solemnly enjoined by most of the state constitutions, and particularly by our own, as a necessary safeguard against the danger of degeneracy, to which republics are liable, as well as other governments, though in a less degree than others. And a fair comparison of the political doctrines not unfrequent at the present day, with those which characterized the epoch of our revolution, and which form the basis of our republican constitutions, will best determine whether the declaratory recurrence here made to those principles ought to be viewed as unseasonable and improper, or as a vigilant discharge of an important duty. The authority of constitutions over governments, and of the sovereignty of the people over constitutions, are truths which are at all times necessary to be kept in mind; and at no time, perhaps, more necessary than at present.

The fourth resolution stands as follows:—[The report quoted the 1798 resolution expressing regret that the federal government had shown a tendency "to enlarge its powers by forced constructions," and prophesying a monarchy as the eventual consequence.]

The *first* question here to be considered is, whether a spirit has, in sundry instances, been manifested by the federal government to enlarge its powers by forced constructions of the constitutional charter.

The General Assembly having declared their opinion, merely, by regretting, in general terms, that forced constructions for enlarging the federal powers have taken place, it does not appear to the committee necessary to go into a specification of every instance to which the resolution may allude. The Alien and Sedition Acts, being particularly named in a succeeding resolution, are of course to be understood as included in the allusion. Omitting others which have less occupied public attention, or been less extensively regarded as unconstitutional, the resolution may be presumed to refer particularly to the bank law, which, from the circumstances of its passage, as well as the latitude of construction on which it is founded, strikes the attention with singular force, and the carriage tax, distinguished also by circumstances in its history having a similar tendency. Those instances alone, if resulting from forced construction, and calculated to enlarge the powers of the federal government,—as the committee cannot but conceive to be the case,—sufficiently warrant this part of the resolution. The committee have not thought it incumbent on them to extend their attention to laws which have been objected to rather as varying the constitutional distribution of powers in the federal government, than as an absolute enlargement of them; because instances of this sort, however important in their principles and tendencies, do not appear to fall strictly within the text under view . . .

That the obvious tendency, and inevitable result, of a consolidation of the states into one sovereignty, would be to transform the republican system of the United States into a monarchy, is a point which seems to have been sufficiently decided by the general sentiment of America. In almost every instance of discussion relating to the consolidation in question, its certain tendency to pave the way to monarchy seems not to have been contested. The prospect of such a consolidation has formed the only topic of controversy. It would be unnecessary, therefore, for the committee to dwell long on the reasons which support the position of the General Assembly. It may not be improper, however, to remark two consequences, evidently flowing from an extension of the federal power to every subject falling within the idea of the "general welfare."

One consequence must be, to enlarge the sphere of discretion allotted to the executive magistrate. Even within the legislative limits properly defined by the Constitution, the difficulty of accommodating legal regulations to a country so great in extent, and so various in its circumstances, had been much felt, and has led to occasional investments of power in the executive, which involve perhaps as large a portion of discretion as can be deemed consistent with the nature of the executive trust. In proportion as the objects of legislative care might be multiplied, would the time allowed for each be diminished, and the difficulty of providing uniform and particular regulations for all be increased. From these sources would necessarily ensue a greater latitude to the agency of that department which is always in existence, and which could best mould regulations of a general nature, so as to suit them to the diversity of particular situations. And it is in this latitude, as a supplement to the deficiency of the laws, that the degree of executive prerogative materially consists.

The other consequence would be, that of an excessive augmentation of the offices, honors, and emoluments, depending on the executive will. Add to the present legitimate stock all those, of every description, which a consolidation of the states would take from them, and turn over to the federal government, and the patronage of the executive would necessarily be as much swelled, in this case, as its prerogative would be in the other.

This disproportionate increase of prerogative and patronage must evidently either enable the chief magistrate of the Union, by quiet means, to secure his reelection from time to time, and finally to regulate the succession as he might please; or, by giving so transcendent an importance to the office, would render the election to it so violent and corrupt, that the public voice itself might call for an hereditary in place of an elective succession. Whichever of these events might follow, the transformation of the republican system of the United States into a monarchy, anticipated by the General Assembly from a consolidation of the states into one sovereignty, would be equally accomplished; and whether it would be into a mixed or an absolute monarchy, might depend on too many contingencies to admit of any certain foresight . . .

[The report continued with a discussion of the arguments against the constitutionality of the Alien and Sedition acts.]

It is deemed to be a sound opinion that the Sedition Act in its definition of some of the crimes created, is an abridgment of the freedom of publication, recognized by principles of the common law in England.

The freedom of the press, under the common law, is, in the defences of the Sedition Act, made to consist in an exemption from all previous restraint on printed publications, by persons authorized to inspect or prohibit them. It appears to the committee that this idea of the freedom of the press can never be admitted to be the American idea of it; since a law inflicting penalties on printed publications would have a similar effect with a law authorizing a previous restraint on them. It would seem a mockery to say that no laws should be passed preventing publications from being made, but that laws might be passed for punishing them in case they should be made.

The essential difference between the British government and the American constitutions will place this subject in the clearest light.

In the British government, the danger of encroachments on the rights of the people is understood to be confined to the executive magistrate. The representatives of the people in the legislature are not only exempt themselves from distrust, but are considered as sufficient guardians of the rights of their constituents against the danger from the executive. Hence it is a principle, that the Parliament is unlimited in its power; or in their own language, is omnipotent. Hence, too, all the ramparts for protecting the rights of the people,—such as their Magna Charta, their bill of rights, &c.,—are not reared against the Parliament, but against the royal prerogative. They are merely legislative precautions against executive usurpation. Under such a government as this, an exemption of the press from previous restraint by licensers appointed by the king, is all the freedom that can be secured to it.

In the United States, the case is altogether different. The people, not the government, possess the absolute sovereignty. The legislature, no less than the executive, is under limitations of power. Encroachments are regarded as possible from the one as well as from the other. Hence, in the United States, the great and essential rights of the people are secured against legislative as well as executive ambition. They are secured, not by laws paramount to laws. This security of the freedom of the press requires that it should be exempt, not only from previous restraint of the executive, as in Great Britain; but from legislative restraint also; and this exemption, to be effectual, must be an exemption, not only from the previous inspection of licensers, but from the subsequent penalty of laws.

The state of the press, therefore, under the common law, cannot, in this point of view, be the standard of its freedom in the United States.

But there is another view under which it may be necessary to consider this subject. It may be alleged that, although the security for the freedom of the press be different in

Great Britain and in this country,—being a legal security only in the former, and a constitutional security in the latter,—and although there may be a further difference, in an extension of the freedom of the press, here, beyond an exemption from previous restraint, to an exemption from subsequent penalties also,—yet the actual legal freedom of the press, under the common law, must determine the degree of freedom which is meant by the terms, and which is constitutionally secured against both previous and subsequent restraints.

The committee are not unaware of the difficulty of all general questions, which may turn on the proper boundary between the liberty and licentiousness of the press. They will leave it, therefore, for consideration only, how far the difference between the nature of the British government, and the nature of the American government, and the practice under the latter, may show the degree of rigor in the former to be inapplicable to, and not obligatory in, the latter.

The nature of governments elective, limited, and responsible, in all their branches, may well be supposed to require a greater freedom of animadversion, than might be tolerated by the genius of such a government as that of Great Britain. In the latter, it is a maxim, that the king—an hereditary, not a responsible magistrate—can do no wrong; and that the legislature, which, in two thirds of its composition, is also hereditary, not responsible, can do what it pleases. In the United States, the executive magistrates are not held to be infallible, nor the legislatures to be omnipotent; and both, being elective, are both responsible. Is it not natural and necessary, under such different circumstances, that a different degree of freedom in the use of the press should be contemplated? . . .

To these observations one fact will be added, which demonstrates that the common law cannot be admitted as the universal expositor of American terms, which may be the same with those contained in that law. The freedom of conscience, and of religion, is found in the same instrument which asserts the freedom of the press. It will never be admitted that the meaning of the former, in the common law of England, is to limit their meaning in the United States . . .

[The report then quoted the resolution citing the acts of the Virginia state ratifying convention.]

To place this resolution in its just light, it will be necessary to recur to the act of ratification by Virginia, which stands in the ensuing form:—

We, the delegates of the people of Virginia, duly elected in pursuance of a recommendation from the General Assembly, and now met in Convention, having fully and freely investigated and discussed the proceedings of the Federal Convention, and being prepared, as well as the most mature deliberation hath enabled us, to decide thereon,—DO, in the name and in behalf of the people of Virginia, declare and make known, that the powers granted under the constitution, being derived from the people of the United States, may be resumed by them whensoever the same shall be perverted to their injury or oppression; and that every power not granted thereby remains with them, and at their will. That, therefore, no right of any denomination can be cancelled, abridged, restrained, or modified, by the Congress, by the senate or the House of Representatives, acting in any capacity, by the President, or any department or officer of the United States, except in those instances in which power is given by the Constitution for those purposes; and that, among other essential rights, the liberty of conscience and of the press cannot be cancelled, abridged, restrained, or modified by any authority of the United States.

Here is an express and solemn declaration by the Convention of the state, that they ratified the Constitution in the sense that no right of any denomination can be cancelled, abridged, restrained, or modified, by the government of the United States, or any part of it, except in those instances in which power is given by the Constitution; and in the sense, particularly, "that among other essential rights, the liberty of conscience and freedom of the press cannot be cancelled, abridged, restrained, or modified, by any authority of the United States."

Under an anxiety to guard more effectually these rights against every possible danger, the Convention, after ratifying the Constitution, proceeded to prefix to certain amendments proposed by them, a declaration of rights, in which are two articles providing, the one for the liberty of conscience, the other for the freedom of speech and of the press.

Similar recommendations having proceeded from a number of other states; and Congress, as has been seen, having, in consequence thereof, and with a view to extend the ground of public confidence, proposed, among other declaratory and restrictive clauses, a clause expressly securing the liberty of conscience and of the press; and Virginia having concurred in the ratifications which made them a part of the Constitution,—it will remain with a candid public to decide whether it would not mark an inconsistency and degeneracy, if an indifference were now shown to a palpable violation of one of those rights—the freedom of the press; and to a precedent, therein, which may be fatal to the other—the free exercise of religion.

[The report quoted the provisions requesting the governor to transmit the 1798 resolutions to other states and to Virginia's congressional delegation, and calling on other legislatures to declare the Alien and Sedition acts unconstitutional.]

The fairness and regularity of the course of proceeding here pursued, have not protected it against objections even from sources too respectable to be disregarded.

It has been said that it belongs to the judiciary of the United States, and not the state legislatures, to declare the meaning of the Federal Constitution.

But a declaration that proceedings of the federal government are not warranted by the Constitution, is a novelty neither among the citizens nor among the legislatures of the states; nor are the citizens or the legislature of Virginia singular in the example of it.

Nor can the declarations of either, whether affirming or denying the constitutionality of measures of the federal government, or whether made before or after judicial decisions thereon, be deemed, in any point of view, an assumption of the office of the judge. The declarations in such cases are expressions of opinion, unaccompanied with any other effect than what they may produce on opinion, by exciting reflection. The expositions of the judiciary, on the other hand, are carried into immediate effect by force. The former may lead to a change in the legislative expression of the general will—possibly to a change in the opinion of the judiciary; the latter enforces the general will, whilst that will and that opinion continue unchanged.

And if there be no impropriety in declaring the unconstitutionality of proceedings in the federal government, where can there be the impropriety of communicating the declaration to other states, and inviting their concurrence in a like declaration? What is allowable for one, must be allowable for all; and a free communication among the states, where the Constitution imposes no restraint, is as allowable among the state governments as among other public bodies or private citizens. This consideration derives a weight that cannot be denied to it, from the relation of the state legislatures to the federal legislature as the immediate constituents of one of its branches.

The legislatures of the states have a right also to originate amendments to the Constitution, by a concurrence of two thirds of the whole number, in applications to Congress for the purpose. When new states are to be formed by a junction of two or more states, or parts of states, the legislatures of the states concerned are, as well as Congress, to concur in the measure. The states have a right also to enter into agreements or compacts, with the consent of Congress. In all such cases a communication among them results from the object which is common to them.

It is lastly to be seen, whether the confidence expressed by the Constitution, that the *necessary and proper measures* would be taken by the other states for cooperating with Virginia in maintaining the rights reserved to the states, or to the people, be in any degree liable to the objections raised against it.

If it be liable to objections, it must be because either the object or the means are objectionable.

The object, being to maintain what the Constitution has ordained, is in itself a laudable object.

The means are expressed in the terms "the necessary and proper measures." A proper object was to be pursued by the means both necessary and proper.

To find an objection, then, it must be shown that some meaning was annexed to these general terms which was not proper; and, for this purpose, either that the means used by the General Assembly were an example of improper means, or that there were no proper means to which the terms could refer.

In the example, given by the state, of declaring the Alien and Sedition Acts to be unconstitutional, and of communicating the declaration to other states, no trace of improper means has appeared. And if the other states had concurred in making a like declaration, supported, too, by the numerous applications flowing immediately from the people, it can scarcely be doubted that these simple means would have been as sufficient as they are unexceptionable.

It is no less certain that other means might have been employed which are strictly within the limits of the Constitution. The legislatures of the states might have made a direct representation to Congress, with a view to obtain a rescinding of the two offensive acts; or they might have represented to their respective senators in Congress their wish that two thirds thereof would propose an explanatory amendment to the Constitution; or two thirds of themselves, if such had been their opinion, might, by an application to Congress, have obtained a convention for the same object.

These several means, though not equally eligible in themselves, nor probably to the states, were all constitutionally open for consideration. And if the General Assembly, after declaring the two acts to be unconstitutional, (the first and most obvious proceeding on the subject), did not undertake to point out to the other states a choice among the further measures that might become necessary and proper, the reserve will not be misconstrued by liberal minds into any culpable imputation.

These observations appear to form a satisfactory reply to every objection which is not founded on a misconception of the terms employed in the resolutions. There is one other, however, which may be of too much importance not to be added. It cannot be forgotten that, among the arguments addressed to those who apprehended danger to liberty from the establishment of the general government over so great a country, the appeal was emphatically made to the intermediate existence of the state governments between the people and that government, to the vigilance with which they would descry the first symptoms of usurpation, and to the promptitude with which they would sound the alarm to the public. This argument was probably not without its effect; and if it was a proper one then to recommend the establishment of a constitution, it must be a proper one now to assist in its interpretation.

The only part of the two concluding resolutions that remains to be noticed, is the repetition, the first, of that warm affection to the Union and its members, and of that scrupulous fidelity to the Constitution, which have been invariably felt by the people of this state. As the proceedings were introduced with these sentiments, they could not be more properly closed than in the same manner. Should there be any so far misled as to call in question the sincerity of these professions, whatever regret may be excited by the error, the General Assembly cannot descend into a discussion of it. Those who have listened to the suggestion can only be left to their own recollection of the part which this state has borne in the establishment of our national independence, or the establishment of our national Constitution, and in maintaining under it the authority and laws of the Union, without a single exception of internal resistance or commotion. By recurring to the facts, they will be able to convince themselves that the representatives of the people of Virginia must be above the necessity of opposing any other shield to attacks on their national patriotism, than their own conscientiousness, and the justice of an enlightened public; who will perceive in the resolutions themselves the strongest evidence of attachment both to the Constitution and the Union, since it is only by maintaining the different governments, and the departments within their respective limits, that the blessings of either can be perpetuated.

The extensive view of the subject, thus taken by the committee, has led them to report to the house, as *the result of the whole*, the following resolution:—

Resolved, That the General Assembly, having carefully and respectfully attended to the proceedings of a number of the states, *in answer to the resolutions of December 21, 1798, and having accurately and fully reexamined and reconsidered the latter, find it to be their indispensable duty* to adhere to the same, as founded in truth, as consonant with the Constitution, and as conducive to its preservation; and more especially to be their duty to renew, as they do hereby renew, their PROTEST against the Alien and Sedition Acts, as palpable and alarming infractions of the Constitution.

Comments

Jefferson and Madison responded to the crisis of 1798 with two of the most important documents in American constitutional history. The Kentucky Resolutions of 1798, in particular, were a brilliant synthesis of pre-Revolutionary Whig opposition to royal (recast, in the American context, as federal) tyranny, the English free-speech tradition, 1790s anti-nationalist concerns to police and preserve the constitutional limits to power, and the notion of the Constitution as a league or compact between sovereign states. The last of these ideas, which in earlier Republican argument had been only one among several themes, was elevated in the "doctrines of '98" to the status of a constitutional meta-principle. From the "fact" of the Constitution's contractual nature, Jefferson and Madison now inferred that federal power was necessarily derivative and limited, that the states retained residuary and inviolable sovereignty, and that the text of the constitutional compact and the intentions of its parties (the states) were the only legitimate bases for constitutional argument.

The two men, to be sure, were not in perfect agreement, though for the rest of their lives they would insist they were. Perhaps most fundamentally they differed over the nature of the compact. Jefferson, like Chief Justice M'Kean in *Cobbett,* conceived of the Constitution as an agreement between each state and all the rest, and drew the logical conclusion that disputes over the amount of power each state had delegated could not be resolved against the state except through the amendment process. It followed, Jefferson thought and the Kentucky Resolutions of 1799 stated, that each state possessed the constitutional power to "nullify" federal laws that were in its opinion unconstitutional. (Neither Jefferson nor the author of the 1799 resolutions specified how the state's constitutional power was to be exercised or what its exact effect might be.) Madison, on the other hand, portrayed the Constitution as a multilateral compact among all the states, and accepted the majoritarian corollary that a state could be bound by the constitutional opinion of the Union as a whole. Although Madison's endorsement of judicial review as a means for safeguarding the Constitution's structures was lukewarm, he clearly distinguished between a court opinion on a constitutional issue, which is "carried into immediate effect by force" and "enforces the general will," and the passage of resolutions by a state legislature, which are mere "expressions of opinion." For Madison, the states' *constitutional* remedies against constitutional oppression were political and indeed electoral.

A second significant difference between Jefferson and Madison lay in their treatment of free speech. Jefferson viewed the Sedition Act's infringement of the First Amendment primarily as an issue of federalism: the Constitution's text demonstrated that the states had retained "to themselves the right of judging how far" freedom of speech could be regulated or curtailed. In contrast, Madison described the act's violation of the right of free speech as especially alarming because of that right's primacy in Anglo-American constitutional thought. Already, at the very beginning of the Republican constitutional tradition, there existed a critical ambiguity: Was the Republican adherence to state sovereignty and to the limitation of federal power a means to the protection of liberty, or an end in itself (or, more darkly, a means to the preservation of slavery, as would be charged by later anti-slavery nationalists)?

Five

The Jeffersonians in Power

The "Revolution of 1800," as the Republicans proudly labeled the federal election that gained for them control of both the presidency and Congress, almost ran aground before it had properly begun. Republican presidential electors, maintaining *too* strict a party discipline, cast exactly the same number of votes for Jefferson and Aaron Burr, which threw the election into the House of Representatives. Jefferson was elected only after repeated balloting and behind-the-scenes efforts by such unlikely advocates as Alexander Hamilton (Hamilton explained to one correspondent that the Republicans were divided into "speculative theorists" and "absolute terrorists"; inasmuch as Jefferson was one of the former, and not personally corrupt, he was preferable to the unpredictable Burr). This near-election of the wrong candidate led to the adoption of the Twelfth Amendment, an event of more than mechanical importance because that amendment was the first formal, constitutional recognition that the Republic would be governed through party politics rather than in a nonpartisan fashion.

Jefferson's first term was enormously successful from a political standpoint. A considerable proportion of the Republican legislative agenda was enacted, with the president playing a vital role in securing its passage (in contrast to the more distant part played by his predecessors). On the national level, the Federalist party's power waned, and its members more and more adopted the terms and presuppositions of Republican constitutionalism. The period, however, was not without its constitutional controversies. Many Republicans doubted the legitimacy of the abolition of the circuit judgeships or of the Louisiana Purchase, however politically desirable both actions were. And the direct legislative assault on the Federalist judiciary failed when the Republican-controlled Senate refused to remove Justice Samuel Chase from office.

Jefferson's second term was much less tranquil. In particular, the Embargo Act (December 21, 1807), which was intended to exert economic pressure on Britain and France to compel their recognition of American neutral rights, proved disastrous to New England's economy and provoked widespread political and constitutional dissatisfaction with the Republican leadership. The administration gradually settled into a siege mentality reminiscent of the Federalist leadership of 1798–1800, and the extraordinary measures it took against perceived danger at home and abroad provoked severe criticism from Federalists and "Old Republicans."

Section A: *The Revolution of 1800: What Is to Be Done?*

Jefferson's first inaugural address, in March 1801, signaled the new president's commitment to a moderate interpretation of the "doctrines of '98" and the Revolution of 1800. He described the intense theoretical and political strife of the last decade as a "difference of opinion . . . not a difference of principle." Although Jefferson privately believed that most of the Federalist leadership was consciously anti-republican, he publicly insisted that "We have called by different names brethren of the same principle. We are all republicans—we are all federalists." Not all of Jefferson's fellow Republicans shared his professed confidence in their political foes or in the constitutional structure as it existed in 1801.

Edmund Pendleton
"The Danger Not Over"
(October 5, 1801)[75]

Pendleton, president of the Virginia Court of Appeals, was one of the most revered lawyers in America. A leading Whig during the Revolutionary period, he supported with reservations the Constitution during the ratification period. Despite good personal relations with Washington, he rapidly became a strong Republican in the 1790s, and backed the Jefferson administration until his death in 1803. As the following newspaper essay (widely read at the time) demonstrates, however, Pendleton regarded the Revolution of 1800 as incomplete without substantial changes in the Constitution's text. The essay enjoyed a prominent place in the revival of states' rights constitutionalism around 1820. Thomas Ritchie, the influential Republican editor of the *Richmond Enquirer*, spoke of the Report of 1800 and of "The Danger Not Over" as, respectively, the Old and New Testaments of his political Bible.

Although one of my age can have little to hope, and less to fear, from forms of government, as rather belonging to the next world than the present; and possibly may be charged with intermedling where he has no interest, when ever he utters opinions concerning social regulations; yet I feel impelled by an anxious desire to promote the happiness of my country, to submit to the public consideration, some reflections on our present political state.

It is far from my intention to damp the public joy, occasioned by the late changes of our public agents, or to disturb the calm which already presages the most beneficial consequences; on the contrary, I consider this event as having arrested a train of measures which were gradually conducting us towards ruin.

These changes will be matter of tenfold congratulation, if we make the proper use of them: If instead of negligently reposing upon the wisdom and integrity, which have already softened even political malice, we seize the opportunity to erect new barriers against folly, fraud and ambition; and to explain such parts of the constitution, as have been already or may be interpreted contrary to the intention of those who adopted it.

This proposition does not argue of want of proper confidence in our present Chief Magistrate, but the contrary. It can be no censure to believe that he has a nobler destiny to fulfill, than that of making his contemporary country-men happy for a few years; and that the rare event of such a character at the head of a nation, imposes on us the sacred duty of seizing the propitious opportunity, to do all in our power to perpetuate that happiness: as to that species of confidence, which would extinguish free enquiry and popular watchfulness, it is never desired by patriotism, nor ought to be yielded by freeman.

In pursuit of our purpose, we ought to keep in mind certain principles which are believed to be sound; to enquire whether they have been violated under the constitution? and then consider how a repetition of those violations may be prevented—As thus,

I.

Government is instituted for the good of the community, and not to gratify avarice or ambition; therefore unnecessary increase of debt—appointment of useless offices, such as stationary ministers to foreign courts, with which we have little connexion, and sixteen additional judges at a time when the business of the Federal Courts had greatly diminished and engaging us in a war abroad, for the sake of advancing party projects at home, are abuses in government.

II.

The chief good derivable from government, is civil liberty; and if government is so constructed, as to enable its administrators to assail that liberty with the several weapons heretofore most fatal to it, the structure is defective; of this sort, standing Armies—Fleets—severe penal laws—War—and a multitude of civil Officers, are universally admitted to be; and if our government can, with ease and impunity, array these forces against social liberty, the constitution is defective.

III.

Peace is undoubtedly that state which proposes to society the best chance for the continuance of freedom and happiness; and the situation of America is such, as to expose her to fewer occasions for war, than any other nation; whilst it also disables her from gaining any thing by war. But if, by indirect means, the executive can involve us in war, not declared by the legislature; if a treaty may be made which will incidentally produce a war, and the legislature are bound to pass all laws necessary to give it full effect; or if the judiciary may determine a war to exist, although the legislature hath refused to declare it; then the constitution is defective, since it admits constructions which pawn our freedom and happiness upon the security of executive patriotism, which is inconsistent with Republican Principles.

IV.

Union is certainly the basis of our political prosperity, and this can only be preserved by confining, with precision, the federal government to the exercise of powers clearly required by the general interest, or respecting foreign nations, and the state governments to objects of a local nature; because the states exhibit such varieties of character and interests, that a consolidated general government would be in a perpetual conflict with state interests, from its want of local knowledge, or from a prevalence of local prejudice or interest, so as certainly to produce civil war and disunion. If then the distinct provinces of the general and state governments are not clearly defined: If the former may assail the latter by penalties, and by absorbing all subjects of taxation—If a system leading to consolidation, may be formed and pursued,—and if, instead of leaving it to the respective states to encourage their agriculture or manufacturers, as their local interest may dictate, the general government may by bountys or protective duties, tax the one to promote the other; then the constitution has not sufficiently provided for the continuance of the union, by securing the rights of the state governments and local interests.

V.

It is necessary for the preservation of Republican government, that the legislative, executive, and judiciary powers should be kept separate and distinct from each other, so that no man, or body of men, shall be authorized to exercise more than one of them at the same time: The Constitution, therefore, in consigning to the Federal Senate, a participation in the powers of each department, violates this important principle, and tends to create in that body, a dangerous aristocracy. And

VI.

An essential principle of representative government is that it be influenced by the will of the people; which will can never be expressed, if their representatives are corrupted, or influenced by hopes of office. If this hope may multiply offices and extend patronage— If the president may nominate to valuable offices, members of the legislature, who shall please him, and displease the people, by increasing his power and patronage—If he may be tempted to use his power and patronage for securing his re-election—and if he may even bestow lucrative diplomas upon judges, whilst they are receiving liberal salaries, paid as the price of their independence and purity; then a risk exists, lest the legislatures should legislate—the judges decide—and the Senate concur in nominations with an eye to those offices—and lest the president may appoint with a view to his re-election; and thus may at length appear the phenomenon, of a government, republican in form, without possessing a single chaste organ for expressing the public will.

Many of these objections were foreseen, when the constitution was ratified, by those who voted for its adoption; but waived then, because of the vast importance of the union, which a rejection might have placed in hazard—Of the provision made for amendments, as trials should discover defects—and the hope that in the mean time, the instrument with all its defects, might produce social happiness, if a proper tone was given to the government, by the several agents, in its operation: But since experience has evinced, that much mischief may be done under an unwise administration; and that even the most valuable parts of the constitution, may be evaded or violated, we ought no longer to rest our security upon the vain hope which depends on the rectitude of fallible men in successive administrations; But now that the union is as firmly established by the general opinion of the citizen, as well can ever hope it to be, it behoves [*sic*] us to bring forward amendments, which may fix it upon principles capable of restraining human frailties.

Having, I trust, shewn the utility and necessity of such efforts at this time, I will adventure to submit to the consideration of my fellow citizens, with great humility and deference, whether it would not be adviseable [*sic*] to have the constitution amended.

1st. By rendering a president ineligible for the next Turn, and transferring from him to the legislature, the appointment of the judges, and stationary foreign ministers; making the stipends of the latter to be no longer discretionary in the president.

2. By depriving the Senate of all executive power; and shortening their term of service, or subjecting its members to removal by their constituents.

3. By rendering members of the legislature and the judges, whilst in office and for a limited time thereafter, incapable of taking any other office whatsoever, (the offices of President and Vice-President excepted); and subjecting the judges to removal by the concurring vote of both houses of Congress.

4. By forming some check upon the abuse of public credit, which, tho' in some instances useful, like Fleets and Armies, may, like those, be carried to extremes dangerous to liberty, and inconsistent with economical government.

5. By instituting a fair mode of impanelling juries.

6. By declaring that no treaty with a foreign nation, so far as it may relate to Peace or War,—to the expenditure of public money—or to commercial regulations, shall be law, until ratified by the legislature; the interval between such treaty and the next meeting of Congress, excepted, so far as it may not relate to the grant of money.

7. By defining prohibited powers so explicitly, as to defy the wiles of construction. If nothing more should be gained, it will be a great acquisition, clearly to interdict laws relating to the freedom of speech,—of the Press—and of religion: To declare that the Common Law of England, or of any other foreign country, in criminal cases, shall not be considered as a law of the United States,—and that treason shall be confined to the cases stated in the constitution, so as not to be extended further, by law, or construction, or by using other terms, such as sedition, &c.; and

8. By marking out with more precision, the distinct powers of the General and State Governments.

In the Virginia Bill of Rights is expressed this inestimable sentiment "That no free Government, or the blessing [of] liberty, can be preserved to any people, but by a firm adherence to justice, moderation, temperance, frugality, and virtue; and by frequent recurrence to fundamental principles." A sentiment produced, no doubt, by the experience of this melancholy truth, "That of men advanced to power, more are inclined to destroy liberty, than to defend it,['] there is of course a continual effort for its destruction, which ought to be met by corresponding efforts for its preservation.

These principles and propositions are most respectfully submitted to my fellow Citizens, with this observation: "That it is only when great and good men are at the head of a nation, that the people can expect to succeed, in forming new barriers to counteract recent encroachments on their rights; and when ever a nation is so supine as to suffer such an opportunity to be lost, they will soon feel "THAT THE DANGER WAS NOT OVER."

St. George Tucker
"View of the Constitution of the United States" (copyrighted on May 9, 1803)[76]

As well as being a prominent Virginia state judge, Tucker was professor of law at William and Mary. From that position, he played a major role in the formulation and dissemination of Republican constitutionalism through his teaching and through the publication in 1803 of the first edition of Blackstone's *Commentaries* with extensive American annotations. "Tucker's Blackstone" was one of the most widely circulated legal texts in early nineteenth-century America; among the lengthy essays that Tucker wrote and appended to the *Commentaries* was a "View of the Constitution," the first academic commentary on the federal Constitution.

. . . I am to consider the nature of that instrument by which the federal government of the United States, has been established, with the manner of its adoption.

The constitution of the United States of America, then, is an original, written, federal, and social compact, freely, voluntarily, and solemnly entered into by the several states of North-America, and ratified by the people thereof, respectively; whereby the several states, and the people thereof, respectively, have bound themselves to each other, and to the federal government of the United States; and by which the federal government is bound to the several states, and to every citizen of the United States . . .

1. It is a compact; by which it is distinguished from a charter, or grant; which is either the act of a superior to an inferior; or is founded upon some consideration moving from one of the parties, to the other, and operates as an exchange, or sale: but here the contracting parties, whether considered as states, in their politic capacity and character; or as individuals, are all equal; nor is there any thing granted from one to another: but each stipulates to part with, and to receive the same thing, precisely, without any distinction or difference in favor of any of the parties. The considerations upon which this compact was founded, and the motives which led to it, as declared in the instrument itself, were, to form a more perfect union than theretofore existed between the confederated states; to establish justice, and ensure domestic tranquility, between them; to provide for their common defence, against foreign force, or such powerful domestic insurrections as might require aid to suppress them; to promote their general welfare; and to secure the blessings of liberty to the people of the United States, and their posterity.

2. It is a federal compact; several sovereign and independent states may unite themselves together by a perpetual confederacy, without each ceasing to be a perfect state. They will together form a federal republic: the deliberations in common will offer no violence to each member, though they may in certain respects put some constraint on the exercise

of it, in virtue of voluntary engagements. The extent, modifications, and objects of the federal authority are mere matters of discretion; so long as the separate organization of the members remains, and from the nature of the compact must continue to exist, both for local and domestic, and for federal purposes; the union is in fact, as well as in theory, an association of states, or, a confederacy . . .

3. It is also, to a certain extent, a social compact; the end of civil society is the procuring for the citizens whatever their necessities require, the conveniences and accommodations of life, and in general, whatever constitutes happiness: with the peaceful possession of property, a method of obtaining justice with security; and in short, a mutual defence against all violence from without. In the act of association, in virtue of which a multitude of men form together a state or nation, each individual is supposed to have entered into engagements with all, to procure the common welfare: and all are supposed to have entered into engagements with each other, to facilitate the means of supplying the necessities of each individual, and to protect and defend him. And this is, what is ordinarily meant by the original contract of society. But a contract of this nature actually existed in a visible form between the citizens of each state, respectively, in their several constitutions; it might therefore be deemed somewhat extraordinary, that in the establishment of a federal re-public, it should have been thought necessary to extend its operation to the persons of individuals, as well as to the states, composing the confederacy. It was apprehended by many, that this innovation would be construed to change the nature of the union, from a confederacy, to a consolidation of the states; that as the tenor of the instrument imported it to be the act of the people, the construction might be made accordingly: an interpretation that would tend to the annihilation of the states, and their authority. That this was the more to be apprehended, since all questions between the states, and the United States, would undergo the final decision of the latter.

4. It is an original compact; whatever political relation existed between the American colonies, antecedent to the revolution, as constituent parts of the British empire, or as dependencies upon it, that relation was completely dissolved and annihilated from that period . . . From the moment of the revolution they became severally independent and sovereign states, possessing all the rights, jurisdictions, and authority, that other sovereign states, however constituted, or by whatever title denominated, possess; and bound by no ties but of their own creation, except such as all other civilized nations are equally bound by, and which together constitute the customary law of nations. A common council of the colonies, under the name of a general congress, had been established by the legislature, or rather conventional authority in the several colonies. The revolutionary war had been begun, and conducted under its auspices; but the first act of union which took place among the states after they became independent, was the confederation between them, which was not ratified until March 1781, near five years from the commencement of their inde-pendence. The powers thereby granted to congress, though very extensive in point of moral obligation upon the several states, were perfectly deficient in the means provided for the practical use of them, as has been already observed. The agency and co-operation of the states, which was requisite to give effect to the measures of congress, not unfre-quently occasioned their total defeat. It became an unanimous opinion that some amend-ments to the existing confederation was absolutely necessary, and after a variety of un-successful attempts for that purpose a general convention was appointed by the legislatures of twelve states, who met, consulted together, prepared, and reported a plan, which contained such an enlargement of the principles of the confederation, as gave the new system the aspect of an entire transformation of the old.

That the student may more clearly apprehend the nature of these objections, it may be proper to illustrate the distinction betwen federal compacts and obligations, and such as are social by one or two examples. A federal compact, alliance, or treaty, is an act of the state, or body politic, and not of an individual; on the contrary, the social contract is understood to mean the act of individuals, about to create, and establish, a state, or body politic, among themselves . . .

[Tucker went on to contrast the Articles of Confederation and the Constitution.]

The mild tone of requisition was exchanged for the active operations of power, and the features of a federal council for those of a national sovereignty. These concessions it was seen were, in many instances, beyond the power of the state legislatures, (limited by their respective constitutions) to make, without the express assent of the people. A convention was therefore summoned, in every state by the authority of their respective legislatures, to consider of the propriety of adopting the proposed plan; and their assent made it binding in each state; and the assent of nine states rendered it obligatory upon all the states adopting it. Here then are all the features of an original compact, not only between the body politic of each state, but also between the people of those states in their highest sovereign capacity.

Whether this original compact be considered as merely federal, or social, and national, it is that instrument by which *power is created* on the one hand, and *obedience exacted* on the other. As federal it is to be construed strictly, in all cases where the antecedent rights of *states* may be drawn in question; as a social compact it ought likewise to receive the same strict construction, wherever the right of personal liberty, or personal security, or of private property may become the subject of dispute; because every person whose liberty or property was thereby rendered subject to the new government, was antecedently a member of a civil society to whose regulations he had submitted himself, and under whose authority and protection he still remains, in all cases not expressly submitted to the new government. The few particular cases in which he submits himself to the new authority, therefore, ought not to be extended beyond the terms of the compact, as it might endanger his obedience to that state to whose laws he still continues to owe obedience; or may subject him to a double loss, or inconvenience for the same cause.

And here it ought to be remembered that no case of *municipal* law can arise under the constitution of the United States, except such as are expressly comprehended in that instrument. For the *municipal* law of one state or nation has no force or obligation in any other nation; and when several states, or nations unite themselves together by a federal compact, each retains its own municipal laws, without admitting or adopting those of any other member of the union, unless there be an article expressly to that effect. The municipal laws of the several American states differ essentially from each other; and as neither is entitled to a preference over the other, on the score of intrinsic superiority, or obligation; and as there is no article in the compact which bestows any such preference upon any, it follows, that the municipal laws of no one state can be resorted to as a general rule for the rest. And as the states, and their respective legislatures are absolutely independent of each other, so neither can any common rule be extracted from their several municipal codes. For, although concurrent laws, or rules may perhaps be met with in their codes, yet it is in the power of their legislatures, respectively to destroy that concurrence at any time, by enacting an entire new law on the subject; so that it may happen that that which is a concurrent law in all the states to-day may cease to be law in one, or more of them to-morrow. Consequently neither the particular municipal law of any one, or more, of the states, nor the concurrent municipal laws of the whole of them, can be considered as the common rule, or measure of justice in the courts of the federal republic; neither hath the federal government any power to establish such a common rule, generally; no such power being granted by the constitution. And the principle is certainly much stronger, that neither the common nor statute law of any other nation, ought to be a standard for the proceedings of this, unless previously made its own by legislative adoption: which, not being permitted by the original compact, by which the government is *created*, any attempt to introduce it, in that or any other mode, would be a manifest breach of the terms of that compact.

Another light in which this subject may be viewed is this. Since each state in becoming a member of a federal republic retains an uncontrolled jurisdiction over all cases of *municipal* law, every grant of jurisdiction to the confederacy, in any such case, is to be considered as special, inasmuch as it derogates from the antecedent rights and jurisdictions of the state making the concession, and therefore ought to be construed strictly, upon the grounds already mentioned. Now, the cases falling under the head of *municipal law,* to which the authority of the federal government extends, are few, definite, and enumerated, and are all carved out of the sovereign authority and former exclusive, and uncontrollable jurisdiction of the *states* respectively: they ought therefore to receive the strictest construction. Otherwise the gradual and sometimes imperceptible usurpations of power, will end in the total disregard of all its intended limitations.

If it be asked, what would be the consequence in case the federal government should exercise powers not warranted by the constitution, the answer seems to be, that where the act of usurpation may immediately affect an individual, the remedy is to be sought by recourse to that judiciary, to which the cognizance of the case properly belongs. Where it may affect a state, the state legislature, whose rights will be invaded by every such act, will be ready to mark the innovation and sound the alarm to the people: and thereby either effect a change in the federal representation, or procure in the mode prescribed by the constitution, further "declaratory and restrictive clauses", by way of amendment thereto. An instance of which may be cited in the conduct of the Massachusetts legislature: who, as soon as that state was sued in the federal court, by an individual, immediately proposed, and procured an amendment to the constitution, declaring that the judicial power of the United States shall not be construed to extend to any suit brought by an individual against a state.

5. It is a written contract; considered as a federal compact, or alliance between the states, there is nothing new or singular in this circumstance, as all national compacts since the invention of letters have probably been reduced to that form: but considered in the light of an original, social, compact, it may be worthy of remark, that a very great lawyer [Blackstone], who wrote but a few years before the American revolution, seems to doubt whether the original contract of society had in any one instance been formally expressed at the first institution of the state. The American revolution seems to have given birth to this new political phenomenon: in every state a written constitution was framed, and adopted by the people, both in their individual and sovereign capacity, and character. By this means, the just distinction between sovereignty, and the government, as rendered familiar to every intelligent mind; the former was found to reside in the *people*, and to be unalienable from them; the latter in their *servants* and *agents:* by this means, also, government was reduced to its elements; its object was defined, its principles ascertained; its power limited, and fixed; its structure organized; and the functions of every part of the machine so clearly designated, as to prevent any interference, so long as the limits of each were observed. The same reasons operated in behalf of similar restrictions in the federal constitution, whether considered as the act of the body politic of the several states, or, the people of the states, respectively, or, of the people of the United States, collectively. Accordingly we find the structure of the government, its several powers and jurisdictions, and the concessions of the several states, generally, pretty accurately defined, and limited. But to guard against encroachments on the powers of the several states, in their politic character, and of the people, both in their individual and sovereign capacity, an amendatory article was added, immediately after the government was organized, declaring; that the powers not delegated to the United States, by the constitution, nor prohibited by it to the states, are reserved to the states, respectively, or to the people. And, still further, to guard the people against constructive usurpations and encroachments on their rights, another article declares; that the enumeration of certain rights in the constitution, shall not be construed to deny, or disparage, others retained by the people. The sum of all which appears to be, that the powers delegated to the federal government, are, in all cases, to receive the most strict construction that the instrument will bear, where the rights of a state or of the people, either collectively, or individually, may be drawn in question . . .

Comment

One of Tucker's primary concerns in the "View" was to translate the great constitutional rhetoric of the Virginia and Kentucky resolutions into straightforward rules of law. The contractual nature of the Constitution, he insisted, created a presumption in favor of state rather than federal power, and the prepolitical nature of personal rights gave rise to a similar presumption against the legitimacy of federal intrusion into "personal liberty or personal security, or . . . private property." "Tucker's Blackstone" popularized the expression "strict construction" to summarize these legal presumptions; it is important to remember that, when used by early Republicans such as Tucker, the notion of "strict construction" was directly and intrinsically connected to the compact theory of the "doctrines of '98."

Section B: *Thomas Jefferson and the Republican Presidency*

Republican constitutionalists in the 1790s opposed expansive readings of presidential power. In part they no doubt were motivated by the obvious expediencies of politics, but their concern over anything reminiscent of kingly prerogative had deep roots in the Whig tradition. Before Jefferson's inauguration, most Federalists—and many Republicans—believed that his Republicanism involved hostility to executive power. Explaining to Hamilton why he could not support Jefferson over Burr during the electoral crisis in early 1801, John Marshall wrote: "Mr. Jefferson appears to me to be a man who will embody himself with the House of Representatives. By weakening the office of President he will increase his personal power." Hamilton repeatedly urged James Bayard, who as Delaware's lone Representative controlled one of the electoral votes in the House, to support Jefferson over Burr. Hamilton explained:

> Perhaps myself the first, at some expence of popularity, to unfold the true character of Jefferson, it is too late for me to become his apologist. Nor can I have any disposition to do it. I admit that his politics are tinctured with fanaticism, that he is too much in earnest in his democracy, that he has been a mischevous enemy to the principle measures of our past administration, that he is crafty & persevering in his objects, that he is not scrupulous about the means of success, nor very mindful of truth, and that he is a contemptible hypocrite. But it is not true as is alleged that he is an enemy to the power of the Executive, nor that he is for confounding all the powers in the House of Rs. It is a fact which I have frequently mentioned that while we were in the administration together he was generally for a large construction of the Executive authority, & not backward to act upon it in cases which coincided with his views. Let it be added, that in his theoretic Ideas he has considered as improper the participations of the Senate in the Executive Authority. I have more than once made the reflection that viewing himself as the

reversioner, he was solicitous to come into possession of a Good Estate.

Thomas Jefferson
Letter to James Monroe
(May 29, 1801)[77]

Early in Jefferson's first administration, his friend Governor Monroe, of Virginia, solicited his opinion on a point of constitutional etiquette: Should the executives of the general and state governments correspond directly (the only proper mode between executive magistrates of equal dignity), or would Jefferson treat the governors as subordinates?

. . . As to the mode of correspondence between the general and particular executives, I do not think myself a good judge. Not because my position gives me any prejudice on the occasion; for, if it be possible to be certainly conscious of anything, I am conscious of feeling no difference between writing to the highest and lowest being on earth, but because I have ever thought that forms should yield to whatever should facilitate business. Comparing the two governments together, it is observable that, in all those cases where the independent or reserved rights of the States are in question, the two executives, if they are to act together, must be exactly co-ordinate; they are, in these cases, each the supreme head of an independent government. In other cases, to wit, those transferred by the Constitution to the General Government, the general executive is certainly pre-ordinate, e.g., in a question respecting the militia and others easily to be recollected. Were there, therefore, to be a stiff adherence to etiquette, I should say that in the former cases the correspondence should be between the two heads, and that in the latter the Governor must be subject to receive orders from the war department as any other subordinate officer would. And were it observed that either party set up unjustifiable pretensions, perhaps the other might be right in opposing them by a tenaciousness of its own rigorous rights. But I think the practice in General Washington's administration was most friendly to business and was absolutely equal, sometimes he wrote to the Governors, and sometimes the heads of departments wrote . . . If this be practiced promiscuously in both classes of cases, each party setting examples of neglecting etiquette, both will stand on equal ground, and convenience alone will dictate through whom any particular communication is to be made. On the whole, I think a free correspondence best and shall never hesitate to write myself to the Governors in every federal case where the occasion presents itself to me particularly . . .

Thomas Jefferson
Letters to Abigail Adams[78]

Abigail Adams and Jefferson corresponded in 1804 in connection with the latter's pardon of those convicted under the Sedition Act of libeling John Adams, an action both Adamses resented.

(July 22, 1804)

. . . I discharged every person under punishment or prosecution under the Sedition Law because I considered, and now consider, that law to be a nullity, as absolute and as palpable as if Congress had ordered us to fall down and worship a golden image, and that it was as much my duty to arrest its execution in every stage as it would have been to have rescued from the fiery furnace those who should have been cast into it for refusing to worship the image. It was accordingly done in every instance without asking what the offenders had done, or against whom they had offended, but whether the pains they were suffering were inflicted under the pretended sedition law . . .

(September 11, 1804)

. . . You seem to think it devolved on the judges to decide on the validity of the Sedition Law. But nothing in the Constitution has given them a right to decide for the executive, more than to the executive to decide for them. Both magistrates are equally independent in the sphere of action assigned to them. The judges, believing the law constitutional, had a right to pass a sentence of fine and imprisonment, because the power was placed in their hands by the Constitution. But the executive, believing the law to be unconstitutional, were bound to remit the execution of it, because that power has been confided to them by the Constitution. That instrument meant that its co-ordinate branches should be checks on each other. But the opinion which gives to the judges the right to decide what laws are constitutional and what not, not only for themselves in their own sphere of action but for the Legislature and executive also in their spheres, would make the judiciary a despotic branch . . .

Thomas Jefferson
Letter to John B. Colvin
(September 20, 1810)[79]

At least once during his presidency, in the purchase of Louisiana, Jefferson took action that he privately considered unconstitutional. Other measures—aspects of his handling of the Burr conspiracy and some of the measures taken to enforce the 1808–9 embargo against commerce with Britain and France—approached the outer limits of Republican constitutionalism. On several occasions during and after his presidency, Jefferson explained his belief that the president at times had a duty even higher than that of preserving the Constitution.

. . . The question you propose, whether circumstances do not sometimes occur which make it a duty in officers of high trust to assume authorities beyond the law, is easy of solution in principle but sometimes embarrassing in practice. A strict observance of the written laws is doubtless *one* of the high duties of a good citizen, but it is not *the highest*. The laws of necessity, of self-preservation, of saving our country when in danger are of higher obligation. To lose our country by a scrupulous adherence to written law would be to lose the law itself, with life, liberty, property, and all those who are enjoying them with us, thus absurdly sacrificing the end to the means. When, in the battle of Germantown, General Washington's army was annoyed from Chew's house, he did not hesitate to plant his cannon against it, although the property of a citizen. When he besieged Yorktown, he leveled the suburbs, feeling that the laws of property must be postponed to the safety of the nation. While the army was before York, the Governor of Virginia took horses, carriages, provisions and even men by force, to enable that army to stay together till it could master the public enemy; and he was justified. A ship at sea in distress for provisions, meets another having abundance, yet refusing a supply; the law of self-preservation authorizes the distressed to take a supply by force. In all these cases, the unwritten laws of necessity, of self-preservation, and of the public safety, control the written laws of meum and tuum. Further to exemplify the principle, I will state an hypothetical case. Suppose it had been made known to the Executive of the Union in the autumn of 1805, that we might have the Floridas for a reasonable sum, that that sum had not indeed been so appropriated by law, but that Congress were to meet within three weeks, and might appropriate it on the first or second day of their session. Ought he, for so great an advantage to his country, to have risked himself by transcending the law and making the purchase? The public advantage offered, in this supposed case, was indeed immense; but a reverence for law, and the probability that the advantage might still be legally accomplished by a delay of only three weeks, were powerful reasons against hazarding the act. But suppose it was foreseen that a John Randolph [a well-known Republican critic of Jefferson] would find means to protract the proceeding on it by Congress, until the ensuing spring, by which time new circumstances would change the mind of the other party. Ought the Executive, in that case, and with that foreknowledge, to have secured the good to his country, and to have trusted to their justice for the transgression of the law? I think he ought, and that the act would have been approved.

From these examples and principles you may see what I think on the question proposed. They do not go to the case of persons charged with petty duties, where consequences are trifling and time allowed for a legal course, nor to authorize them to take such cases out of the written law. In these, the example of over-leaping the law is of greater evil than a strict adherence to its imperfect provisions. It is incumbent on those only who accept of great charges to risk themselves on great occasions, when the safety of a nation or some of its very high interests are at stake . . .

An officer is bound to obey orders; yet he would be a bad one who should do it in cases for which they were not intended, and which involved the most important consequences. The line of discrimination between cases may be difficult; but the good officer is bound to draw it at his own peril, and throw himself on the justice of his country and the rectitude of his motives.

Comment

The central principle in Jefferson's vision of the presidency was his belief in that officer's direct responsibility to the Constitution and to the people to act on its and their behalf. Jefferson's tactful but firm assertion of his superiority to state governors in "federal cases" in his letter to Monroe marked the beginning of a consistent defense of the president's authority to act, in his constitutional sphere, independently of the approbation of state governments. In his Sedition Act pardons and his refusal to concede the executive's amenability to judicial process (see below), Jefferson asserted presidential independence from the constitutional opinions of the federal courts. The president's duty to exercise his own constitutional judgment, furthermore, was itself subordinate to his overriding obligation to protect the nation, an obligation that Jefferson believed had required him to transcend even the Constitution in service to the Constitution's creators.

Section C: *The Republicans and the Federal Courts*

The lame-duck Federalist Congress that sat in the winter of 1800–1801 amended the Judiciary Act of 1789 in a variety of ways, most importantly by redesigning the structure of the federal courts. In place of the 1789 act's clumsy provision that the circuit courts (which had both trial and appellate duties) be staffed by local district judges and Supreme Court justices, the 1801 act created sixteen new circuit judgeships. This substantially parallels the present system, and most modern scholars have regarded the change as an improvement on the original scheme.

But the act had a political dimension as well. The new judgeships, as well as other new officers created by the 1801 act, could be filled by outgoing President Adams and confirmed by the Federalist Senate. In the short time remaining before Jefferson's inauguration, Adams proceeded to do so, prompting Republicans to label the statute the "Midnight Judges Act." When Jefferson took office, he and the Republican congressional leadership regarded the new Federalist officers as a major target of "remedial" action, and on his own authority Jefferson instructed Secretary of State Madison to retain several commissions that the outgoing president had signed but not delivered. This action, of course, led to *Marbury v. Madison* (1803), in which the Supreme Court denied one of Adams's appointees relief on the ground that the section of the 1789 act giving the Court jurisdiction over the case was unconstitutional. Of far greater importance at the time was the effort to repeal the 1801 act, abolish the new circuit judgeships, and thereby remove the new judges from office. The Federalists, and some Republicans, regarded this as a direct assault on the independence of the judiciary and a violation of article three. In the end, the repeal bill was enacted, and then challenged in federal court.

Gouverneur Morris
Speech in the U.S. Senate
(January 8, 1802)[80]

. . . What will be the effect of the desired repeal? Will it not be a declaration to the remaining judges that they hold their offices subject to your will and pleasure? And what will be the result of this? It will be, that the check established by the Constitution, wished for by the people, and necessary in every contemplation of common sense, is destroyed. It had been said, and truly too, that Governments are made to provide against the follies and vices of men. For to suppose that Governments rest upon reason is a pitiful solecism. If mankind were reasonable, they would want no Government. Hence, checks are required in the distribution of power among those who are to exercise it for the benefit of the people. Did the people of America vest all powers in the Legislature? No; they had vested in the judges a check intended to be efficient—a check of the first necessity, to prevent an invasion of the Constitution by unconstitutional laws—a check which might prevent any faction from intimidating or annihilating the tribunals themselves.

On this ground, . . . I stand to arrest the victory meditated over the Constitution of my country; a victory meditated by those who wish to prostrate that Constitution for the furtherance of their own ambitious views. Not of him who had recommended this measure, nor of those who now urged it—for, on his uprightness and their uprightness, I have the fullest reliance—but of those in the background who have further and higher objects. Those troops that protect the outworks are to be first dismissed. Those posts which present the strongest barriers are first to be taken, and then the Constitution becomes an easy prey.

Let us then, secondly, consider whether we have constitutionally a power to repeal this law. [Here Morris quoted article three section one of the Constitution.] I have heard a verbal criticism about the words shall and may, which appeared the more unnecessary to me as the same word shall is applied to both members of the section. For it says "the judicial power, &c., shall be vested in one Supreme Court and such inferior courts as the Congress may, from time to time ordain and establish." The Legislature, therefore, had without doubt the right of determining, in the first instance, what inferior courts should be established; but when established, the words are imperative, a part of the judicial power shall vest in them. And "the judges shall hold their offices during good behaviour." They shall receive a compensation which shall not be diminished during their continuance in office. Therefore, whether the remarks be applied to the tenure of office or the quantum of compensation, the Constitution is equally imperative. After this exposition, gentlemen are welcome to any advantage to be derived from the criticism on shall and may.

But another criticism, which but for its serious effects I would call pleasant, has been made, the amount of which is: you shall not take the man from the office, but you may take the office from the man; you shall not drown him, but you may sink his boat under him; you shall not put him to death, but you may take away his life. The Constitution secures to a judge his office; says he shall hold it, that is, it shall not be taken from him during good behaviour; the Legislature shall not diminish, though their bounty may increase, his salary; the Constitution provides perfectly for the inviolability of his tenure. But yet we may destroy the office which we cannot take away, as if the destruction of the office would not as effectually deprive him of it as the grant to another person. It is admitted that no power derived from the Constitution can deprive him of the office, and yet it is contended that by repeal of the law that office may be destroyed. Is not this absurd?

It had been said, that whatever one Legislature can do another can undo; because no Legislature can bind its successor, and therefore that whatever we make we can destroy. This I deny on the ground of reason, and on that of the Constitution. What! can a man destroy his own children? Can you annul your own compacts? Can you annihilate the national debt? When you have by law created a political existence, can you, by repealing the law, dissolve the corporation you had made? When by your laws you give to an individual any right whatever, can you by subsequent law rightfully take it away? No. When you make a compact you are bound by it. When you make a promise you must perform it.

Establish the contrary doctrine and what follows? The whim of the moment becomes the law of the land; your country will be looked upon as a den of robbers; every honest man will fly your shores. Who will trust you, when you are the first to violate your own contracts? The position, therefore, that the Legislature may rightfully repeal every law made by a preceding Legislature, when tested by reason, is untrue. And it is equally untrue when compared with the precepts of the Constitution; for what does the Constitution say? You shall make no ex post facto law. Is not this an ex post facto law?

Aaron Burr
Letter to Barnabus Bidwell
(February 1, 1802)[81]

As vice-president, Burr was the presiding officer of the Senate, where John Breckenridge, of Kentucky, introduced the repeal bill. Burr played an ambiguous role during the legislative proceedings, on one occasion casting a tie-breaking vote to preserve the bill, on

another sending the bill to a select committee with a Federalist majority. His private correspondence suggests that his behavior was motivated, at least in part, by scruples about the bill's legitimacy. Bidwell was a Republican state legislator in Massachusetts.

Dear Sir

The Newspapers will have shewn you the position of the Bill now before the Senate for the Repeal of the act of last session establishing a new Judiciary System: and that the bill when on it's third Reading was by the Casting Vote of the V[ice]. P[resident], referred to a Select Committee—this day Notice has been given that a motion to discharge that Committee will be made tomorrow—It should be noted that the arrival of Mr. Bradley has given a vote to the Republican Side; hence it may be presumed that the Committee will be discharged and that the bill will pass the Senate tomorrow: and that in the Course of three Weeks it will become a law—I state this however as mere Conjecture.

The Constitutional right & power of Abolishing one Judiciary System & establishing another, cannot be doubted—The power thus to deprive Judges of their offices and Salaries must also be admitted: but whether it would be constitutionally Moral, if I may use the expression, and if so, whether it would be politic & expedient, are questions on which I could wish to be further advised—Your opinion on these points would be particularly acceptable—

Barnabus Bidwell
Letter to Aaron Burr
(February 14, 1802)[82]

Dear Sir:

The last Mail presented me your favour of Feb. 1st. for which you have my cordial thanks. I had before seen that the Bill for the repeal of the act of last Feby. establishing a Judiciary System, was, on its third reading, by the casting vote of the Vice-President, referred to a Select-Committee. The decision of the Vice-President in favour of a Committment has received the general approbation of the Republicans here, as indicating a wish to give every opportunity of considering and maturing the Bill, and not hazarding any thing by such a delay. But the general, and so far as I at present recollect, the universal opinion of the Republicans, of my circle of acquaintance here, is in favour of the measure of a Repeal. No doubt exists here of its constitutionality. On that point, the sentiments of both parties in Massts seem to be pledged. By our Constitution the tenure of judicial office is during good behaviour, extending to our Courts of Common Pleas, as well as to the Supreme Jud. Court. Several years past efforts were made to abolish the Courts of Common Pleas, in order to establish a system of Circuit Courts, to consist of professional men, with Salaries, instead of the existing Judges, with perquisites but without Salaries. These efforts were repeated. And altho they did not prevail; yet both the advocates & opposers of the proposed Reform, agreed in the constitutional right of the Legislature on the subject. That right has never been denied or doubted here; and the objection in your Senate strikes us as the mere display of ingenuity, without any solid foundation. Various considerations satisfy us of the expediency of the measure. Although in expressing an opinion on this subject, I feel the reproach due to the School-man reading Hannibal a lecture upon the art of war; yet, in compliance with a request, which has the force of a command, I will mention two or three reasons which prevail with me & those with whom I am on terms of political intimacy in this place. 1st. The Repeal is not an innovation, but a Restoration of the former state of things. 2ndly. It is in correspondence with the System of Oeconomy & simplification:—attempted by the present Administration & Republican majorities in Congress and desired & expected by Republicans in all parts of the country. 3rdly. It will check that predominance of judiciary influence on the Side of the federal party which has been felt and lamented by all the friends of impartial justice and equal rights. Federalism has predominated in our national & too much in our State Judiciaries: and that circumstance has operated to federalise the Profession of Lawyers in all of the States. Young men, coming upon the Stage, are insensibly influenced by examples and official impressions; and a political bias is the natural consequence. That effect is proportioned to its cause. The additional judiciary was an enlargement of the sphere of official federalism, & in that point of view objectionable. 4thly. The system was so obviously the offspring of party, that the new Judges had reason to expect its repeal, & have, therefore, less reason to complain. For these, among other reasons, I hope the Bill will ultimately pass. With great respect I am, Dear Sir, your friend & humble Servant.

James A. Bayard
Speech in the U.S. House of Representatives
(February 20, 1802)[83]

Upon the main question, said Mr. B., whether the judges hold their offices at the will of the Legislature, an argument of great weight and according to my humble judgment of irresistible force, still remains. The Legislative power of the Government is not absolute, but limited. If it be doubtful whether the Legislature can do what the Constitution does not explicitly authorize; yet there can be no question that they cannot do what the Constitution expressly prohibits. To maintain, therefore, the Constitution, the judges are a check upon the Legislature. The doctrine I know is denied [by certain Republican legislators during the repeal-bill debates], and it is therefore incumbent upon me to show that it is sound.

It was once thought by gentlemen who now deny the principle, that the safety of the citizen and of the States rested upon the power of the judges to declare an unconstitutional law void. How vain is a paper restriction if it confers neither power nor right! Of what importance is it to say Congress are prohibited from doing certain acts, if no legitimate authority exists in the country to decide whether an act done is a prohibited act? Do gentlemen perceive the consequences which would follow from establishing the principle that Congress have the exclusive right to decide upon their own powers? This principle admitted, does any Constitution remain? Does not the power of the Legislature become absolute and omnipotent? Can you talk to them of transgressing their powers when no one has a right to judge of those powers but themselves? They do what is not authorized, they do what is inhibited, nay, at every step they trample the Constitution under foot; yet their acts are lawful and binding, and it is treason to resist them. How ill, sir, do the doctrines and professions of these gentlemen agree! They tell us they are friendly to the existence of the States; that they are the friends of a federative, but the enemies of a consolidated, General Government, and yet, sir, to accomplish a paltry subject, they are willing to settle a principle which, beyond all doubt would eventually plant a consolidated Government with unlimited power upon the ruins of the State governments. Nothing can be more absurd than to contend that there is a practical restraint upon a political body who are answerable to none but themselves for the violation of the restraint, and who can derive from the very act of violation undeniable justification of their conduct.

If, said Mr. B., you mean to have a constitution, you must discover a power to which the acknowledged right is attached of pronouncing the invalidity of the acts of the Legislature which contravene the instrument. Does the power reside in the States? Has the Legislature of a State a right to declare an act of Congress void? This would be erring upon the opposite extreme. It would be placing the General Government at the feet of the State governments. It would be allowing one member of the Union to control all the rest.

It would inevitably lead to civil dissension and a dissolution of the General Government. Will it be pretended that the State courts have the exclusive right of deciding upon the validity of our laws? I admit that they have the right to declare an act of Congress void. But this right they enjoy in practice, and it ever essentially must exist, subject to the revision and control of the courts of the United States. If the State courts definitively possessed the right of declaring the invalidity of the laws of this Government, it would bring us in subjection to the States. The judges of those courts being bound by the laws of the State, if a State declared an act of Congress unconstitutional, the law of the State would oblige its courts to determine the law invalid. This principle would also destroy the uniformity of obligation upon all the States, which should attend every law of this Government. If a law were declared void in one State, it would exempt the citizens of that State from its operation whilst obedience was yielded to it in the other States. I go further and say, if the States or State courts had a final power of annulling the acts of this Government, its miserable and precarious existence would not be worth the trouble of a moment to preserve. It would endure but a short time as a subject of derision, and, wasting into an empty shadow, would quickly vanish from our sight.

Let me now ask if the power to decide upon the validity of our laws resides with the people? Gentlemen cannot deny this right to the people. I admit that they possess it. But if, at the same time, it does not belong to the courts of the United States, where does it lead the people? It leads them to the gallows. Let us suppose that Congress, forgetful of the limits of their authority, pass an unconstitutional law. They lay a direct tax upon one State and impose none upon the others. The people of the State taxed contest the validity of the law. They forcibly resist its execution. They are brought by the Executive authority before the courts upon charges of treason. The law is unconstitutional, the people have done right, but the courts are bound by the law and obliged to pronounce upon them the sentence which it inflicts. Deny to the courts of the United States the power of judging upon the constitutionality of our laws, and it is vain to talk of its existing elsewhere. The infractors of the laws are brought before these courts, and if the courts are implicitly bound, the invalidity of the laws can be no defence.

There is, however, Mr. Chairman, still a stronger ground of argument upon this subject. I shall select one or two cases to illustrate it. Congress are prohibited from passing a bill of attainder; it is also declared in the Constitution that "no attainder of treason shall work corruption of blood or forfeiture, except during the life of the party attainted." Let us suppose that Congress pass a bill of attainder, or they enact that any one attainted of treason shall forfeit to the use of the United States all the estate which he held in any lands or tenements. The party attainted is seized and brought before a federal court and an award of execution passed against him. He opens the Constitution and points to this line, "no bill of attainder or *ex post facto* law shall be passed." The attorney for the United States reads the bill of attainder.

The courts are bound to decide, but they have only the alternative of pronouncing the law or the Constitution invalid. It is left to them only to say that the law vacates the Constitution, or the Constitution avoids the law. So in the other case stated, the heir, after the death of his ancestor, brings his ejectment in one of the courts of the United States to recover his inheritance. The law by which it is confiscated is shown. The Constitution gave no power to pass such a law. On the contrary, it expressly denied it to the Government. The title of the heir is rested on the Constitution, the title of the Government on the law. The effect of one destroys the effect of the other; the court must determine which is effectual.

There are many other cases, Mr. Chairman, of a similar nature to which I might allude. There is the case of the privilege of habeas corpus, which cannot be suspended but in times of rebellion or of invasion. Suppose a law prohibiting the issuing of the writ at a moment of profound peace. If in such case the writ were demanded of a court, could they say, it is true the Legislature were restrained from passing the law, suspending the privilege of this writ at such a time as that which now exists, but their mighty power has broken the bonds of the Constitution and fettered the authority of the court. I am not, sir, disposed to vaunt, but standing on this ground I throw the gauntlet to any champion upon the other side. I call upon them to maintain that in a collision between a law and the Constitution, the judges are bound to support the law, and annul the Constitution. Can the gentlemen relieve themselves from this dilemma. Will they say, though a judge has no power to pronounce a law void, he has a power to declare the Constitution valid.

The doctrine for which I am contending is not only clearly inferable from the plain language of the Constitution, but by law has been expressly declared and established in practice since the existence of the Government.

The second section of third article of the Constitution expressly extends the judicial power to all cases arising under the Constitution, the laws, &c. The provision in the second clause of the sixth article leaves nothing to doubt. "This Constitution, and the laws of the United States which shall be made in pursuance thereof, &c. shall be the supreme law of the land." The Constitution is absolutely the supreme law. Not so the acts of the Legislature. Such only are the law of the land as are made in pursuance of the Constitution.

I beg the indulgence of the Committee one moment, while I read the following provision from the twenty-fifth section of the judicial act of the year seventeen hundred and eighty-nine:

"A final judgment or decree in any suit in the highest court of law or equity of a State in which a decision in the suit could be had, where is drawn in question the validity of a treaty or statute of, or an authority exercised under, the United States, and the decision is against their validity, &c. may be reexamined and reversed or affirmed in the Supreme Court of the United States, upon a writ of error."

Thus, as early as the year 1789, among the first acts of the Government, the Legislature explicitly recognised the right of a State court to declare a treaty, a statute, and authority exercised under the United States, void, subject to the revision of the Supreme Court of the United States; and it has expressly given the final power to the Supreme Court to affirm a judgment which is against the validity either of a treaty, statute, or an authority of the Government.

I humbly trust, Mr. Chairman, that I have given abundant proofs from the nature of our Government, from the language of the Constitution, and from Legislative acknowledgement, that the judges of our courts have the power to judge and determine upon the constitutionality of our laws.

Joseph H. Nicholson
Speech in the U.S. House of Representatives
(February 27, 1802)[84]

We say that we have the same right to repeal the law establishing inferior courts that we have to repeal the law establishing post offices and post roads, laying taxes, or raising armies. This right would not be denied but for the construction given to that part of the Constitution which declares that "the judges both of the supreme and inferior courts shall hold their offices during good behavior."

The arguments of gentlemen, generally, have been directed against a position that we never meant to contend for: against the right to remove the judges in any other manner than by impeachment. This right we have never insisted on; we have never in the most distant manner contended that the Constitution vested us with the same power that the Parliament of England have, or that is given to the Legislatures of Pennsylvania, Delaware, New Jersey, and some others.

Our doctrine is that every Congress has a right to repeal any law passed by its predecessors, except in cases where the Constitution imposes a prohibition. We have been told that we cannot repeal a law fixing the President's salary during the period for which he was elected. This is admitted, because it is so expressly declared in the Constitution; nor is the necessity so imperious, because at the expiration of every four years, it is in the power of Congress to regulate it anew, as their judgments may dictate. Neither can we diminish the salary of a judge so long as he continues in office, because in this particular the Constitution is express likewise. But we do contend that we have absolute, uncontrolled right to abolish all offices which have been created by Congress, when in our judgment those offices are unnecessary and are productive of a useless expense.

Let us examine the objections which have been raised to this upon that part of the Constitution in which it is said that "the judges both of the supreme and inferior courts shall hold their offices during good behaviour, and shall receive, at stated times, a compensation for their services, which shall not be diminished during their continuance in office."

It has already been stated by some of my friends, and I shall not therefore dwell upon it, that the prohibition contained in these words was of two kinds: the one applying to the Legislature, and prohibiting a diminution of salary; the other applying to the Executive, and forbidding a removal from office. The first prohibition our adversaries readily admit, but the second, they say, applies as well to the Legislature as to the Executive; I should agree to this, too, were there any necessity for it, but it is not pretended by us that we have the right to remove from office any officer whatsoever—not only a judge, but even a revenue officer; there would, therefore, be no necessity for imposing a restriction upon Congress in relation to a judge any more than in relation to an officer concerned in the collection of revenue. They are each appointed by the president and Senate, but the Executive officer holds his place at the will of the President, the judge holds his office during good behaviour, and neither [is] subject to removal by the Legislature.

The term good behaviour is said to secure to the judge an estate for life in his office, determinable only upon impeachment for an conviction of bribery, corruption, and other high crimes and misdemeanors, and that inasmuch as his good conduct is the tenure by which he holds his office, he cannot be deprived of it so long as he demeans himself well.

Your supervisors who superintend the collection of your excise duties are appointed by the President and Senate, and hold their offices under the Constitution, not during good behaviour but during the will and pleasure of the President. The tenure by which [one of them] holds his office is completely beyond the power of the Legislature, and they cannot remove him. So long as he can secure the good will of the President, he is to hold his office against the whole world. It is as sacred, in relation to the authority of Congress, as that of a judge. They both hold their offices independent of the Legislature; the one during good behaviour, the other during the pleasure of the President. It is not in our power to remove an excise officer so long as his office continues, any more than to remove a judge, so long as his office continues. The authority vested in us is entirely Legislative, and has nothing to do with the Executive power of removal. Yet is there any man on earth can say that we have not a Constitutional right to repeal the laws laying excise duties, by which the office of supervisor is created? And can any one say that we can remove the supervisor in any other manner than by repealing the law?

We do not contend for the right to remove the judge any more than for the right to remove the supervisor, neither of which we can do, each holding his office independent of us; but we allege that the tenure by which either holds his office cannot prohibit us from repealing a law by which the office is created . . .

I am aware that I may be told that the President, in giving his sanction to the law, at the same time, impliedly signifies his consent to the removal of the officer. But permit me to suppose that the President refuses his signature to the law, and tells you that these officers hold their commissions independent of you, and therefore you have no right to dismiss them; that the Constitution authorizes them to hold their places during his will and pleasure, and that it is his will and pleasure [that] they shall continue in office. Here the tenure is as strong and inviolable by the Legislative power as the tenure of the judge.

Yet Congress may, notwithstanding, afterwards pass the law by the concurrence of two-thirds, and destroy this sacred tenure of office.

If, then, the tenure of office in the one case cannot destroy the right to repeal, why shall it destroy it in the other? Both tenures are equally independent of Legislative control—the one securing an estate defeasible by misbehaviour, the other securing an estate defeasible by the will of the President; but neither dependent on Congress for continuance in office, so long as the office itself exists. Gentlemen say we cannot do that by indirect means which we cannot do directly; that is, that we cannot remove a judge by repealing this law, inasmuch as we cannot remove him by direct means. But I have proved beyond the possibility of doubt that we may indirectly remove an excise officer by repealing the law under which he was appointed, although we have no authority to remove him in any direct manner. If the principle laid down by gentlemen is not true in the one case, it cannot be true in the other.

For my own part, Mr. Chairman, I think no doubt can be entertained that the power of repealing, as well as of enacting laws, is inherent in every Legislature. The Legislative authority would be incomplete without it. If you deny the existence of this power, you suppose a perfection in man which he can never attain. You shut the door against a retraction of error by refusing him the benefit of reflection and experience. You deny to the great body of the people all the essential advantages for which they entered into society. This House is composed of members coming from every quarter of the Union, supposed to bring with them the feelings and to be acquainted with the interests of their constituents. If the feelings and the interests of the nation require that new laws should be enacted, that existing laws should be modified, or that useless and unnecessary laws should be repealed, they have reserved this power to themselves by declaring that it should be exercised by persons freely chosen for a limited period to represent them in the National Legislature.

Comment

The primary Federalist objection to the repeal bill was that it violated the Constitution's guarantee to federal judges of tenure during good behavior. Although most Republicans accepted the counter-argument that the bill did not remove the circuit judges from office but merely abolished the offices themselves, the formulation and expediency of this reasoning disturbed some of them (note Burr's query about the constitutional "morality" of the bill). Federalists such as Congressman Bayard also reminded the bill's supporters of Republican demands only a few years previously that the courts declare the Sedition Act unconstitutional. Judges whose positions might be legislated out from under them hardly could play the role in maintaining the Constitution that Republicans and Federalists alike envisioned for them (and, it was implied, might resist the repeal bill by invoking the power of judicial review).

Stuart v. Laird
5 U.S. (1 Cranch) 299 (Mar. 2, 1803)

John Laird obtained a judgment against Hugh Stuart in a contract action governed by Virginia law in one of the new, independently staffed circuit courts (the Fourth Circuit) established by the 1801 Judiciary Act. After the act was repealed, Stuart resisted enforce-

ment of the judgment in the revived circuit court (the Fifth, on which John Marshall served as circuit-riding justice) on the ground that the 1802 repeal act was unconstitutional.

Charles Lee, for [Stuart]. The act of assembly of Virginia, which gives this summary remedy upon forthcoming bonds, allows the motion for judgment to be made only to the same court from which the execution issued. In this case, the execution issued from the court of the United States for the fourth circuit, in the eastern Virginia district, composed of Judges Key, Taylor and McGill. The motion was made to the court of the United States for the fifth circuit, in the Virginia district, holden by the Chief Justice of the United States.

This is not the same court from which the execution issued. The motion, therefore, in this court, was not regular, unless it made so by the [Judiciary Repeal] acts . . .

The court of the fifth circuit ought not to have taken cognisance of the motion . . . If the Repeal acts of 1802 . . . are constitutional, then it is admitted, there is no error in the judgment; because, in that case, the courts ceased to exist, the judges were constitutionally removed, and the transfer from one court to the other was legal. But if those acts are unconstitutional, then the court of the fourth circuit still exists, the judges were not removed, and the transfer of jurisdiction did not take place. The legislature did not intend to transfer causes from one existing court to another. If, then, the courts still exist, the causes not being intended to be removed from existing courts, were not removed.

But we contend that those acts were unconstitutional so far as they apply to this cause. 1st. The first act (March 8th, 1802) is unconstitutional, inasmuch as it goes to deprive the courts of all their power and jurisdiction, and to displace judges who have been guilty of no misbehavior in their offices. By the constitution, the judges, both of the supreme and the inferior courts, are to hold their offices during good behavior. So much has been recently said, and written, and published upon this subject, that it is irksome to repeat arguments which are now familiar to every one. There is no difference between the tenure of office of a judge of the supreme court and that of a judge of an inferior court. The reason of that tenure, to wit, the independence of the judge, is the same in both cases; indeed, the reason applies more strongly to the case of the inferior judges, because to them are exclusively assigned cases of life and death.

It is admitted, that congress have the power to modify, increase or diminish the power of the courts and the judges. But that is a power totally different from the power to destroy the courts, and to deprive them of all power and jurisdiction. The one is permitted by the constitution, the other is restrained by the regard which the constitution pays to the independence of the judges. They may modify the courts, but they cannot destroy them, if thereby they deprive a judge of his office. This provision of the constitution was intended to place the judges not only beyond the reach of executive power, of which the people are always jealous, but also to shield them from the attack of that party spirit which always predominates in popular assemblies.

It is admitted, that the powers of courts and judges may be altered and modified, but cannot be totally withdrawn. By the repealing law, the powers of both are entirely taken away.

But the laws are also unconstitutional, because they impose new duties upon the judges of the supreme court, and thereby infringe their independence; and because they are a legislative, instead of an executive appointment of judges to certain courts. By the constitution, all civil officers of the United States, including judges, are to be nominated and appointed by the president, by and with the advice and consent of the senate, and are to be commissioned by the president. The act of 29th April, 1802, appoints the "present Chief Justice of the supreme court," a judge of the court thereby established. He might as well have been appointed a judge of the circuit court of the district of Columbia, or the Mississippi territory. Besides, as judge of the supreme court, he could not exercise the duties or jurisdiction assigned to the court of the fifth circuit, because, by the constitution of the United States, the supreme court has only appellate jurisdiction; except in the two cases where a state or a foreign minister shall be a party. That jurisdiction of the supreme court, therefore, being appellate only, no judge of that court, as such, is authorized to hold a court of original jurisdiction. No act of congress can extend the original jurisdiction of the supreme court, beyond the bounds limited by the constitution.

A degree of respect is certainly due to precedents and past practice. If it be said, that the practice from the year 1789 to 1801 is against us; we answer, that the practice was wrong, that it crept in unawares, without consideration and without opposition; congress at last saw the error, and in 1801 they corrected it, and placed the judicial system on that ground upon which it ought always to have stood. By the [Judiciary Act] of 1801, the precedent was broken, so that now precedents are both ways. If there are twelve years' practice against us, there is one year for us. There has never been a judicial decision upon the subject. If the construction is as we contend, then the court below had no jurisdiction. The power of congress to transfer causes from one court to another is admitted; but if the [Repeal] acts of March and April 1802, are totally unconstitutional, they are void; the causes have not been transferred, and the court of the fourth circuit still exists, with all its powers and jurisdiction.

Gantt, for [Laird]. No error is relied on but the want of jurisdiction. It is admitted, that congress have power to transfer the jurisdiction of causes from one inferior court to another; and therefore, the question whether they have the power to deprive a judge of his office, does not belong to this case; has nothing at all to do with it. But admitting, for the sake of argument, that congress have not the latter power, yet an act may be constitutional in part, and unconstitutional in part. Congress have an express power, by the constitution, to constitute, and from time to time to ordain and establish tribunals inferior to the supreme court. The tenure of office may be a restraint in part to the exercise of this power, but cannot take away altogether the right to alter and modify existing courts.

As to the objection that the law of 1789 is unconstitutional, inasmuch as it gives circuit powers, or original jurisdiction, to judges of the supreme court; it is most probable, that the members of the first congress, many of them having been members of the convention which formed the constitution, best knew its meaning and true construction. But if they were mistaken, yet the acquiescence of the judges, and of the people, under that construction, has given it a sanction which ought not now to be questioned.

Lee, in reply. The acts of 1801 and 1802 were not alike, in abolishing the circuit courts. The former, in abolishing the then existing courts, did not turn the judges out of office, nor in any degree affect their independence; but the act of 1802 strikes off sixteen judges, at a stroke, drives them from their offices, and assigns their duties to others. An error was committed in 1789. That act was unconstitutional, but the act of 1801 restored the system to its constitutional limits. We now contend for the pure construction of the constitution, and hope it will be established, notwithstanding the precedent to the contrary.

The CHIEF JUSTICE, having tried the cause in the court below, declined giving an opinion.

PATTERSON [Paterson], J. (Judge Cushing being absent on account of ill health), delivered the opinion of the court.

Two reasons have been assigned by counsel for reversing the judgment on the forthcoming bond: 1. That as the bond was given for the delivery of property levied on by virtue of an execution issuing out of, and returnable to, a court for the fourth circuit, no other court could legally proceed upon the said bond. This is true, if there be no statutable provision to direct and authorize such proceeding. Congress have constitutional authority to establish, from time to time, such inferior tribunals as they may think proper; and to transfer a cause from one such tribunal to another. In this last particular, there are no words in the constitution to prohibit or restrain the exercise of legislative power. The present is a case of this kind. It is nothing more than the removal of the suit brought by Stuart against Laird, from the court of the fourth circuit to the court of the fifth circuit, which is authorized to proceed upon and carry it into full effect. This is apparent from the 9th section of the act entitled, "An act to amend the judicial system of the United States," passed the 29th of April 1802. The forthcoming bond is an appendage to the cause, or rather a component part of the proceedings.

2d. Another reason for reversal is, that the judges of the supreme court have no right to sit as circuit judges, not being appointed as such, or, in other words, that they ought to have distinct commissions for that purpose. To this objection, which is of recent date, it is sufficient to observe, that practice, and acquiescence under it, for a period of several years, commencing with the organization of the judicial system, affords an irresistible answer, and has indeed fixed the construction. It is a contemporary interpretation of the most forcible nature. This practical exposition is too strong and obstinate to be shaken or controlled. Of course, the question is at rest, and ought not now to be disturbed.

Judgement affirmed

Comment

Paterson avoided directly addressing the claim that the 1802 act had violated the constitutional guaranty of judicial tenure during good behavior, but his opinion for the Court signaled that body's acceptance of the repeal legislation.

Six

The First Years of the Marshall Court

During Jefferson's administration, the U.S. Supreme Court was substantially in eclipse. The Court acquiesced in the Republicans' repeal of the "Midnight Judges Act" and took no action to aid the Adams appointees whose commissions Jefferson withheld. Justice Samuel Chase eventually provoked his own impeachment by his partisan attacks on the Republicans from the bench. The other justices took a much lower profile, and the new chief justice, John Marshall, was widely regarded by nationalist Federalists as a political trimmer tainted by opposition ideas about the Constitution.

Oliver Wolcott
Letter to Fisher Ames
(December 29, 1799)[85]

Marshall's disavowal of the Alien and Sedition acts and his subsequent election to the House deepened nationalist concerns over his potential role in Congress. Already in October 1798, George Cabot had warned Timothy Pickering that Marshall "has much to learn on the subject of a practicable system of free government for the United States." The following April, Cabot wrote Rufus King that Marshall "ought not to be attacked in the [Federalist] newspapers" because his "mind and disposition" were sound; Cabot did not deny, however, that Marshall's constitutional opinions were affected by "the influence of the atmosphere of Virginia, which doubtless makes everyone who breathes it visionary and, upon the subject of free government, incredibly credulous." Fisher Ames was less willing to forgive Marshall's public criticism of the Sedition Act of 1798: "Excuses may palliate; future zeal in the cause may partially atone; but his character is done for . . . False Federalists or such as act wrong from false fears should be dealt hardly with, if I were Jupiter Tonans." On Marshall's arrival in Philadelphia for the first session of the Sixth Congress, Oliver Wolcott wrote Ames his impressions of Marshall:

. . . A number of distinguished men appear from the southward, who are not pledged by any act to support the system of the last Congress; these men will pay great respect to the opinions of General Marshall; he is doubtless a man of virtue and distinguished talents, but he will think much of the State of Virginia, and is too much disposed to govern the world according to rules of logic; he will read and expound the Constitution as if it were a penal statute, and will sometimes be embarrassed with doubts of which his friends will not perceive the importance . . .

John Marshall
Speech in the U.S. House of Representatives
(March 7, 1800)[86]

Congressman Marshall's performance in Congress was as erratic as Wolcott had feared. Although Marshall was supportive of President Adams and generally endorsed Federalist legislation, he sometimes displayed in important situations what Wolcott and others regarded as Virginian and "visionary" biases. Marshall, for example, labored successfully to include a provision for the right to a jury trial in a proposed bankruptcy act, an idea opposed by most Federalists and supported by Republicans. He opposed a Federalist attempt to create a joint committee that would give the Federalist-controlled Congress authority to determine the electoral outcome of the 1800 election. Most significantly, from the standpoint of political symbolism, he initially voted to repeal the Sedition Act of 1798, and then joined the Republicans in voting against repeal when an amendment to the repeal bill was added that would have recognized federal common-law jurisdiction over seditious libel. In the speech excerpted below, Marshall insisted on a narrowing definition of the powers of the federal courts.

. . . By the constitution, the judicial power of the United States is extended to all *cases in law and equity* arising under the constitution, laws and treaties of the United States; but the resolutions under discussion declare the judicial power to extend to *all questions* arising under the constitution, treaties and laws of the United States. The difference between the constitution and the resolutions was material and apparent. A case in law or equity was a term well understood, and of limited signification. It was a controversy between parties which had taken a shape for judicial decision. If the judicial power extended to every *question* under the constitution it would involve almost every subject proper for legislative discussion and decision; if to every *question* under the laws and treaties of the United States it would involve almost every subject on which the executive could act. The division of power which the gentleman had stated, could exist no longer, and the other departments would be swallowed up by the judiciary. But it was apparent that the resolutions had essentially misrepresented the constitution. He did not charge the gentleman from New York, with intentional misrepresentation; he would not attribute to him such an artifice in any case, much less in a case where detection was so easy and so certain. Yet this substantial departure from the constitution, in resolutions affecting substantially to unite it, was not the less worthy of remark for being unintentional. It manifested the course of reasoning by which the gentleman had himself been misled, and his judgment betrayed into the opinions those resolutions expressed.

By extending the judicial power to all *cases in law and equity*, the constitution had never been understood, to confer on that department, any political power whatever. To come within this description, a question must assume a legal form, for forensic litigation, and judicial decision. There must be parties to come into court, who can be reached by its process, and bound by its power; whose rights admit of ultimate decision by a tribunal to which they are bound to submit . . .

Theodore Sedgwick
Letter to Rufus King
(May 11, 1800)[87]

After working with Marshall for a congressional session, Speaker of the House Theodore Sedgwick gave him a mixed review.

...Marshall was looked up to as the man whose great and commanding genius was to enlighten & direct the national councils. This was the general sentiment, while some, and those of no inconsiderable importance, calculating on his foolish declaration, relative to the alien & sedition laws, thought him temporizing while others deemed him feeble.

None had in my opinion justly appreciated his character. As his character has stamped itself on the measures of the present session, I am desirous of letting you know how I view it.

He is a man of very affectionate disposition, a great simplicity of manners and honest & honorable in all his conduct.

He is attached to pleasures, with convivial habits strongly fixed.

He is indolent, therefore; and indisposed to take part in the common business of the house.

He has a strong attachment to popularity but indisposed to sacrifice to it his integrity; hence it is that he is disposed on all popular subjects to feel the public pulse and hence results indecision and *an obsession* of doubt.

Doubts suggested by him create in more feeble minds those which are irremovable. He is disposed ... to express great respect for the sovereign people and to quote their opinions as an evidence of the truth.

The latter is of all things the most destructive of personal independence & of that weight of character which a great man ought to possess.

This gentleman, when aroused, has strong reasoning powers; they are almost unequalled. But before they are excited, he has frequently, nearly, destroyed any impression from them ...

John Marshall
Letter to St. George Tucker
(November 27, 1800)[88]

In early 1800 a pamphlet on "How Far the Common Law of England Is the Law of the Federal Government" appeared. Although unsigned, it was known to be written by St. George Tucker, judge of the Virginia General Court, professor of law at William and Mary, and prominent Republican jurist. The pamphlet predictably denied that "any grant of general jurisdiction in cases at common law" had been conferred on the federal courts by the Constitution, though Tucker conceded that, in cases where the federal court otherwise had jurisdiction, it might look to the "maxims and rules of proceedings" of the common law in order to "govern and direct the course of proceeding." Tucker politely sent his friend the Federalist John Marshall a copy of the pamphlet, and Marshall replied:

Dear Sir:

I had the pleasure a few days past of receiving a pamphlet written by you on the question how far the common law is the law of the United States for which I thank you. I have read it with attention & you will perhaps be surprised at my saying that I do not suppose we should essentially disagree. In political controversy it often happens that the precise opinion of the adversary is not understood, & that we are at much labor to disprove propositions which have never been maintained. A stronger evidence of this cannot I think be given than the manner in which the references to the common law have been treated. The opinion which has been controverted is, that the common law of England has not been adopted as the common law of America by the constitution of the United States. I do not believe one man can be found who maintains the affirmative of this proposition. Neither in public nor in private have I ever heard it advocated, & I am as entirely confident as I can be at anything of the sort, that it never has been advocated. This strange & absurd doctrine was first attributed to the judiciary of the United States by some frothy newspaper publications which appeared in Richmond something more than twelve months past, but I never suspected that an attempt would be made to represent this as a serious opinion entertained by respectable men, until I saw the argument contained in the report of a committee of the house of Delegates in Virginia [the Report of 1800]. You will pardon me for saying that notwithstanding the respectability of the author of this report, I could not read the part of it respecting the common law without being reminded of a ludicrous story told by Mr. Mason in the house of Delegates in Williamsburg of a man who amused himself by taking such a position as to cast his shadow on a wall & then butt at it as at a real enemy. So this report has gratuitously attributed to certain gentlemen an opinion never entertained & has thus very gravely demonstrated that the opinion is founded in error.

What the precise opinion entertained on this subject may be I do not profess to know but I believe that in the general definition of the principle sensible men of the two parties would not disagree very materially. In the application of principles there would perhaps be more difference than in this definition.

With respect to the case of Isaac Williams which you have mentioned in a note, I cannot believe that you & Judge Ellesworth (if I understand that case rightly) would disagree. Isaac Williams was prosecuted on two separate indictments—the one for privateering under a French commission against the British & the other for privateering under the same commission against his own countrymen. He was found guilty on both indictments. In the one case he was guilty of an offense against a public treaty of the United States & in other of an offense against the United States on the high seas. I believe it is not controverted that both these crimes are clearly punishable in the federal courts. The defence set up, so far as I understand it, was that by taking a commission in the service of France which was itself a [statutory] crime, Isaac Williams withdrew himself from the cognizance of our courts by ceasing to be an American citizen. I mistake your opinions very much if you would have countenanced this defence.

In the case of Williams the common law [which rejected the right of unilateral expatriation] was not relied on as giving the court jurisdiction, but came in incidentally as part of the law of a case of which the court had complete & exclusive possession. I do not understand you as questioning the propriety of thus applying the common law, not of England, but of our own country.

My own opinion is that our ancestors brought with them the laws of England both statute & common law as existing at the settlement of each colony, so far as they were applicable to our situation.

That on our revolution the preexisting law of each state remained so far as it was not changed either expressly or necessarily by the nature of the governments which we adopted.

That on adopting the existing constitution of the United States the common & statute law of each state would apply themselves to magistrates of the general as well as to magistrates of the particular government. I do not recollect ever to have heard the opinions of a leading gentleman of the opposition which conflict with these. Mr. Gallatin in a very acute speech on the sedition law was understood by me to avow them. On the other side it was contended, not that the common law gave the courts jurisdiction in cases of sedition but that the constitution gave it.

Comment

As Marshall shrewdly observed, the 1798–1800 debate over a federal common law was bedeviled by persistent confusion over exactly what was, or was not, being affirmed or denied. The statement "there is a federal common law" could and did bear several distinct meanings. The most expansive nationalist position was to suggest that the English common law was adopted in its entirety by the Constitution or by the national character of the federal government, thus giving federal courts both jurisdiction and substantive law to apply even in the absence of any congressional action. Republicans like Tucker often accused Federalists of holding this view, and in this letter Marshall vigorously denied that it was "a serious opinion entertained by respectable men." (A few years later, in *Clarke v. Bazadone*, Marshall, as chief justice, would be presented with precisely this argument as to Supreme Court jurisdiction.) Most nationalists, however, believed that the *statutory* jurisdiction accorded federal circuit courts by the 1789 Judiciary Act permitted these courts to use common-law definitions of nonstatutory offenses against federal authority. In the preceding letter, Marshall seems to be denying the existence of nonstatutory federal crimes, and to be confining the common law's role to that of an interpretive tool for the construction of the Constitution and federal statutes, a view essentially identical to that of Republicans Tucker and Albert Gallatin.

The Limits of Jurisdiction

For modern lawyers, *Marbury v. Madison* is the towering constitutional decision of the early Marshall Court because it is now treated as the case "establishing" judicial review. As has been noted, however, by 1800 the legitimacy of judicial review (if not its precise relationship to constitutional decision-making by other branches) was relatively uncontroversial. In its original setting, *Marbury* was significant for two quite different reasons. The case's place in the struggle to determine the judiciary's power to control executive lawlessness (as perceived by the courts) is addressed in Chapter 8 below; here the focus is on its importance as one indication of the early Marshall Court's attitude toward its own jurisdiction.

High Federalists such as Wolcott had feared that Marshall would take a narrow word-and-logic-chopping approach to constitutional questions, and Marshall himself had displayed a real concern to preserve the constitutional and statutory limits on federal-court jurisdiction. In a series of cases beginning with *Marbury*, the early Marshall Court declined to exercise jurisdiction with which it arguably was entrusted. Even *Stuart*, where the Court refused to rule unconstitutional the 1802 repeal act, fits the pattern: by upholding the constitutionality of their statutory obligation to ride circuit, the justices accepted Congress's power to control federal court jurisdiction.

Marbury v. Madison
5 U.S. (1 Cranch) 137 (Feb. 24, 1803)

Secretary of State John Marshall failed to deliver a sealed commission as a federal justice of the peace to William Marbury prior to the end of the Adams administration, and on

coming into office President Jefferson ordered the new secretary of state, James Madison, to withhold any commissions of "midnight" appointees still in the executive's possession. Marbury sought a writ of *mandamus* against Madison from the Supreme Court, acting under its original jurisdiction. Marshall first concluded that Marbury was entitled to the commission and to judicial aid in procuring it. Marshall then turned to the question of the Court's jurisdiction:

Chief Justice MARSHALL delivered the opinion of the Court: . . .

This, then, is a plain case for a *mandamus*, either to deliver the commission, or a copy of it from the record; and it only remains to be inquired, whether it can issue from this court?

The act to establish the judicial courts of the United States authorizes the supreme court, "to issue writs of *mandamus*, in cases warranted by the principles and usages of law, to any courts appointed or persons holding office, under the authority of the United States." The secretary of state, being a person holding an office under the authority of the United States, is precisely within the letter of this description; and if this court is not authorized to issue a writ of *mandamus* to such an officer, it must be because the law is unconstitutional, and therefore, absolutely incapable of conferring the authority, and assigning the duties which its words purport to confer and assign.

The constitution vests the whole judicial power of the United States in one supreme court, and such inferior courts as congress shall, from time to time, ordain and establish. This power is expressly extended to all cases arising under the laws of the United States; and consequently, in some form, may be exercised over the present case; because the right claimed is given by a law of the United States.

In the distribution of this power, it is declared, that "the supreme court shall have original jurisdiction, in all cases affecting ambassadors, other public ministers and consuls, and those in which a state shall be a party. In all other cases, the supreme court shall have appellate jurisdiction." It has been insisted, at the bar, that as the original grant of jurisdiction to the supreme and inferior courts, is general, and the clause, assigning original jurisdiction to the supreme court, contains no negative or restrictive words, the power remains to the legislature, to assign original jurisdiction to that court, in other cases than those specified in the article which has been recited; provided those cases belong to the judicial power of the United States.

If it had been intended to leave it in the discretion of the legislature, to apportion the judicial power between the supreme and inferior courts, according to the will of that body, it would certainly have been useless to have proceeded further than to have defined the judicial power, and the tribunals in which it should be vested. The subsequent part of the section is mere surplusage—is entirely without meaning, if such is to be the construction. If congress remains at liberty to give this court appellate jurisdiction, where the constitution has declared their jurisdiction shall be original; and original jurisdiction where the constitution has declared it shall be appellate; the distribution of jurisdiction, made in the constitution, is form without substance. Affirmative words are often, in their operation, negative of other objects than those affirmed; and in this case, a negative or exclusive sense must be given to them, or they have no operation at all.

It cannot be presumed, that any clause in the constitution is intended to be without effect; and therefore, such a construction is inadmissible, unless the words require it. If the solicitude of the convention, respecting our peace with foreign powers, induced a provision that the supreme court should take original jurisdiction in cases which might be supposed to affect them; yet the clause would have proceeded no further than to provide for such cases, if no further restriction on the powers of congress had been intended. That they should have appellate jurisdiction in all other cases, with such exceptions as congress might make, is no restriction; unless the words be deemed exclusive of original jurisdiction.

When an instrument organizing, fundamentally, a judicial system, divides it into one supreme, and so many inferior courts as the legislature may ordain and establish; then enumerates its powers, and proceeds so far to distribute them, as to define the jurisdiction of the supreme court, by declaring the cases in which it shall take original jurisdiction, and that in others it shall take appellate jurisdiction, the plain import of the words seems to be, that in one class of cases, its jurisdiction is original, and not appellate; in the other, it is appellate, and not original. If any other construction would render the clause inoperative, that is an additional reason for rejecting such other construction, and for adhering to their obvious meaning. To enable this court, then, to issue a *mandamus*, it must be shown to be an exercise of appellate jurisdiction, or to be necessary to enable them to exercise appellate jurisdiction.

It has been stated at the bar, that the appellate jurisdiction may be exercised in a variety of forms, and that if it be the will of the legislature that a *mandamus* should be used for that purpose, that will must be obeyed. This is true, yet the jurisdiction must be appellate, not original. It is the essential criterion of appellate jurisdiction, that it revises and corrects the proceedings in a cause already instituted, and does not create that cause. Although, therefore, a *mandamus* may be directed to courts, yet to issue such a writ to an officer, for the delivery of a paper, is, in effect, the same as to sustain an original action for that paper, and therefore, seems not to belong to appellate, but to original jurisdiction. Neither is it necessary in such a case as this, to enable the court to exercise its appellate jurisdiction. The authority, therefore, given to the supreme court by the act establishing the judicial courts of the United States, to issue writs of *mandamus* to public officers, appears not to be warranted by the constitution; and it becomes necessary to inquire, whether a jurisdiction so conferred can be exercised.

The question, whether an act, repugnant to the constitution, can become the law of the land, is a question deeply interesting to the United States; but, happily, not of an intricacy proportioned to its interest. It seems only necessary to recognize certain principles, supposed to have been long and well established, to decide it. That the people have an original right to establish, for their future government, such principles as, in their opinion, shall most conduce to their own happiness, is the basis on which the whole American fabric has been erected. The exercise of this original right is a very great exertion; nor can it, nor ought it, to be frequently repeated. The principles, therefore, so established, are deemed fundamental; and as the authority from which they proceed is supreme, and can seldom act, they are designed to be permanent.

This original and supreme will organizes the government, and assigns to different departments their respective powers. It may either stop here, or establish certain limits not to be transcended by those departments. The government of the United States is of the latter description. The powers of the legislature are defined and limited; and that those limits may not be mistaken or forgotten, the constitution is written. To what purpose are powers limited, and to what purpose is that limitation committed to writing, if these limits may, at any time, be passed by those intended to be restrained? The distinction between a government with limited and unlimited powers is abolished, if those limits do not confine the persons on whom they are imposed, and if acts prohibited and acts allowed, are of equal obligation. It is a proposition too plain to be contested, that the constitution controls any legislative act repugnant to it; or that the legislature may alter the constitution by an ordinary act.

Between these alternatives, there is no middle ground. The constitution is either a superior paramount law, unchangeable by ordinary means, or it is on a level with ordinary legislative acts, and, like other acts, is alterable when the legislature shall please to alter it. If the former part of the alternative be true, then a legislative act, contrary to the constitution, is not law: if the latter part be true, then written constitutions are absurd attempts, on the part of the people, to limit a power, in its own nature, illimitable.

Certainly, all those who have framed written constitutions contemplate them as forming the fundamental and paramount law of the nation, and consequently, the theory of every such government must be, that an act of the legislature, repugnant to the constitution, is void. This theory is essentially attached to a written constitution, and is, consequently, to be considered, by this court, as one of the fundamental principles of our society. It is not, therefore, to be lost sight of, in the further consideration of this subject.

If an act of the legislature, repugnant to the constitution, is void, does it, notwithstanding its invalidity, bind the courts, and oblige them to give it effect? Or, in other words, though it be not law, does it constitute a rule as operative as if it was a law? This would be to overthrow, in fact, what was established in theory; and would seem, at first view, an absurdity too gross to be insisted on. It shall, however, receive a more attentive consideration.

It is emphatically, the province and duty of the judicial department, to say what the law is. Those who apply the rule to particular cases, must of necessity expound and interpret that rule. If two laws conflict with each other, the courts must decide on the operation of each. So, if a law be in opposition to the constitution; if both the law and the constitution apply to a particular case, so that the court must either decide that case, conformable to the law, disregarding the constitution; or conformable to the constitution, disregarding the law; the court must determine which of these conflicting rules governs the case; this is of the very essence of judicial duty. If then, the courts are to regard the constitution, and the constitution is superior to any ordinary act of the legislature, the constitution, and not such ordinary act, must govern the case to which they both apply.

Those, then, who controvert the principle, that the constitution is to be considered, in court, as a paramount law, are reduced to the necessity of maintaining that courts must close their eyes on the constitution, and see only the law. This doctrine would subvert the very foundation of all written constitutions. It would declare that an act which, according to the principles and theory of our government, is entirely void, is yet, in practice, completely obligatory. It would declare, that if the legislature shall do what is expressly forbidden, such act, notwithstanding the express prohibition, is in reality effectual. It would be giving to the legislature a practical and real omnipotence, with the same breath which professes to restrict their powers within narrow limits. It is prescribing limits, and declaring that those limits may be passed at pleasure. That it thus reduces to nothing, what we have deemed the greatest improvement on political institutions, a written constitution, would, of itself, be sufficient, in America, where written constitutions have been viewed with so much reverence, for rejecting the construction. But the peculiar expressions of the constitution of the United States furnish additional arguments in favor of its rejection. The judicial power of the United States is extended to all cases arising under the constitution. Could it be the intention of those who gave this power, to say, that in using it, the constitution should not be looked into? That a case arising under the constitution should be decided, without examining the instrument under which it arises? This is too extravagant to be maintained. In some cases, then, the constitution must be looked into by the judges. And if they can open it at all, what part of it are they forbidden to read or to obey?

. . . [I]t is apparent, that the framers of the constitution contemplated that instrument as a rule for the government of courts, as well as of the legislature. Why otherwise does it direct the judges to take an oath to support it? This oath certainly applies in an especial manner, to their conduct in their official character. How immoral to impose it on them, if they were to be used as the instruments, and the knowing instruments, for violating what they swear to support!

The oath of office, too, imposed by the legislature, is completely demonstrative of the legislative opinion on this subject. It is in these words: "I do solemnly swear, that I will administer justice, without respect to persons, and do equal right to the poor and to the rich; and that I will faithfully and impartially discharge all the duties incumbent on me as ———, according to the best of my abilities and understanding, agreeably to the constitution and laws of the United States." Why does a judge swear to discharge his duties agreeably to the constitution of the United States, if that constitution forms no rule for his government? if it is closed upon him and cannot be inspected by him? If such be the real state of things, this is worse than solemn mockery. To prescribe, or to take this oath, becomes equally a crime.

It is also not entirely unworthy of observation, that in declaring what shall be the supreme law of the land, the constitution itself is first mentioned; and not the laws of the United States, generally, but those only which shall be made in pursuance of the constitution, have that rank.

Thus, the particular phraseology of the constitution of the United States confirms and strengthens the principle, supposed to be essential to all written constitutions, that a law repugnant to the constitution is void; and that courts, as well as other departments, are bound by that instrument.

Comment

In asserting the power to declare congressional statutes void because un-constitutional, Marshall adopted a rationale for the power very similar to that propounded by Judge Nelson in *Kamper v. Hawkins* or Congressman Bayard in the 1802 debates over the bill to repeal the "Midnight Judges Act." Unlike Roane and Tucker in *Kamper*, Marshall did not appear to assert any special judicial commission to defend the Constitution: judicial review, as he de-scribed it, was no more than what the judges' duty and oath required of them in the ordinary course of deciding which rule of law governed a particular case. The institutional modesty of Marshall's argument, however, may have obscured deeper similarities between his views and those of Tucker. The latter had drawn a close connection between the (Virginia) constitution's written character, its consequent availability as positive law, and the "duty and office of the judiciary . . . to expound *what the law is.*" Marshall made the same associations, but left it unclear as to whether he accepted Tucker's further conclusions that constitutional interpretation was "exclusively" a judicial func-tion and that the interpretations of the highest court in a jurisdiction were to be taken "as expounding, in their truest sense," the constitution.

Modern scholars sometimes criticize Marshall's interpretation of article three's allocation of federal jurisdiction as forced, and they often label his reading of the Judiciary Act as unnecessary or implausible. In Marshall's own context, neither criticism is entirely apposite. Rigid distinctions between var-ious kinds of jurisdiction were common in the founding era (compare *Kamper*); and Marshall's construction of the Judiciary Act treated it, not unrealistically, as an attempt to give the Supreme Court a general supervisory power similar to that exercised by the Court of King's Bench.

Clarke v. Bazadone
5 U.S. (1 Cranch) 211 (Feb. 1803)

This was a writ of error issued from this court to the general court for the territory northwest of the river Ohio, to reverse a judgment rendered in that court against Clarke, the plaintiff in error, in favor of Bazadone, on a foreign attachment, for $12,200 damages, and $95.30 costs.

The general court of the North-western Territory was established by the ordinance of the old congress, under the confederation, and the principal question was, whether a writ of error would lie from this court to the general court of that territory? There was no appearance for the defendant in error.

[*Mason*], for the plaintiff in error, contended: 1st. That this court possesses a general superintending power over all the other courts of the United States, resulting from the nature of a supreme court, independent of any express provisions of the constitution or laws of the United States. 2d. That this court has the power, under the constitution of the United States.

1. It is a general principle, that the proceedings of an inferior tribunal are to be corrected by the superior, unless the latter is expressly restrained from exercising such a control. This is a principle of the laws of that country from which we derive most of our principles of jurisprudence, and is so intimately connected with them, that it is difficult to separate them.

In the Saxon times, the Wittenagemote was the supreme court, and had the general superintendence. But in the time of William the Conqueror, the *aula regis* was established as the sovereign court of the kingdom, and to that court devolved all the former judicial power of the Wittenagemote; the power of superintending the other courts was derived from the principle of supremacy. A writ of error is a commission to judges of a superior court, by which they are authorized to examine the record, upon which a judgment was given in an inferior court, and on such examination, to reverse or affirm the same, according to law. The court of king's bench superintends the proceedings of all other inferior courts, and by the plenitude of its power corrects the errors of those courts; hence it is, that a writ of error lies in that court, to a judgment given in the king's bench in Ireland. And upon a judgment in Calais, when under the subjection of the king of England, a writ of error lay in the king's bench. A writ of error would have laid to the king's bench from these colonies, before the revolution, but for the particular provisions of charters, &c. Wherever a new jurisdiction is erected by act of parliament, and the court acts as a court of record, according to the course of the common law, a writ of error lies on their judgments. The power is inherent in every superior court, to revise the judgments of its inferior.

2. By the constitution of the United States, Art. III, the judicial power is vested in one supreme court, and such inferior courts as congress shall, from time to time, ordain and establish; and shall extend to all cases arising under the constitution and laws of the United States, and to controversies in which the United States shall be a party. And the supreme court is to have appellate jurisdiction, in all these cases, with such exceptions, and under such regulations, as congress shall make. Congress has made no exception of the present case; and no regulation of congress was necessary to give this court the appellate power. It derives it from the constitution itself.

This is a case arising under the laws of the United States. The very existence of the court whose judgments is complained of, is derived from the United States. The laws adopted for the Northwestern Territory derive their whole obligatory effect from the ordinance of the old congress, and are, in fact, laws of the United States, although copied from state laws. All power and authority exercised in that territory have emanated from the United States; and all offences there committed are against the authority of the United States.

If, then, this is a case, by the constitution, cognisable by the judicial authority of the United States; if, by the constitution, this court has appellate jurisdiction in all such cases, and if this case is not within any exception made by the constitution, or by any act of congress, nothing is wanting but to devise a mode to bring the cause before this court. The writ of error is the common and well-known process in like cases, and by the 14th section of the judiciary act of 1789, every court of the United States is expressly authorized "to issue writs of *scire facias*, *habeas corpus*, and all other writs not specifically provided for by statute, which may be necessary for the exercise of their respective jurisdictions, and agreeable to the principles and usages of law." If, then, the court has jurisdiction, no difficulty can occur as to a mode of exercising it.

THE COURT quashed the writ of error, on the ground, that the act of congress had not authorized an appeal or writ of error from the general court of the Northwestern Territory, and, therefore, although from the manifest errors on the face of the record, they felt every disposition to support the writ of error, they were of opinion, they could not take cognisance [*sic*] of the case.

Comment

Clarke continued the Marshall Court's limitation of its jurisdiction to constitutional grants of jurisdiction by Congress. The Court's abrupt dismissal of counsel's argument that it could exercise a general supervisory power like that of the King's Bench was an implicit repudiation of part of the nationalist constitutionalism of the 1790s: in the opinion of the Court, federal-court jurisdiction was not co-extensive by definition with the reach of congressional power.

Hepburn v. Ellzey
6 U.S. (2 Cranch) 443 (Feb. 1805)

This was a question certified from the Circuit Court for the fifth circuit, holden in the Virginia district, on which the opinions of the judges of that court were opposed.

The certificate set forth that "in this cause it occurred as a question, whether Hepburn & Dundas, the plaintiffs in this cause, who are citizens and residents of the district of Columbia, and are so stated in the pleadings, can maintain an action in this court against the defendant, who is a citizen and inhabitant of the commonwealth of Virginia, and is also stated so to be in the pleadings, or whether, for want of jurisdiction, the said suit ought not to be dismissed."

E. J. Lee, for the plaintiffs.—This question arises under the 2d section of the 3d article of the constitution of the United States, which defines the jurisdiction of the courts of the United States. The particular words of the section which apply to the question, are those declaring that the jurisdiction of the courts of the United States shall extend "to controversies between citizens of different states." If such words are used in the constitution as, according to their literal meaning, will give jurisdiction to the court, it is all that is necessary to be established.

It is essential, in determining this question, to ascertain the import of the term "states," which, in itself, is a vague expression. It will sometimes mean an extent of country within certain limits, within which the authority of the neighboring country cannot be lawfully exercised. It sometimes means the government which is established in separate parts of a territory occupied by a political society. It may also be said to be a society by which a multitude of people unite together under the dependence of a superior power for protection. And sometimes, it means a multitude of people united by a communion of interest and by common laws. This is the definition given by Cicero.

Either of the above definitions will bring the district within the meaning of the constitution. It is certainly such an extent of country as excludes from within its limits the force and operation of the laws of the governments which adjoin it. There exists within it a political society, with a government over it. That government, for all general concerns of the society, is the congress and President of the United States. And as to its local concerns, there are subordinate authorities under the superintendence of the national government. This political society is dependent upon the superior power of the United States.

It is not essential to the formation of a state, that the members of it should have the power, in all cases, of electing their own officers; but it is sufficient that there are certain rules laid down either by themselves, or those by whom they have submitted to be governed, for their conduct.

The people of the district are governed by a power to which they have freely submitted. They do not possess, in as great degree, the rights of sovereignty, as those people who inhabit the states. And if the free exercise of all the rights of sovereignty, uncontrolled by any other power, is essential in the formation of a state, none of those sections of the country which form the United States are entitled strictly to the appellation of a "state;" for there are certain rights of sovereignty which they cannot exercise in their state capacity, such as regulating commerce, making peace and war, &c.

The term "states," as used in the constitution, may, according to the subject-matter, be understood in either of the above senses. It has been understood by a majority of the judges of this court, in the case of *Chisholm's Executors v. State of Georgia*, to mean the government.

The idea, that those territories which are under the exclusive government of the United States, are to be considered in some respects as included in the term "states," as used in the constitution, is supported by the acts of congress. In the 2d paragraph of the 2d section of the 4th article of the constitution, it is declared, that "a person charged in any state with treason, felony or other crime, who shall flee from justice and be found in another state, shall, on demand of the executive authority of the state from which he fled, be delivered up to be removed to the state having jurisdiction of the crime." It is also declared in the same article of the constitution, that "no person held to service or labor in one state, under the laws thereof, escaping into another, shall, in consequence of any law or regulation therein, be discharged from such service or labor, but shall be delivered up on claim of the party to whom such service or labor may be due."

Congress, in prescribing the mode of executing the powers contained in these clauses of the constitution, passed a law . . . which declares, "that whenever the executive authority of any state in the union, or of either of the territories northwest or south of the river Ohio, shall demand any person as a fugitive from justice, of the executive authority of any such state or territory to which such person shall have fled," and shall produce such evidence of the fact as is prescribed by the act, the person so escaping shall be surrendered, &c. A similar provision, with respect to persons held to labor or service under the laws of the states or territories, is contained in the same act of congress.

If these territories are not, as to some purposes, included in the term "states," used in the above clauses of the constitution, congress could not constitutionally pass a law making it the duty of the executive of a state to comply with such a requisition of the executive of one of those territories. If they are thus included, why may they not also be included in that part of the constitution which uses the same term, "states," in defining the jurisdiction of the courts? The citizens of the territories are subject to the same evil, if they are obliged to resort to the state courts, which was intended to be remedied by that clause of the constitution which authorizes citizens of different states to resort to the federal courts. And if, being within the same evil, authorized congress to give a latitude to the term "states," in one part of the constitution, the same reason will authorize the same construction of the same term in another part.

The words of the constitution only authorize such a requisition to be made by the executive of a state, upon the executive of another state. It must, therefore, be acknowledged, either that the territories are included in the term states, or that the act of congress is unconstitutional. As a further proof of the same construction of the word state, congress, by the 6th section of the act supplementary to the act concerning the district of Columbia, have enacted, that in all cases where the constitution or laws of the United States provide that criminals and fugitives from justice, or persons held to labor in any state, escaping into another state, shall be delivered up, the chief justice of the said district shall be, and he is hereby required to cause to be apprehended and delivered up such criminal, &c., who shall be found within the district.

Independently of these considerations, it seems to be agreeable to the first principles of government, that all persons who are under the peculiar and exclusive government and protection of a particular power, have, as it were, a natural claim upon that power for protection and redress of wrongs. And that the courts of the United States are the most proper tribunals to which the people of the District of Columbia can apply for redress, in all cases where the aggressor can be found within the jurisdiction of those courts. It seems to be a denial of that protection which the United States are bound to afford to those who reside under their exclusive jurisdiction, to say, that because you may sue your debtor in a foreign tribunal (if I may use the expression), therefore, you shall not resort to our own courts, although your debtor may be found within our jurisdiction. The framers of the constitution could never have supposed it necessary to declare, in express terms, that the courts of the United States should have power to hear and decide on the complaints of one of the citizens of those districts that were under the exclusive government and care of the United States, to whom alone allegiance was due. They could not have intended to deny to that part of the citizens of the United States who inhabit the territories, the privileges which are granted to citizens of particular States, and even to foreigners; especially, the right of resorting to an impartial tribunal of justice. When they permitted aliens to resort either to the state or to the federal courts, they could not mean to confine one of their own exclusive citizens to a remedy in the state courts alone. It would be strange, that those citizens who owe no allegiance but to the United States, should be debarred from going into the courts of the United States for redress, when that privilege is granted to others, in like circumstances, who owe allegiance to a foreign, or to a state government.

C. Lee, contra.—This is a new question, which has arisen in consequence of the cession of the district of Columbia, by the States of Virginia and Maryland, to the United States.

The words of the constitution do not take in the case, and the act of congress is also too narrow. The constitution is a limited grant of power. Nothing is to be presumed but what is expressed.

It is contended, that a citizen of the district of Columbia is a citizen of a state. It is said, that he is a citizen of the United States, and not being a citizen of the same state with the defendant, he must be a citizen of a different state. But there may be a citizen of the United States, who is not a citizen of any one of the states. The expression a citizen of a state, has a constitutional meaning. The states are not absolutely sovereigns, but (if I may use the expression) they are demi-sovereigns. The word state has a meaning peculiar to the United States. It means, a certain political society forming a constituent part of the union. There can be no state, unless it be entitled to a representation in the senate. It must have its separate executive, legislative and judicial powers. The term may also comprehend a number of other ideas.

Even if the constitution of the United States authorizes a more enlarged jurisdiction than the judiciary act of 1789 has given, yet the court can take no jurisdiction which is not given by the act. I, therefore, call for the law which gives a jurisdiction in this case. The jurisdiction given to the federal courts, in cases between citizens of different states, was, at the time of the adoption of the constitution, supposed to be of very little importance to the people.

In no case from any one of the territories has this court ever considered itself as having jurisdiction; and in that of *Clarke v. Bazadone* the writ of error was quashed, because the act of congress had not given this court appellate jurisdiction in cases from the territories.

This is not a case between citizens of different States, within the meaning of the constitution. And in the case of *Bingham v. Cabot* [1798] it was decided by this court, that the courts of the United States were courts of limited jurisdiction, and that it must appear upon the record, that the parties were citizens of different States, in order to support the jurisdiction.

E. J. Lee, in reply.—A law was not necessary to give the federal courts that jurisdiction which is provided for by the constitution. It was only necessary to limit the amount of the claims which should come before the different inferior courts. If a demand should be made by the executive power of the district of Columbia, upon the executive of a state to deliver up a fugitive from justice, the constitution would apply, and oblige the state executive to respect the demand. If the term state is to have the limited construction contended for by the opposite counsel, the citizens of Columbia will be deprived of the general rights of citizens of the United States. They will be in a worse condition than aliens.

By the 4th article of the constitution of the United States, §1, "Full faith and credit shall be given, in each state, to the public acts, records and judicial proceedings on every other state." If the district of Columbia is not to be considered as a state for this purpose, there is no obligation upon the states to give faith or credit to the records or judicial proceedings of this district. But congress, in carrying into effect this provision of the constitution . . . has expressly declared, that it "shall apply as well to the public acts," &c., "of the respective territories of the United States, and countries subject to the jurisdiction of the United States, as to the public acts," &c., "of the several States," thereby giving another clear legislative construction to the word states, conformable to that for which we contend.

Again, by the 9th section of the 1st article of the constitution of the United States, "no tax or duty shall be laid on articles exported from any state." Can congress lay a tax or duty on articles exported from the district of Columbia, without a violation of the constitution? By the same section, "no preference shall be given by any regulation of commerce or revenue to the ports of one state over those of another." Can congress constitutionally give a preference to the ports of the district of Columbia over those of any of the States? The same section says, "nor shall vessels bound to or from one state be obliged to enter, clear or pay duties on another." Can vessels sailing to or from the district of Columbia be obliged to enter, clear or pay duties in Maryland or Virginia? Yet all this may be done, if the rigid construction contended for, be given to the word *state*.

It is true, that the citizens of Columbia are not entitled to the elective franchise, in as full a manner as the citizens of states. They have no vote in the choice of president, vice-president, senators and representatives in congress. But in this, they are not singular. More than seven-eighths of the free white inhabitants of Virginia are in the same situation. Of the white population of Virginia, one-half are females; half of the males probably are under age; and not more than one-half of the residue are freeholders, and entitled to vote at elections. The same case happens in some degree in all the states. A great majority are not entitled to vote. But in every other respect, the citizens of Columbia are entitled to all the privileges and immunities of citizens of the United States.

MARSHALL, Ch. J., delivered the opinion of the court.—The question in this case is, whether the plaintiffs, as residents of the district of Columbia, can maintain an action in the circuit court of the United States for the district of Virginia. This depends on the act of congress describing the jurisdiction of that court. That act gives jurisdiction to the circuit courts in cases between a citizen of the state in which the suit is brought, and a citizen of another state. To support the jurisdiction in this case, therefore, it must appear that Columbia is a state.

On the part of the plaintiffs, it has been urged, that Columbia is a distinct political society; and is, therefore, "a state," according to the definitions of writers on general law. This is true. But as the act of congress obviously uses the word "state" in reference to that term as used in the constitution, it becomes necessary to inquire whether Columbia is a state in the sense of that instrument. The result of that examination is a conviction that the members of the American confederacy only are the states contemplated in the constitution.

The house of representatives is to be composed of members chosen by the people of the several states; and each state shall have at least one representative. The senate of the United States shall be composed of two senators from each state. Each state shall appoint, for the election of the executive, a number of electors equal to its whole number of senators and representatives. These clauses show that the word state is used in the constitution as designating a member of the union, and excludes from the term the signification attached to it by writers on the law of nations. When the same term which has been used plainly in this limited sense, in the articles respecting the legislative and executive departments, is also employed in that which respects the judicial department, it must be understood as retaining the sense originally given to it.

Other passages from the constitution have been cited by the plaintiffs, to show that the term state is sometimes used in its more enlarged sense. But on examining the passages quoted, they do not prove what was to be shown by them.

It is true, that as citizens of the United States, and of that particular district which is subject to the jurisdiction of congress, it is extraordinary, that the courts of the United States, which are open to aliens, and to the citizens of every state in the union, should be closed upon them. But this is a subject for legislative, not for judicial consideration.

The opinion to be certified to the circuit court is, that that court has no jurisdiction in the case.

Comment

Nationalist constitutionalism in the 1790s generally denied any special status in American political metaphysics to the states. For the nationalists, the United States was both the fundamental societal body and the locus of ultimate sovereignty. The Republican "doctrines of '98" exactly reversed these opinions. *Hepburn v. Ellzey* indicated the early Marshall Court's basic acceptance of the Republican claim that "the members of the American confederacy" enjoyed a special constitutional status.

United States v. Fisher
6 U.S. (2 Cranch) 358 (Feb. 1805)

A federal statute, read literally, gave claims of the United States priority in the distribution of insolvent estates. The assignees of persons adjudged bankrupt under the Federal Bankruptcy Act of 1800 resisted the government's claim to priority, arguing that giving the government priority in all cases of insolvency would make "the prerogative of the United States . . . exceed that of the King of England." At most, they contended, the statute should extend to cases involving revenue officers under bond to the government, for if read literally the statute was unconstitutional.

Ingersoll [for the assignees]:
If liens general or specific, if judgments and mortgages are to be set aside by the prerogative of the United States, it will be to impair the obligation of contracts by an *ex post facto* law.

Under what clause of the constitution is such a power given to Congress? Is it under the general power to make all laws necessary and proper for carrying into execution the particular powers specified? If so, where is the necessity, or where the propriety, of such a provision, and to the exercise of what other power is it necessary?

But it is in direct violation of the constitution, inasmuch as it deprives the debtor of his trial by jury, without his consent.

JOHNSON, J. Do you admit the law . . . to be constitutional as to revenue officers?

Ingersoll: We neither admit nor deny it as to them; but we deny the power of Congress to give the United States a preference in all cases of persons who may become indebted to them in every possible manner . . .

[John Marshall's opinion sustaining the government's claim first insisted on a literal reading of the statutory language. He then addressed the question of constitutionality in his first significant opinion respecting the reach of Congress's substantive law-making powers.]

MARSHALL, *Ch. J.*, delivered the opinion of the Court:

. . . If the act has attempted to give the United States a preference in the case before the court, it remains to inquire whether the constitution obstructs its operation.

To the general observations made on this subject, it will only be observed, that as the court can never be unmindful of the solemn duty imposed on the judicial department when a claim is supported by an act which conflicts with the constitution, so the court can never be unmindful of its duty to obey laws which are authorized by that instrument.

In the case at bar, the preference claimed by the United States is not prohibited; but it has been truly said that under a constitution conferring specific powers, the power contended for must be granted, or it cannot be exercised.

It is claimed under the authority to make all laws which shall be necessary and proper to carry into execution the powers vested by the constitution in the government of the United States, or in any department or officer thereof.

In construing this clause it would be incorrect, and would produce endless difficulties, if the opinion should be maintained that no law was authorized which was not indispensably necessary to give effect to a specific power.

Where various systems might be adopted for that purpose, it might be said with respect to each, that it was not necessary, because the end might be obtained by other means. Congress must possess the choice of means, and must be empowered to use any means which are in fact conducive to the exercise of a power granted by the constitution.

The government is to pay the debt of the union, and must be authorized to use the means which appear to itself most eligible to effect that object. It has, consequently, a right to make remittances by bills or otherwise, and to take those precautions which will render the transaction safe.

This claim of priority on the part of the United States will, it has been said, interfere with the right of the state sovereignties respecting the dignity of debts, and will defeat the measures they have a right to adopt to secure themselves against delinquencies on the part of their own revenue officers.

But this is an objection to the constitution itself; the mischief suggested, so far as it can really happen, is the necessary consequence of the supremacy of the laws of the United States on all subjects to which the legislative power of Congress extends . . .

The majority of this court is of opinion that the United States are entitled to that priority, and, therefore, the judgment of the circuit court is to be reversed, and the cause to be remanded for further proceedings.

Judgment reversed.

[Justice Bushrod Washington had presided over the circuit court whose judgment the Supreme Court reversed in *Fisher*, and so he declined to take part in the Court's deliberations. He nevertheless restated the opinion he had given below holding that the act was not to be read literally.]

WASHINGTON, *J.*:

. . . The sovereign, may, in the exercise of his powers, secure to himself this exclusive privilege of being preferred to the citizens, but this is not evidence that the claim is sanctioned by the principles of immutable justice. If this right is asserted, individuals must submit; but I do not find it in my conscience to go further in advancement of the claim, than the words of the law fairly interpreted, in relation to the whole law, compel me. But I do not thin[k] that Congress meant to exercise their power to the extent contended for. First, because in every other section of the law they have declared a different intent; and, secondly, because it would not only be productive of the most cruel injustice to individuals, but would tend to destroy, more than any other act I can imagine, all confidence between man and man. The preference claimed is not only unequal in respect to private citizens, but is of a nature against which the most prudent man cannot guard himself. As to public officers, and receivers of public money of all descriptions, they are, or may be known as such; and any person dealing with them does it at the peril of being postponed to any debts his debtor may owe to the United States, should he become unfortunate. He acts with his eyes open, and has it in his power to calculate the risk he is willing to run.

But if this preference exists in every possible case of contracts between the United States and an individual, there is no means by which any man can be apprised of his danger in dealing with the same person . . .

Comment

Marshall's opinion in *Fisher* used nationalist rhetoric to reach an end compatible with Republican principles. Marshall refused to require a relation of strict necessity between a legitimate implied power and an enumerated one, and he adopted Hamiltonian language recognizing Congress's discretion "to use any means which are in fact conducive to the exercise of a power granted by the constitution." The result in *Fisher*, on the other hand, differed little from the decision of the Republican state judges in *Woodson v. Randolph* in the generosity with which it viewed congressional power, and little attention was paid to the decision.

William Johnson
Letter to Thomas Jefferson
(December 10, 1822)[89]

President Jefferson's first appointment to the Supreme Court was William Johnson, a Republican state judge from South Carolina. Many years later, the two men corresponded about the early years of the Marshall Court.

. . . While I was on our state-bench I was accustomed to delivering seriatim opinions in our appellate court, and was not a little surprised to find our Chief Justice in the Supreme Court delivering all the opinions in cases in which he sat, even in some instances when contrary to his own judgment and vote. But I remonstrated in vain; the answer was he is willing to take the trouble and it is a mark of respect to him. I soon however found out the real cause. Cushing was incompetent. Chase could not be got to think or write— Patterson [Paterson] was a slow man and willingly declined the trouble and the other two judges [Marshall and Washington] you know are commonly estimated as one judge . . .

Some case soon occurred in which I differed from my brethren and I thought it a thing of course to deliver my opinion. But, during the rest of the session I had heard nothing but lectures on the indecency of judges cutting at each other, and the loss of reputation which the Virginia appellate court had sustained by pursuing such a course. At length I found that I must either submit to circumstances or become such a cypher in our consultations as to effect no good at all. I therefore bent to the current, and persevered until I got them to adopt the course they now pursue, which is to appoint someone to deliver the opinion of the majority, but leave it to the discretion of the rest of the judges to record their opinions or not ad libitum [at pleasure] . . .

Seven

Civil Liberty and American Constitutionalism during Jefferson's Administration

Section A: *Religious and Personal Freedom in the Virginia Court of Appeals*

One of the best-known American courts of the 1790s and early 1800s was Virginia's highest civil court, the court of appeals. After the death of Edmund Pendleton in 1803, furthermore, that court was dominated for several years by the very forceful and very Jeffersonian jurists Spencer Roane and St. George Tucker.

Virginia Declaration of Rights
(adopted in convention on June 12, 1776)[90]

The convention that acted as Virginia's revolutionary government in 1776 first adopted a bill of rights and a constitution and then acted as the commonwealth's legislature. Some Virginia lawyers (including Thomas Jefferson himself) believed or feared that this placed the state's constitutional instruments on no higher political ground than ordinary legislative acts, though a majority, including the state judiciary, disagreed, and held the constitution and bill of rights to be paramount law.

Section 1. That all men are by nature equally free and independent, and have certain inherent rights, of which, when they enter into a state of society, they cannot, by any compact, deprive or divest their posterity; namely, the enjoyment of life and liberty, with the means of acquiring and possessing property, and pursuing and obtaining happiness and safety . . .

Section 4. That no man, or set of men, are entitled to exclusive or separate emoluments or privileges from the community, but in consideration of public services; which, not being descendible, neither ought the offices of magistrate, legislator, or judge to be hereditary . . .

Section 15. That no free government, or the blessings of liberty, can be preserved to any people but by a firm adherence to justice, moderation, temperance, frugality, and virtue, and by frequent recurrence to fundamental principles.

Section 16. That religion, or the duty which we owe to our Creator, and the manner of discharging it, can be directed only by reason and conviction, not by force or violence;

and therefore all men are equally entitled to the free exercise of religion, according to the dictates of conscience; and that it is the mutual duty of all to practise Christian forbearance, love, and charity towards each other.

Turpin v. Locket
6 Call. 113 (Va. May 1804)

Perhaps the most hotly debated political and legal question in post-Revolutionary Virginia involved the status of the glebe lands (farmlands provided for the upkeep of parsons) of the pre-Revolutionary established church. A series of conflicting legislative pronouncements culminated in an act of 1802 that declared earlier statutes vesting the lands in the Episcopal church unconstitutional and instructed the local governments to sell "vacant" glebes (that is, lands in parishes without a resident Episcopal parson) and to use the proceeds for poor relief.

The 1802 act was challenged on constitutional grounds by the vestry (the church governing body) of Manchester parish, but Chancellor George Wythe sustained the act's constitutionality. On review, the court of appeals was prepared to reverse Wythe's decision (by a 3–1 vote, with Spencer Roane, now an appeals-court judge, dissenting). However, the night before its decision in the church's favor was to be announced, President Pendleton died. The remaining majority judges agreed to schedule reargument so that the case could be decided by a full bench. The man subsequently appointed to the Court was St. George Tucker.

The attorneys for the overseers of the poor invoked the state's "Act for Establishing Religious Freedom," which was drafted by Jefferson in 1777 and enacted in January 1786. The act stated: "No man shall be compelled to frequent or support any religious worship, place or ministry whatever."

Turpin and others, as vestry men and church wardens of the parish of Manchester, in the county of Chesterfield, exhibited their bill against the overseers of the poor, in the court of chancery, stating, That some of them were members of the church of England, in Virginia, before the declaration of independence; others were of the vestry of that church at the same era; and others of the same vestry when the act of assembly, incorporating the protestant episcopal church, passed in October 1784: At which time the said church was a subsisting religious society, in possession of the glebes formerly belonging to them. That the glebe in question was purchased in pursuance of the act of 1748, the contributions for which were raised, if not altogether, at least with a very small exception, from the followers of the same communion, many of whom have left descendants, or representatives still residing in the parish, and still adhering to the essential principles of that church. That the purchase of the glebe was for the benefit of the religious society, called the church of England, to be applied to the use of its ministers, but continuing as the property of the said society, even when there was no incumbent. That no member of the convention in 1776, ventured to suggest the deprivation of the church property; and that the act of November 1776 [which expressly recognized the church's right to the glebes] be considered as a contemporaneous exposition of the new constitution, so as plainly to mark the distinction between an establishment with power to create future burthens, and the rights of the church of England to the property already acquired. That the church of England and the protestant episcopal church were, in effect, the same, and that the acts of assembly, which recognized the identity, confirmed the property, which formerly belonged to the church of England, to the protestant episcopal church; and being a vested right, it could not be taken away by the repeal of those acts . . .

The defendants put in an answer[:] That the revolution abolished the church of England, which was part of the British government. That the pretensions of the complainants extended to an establishment, which was inconsistent with the bill of rights. That the property in question had been purchased for the benefit of the church; ceased with it; and revested in the community. That it was admitted, even by the English law, that an act of parliament might change the national religion; and that was completely done, in this country, by the bill of rights. That if the supposed identity between the protestant episcopal church and the church of England was real, that would not protect the property, which was purchased by the joint contribution of the whole community, now divided into various sects, and each having an equal interest in the subject. But that the churches were in fact different; the church of England having been established by law; and the protestant episcopal church by voluntary association. That the difference was, in effect, admitted by the members of the protestant episcopal church themselves when they petitioned, in the year 1784, for the act of incorporation, on the ground that the church of England had been abolished, and that the protestant episcopal church had no legal existence. That all the acts of assembly insisted on by the complainants were unconstitutional; and therefore had been repealed in the spirit of the act of 1785, for establishing religious freedom, which contained a true exposition of the bill of rights. That the glebe in question was vacant, and without an incumbent; and that, the property in the glebe being in the people at large, the assembly might constitutionally dispose of it. That upon the dissolution of the church of England, no artificial proprietor of the glebe was left; and therefore when the protestant episcopal church petitioned for the act of incorporation in 1784, they had no property in the subject upon which that law could operate . . .

TUCKER, Judge . . . This is a question which I most sincerely regret has ever been agitated. At the commencement of our happy revolution, that reverend body of men, who then filled the pulpits in this country, far from inculcating the doctrines of passive obedience and non-resistance to the invaders of the rights of their country, were zealous in her cause, and not only by precept and exhortation, but even by example in numerous instances, demonstrated that no selfish considerations of the possible consequences of a change of government, could influence them to swerve from that noble attachment to the liberties of their country, which communicated zeal and energy to others; And, if ever men in their station deserved the esteem of their country, that meed was due to the established church in Virginia, at that period. That the convention did not explicitly provide for the security of their rights by a constitutional declaration, is an omission, of which I pretend not to know, or to assign, the cause.

Nor can I less regret, that this question, on which the legislature were so repeatedly urged to pass a law, was so long, and so repeatedly avoided and procrastinated by them, that the reasons which might have operated with those who had participated in the debates in the convention, have either been totally forgotten, or are still remembered, only by a few, who have either retreated from the service of their country, or have been appointed to serve her in some other department. But most of all, I regret that this truly important question did not receive that solemn discussion and decision, which it was intended it should have received, on the very day that robbed Virginia of the oldest, and one of the most distinguished characters [Pendleton] that remained of those who held a place in her revolutionary councils and of judicial talents; which will ever mark that day in the calendar of unfortunate events. A decision, at that time, would probably have reconciled the doubts of all who doubted; and would have produced acquiescence, at least, in those who were not convinced.

. . . [Under] the former laws and constitution of the colony of Virginia, the parson, and the vestry were considered as part of the general body politic, or state; and not as a mere private incorporation, with capacity to hold lands, to a certain amount, for a special purpose: The former being a branch of the hierarchy of the monarchical constitution, and engrafted upon the government itself; whereas, the latter were, at most, an eleemosinary [sic] body, for private, although in some measure, spiritual purposes: and that the acceptance of such a private foundation, in lieu of their former privileges, immediately connected with the government itself, must be construed as a total surrender of their former state; and an acceptance of an entirely new, and essentially different, constitution of incorporation . . .

[Deciding the present case] is an unpleasant, and in some respects an arduous, task; for surely no task can be more arduous than that of reconciling the conflicting, and even opposite, acts of the legislative body. If they cannot be reconciled to each other, it will be our duty to pronounce those to be valid, which are most easily reconcileable to the dictates of moral justice, and the principles of the constitution of this commonwealth.

Two principles, neither of which can, or ought to be, shaken by this court, or by any authority in the state, are to be found in our bill of rights. *Art.* 1 and 16.

First, that the right of private property; and,

Secondly, that the right of conscience in matters of religion, shall be held sacred and inviolate.

A third principle, scarcely inferior in point of importance, and not inferior in point of obligation is, That no man, or set of men, are entitled to exclusive or separate emoluments or privileges from the community, but in consideration of public services. *Art.* 4.

What are *public services*?

Such, in which the community have, or may be presumed to have, a common interest.

Can the dissenters from the protestant episcopal church (infinitely more numerous than the adherents to that church) be presumed to have a common interest, with them, in the promulgation of religious tenets, of which they disapprove, and from which they avowedly dissent?

If this be the fact, of which I believe no doubt is entertained, are the members of the protestant episcopal church entitled to receive from the community at large, exclusive, or separate emoluments, for teaching doctrines, from which a majority of the community dissent, as the rents and profits of the glebes must be considered as an annual stipend paid by the commonwealth to the ministers of the protestant episcopal church?

If the legislature had thought proper to appropriate the glebes and churches purchased and built, at the expense of all the parishioners, in each parish, for the use of such minister, or teacher of religion as a majority of the parish should choose, without regard to sects or denominations of religion, whether christian, jew, mahometan or other whatsoever, this article, I apprehend, would not have stood in the way of such a general appropriation. But where one religious society (inferior in numbers to several others, and perhaps to any other) receive exclusively a bounty from the state, such exclusive bounty, so long as it remains exclusive, must, I conceive, appear to be granted in opposition both to the letter and spirit of the article. And if it be, the grant is void.

This interpretation does not, I apprehend, in the least, interfere with, or violate that fundamental principle of our constitution, that private property shall be sacred and inviolable.

The glebes, as such, were never private property. They were purchased at the common expense of the whole parish, and (according to the prevailing maxim of the government at that time) for the common benefit of all the parishioners, without distinction.

The revolution put an entire period to the maxim, that "mankind may be benefitted by the promulgation of religious doctrine, from which they wholly dissent."

From that moment, the promulgation of the religious doctrines of any religious sect ceased to be a common benefit to the community.

But the incumbents of the respective parishes had acquired legal rights, under the existing laws, which the legislature were too just to violate. A life, or lives in being, would not long retard the operation of any plan, which might be recommended by the change of constitution, and of principle, which had taken place. Besides, those incumbents who, upon the faith of the existing constitution and laws, had qualified themselves for the function to which they were elected, and renounced all other pursuits on that account, had acquired a moral right to be continued in the enjoyment of their legal estates, thus acquired.

So far as any act of the legislature has operated for that purpose, it may be considered as pursuing the injunctions of moral justice, and of the first article of our bill of rights. Beyond that point, I conceive every such act to have been void.

If one act of the legislature be void, as repugnant to the constitution, a subsequent act, declaring such repugnant act to be void, and repealing it accordingly, cannot be contrary to the constitution in that respect.

The act of 1798, repealing the act for incorporating the protestant episcopal church, and several others relating to the glebes, therefore, is not itself unconstitutional.

The consequence is, that the newly incorporated bodies, incorporated, authorized, and continued by those acts respectively, have no longer any legal existence, being entirely dissolved.

It follows that the plaintiffs, as vestrymen, have not any legal title to the glebe.

If the legislature, without any consideration whatever, but merely *meromotu*, grant lands to a private person, in his natural capacity, without any fraud, or fault on his part, such donation I hold to be irrecoverable, under the first article of the bill of rights. But where the legislature creates an artificial person, and endows that artificial person with certain rights and privileges, either in respect to property, or otherwise, this must be intended as having some relation to the community at large; and the consideration upon which such artificial body was created, or endowed with all, any, or either of its rights and privileges, seems to be examinable, as well by the legislature itself, as by the courts of justice. And if such creation, or endowment, be either unconstitutional, or merely impolitic, and unadvised, the legislature, I apprehend, is competent to amend, or repeal its own act, provided it do not annul, or avoid any private right, which may have been legally acquired by any individual in his natural capacity, under such act: whereas a court of justice can only pronounce the act void so far as it contains any thing, which the constitution of the commonwealth prohibits the grant of.

The legislature, therefore, I conceive, were competent to the repeal of the act for incorporating the protestant episcopal church; and of all other acts vesting, in that church, the property theretofore belonging to the church by law established, so far as they have repealed them. But if by such repeal they may be supposed to have offered an injury to the legal, or vested, rights of any individual, such rights cannot be affected by the act of repeal: and the parties are still at full liberty to defend those rights in a course of law . . . I am therefore of opinion that the bill was properly dismissed, and that the decree ought to be affirmed.

ROANE, Judge . . . [I]t appears, that both the salaries and glebes were derived from the government to the *ministers* of the established church. Those ministers were only known in that character, and in that of *private* persons. It would be ridiculous to attempt to shew, that the grant was not made to them in their private character. It was then only made to those ministers in their character of ministers of the national church. It was not made to them as ministers of a mere religious society, having certain doctrines and tenets. The then government did think an establishment necessary, as a part of the political system, and that the public good was promoted by the coercion and monopoly incident to such establishment. On this ground, only, however mistaken, however abhorrent to our present ideas, could the government of our country have justified the application of public property to the use of a particular religious society, or of the ministers of that society . . . Without contending for the omnipotence of parliament, or even of the people in a state of revolution; without asserting a right, in either, to do injustice or destroy the rights of property, I may at least assert, that the just powers of the latter, are equal to those of the former. I suppose, also, it will be readily conceded, that an act of either, entirely and substantially inconsistent with the existence of the corporation, is as much a dissolution of it, as a dissolution by express words. I am willing to admit, also, that a dissolution may be partial, as well as total: *partial*, in so far as the corporation may be dissolved, by express words, or by the effect of the act at variance with it. This position is a concession in favour of the episcopal church, as it admits that the society of the church of England (if it were a corporation), however it may be, upon the point in question, might survive the wreck of the revolution, in relation to lawful or indifferent matters; not only (for example) the rights of doctrine and worship, which it holds in common with other societies, but such rights of property as appertain to it as a mere religious society, and do not contravene any constitutional principles.

...I [now] will consider the effect of the revolution, and the principles of the constitution, upon the subject in question: when I speak of the effect of the revolution, I know I stand upon an important ground. I know, also, the danger of different inferences being drawn, from this source, owing to the different *media* through which they pass. I know that some men have more fervour than others; more sensibility in the cause of equal rights. I know that, from this cause, the inferences to be drawn from this source, will, unavoidably, be *tinged* and diversified. But there are certain cardinal points, upon which all men must agree. It must, I presume, be admitted by all, that, that memorable event, established, in America, the reign of equal justice, delivered our dissenting brethren, from the tyranny exercised over them, and exempted the rights of conscience, from the power of the civil magistrate. If in aid of these great principles of the revolution, the expressions, or the clear principles of the constitution, are to be found, then indeed we have attained to the acme of human sanction. This desideratum appears to me to exist in the present case. Our bill of rights, on a large and liberal view, comes full up to the point of liberating dissenters from future contributions: and when we reflect, that an instrument of this kind, exists not in detail, and only declares, in general, the great principles of free government, it is supposed, that the 4th and 16th articles thereof are almost expressly in point: at least they give us great principles which are decisive of the present question. There is not a human being who can read those articles, and justify, as constitutional, future exactions from dissenters. This has been universally admitted, from the beginning, in relation to the salaries; but a difference is set up, in relation to the glebes. I confess, as I have already said, that I cannot see a difference. They stand upon the same *reason*, if not precisely upon the same ground; and it must be readily conceded, that the *reason* of an instrument of this kind, must emphatically apply. The claim of *post revolutionary* salary, by even a contemporary incumbent, is justly abandoned by the appellants' counsel: but the case embraced by the act of 1802, of a *vacant glebe*, is infinitely less strong. It does not invade the interest of an *existing* incumbent. It only intercepts the *contingent* and *possible* title, which might have accrued to *some future* minister as *successor* to the last incumbent. In this view, his remote, contingent, and possible claim, stands reprobated, as a source of title, by the uniform decisions of this court...

The important effect now supposed, has been wrought by the revolution. The property in question, for want of an adequate grantee, has reverted to the grantor. If you please, the corporate character of the grantee is destroyed, by the effect of the revolution: it is destroyed, to say the least, as to property taken from strangers to the established church, by coercion, and held from them by violence: it is destroyed, as to the subject in question: That memorable event has tumbled to the ground, the then *national* church, together with its colleague, the government: It has not tumbled to the ground, and I trust never will, the pure and excellent system of that church, considered as a society of christians; but that towering and powerful hierarchy, whose progress was not to be arrested, by even the mild and tolerant principles of the episcopal persuasion: that overwhelming hierarchy, which levelled to the dust, every vestige of religious *liberty*!

Let me not be supposed, sir, to denounce this hierarchy, with too much severity. Is it not known to every sciolist in our laws, that *it* procured the enaction of a statute, for *silencing*, and even *banishing* non-conforming ministers? Is it not known to every member of this court, that even in the dawn of our struggle against Britain, for *civil* liberty, many meek and pious teachers of the gospel were imprisoned, persecuted, and treated as criminals?

The only crime of these men, was, their worshipping God according to the dictates of their own consciences! There is not a gentleman old enough to know the fact, who has not seen ministers of the gospel of Christ, teaching their doctrines through the grated windows of a prison! I mention these things, but to shew the character and tendencies of the hierarchal government; the utter annihilation which then existed, of every semblance of religious liberty!

The revolution, however, has brought down this powerful hierarchy to the standard of free and equal government: the cause of the grant has ceased; and it becomes unlawful for the church or corporation to act up to the end for which it was established. In this view, of a reversion of the glebe lands, to the government, for the benefit of the people, any *after* disposition or continuation of them, by law, or by *construction*, to the use of a particular society, is, in fact, equally with the levies of salaries, a *coercive* contribution from the dissenters: it stands precisely on a common ground with such levy: it is, equally with it, in the teeth of the bill of rights: it is moreover equally with it in direct hostility with the *noble* principle, declared in the preamble of the act of November 1776, which I shall presently particularly recite.

It is urged on us, with great vehemence, by the appellants' counsel that this is a *vested* right, and not to be divested, even by the effect of the revolution. I shall not be among those, who assert a right in the government, or even in the people, to violate private rights, and perpetrate injustice. The just end and object of all governments, and all revolutions, reprobate this idea. I trust I shall not be more tardy, that those who are more loud and clamorous, to respect the vested rights of individuals, or societies . . . But the question here is, in whom the property in question is vested? I may be mistaken in my application and inference, but I bow implicitly to the principle. I apprehend, however, that this position respecting the inviolability of vested rights, only extends to such private and *perfect* rights, as are not hostile to the principles of the government: such as are unconnected with, and depend not upon, the existence of the government. Such rights, or emoluments, as are inseparably connected with, and depend upon the government, must stand or fall therewith. Neither the government nor the individual can be supposed to have contemplated a revolution, when they contracted; a state of things, which disfranchies [*sic*] the government, and puts it out of its power to perform the contract on its part. Under a contrary construction, the individual must either receive his emolument, as a sinecure, his duties, in consideration of which it was given, being withdrawn, or rendered unlawful, or the then system of government be kept *up* for the purpose of continuing to the individual the complete enjoyment of the contract.

This last idea is outrageous, and deeply affects the expediency, almost under any circumstances, of asserting the right of reform and revolution. A very familiar and analogous case occurs, to exemplify my ideas. By the Virginia constitution, our judges hold their offices and salaries, during good behaviour. They cannot, during the existence of the constitution, be deprived of either, without a breach of such behaviour. But if the people choose to reform the government, and render their services unnecessary, no man will contend that they shall receive their salaries for nothing: none will contend, that these men remain judges, or retain their salaries, in that event, although the new judiciary system, be precisely similar to the old: none will assert, that for the sake of perpetuating to those officers, their emoluments, a system of government shall be kept up, which is injurious to the interests and hostile to the wishes of the people. But the case in question, although it has received, did not require, the intervention of a revolution to effect an extinguishment. The admitted right of the then government to change the established religion; the admitted, nay I might almost say, the *boasted*, omnipotence of parliament, was competent to put down, by *law*, a system, and its appendages, which, the legislature itself had set up. Granting, which is the most that could be contended for, that the legislature should have permitted the *life interest* of the then incumbents to run out, in tenderness to those who engaged in their functions, under a reasonable expectation of the continuance of the then system, that body certainly possessed full power to intercept the *contingent* and *possible* claims of their "successors." It is asking but a small boon, that the same effect shall be given to the revolution; to a revolution, founded on principles utterly subversive of ecclesiastical coercion and monopoly.

It remains lastly to consider the effect of the laws posterior to the revolution, upon the question before us. The act of November 1776, in the clause so much relied on, (if my view of the subject is right), is in direct hostility, not only with the spirit of the bill of rights, but with the spirit declared in its own preamble. That preamble recites, "that it is contrary to the principles of reason and justice, that any should be compelled to *contribute* to the maintenance of a church, with which their consciences will not permit them to join, and from which they can, therefore, receive no benefit." This inconsistency, considering its illustrious parentage, could only have arisen, from the embarrassment in which that legislature was placed, according to the information of one of the appellants' counsel in the former argument; from the duress, I had almost said, under which they then stood; and from the necessity they were then under, to eventuate in some such act as that, as the "price of peace," between the contending parties. This pressure, however, did not compel them, as there was no necessity for it, to renounce in their *preamble*, principles, which, as members of the convention, they had so nobly and recently established . . . These considerations, while they exempt from all possible blame, that respectable assembly, for enacting a commentary, so hostile to their own excellent text, certainly weaken the authority of that act, as a cotemporaneous [sic] exposition of the constitution. This memorable act provides, that all dissenters from "the church by law established," shall be exempt, &c. from levies, &c. for supporting "the said church as it *now is* or hereafter may be established, and its ministers." I beg your attention, sir, to these remarkable expressions. Do gentlemen contend, that in this *portrait* of the *character* of the church, this act is a just exposition of the constitution? Has the constitution permitted the "established church" to continue, or does it tolerate a legislative right to establish a particular church? No, sir, I believe not. The most that has ever been contended for, by any the least liberal of our fellow citizens, is a legislative right to erect a general establishment of religion. Shall an act thus marked with a want of knowledge of our constitution, or of respect for its clearest principles, be considered, by this court, as a safe and proper guide, in the exposition of that instrument? I think not. This act of November 1776, so far as it makes a reservation of the several glebes, must either be considered as declaratory of the then law, on that subject, or as investing the episcopal society therewith. In the first view, it is only by a legislative construction of the law and constitution on this subject, which, however respectable, (but that respectability is much impaired by the errors and inconsistency, just stated), must yield to that of the judiciary: in the second view, it is unconstitutional . . .

If it be said that the acts of 1776 and 1784 have forestalled the act of 1802, by investing the glebes in the protestant episcopal church, I answer that the bill of rights had previously forestalled them, by interdicting grants of public property to individuals or societies, except in consideration of public service: and by inhibiting the legislature from favouring or endowing one religious society in preference to others. The act of 1802 has only put aside the infractions of the constitution, contained in the two former acts. While we are upon the subject of cotemporaneous [sic] exposition, why do not the appellants' counsel give us credit for the act of the same session, docking entails? That act has assailed what may be considered by some, as a *private* and *perfect* right; a right not held from the government, nor dependent on it; a right *vested in interest*, and only postponed in enjoyment; vested also in persons *in esse*, and who were ascertained and known. In all these respects the case affected by that act is infinitely more strong, than the case before us. In this case the right is not perfect but dependent; dependent upon the existence of the law and the government, and held from them; and the person for whom it is set up, is unknown and wholly uncertain: he is, in the emphatical language of our late venerable president, in the case of *Carter v. Tyler*, a person "in the clouds:" that expression, there applied to an existing remainderman in tail, is infinitely more applicable to the *possible* "successor" to a late incumbent. And on what grounds was the act of entails passed? Its preamble recites reasons of *inconvenience and impolicy* only. No constitutional repugnance is there assigned; and if any did exist, it is infinitely less strong, than that which intercepts the present claim. I consider that act as a high authority. It was passed by the same legislature who passed the other act alluded to; and that legislature being free, in this instance, from that embarrassment which besieged them while acting upon the subject of the glebes, the authority of the former act, probably deserves more consideration than that of the latter;

the non-existence too, of those errors and inconsistencies in the former act, which mark the latter, decidedly determines its preference. Besides, the act of entails has always been acquiesced in: it has received the sanction of our courts: and in the case of *Carter v. Tyler*, it received the sanction of this court, upon great consideration. Is it not then a high authority? That act, to say the least, destroyed the "possibility" of an interest; but the claim now set up, as paramount to the power of the legislature, is less than a "possibility." The legislature in passing, and the judiciary in supporting, the act of entails, must have taken an infinitely bolder ground than is necessary to be occupied on the present occasion. Here, the doctrines of the common law, in its ordinary acceptation, and giving to the revolution the mere effect of dissolving the corporation, suffice for our purpose: But in that case, the legislature proceeded upon great principles. We were thrown into a new situation; we held the ground of a free and equal government; and the codes and doctrines of dark and arbitrary times, tending to hereditary influence and excessive wealth, were thrown aside, and disregarded. But I must pause: I am entering into an extensive field: I wish not to prejudge, or anticipate any thing.

In expounding the acts of the convention of 1776, I have adhered to those instruments themselves. I reject all extraneous sources of information. I reject them, in relation to the bill of rights, because those ephemeral circumstances do not apply to great principles, pertaining to our latest posterity. I would receive, with more caution, the legislative exposition of the constitution, contained in the act of November 1776, because the dignity of legislative exposition is lessened, if not *lost*, when the legislature enacting and expounding is the same. Such an exposition, considered as a judicial decision, seems to contravene great principles. It contravenes that principle requiring a separation of the legislative and judicial departments. The effect of this principle reaches *every* legislative exposition, more or less; but an union of the powers of *passing* and executing laws in the same persons, forms no contemptible definition of despotism. But although I deem it right to reject all extraneous information in forming my conclusion upon the constitution, I have, as a matter of curiosity, examined the journals of the convention touching the present subject. I can find in them nothing varying the construction, arising from the instrument itself. In the session of the convention, only one solitary petition on the subject of religious rights was presented. The grievances of the dissenters, great as they were, seemed lost in the greater grievance of America. But if it were otherwise; if any expressions, contained in the journals of those times, seemed to depart from the spirit breathed in their more solemn and deliberate acts, I should attempt to apologize for that illustrious assembly. I should rather impute them to the infirmities of our nature; to the resumption of their empire, by ancient habits and prejudices. I should readily excuse a bias, which in the infantine state of free government, may have been *only* overborne, by the noble effort, by the sublime enthusiasm, which produced the act of government; by that noble fervour, which must animate all men, engaged in the most noble and important of human transactions. But these patriots require no apology. Their work speaks for itself. It will go down to posterity, and receive the grateful applause of one of the most enlightened and happy of nations. The magnitude of this subject almost carries me beyond the cool deliberation which ought to preside in this place. But I am sure the congenial feelings of those who hear me will readily excuse me . . .

We were exhorted by one of the appellants' counsel, at the former argument, and the substance is repeated in the last, "to put deism to fight, and restore the altars of our forefathers." If there is a league, of deists or others, in the legislature or elsewhere, to overturn religion, or impair morality, it is to me a subject of the *deepest* regret. I can never cease to believe, that these are the *firmest* pillars of civil society, the *surest* basis of human happiness. For myself, I am now called to discharge a painful duty. That duty must not be obstructed, by any sympathies, or partialities of mine. While sitting in this seat, the stern maxims of judicial independence, scarcely permit me to *recognize* in the respectable society now before us, the revered patron of my early youth, the depositary [*sic*] of my best wishes.

CARRINGTON, Judge, and LYONS, President . . . We are . . . clear upon the merits. For it has been frequently decided by the court, that unconstitutional laws are void; and we think the statute, now under consideration, is of that class.

It is a mistake to suppose, that the church, here, was identified with that of the mother country, and had no capacity to hold lands.

For although the church of England was the prototype, it certainly was not the actual church of Virginia; which was founded by the local legislature; and its structure and capacities are to be sought for in the laws of the colony only . . .

The question then is, what effect the revolution had upon the property of the church?

It was contended by the counsel for the appellees, That, if the church had capacity to hold lands before the date of independence, that event destroyed it; and that, upon the dissolution, the glebes devolved upon the commonwealth. But revolutions are intended to preserve, not to take away rights: Nor was it ever pretended, that an alteration, in the form of a government, affected private property. Such a consequence would prevent all revolutions, as no set of men would ever unite in a measure productive of such fatal effects; and therefore we unhesitatingly pronounce, that the revolution did not produce that result.

A distinction was attempted, however, between a natural person and an artificial body: The right of the first being admitted; that of the latter denied: But there is, in fact, no such distinction. For property being a civil institution, the right to it is, in all cases, conferred by law: Which applies as forcibly to a society, as to an individual; and the change of a government no more affects the claims of the one, than those of the other.

But to obviate this, it was urged, That, although the revolution did not produce the effect directly, it did indirectly; and the reasons assigned for it were, 1. That the society was dissolved, as the king, one of its integral parts, was gone. 2. That incorporated religious societies are contrary to the sixteenth article of the bill of rights. 3. That the profits of the glebes are emoluments, which one religious society cannot take to its separate use, without a violation of the fourth article of that instrument.

Neither of these propositions is true:

Not that which relates to the abolition of the kingly office.

Because the king was not an integral part of the established church. For he was never declared to be so by any law; and he exercised no acts with regard to the institution, except as one of the component parts of the general legislature of the colony . . .

Not that with respect to the sixteenth article of the bill of rights:

Because there is nothing in that article, which forbids the continuation of the establishment, or the incorporation of religious societies. For the whole relates to the rights of conscience, and the mutual charities which men owe each other.

Not that with respect to the fourth article of the bill of rights . . .

Because the whole article, according to grammatical and legal construction, relates to magistrates, legislators and judges only.

For, in the first place, the words, *"public services,"* are equivocal, as they apply not only to officers concerned in the general administration of government, but to subordinate agents, acting for the benefit of the community also; as, for instance, to public teachers, and other occupations, conducive directly, or indirectly, to the public benefit. And, although this particular church was not the only one in the state, and therefore so far the right might be said to be partial, yet that forms no objection to the principle, as similar benefits may be conferred on the rest, so as to produce general equality. For the grant of a small piece of land to any religious society, to support a minister to teach the principles of christianity, would be a grant for a public purpose; not only upon the reason of the thing, but upon the expression and meaning of the last article of the bill of rights: which declares, "that no government, or the blessing of liberty, can be preserved to any people, but by a firm adherence to justice, moderation, temperance, frugality, and virtue;" and "that it is the mutual duty of all to practice *christian* forbearance, love and charity towards each other:" [Lyons and Carrington have completed the last two sections of the Virginia Bill of

Rights] which latter words shew, that the *christian* religion was that which was contemplated throughout the whole article, as none but *christians* would be conversant in the principles and duties prescribed by it. But, if adherence to such principles, and the exercise of such duties, be indispensable to the preservation of liberty and the happiness of people, it is obvious, that a reasonable grant to a religious society, for the purpose of inculcating them, would not, (more than to a college, or other seminary of learning,) be unconstitutional. And, accordingly, it never has been disputed, that the property of the college of William & Mary continued inviolable after the revolution, notwithstanding their possessions were donations by the crown, out of the public domain, and the members not officers of government, rendering *public services* to the state: and notwithstanding, too, one of the professorships, that of divinity, was devoted to the doctrines of the established church; the preparing ministers for which was one main object for establishing the college, as avowed in several of the early statutes, and the charter made in conformity to them ... Which seems to put the question at rest.

But, independent of this, the remark is correct, that, in political language, *emoluments* and *privileges* most naturally apply to the rewards given to those concerned as officers of government, in the general administration of public affairs: and that they were so understood, in this article, is obvious. For they are connected with the words *public services;* which, by the subsequent parts of the sentence, are transferred to the three great departments of government, namely, the executive, legislative and judiciary ... The fair interpretation, therefore, is, that *"emoluments"* and *"privileges,"* (which are the rewards for services by officers administering the government,) not being descendible, the offices, from which the *services* were to proceed, ought not to be hereditary. In this view, which is most consistent with the context, and general intent, of the article, the case is nothing more than the ordinary course of explaining the generality of the preceding words, by those which follow; and confining the operation of the first, to the specific terms of the latter. Which interpretation has the additional advantage, that it preserves and gives effect to all the words in the article; whereas the other virtually suppresses the intervening words, (*"which not being descendible,"*) to the injury of the sentence; and, therefore, ought to be repudiated ...

[A]ny other construction would be attended with the most inconvenient consequences, as it would take, from the legislature, the power of making a gift either to a community, or an individual, unless engaged in some public service, although the occasions of society often require legislative grants for purposes wholly individual, or partial, in their nature.

Upon no sound construction, therefore, of the bill of rights, compared with the laws antecedent to the revolution, can the church be considered as dissolved by that event, or divested of its property, in consequence of it: and the uniform interpretation and practice of the country have been agreeable to this opinion. [Carrington and Lyons then discussed the various postrevolutionary statutes addressing the status and property of the Episcopal church.]

As far, then, as construction and practice, both ancient and modern, can settle any question, this appears to be settled.

But it was said, that neither the convention, nor the legislature, could alter the constitution; or give it a meaning which the words would not bear.

To which we answer,

1. That if that position were true to the whole extent, it would not affect the case; because we have, already, endeavoured to shew, that the construction and practice were in strict accordance, with the intent and letter of the instrument; and, therefore, that the case, supposed by the position, does not exist on the present occasion.

2. That the constitution, and the subsequent acts of the convention, stand upon the same ground. For both depend upon the acquiescence of the people, as the convention was not deputed to make the constitution; or to pass laws under it; and, therefore, if the people acquiesced under the constitution, they acquiesced in the interpretation also.

3. That written constitutions are, like other instruments, subject to construction; and, when expounded, the exposition, after long acquiescence, becomes, as it were, part of the instrument; and can, no more, be departed from, than that.

4. That it is unimportant, therefore, whether the legislature can, or cannot, now, bestow *other* property, upon religious societies; for, either way, their contemporaneous and subsequent decisions amount to so many recognitions of the first interpretation by the convention, that the church continued; and that the then existing glebes belonged to it. Which, as before observed, makes, in effect, the construction, as to those subjects, part of the instrument . . .

Upon the whole, we think, that the church had a right to the glebes, at the date of the revolution; that, that event had no effect upon the title; that nothing has happened since to divest it; that the act of 1802 is unconstitutional; and that the injunction ought to have been awarded. But, as the other judges are of a different opinion, the decree of the chancellor stands, and is to be affirmed, as upon a division of the court.

Comment

Turpin raised two constitutional issues of great importance. Substantively, the case involved the meaning of religious freedom in a constitutional system that, both on the state and on the federal level, purported to guarantee such freedom. Judges Tucker and Roane viewed the Revolution as marking a sharp divide between a colonial polity of "towering and powerful hierarchy" in church and state and a post-Revolutionary Virginia in which all coercive structures and legal systems were subjected to "the standard of free and equal government." From this perspective, the colonial established church and the contemporaneous Episcopal church were radically distinct bodies, and the latter had no legal claim to the former's repudiated privileges.

President Lyons and Judge Carrington, in contrast, took a narrow view of the Revolution's meaning. For them, the pre-Revolutionary order had been neither as alien nor as politically evil as their colleagues portrayed it. The colonial established church, they admitted, was defective in that it discriminated among *Christians*, but its recognition of Christianity-in-general was not an infringement of liberty. Nor was the church qua church part of the government, and from the latter proposition Lyons and Carrington concluded logically that *Turpin* involved a legislative attack on vested rights rather than a legislative vindication of the rights of conscience.

Turpin also involved a far-reaching disagreement over the nature of constitutional interpretation. As in *Kamper v. Hawkins*, Tucker and Roane asserted the superiority of judicial over legislative exposition of the Constitution, and the legitimacy of judges considering extratextual principles ("the dictates of moral justice," "the spirit of the bill of rights") as well as the letter of the text. Lyons and Carrington rested their views on the dignity of the 1776 pro-church legislation as a legislative interpretation of the Virginia Bill of Rights, contemporaneous with the adoption of the bill of rights, which had become through "long acquiescence . . . part of the instrument."

Roane, a strong advocate of the Republican interpretation of the federal Constitution, took the opportunity to make an unmistakable if implicit defense of congressional repeal of the 1801 Judiciary Act, an issue on which his constitutional ally Tucker was ambivalent.

Hudgins v. Wright
1 Hen. & Munf. 133 (Va. Nov. 11, 1806)

Republican constitutional thought purported to rest on, and to be centrally concerned with, protecting the rights of humanity. *Turpin v. Locket* was viewed by people such as Jefferson as a triumph of religious freedom and civil equality. In 1806 the Virginia Court of Appeals was confronted with an even more difficult conflict between traditional practice and Republican principle: the place of human slavery in the American "empire for liberty" (Jefferson's words). *Hudgins v. Wright* was a suit for their freedom brought by the Wrights, whose master (Hudgins) was planning to "send" them—almost certainly sell them—out of state. Chancellor George Wythe, always the most radical legal thinker among the Republicans, held for the Wrights in an opinion (unfortunately lost) that excited great public interest and concern. Hudgins appealed to a court dominated by two fervent anti-slavery activists, Tucker and Roane.

The appellees, in this case, which was an appeal from the High Court of Chancery, were permitted to sue *in forma pauperis*. The appellant, being about to send them out of the State, a writ of *ne exeat* was obtained from the Chancellor, on the ground that they were entitled to freedom.—In their bill, they asserted this right as having been descended, in the maternal line, from a free *Indian* woman; but their genealogy was very imperfectly stated. The time of the birth of the youngest was established by the testimony; and the characteristic features, the complexion, the hair and eyes, were proven to have been the same with those of whites. Their genealogy was traced back by the evidence taken in the cause, (though different from that mentioned in the bill,) through female ancestors, to an old *Indian* called *Butterwood Nan*. One of the witnesses who had seen her, describes her as an old *Indian*. Others prove, that her daughter *Hannah* had long black hair, was of the right Indian copper colour, and was generally called an *Indian* by the neighbours, who said she might recover her freedom, if she would sue for it; and all those witnesses deposed that they had often seen *Indians*. Another witness, (*Robert Temple*), whose deposition was taken on the part of the appellant, proves that the father of *Butterwood Nan* was said to have been an *Indian*, but he is silent as to her mother.

On the hearing, the late Chancellor, perceiving from his own view, that the youngest of the appellees was perfectly white, and that there were gradual shades of difference in colour between the grand-mother, mother, and grand-daughter, (all of whom were before the Court,) and considering the evidence of the cause, determined that the appellees were entitled to their freedom; and, moreover, on the ground that freedom is the birth-right of every human being, which sentiment is strongly inculcated by the first article of our "political catechism," the bill of rights —he laid it down as a general position, that whenever one person claims to hold another in slavery, the *onus probandi* lies on the claimant.

Randolph, for the appellant. The ground on which the appellees claim their freedom, is, that they are lineally descended from a free Indian woman. On the other side, it is contended, that they are descended from a negro woman by an Indian. Although the circumstance of their being white operated on the mind of the Chancellor, who decreed their freedom; yet as the whole of the testimony proved them to have been descended from a slave, the presumption on which that decree was founded must fail.

Whether they are white or not, cannot appear to this Court from the record. They have asserted their right to freedom on very different grounds; and have not, in their evidence, made out the genealogy stated in their bill.

If they could derive their descent from Indians in the maternal line, still it will be found, from the evidence, that their female ancestor was brought into this country between the years 1679 and 1705, and under the laws then in force, might have been a slave . . .

George K. Taylor, for the appellees. This is not a common case of mere *blacks* suing for their freedom; but of persons perfectly *white*. The peculiar circumstances under which the bill was drawn, will readily account for any inaccuracies which may appear in stating the genealogy of the appellees. But would it have been prudent, or even necessary, to delay the cause, by an amended bill?

He [Taylor] then took a circumstantial view of the evidence, and inferred, that it clearly proved the appellees to have descended from an *Indian stock*: all the witnesses deposed to the fact that the female ancestor under whom they claimed was "of the right *Indian* copper colour," with long black hair; that she was called an Indian in her master's family, and by the neighbours generally, who said she might get her freedom, if she would sue for it; and many of them had *often* seen *Indians*. What more than strong characteristic features would be required, to prove a person *white*?

If, in fact, the appellees are descended from Indians, it is incumbent on the appellant to prove that they are slaves; the appellees are not bound to prove the contrary.

From the beginning of the world till the year 1679, all *Indians* were, in *fact* as well as *right*, free persons. In that year an act passed declaring *Indian* prisoners taken in war to be slaves: and in 1682, another, that *Indians* sold to us by neighbouring *Indians* and others trading with us should be slaves. These acts remained in force (till 1691, as supposed by one of the Judges, or at farthest) till 1705, when it has been decided they were repealed.

As *all Indians* were free, except those brought into this country within the periods and under the circumstances just mentioned, the appellant must bring the appellees within those *exceptions*, to be entitled to their services as slaves.—Not a case can be shewn from the books, where a person claiming under an exception must not bring himself within it . . .

Randolph, in reply. The circumstances of the appellees' being *white*, has been mentioned, more to excite the feelings of the Court as *men*, than to address them as *Judges*.

In deciding upon the rights of *property*, those rules which have been established are not to be departed from, because *freedom* is in question . . .

Judge TUCKER. In this case, the paupers claim their freedom as being descended from Indians entitled to their freedom. They have set forth their pedigree in the bill, which the evidence proves to be fallacious. But as there is no *Herald's Office* in this country, nor even a *Register* of births for any but white persons, and those *Registers* are either all lost, or of all records probably the most imperfect, our Legislature, even in a writ of *praecipe quod reddat*, has very justly dispensed with the old common law precision required in a *writ of right*, and the reason for dispensing with it in the present case, is a thousand times stronger. In a claim for freedom, like a claim for money had and received, the plaintiff may well be permitted to make out his case on the trial according to the evidence.

What then is the evidence in this case? Unequivocal proof adduced perhaps by the defendant, that the plaintiffs are in the maternal line descended from *Butterwood Nan*, an old *Indian woman*;—that she was 60 years old, or upwards, in the year 1755;—that it was always understood, as the witness *Robert Temple* says, that her *father was an Indian*, though he cautiously avoids saying he knew, or ever heard, who, or what, her mother was. The other witness *Mary Wilkinson*, the only one except *Robert Temple* who had ever seen her, describes her as an *old Indian*: and her testimony is strengthened by that of the other witnesses, who depose that her daughter *Hannah* had long black hair, was of a copper complexion, and generally called an *Indian* among the neighbours;—a circumstance which would not well have happened, if her mother had not had an equal, or perhaps a larger portion of *Indian* blood in her veins . . .

In aid of the other evidence, the Chancellor decided upon his own view. This, with the principles laid down in the decree, has been loudly complained of . . .

I draw this conclusion, that all *American Indians* are *prima facie* FREE: and that where the fact of their nativity and descent, in a *maternal* line, is satisfactorily established, the burthen of proof thereafter lies upon the party claiming to hold them as slaves. To effect which, according to my opinion, he must prove the progenitrix of the party claiming to be free, to have been brought into *Virginia*, and made a slave between the passage of the act of 1679, and its repeal in 1691.

All *white persons* are and ever have been FREE in this country. If one *evidently white*, be notwithstanding claimed as a slave, the proof lies on the party claiming to make the other his slave . . .

Suppose three persons, a black or mulatto man or woman with a flat nose and woolly head; a copper-coloured person with long jetty black, straight hair; and one with a fair complexion, brown hair, not woolly nor inclining thereto, with a prominent Roman nose, were brought together before a Judge upon a writ of *Habeas Corpus*, on the ground of false imprisonment and detention in slavery: that the only evidence which the person detaining them in his custody could produce was an authenticated bill of sale from another person, and that the parties themselves were unable to produce any evidence concerning themselves, whence they came, &c. &c. How must a Judge act in such a case? I answer he must judge from his own view. He must discharge the white person and the *Indian* out of custody, taking surety, if the circumstances of the case should appear to authorise it, that they should not depart the state within a reasonable time, that the holder may have an opportunity of asserting and proving them to be lineally descended in the maternal line from a female *African* slave; and he must redeliver the black or mulatto person, with the flat nose and woolly hair to the person claiming to hold him or her as a slave, unless the black person or mulatto could procure some person to be bound for him, to produce proof of his descent, in the maternal line, from a *free female ancestor*.–But if no such caution should be required on either side, but the whole case be left with the Judge, he must deliver the former out of custody, and permit the latter to remain in slavery, until he could produce proofs of his right to freedom. This case shews my interpretation how far the *onus probandi* may be shifted from one party to the other: and is, I trust, a sufficient comment upon the case to shew that I do not concur with the Chancellor in his reasoning on the operation of the first clause of the Bill of Rights, which was notoriously framed with a cautious eye to this subject, and was meant to embrace the case of free citizens, or aliens only; and not by a side wind to overturn the rights of property, and give freedom to those very people whom we have been compelled from imperious circumstances to retain, generally, in the same state of bondage that they were in at the revolution, in which they had no *concern, agency or interest*. But notwithstanding this difference of opinion from the Chancellor, I heartily concur with him in pronouncing the appellees *absolutely free*; and am therefore of opinion that the decree be affirmed.

Judge ROANE . . . In the case of a person visibly appearing to be a negro, the presumption is, in this country, that he is a slave, and it is incumbent on him to make out his right to freedom: but in the case of a person visibly appearing to be a white man, or an *Indian*, the presumption is that he is free, and it is necessary for his adversary to shew that he is a slave.

In the present case it is not and cannot be denied that the appellees have entirely the *appearance* of white people: and how does the appellant attempt to deprive them of the blessing of liberty to which all such persons are entitled? He brings no testimony to shew that any ancestor in the female line was a *negro* slave or even an *Indian rightfully* held in slavery. Length of time shall not bar the right to freedom of those who, *prima facie*, are free, and whose poverty and oppression, (to say nothing of the rigorous principles of former times on this subject,) has prevented an attempt to assert their rights. But in the case before us, there has been no acquiescence. It is proved that John, (a brother of *Hannah*,) brought a suit to recover his freedom; and that *Hannah* herself made an almost continual claim as to her right of freedom, insomuch that she was threatened to be whipped by her master for mentioning the subject. It is also proved by *Francis Temple* (perhaps the brother of *Robert*) that the people in the neighbourhood said "that if she would try for her freedom she would get it." This general reputation and opinion of the neighbourhood is certainly entitled to some credit: it goes to repel the idea that the given female ancestor of *Hannah* was a lawful slave; it goes to confirm the other strong testimony as to *Hannah's* appearance as an *Indian*. It is not to be believed but that some of the neighbours would have sworn to that concerning which they all agreed in opinion; and, if so, *Hannah* might, on their testimony, have perhaps obtained her freedom, had those times been as just and liberal on the subject of slavery as the present . . .

Judges FLEMING, CARRINGTON, and LYONS, President, concurring, the latter delivered the decree of the Court as follows:

This Court, not approving of the Chancellor's principles and reasoning in his decree made in this cause, except so far as the same relates to white persons and native *American Indians*, but entirely disapproving thereof, so far as the same relates to native *Africans* and their descendants, who have been and are now held as slaves by the citizens of this state, and discovering no other error in the said decree, affirms the same.

Comment

Chancellor Wythe's decision at the trial in *Hudgins* was a daring attempt to blend Republican idealism, constitutional text, and legal caution. Wythe did not hold that the Wrights were free simply because slavery violated natural justice or because they had a natural right to liberty, though few if any Republicans would have denied either proposition. Nor did Wythe claim that the positive language of freedom contained in the Virginia Bill of Rights (and in other American constitutional documents) abolished slavery of its own force. Instead, he held that the bill of rights, read against the background of natural justice, established a legal presumption in favor of the freedom of every person. Shifting the burden of proof in suits for freedom was no mere legal technicality, as the public response to Wythe's opinion revealed; the fragmentary state of public records in Virginia would have instantly rendered many claims to property in slaves indefensible.

The state court of appeals substantially rejected Wythe's attempt to join Republican political morality and Republican law and did so on explicitly racial grounds. Wythe's presumption of freedom was legally proper, the court acknowledged, when those asserting their liberty were in fact white (or Native American) in appearance, and the reverse was true when the claimants seemed to be black. Such a racial distinction did not rest easily with the political ideals that the judges, Tucker and Roane in particular, espoused. Tucker attempted to justify the anomaly with a claim of necessity and a denial that black Americans had any "concern, agency or interest" in the Revolution that established American freedom. In doing so, he distanced the legal question of slavery (an institution he sincerely despised) from the libertarian and revolutionary principles that he treated as relevant in other constitutional disputes.

Section B: *Freedom of the Press in the New York Supreme Court*

During the period of the Alien and Sedition acts crisis, a number of Republican lawyers defended extraordinarily broad definitions of the constitutional guarantees of speech and press freedom. After 1801, however, Republican enthusiasm for a libertarian view of those rights tended to decline.

Alexander Hamilton
Oral Argument in *People v. Croswell*
(N.Y. Feb. 13, 1804)[91]

Harry Croswell, a printer, was indicted in a New York state court for libeling President Jefferson in his newspaper *The Wasp*. The prosecution presented evidence that the paper had published stories accusing Jefferson of having paid printers to libel Presidents Washington and Adams; and the judge instructed the jurors that their only duty was to determine whether Croswell published the stories, and whether the stories referred to Washington, Adams, and Jefferson. The truth or falsity of the libel and the malice *vel non* of the publisher were, according to the judge, exclusively matters for the court. The jury returned a guilty verdict and Croswell appealed. Before the New York Supreme Court (then an appellate court), Croswell's counsel was Alexander Hamilton. After considerable, and confusing, internal debate, the court divided evenly. Republican Justices Lewis and Livingston voted against Croswell's appeal, and Republican Thompson and Federalist Kent accepted Hamilton's free-press argument. The case itself ended inconclusively (the prosecution never attempted to have Croswell sentenced), but Hamilton's argument, published as a pamphlet, was widely read.

. . . [B]efore I advance to the full discussion of this question, it may be necessary for the safety and accuracy of investigation, a little to define what this liberty of the press is, for which we contend, and which the present doctrines of those opposed to us, are, in our opinions, calculated to destroy.

The Liberty of the Press consists, in my idea, in publishing the truth, from good motives and for justifiable ends, though it reflect on government, on magistrates, or individuals. If it be not allowed, it excludes the privilege of canvassing men, and our rulers. It is in vain to say, you may canvass measures. This is impossible without the right of looking to men. To say that measures can be discussed, and that there shall be no bearing on those, who are the authors of those measures, cannot be done. The very end and reason of discussion would be destroyed. Of what consequence to shew its object? Why is it to be thus demonstrated, if not to show too, who is the author? Is it essential to say, not only that the measure is bad and deleterious, but to hold up to the people who is the author, that, in this our free and elective government, he may be removed from the seat of power. If this be not to be done, then in vain will the voice of the people be raised against the inroads of tyranny. For, let a party but get into power, they may go on from step to step, and in *spite* of canvassing their measures, fix themselves firmly in their seats, especially as they are never to be reproached for what they have done. This abstract mode, in practice can never be carried into effect. But, if under the qualifications I have mentioned, the power be allowed, the liberty for which I contend will operate as a salutary check. In speaking thus for the Freedom of the Press, I do not say there ought to be an unbridled licence; or that the characters of men who are good, will naturally tend eternally to support themselves. I do not stand here to say that no shackles are to be laid on this licence . . .

I contend for the liberty of publishing truth, with good motives and for justifiable ends, even though it reflect on government, magistrates, or private persons. I contend for it under the restraint of our tribunals–When this is exceeded, let them interpose and punish. When, however, we do look at consequences, let me ask whether it is right that a permanent body of men, appointed by the executive, and, in some degree, always connected with it, should exclusively have the power of deciding on what shall constitute a libel on our rulers, or that they shall share it, united with a changeable body of men, chosen by the people. Let our Juries still be selected, as they now are, by lot. But it cannot be denied, that every permanent body of men is, more or less, liable to be influenced by the spirit of the existing administration: that such a body may be liable to corruption, and that they may be inclined to lean over towards party modes. No man can think more highly of our judges, and I may say personally so, of those who now preside, than myself; but I must forget what human nature is, and what her history has taught us, that permanent bodies may be so corrupted, before I can venture to assert that it cannot be. As then it may be, I do not think it safe thus to compromit [*sic*] our independence. For though, as individuals, they may be interested in the general welfare, yet, if once they enter into the views of government, their power may be converted into the engine of oppression. It is in vain to say that allowing them this exclusive right to declare the law, on what the Jury has found, can work no ill; for, by this privilege they can assume and modify the fact, so as to make the most innocent publication libellous. It is therefore not a security to say, that this exclusive power will but follow the law. It must be with the Jury to decide on the intent,— they must in certain cases be permitted to judge of the law, and pronounce on the combined matter of law and of fact . . .

My definition of libel is . . . this: I would call it a slanderous or ridiculous writing, picture, or sign, with a malicious or mischievous design or intent, towards government, magistrates, or individuals. If this definition does not embrace all that may be so called, does it not cover enough for every beneficial purpose of justice? If it have a good intent, it ought not to be a libel, for it then is an innocent transaction; and it ought to have this intent, against which the jury have it in their discretion to pronounce. It shews itself to us as a sentence of fact. Crime is a matter of fact by the code of our jurisprudence. In my opinion, every specific case is a matter of fact, for the law gives the definition. It is some act in violation of law. When we come to investigate, every crime includes an intent. Murder consists in killing a man with malice prepense. Manslaughter, in doing it without malice, and at the moment of an impulse of passion. Killing may even be justifiable if not praise-worthy, as in defence of chastity about to be violated. In these cases the crime is defined, and the intent is always the necessary ingredient. The crime is matter of law as far as definition is concerned; fact, as far as we are to determine its existence . . .

Suppose a man should enter the apartments of the King, this in itself is harmless, but if he do it with an intent to assassinate, it is treason. To whom must this be made to appear in order to induce conviction? to the Jury. Let it rather be said that crime depends on intent, and intent is one parcel of the fact. Unless therefore it can be shewn that there is some specific character of libel, that will apply in all cases, intent, tendency, and quality, must all be matters of fact for a Jury. There is therefore nothing which can be libel, independent of circumst[a]nces; nothing which can be so called in opposition to time and circumstances . . .

. . . I must examine how far truth is to be given in evidence. This depends on the intent's being a crime. Its being a truth is a reason to infer that there was no design to injure another. Thus not to decide on it, would be injustice, as it may be material in ascertaining the intent. It is impossible to say that to judge of the quality and nature of an act, the truth is immaterial. It is inherent in the nature of things, that the assertion of truth cannot be a crime. In all systems of law this is a general axiom . . . [But] whether the truth be a justification, will depend on the motives with which it was published.

Personal defects can be made public only to make a man disliked. Here then it will not be excused: it might however be given in evidence to the libellous degree. Still however it is a subject of enquiry. There may be a fair and honest exposure. But if he uses the weapon of truth wantonly; if for the purpose of disturbing the peace of families; if for relating that which does not appertain to official conduct, so far we say the doctrine of our opponents is correct . . .

. . . I am inclined to think courts may go thus far [to hold that truth is a defense to a libel prosecution], for it is absolutely essential to right and security that the truth should be admitted. To be sure this may lead to the purposes suggested [i.e., truthful statements about public officials that are relevant to evaluation of their public activities]. But my reply is, that government is to be thus treated, if it furnish reasons for calumny. I affirm that in the general course of things, the disclosure of truth is right and prudent, when liable to the checks I have been willing it should receive as an object of animadversion.

It cannot be dangerous to government, though it may work partial difficulties. If it be not allowed, the people will stand liable to encroachments on their rights. It is evident that if you cannot apply this mitigated doctrine for which I speak, to the cases of libels here, you must for ever remain ignorant of what your rulers do. I never can think this ought to be; I never did think the truth was a crime; I am glad the day is come in which it is to be decided; for my soul has ever abhorred the thought, that a free man dared not speak the truth; I have for ever rejoiced when this question has been brought forward . . .

[The jury has,] it is said, the power to decide in criminal [cases], on the law and the fact. They have then the right, because they cannot be restricted in its exercise; and in politics, power, and right are equivalent. To prove it, what shall we say to this case? Suppose the legislature to have laid a tax, which by the Constitution, they certainly are entitled to impose, yet still the legislature may be guilty of oppression; but who can prevent them, or say they have not authority to raise taxes. Legal power then is the decisive effect of certain acts without controul. It is agreed that the Jury may decide against the direction of the Court, and that their verdict of acquittal cannot be impeached, but must have its effect. This, then I take to be the criterion, that the Constitution has lodged the power with them, and they have the right to execise it. For this I could cite authorities. It is nothing to say, in opposition, to this, that they, if they act wrong, are to answer between God and their consciences. This may be said of the legislature, and yet nevertheless they have the power and the right of taxation. I do not mean to admit, that it would be proper for Jurors thus to conduct themselves, but only to shew that the Jury do possess the legal right of determining on the law and the fact. What then do I conceive to be true doctrine. That in the general distribution of power in our Constitution it is the province of the Jury to speak to fact, yet in criminal cases the consequences and tendency of acts, the law and the fact are always blended. As far as the safety of the citizen is concerned, it is necessary that the Jury shall be permitted to speak to both . . .

Comment

Hamilton's argument in *Croswell*, though technically unsuccessful in that case, stated what became the standard legal doctrine of criminal libel in American courts for over a century: the truth of the alleged libel was admissible as a defense, though not an absolute one; the jury's right to rule on the question of malice or intent was recognized; and the constitutional values of free speech and press were treated as the background to the American common-law definition of libel, rather than as a separate and superordinate source of legal rules. This approach to the crime of libel was essentially identical with that embodied in the Sedition Act of 1798, and to that extent the free-speech theme of the Revolution of 1800 was betrayed or abandoned by its own supporters. The Republican contribution to the law of press freedom was not wholly lost, however, for the Supreme Court eventually endorsed the denial of a federal common law of crimes, and thus disavowed an inherent federal judicial power to punish criticism of government.

More far-reaching was the contribution of the "doctrines of '98" to American political culture. Until World War I, no Congress challenged the Republican rejection of congressional power to criminalize seditious libel, and state criminal prosecutions for libel sharply diminished after 1810. The Republican antipathy toward governmental interference with free speech in *Croswell*, represented by the arch-Federalist Hamilton, outlasted the Republican opportunism that led to the prosecution of Harry Croswell.

Section C: Women's Citizenship in the Massachusetts Supreme Judicial Court

The social and intellectual ferment following the Revolution affected even that most deeply rooted of social institutions, the place of women in society. Abigail Adams's famous demand that republican lawmakers address the legal disabilities to which common law traditionally subjected women was echoed by St. George Tucker, who observed in an 1809 opinion, that "natural justice respects not the difference of persons or of sexes" (*Claiborne v. Henderson*). As with questions of race, however, abstract views of natural justice or republican principle did not translate automatically into constitutional norms.

Martin v. Commonwealth
1 Mass. 347 (Mar. 1805)

A Revolutionary-era Massachusetts statute known as the Absentee Act provided for the forfeiture of the estates of loyalist "inhabitants and members," that is, citizens, of the state who left it during the war. In 1781 a state trial court ordered the seizure of property belonging to a married couple, William and Anna Martin, under the act. Over two decades later, the Martins' son and heir James Martin requested the state high court to reverse the 1781 decision. One of his arguments was that the estate of his mother was not liable to confiscation under the act because she was a married woman (a *feme covert*).

G. BLAKE [for Martin] . . . As to the *fourth* error assigned, *femes-covert* are not within the statute. They are not within the *letter* of the act; almost all the provisions of the act are masculine; nothing is said about females, excepting where provision is made for their dower. It is admitted that there are cases where statutes will extend to females, where the expressions are similar to those used in this act. But it is manifest from the act itself that women were not *intended* to be included under the general description of persons mentioned.

The *first sect.* of the act says "that every *inhabitant* and *member* of the state who," &c. Upon the strict principles of law, a *feme-covert* is not a member; has no *political* relation to the state any more than an alien; upon the most rigid and illiberal construction of the words, she cannot be a member within the meaning of the statute . . . The legislature *intended* to exclude *femes-covert* and infants from the operation of the act; otherwise the word *inhabitant* would have been used alone, and not coupled with the word *member*. This construction is strengthened by the provision in the same (*the first*) *sect.* of the act respecting an oath of allegiance. A *feme-covert* was never holden to take an oath of allegiance. The statute is highly penal; the Court therefore will not extend it beyond the *express* words, or *obvious* meaning, by an equitable construction. The preamble is a key to unlock the meaning. What says the preamble? "Whereas every government hath a right to command the *personal services* of all its *members*, whenever the *exigences [sic] of the state* shall require it, especially in times of an impending or *actual invasion*, no *member* thereof can then withdraw *himself* from the jurisdiction of the government, and thereby deprive it of *his personal services*, without justly incurring the forfeiture of all his property, rights and liberties holden under and derived from that constitution of government, to the support of which *he* hath refused to afford *his* aid and assistance; and whereas the king of *Great Britain* did cause, &c.&c., whereupon it became the indispensable duty of all *the people* of said states forthwith to *unite in defence* of their common freedom, and *by arms* to oppose the fleets and armies of the said king; yet, nevertheless, divers of the *members* of this and of the other *United States* of America, evilly disposed, or regardless of their duty towards their country, did withdraw themselves, &c.&c., aiding or giving encouragement and countenance to the operations of the fleets and armies of the said king against the United States aforesaid."

It is impossible to read the preamble of the statute without seeing the object and intention of the act. The object was not to punish, but to retain the physical force of the state, as is evident from the expression, *personal services in times of actual invasion*, opposing *by arms*, aiding the enemy, &c. How much physical force is retained by retaining married women? What are the *personal services* they are to render in opposing by force an actual invasion? What aid can they give to an enemy? So far are women from being of service in the defence of a country against the attacks of an enemy, that it is frequently thought expedient to send them out of the way, lest they impede the operations of their own party . . . And can it be supposed, in the case before the Court, that the legislature contemplated the case of a wife withdrawing with her husband? It ought not to be, and surely was not intended that she should be exposed to the loss of all her property for withdrawing from the government with her husband. If he commanded it, she was bound to obey him, by a law paramount to all other laws—the law of God.

The Attorney General: . . . Under the *fourth* error originally assigned, it has been contended by the counsel for the plaintiff that the statute did not extend to *femes-covert*. And it is said that the *words* of the act do not include them, because the words are in the masculine gender; that they are *him, his,* &c. The same reasoning would go to prove that the *constitution* of the commonwealth does not extend to women—secures them no rights, no privileges; for it has no words in the feminine gender; it would prove that a great variety of crimes, made so by statute, could not be committed by women, because the statutes had used only the words *him and his*. It also said that a *feme-covert* is not an inhabitant and member of the state. Surely a *feme-covert* can be an inhabitant in every sense of the word. Who are members of the body politic? are not all the *citizens*, members; infants, idiots, insane, or whatever may be their *relative* situations in society? Cannot a *feme-covert* levy war and conspire to levy war? She certainly can commit treason; and if so, there is no one act mentioned in the statute which she is not capable of performing . . .

SEDGWICK, J. . . . The preamble of the statute has described the persons whom it intended to bring within it. It is that member who "withdraws himself from the jurisdiction of the government, and, thereby deprives it of the benefit of his personal services." A *wife* who left the country in the company of her husband did not *withdraw* herself; but was, if I may so express it, withdrawn by him. She did not deprive the government of the benefit of her personal services; she had none to render; none were exacted of her. "The member who so withdraws, incurs," says the preamble, "the forfeiture of all his property, rights, and liberties, holden under and derived from that constitution of government, to the support of which he has refused to afford his aid and assistance." Can any one believe it was the intention of the legislature to demand of *femes-covert* their *aid and assistance* in the support of their constitution of government? This preamble then goes on to particularize the violation of our rights by our former sovereign, and proceeds to declare that it thereupon "became the indispensable duty of all the *people* of said states forthwith to unite in defence of their common freedom, and by arms to oppose the fleets and armies of the said king; yet, nevertheless, divers of the members of this, and of the other United States of America, evilly disposed, or regardless of their duty towards their country, did withdraw themselves," &c. Now it is unquestionably true that the members here spoken of as "evilly disposed" are included in the people above mentioned. What then was the duty of these evilly-disposed persons, for a violation of which they were to be cut off from the community to which they had belonged, and rendered aliens to it? It was "to unite in defence of their common freedom, and *by arms* to oppose" an invading enemy. And can it be supposed to have been the intention of the legislature to exact the performance of this duty from wives, in opposition to the will and command of their husbands? Can it be believed that a humane and just legislature ever intended that wives should be subjected to the horrid alternative of, either, on the one hand, separating from their husbands and disobeying them, or, on the other, of sacrificing their property? It is impossible for me to suppose that such was ever their intention . . .

Comment

Early American political discourse systematically rejected any attempt to treat questions concerning the status and rights of women as constitutional in significance. Like slaves, whom the Virginia judges in *Hudgins v. Wright* treated as no part of the body that carried out the Revolution and secured its benefits, women were treated as a burden on the state rather than as a benefit to it. Even though few people would have denied that American women, married or not, were in some sense citizens, they were treated almost uniformly as servants of their parents or husbands rather than as "members" of the polity.

Eight

The Rule of Law and the Powers of the Judiciary

Marbury v. Madison
5 U.S. (1 Cranch) 137 (Feb. 24, 1803)

President Adams appointed William Marbury a federal magistrate under the 1801 Judiciary Act. Marbury, like several other "midnight" appointees, did not receive his commission before Adams left office. The new president believed that actual delivery of the commissions would have been legally necessary to perfect the appointments, and therefore ordered Secretary of State Madison to withhold the commissions from their Federalist recipients. Marbury then sought a writ of mandamus from the Supreme Court to compel Madison to deliver his commission. The Court held its statutory jurisdiction over the case to be in violation of the Constitution and dismissed Marbury's suit. This exercise of judicial review was not, however, the major significance of the case in 1803. Far more important to Marbury's contemporaries was Marshall's assertion that a federal court with constitutional jurisdiction would have the authority to compel action by a member of the executive cabinet.

MARSHALL, *Chief Justice*: . . . The appointment being, under the constitution, to be made by the president, personally, the delivery of the deed of appointment, if necessary to its completion, must be made by the president also. It is not necessary, that the delivery should be made personally to the grantee of the office: it never is so made. The law would seem to contemplate, that it should be made to the secretary of state, since it directs the secretary to affix the seal to the commission after it shall have been signed by the president. If, then, the act of delivery be necessary to give validity to the commission, it has been delivered, when executed and given to the secretary, for the purpose of being sealed, recorded and transmitted to the party.

But in all cases of letters-patent, certain solemnities are required by law, which solemnities are the evidences of the validity of the instrument: a formal delivery to the person is not among them. In cases of commissions, the sign manual of the president, and the seal of the United States are those solemnities. This objection, therefore, does not touch the case.

It has also occurred as possible, and barely possible, that the transmission of the commission, and the acceptance thereof, might be deemed necessary to complete the right of the plaintiff. The transmission of the commission is a practice, directed by convenience, but not by law. It cannot, therefore, be necessary to constitute the appointment, which must precede it, and which is the mere act of the president. If the executive required that every person appointed to an office should himself take means to procure his commission, the appointment would not be the less valid on that account. The appointment is the sole act of the president; the transmission of the commission is the sole act of the officer to whom that duty is assigned, and may be accelerated or retarded by circumstances which can have no influence on the appointment. A commission is transmitted to a person already appointed; not to a person to be appointed or not, as the letter inclosing the commission should happen to get into the post-office and reach him in safety, or to miscarry . . .

Mr. Marbury, then, since his commission was signed by the president, and sealed by the secretary of state, was appointed; and as the law creating the office, gave the officer a right to hold for five years, independent of the executive, the appointment was not revocable, but vested in the officer legal rights, which are protected by the laws of his country. To withhold his commission, therefore, is an act deemed by the court not warranted by law, but violative of a vested legal right.

This brings us to the second inquiry; which is: If he has a right, and that right has been violated, do the laws of his country afford him a remedy? The very essence of civil liberty certainly consists in the right of every individual to claim the protection of the laws, whenever he receives an injury. One of the first duties of government is to afford that protection. In Great Britain, the king himself is sued in the respectful form of a petition, and he never fails to comply with the judgment of his court . . .

The government of the United States has been emphatically termed a government of laws, and not of men. It will certainly cease to deserve this high appellation, if the laws furnish no remedy for the violation of a vested legal right. If this obloquy is to be cast on the jurisprudence of our country, it must arise from the peculiar character of the case.

It behooves us, then, to inquire whether there be in its composition any ingredient which shall exempt it from legal investigation, or exclude the injured party from legal redress . . .

Is it in the nature of the transaction? Is the act of delivering or withholding a commission to be considered as a mere political act, belonging to the executive department alone, for the performance of which, entire confidence is placed by our constitution in the supreme executive; and for any misconduct respecting which, the injured individual has no remedy? That there may be such cases is not to be questioned; but that every act of duty, to be performed in any of the great departments of government, constitutes such a case, is not to be admitted . . .

It follows, then, that the question, whether the legality of an act of the head of a department be examinable in a court of justice or not, must always depend on the nature of that act. If some acts be examinable, and others not, there must be some rule of law to guide the court in the exercise of its jurisdiction. In some instances, there may be difficulty in applying the rule to particular cases; but there cannot, it is believed, be much difficulty in laying down the rule.

By the constitution of the United States, the president is invested with certain important political powers, in the exercise of which he is to use his own discretion, and is accountable only to his country in his political character, and to his own conscience. To aid him in the performance of these duties, he is authorized to appoint certain officers, who act by his authority, and in conformity with his orders. In such cases, their acts are his acts; and whatever opinion may be entertained of the manner in which executive discretion may be used, still there exists, and can exist, no power to control that discretion. The subjects are political: they respect the nation, not individual rights, and being entrusted to the executive, the decision of the executive is conclusive. The application of this remark will be perceived, by adverting to the act of congress for establishing the department of foreign affairs. This officer, as his duties were prescribed by that act, is to conform precisely to the will of the president: he is the mere organ by whom that will is communicated. The acts of such an officer, as an officer, can never be examinable by the courts. But when the legislature proceeds to impose on that officer other duties; when he is directed peremptorily to perform certain acts when the rights of individuals are dependent on the performance of those acts; he is so far the officer of the law; is amenable to the laws for his conduct; and cannot, at his discretion, sport away the vested rights of others.

The conclusion from this reasoning is, that where the heads of departments are the political or confidential agents of the executive, merely to execute the will of the president, or rather to act in cases in which the executive possesses a constitutional or legal discretion, nothing can be more perfectly clear, than that their acts are only politically examinable. But where a specific duty is assigned by law, and individual rights depend upon the performance of that duty, it seems equally clear, that the individual who considers himself injured, has a right to resort to the laws of his country for a remedy.

If this be the rule, let us inquire, how it applies to the case under the consideration of the court. The power of nominating to the senate, and the power of appointing the person nominated, are political powers, to be exercised by the president, according to his own discretion. When he has made an appointment, he has exercised his whole power, and his discretion has been completely applied to the case. If, by law, the officer be removable at the will of the president, then a new appointment may be immediately made, and the rights of the officer are terminated. But as a fact which has existed, cannot be made never to have existed, the appointment cannot be annihilated; and consequently, if the officer is by law not removable at the will of the president, the rights he has acquired are protected by the law, and are not resumable by the president. They cannot be extinguished by executive authority, and he has the privilege of asserting them in like manner, as if they had been derived from any other source.

The question whether a right has vested or not, is, in its nature, judicial, and must be tried by the judicial authority. If, for example, Mr. Marbury had taken the oaths of a magistrate, and proceeded to act as one; in consequence of which, a suit has been instituted against him, in which his defence had depended on his being a magistrate, the validity of his appointment must have been determined by judicial authority. So, if he conceives that, by virtue of his appointment, he has a legal right either to the commission which has been made out for him, or to a copy of that commission, it is equally a question examinable in a court, and the decision of the court upon it must depend on the opinion entertained of his appointment. That question has been discussed, and the opinion is, that the latest point of time which can be taken as that at which the appointment was complete, and evidenced, was when, after the signature of the president, the seal of the United States was affixed to the commission.

It is, then, the opinion of the Court: 1st. That by signing the commission of Mr. Marbury, the President of the United States appointed him a justice of peace for the county of Washington, in the district of Columbia; and that the seal of the United States, affixed thereto by the secretary of state, is conclusive testimony of the verity of the signature, and of the completion of the appointment; and that the appointment conferred on him a legal right to the office for the space of five years. 2d. That, having this legal title to the office, he has a consequent right to the commission; a refusal to deliver which is a plain violation of that right, for which the laws of his country afford him a remedy...

Comment

Marshall's discussion of Marbury's claim joined several key concepts of early constitutionalism. Marshall first concluded that Marbury had a vested right to the privileges of his appointment. The appointment was complete when the commission was signed and sealed in the Court's—though not the president's—legal opinion and this constituted a legal fact that the most extensive executive discretion could not change. Marshall thereby arrayed Marbury and the universally respected idea of vested rights against Jefferson and the notion of governmental discretion that was so odious to many Americans and especially Republicans. That the protection of property was one of "the first duties of government" was a commonplace in Anglo-American political discourse. Marshall could conclude with ease, then, that American jurisprudence afforded Marbury some efficacious remedy; and, in a section of the opinion that is omitted, the chief justice identified the writ of mandamus, by which common-law courts directly commanded official action, as the proper remedy.

Marshall then turned to one of the central themes of early constitutional history: the relationship between the domain of politics and the sphere of law. Political decisions, according to the chief justice, were the subject of legislative or executive discretion; they were "examinable" only by the electoral process and the decision-maker's own conscience. Decisions affecting legal rights were "examinable in a court" applying judicially pronounced rules; the courts enforced those rules by peremptory commands. Any issue involving a claim of vested right involved by definition a question of law rather than discretion. Marshall treated these two spheres of decision and their quite distinct rules of operation as implying distinctly different institutional consequences. The political decisions of a political branch were final as were the legal decisions of the judiciary. This formulation neatly preserved both a constitutional-review function for the president (and, implicitly, Congress) *and* the finality of judicial decisions in cases falling within a court's jurisdiction. The president had the right and responsibility to interpret the Constitution when exercising his discretion, as in deciding whether to sign or veto a bill. On the other hand, he had no discretion at all in dealing with legal matters of right, as to which any court of competent jurisdiction could impose a duty even on the executive to act at the court's behest.

Thomas Jefferson
Letter to George Hay
(June 2, 1807)[92]

Hay was the United States attorney who conducted the prosecution of Aaron Burr for treason. During his extensive correspondence with Hay about the course of the prosecution, Jefferson restated his view of the executive branch's authority to interpret the Constitution (and the laws generally) and to act on that interpretation notwithstanding a contrary interpretation by the courts.

Dear Sir,—While Burr's case is depending before the court, I will trouble you, from time to time, with what occurs to me. I observe that the case of Marbury v. Madison has been cited, and I think it material to stop at the threshold the citing that case as authority, and to have it denied to be law. 1. Because the judges, in the outset, disclaimed all cognizance of the case, altho they then went on to say what would have been their opinion, had they had cognizance of it. This, then, was confessedly an extrajudicial opinion, and, as such, of no authority. 2. Because, had it been judicially pronounced, it would have been against law; for to a commission, a deed, a bond, *delivery* is essential to give validity. Until, therefore, the commission is delivered out of the hands of the Executive & his agents, it is not his deed. He may withhold or cancel it at pleasure, as he might his private deed in the same situation. The constitution intended that the three great branches of the government should be co-ordinate, and independent of each other. As to acts, therefore, which are to be done by either, it has given no controul to another branch. A judge, I presume, cannot sit on a bench without a commission, or a record of a commission; &

the Constitution having given to the judiciary branch no means of compelling the executive either to *deliver* a commission, or to make a record of it, shews it did not intend to give the judiciary that controul over the executive, but that it should remain in the power of the latter to do it or not. Where different branches have to act in their respective lines, finally & without appeal, under any law, they may give to it different and opposite constructions . . . In the cases of Callendar & some others, the judges determined the sedition act was valid under the Constitution, and exercised their regular powers of sentencing them to fine & imprisonment. But the executive [Jefferson] determined the sedition act was a nullity under the Constitution, and exercised his regular power of prohibiting the execution of the sentence . . .

On this construction I have hitherto acted; on this I shall ever act, and maintain it with the powers of the government, against any control which may be attempted by the judges, in subversion of the independence of the executive & Senate within their peculiar department. I presume, therefore, that in a case where our decision is by the Constitution the supreme one, & that which can be carried into effect, it is the constitutionally authoritative one, and that by the judges was *coram non judice*, & unauthoritative, because it cannot be carried into effect. I have long wished for a proper occasion to have the gratuitous opinion in Marbury v. Madison brought before the public, & denounced as not law; & I think the present a fortunate one, because it occupies such a place in the public attention. I should be glad, therefore, if, in noticing that case, you could take occasion to express the determination of the executive, that the doctrines of that case were given extrajudicially & against law, and that their reverse will be the rule of action with the executive . . .

Little v. Barreme
6 U.S. (2 Cranch) 170 (Feb. 27, 1804)

During the naval quasi-war with France in 1798–1800, an American frigate commanded by a Captain Little captured *The Flying Fish*, brought her into an American port, and sought her condemnation by the federal district court. The ship's owners counter-claimed for damages against Little. A congressional statute authorized the president to instruct the navy to seize American ships bound to French ports, and the president through the secretary of the navy had ordered the seizure of vessels sailing from French ports as well. The district court found that *The Flying Fish* was in fact Danish, and had been sailing from rather than to a French port. It therefore refused to condemn her, but it also denied the owners damages because Little had probable cause to think The *Flying Fish* was American. The circuit court, however, held the owners entitled to damages on the ground that Congress had authorized seizure, even of an American vessel, only when bound to (not from) a French port.

MARSHALL, *Chief Justice*, now delivered the opinion of the Court . . .

It is by no means clear that the president of the United States, whose high duty it is to "take care that the laws be faithfully executed," and who is commander in chief of the armies and navies of the United States, might not, without any special authority for that purpose, in the then existing state of things, have empowered the officers commanding armed vessels of the United States, to seize and send into port for adjudication, American vessels which were forfeited by being engaged in this illicit commerce. But when it is observed . . . that the 5th section [of the statute] gives a special authority to seize on the high seas and limits that authority to the seizure of vessels bound or sailing to a French port, the legislature seem to have prescribed that the manner in which this law shall be carried into execution, was to exclude a seizure of any vessel not bound *to* a French port. Of consequence, however strong the circumstances might be, which induced Captain

Little to suspect *The Flying Fish* to be an American vessel, they could not excuse the detention of her, since he would not have been authorized to detain her had she been really American.

It was so obvious, that if only vessels sailing to a French port could be seized on the high seas, that the law would be very often evaded, that this act of congress appears to have received a different construction from the executive of the United States; a construction much better calculated to give it effect.

A copy of this act was transmitted by the secretary of the navy, to the captains of the armed vessels, who were ordered to consider the 5th section as a part of their instructions. The same letter contained the following clause:

> A proper discharge of the important duties enjoined on you, arising out of this act, will require the exercise of a sound and an impartial judgment. You are not only to do all that in you lies, to prevent all intercourse, whether direct or circuitous, between the ports of the United States and those of France or her dependencies, where the vessels are apparently as well as really American, and protected by American papers only, but you are to be vigilant that vessels of cargoes, really American, but covered by Danish or other foreign papers, and bound to or from French ports, do not escape you.

These orders, given by the executive, under the construction of the act of congress made by the department to which its execution was assigned, enjoin the seizure of American vessels sailing from a French port. Is the officer who obeys them liable for damages sustained by this misconstruction of the act, or will his orders excuse him? If his instructions afford him no protection, then the law must take its course, and he must pay such damages as are legally awarded against him; if they excuse an act, not otherwise excusable, it would then be necessary to inquire, whether this is a case in which the probable cause which existed to induce a suspicion that the vessel was American, would excuse the captor from damages when the vessel appeared in fact to be neutral.

I confess, the first bias of my mind was very strong in favour of the opinion, that though the instructions of the executive could not give a right, they might yet excuse from damages. I was much inclined to think, that a distinction ought to be taken between acts of civil and those of military officers; and between proceedings within the body of the country and those on the high seas. That implicit obedience which military men usually pay to the orders of their superiors, which indeed is indispensably necessary to every military system, appeared to me strongly to imply the principle that those orders, if not to perform a prohibited act, ought to justify the person whose general duty it is to obey them, and who is placed by the laws of his country in a situation which in general requires that he should obey them. I was strongly inclined to think that, where, in consequence of orders from the legitimate authority, a vessel is seized, with pure intention, the claim of the injured party for damages would be against that government from which the orders proceeded, and would be a proper subject for negotiation. But I have been convinced that I was mistaken, and I have receded from this first opinion. I acquiesce in that of my brethren, which is, that the instructions cannot change the nature of the transaction, or legalize an act which, without those instructions, would have been a plain trespass.

It becomes, therefore, unnecessary to inquire whether the probable cause afforded by the conduct of *The Flying Fish* to suspect her of being an American, would excuse Captain Little from damages for having seized and sent her into port, since, had she been an American, the seizure would have been unlawful.

Captain Little, then, must be answerable in damages to the owner of this neutral vessel, and as the account taken by order of the circuit court is not objectionable on its face, and has not been excepted to by counsel before the proper tribunal, this court can receive no objection to it.

There appears, then, to be no error in the judgment of the circuit court, and it must be affirmed with costs.

Comment

In the case of *The Flying Fish*, the Supreme Court upheld the continuing validity of an important legal doctrine of the colonial Whigs: the amenability of executive officers to damage actions for violations of the law in the exercise of their official duties. Some American lawyers, among them John Marshall, had assumed that the colonial rule had been a legal counterweight to the general independence of the British Crown from the popular will, and therefore was obsolescent in the Republic. Executive officers acting under orders from the president, in this view, should enjoy immunity against suit because their superior was amenable for abuses to the electoral and impeachment processes. Marshall's colleagues, however, insisted that this traditional tool for imposing the rule of law on the executive was not abolished by the Constitution or American republicanism.

United States v. Smith
27 Fed. Cas. 1192 (C.C.D.N.Y. July 15, 1806)

William S. Smith was indicted for outfitting a military expedition to be carried out against Spain's American possessions in violation of a federal statute making such filibustering a crime. In his defense, Smith argued that his activities had been undertaken with the knowledge and approval of President Jefferson, and he subpoenaed the secretaries of state and the navy as well as two State Department officials to testify to this effect. When Madison and the other officials did not attend pursuant to the subpoenas, Smith's attorneys moved for the circuit court to proceed to enforce its process against Madison and the others, and for the trial to be postponed.

PATTERSON [Paterson], Circuit Justice, informed the bar, that the court had received a letter from Messrs. Madison, Dearborne and R. Smith, informing that they would not be able to attend. The letter was in these words: "To the Honorable the Judges of the Circuit Court of the District of New York: We have been summoned to appear, on the 14th day of this month, before a special circuit court of the United States for the district of New York, to testify on the part of William S. Smith and Samuel G. Ogden . . . Sensible of all the attention due to the writs of subpoena issued in these cases, it is with regret we have to state to the court, that the president of the United States, taking into view the state of our public affairs, has specially signified to us that our official duties cannot, consistently therewith, be at this juncture dispensed with. The court, we trust, will be pleased to accept this as a satisfactory explanation of our failure to give the personal attendance required. And as it must be uncertain whether, at any subsequent period, the absence of heads of departments, at such a distance from the scene of their official duties, may not equally happen to interfere with them, we respectfully submit, whether the objects of the parties in this case may not be reconciled with public considerations by a commission issued, with the consent of their counsel and that of the district attorney of the United States, for the purpose of taking, in that mode, our respective testimonies. We have the honor to be, with the greatest respect, your most obedient servants. James Madison, H. Dearborne. R. Smith. City of Washington, 8th of July, 1806." . . .

Pierpont Edwards [for the United States]. When the attachment [the procedure to enforce the subpoenas] is argued, we shall not take the ground of privilege for the executive officers of the government. I know the district attorney would disdain to rest himself on such a pretext . . .

Cadwallader D. Colden [for the defendant]. . . . I proceed to inquire whether Mr. Madison and the other heads of departments have offered a sufficient excuse for this disobedience to the process of the court, by saying they are members of the executive government—whether these dignified sounds elevate them above the constitution and laws.

The general rule is that all persons are bound to give testimony. I have no book from which to read this rule; but I think it is written by the finger of God on the heart of every man. True it is that the necessities of society have introduced one exception, and but one: and that is where a person in the capacity of counsellor or attorney, represents another. This exception is most strictly confined to this relationship.

But it may be said that there are certain political motives which should induce the court to excuse the secretary of state and other heads of departments from giving testimony. That, were they to be examined as witnesses they might disclose state secrets! If I were to admit that there are certain secrets between the president and his secretaries which they would not wish to be disclosed (and I have no doubt there are many such), or which ought not to be disclosed, still the witnesses who have been duly summoned owe obedience to the process of the court; they must appear and be sworn, and when on their oaths, they may avail themselves of this excuse if questions are put to them which they ought not to answer. But the court must judge, and not the witnesses, whether they shall or shall not answer. Much less shall the witnesses be allowed to determine for themselves whether they will be obedient to a mandate of the judicial authority. Such was the determination of the supreme court of the United States in the case of Marbury v. Madison.

Thomas A. Emmett [for the defendant]. Another question has been raised. It has been insinuated rather than explicitly expressed, by one of the counsel for the prosecution, that those witnesses could not be coerced to appear. If hereby is meant to be asserted any peculiar privilege of office, certainly such claim cannot be made by Doctor Thornton or Mr. Wagner [the State Department employees]. Nor is there such a privilege attached to any of the offices [cabinet posts] held by the other witnesses. It is a strange doctrine in this free country, where the constitution and laws have accurately marked out the rights and privileges belonging to every office. Privileges of exemption from those duties to which every citizen is liable as such, must be clearly shown, and the law by which they are authorized must be produced.

PATTERSON, [Paterson], Circuit Justice. You may save yourself the trouble of arguing that point; the witnesses may undoubtedly be compelled to appear . . .

Emmett . . . Let us suppose that we could prove that the acts charged against the defendant were done by the express order of the president of the United States; would not such an order be a complete justification? That the president might have authority to give such an order cannot be questioned. Congress have the power of declaring war; and when that is done, the president is to act under it, and may authorize any military or hostile measure against the enemy. If it be said that there was no declaration by congress, it is sufficient for us to answer that there might have been. The constitution does not require that a declaration of war should be made public; it would be absurd to suppose that it did, and thereby the executive of this country was to be deprived of all chance of taking an enemy by surprise, or of the advantage of secret measures of defence or offence. It is well known, that at the time General Miranda's expedition was set on foot, congress was sitting with closed doors, and might have, nay, it was universally believed they had, declared war against Spain. If they had done so, the president would have had constitutional authority to sanction the acts for which the defendant is now to answer; and will it be said that the individual acting under the order or sanction of the chief magistrate of the country, who might have had authority to give that sanction, shall be answerable criminally for what he has done pursuant to that order? Must he inquire whether the chief magistrate was or was not authorized to give the order, and must the defendant be punished if it turns out that the president has acted illegally? No; it would be an oppressive and tyrannical doctrine to say the defendant may be charged with a crime under such circumstances. The defendant had only to inquire whether the president gave him an order which might be within the scope and limits of his constitutional functions, and if it was so, the defendant cannot be punished for his obedience. I will not take up the time of the court longer on this part of the subject, or detain it with any argument to show that when we have proved that the defendant acted with the knowledge, consent, and approbation of the president of the United States, it must be equivalent to proving that he acted under an express order.

But let us suppose that the testimony we offer would not make out a justification according to the strict legal acceptation of that term; still we say it would form such an excuse for the defendant as would entitle him to a verdict of acquittal. If the defendant can satisfy the jury by the testimony of the witnesses whom he now calls, that he had no intention to disobey the laws, but on the contrary that he thought, and had reason to think, that his conduct was sanctioned by their authority; and that he would merit the approbation of his government, and the applause of his countrymen, he will not, he ought not, to be convicted. Where there is no intent to do wrong, there can be no crime. This is a principle not derived to us from tradition or record; it is in the heart of every man, is imbibed with our reason, and cannot be obliterated while a sense of justice, or knowledge of right and wrong is retained.

I expect to hear it said, that if this principle be applicable to all cases, then an ignorance of the law will always be an excuse for an offence. Sir, I say it will be so whenever a defendant may have it in his power clearly to demonstrate that he was ignorant. As if a law should this day be passed at Washington against the exportation of arms, and a person tomorrow, before he could possibly have knowledge of the existence of such a law, should make a shipment contrary to the prohibition, I say no jury on earth would convict a defendant under such circumstances. No court on earth would tell a jury, that in such a case, they ought to convict.

PATTERSON [Paterson], Circuit Justice. . . . The first question is, whether the facts stated in the defendant's affidavit be material, or ought to be given in evidence, if the witnesses were now in court, and ready to testify to their truth? Does the affidavit disclose sufficient matter to induce the court to put off the trial [to allow enforcement of the subpoenas supported by the affidavit]? As judges, it is our duty to administer justice according to law. We ought to have no will, no mind, but a legal will and mind. The law, like the beneficent author of our existence, is no respecter of persons; it is inflexible and even-handed, and should not be subservient to any improper considerations or views. This ought to be the case particularly in the United States, which we have been always led to consider as a government not of men, but of laws, of which the constitution is the basis.

The evidence which is offered to a court must be pertinent to the issue, or in some proper manner connected with it. It must relate and be applied to the particular fact or charge in controversy, so as to constitute a legal ground to support, or a legal ground to resist the prosecution . . . If the evidence be not pertinent, nor the witnesses material, the court ought not to receive either. Let us test the affidavit of the defendant by this principle or rule. The defendant is indicted for providing the means, to wit, men and money, for a military enterprise against the dominions of the king of Spain, with whom the United States are at peace, against the form of a statute in such case made and provided. He has pleaded not guilty; and to evince his innocence, to justify his infraction of the act of congress, or to purge his guilt, he offers evidence to prove, that this military enterprise was begun, prepared, and set on foot with the knowledge and approbation of the executive department of our government. Sitting here in our judicial capacities, we should listen with caution to a suggestion of this kind, because the president of the United States is bound by the constitution to "take care that the laws be faithfully executed." These are the words of the instrument; and, therefore, it is to be presumed that he would not countenance the violation of any statute, and particularly if such violation consisted in expeditions of a warlike nature against friendly powers. The law, indeed, presumes, that every officer faithfully executes his duties, until the contrary be proved. And, besides the constitutional provision just mentioned, the seventh section of the act under consideration expressly declares, that it shall be lawful for the president of the United States, or such other person as he shall have empowered for that purpose, to employ such part of the land or naval forces of the United States, or of the militia thereof, as shall be judged necessary for the purpose of preventing the carrying on of any such expedition or enterprise from the territories of the United States against the territories or dominions of a foreign prince or state with whom the United States are at peace . . .

This fifth section, which prohibits military enterprises against nations with which the United States are at peace, imparts no dispensing power to the president. Does the constitution give it? Far from it, for it explicitly directs that he shall "take care that the laws be faithfully executed." This instrument, which measures out the powers and defines the duties of the president, does not vest in him any authority to set on foot a military expedition against a nation with which the United States are at peace. And if a private individual, even with the knowledge and approbation of this high and preeminent officer of our government, should set foot on such a military expedition, how can he expect to be exonerated from the obligation of the law? Who holds the power of dispensation? True, a nolle prosequi may be entered, a pardon may be granted; but these presume criminality, presume guilt, presume amenability to judicial investigation and punishment, which are very different from a power to dispense with the law.

Supposing then that every syllable of the affidavit is true, of what avail can it be on the present occasion? Of what use or benefit can it be to the defendant in a court of law? Does it speak by way of justification? The president of the United States cannot control the statute, nor dispense with its execution, and still less can he authorize a person to do what the law forbids. If he could, it would render the execution of the laws dependent on his will and pleasure; which is a doctrine that has not been set up, and will not meet with any supporters in our government. In this particular, the law is paramount. Who has dominion over it? None but the legislature; and even they are not without their limitation in our republic. Will it be pretended that the president could rightfully grant a dispensation and license to any of our citizens to carry on a war against a nation with whom the United States are at peace? Ingenious and learned counsel may imagine, and put a number of cases in the wide field of conjecture; but we are to take facts as we find them, and to argue from the existing state of things at the time. If we were at war with Spain, there is an end to the indictment; but, if at peace, what individual could lawfully make war or carry on a military expedition against the dominions of his Catholic majesty? The indictment is founded on a state of peace, and such state is presumed to continue until the contrary appears. A state of war is not set up in the affidavit. If, then, the president knew and approved of the military expedition set forth in the indictment against a prince with whom we are at peace, it would not justify the defendant in a court of law, nor discharge him from the binding force of the act of congress; because the president does not possess a dispensing power. Does he possess the power of making war? That power is exclusively vested in congress; for, by the eighth section of the 1st article of the constitution, it is ordained, that congress shall have power to declare war, grant letters of marque and reprisal, raise and support armies, provide and maintain a navy, and to provide for calling forth the militia to execute the laws of the Union, suppress insurrections, and repel invasions . . . It appearing, then, that the testimony of Mr. Madison, Mr. Smith, Mr. Wagner, and Mr. Thornton, as stated in the defendant's affidavit, is not pertinent to the issue, nor material by way of justification or defence against the facts charged in the indictment, their absence cannot operate as a legal excuse to put off the trial.

But it has been contended, that if the testimony offered should not amount to a justification, it will amount to a mitigation of the punishment, and ought to pass to the jury for the sake of reaching the ears of the judges. I take this to be incorrect in principle, so far as it regards criminal prosecutions. Why suffer evidence to go to the jury, that is not pertinent to the issue; that will not justify the defendant, nor prove his innocence, nor purge his guilt? Is it that the court may instruct the jury that they must not regard such evidence, because it is irrelevant? This would be the work of supererogation and inutility. Nor is this all; the evidence may warp their opinion, may mislead their judgment, and induce them to find an erroneous verdict . . .

[Smith was convicted.]

Comment

William Smith's defense raised two important constitutional questions. The first was the ability of the courts to require executive officers to assist in the conduct of a criminal trial. By ruling the intended testimony irrelevant, the circuit court avoided a direct confrontation with the administration over the refusal of Madison and others to obey the subpoenas. Justice Paterson nonetheless stated the judges' view unequivocally: "The witnesses may undoubtedly be compelled to appear." Paterson's constitutional confidence was a striking assertion of the understanding of executive-judicial relations that had been emerging gradually since *Marbury* in 1803. Where courts possessed jurisdiction and were applying law, Paterson implied, executive officers were mere citizens, as liable as any others to judicial command. The prosecutors, interestingly, justified the recalcitrance of Madison and the others on evidentiary grounds, and emphatically disavowed any claim of executive privilege.

In *United States v. Smith*, Paterson also reencountered the question of discretion versus law with which the Supreme Court had dealt in *Marbury*. Paterson treated Smith's argument that presidential approbation of his military adventurism was a defense against prosecution as a revival of the old assertion by the Stuart kings of a power to "dispense" with the execution of statutes. Whig tradition long had identified that claim as one of the Stuarts' most arrogant and oppressive aggressions against liberty and parliamentary authority; Paterson's opinion in *Smith* repeatedly alluded to this tradition and cleverly cast Thomas Jefferson in the role of James II.

United States v. Burr
25 Fed. Cas. 30 (C.C.D.Va. June 13, 1807)

During the prosecution of Burr for treason, he requested the circuit court to issue a subpoena *duces tecum* to President Jefferson to compel the latter to appear in court and produce various documents that were in Jefferson's custody as president. The United States attorney, George Hay, resisted the motion.

MARSHALL, *Chief Justice*. The object of the motion now to be decided is to obtain copies of certain orders, understood to have been issued to the land and naval officers of the United States for the apprehension of the accused, and an original letter from General Wilkinson to the president in relation to the accused, with the answer of the president to that letter, which papers are supposed to be material to the defence. As the legal mode of effecting this object, a motion is made for a subpoena duces tecum, to be directed to the president of the United States. In opposition to this motion, a preliminary point has been made by the counsel for the prosecution. It has been insisted by them that, until the grand jury shall have found a true bill, the party accused is not entitled to subpoenas nor to the aid of the court to obtain his testimony. [A lengthy discussion of a defendant's right to the assistance of the court's process under the common law and the Sixth Amendment is omitted.]

Upon immemorial usage . . . then, and upon what is deemed a sound construction of the constitution and law of the land, the court is of the opinion that any person charged with a crime in the courts of the United States has a right, before as well as after indictment, to the process of the court to compel the attendance of his witnesses. Much delay and much inconvenience may be avoided by this construction; no mischief, which is perceived, can be produced by it. The process would only issue when, according to the ordinary course of proceeding, the indictment would be tried at the term to which the subpoena is made returnable; so that it becomes incumbent on the accused to be ready for his trial at that term.

This point being disposed of, it remains to inquire whether a subpoena duces tecum can be directed to the president of the United States, and whether it ought to be directed in this case? This question originally consisted of two parts. It was at first doubted whether a subpoena could issue, in any case, to the chief magistrate of the nation; and if it could, whether that subpoena could do more than direct his personal attendance; whether it could direct him to bring with him a paper which was to constitute the gist of his testimony.

While the argument was opening, the attorney for the United States avowed his opinion that a general subpoena might issue to the president; but not a subpoena duces tecum. This terminated the argument on that part of the question. The court, however, has thought it necessary to state briefly the foundation of its opinion, that such a subpoena may issue. In the provisions of the constitution, and of the statute, which give to the accused a right to the compulsory process of the court, there is no exception whatever. The obligation, therefore, of those provisions is general; and it would seem that no person could claim an exemption from them, but one who would not be a witness. At any rate, if an exception to the general principle exist, it must be looked for in the law of evidence.

The exceptions furnished by the law of evidence (with only one reservation), so far as they are personal, are of those only whose testimony could not be received. The single reservation alluded to is the case of the king. Although he may, perhaps, give testimony, it is said to be incompatible with his dignity to appear under the process of the court. Of the many points of difference which exist between the first magistrate in England and the first magistrate of the United States, in respect to the personal dignity conferred on them by the constitutions of their respective nations, the court will only select and mention two.

It is a principle of the English constitution that the king can do no wrong, that no blame can be imputed to him, that he cannot be named in debate. By the constitution of the United States, the president, as well as any other officer of the government, may be impeached, and may be removed from office on high crimes and misdemeanors. By the constitution of Great Britain, the crown is hereditary, and the monarch can never be a subject. By that of the United States, the president is elected from the mass of the people, and, on the expiration of the time for which he is elected, returns to the mass of the people again. How essentially this difference of circumstances must vary the policy of the laws of the two countries, in reference to the personal dignity of the executive chief, will be perceived by every person.

In this respect, the first magistrate of the Union may more properly be likened to the first magistrate of a state; at any rate, under the former Confederation; and it is not known ever to have been doubted, but that the chief magistrate of a state might be served with a subpoena ad testificandum. If, in any court of the United States, it has ever been decided that a subpoena cannot issue to the president, that decision is unknown to this court.

If, upon any principle, the president could be construed to stand exempt from the general provisions of the constitution, it would be, because his duties as chief magistrate demand his whole time for national objects. But it is apparent that this demand is not unremitting; and, if it should exist at the time when his attendance on a court is required, it would be shown on the return of the subpoena, and would rather constitute a reason for not obeying the process of the court than a reason against its being issued.

In point of fact it cannot be doubted that the people of England have the same interest in the service of the executive government, that is, of the cabinet counsel, that the American people have in the service of the executive of the United States, and that their duties are as arduous and as unremitting. Yet it has never been alleged, that a subpoena might not be directed to them. It cannot be denied that to issue a subpoena to a person filling the exalted position of the chief magistrate is a duty which would be dispensed with more cheerfully than it would be performed; but, if it be a duty, the court can have no choice in the case.

If, then, as is admitted by the counsel for the United States a subpoena may issue to the president, the accused is entitled to it of course; and whatever difference may exist with respect to the power to compel the same obedience to the process, as if it had been directed to a private citizen, there exists no difference with respect to the right to obtain it. The guard, furnished to this high officer, to protect him from being harassed by vexatious and unnecessary subpoenas, is to be looked for in the conduct of a court after those subpoenas have issued; not in any circumstance which is to precede their being issued.

If, in being summoned to give his personal attendance to testify, the law does not discriminate between the president and a private citizen, what foundation is there for the opinion that this difference is created by the circumstance that his testimony depends on a paper in his possession, not on facts which have come to his knowledge otherwise than by writing? The court can perceive no foundation for such an opinion. The propriety of introducing any paper into a case, as testimony, must depend on the character of the paper, not on the character of the person who holds it.

A subpoena duces tecum, then, may issue to any person to whom an ordinary subpoena may issue, directing him to bring any paper of which the party praying it has a right to avail himself as testimony; if, indeed, that be the necessary process for obtaining the view of such a paper. When this subject was suddenly introduced, the court felt some doubt concerning the propriety of directing a subpoena to the chief magistrate, and some doubt also concerning the propriety of directing any paper in his possession, not public in its nature, to be exhibited in court. The impression that the questions which might arise in consequence of such process, were more proper for discussion on the return of the process than on its issuing, was then strong on the mind of the judges; but the circumspection with which they would take any step which would in any manner relate to that high personage, prevented their yielding readily to those impressions, and induced the request that those points, if not admitted, might be argued. The result of that argument is a confirmation of the impression originally entertained.

The court can perceive no legal objection to issuing a subpoena duces tecum to any person whatever, provided the case be such as to justify the process. This is said to be a motion to the discretion of the court. This is true. But a motion to its discretion is a motion, not to its inclination, but to its judgment; and its judgment is to be guided by sound legal principles. A subpoena duces tecum varies from an ordinary subpoena only in this; that a witness is summoned for the purpose of bringing with him a paper in his custody. In some of our sister states whose system of jurisprudence is erected on the same foundation with our own, this process, we learn, issues of course. In this state it issues, not absolutely of course, but with leave of the court.

No case, however, exists as is believed, in which the motion has been founded on an affidavit, in which it has been denied, or in which it has been opposed. It has been truly observed that the opposite party can, regularly, take no more interest in the awarding a subpoena duces tecum than in awarding an ordinary subpoena. In either case he may object to any delay, the grant of which may be implied in granting the subpoena; but he can no more object regularly to the legal means of obtaining testimony, which exists in the papers, than in the mind of the person who may be summoned. If no inconvenience can be sustained by the opposite party, he can only oppose the motion in the character of an amicus curiae, to prevent the court from making an improper order, or from burthening some officer by compelling an unnecessary attendance.

This court would certainly be very unwilling to say that upon fair construction the constitutional and legal right to obtain its process, to compel the attendance of witnesses, does not extend to their bringing with them such papers as may be material in the defence. The literal distinction which exists between the cases is too much attenuated to be countenanced in the tribunals of a just and humane nation. If, then, the subpoena be issued without inquiry into the manner of its application, it would seem to trench on the privileges which the constitution extends to the accused; it would seem to reduce his means of defence within narrower limits than is designed by the fundamental law of our country, if an overstrained rigor should be used with respect to his right to apply for papers deemed by himself to be material.

In the one case the accused is made the absolute judge of the testimony to be summoned; if, in the other he is not a judge, absolutely for himself, his judgment ought to be controlled only so far as it is apparent that he means to exercise his privileges not really in his own defence, but for purposes which the court ought to discountenance. The court ought not to lend its aid to motions obviously designed to manifest disrespect to the government; but the court has no right to refuse its aid to motions for papers to which the accused may be entitled, and which may be material in his defence.

These observations are made to show the nature of the discretion which may be exercised. If it be apparent that the papers are irrelative to the case, or that for state reasons they cannot be introduced into the defence, the subpoena duces tecum would be useless. But, if this be not apparent, if they may be important in the defence, if they may be safely read at the trial, would it not be a blot in the page which records the judicial proceedings of this country, if, in a case of such serious import as this, the accused should be denied the use of them? . . .

The second objection is, that the letter contains matter which ought not to be disclosed. That there may be matter, the production of which the court would not require, is certain; but, in a capital case, that the accused ought, in some form, to have the benefit of it, if it were really essential to his defence, is a position which the court would very reluctantly deny. It ought not to be believed that the department which superintends prosecutions in criminal cases, would be inclined to withhold it.

What ought to be done under such circumstances presents a delicate question, the discussion of which, it is hoped, will never be rendered necessary in this country. At present it need only be said that the question does not occur at this time. There is certainly nothing before the court which shows that the letter in question contains any matter the disclosure of which would endanger the public safety. If it does contain such matter, the fact may appear before the disclosure is made. If it does contain any matter which it would be imprudent to disclose, which it is not the wish of the executive to disclose, such matter, if it be not immediately and essentially applicable to the point, will, of course, be suppressed.

It is not easy to conceive that so much of the letter as relates to the conduct of the accused can be a subject of delicacy with the president. Everything of this kind, however, will have its due consideration on the return of the subpoena . . .

Much has been said about the disrespect to the chief magistrate, which is implied by this motion, and by such a decision of it as the law is believed to require. These observations will be very truly answered by the declaration that this court feels many, perhaps, peculiar motives for manifesting as guarded a respect for the chief magistrate of the Union as is compatible with its official duties.

To go beyond these would exhibit a conduct which would deserve some other appellation than the term respect. It is not for the court to anticipate the event of the present prosecution. Should it terminate as is expected on the part of the United States, all those who are concerned in it should certainly regret that a paper which the accused believed to be essential to his defence, which may, for aught that now appears, be essential, had been withheld from him.

I will not say, that this circumstance would, in any degree, tarnish the reputation of the government; but I will say, that it would justly tarnish the reputation of the court which had given its sanction to its being withheld. Might I be permitted to utter one sentiment, with respect to myself, it would be to deplore, most earnestly, the occasion which should compel me to look back on any part of my official conduct with so much self-reproach as I should feel, could I declare, on the information now possessed, that the accused is not entitled to the letter in question, if it should be really important to him . . .

Thomas Jefferson
Letters to George Hay

(June 12, 1807)[93]

Sir: In answering your letter of the 9th, which desired a communication of one to me from General Wilkinson, specified by its date, I informed you in mine of the 12th that I had delivered it, with all other papers respecting the charges against Aaron Burr, to the attorney general when he went to Richmond; that I had supposed he had left them in your possession, but would immediately write to him, if he had not, to forward that particular letter without delay. I wrote to him accordingly on the same day, but having no answer I know not whether he has forwarded the letter. I stated in the same letter that I had desired the secretary of war to examine his office in order to comply with your further request to furnish copies of the orders which had been given respecting Aaron Burr and his property; and, in a subsequent letter of the same day, I forwarded you copies of two letters from the secretary at war, which appeared to be within the description expressed in your letter. The order from the secretary of the navy you said you were in possession of.

The receipt of these papers has, I presume, so far anticipated, and others this day forwarded, will have substantially fulfilled the object of a subpoena from the district court of Richmond, requiring that those officers and myself should attend the court in Richmond, with the letter of General Wilkinson, the answer to that letter, and the orders of the department of war and the navy therein generally described. No answer to General Wilkinson's letter, other than a mere acknowledgement of its receipt in a letter written for a different purpose, was ever written by myself or any other.

To these communications of papers I will add, that if the defendant suppose there are any facts within the knowledge of the heads of departments or of myself, which can be useful for his defence, from a desire of doing anything our situation will permit in furtherance of justice, we shall be ready to give him the benefit of it, by way of deposition through any persons whom the court shall authorize to take our testimony at this place. I know indeed that this cannot be done but by consent of parties, and I therefore authorize you to give consent on the part of the United States. Mr. Burr's consent will be given of course, if he suppose the testimony useful.

As to our personal attendance at Richmond, I am persuaded the court is sensible that paramount duties to the nation at large control the obligation of compliance with its summons in this case, as it would should we receive a similar one to attend the trials of Blennerhassett and others in Mississippi territory, those instituted at St. Louis and other places on the western waters, or at any place other than the seat of government [this reference is to prosecutions brought against other suspected participants in Burr's conspiracy]. To comply with such calls would leave the nation without an executive branch, whose agency nevertheless is understood to be so constantly necessary that it is the sole branch which the constitution requires to be always in function. It could not, then, intend that it should be withdrawn from its station by any co-ordinate authority.

With respect to papers, there is certainly a public and private side to our offices. To the former belong grants of land, patents for inventions, certain commissions, proclamations, and other papers patent in their nature. To the other belong mere executive proceedings. All nations have found it necessary that, for the advantageous conduct of their affairs, some of these proceedings, at least, should remain known to their executive functionary only. He, of course, from the nature of the case, must be the sole judge of which of them the public interest will permit publication.

Hence, under our constitution, in requests of papers from the legislative to the executive branch, an exception is carefully expressed, 'as to those which he may deem the public welfare may require not to be disclosed,' as you will see in the inclosed resolution of the house of representatives, which produced the message of January 22d, respecting this case. The respect mutually due between the constituted authorities in their official intercourse, as well as sincere dispositions to do for every one what is just, will always insure from the executive, in exercising the duty of discrimination confided to him, the same candor and integrity to which the nation has, in like manner, trusted in the disposal of its judiciary authorities. Considering you as the organ for communicating these sentiments to the court, I address them to you for that purpose, and salute you with esteem and respect.

(June 20, 1807)

...I did not see till last night the opinion of the Judge on the *subpoena duces tecum* against the President. Considering the question there as *coram non judice*, I did not read his argument with much attention. Yet I saw readily enough, that, as is usual where an opinion is to be supported, right or wrong, he dwells much on smaller objections and passes over those which are solid. Laying down the position generally, that all persons owe obedience to subpoenas, he admits no exception unless it can be produced in his law books. But if the Constitution enjoins on a particular officer to be always engaged in a particular set of duties imposed on him, does not this supersede the general law, subjecting him to minor duties inconsistent with these? The Constitution enjoins his constant agency in the concerns of 6 millions of people. Is the law paramount to this, which calls on him on behalf of a single one? Let us apply the Judge's own doctrine to the case of himself & his brethren. The sheriff of Henrico summons him from the bench, to quell a riot somewhere in his county. The federal judge is, by the general law, a part of the *posse* of the State sheriff. Would the Judge abandon major duties to perform lesser ones? Again; the court of Orleans or Maine commands, by subpoenas, the attendance of all the judges of the Supreme court. Would they abandon their posts as judges, and the interests of millions committed to them, to serve the purposes of a single individual? The leading principle of our Constitution is the independence of the Legislature, executive and judiciary of each other, and none are more jealous of this than the judiciary. But would the executive be independent of the judiciary, if he were subject to the commands of the latter, & to imprisonment for disobedience; if the several courts could bandy him from pillar to post, keep him constantly trudging from north to south & east to west, and withdraw him entirely from his constitutional duties? The intention of the Constitution, that each branch should be independent of the others, is further manifested by the means it has furnished to each, to protect itself from enterprises of force attempted on them by the others, and to none has it given more effectual or diversified means than to the executive. Again; because ministers can go into a court in London as witnesses, without interruption to their executive duties, it is inferred that they would go to a court 1000 or 1500 miles off, and that ours are to be dragged from Maine to Orleans by every criminal who will swear that their testimony "may be of use to him." The Judge says, "it is apparent that the President's duties as chief magistrate do not demand his whole time, & are not unremitting." If he alludes to our annual retirement from the seat of government, during the sickly season, he should be told that such arrangements are made for carrying on the public business, at and between the several stations we take, that it goes on as unremittingly there, as if we were at the seat of government . . .

Comment

Burr's prosecution for treason presented in stark terms the question of the constitutional relationship between the executive and the courts. Burr's motion for a subpoena to be issued to Thomas Jefferson raised the astounding if unlikely possibility of the chief justice ordering a federal marshal to arrest the president to compel his obedience. Somewhat less luridly, the motion compelled the Jefferson administration to argue formally to a court the principle underlying its willingness to disobey judicial process in *Marbury* and *Smith*: the claim that the judiciary had no power to compel action by the coordinate executive authority. Conversely, given their affirmative decision as to the relevance of the papers Burr's motion demanded, Marshall and his colleague, district judge Cyrus Griffin, could not take the path the courts followed in *Marbury* and *Smith* of theoretically asserting a power that they then declined to exercise. The Burr subpoena, finally, touched on the difference between the legal discretion of the judge and the extralegal discretion of the president.

Perhaps unsurprisingly, both Marshall and Jefferson attempted to combine adherence to constitutional principle with pragmatic compromise. Marshall's opinion was similar in form to his discussion of the mandamus issue in *Marbury*. The chief justice established at length a criminal defendant's general right to receive judicial assistance in obtaining witnesses, and then denied the existence of any relevant exception to the rule that would affect Burr's motion. In particular, Marshall (like Paterson in *Smith*) raised but rejected an analogy between the president and the British monarch. In response to prosecutor Hay's argument that holding the president liable to process could interfere with execution of his constitutional duties, the chief justice invoked the courts' power to deny vexatious motions and suppress evidence the publication of which might harm the national interests. Marshall was insistent on the Court's respect for "the chief magistrate of the Union" and vague about the Court's power to enforce its process against an unwilling president.

The administrations's primary attack on the subpoena motion in court was an argument from inconvenience: to acknowledge a legal duty to obey the subpoena would leave the president and other high executive officers, whom "the Constitution enjoins . . . to be always engaged" in their duties, potentially unable to fulfill those duties. Jefferson's deeper concern, however, rested on his views of constitutional structure. For him, the Constitution vested in both president and courts independence of the other branches as well as discretion in the exercise of their respective duties. Both were responsible directly to the people, and in exercising "the duty of discrimination" were controlled (under ordinary circumstances) only by their own "candor and integrity." From this standpoint, Burr's claim that the circuit court could compel Jefferson to act was a brazen argument for judicial supremacy, a plea for Marshall to substitute his discretion for Jefferson's in an area within the latter's competence.

Marshall's rejoinder rested on drawing a sharp distinction between executive and judicial discretion. Many of the most important executive powers, as Marshall had written in *Marbury*, were "political" in nature, and as such involved the exercise of "the will of the President." In acting with discretion, the president was to consult his personal "conscience" and wisdom. Courts, in contrast, never acted at the personal will of the judges, and were not free to consult the judges' private opinions. A motion for a subpoena in Virginia was "a motion to the discretion of the court." But "discretion" in the judicial context referred to the judges' application of legal rules to specific cases: "a motion to its discretion is a motion, not to its inclination, but to its judgment; and its judgment is to be guided by sound legal principles." Declaring the president amenable to judicial process did not substitute one official's will for another's, as Jefferson believed, but merely acknowledged the rule of law over both judge and executive.

The Constitution and Jefferson's Embargo

In June 1807 the British warship *Leopard* attacked the American frigate *Chesapeake*, killing or capturing a number of American seamen. The attack was the culmination of many months of increasing tension on the high seas between Britain, locked in a life-and-death struggle with Napoleonic France, and the United States. The American response to the *Chesapeake* incident, and to the ongoing depredations on American shipping both by the Royal Navy and by French privateers, was the passage by Congress, in December 1807, of an embargo on trade with the European belligerents. The embargo was extremely unpopular in the Northeast, and was widely disobeyed despite increasingly vigorous enforcement by the Jefferson administration and by the United States Navy. Congress eventually revised the embargo statute to give federal port collectors the power to detain for presidential consideration vessels ostensibly bound for American ports whenever in the collector's opinion a vessel's master intended to flout the embargo. In a subsequent circular to the collectors, Secretary of the Treasury Gallatin listed "excessive shipments of certain commodities" such as rice, flour, and cotton as per se grounds for detention, and informed them that the president desired all such vessels to be automatically detained.

Gilchrist v. Collector of Charleston
10 Fed. Cas. 355 (C.C.D.S.C. May 28, 1808)

Adam Gilchrist's freighter *Resource* was prepared to sail from Charleston loaded with rice and cotton and was ostensibly bound for Baltimore. The Charleston collector, Simeon Theus, believed himself constrained to deny Gilchrist clearance papers by the Gallatin circular. Gilchrist then applied to the federal circuit court for a writ of mandamus compelling Theus to issue the papers. Presiding was Supreme Court Justice William Johnson, a native South Carolinian and Jefferson's first appointment to the high court.

JOHNSON, *Circuit Justice* . . . The affidavit, upon which this motion is founded, states, that the ship Resource is ballasted with 140 barrels of rice, under a load of cotton, and is destined for the port of Baltimore. The collector, in his return to the rule, acknowledges, that he believes the port of Baltimore to be her real destination; and that, if he had no other rule of conduct but the 11th section of the act supplementary to the embargo act, he would not detain her; but urges in excuse, for refusing her a clearance, a letter from the secretary of the treasury. It is not denied that if the petitioners be legally entitled to a clearance, this court may interpose its authority, by the writ of mandamus, to compel the collector to grant it. The only questions, therefore, will be, whether the section of the act alluded to, authorizes the detention of the vessel; and if it does not, whether the instructions of the president, through the secretary of the treasury, unsupported by act of the congress, will justify the collector in that detention. On the latter question there can be no doubt. The officers of our government, from the highest to the lowest, are equally subjected to legal restraint; and it is confidently believed that all of them feel themselves equally incapable, as well from law as inclination, to attempt an unsanctioned encroachment upon individual liberty. In the letter alluded to, Mr. Gallatin speaks only in the language of recommendation, not of command; at the utmost the collector could only plead the influence of advice, and not the authority of the treasury department in his justification. In the act of congress there is no ambiguity. The object is to prevent evasions of the embargo act, by vessels which sail ostensibly for some port in the United States, when their real destination is to some other port or place. The granting of clearances is left absolutely to the discretion of the collector; the right of detaining in cases which excite suspicion is given him, with a reference to the will of the executive. Congress might have vested this discretion in the president, the secretary of the treasury, or any other officer, in which they thought proper to vest it; but, having vested the right of granting or refusing in the collector, with an appeal to the president only in case of refusal–the right of granting clearances remains in him unimpaired and unrestricted.

It does not appear to us that the instructions from the treasury department are intended to reach this case. The recommendation not to grant clearances on shipments of provisions appears by the context to be restricted by two provisos, evidently pointed at by the reasons assigned for that recommendation. First, if intended for a place where they are not wanted for consumption, or we suppose, where supplies of the same article can be had from the state or neighbourhood in which such place is situated. Secondly, for a port that usually exports that article. Now with regard to the article of rice, it is impossible to say how much the city of Baltimore will want for its consumption, as they have no internal supplies, and as the three Southern states alone are exporters of that article. Shipments of rice from Baltimore to Charleston might create suspicion, but not such shipments from Charleston to Baltimore. We are of opinion that the act of congress does not authorize the detention of this vessel. That without the sanction of law, the collector is not justified by the instructions of the executive, in increasing restraints upon commerce, even if this case had been contemplated by the letter alluded to; but that from a temperate consideration of that letter, this case does not appear to come within the spirit and meaning of the instructions which it contains.

A writ of mandamus was issued accordingly, commanding the collector to grant a clearance to the Resource.

Johnson's decision in *Gilchrist* received national attention. Federalist newspapers praised Johnson: the *Gazette of the United States* (Philadelphia) commented that it

> gives us great pleasure to find that Judge Johnson has sufficient integrity and independence to make the laws of the land and not the will of the Executive the rule of his judicial conduct. Nothing in the conduct of the present Administration is so alarming to the liberty and independence of the country as the repeated attempts they are making to give to Executive proclamations and circular letters the force and effect of law. If the President could once get the control that he wishes and that his partisans wish to give him over the Court, the power of Congress would become as nugatory in this country as that of Bonaparte's Senate is in France, and Presidential mandates would constitute the law of the land.

Republican papers replied with vigorous assaults on the federal courts. The Philadelphia *Aurora* introduced Johnson's opinion with a bitter preamble:

> The following extraordinary case will be read with the greatest astonishment. It affords another memorable example of the profligacy of the Judiciary, who will give to the law an explanation perverting its intention and in violation of the most sacred rights and best policy of the Nation and Government... It is an additional proof of the monstrous absurdity of what is called the independence of the Judges. They are, in fact, so independent of control and of every other tie but that of their own perverse will, against the very principles of the government, that unless their tenure of office is altered and that corps brought to some sort of responsibility, they must in the end destroy the government. If the laws and policy of the Nation are to be set aside upon a quibble, if the very principles of peace and war are to be involved in the wretched subterfuges and equivocations of this subtle class of men, what avails all the superiority of a representative government which cannot check or chastise the crimes of such a class.

Caesar Rodney
Letter to Thomas Jefferson
(July 15, 1808)[94]

President Jefferson regarded the *Gilchrist* decision, coming from a Republican judge and out of the Republican and hawkish South, as a disastrous blow to his attempts to enforce the embargo in Federalist, anti-embargo New England. The administration's public response took the form of a letter from Attorney General Rodney to Jefferson himself, published in the newspapers.

Sir: I have read and considered the papers and documents referred to me relative to the case of a mandamus, issued by the circuit court of the United States for the district of South Carolina, to compel the collector of the port of Charleston to grant clearances to certain vessels. The first question that naturally presents itself, is, whether the court possessed the power of issuing a mandamus in such a case. A mandamus in England is styled a "prerogative writ," and in that country is awarded solely and exclusively by the court of king's bench. The constitution and laws of the United States establish our judicial system. To these we must refer, in order to ascertain the jurisdiction of the respective courts, the extent of their powers, and the limits of their authority. The "act to establish the judicial courts of the United States," passed the 24th September, 1789, declares and defines the jurisdiction of the several courts thereby created, and among these the jurisdiction of the circuit courts. Upon a careful and attentive perusal, it will be found to delegate to the circuit courts no power to issue writs of mandamus. In the thirteenth section of that act, this authority is expressly given to the supreme court of the United States . . . An authority given, perhaps, because its jurisdiction extended all over the United States. The fourteenth section, immediately succeeding that which gives this authority, in plain and positive terms, to the supreme court, solely, if not exclusively, (and the affirmative frequently, and in this case justly, I think, implies a negative) contains the following provision. "All the before mentioned courts of the United States, (including the supreme as well as the circuit and district courts) shall have power to issue writs of scire facias, habeas corpus, and all other writs not specially provided for by the statute, which may be necessary for the exercise of their respective jurisdictions." This clause cannot affect the case, I conceive. The mandamus is a writ which, we have seen, is specially provided for by law. This section was evidently not designed to give any additional jurisdiction to either of the courts, but merely the means of executing that jurisdiction already granted to them respectively. The issuing of a mandamus in the case under consideration was an act of original jurisdiction. Precisely as much so, as it would have been in the supreme court, to have exercised the power in the case of Marbury v. Madison. In that case the supreme court declared, that to issue a mandamus to the secretary of state, would be, to exercise an original jurisdiction, not given by the constitution; and which could not be granted by congress. The constitution having enumerated or declared the particular cases in which the supreme court should exercise original jurisdiction, though there were no negative expressions, the affirmative, they considered, implied them. It was on this principle alone they refused to exert their authority.

The practice, I believe, has uniformly been, so far as I can trace it from the books of reports that have been published, or from recollection and experience on the subject, to apply to the supreme court for a mandamus. This court it is true have determined not to issue the writ, when it would be an act of original jurisdiction. But this I apprehend, can afford no ground for the circuit court's assuming an authority which the supreme court have declined, unless by a legislative act the power be delegated to them. This power is not inherent nor necessarily incidental to a court of justice, even of general jurisdiction . . .

It is scarcely necessary to remark, that when a court has no jurisdiction, even consent will not give it; and much less the mere tacit acquiescence of a party, in not denying their authority. Independent of this serious and conclusive objective to the proceeding adopted by the court there are others entitled to consideration. For supposing the court did not err in the exercise of jurisdiction, and admitting the British doctrines on the subject without restriction or limitation could be extended to this country, there are legal exceptions to the course they have pursued, supported by English authority. In the first place, the law gave the collector complete discretion over the subject. According to the opinion he might form, he possessed competent authority to grant or refuse a clearance. And I apprehend where the law has left this discretion in an officer, the court, agreeably to the British practice and precedents, ought not to interpose by way of mandamus. Secondly. In this case there was a controlling power in the chief magistrate of the United States. There was in fact, an express appeal given to the president by the very words of the act of congress, which authorizes the collectors to detain vessels "until the decision of the president of the United States be had there upon." By the mandamus the reference to the president is taken away; and the collector is commanded to clear the vessel without delay. Agreeably to the English authorities under such circumstances, it is not the course I believe to issue a mandamus. Thirdly. The parties, it seems, had their legal remedy against the collector; and it is not usual if not unprecedented, to grant a mandamus in such a case. Fourthly.

A mandamus is not issued to a mere ministerial officer to compel him to his duty. The court will leave the parties to their remedy by action, or even by indictment . . .

It results from this view of the subject, that the mandamus, issued by the circuit court for the district of South Carolina, was not warranted by any power vested in the circuit courts by statute, nor by any power necessarily incident to courts, nor countenanced by any analogy between the circuit courts, and the court of king's bench; the only court in that country possessing the power of issuing such writs. And it further appears, that even the court of king's bench, for the reasons assigned, would not agreeably to their practice and principles, have interfered in the present case by mandamus. It might perhaps with propriety be added, that there does not appear in the constitution of the United States any thing which favours an indefinite extension of the jurisdiction of courts, over the ministerial officers within the executive department. On the contrary, the careful discrimination which is marked between the several departments should dictate great circumspection to each, in the exercise of powers having any relation to the other. The courts are indubitably the source of legal redress for wrongs committed by ministerial officers; none of whom are above the law. This redress is to be administered by due and legal process in the ordinary way. For there appears to be a material and obvious distinction, between a course of proceeding which redresses a wrong committed by an executive officer, and an interposition by a mandatory writ, taking the executive authority out of the hands of the president, and prescribing the course, which he and the agents of any department must pursue. In one case the executive is left free to act in his proper sphere, but it is held to strict responsibility; in the other all responsibility is taken away; and he acts agreeably to judicial mandate. Writs of this kind if made applicable to officers indiscriminately, and acts purely ministerial and executive in their nature, would necessarily have the effect of transferring the powers vested in one department to another department. If in a case like the present, where the law vests a duty and a discretion in an executive officer, a court can not only administer redress against the misuse of the authority, but previously direct the use to be made of it, it would seem that under the name of a judicial power, an executive function is necessarily assumed, and that part of the constitution perhaps defeated, which makes it the duty of the president to take care that the laws be faithfully executed. I do not see any clear limitation to this doctrine, which would prevent the courts from compelling by mandamus all the executive officers; all subordinate to the president at least, whether charged with legal duties in the treasury or other department, to execute the same according to the opinion of the judiciary and contrary to that of the executive. And it is evident that the confusion arising will be greatly increased by the exercise of such a power by a number of separate courts of local jurisdiction, whose proceedings would have complete and final effect, without an opportunity of control by the supreme court. So many branches of the judiciary, acting within their respective districts, their courses might be different; and different rules of action might be prescribed for the citizens of the different stages, instead of that unity of administration which the constitution meant to secure by placing the executive power for them all, in the same head. What, too, becomes of the responsibility of the executive to the court of impeachment, and to the nation? Is he to remain responsible for acts done by command of another department? or is the nation to lose the security of that responsibility altogether? From these and other considerations, were this branch of the subject to be pursued, it might be inferred, that the constitution of the United States, by the distribution of the powers of our government to different departments, ascribing the executive duties to one, and the judiciary to another, controls any principles of the English law, which would authorize either to enter into the department of the other, to annul the powers of that other, and to assume the direction of its operations to itself . . .

Like Johnson's decision, Rodney's letter was the subject of widespread journalistic comment. Republican papers praised Rodney's reading of the law, and the Federalist press criticized the letter as an executive usurpation of judicial authority.

William Johnson
Public Statement
(August 26, 1808)[95]

Johnson defended himself against Rodney's attack in the newspapers.

In a Charleston paper, received by the last mail, I have perused a letter addressed by the attorney general of the United States to the president, relative to the proceedings of the circuit court of South Carolina, in the case of The Resource. That the president should have consulted that officer upon a legal subject, is perfectly consistent with the relation subsisting between their respective stations; and as long as the result of that consultation was confined to the cabinet, there had occurred nothing inconsistent with the relation between the executive and judicial departments. But when that opinion is published to the world, under the sanction of the president, an act so unprecedented in the history of executive conduct could be intended for no other purpose than to secure the public opinion on the side of the executive and in opposition to the judiciary. Under this impression I feel myself compelled, as the presiding judge of the court, whose decision is the subject of the attorney general's animadversions, to attempt a vindication of, or at least an apology for that decision. So long as its merits were the subject of mere newspaper discussion, I felt myself under no concern about the opinion that the public might form of it. The official acts of men in office are proper subjects for newspaper remarks. The opinion that cannot withstand a free and candid investigation must be erroneous. It is true that a judge may, without vanity, entertain a doubt of the competency of some of the editors of newspapers to discuss a difficult legal question; yet no editorial or anonymous animadversions, however they may have been characterized by illiberality or ignorance, should ever have induced me to intrude these observations upon the public. But when a bias is attempted to be given to public opinion by the overbearing influence of high office, and the reputation of ability and information, the ground is changed; and to be silent could only result from being borne down by weight of reasoning or awed by power. I should regret exceedingly should I err in attributing to the president the publication of the attorney general's letter. I do so because, from the nature of the case, it is impossible to think otherwise. There is no reason to suppose that the attorney general would have published it at all; or at least not without the command or permission of the president. That the attorney general should have formed conclusions differing from those of the court, is the most natural thing imaginable. It proceeds from the assumption of erroneous premises. The writ of mandamus in a case analogous to that of The Resource is not provided for by law. The collector had not an unlimited discretion in granting or refusing a clearance. There was not a general appeal to the will of the chief magistrate. Nor does the court found its right to issue the mandamus upon an analogy drawn from the courts of Great Britain. Upon the affirmation of these propositions the opinion of the attorney general appears to be predicated. In addition to which he would seem to have misapprehended the purport of the decision of the supreme court in the case of Marbury v. Madison, and to have drawn reasons from inconvenience, which may prove a great deal too much for the public security; and which have already met with the disapprobation of the supreme court in the before mentioned case . . .

[The embargo act,] although from a superficial view it may seem otherwise, really authorizes no restraint whatever upon the commercial intercourse of the several states, or of any state within itself. It is not a vessel really bound from one port or place in the United States to another, that the collector is authorized to detain, for that is no violation of the embargo act; but those which are only ostensibly bound from one port to another, within the United States when their real destination is to some other port or place, or to do some act in violation of the laws imposing an embargo. I assume it as an incontestable proposition, that every inhabitant of the United States has a perfect right to carry on commerce from one port to another, unless restricted by law; that no officer of our government can legally restrict him in the exercise of that right, except in cases specified by law. I would as soon attempt to prove his right to the air that he breathes, or the food that he consumes, as to support these doctrines by a course of reasoning; nor is it less clear, that in all cases of uninterdicted commerce, the collector is bound to grant a clearance whenever the forms imposed by law have been complied with. It is the obligation on him correlative to the right of the citizen . . . [Johnson discussed "the embarrassment" the case had caused for Collector Theus, caught between his own belief that The Resource was entitled to sail under the statute, and the apparent command of his superiors to detain it.]

The jurisdiction of the court, as is properly observed by the attorney general, must depend upon the constitution and laws of the United States. We disclaim all pretensions to any other origin of our jurisdiction, especially the unpopular grounds of prerogative and analogy to the king's bench. That judicial power, which the constitution vests in the United States, and the United States in its courts, is all that its courts pretend to exercise. In the constitution it is laid down, that "the judicial power of the United States shall extend to all cases in law or equity, arising under this constitution and laws of the United States, and treaties made, or which shall be made," etc. The term "judicial power" conveys the idea, both of exercising the faculty of judging and of applying physical force to give effect to a decision. The term "power" could with no propriety be applied, nor could the judiciary be denominated a department of government, without the means of enforcing its decrees. In a country where laws govern, courts of justice necessarily are the medium of action and reaction between the government and the governed. The basis of individual security and the bond of union between the ruler and the citizen must ever be found in a judiciary sufficiently independent to disregard the will of power, and sufficiently energetic to secure to the citizen the full enjoyment of his rights. To establish such a one was evidently the object of the constitution. But to what purpose establish a judiciary, with power to take cognizance of certain questions of right, but not power to afford such redress as the case evidently requires? Suppose congress had vested in the circuit court a certain jurisdiction, without prescribing by what forms that jurisdiction should be exercised; would it not follow that the court must itself adopt a mode of proceeding adapted to the exigency of each case? It must do so, or refuse to act. One thing, at least, cannot be denied: that the power of congress was competent to authorize the circuit court to issue the writ of mandamus. From this it would follow, that issuing that writ is a mere incident to the judicial power, and not in itself a distinct branch of jurisdiction; for the constitution nowhere expressly vests in the United States the power to issue that writ, or any other. And if a mere incident, I see no reason why it should not follow with the principal jurisdiction, when vested by congress in its courts . . . In [*Marbury v. Madison*] the court did not decide, as the attorney general seems to suppose, that issuing a mandamus was an exercise of jurisdiction not within the scope of the judicial powers of the United States. On the contrary, they expressly declare the power and the propriety of the courts issuing it in many cases which may occur. But except in cases where a foreign minister or a state is a party, the supreme court is restricted to the exercise of an appellate jurisdiction; and its decision was, that the act of congress, so far as it was intended to vest that court with power to issue the writ of mandamus in a case partaking of the nature of original jurisdiction, was unconstitutional and void. A void law I presume is no law; and it would follow therefore that the writ of mandamus, in those cases of original jurisdiction, which cannot constitutionally be submitted to the supreme court, comes fully within the description of a writ not otherwise provided for by law . . .

. . . Some other observations of the attorney general remain to be noticed, viz. that in giving redress by the process of mandamus, the courts may extend their claim to jurisdiction, to a general usurpation of power over the ministerial officers in the executive department; that it is a mode of proceeding which takes away from the government the benefit of appeal, and interferes with the responsibility to which officers of government are subject by impeachment. With regard to the first of these observations, it is evident that the attorney general mistakes the object against which his complaint should be directed. The courts do not pretend to impose any restraint upon any officer of government, but what results from a just construction of the laws of the United States. Of these laws the courts are the constitutional expositors; and every department of government must submit to their exposition; for laws have no legal meaning but what is given them by the courts to whose exposition they are submitted. It is against the law, therefore, and not the courts, that the executive should urge the charge of usurpation and restraint; a restraint which may at times be productive of inconveniences, but which is certainly very consistent with the nature of our government: one which it is very possible the president may have deserved the plaudits of his country for having transcended, in ordering detentions not within the embargo acts, but which notwithstanding it is the duty of our courts to encounter the odium of imposing. Let us take this argument together with that which relates to the liability of officers to impeachment, and some others which are used by the attorney general, into one view; and to what conclusions do they lead us? The president is liable to impeachment; he is therefore not to be restrained by the courts. The collector and every other officer, with equal propriety, who holds his office at the will of the president, are his agents, mere ministers of his will; therefore they are not to be restrained by the process of the courts. The power given to them is power given to him; in subordination to his will they must exercise it. He is charged with the general execution of the laws; and the security of the citizen lies in his liability to impeachment, or in an action for damages against the collector. This would indeed be an improvement on presidential patronage. It would be organizing a band, which in the hands of an unprincipled and intrepid president (and we may have the misfortune to see such a one elevated to that post) could be directed with an effect, but once paralleled in history. If these arguments have any force at all, as directed against the correctness of the circuit court's issuing the writ of mandamus, they would have equal weight to prove the impropriety of permitting them to issue the writ of habeas corpus; which is but an analogous protection to another class of individual rights, and might be urged to show that the whole executive department, in all its ramifications, civil, military and naval, should be left absolutely at large, in their conduct to individuals. What benefit results to the ruined citizen from the impeachment of the president, could we suppose it in the power of any individual to effect it? or what security from an action against a public officer whose circumstances may be desperate? But such is not the genius of our constitution. The law assigns every one his duty and his rights; and for enforcing the one and maintaining the other, courts of justice are instituted . . .

The argument drawn from the liability of the officers of government to impeachment, I cannot help thinking unhappily applied in another view. If an officer attempt an act inconsistent with the duties of his station, it is presumed that the failure of the attempt would not exempt him from liability to impeachment. Should a president head a conspiracy for the usurpation of absolute power, it is hoped that no one will contend that defeating his machinations would restore him to innocence. If, in the present instance, the owner of The Resource had been ordered to be hanged, instead of ordering his vessel to be detained, and the courts of this district had rescued him from executive power, it is presumed that the attorney general would not contend, that the liability to impeachment was done away; although he would find no difficulty in showing that it was a case analogous to that of the mandamus; of the violation of that careful discrimination which is marked between the several departments by the constitution. The objection, "that this mode of proceeding takes away the right of appeal," is but slightly touched upon by the attorney general; and probably, because, in revolving the subject, he perceived that it is no objection to the exercise of jurisdiction in the circuit courts of the United States, that there is no appeal from their decisions; as they actually possess and exercise a very extensive jurisdiction without appeal . . .

I will dismiss this subject with two additional remarks. The courts of the United States never have laid claim to a controlling power over officers vested by law with an absolute discretion, not inconsistent with the constitution; for in such a case, the officer is himself the paramount judge and arbiter of his own actions. Now would they, for the same reason, undertake to control the acts of an officer who is a mere agent of the executive or any other department, in the performance of whatever may be constitutionally, and is by law, submitted to the discretion of that department; for in that case, the process of the court should be directed to the head of the department, or it should not issue at all. In such cases there is an evident propriety in leaving an injured individual to his action for damages; as it is only upon evidence of express malice or daring disregard to propriety, that this action could be maintained. In such a case, the authority is complete; but the motive is censurable. The courts will not interfere to prevent the act; because the law authorizes it. But as the law did not authorize it for individual oppression, they will give damages to the individual who suffers by the wanton exercise of a legal power. This subject was very fully considered in the case of Marbury v. Madison; and to pursue it further, I should do little more than repeat the words of the court in that case. The discrimination between the cases in which a mandamus might, and might not issue to the secretary of state, will point out to those who consider it, the limitation to this doctrine in the idea of the judiciary . . .

. . . It is very possible that the court may have erred in their decision. It is enough, however, and all that a judge, who had understanding enough to be conscious of his own fallibility, can pretend to, that there existed grounds at least specious for the issuing of the mandamus. Though the laws had not vested the power, the submission of the officers of government would, at least, excuse the act of the court. There never existed a stronger case for calling forth the powers of a court; and whatever censure the executive sanction may draw upon us, nothing can deprive us of the consciousness of having acted with firmness, impartiality and an honest intention to discharge our duty. Indeed there is one remark relative to the attorney general's letter, which cannot have escaped the notice of the most superficial observer. The principal question, that on which it would seem that the executive was most interested to secure the public approbation, viz. the legality of the instructions given to the collector, is completely put aside; while the public attention is fixed upon another more abstruse and admitting of a greater variety of opinion. It may be possible to prove the court wrong in interposing its authority; but certainly establishing the point of their want of jurisdiction will not prove the legality of the instructions given to the collector. The argument is not that the executive have done right, but that the judiciary had no power to prevent their doing wrong . . .

Comment

The debate between Justice Johnson and Atttorney General Rodney took place on three different levels. The immediate legal questions were the legal force of the Gallatin circular and the legitimacy of the court's writ of mandamus to Collector Theus. As Johnson noted in his reply to Rodney, the latter chose to criticize the circuit court's assertion of jurisdiction rather than to defend the circular's legality; and in fact Johnson's interpretation of the embargo act was in accord with contemporaneous norms of statutory construction.

At a deeper level, Johnson and Rodney were contesting the existence of inherent powers in, respectively, the executive and the courts. Rodney accused Johnson of exercising an authority neither granted the circuit court by the Judiciary Act nor "necessarily incident to courts." (Rodney made the latter point by referring to England, where only one of the three great common-law courts, King's Bench, could issue writs of mandamus.) Because he found no statutory authority for the Gallatin circular, Johnson in turn analyzed the executive's actions as an implicit assertion of inherent legal authority, and then vigorously denied the existence of such authority. In the absence of legislative authorization, no executive officer possessed any legal power to "encroach upon individual liberty." Both Rodney's and Johnson's arguments were authentically Republican in their denial of extratextual and undelegated governmental power. The different conclusions they reached stemmed from a still more fundamental level of disagreement.

Rodney's attack on the writ of mandamus rested on a thoroughly Jeffersonian insistence on the Constitution's "careful discrimination between the branches of government." The attorney general did not deny the personal liability of executive officers for illegal acts, but he regarded a judicial order to such an officer in the latter's official capacity as a usurpation of executive power, "taking the executive authority out of the hands of the president." Under the Constitution, all executive powers were to be exercised by or under the supervision of the president, who was in turn subject to popular control by the electoral or impeachment processes. Judicial interference in executive actions would destroy the unity and responsibility of "administration" the Constitution had created.

Johnson did not deny the existence of areas in which executive officers possessed "an absolute discretion" with which courts could not directly interfere, but he confined such areas to those created "by law . . . not inconsistent with the constitution." Because Johnson shared the view of other Republican judges such as Tucker and Roane that "courts are the constitutional expositors" of all law, this reservation left the definition of the executive's sphere of discretion to the courts, and not to the executive's independent constitutional judgment. The issuance of a writ of mandamus to an executive officer where that officer did not enjoy absolute discretion was thus not interference by one magistrate in another's domain, but instead the restraint of law itself.

United States v. The William
28 Fed. Cas. 614 (D. Mass. Oct. 3, 1808)

The *Gilchrist* controversy occurred over the summer of 1808. At the same time, another judicially imposed publicity disaster for the Republican administration appeared to be developing in Massachusetts, where a direct constitutional assault on the entire embargo scheme was being mounted in the federal district court before a staunchly Federalist Judge, John Davis.

DAVIS, District Judge. This libel is founded on the act of congress passed 22d December, 1807 intitled, "An act laying an embargo on all ships and vessels in the ports and harbors of the United States," and on the first supplementary act, passed January 9th, 1808. The libel alleges, that sundry enumerated goods, wares and merchandize, on the 17th day of March last, on the high seas, were put, from said brigantine on board another vessel, called the Nancy; and also, that other goods, wares and merchandize, on the 11th day of

May last, at Lynn, in said district, were put, from said brigantine, on board another vessel, called the Mary, with intent, that said goods, wares and merchandize should be transported to some foreign port or place, contrary to the acts aforesaid, by which, it is alleged, that said brigantine is forfeited.

It has been contended, by the counsel for the claimants, Benj. Ireson and others . . . 1st That the facts, appearing in evidence, do not present a case, within the true intent and meaning of the acts aforesaid. 2d. That the acts, on which a forfeiture is claimed, are unconstitutional. [Davis postponed a ruling on the claimants' factual arguments.] But it appears to be necessary to declare an opinion on the constitutional question, which has been so fully discussed, especially as the objection, if available, equally applies to many other cases before the court. Under these circumstances, I have considered it expedient, and indeed an incumbent duty, to give an opinion on this great and interesting question; though an entire decision on the case, in which it was presented and argued, is, for the reasons suggested, postponed . . .

My views of the constitutional question, which has been raised in this case, will be confined to the acts relative to navigation, and to exportation by sea. On those, only, do the cases before the court depend; and it is obviously incumbent on a judge to confine himself to the actual case, presented for trial, and its inseparable incidents, and to avoid pronouncing premature decisions on extraneous questions. The prohibition of exportation by land, can, properly, come into view, only as it may tend to explain those provisions, on which I am called to decide, and to indicate their character. In the whole course of the interesting argument on this great question, and in all my reflections upon the subject, I have been deeply sensible of the solemn weight and magnitude of the inquiry. The unusual press of business, at this term, and the application of the recent acts to the numerous cases presented for trial, must have given full occupation to the mind, if supposed to be solicitous for a correct discharge of duty; and I could have wished, that this paramount question of constitutionality, when gentlemen had determined to rely on it, should have been reserved for the higher tribunals of the nation. But, on this subject, it was not for me to choose. A comparison of the law with the constitution is the right of the citizen. Those who deny this right, and the duty of the court resulting from it, must regard with strange indifference, a precious security to the individual, and have studied, to little profit, the peculiar genius and structure of our limited government.

Objections to an act of congress, on the ground of constitutionality, may be referred to the following heads: (1) A repugnancy to some of the exceptions or restrictions to the legislative authority, expressed in the constitution of the United States. (2) A repugnancy to some of the affirmative provisions, in the constitution. (3) A want of conformity to the powers vested in the legislature, by the constitution; or that the act in question is not authorised by any of those powers.

As an instance under the first head, we may suppose an act, contravening the restrictive clause in the constitution, "No bill of attainder or ex post facto law shall be passed." An act repugnant to the declaration that, "the trial of all crimes, except in cases of impeachment, shall be by jury" would afford an example under the second head. Contraventions of this description, when clearly described and determined, could be of no legal effect; and it would appear to be the duty of the national courts, conformably to their specified authority by the constitution, and pursuant to the oath of office, to regard the acts, containing such repugnancies, to be so far void. It does not appear nor is it, as I recollect, contended, that the acts under consideration, are liable to objections of this description. They contravene none of the exceptions or restrictions, expressed in the constitution, nor is it made to appear, that they are repugnant to any of its affirmative declarations. At least, this is true of the primary provisions. If any of the auxiliary regulations, in the supplementary acts, applying to the coasting trade, are liable to objections of this nature, they will be separately considered. Some of those regulations, it is argued, contravene that restriction on the powers of congress, which provides, that "vessels bound to, or from, one state, shall not be obliged to enter, clear, or pay duties in another." If this objection be available, it equally applies to the regulations in the coasting act, early adopted after the organization of the government; and which have since been in uniform operation, without meeting an objection of this sort. There is a degree of ambiguity in the expression, which seems to countenance the construction suggested in the argument; but the true construction avoids the objection. It was intended, as I understand it, to prevent vessels bound to, or from, a port, in any state, being obliged to enter, clear, or pay duties in any state, other than that, to, or from which, they should be proceeding. One of the amendments proposed by the state of North Carolina, suggests the following substitute for the clause we are now considering. "Nor shall vessels, bound to a particular state, be obliged to enter or pay duties in any other; nor, when bound from any one of the states, be obliged to clear in another." This reading would give a clearer expression of, what must be considered, the true meaning of the clause as it now stands. The objections, on the ground of unconstitutionality, to the acts in question, are thus limited to the third head; a defect of constitutional power, in the congress of the United States, to enact them. On this ground has the argument proceeded, and it is contended, that congress have not power or authority, by the constitution of the United States thus to interdict commercial intercourse with foreign nations. On this head, a preliminary inquiry, of material importance, presents [itself]: What is the power or authority of the court, relative to an objection of this description? Or, in other words, is a mere exceeding of the powers of congress, in legislation, without a repugnancy to express provisions of the constitution, among the proper objects of cognizance in the federal judiciary?

In the consideration of this preliminary question, I shall first recur to judicial determinations and opinions for light and guidance. In the year 1792, congress passed an act, relative to the claims of invalids, for pensions, which required the intervention, in a qualified manner, of the circuit courts. The judges of three of the circuit courts declined the execution of the act, and assigned their reasons, to the president of the United States. The objections were, that the business, assigned to the courts by the act, was not of a judicial nature; and that their judgments, or opinions, (which they considered as judgments) were, by the act, subjected to revision and controul by the legislature, and by an officer of the executive department. Though they declined acting as courts under the act, they expressed a willingness, for the accommodation of applicants, to consider themselves as commissioners; but congress, at a subsequent session, repealed the objectionable clauses, and made other provision, for determining the claims of applicants for pensions [Hayburn's Case]. In the case of Vanhorne's Lessee v. Dorrance, in the circuit court of Pennsylvania, April term 1795, Judge Paterson pronounced an act of Pennsylvania, called, the "Quieting and Confirming Act," to be null and void, as repugnant to the constitution of that state. In the supreme court of the United States, February term, 1796, in the case of Hylton v. U.S., the constitutionality of the act, "laying duties on carriages," was discussed and determined. The point, in controversy, depended on the meaning of the terms "direct tax," in the constitution. It was contended, by the counsel for the plaintiff in error, that the tax on carriages was a direct tax, and, not being laid according to the census, as direct taxes are, by the constitution, required to be laid, that the law was void. The court were, unanimously, of opinion, that the tax on carriages was not a direct tax; of course, the question of the validity of an act, repugnant to an express clause in the constitution, was not determined. Judge Paterson, however, gave his opinion, on this point. "If it be a direct tax, it is unconstitutional; because it has been laid pursuant to the rule of uniformity, and not to the rule of apportionment." Judge Chase observed: "As I do not think the tax on carriages is a direct tax, it is unnecessary, at this time, for me to determine, whether the court constitutionally possesses the power to declare an act of congress void, on the ground of its being made contrary to, or in violation of the constitution; but if the court have such power, I am free to declare, that I will never exercise it but in a very clear case." Justices Iredell, Wilson and Cushing all concurred with their associates, that the tax on carriages was not a direct tax, but gave no intimation of their opinions, if it had been of that denomination. In the same court, August term, 1798, in the action Calder v. Bull, the question was, as to the validity of an act of the legislature of Connecticut, setting aside a decree of a court of probate, and granting a new hearing. It was contended, that it was an ex post facto law, and, as such, prohibited by the constitution of the United States. The court were of opinion, that the law in question was not an ex post facto law, and, of course, there was no contravention of the constitution. Judge Chase avoided giving an opinion, whether the court had jurisdiction to decide, that any law made by congress, contrary to the constitution of the United States, be void. Judge Iredell was more explicit. "It has been the policy," said he, "of all the American states, which have individually framed their state constitutions, since the Revolution, and of the people of the United States, when they framed the federal constitution, to define, with precision, the objects of the legislative power, and to restrain its exercise, within marked and settled boundaries. If any act of congress, or of the legislature of a state, violates those constitutional provisions, it is unquestionably void; though, I admit, that, as the authority to declare it void, is of a delicate and awful nature, the court will never resort to that authority, but in a clear and urgent case." The last case, which I shall cite, is U.S. v. Callender, in the circuit court in Virginia, May term, 1800, on the additional act "for the punishment of certain crimes against the United States," commonly called the sedition law. The counsel for the traverser offered to argue to the jury, that the law was unconstitutional. In overruling this motion, and in assigning his reasons, Judge Chase made the following observations, which appear to be pertinent to the present inquiry: "No citizen of knowledge and information, unless under the influence of passion or prejudice, will believe, without very strong and indubitable proof, that congress will, intentionally, make any known violation of the federal constitution and their sacred trust. I admit, that the constitution contemplates that congress may, from inattention, or error in judgment, pass a law prohibited by the constitution, and, therefore, it has provided a peaceable, safe, and adequate remedy. If such a case should happen, the mode of redress is pointed out in the constitution, and no other mode can be adopted, without a manifest infraction of it. Every man must admit, that the power of deciding the constitutionality of any law of the United States, (or of any particular state) is one of the greatest and most important powers the people could grant. Such power is restrictive of the legislative power of the Union, and also of the several states, not absolute and unlimited, but confined to such cases only, where the law in question shall clearly appear to have been prohibited by the federal constitution, and not in any doubtful case." The immediate question that the learned judge was then considering was, whether the power of determining the constitutionality of the law belonged, exclusively, to the court, or whether it could be rightfully exercised by a jury. His remaining observations, appearing in the published account of the trial, more especially apply to that question.

None of these cases decide the point now under consideration. By one of them, we have a decision against a state law, produced as a ground of title, as being repugnant to the constitution of the state. In another, we have the opinion of Judge Paterson, that a law of the United States, would, upon a certain construction, be repugnant to the constitution, and void. In the Connecticut case, we have Judge Iredell's opinion, that an act of congress, or of the legislature of any state, may be declared void by the court, if it violate constitutional provisions. Judge Chase, in those cases, speaks with great caution, on this head, it not being necessary to decide the point. In Callender's trial he is more explicit, and I understand him to admit the power of the court to disregard a statute, repugnant to the restrictions, in the constitution, on the authority of congress, and on that of the state legislatures. In none of the cases have we a decision, nor an opinion, as to the power of the court, where the objection to a statute is grounded, not on a repugnancy to express provisions, but on a supposed undue extension of a given power. The first case is of a peculiar nature, and no conclusive inference can be drawn from it, of the opinion of the court, relative to the point now under consideration. The law was not declared void, but the court declined acting upon it, except in a qualified manner, as commissioners. Their views and determinations on the subject, have reference to the nature of the judicial authority, and to the preservation of their constitutional independency, against encroachment.

Finding no direct judicial authority on the point, I shall next adduce opinions and reasonings from a less authoritative source, but still highly respectable . . . The work to which I refer, is that admirable commentary on the constitution of the United States, intitled, "The Federalist," the author of which is pronounced by one of our learned judges [Chase, in *Calder v. Bull*], to be superior to Blackstone, or his successor Woodeson, for extensive and accurate knowledge of the true principles of government. If we love and cherish that constitution, we shall highly esteem this excellent commentary on that precious instrument. If that great political temple command our admiration, we shall follow, with improvement and delight, this luminous guide, through all its fair apartments . . . [Davis then quoted extensively from various numbers of "The Federalist."]

These extracts give a clear and satisfactory view of the opinions entertained by the writer, or writers, of those papers, on this topic; and it is evident, that the judicial authority, is, in their estimation, precisely limited, in regard to deciding on the validity of legislative acts; and that the power to declare them void exists, only, in cases of contravention, opposition or repugnancy, to some express restrictions or provision contained in the constitution. The examples and the argument apply only to cases of legislative action, which their powers forbid; not to those, which their powers may be supposed not to authorize. This is further manifest from observations, variously interspersed, in those writings, relative to a supposed abuse or exceeding of powers, by the legislature; or, in other words, to an act of usurpation. In the first place, there is a strong conviction expressed, that no such case can or will occur, in a government so organized, and where such strong sympathies will exist, between the representatives and their constituents. That the government is in the hands of the representatives of the people, is pronounced to be, "the essential and only efficacious security for the rights and privileges of the people, which is attainable in civil society." But, should usurpation rear its head; should the unnatural case ever occur, when the representatives of the people should betray their constituents, we are referred, for consolation and remedy, to the power and vigilance of the state governments; to publick opinion; to the active agency of the people in their elections; to that perpetual dependence on the people, which is the primary controul on the government; "to the vigilant and manly spirit, which actuates the people of America, a spirit which nourishes freedom, and, in return, is nourished by it;" and, in case of desperate extremities, for which no system of government can provide, "to that original right of self-defence, which is paramount to all positive forms of government." In one passage, indeed, where the writer is speaking of the resort, in case of a supposed usurpation, we are referred to the judiciary and to the executive, as well as to the people, without any discrimination of the circumstances to which the different sources of remedy would be applicable. "In the first instance," says the writer, "the success of the usurpation will depend on the executive and judiciary departments, which are to expound and to give effect to the legislative acts; and, in the last resort, a remedy must be obtained from the people, who can, by the election of more faithful representatives, annul the acts of the usurpers." This passage may be so construed, as to be consistent with those before cited; but, if irreconcilable, with the doctrines so clearly expressed in other places, we must account for any supposed diversity of sentiment, from the circumstance, that those valuable papers were not all from the same pen. Cases might be put, of acts, so manifestly without the sphere of objects, committed to the national government, that the judiciary branch might be competent to pronounce them invalid, not as repugnant to any particular clause of the constitution, but to its whole expressed design and tenour. "The propriety of a law," says the writer, "so frequently quoted, must always be determined by the nature of the powers upon which it is founded. Suppose, by some forced construction of its authority (which indeed cannot be easily imagined) the federal legislature should attempt to vary the law of descent in any state; would it not be evident, that, in making such an attempt, it had exceeded its jurisdiction, and infringed upon that of the state?" Here would be an obvious assumption of a new power, not to be found in the constitution, and it is distinguishable from an improper exercise, or undue extension, of a power given . . .

It is a recommendation of these views of the constitutional powers of the judiciary, relative to legislative acts, that they reduce it to that precision and certainty, which is so desirable, in reference to judicial deliberations; and avoid those manifest grounds or occasions of irreconcilable collision, between the judiciary and legislative departments, which might otherwise prevail. Affirmative provisions and express restrictions, contained in the constitution, are sufficiently definite to render decisions, probably in all cases, satisfactory; and the interferences of the judiciary with the legislature, to use the language of the constitution, would be reduced to "cases," easily to be understood, and, in which the superior, commanding, will of the people, who established the instrument, would be clearly and peremptorily expressed. To extend this censorial power further, and especially to extend it to the degree, contended for in the objections to the act now under consideration, would be found extremely difficult, if not impracticable, in execution. To determine where the legitimate exercise of discretion ends, and usurpation begins, would be a task most delicate and arduous. It would, in many instances, be extremely difficult to settle it, even in a single body. It would be much more so, if to be adjusted by two independent bodies, especially if those bodies, from the nature of their constitution, must proceed by different rules. Before a court can determine, whether a given act of congress, bearing relation to a power with which it is vested, be a legitimate exercise of that power, or transcend it, the degree of legislative discretion, admissible in the case, must first be determined. Legal discretion is limited. It is thus defined by lord Coke, "Discretio est discernere, per legem, quid sit justum." Political discretion has a far wider range. It embraces, combines and considers, all circumstances, events and projects, foreign or domestick, that can affect the national interests. Legal discretion has not the means of ascertaining the grounds, on which political discretion may have proceeded. It seems admitted, that necessity might justify the acts in question. But how shall legal discussion determine, that political discretion, surveying the vast concerns committed to its trust, and the movements of conflicting nations, has not perceived such necessity to exist? Considerations of this nature have induced a doubt of the competency, or constitutional authority of the court, to decide an act invalid, in a case of this description. On the precise extent, however, of the power of the court, I do not give a definite opinion; my view of the main question, submitted by the counsel, in this case, rendered such a decision unnecessary. I now proceed to the examination of that question. It will be perceived, that some of the considerations, suggested under the last head, have an application to the remaining inquiry, and, it is acknowledged, that they had an influence in forming my determination.

It is contended, that congress is not invested with powers, by the constitution, to enact laws, so general and so unlimited, relative to commercial intercourse with foreign nations, as those now under consideration. It is well understood, that the depressed state of American commerce, and complete experience of the inefficacy of state regulations, to apply a remedy, were among the great, procuring causes of the federal constitution. It was manifest, that other objects, of equal importance, were exclusively proper for national jurisdiction; and that under national management and controul, alone, could they be advantageously and efficaciously conducted. The constitution specifies those objects. A national sovereignty is created. Not an unlimited sovereignty, but a sovereignty, as to the objects surrendered and specified, limited only by the qualifications and restrictions, expressed in the constitution. Commerce is one of those objects. The care, protection, management and controul, of this great national concern, is, in my opinion, vested by the constitution, in the congress of the United States; and their power is sovereign, relative to commercial intercourse, qualified by the limitations and restrictions, expressed in that instrument, and by the treaty making power of the president and senate. "Congress shall have power to regulate commerce with foreign nations, and among the several states, and with the Indian tribes." Such is the declaration in the constitution. Stress has been laid, in the argument, on the word "regulate," as implying, in itself, a limitation. Power to regulate, it is said, cannot be understood to give a power to annihilate. To this it may be replied, that the acts under consideration, though of very ample extent, do not operate as a prohibition of all foreign commerce. It will be admitted that partial prohibitions are authorized by the expression; and how shall the degree, or extent, of the prohibition be adjusted, but by the discretion of the national government, to whom the subject appears to be committed? Besides, if we insist on the exact and critical meaning of the word "regulate," we must, to be consistent, be equally critical with the substantial term "commerce." The term does not necessarily include shipping or navigation; much less does it include the fisheries. Yet it never has been contended, that they are not the proper objects of national regulation; and several acts of congress have been made respecting them. It may be replied, that these are incidents to commerce, and intimately connected with it; and that congress, in legislating respecting them, sat under the authority, given them by the constitution, to make all laws necessary and proper, for carrying into execution the enumerated powers. Let this be admitted; and are they not at liberty, also, to consider the present prohibitory system, as necessary and proper to an eventual beneficial regulation? I say nothing of the policy of the expedient. It is not within my province. But, on the abstract question of constitutional power, I see nothing to prohibit or restrain the measure.

Further, the power to regulate commerce is not to be confined to the adoption of measures, exclusively beneficial to commerce itself, or tending to its advancement; but, in our national system, as in all modern sovereignties, it is also to be considered as an instrument for other purposes of general policy and interest. The mode of its management is a consideration of great delicacy and importance; but, the national right, or power, under the constitution, to adapt regulations of commerce to other purposes, than the mere advancement of commerce, appears to me unquestionable. Great Britain is styled, eminently, a commercial nation; but commerce is, in fact, a subordinate branch of her national policy, compared with other objects . . . The situation of the United States, in ordinary times, might render legislative interferences, relative to commerce, less necessary; but the capacity and power of managing and directing it, for the advancement of great national purposes, seems an important ingredient of sovereignty. It was perceived that, under the power of regulating commerce, congress would be authorized to abridge it, in favour of the great principles of humanity and justice. Hence the introduction of a clause, in the constitution, so framed, as to interdict a prohibition of the slave trade, until 1808. Massachusetts and New York proposed a stipulation that should prevent the erection of commercial companies, with exclusive advantages. Virginia and North Carolina suggested an amendment, that "no navigation law, or law regulating commerce, should be passed, without the consent of two thirds of the members present, in both houses." These proposed amendments were not adopted, but they manifest the public conceptions, at the time, of the extent of the powers of congress, relative to commerce.

It has been said, in the argument, that the large commercial states, such as New York and Massachusetts, would never have consented to the grant of power, relative to commerce, if supposed capable of the extent now claimed. On this point, it is believed, there was no misunderstanding. The necessity of a competent national government was manifest. Its essential characteristics were considered and well understood; and all intelligent men perceived, that a power to advance and protect the national interest, necessarily involved a power, that might be abused . . .

If it be admitted that national regulations relative to commerce, may apply it as an instrument, and are not necessarily confined to its direct aid and advancement, the sphere of legislative discretion is, of course, more widely extended; and, in time of war, or of great impending peril, it must take a still more expanded range. Congress has power to declare war. It, of course, has power to prepare for war; and the time, the manner, and the measure, in the application of constitutional means, seems to be left to its wisdom and discretion. Foreign intercourse becomes, in such times, a subject of peculiar interest, and its regulation forms an obvious and essential branch of the federal administration. In the year 1798, when aggressions from France became insupportable, a non-intercourse law, relative to that nation and her dependencies, was enacted; partial hostilities, for a time, prevailed; but no war was declared. I have never understood, that the power of congress to adopt that course of proceeding was questioned. It seems to have been admitted, in the argument, that state necessity might justify a limited embargo, or suspension of all foreign commerce; but if congress have the power, for purposes of safety, of preparation, or counteraction, to suspend commercial intercourse with foreign nations, where do we find them limited as to the duration, more than as to the manner and extent of the measure? Must we understand the nation as saying to their government: "We look to you for protection and security, against all foreign aggressions. For this purpose, we give you the controul of commerce; but, you shall always limit the time, during which this instrument is to be used. This shield of defence you may, on emergent occasions, employ; but you shall always announce to us and to the world, the moment when it shall drop from your hands."

It is apparent, that cases may occur, in which the indefinite character of a law, as to its termination, may be essential to its efficacious operation. In this connexion, I would notice the internal indications, exhibited by the acts themselves, relative to their duration. In addition to the authority given to the president to suspend the acts, upon the contingency of certain events, we have evidence, from the very nature of their provisions, that they cannot be designed to be perpetual. An entire prohibition of exportation, unaccompanied with any restriction on importations, could never be intended for a permanent system; though the laws, in a technical view, may be denominated perpetual, containing no specification of the time when they shall expire. In illustration of their argument, gentlemen have supposed a strong case; a prohibition of the future cultivation of corn, in the United States. It would not be admitted, I presume, that an act, so extravagant, would be constitutional, though not perpetual, but confined to a single season. And why? Because it would be, most manifestly, without the limits of the federal jurisdiction, and relative to an object, or concern, not committed to its management. If an embargo, or suspension of commerce, of any description, be within the powers of congress, the terms and modifications of the measure must also be within their discretion. If the measure be referred to state necessity, the body that is authorized to determine on the existence of such necessity, must, also, be competent so to modify the means, as to adapt them to the exigency. It is said, that such a law is in contravention of unalienable rights; and we have had quotations from elementary writers, and from the bills of rights of the state constitutions, in support of this position. The doctrines and declarations of those respectable writers, and in those venerable instruments, are not to be slighted; but we are to leave the wide field of general reasonings and abstract principles, and are to consider the construction and operation of an express compact, a government of convention. The general position is incontestible, that all that is not surrendered by the constitution, is retained. The amendment which expresses this, is for greater security; but such would have been the true construction, without the amendment. Still, it remains to be determined, and it is often a question of some difficulty, what is given? By the second article of the confederation, congress were prohibited the exercise of any power not expressly delegated. A similar qualification was suggested, in one of the amendments proposed by the state of New-Hampshire, to the new constitution. The phraseology, indeed, was strengthened; and congress were to be prohibited from the exercise of powers, not expressly and particularly delegated. Such expressions were not adopted . . . It is wisely left as it is; and the true sense and meaning of the instrument is to be determined by just construction; guided and governed by good sense and honest intentions. Under the confederation, congress could have no agency relative to foreign commerce, but through the medium of treaties; and, by the ninth article, it was stipulated, that no treaty of commerce should be made, whereby the legislative power of the respective states, should be restrained, from imposing such imposts and duties on foreigners, as their own people were subjected to, "or from prohibiting the exportation of any species of goods or commodities whatsoever." Here we find an express reservation to the state legislatures of the power to pass prohibitory commercial laws, and, as respects exportations, without any limitations. Some of them exercised this power. In Massachusetts, it was carried to considerable extent, with marked determination, but to no sensible good effect. One of the prohibitory acts of that state, passed in 1786, was for the express "encouragement of the agriculture and manufacturers in our own country." The other, which was a counteracting law, had no definite limitation, but was to continue in force, until congress should be vested with competent powers, and should have passed an ordinance for the regulation of the commerce of the states. Unless congress, by the constitution, possess the power in question, it still exists in the state legislatures—but this has never been claimed or pretended, since the adoption of the federal constitution; and the exercise of such a power by the states, would be manifestly inconsistent with the power, vested by the people in congress, "to regulate commerce." Hence I infer, that the power, reserved to the states by the articles of confederation, is surrendered to congress, by the constitution; unless we suppose, that, by some strange process, it has been merged or extinguished, and now exists no where.

The propriety of this power, on the present construction, may be further evinced, by contemplating the operation of specific limitations or restrictions, which it might be proposed to apply. Will it be said, that the amendment, proposed by Virginia and North Carolina, would be an improvement in the instrument of government? Such a provision might prevent the adoption of exceptionable regulations; but, it would be equally operative in defeating those that it would be salutary; and would disable the majority of the nation from deciding on the best means of advancing its prosperity. To avoid such a system, as is now in operation, shall the people expressly provide, as a limitation to the power of regulating commerce, that it shall not extend to a total prohibition; or but for a limited time? Nothing would be gained by such restrictions. A prohibition might still be so nearly total, or extend to such a length of time, without violation of the restriction, as to be equivalent, in practical effect, to the present arrangement. Or will it be said, that the judiciary should then be called upon to decide the law void, though not repugnant to the terms of the restriction, and to consider exceptions from the prohibition, as, in the common case of a fraudulent deed, to be merely colourable? Loose and general restrictions would be ineffective, or, at best, merely directory. If particular and precise, they would evince an indiscreet attempt to anticipate the immense extent and variety of national exigencies, and would not be suitable appendages to a power, which, in its exercise, must depend on contingencies, and, from its nature and object, must be general. A particular mischief or inconvenience, contemplated in framing such limitations, might be avoided; but they would also injuriously fetter the national councils, and prevent the application of adequate provisions for the publick safety and happiness, according to the ever varying emergencies of national affairs. Let us not insist on a security, which the nature of human concerns will not permit. More effectual guards against abuse, more complete security for civil and political liberty, and for private right, are not, perhaps, afforded to any nation than to the people of the United States. These views of the national powers are not new. I have only given a more distinct exhibition of habitual impressions, coeval, in my mind, with the constitution. Upon these considerations, I am bound to overrule the objections to the acts in question, which I shall proceed to apply to the cases before the court, believing them to be constitutional laws.

Comment

Davis's opinion in *The William* was a concise formulation of the place of judicial review in the nationalist understanding of the Constitution. Davis sharply distinguished between challenges to congressional statutes based on express restrictions (or restrictions implied by affirmative provisions such as that mandating criminal trial by jury) in the constitutional text, and challenges that asserted "a mere exceeding of the powers of Congress." The former were judicially cognizable because the text's "affirmative provisions and express restrictions . . . are sufficiently definite" to provide courts with adequate standards for measuring the conformity of a statute to the Constitution. In cases where Congress was alleged to have exceeded or abused its delegated powers, however, the exercise of judicial review would require a court to determine "the degree of legislative discretion, admissible in the case." Given the differing information available to judges and legislators, their different modes of proceeding, and the public need to accord Congress broad discretion to act in the national interest, Davis regarded the judiciary as incompetent to "determine where the legitimate exercise of discretion ends, and usurpation begins." The only practicable and constitutional remedy in such a situation lay in the electoral responsibility of Congress.

Davis admitted an apparent exception to his exclusion of judicial review from cases of congressional overreaching. One might imagine a statute (a total ban on the cultivation of corn, for example) that was "so manifestly without the sphere" of federal authority "that the judiciary branch might be competent to pronounce them invalid." This exception, however, was for Davis more a theoretical possibility than a likely case, and no statute "bearing relation to a power with which [Congress] is vested" would fall within it.

Turning to the specific case of the embargo, Davis noted that Congress clearly was vested with control over commerce with foreign countries, and therefore enjoyed "sovereignty . . . limited only by the qualifications and restrictions expressed in the constitution." It followed from this sovereignty that Congress could employ its commerce power not only to aid commerce itself, but also as "an instrument for other purposes of general policy." The embargo, therefore, was a legitimate exercise of Congress's discretion to employ a delegated power to achieve delegated ends (the conduct of the nation's foreign policy).

It was ironic that the Jefferson administration's embargo was dealt its most serious legal blow by the first Republican justice and sustained by a New England Federalist judge, particularly because the two men's opinions were authentic expressions of Republican and nationalist thought, respectively. For Johnson, the very point of the Constitution was to bind down government by the written rules of law, and in the interests of preserving the rights of "individual liberty." Davis, on the other hand, found no room for the "general reasonings and abstract principles" of "unalienable rights" in construing governmental powers granted by "an express compact." The Constitution's purpose was to enable government to protect "the publick safety and happiness" in "the ever varying emergencies of national affairs."

Nine

The Disintegration of the "Republican Ascendancy"

Thomas Jefferson's departure from office in March 1809 marked an irrevocable breakdown of agreement over the meaning of the "Republican Ascendancy." States' rights "Old Republicans" had become increasingly unhappy with what they perceived as Jefferson's compromises of principle, and they viewed his successor Madison as an open apostate. States' rights agitation, in turn, increasingly appeared to Madison and the Republican party leadership as a defense not of liberty but of lawlessness and disunion. This renewal of bitter constitutional disagreement took place as the United States lurched from confrontation to war with Great Britain.

Section A: *James Madison and the Constitutional Role of the Presidency*

The Olmstead Affair

President Madison's first constitutional crisis had its origins in events that took place long before his inauguration. In September 1778 the British sloop *Active* had been brought into Philadelphia as a prize, but an immediate dispute arose over who was entitled to the proceeds of its sale. While the *Active* had been en route from Jamaica to British-occupied New York, a group of impressed American sailors led by Gideon Olmstead seized the vessel and set sail for a New Jersey port. Before reaching safe harbor, however, the *Active* was overtaken and captured by a Pennsylvania state warship, the *Convention*, which compelled Olmstead and his fellows to sail to Philadelphia.

In proceedings before a state court, the *Convention*'s master, Olmstead's group, and the captain of the American privateer *Le Gerard* all laid claim to the proceeds of the *Active*'s sale. A jury found that the Olmstead party had not been in complete control of the sloop when the *Convention* seized her; and, in accordance with its verdict, the court divided the prize money into four parts and awarded one quarter each to the masters of the *Convention* and the *Le Gerard*, to the commonwealth of Pennsylvania as owner of the *Convention*, and to Olmstead and his comrades.

The latter group appealed to the commission of appeals in prize cases established by the Continental Congress and recognized by Pennsylvania statute. This federal appellate body ruled Olmstead and company entitled to the entire proceeds, but the Pennsylvania trial court refused to obey its judgment because state law forbade appeals in admiralty cases based solely on questions of fact. Instead, the state court deposited the commonwealth's share of the prize money with the state treasurer, David Rittenhouse, who made bond to guarantee the sum. The money came into the hands of Rittenhouse's two daughters (and executrices) after his death in 1796.

After the ratification of the Constitution, Olmstead and three others sought to enforce the judgment of the old appellate commission in the new federal district court. In 1803 United States District Judge Richard Peters ruled that the state's share of the prize money should be delivered to the plaintiffs, and in response the state legislature passed a statute calling on Rittenhouse's daughters to deliver the money to the state. On advice of counsel, the executrices obeyed neither order.

In May 1807 Olmstead's attorney requested the district court to enforce its decree. This Judge Peters declined to do. As he explained in his answer to a Supreme Court order:

> But from prudential, more than other motives, I deemed it best to avoid embroiling the government of the United States and that of Pennsylvania (if the latter government should choose so to do), on a question which has rested on my single opinion, so far as it is touched by my decree: and under the influence of this sentiment, I have withheld the process required . . . There being no other legal mode of obtaining the decision of the superior tribunal of the United States (the only jurisdiction by which the judgments of inferior courts of the United States can be finally rectified or judicially annulled), I have thought it proper, and under all circumstances, fully justifiable, to obtain that decision, by placing the case under the cognisance of your honorable court, in its present form. On the merits and justice of the claim of [Olmstead and his companions], I have no doubt; but remain of the same opinion, I have mentioned in my decree.

Olmstead's lawyer then sought a writ of mandamus from the Supreme Court to compel Peters to enforce his decision. In February 1809, shortly before Madison took office, the Court announced its decision:

United States v. Peters
9 U. S. (5 Cranch) 115 (Feb. 20, 1809)

Marshall, Ch. J., delivered the opinion of the court as follows:—With great attention, and with serious concern, the court has considered the return made by the judge for the district of Pennsylvania to the mandamus directing him to exercise the sentence pronounced by him in the case of *Gideon Olmstead and others v. Rittenhouse's Executrices*, or to show cause for not so doing. The cause shown is an act of the legislature of Pennsylvania, passed subsequent to the rendition of his sentence. This act authorizes and requires the governor to demand, for the use of the state of Pennsylvania, the money which had been decreed to Gideon Olmstead and others; and which was in the hands of the executrices of David Rittenhouse; and in default of payment, to direct the attorney-general to institute a suit for the recovery thereof. This act further authorizes and requires the governor to use any further means he may think necessary for the protection of what it denominates "the just rights of the state," and also to protect the person and properties of the said executrices of David Rittenhouse, deceased, against any process whatever, issued out of any federal court, in consequence of their obedience to the requisition of the said act.

If the legislatures of the several states may, at will, annul the judgments of the courts of the United States, and destroy the rights acquired under those judgments, the constitution itself becomes a solemn mockery; and the nation is deprived of the means of enforcing its laws by the instrumentality of its own tribunals. So fatal a result must be deprecated by all, and the people of Pennsylvania, not less than the citizens of every other state, must feel a deep interest in resisting principles so destructive of the Union and in averting consequences so fatal to themselves.

The act in question does not, in terms, assert the universal right of the state to interpose in every case whatever; but assigns, as a motive for its interposition in this particular case, that the sentence, the execution of which it prohibits, was rendered in a cause over which the federal courts have no jurisdiction.

If the ultimate right to determine the jurisdiction of the courts of the Union is placed by the constitution in the several state legislatures, then this act concludes the subject; but if that power necessarily resides in the supreme judicial tribunal of the nation, then the jurisdiction of the district court of Pennsylvania, over the case in which that jurisdiction was exercised, ought to be most deliberately examined; and the act of Pennsylvania, with whatever respect it may be considered, cannot be permitted to prejudice the question . . .

It is contended, that the federal courts were deprived of jurisdiction in this cause, by that amendment of the constitution, which exempts states from being sued in those courts by individuals. This amendment declares, "that the judicial power of the United States shall not be construed to extend to any suit, in law or equity, commenced or prosecuted against one of the United States by citizens of another state, or by citizens or subjects of any foreign state."

The right of a state to assert, as plaintiff, any interest it may have in a subject, which forms the matter of controversy between individuals, in one of the courts of the United States, is not affected by this amendment; nor can it be so construed as to oust the court of its jurisdiction, should such claim be suggested. The amendment simply provides, that no suit shall be commenced or prosecuted against a state. The state cannot be made a defendant to a suit brought by an individual; but it remains the duty of the courts of the United States to decide all cases brought before them by citizens of one state against citizens of a different state, where a state is not necessarily a defendant. In this case, the suit was not instituted against the state, or its treasurer, but against the executrices of David Rittenhouse, for the proceeds of a vessel condemned in the court of admiralty, which were admitted to be in their possession. If these proceeds had been the actual property of Pennsylvania, however wrongfully acquired, the disclosure of that fact would have presented a case on which it is necessary to give an opinion; but it certainly can never be alleged, that a mere suggestion of title in a state, to property in possession of an individual, must arrest the proceedings of the court, and prevent their looking into the suggestion, and examining the validity of the title.

If the suggestion in this case be examined, it is deemed perfectly clear, that no title whatever to the certificates in question was vested in the state of Pennsylvania.

By the highest judicial authority of the nation, it has been long since decided, that the court of appeals erected by [the Continental Congress] had full authority to revise and correct the sentences of the courts of admiralty of the several states, in prize causes. That question, therefore, is at rest. Consequently, the decision of the court of appeals in this case annulled the sentence of the court of admiralty, and extinguished the interest of the state of Pennsylvania in the Active and her cargo, which was acquired by that sentence. The full right to that property was immediately vested in the claimants, who might rightfully pursue it, into whosesoever [*sic*] hands it might come . . . [T]he property, which represented the Active and her cargo, was in possession not of the state of Pennsylvania, but of David Rittenhouse, as an individual; after whose death, it passed, like other property, to his representatives.

Since, then, the state of Pennsylvania had neither possession of, nor right to, the property on which the sentence of the district court was pronounced, and since the suit was neither commenced nor prosecuted against that state, there remains no pretext for the allegation, that the case is within that amendment of the constitution which has been cited; and consequently, the state of Pennsylvania can possess no constitutional right to resist the legal process which may be directed in this cause.

It will be readily conceived, that the order which this court is enjoined to make by the high obligations of duty and of law, is not made without regret at the necessity which has induced the application. But it is a solemn duty, and therefore, must be performed. A peremptory *mandamus* must be awarded.

Resolutions
Pennsylvania General Assembly
(adopted on April 3, 1809)[96]

The Pennsylvania authorities reacted vigorously and hostilely to the Supreme Court's decision. On March 6, two days after Madison became president, the Republican-controlled Pennsylvania legislature received a committee report recommending that it approve a series of resolutions denouncing federal-court jurisdiction over issues of state authority and proposing a constitutional amendment to establish an "impartial tribunal . . . to determine disputes between the General and State Governments."

That, as a member of the Federal Union, the Legislature of Pennsylvania acknowledges the supremacy, and will cheerfully submit to the authority, of the General Government, as far as that authority is delegated by the Constitution of the United States. But, whilst they yield to this authority, when exercised within constitutional limits, they trust they will be not considered as acting hostile to the General Government, when, as *guardians of the State rights*, they cannot permit an infringement of those rights, by an unconstitutional exercise of power in the United States' courts.

. . . [I]t is to be lamented, that no provision is made, in the Constitution, for determining disputes between *General* and *State* Governments, by an impartial tribunal, when such cases occur. The Legislature is seriously impressed with the insecurity of the State Rights, if the Courts of United States are permitted to give unlimited extension to their power, in deciding on those Rights . . . That, should the independence of the States, as secured by the Constitution, be destroyed, the liberties of the People, in so extensive a country, cannot long survive. To suffer the United States Courts to decide on State Rights, will, from a bias in favor of power, necessarily destroy the Federal Part of our Government: and, whenever the Government of the United States becomes consolidated, we may learn from the history of Nations, what will be the event.

Concurrently with the legislature's actions, Republican Governor Simon Snyder ordered state militia General Michael Bright to prevent federal action against Rittenhouse's daughters. When the United States marshal attempted to serve papers on the executrices, Bright's militia repeatedly stopped him. The marshal then prepared to summon a federal *posse comitatus* "to suppress the force and arms embodied, in opposition to the constitution"; and a federal grand jury indicted Bright and several other members of the militia.

Armed conflict between state and federal authorities was averted, however, by state hesitation and a combination of federal firmness and tact. The state Republican party was divided over Governor Snyder's policy of defiance, and an April 4 statute ambiguously approved his activation of the militia while appropriating $18,000 "to meet all contingent expences" relating to the Olmstead affair. Snyder in turn sought to enlist Republican President Madison in his defense of states' rights:

Simon Snyder
Letter to James Madison
(April 6, 1809)[97]

Sir,

In discharge of a Legislative injunction, I transmit to you the proceedings of the General Assembly, on the long litigated cause of Gideon Olmstead and others, versus Elizabeth Sergeant and Esther Waters, executrices of David Rittenhouse, deceased, late Treasurer of Pennsylvania . . .

While I deeply deplore the circumstance which has led to this correspondence, I am consoled with the pleasing idea, that the chief magistracy of the Union is confided to a man who merits, and who possesses so great a portion of the esteem and the confidence of a vast majority of the citizens of the United States; who is *so* intimately acquainted with the principles of the Federal constitution, and who is no less disposed to protect the sovereignty and independence of the several states, as guaranteed to them, than to defend the rights and legitimate powers of the General government; who will justly discriminate between opposition to the constitution and laws of the United States, and that of resisting the decree of a Judge, founded, as it is conceived, in a usurpation of power and jurisdiction, not delegated to him by either, and who is equally solicitous, with myself, to preserve the Union of the States, and to adjust the present unhappy collision of the two governments in such a manner as will be equally honorable to them both.

Permit me to add, in addition to the Act I have done as the Chief magistrate of the State of Pennsylvania, to assure you, Sir, as an individual, of my full confidence in the wisdom, justice and integrity of the present administration of the General government, and my fixed determination, in my public, as well as in my private capacity, to support it in all constitutional measures it may adopt . . .

James Madison
Letter to Simon Snyder
(April 13, 1809)[98]

Sir,

I have received your letter of the 6th. instant, accompanied by certain Acts of the Legislature of Pennsylvania; which will be laid before Congress, according to the desire expressed.

Considering our respective relations to the subject of these communications, it would be unnecessary, if not improper, to enter into any examination of some of the questions connected with it. It is sufficient, in the actual posture of the case, to remark that the Executive of the U. States, is not only unauthorized to prevent the execution of a Decree sanctioned by the Supreme Court of the U. States, but is expressly enjoined by Statute, to carry into effect any such decree, where opposition may be made to it. It is a propitious circumstance therefore, that whilst no legal discretion lies with the Executive of the U. States to decline steps which might lead to a very painful issue, a provision has been made by the Legislative Act transmitted by you, adequate to a removal of the existing difficulty. And I feel great pleasure in assuring myself, that the authority which it gives will be exercised in a spirit corresponding with the patriotic character of the State over which you preside. Be pleased, Sir, to accept assurances of my respectful consideration.

State resistance to the federal court decree rapidly crumbled. The United States marshal succeeded in arresting Rittenhouse's daughters, and the state chief justice, William Tighlman, denied their petition for release by writ of habeas corpus. Bright and the other militiamen indicted were arrested and convicted, and President Madison subsequently pardoned them.

Comment

The Olmstead affair presented the Supreme Court and President Madison with a perplexing tangle of constitutional problems. Pennsylvania's argument against enforcement of the federal judgments rested on premises of impeccably Republican origin. The original, pre-1787 judgment arguably had violated a great Anglo-American bulwark of liberty, trial by jury, by substituting the decision of judges for jurors on a factual issue. The seizure of state property by authority of a federal decree was a blatant intrusion into state sovereignty similar to that which the Court attempted in *Chisholm v. Georgia* and the Eleventh Amendment repudiated. In contrast, the state legislature's attempts to "interpose" its authority clearly echoed the Virginia and Kentucky resolutions, and Governor Snyder's request for Madison's aid implicitly invoked Jefferson's unwavering insistence that the president was entitled and obligated to exercise independent judgment in constitutional matters. The response of the Court and president to Pennsylvania's challenge foreshadowed and shaped the contours of Republican constitutionalism in its second decade of ascendancy.

John Marshall's opinion for the Court rejected the state's specific arguments while avoiding any direct statement on Pennsylvania's invocation of broader Republican principles. Marshall barely noticed the original dispute over the right of trial by jury. He reminded his hearers that the proceedings were originally in admiralty, an area of law in which neither tradition nor constitutional rule required trial by jury, and that it was settled law that the old appeals commission had "full authority to revise and correct" state admiralty judgments.

Marshall spent more time addressing Pennsylvania's claim that it merely was arresting an assertion of jurisdiction by the federal courts in violation of the Eleventh Amendment. Olmstead's action did not subject the state to judicial process nor its treasury to the federal marshal: Rittenhouse's daughters were the defendants and the possessors of the property in dispute. The Eleventh Amendment's limitation on jurisdiction, therefore, was inapplicable, and Peters's award of the monies to the plaintiffs rather than to the state was the product of his obedience to the constitutional "duty of the courts of the United States to decide all cases" falling under their diversity jurisdiction. *Peters*, Marshall insisted, need not involve any great political questions of federalism: it was, rather, a routine application of the laws of jurisdiction and the enforcement of judgments. By defying the federal decree, on the other hand, Pennsylvania had raised the question of the Constitution's grant of judicial power to the federal government. The state was not interposing its authority to shelter liberty from tyranny, but was intruding into the Supreme Court's orderly and constitutionally indisputable power to regulate the jurisdiction of lower federal courts. Marshall was careful not to pronounce a blanket rejection of the idea of state interposition; at least as a rhetorical matter, he described his rejection of a state "constitutional right to resist the legal process . . . in this cause" as a consequence of the specific holding that the Eleventh Amendment did not apply.

Madison's response to Snyder muffled by its brevity the importance of the constitutional principle the president was articulating. Without denying his duty to exercise constitutional judgment (a duty Madison took seriously), Madison bluntly denied its applicability to the dispute between Pennsylvania and the Court. As "the Executive of the U. States," Madison's sole duty was to execute the Court's decree in the event of resistance. In such circumstances, Madison's personal views of the constitutional issues involved were irrelevant: "It would be unnecessary, if not improper," to discuss them, he wrote.

Madison's decision to support the Court in the Olmstead affair resolved a significant ambiguity left over from his predecessor's conflicts with the courts. After *Peters*, the Republican presidents consistently denied any discretion to refuse to enforce or obey specific judicial decisions. Jefferson's assertion of the president's constitutional independence from the judiciary was now clearly complemented by Madison's recognition of the president's constitutional obligation to uphold judicial authority within its sphere of activity.

James Madison
Message to the U.S. House of Representatives
(February 21, 1811)[99]

To the House of Representatives of the United States:
Having examined and considered the bill, entitled "An act incorporating the Protestant Episcopal Church in the town of Alexandria, in the District of Columbia," I now return the bill to the House of Representatives," in which it originated, with the following objections:

Because the bill exceeds the rightful authority to which Governments are limited, by the essential distinction between civil and religious functions, and violates, in particular, the article of the Constitution of the United States, which declares, that "Congress shall make no law respecting a religious establishment." The bill enacts into, and establishes by law, sundry rules and proceedings relative purely to the organization and polity of the church incorporated, and comprehending even the election and removal of the Minister of the same; so that no change could be made therein by the particular society, or by the general church of which it is a member, and whose authority it recognises. This particular church, therefore, would so far be a religious establishment by law; a legal force and sanction being given to certain articles in its constitution and administration. Nor can it be considered, that the articles thus established are to be taken as the descriptive criteria only of the corporate identity of the society, inasmuch as this identity must depend on other characteristics; as the regulations established are generally unessential, and alterable according to the principles and canons, by which churches of that denomination govern themselves; and as the injunctions and prohibitions contained in the regulations, would be enforced by the penal consequences applicable to a violation of them, according to the local law:

Because the bill vests in the said incorporated church an authority to provide for the support of the poor, and the education of poor children of the same; an authority which being altogether superfluous, if the provision is to be the result of opious charity, would be a precedent for giving to religious societies, as such, a legal agency in carrying into effect a public and civil duty.

Comment

Although he accepted the finality of judicial interpretations of the Constitution in cases within the courts' jurisdiction, Madison agreed with Jefferson that the president enjoyed independent interpretive authority and responsibility in other situations. On several occasions during his presidency, Madison vetoed on constitutional grounds bills that Congress had enacted, in the case of the 1811 church incorporation bill because in his view it violated the strict separation of church and state mandated both by general principles and by the First Amendment.

Laban Wheaton
Speech in the U.S. House of Representatives
(February 21, 1811)[100]

. . . He [Wheaton] did not imagine that they were to assume the objections of the President to be valid and of course to dismiss the bill. They had a duty to perform as well as the President. He had performed his duty in the case presented for consideration. And would gentlemen assume it as a correct position because the bill was objected to by the President that the House ought not to act understandingly? This was not a correct principle. In his view the objections made by the President to this bill were altogether futile. Mr. W. said he did not consider this bill any infringement of the Constitution. If it was, both branches of the Legislature, since the commencement of the Government, had been guilty of such infringement. It could not be said, indeed, that they had been guilty of doing much about religion; but they had at every session appointed Chaplains, to be of different denominations, to interchange weekly between the two Houses. Now, if a bill for regulating the funds of a religious society could be an infringement of the Constitution, the two Houses had so far infringed it by electing, paying or contracting with their Chaplains; for so far it established two different denominations of religion. Mr. W. deemed this question of very great consequence. Were the people of this District never to have any religion? Was it to be entirely excluded from these ten miles of square? He should be afraid to come if that were to be the case. The want of time was no sufficient reason against giving this subject a mature consideration. What was done ought to be well done.

The Orono
18 Fed. Cas. 830 (C.C.D. Mass. May 1812)

President Madison's relationship with the federal judiciary was much more positive than President Jefferson's had been. The courts, nonetheless, sometimes found occasion to continue their struggle to impose legal constraints on executive actions.

On March 1, 1809, President Jefferson had signed a Non-Intercourse Act banning commerce with France and Britain, but permitting the president, by proclamation, to reopen trade with either country upon its decision to cease interference with neutral shipping. On April 19 President Madison suspended the act's ban on commerce with Britain because he had been assured by the British minister, David Erskine, that the latter's government was going to comply with the act's requirements. By the beginning of August, however, Madison learned that the British government had repudiated Erskine's representations. So on August 9 the president revoked his April proclamation, and closed off trade with Britain once more. This revival of the embargo was not sanctioned explicitly by the text of the Non-Intercourse Act.

Prior to the expiration of the act, but after Madison's April proclamation reopening trade with Britain, the American schooner *Orono* took on board a cargo of rum and molasses at a British port in the West Indies. The United States subsequently attempted to seize the *Orono* under the act and Madison's August proclamation.

STORY, Circuit Justice. . . . [It is argued by] the United States, that this proclamation [of April 19, opening trade with Britain] being founded on a mistake of fact [that Erskine's assurances were accurate], had no legal effect, and was merely void. Whether it was so founded in mistake, is not for the court to determine. It does not belong to the court to superintend the acts of the executive, nor to decide on circumstances left to his sole discretion. So far as applies to courts of justice, the president's proclamation, being founded on the law, is to be considered as duly and properly issued, and of course as completely suspending the act of 1 March, 1809, as to Great Britain and her dependencies . . .

The next question is, whether the proclamation of the president of the United States, of 9th August, 1809, revived the act of March 1, 1809, against Great Britain and her dependencies; for if it did not, then clearly the Orono has been guilty of no offence. I take it to be an incontestable principle, that the president has no common law prerogative to interdict commercial intercourse with any nation; or revive any act, whose operation has expired. His authority for this purpose must be derived from some positive law; and when that is once found to exist, the court have nothing to do with the manner and circumstances under which it is exercised. The only law produced for this purpose is the eleventh section of the act of March 1, 1809, and first and third sections of [the] Act [of] June 28, 1809, which refer to the former provision. Now, the eleventh section contains no authority whatsoever to enable the president to revive that act, when once it had been suspended, as to either nation. The authority given is exclusively confined to the revocation of the act. For the executive department of the government, this court entertain the most entire respect; and amidst the multiplicity of cares in that department, it may, without any violation of decorum, be presumed, that sometimes there may be an inaccurate construction of a law. It is our duty to expound the laws as we find them in the records of state; and we cannot, when called upon by the citizens of the country, refuse our opinion, however it may differ from that of very great authorities. I do not perceive any reasonable ground to imply an authority in the president to revive this act, and I must therefore, with whatever reluctance, pronounce it to have been, as to this purpose, invalid . . .

Comment

As in *Gilchrist v. Collector of Charleston*, a Republican justice insisted that the president's powers derived from specific, textual grants, or did not exist at all. Neither the Constitution nor the nature of executive power afforded the president "prerogative" and discretionary powers of a quasi-royal type.

Section B: *Adhering to the "Doctrines of '98"*

The Constitutionality of a National Bank Bill Revisited

With the expiration of the charter of the Bank of the United States approaching, Madison's administration attempted to obtain its renewal, motivated by a recognition of the bank's central role in both the federal government's fiscal activities and the national economy. The renewal bill was opposed by a combination of Republicans who objected on constitutional grounds and Federalist defenders of state banks.

Resolutions
Pennsylvania General Assembly
(adopted on January 11, 1811)[101]

The people of the United States by the adoption of the federal constitution established a general government for special purposes, reserving to themselves respectively, the rights and authorities not delegated in that instrument. To the compact thereby created, each state acceded in its character as a state, and is a party. The act of union thus entered into being to all intents and purposes a treaty between sovereign states, the general government by this treaty was not constituted the exclusive or final judge of the powers it was to exercise; for if it were so to judge then its judgment and not the constitution would be the measure of its authority.

Should the general government in any of its departments violate the provisions of the constitution, it rests with the states, and with the people, to apply suitable remedies.

With these impressions, the legislature of Pennsylvania, ever solicitous to secure an administration of the federal and state governments, conformably to the true spirit of their respective constitutions, feel it their duty to express their sentiments upon an important subject now before congress, viz., the continuance or establishment of a bank. From a careful review of the powers vested in the general government, they have the most positive conviction that the authority to grant charters of incorporation, within the jurisdiction of any state without the consent thereof is not recognized in that instrument, either expressly, or by a warrantable implication; Therefore,

Resolved, By the Senate and House of Representatives of the Commonwealth of Pennsylvania, in General Assembly met, That the senators of this state in the senate of the United States, be, and they are hereby instructed, and the representatives of this state in the house of representatives of the United States be, and they hereby are requested to use every exertion in their power, to prevent the charter of the bank of the United States from being designed to have operation within the jurisdiction of any state, without first having obtained the consent of the legislature of such state.

Resolved, That the governor be, and he hereby is requested to forward a copy of the above preamble and resolution, to each of the senators and representatives of this state, in the Congress of the United States.

[*Note:* Most state legislatures in the early nineteenth century claimed the right to "instruct" the state's United States senators by binding instructions. Many, although not all, senators denied the existence of the right, even though it was not unknown for a defiant individual to resign as a point of honor rather than to obey or disobey a legislative instruction.]

The Virginia legislature, on January 22, approved a resolution labeling renewal of the bank "not only unconstitutional, but a dangerous encroachment on the sovereignty of the states."

Peter B. Porter
Speech in the U.S. House of Representatives
(January 18, 1811)[102]

... The mode of reasoning adopted by General [Alexander] Hamilton and the other advocates of implied powers is this: They first search for the end or object for which a particular power is given; and this object will be an immediate or ultimate one, as may best suit the purpose of the argument. Having ascertained the end or object, they abandon the power; or, rather, they confound the power and the object of it together and make the attainment of the object and the execution of the power given to accomplish it, convertible terms. Whatever, they say, attains the object for which any power is given, is an execution of that power.

... The Constitution of the United States is not, as such reasoning supposes it to be, a mere general designation of the ends or objects for which the Federal Government was established, and leaving to Congress a discretion as to the means or powers by which those ends shall be brought about. But the Constitution is a specification of the powers or means themselves by which certain objects are to be accomplished. The powers of the Constitution, carried into execution according to the strict terms and import of them, are the appropriate means and the only means within the reach of this Government for the attainment of its ends.

It is true, as the Constitution declares, and it would be equally true if the Constitution did not declare it, that Congress have a right to pass all laws necessary and proper for executing the delegated powers; but this gives no latitude of discretion on the selection of means or powers. A power given to Congress in its legislative capacity, without the right to pass laws to execute it, would be nugatory; would be no power at all. It would be a solecism in language to call it a power. A power to lay and collect taxes carries with it a right to make laws for that purpose; but they must be laws to lay and collect taxes and not laws to incorporate banks. If you undertake to justify a law under a particular power you must show the incidentality and applicability of the law to the power itself, and not merely its relation to any supposed end which is to be accomplished by its exercise. You must show that the plain, direct, ostensible, primary object and tendency of your law is to execute the power, and not that it will tend to facilitate the execution of it. It is not less absurd than it is dangerous, first to assume some great, distinct and independent power unknown to the Constitution and violating the rights of the States; and then, to attempt to justify it by a reference to, some remote, indirect, collateral tendency which the exercise of it may have towards facilitating the execution of some known and acknowledged power.

This word facilitate has become a very fashionable word in the construction of powers; but, sir, it is a dangerous one; it means more than we are aware of. To do a thing and to facilitate the doing of it, are distinct operations; they are distinct means; they are distinct powers. The Constitution has expressly given to Congress the power to do certain things; and it has, as explicitly, withheld from them the power to do every other thing. The power to lay and collect taxes is one thing; and the power to establish banks, involving in its exercise the regulation of the internal domestic economy of the States, is another and totally distinct thing; and the one is therefore not included in the other.

Again, sir, it is contended that the right to incorporate a bank is implied in the power to regulate trade and intercourse between the several States. It is said to be so inasmuch as it creates a paper currency, which furnishes a convenient and common circulating medium of trade between the several States. Money, sir, has nothing more to do with trade than that it furnishes a medium or representative of the value of the articles employed in trade. The only office of bank bills is to represent money. Now, if it be a regulation of trade to create the representative articles or subjects of trade, a fortiori, will it be a regulation of trade to create the articles or subjects themselves. By this reasoning then you may justify the right of Congress to establish manufacturing and agricultural companies within the several States; because the direct object and effect of these would be to increase manufactures and agricultural products, which are the known and common subjects of trade. You might with more propriety say that under the power to regulate trade between the State, we have a right to incorporate canal companies; because canals would tend directly to open, facilitate and encourage trade and intercourse between the several States; and, in my humble opinion, sir, canals would furnish a much more salutary, direct and efficacious means for enabling the great body of the people to pay their taxes than is furnished by banks. But, sir, these various powers have never been claimed by the Federal Government; and, much as I am known to favor that particular species of internal improvement, I would never vote to incorporate a company for the purpose of opening a canal through any State, without first obtaining the consent of that State whose territorial rights would be affected by it. There can be no question but canal companies, and agricultural companies, and manufacturing companies, and banking companies may all tend more or less to facilitate the operations of trade; but they have nothing to do with the political regulations of trade; and such only come within the scope of the powers of Congress . . .

But, Mr. Chairman, . . . a new argument [has been advanced] in support of the constitutionality of this bank—an argument not deduced from the provisions of the Constitution itself but founded on prescription. [The supporters of the renewal bill] tell us that this bank was originally incorporated by a Congress fully competent and qualified to decide on its constitutionality; that its existence is almost coeval with the Government; that it has been countenanced by all succeeding Administrations; that laws have been passed to enforce the provisions of the original charter; and therefore the Constitutional question must be considered as settled, adjudicated, and at rest.

Whatever may be the opinion of the gentlemen of the *long robe*, I cannot for myself yield to this doctrine of *prescriptive* Constitutional rights. It may answer in England where they have no constitution; or where, rather, as they choose to explain it, immemorial usage or prescription are evidence of what their Constitution is. It may do in Connecticut—(it is not my design to derogate from the respectability of that State, nor of its institutions)—it may be good doctrine in Connecticut, where ancient customs and *steady habits* are their constitution. But, sir, the doctrine should never be tolerated in this House, where every member has a *printed Constitution* on his table before him—a Constitution drawn up with the greatest care and deliberation; with the utmost attention to perspicuity and precision. A Constitution, the injunctions of which, as we in our best judgments shall understand them and not as they shall be interpreted to us by others, we are solemnly bound, by our oaths, to obey.

It is true that this bank was originally established by a Congress competent to judge of its constitutionality. It is equally true that a respectable minority of that Congress opposed the passage of the law on the ground of its unconstitutionality; and if I have been rightly informed, it is also true that the then President, General Washington, in giving his sanction to that law did it with more doubt and hesitation than almost any other act of his Administration.

It is true that subsequent Congresses of different political complexions have passed laws enforcing the provisions of the original charter; and that no attempts have been made to repeal it. But it is equally true that all this might be done away with the most perfect propriety and consistency, although they totally disbelieved in its constitutionality. I need not state to this House, that this is not a law in the ordinary course of legislation—a law prescribing a common rule of conduct for the government of the citizens of the United States at large—liable to be repealed at any time; and the obligations of which would cease with its repeal. This, sir, is not the nature of the law, but it is a law in the nature of a contract between the Government and certain individuals, and the existence of it was extended to twenty years. The moment this contract was made, and its operations commenced, private rights were vested; and it would have been a breach of national faith to have repealed it. The original Congress had the same right that we have to judge of the constitutionality of a law; and having, under that right, passed this law or made this contract, we are bound to carry it, as a contract, into execution. As a contract, every successive Congress, of whatever materials composed, is one party to it; and it is well known that a party cannot violate the obligations of his own contract; but, on the contrary, is bound to carry them into effect. It was competent in the State governments to have opposed the execution on the ground of its unconstitutionality; but, perhaps under all circumstances, they acted a wise and discreet part in not attempting it. The national faith was pledged in the passage of this law. The national credit, which it was at that time and which indeed it is at all times of the first importance to support, was at stake on the faithful execution of this contract; and it was better to suffer for twenty years, under an unconstitutional law, rather than to attempt so violent a remedy—a remedy which would have crippled the credit of the nation in its infancy.

But, sir, because these were proper considerations with our predecessors and the States to suffer the continuance of this law, does it follow that now, when that law has expired by its own limitation, when the obligations of that contract are complied with and discharged, when the national faith is emancipated, that they are motives for us to make a new unconstitutional charter? No, sir. The question now is a question *de novo*. It is a question of conscience in the interpretation of the letter and spirit of the Constitution; unembarrassed by any collateral considerations; and as such I shall feel bound to vote upon it. It is the province of the Executive and judicial departments to explain and direct the practical operation of each particular law; and I must submit to the decisions. But the commentaries of courts are not to furnish the principles upon which I am afterwards to legislate. It is to this book (the Constitution) so justly dear to us all, and not to the books of reports, that we must look as a guide to direct us in the path of our oath and our duty . . .

William H. Crawford
Speech in the U.S. Senate
(February 11, 1811)[103]

. . . The right to erect light-houses is exercised because the commerce of the nation or the collection of duties is greatly facilitated by that means; and, sir, the right to create a bank is exercised because the collection of your revenue and the safekeeping and easy and speedy transmission of your public money is not simply facilitated, but because these important objects are more perfectly secured by the erection of a bank than they can be by any other means in the power of human imagination to devise. We say, therefore, in the words of the Constitution, that a bank is necessary and proper to enable the Government to carry into complete effect the right to lay and collect taxes, imposts, duties, and excises. We do not say that the existence of the Government absolutely depends upon the operations of a bank, but that a national bank enables the Government to manage its fiscal concerns more advantageously than it could do by any other means. The terms necessary and proper, according to the construction given to every part of the Constitution, imposes no limitation upon the powers previously delegated. If these words had been omitted in the clause giving authority to pass laws to carry into execution the powers vested by the Constitution in the National Government, still Congress would have been bound to pass laws which were necessary and proper, and not such as were unnecessary and improper . . .

The original powers granted to the Government by the Constitution can never change with the varying circumstances of the country, but the means by which those powers are to be carried into effect must necessarily vary with the varying state and circumstances of the nation. We are, when acting to-day, not to inquire what means were necessary and proper twenty years ago, not what were necessary and proper at the organization of the Government, but our inquiry must be, what means are necessary and proper this day. The Constitution, in relation to the means by which its powers are to be executed, is one eternal *now*. The state of things now, the precise point of time when we are called upon to act, must determine our choice in the selection of means to execute the delegated powers . . .

James Lloyd
Speech in the U.S. Senate
(February 12, 1811)[104]

. . . It is impossible for the ingenuity of man to devise any written system of Government which, after a lapse of time, extension of empire, or change of circumstances, shall be able to carry its own provision into operation—hence, sir, the indispensable necessity of implied or resulting powers, and hence the provision in the Constitution that the Government should exercise such additional powers as were necessary to carry those that had been delegated into effect. Sir, if this country goes on increasing and extending in the ratio it has done, it is not impossible that hereafter, to provide for all the new cases that may rise under this new state of things, the defined powers may prove only a text and the implied or resulting powers may furnish the sermon to it . . .

Henry Clay
Speech in the U.S. Senate
(February 15, 1811)[105]

... Gentlemen contend that the construction which they give to the Constitution has been acquiesced in by all parties, and under all Administrations; and they rely particularly on an act which passed in 1804 for extending a branch to New Orleans, and another act, of 1807, for punishing those who should forge or utter forged paper of the bank...

When gentlemen attempt to carry this measure upon the ground of acquiescence or precedent, do they forget that we are not in Westminster Hall? In courts of justice the utility of uniformity of decision exacts of the judge a conformity to the adjudication of his predecessor. In the interpretation and administration of the law this practice is wise and proper; and without it, everything depending upon the caprice of the judge, we should have no security for our dearest rights. It is far otherwise when applied to the source of legislation. Here no rule exists but the Constitution; and to legislate upon the ground merely that our predecessors thought themselves authorized, under similar circumstances, to legislate, is to sanctify error and perpetuate usurpation. But if we are to be subjected to the trammels of precedents, I claim, on the other hand, the benefit of the restrictions under which the intelligent judge cautiously receives them. It is an established rule that to give to a previous adjudication any effect, the mind of the judge who pronounced it must have been awakened to the subject, and it must have been a deliberate opinion formed after full argument. In technical language, it must not have been *sub silentio*. Now, the acts of 1804 and 1807, relied upon as pledges for the rechartering of this company, passed not only without any discussions whatever of the Constitutional power of Congress to establish a bank, but I venture to say, without a single member having had his attention drawn to this question. I had the honor of a seat in the Senate when the latter law passed; probably voted for it; and I declare, with the utmost sincerity, that I never once thought of that point; and I appeal confidently to every honorable member who was then present to say if that was not his situation.

This doctrine of precedents, applied to the Legislature, appears to me to be fraught with the most mischievous consequences. The great advantage of our system of government over all others is, that we have a written Constitution defining its limits and prescribing its authorities; and that, however for a time faction may convulse the nation and passion and party prejudice sway its functionaries, the season of reflection will recur, when calmly retracing their deeds, all aberrations from fundamental principle will be corrected. But once substitute practice for principle, the expositions of the Constitution for the text of the Constitution, and in vain shall we look for the instrument in the instrument itself. It will be as diffused and intangible as the pretended Constitution of England; and it must be sought for in the statute book, in the fugitive journals of Congress, and in reports of the Secretary of the Treasury. What would be our condition if we were to take the interpretations given to that sacred book, which is or ought to be the criterion of our faith, for the book itself? We should find the Holy Bible buried beneath the interpretations, glosses, and comments of councils, synods, and learned divines, which have produced swarms of intolerant and furious sects, partaking less of the mildness and meekness of their origin than of a vindictive spirit of hostility towards each other. They ought to afford us a solemn warning to make that Constitution, which we have sworn to support, our invariable guide...

John Pope
Speech in the U.S. Senate
(February 15, 1811)[106]

... Much alarm and delusion have been artfully spread through the country about a violation of the Constitution and a consequent destruction of our republican institutions. I fear the people are unfortunately led to believe that the security of their liberty depends too much upon paper barriers, and too little upon their own virtue and intelligence. It appears to me that the Constitution is occasionally made a mere stalking horse to serve the purposes of unprincipled demagogues and pretended lovers of the people to get into power to the exclusion of honest men. They, with great address, distract and inflame the public mind about some nice Constitutional question or abstract proposition and thereby bring the people to decide, not which candidate is the most entitled to their confidence, but who rides the finest electioneering hobby.

We are misled very much, I believe, by theories and terms more applicable to other Governments than our own. In Great Britain they speak with great propriety of the Government and people, because there is in that country an immense power independent of the people. But here, where every public functionary is responsible to, and the Government in the hands of a majority of the people, those terms do not appear to me applicable in the sense in which they are used in other countries.

My reflections and practical observations on the Government incline me to the opinion that, with regard to measures of general policy not assailing individual liberty or right or the independence of any State, there is not that danger to be apprehended from a liberal construction of the Constitution which gentlemen seem to imagine. So long as the Government is in the hands of the people, measures affecting the whole nation, if oppressive or inconvenient, will be resisted and corrected by the public feeling and opinion. This is not mere theory. Look at the State of Connecticut, one of the best regulated democracies in ancient or modern times, whose Legislature is as omnipotent as the British Parliament. What people enjoy more real liberty and independence? In what country is to be found more practical, intelligent republicanism? Those principles which secure the rights of the citizen and the responsibility of their public servants are held sacred, but the Legislature is, I believe, unrestricted with regard to measures of general policy.

It is a truth which ought to be deeply impressed on the American mind, that the preservation of this republican system depends more upon the virtue and intelligence of the people and the responsibility of their public servants, than paper restrictions ...

The renewal bill finally was defeated in the Senate, where Vice-President George Clinton cast a tie-breaking vote against the bank on constitutional grounds.

Comment

The Republican national leadership supported renewal of the bank's charter with some embarrassment because this provided political ammunition for Republican critics who had long been accusing the Madison administration of crypto-Federalism. Supporters of the renewal bill usually claimed that they were acting consistently with the principles of '98 and with the opposition to the original 1791 act. Changed circumstances, they argued, rendered the bank "necessary and proper" to execute the powers delegated to Congress *in 1811*, regardless of whether the 1791 bill had satisfied the constitutional requirement *then.* Republican critics responded that this was the same long-repudiated argument of the Hamiltonian nationalists that Congress could look to the Constitution's general purposes rather than its specific enumerations of authority in determining the constitutionality of legislation.

Other supporters of renewal contended that, because "the Government [was] in the hands of the people" in the era of the "Republican Ascendancy," hypercritical readings of Congress's constitutional authority were unnecessary and inappropriate. Proposed legislation that attacked neither individual liberty nor the prerogatives of the states posed no threat to a "republican system," the real security of which was in the people's virtue and the legislators' responsibility. Critics noted in turn (with complete accuracy) that one of the primary themes of the Republicanism of 1798–1800 was a rejection of "confidence" in government.

Perhaps the most interesting aspect of the 1811 debate concerned the role of precedent in constitutional interpretation. The renewal bill's advocates pointed to the acceptance of the bank's legal existence by Congress, executive, courts, and people for two decades. Even if the argument against the bank's constitutionality had been the better one in 1791, an unbroken history of acquiescence in it had settled in its favor the interpretation of the Constitution held by the nation. The Republican opposition bitterly denounced this argument as a transmutation of the "printed Constitution" of Republicanism into an imitation of "the pretended Constitution of England," by which government obtained power simply by seizing it. The great Republican doctrine of invoking the constitutional text in order to correct constitutional error would be rendered impossible if precedent usurped the place of the Constitution itself.

In addition to denying the authority of precedent in establishing constitutional principle, some of the bill's opponents explained acquiescence in the first Bank Act as the product of fidelity rather than disobedience to constitutional principle. Once the bank commenced operation, "private rights were vested," and both the national faith and the national credit required observance of the contract to which Congress (mistakenly) had pledged the country.

United States v. Hudson & Goodwin
11 U.S. (7 Cranch) 32 (Feb. 13, 1812)

Hudson and Goodwin were Federalist journalists who were prosecuted for the common-law offense of seditious libel by a Republican United States attorney in federal court.

This was a case certified from the Circuit Court for the district of Connecticut, in which, upon argument of a general demurrer to an indictment for a libel on the president and congress of the United States, contained in the *Connecticut Currant*, of the 7th day of May 1806, charging them with having in secret voted $2,000,000 as a present to Bonaparte, for leave to make a treaty with Spain. The judges of that court were divided in opinion upon the question, whether the circuit court of the United States had a common-law jurisdiction in cases of libel?

Pinkney, Attorney-General, in behalf of the United States, and *Dana*, for the defendants, declined arguing the case.

The Court, having taken time to consider, the following opinion was delivered (on the last day of the term, all the judges being present) by JOHNSON, J.—The only question which this case presents is, whether the circuit courts of the United States can exercise a common-law jurisdiction in criminal cases. We state it thus broadly, because a decision on a case of libel will apply to every case in which jurisdiction is not vested in those courts by statute.

Although this question is brought up now, for the first time, to be decided by this court, we consider it as having been long since settled in public opinion. In no other case, for many years, has this jurisdiction been asserted; and the general acquiescence of legal men shows the prevalence of opinion in favor of the negative of the proposition.

The course of reasoning which leads to this conclusion is simple, obvious, and admits of but little illustration. The powers of the general government are made up of concessions from the several states—whatever is not expressly given to the former, the latter expressly reserve. The judicial power of the United States is a constituent part of those concessions; that power is to be exercised by courts organized for the purpose; and brought into existence by an effort of the legislative power of the Union. Of all the courts which the United States may, under their general powers, constitute, one only, the supreme court, possesses jurisdiction derived immediately from the constitution, and of which the legislative power cannot deprive it. All other courts created by the general government possess no jurisdiction but what is given them by the power that creates them, and can be vested with none but what the power ceded to the general government will authorize them to confer.

It is not necessary to inquire, whether the general government, in any and to what extent, possesses the power of conferring on its courts a jurisdiction in cases similar to the present; it is enough, that such jurisdiction has not been conferred by any legislative act, if it does not result to those courts as a consequence of their creation. And such is the opinion of the majority of this court; for the power which congress possess to create courts of inferior jurisdiction, necessarily implies the power to limit the jurisdiction of those courts to particular objects; and when a court is created, and its operations confined to certain specific objects, with what propriety can it assume to itself a jurisdiction, much more extended, in its nature very indefinite, applicable to a great variety of subjects, varying in every state in the Union and with regard to which there exists no definite criterion of distribution between the district and circuit courts of the same district.

The only ground on which it has ever been contended that this jurisdiction could be maintained is, that, upon the formation of any political body, an implied power to preserve its own existence and promote the end and object of its creation, necessarily results to it. But, without examining how far this consideration is applicable to the peculiar character of our constitution, it may be remarked that it is a principle by no means peculiar to the common law. It is coeval, probably, with the first formation of a limited government; belongs to a system of universal law, and may as well support the assumption of many other powers as those more peculiarly acknowledged by the common law of England.

But if admitted as applicable to the state of things in this country, the consequence would not result from it, which is here contended for. If it may communicate certain implied powers to the general government, it would not follow, that the courts of that government are vested with jurisdiction over any particular act done by an individual, in supposed violation of the peace and dignity of the sovereign power. The legislative authority of the Union must first make an act a crime, affix a punishment to it, and declare the court that shall have jurisdiction of the offense.

Certain implied powers must necessarily result to our courts of justice, from the nature of their institution. But jurisdiction of crimes against the state is not among those powers. To fine for contempt, imprison for contumacy, enforce the observance of order, &c., are powers which cannot be dispensed within a court, because they are necessary to the exercise of all others: and so far our courts, no doubt, possess powers not immediately derived from statute; but all exercise of criminal jurisdiction in common-law cases, we are of opinion, is not within their implied powers.

Comment

Hudson & Goodwin did not quite settle the question, so hotly debated in 1798–1800, of a federal common law of crimes. In 1816, a common-law prosecution was brought in the Massachusetts federal circuit court against the rescuers of a vessel captured by American privateers, and Justice Story (who approved of federal common-law jurisdiction) and the district judge certified the question of their jurisdiction to the Supreme Court. Attorney General Richard Rush followed predecessor William Pinkney's precedent in 1812 and declined to argue the case; no attorney appeared for the defendants. Speaking for the Court, Justice Johnson acknowledged disagreement among the justices on the issue, but stated that, in the absence of argument by counsel, the Court did not choose to "draw [*Hudson & Goodwin*] into doubt." *United States v. Coolidge*. After *Coolidge*, the Republican rejection of a federal common law of crimes was unchallenged.

Ten

Legislative Power and Vested Rights

Currie's Administrators v. Mutual Assurance Society
4 Hen. & Munf. 315 (Va. Nov. 1809)

In 1794 the Virginia General Assembly erected legislation incorporating the Mutual Assurance Society, a fire-insurance association. Under the terms of the charter, all members
of the society contributed to a common fund from which all insured losses were paid.
The much greater risk of fire to town-dwellers led to dissatisfaction with this arrangement,
and in 1805, at the request of a majority of the society's members, the legislature amended
the charter. Among other changes, the 1805 act authorized the creation of separate funds
for town and rural members so that premiums from each group could be applied to losses
in that group only. When the reorganized society then demanded an additional premium
from town-dwellers, one of them (Dr. James Currie) refused, and the society sued him
for the premium. The state trial court gave judgment for the society, and Currie appealed.
While the appeal was pending, he died and the case was continued by the administrators
of his estate.

George K. Taylor and *Call*, for [Currie's administrators,] argued, that the legislature could
not lawfully increase *Currie's* risk without his consent.

Although the original act of incorporation was, in *form*, a *law*, yet in *effect*, it was a mere
compact or *agreement* . . .

The act of 1794 being a contract between the state and the original adventurers, the
obligation of such contract cannot be impaired by the state without a violation of the
constitution of the *United States*. The obligation is impaired, when the legislature say that
repartition shall be made among a *part*, and not the *whole* of the members, as was prescribed
by one of the fundamental rules of the original charter . . .

George Hay [for the society]:

. . . The act of 1794 is called a charter; but the act of 1805 is called a law. This difference
in the denomination of the two legislative acts, which seems to be made without any
design, is a stroke of great policy. If words are properly called things, names, especially
in legal science, may with still greater propriety be called so. This truth is exemplified in
this case. By calling the first act a charter, and the second a law, the counsel for the
appellants thought that they secured to themselves the power of declaiming against a
violation by law of chartered rights. But it is too clear to be disputed, that if the act of
1794 be a charter, and I conclude that it is, the act of 1805 is a charter also, by which the
first is amended; and what is more, amended at the prayer and application of the incorporated body. How much is the force of these arguments already diminished by thus
calling the acts of the legislature by the names which really belong to them?

But we will examine separately the two arguments just stated. The first assumes a point,
which cannot be conceded. A charter is not a compact between the state and the grantee
of the charter. On the part of the state there is no contract express or implied. The state
is not bound either to give to, or to receive, to do, or to abstain from doing, anything.
On the part of the society, there is no obligation to the state. On what ground, then, can
it be said that there is a contract, when neither of the parties enter into any sort of obligation.

The idea is absurd. The real character of the act of 1794, is this; it is in truth a charter of incorporation; a grant of certain rights for the benefit of the grantees only; a law authorizing certain persons to become insurers for each other, and to adopt measures adequate to the accomplishment of their plan . . .

Even if the contracts in question were in some degree changed by the act of 1805, the 10th section of the [first] article of the Constitution of the *United States*, could not be brought to bear upon the subject; because in the first place the obligation of the contract is not impaired, and in the next, the clause under consideration could never have been intended for a case of this description. The object was to prevent the states from passing laws, as they had done, affecting contracts between individuals; such, for instance, as making lands a tender in payment of debts, or suspending executions; but not to prevent a legislature from changing a charter at the request of the persons chartered. Suppose, when this section was submitted to the convention, a proviso had been proposed, excepting from its operation cases like the present; would not this proposition have been rejected, on the ground that it was unnecessary, the point excepted not being within the purview of the section? . . .

Judge ROANE. . . . In order to shew that the act in question is no *law*, and therefore, it is further urged, is a *compact*, and as such is beyond the power of a succeeding legislature, *Blackstone's* definition of municipal law has been relied on. Municipal law is defined by him to be "a *rule* of civil conduct prescribed by the *supreme* power of the state, *commanding* what is right, and prohibiting what is wrong;" and it is argued, that the act in question is no *law*, under this definition, for want of the *generality* implied by the term "rule," and because it is said to be not so much in the nature of a command by the legislature, as of a promise or contract proceeding from it. When we consider, that mere private statutes and acts of parliament, are (even by this writer himself) universally classed among the municipal laws of *England*; nay, even that the *particular customs* of that kingdom, are admitted to form a part of the municipal code, it is evident, that this definition of municipal law, is by far too limited and narrow. I would rather adopt the definition of *Justinian*, that civil (or municipal) law, is, "*quod quisque sibi populus constituit*;" bounded only in this country in relation to legislative acts, by the constitutions of the general and state governments; and limited also by considerations of *justice*. It was argued by respectable member of the bar, that the legislature had a right to pass any law, however just, or unjust, reasonable, or unreasonable. This is a position which even the courtly Judge *Blackstone* was scarcely hardy enough to contend for, under the doctrine of the boasted *omnipotence* of parliament. What is this, but to lay prostrate, at the footstool of the legislature, all our rights of person and of property, and abandon those great objects, for the protection of which, alone, all free governments have been instituted?

For my part, I will not outrage the character of any civilized people, by supposing them to have met in legislature, upon any other ground, than that of morality and justice. In this country, in particular, I will never forget, "that no free government, or the blessing of liberty, can be preserved to any people, but by a firm adherence to *justice*, moderation, temperance, frugality, and virtue, and by frequent recurrence to fundamental principles." [Virginia Declaration of Rights, section 15] must add, however, that when any legislative act is to be questioned, on the ground of conflicting with the superior acts of the *people*, or of invading the vested rights of individuals, the case ought to be palpable and clear: in an equivocal or equiponderant case, it ought not easily to be admitted, that the immediate representatives of the people, representing as well the justice as the wisdom of the nation, have forgotten the great injunctions under which they are called to act. In such case, it ought rather to be believed, that the *judging* power is mistaken.

With respect to acts of incorporation, they ought never to be passed, but in consideration of services to be rendered to the public. This is the principle on which such charters are granted even in *England*; and it holds *a fortiori* in this country, as our bill of rights interdicts all "exclusive and separate emoluments or privileges from the community, but in consideration of public services" [Virginia Declaration of Rights, section 4]. It may be often *convenient* for a set of associated individuals, to have the privileges of a corporation bestowed upon them; but if their object is merely *private* or selfish; if it is detrimental to, or not promotive of, the public good, they have no adequate claim upon the legislature for the privilege. But as it is possible that the legislature may be imposed upon in the first instance; and as the public good and the interest of the associated body, may, in the progress of time, by the gradual and natural working of events, be thrown entirely asunder, the question presents itself, whether, under such and similar circumstances, the hands of a succeeding legislature are tied up from revoking the privilege. My answer is, that they are not. In the first case, no consideration of public service ever *existed*, and in the last, none *continues* to justify the privilege. It is the character of a legislative act to be *repealable* by a succeeding legislature; nor can a preceding legislature limit the power of its successor, on the mere ground of volition only. That effect can only arise from a state of things involving public utility, which includes the observance of *justice* and good faith towards all men.

These ideas are not new; they are entirely sanctioned by the *sublime* act of our legislature, "for establishing religious freedom." That act, after having declared and asserted certain *self-evident* principles, touching the rights of religious freedom, concludes in this manner "And though we well know that this assembly, elected by the people for the *ordinary* purposes of legislation only, have no power to restrain the acts of succeeding assemblies, constituted with powers *equal to our own*, and that, therefore, to declare this act irrevocable, would be of *no effect* in law, yet we are free to declare, that the rights hereby asserted, are of the *natural rights* of mankind, and that if any act shall be hereafter passed, to repeal the present, or to narrow its operation, such act will be *an infringement of natural right*." Conforming to the principles declared in this luminous exposition, I infer, irresistibly, that the power of a succeeding legislature is bounded only, (and that in cases of no *equivocal* complexion,) by the principles and provisions of the constitution and bill of rights, and by those great rights and principles, for the preservation of which all just governments are founded. It is not my intention to go into *detail* on the present subject; but the power of the succeeding legislature is neither to be limited by a state of things, which (as aforesaid) leaves no beneficial result whatsoever, to the community, nor by those petty inequalities and injuries, which arise to *some* individuals or classes of men, under every general regulation whatsoever. I will not say that the reason of the law ceasing, the law itself ought to continue; nor that we are to expect entire and exact justice, under any system whatsoever.

Under the actual case before us, I might, *perhaps*, have spared myself the necessity of this discussion. The principle stated in the act of 1794, which is supposed to have interdicted the separation in question, is couched in terms extremely abstract and *general*. While other principles declared by this act, have clearly and expressly confined the benefits of the institution to *citizens* of this state, and limited insurances to losses occasioned *accidentally by fire*; while it is clearly provided that retribution is to be made by the *insured*, and *that* according to the sum insured, the principle now immediately in question does not seem to prohibit a division or distribution of the members, or their interests into classes, or districts. There was no motive for a restriction upon the society in this particular, especially in an institution of the first impression; and there is no reasonable fear of abuse by the society, of a power equally useful to all, and liable to produce injustice in one quarter as well as another. It was deemed proper to allow to the society the benefit of experience; and as other powers of a character as important as the one before us, were confessedly granted to the society at large, wherefore should this be withheld?

... The act of 1805, if it has produced any injustice at all to any class of subscribers, has fallen short of that crying grade of injustice, which alone can disarm the act of its operation. The society itself, at least, considered this, on the contrary, as a measure essential to the equalization of the risks; and, in this respect, I see no cause to differ from them in opinion.

By referring to the principle of our law respecting corporations, the foregoing results will be fully justified. Those *artificial* persons are rendered necessary in the law from the inconvenience, if not impracticability of keeping alive the rights of associated bodies, by devolving them on one series of individuals after another. The effect of them is, to consolidate the will of the whole, which is collected from the sense of the *majority* of those who constitute them. This decision by a *majority* is a fundamental law of corporations in this country and in England; in which respect our law differs from the civil law; it requiring the concurrence of two thirds of the whole members. It is also a fundamental principle of corporations, that this *majority* may establish rules and regulations for the corporation, (which are considered as a sort of *municipal* law for the body corporate,) subject only to a superior and fundamental law which may have been prescribed by the founder thereof, or by the legislature which grants the privilege–perhaps, also, these petty legislatures ought further to be limited by all those considerations, (including the due observance of justice,) which I have endeavoured to shew, ought to bound the proceedings of all legislatures whatsoever. If, however, there be no such paramount law, or overruling principle, the mere will of the *majority* is competent to *any* regulation. I have endeavoured to shew, that no principle exists in the case before us to answer the foregoing character; that the one suggested is entirely abstract and indefinite as to the point in question; and that it does not appear that any injustice has arisen, or can be reasonably expected to arise, from carrying the measure in question into operation . . . In every view of this case, therefore, I am of opinion, that the judgment of the District Court is correct, and ought to be affirmed.

The Yazoo Affair

In January 1795 the Georgia legislature enacted a statute authorizing the sale of vast areas of land in the western part of the state (in effect, most of modern Mississippi and much of Alabama) to several land-speculation companies. The sales were at remarkably low prices; for example, the Georgia Mississippi Company paid $155,000 for 11 million acres. A storm of protest followed, and in the fall elections the incumbents were swept out of office and replaced by "anti-Yazoo" men. Although the new legislature proceeded to repeal the 1795 grants as unconstitutional and procured by corruption, the land companies rapidly disposed of much of their holdings to third parties, particularly in the Northeastern United States.

Alexander Hamilton
Opinion of Counsel
(March 25, 1796)[107]

As counsel to New Yorkers interested in purchasing Yazoo land, Hamilton was asked to render a formal opinion on the validity of Georgia's attempted revocation of the land grants. His opinion was published in 1799 by a "pro-Yazoo" politician.

CASE

The legislature of the state of Georgia, by an act of the 7th January, 1795, directed a sale to be made of a certain tract of land, therein described to James Gunn and others, by the name of the Georgia company, upon certain conditions therein specified. The sale was made pursuant to the act; the conditions of the sale were performed by the purchasers, and a regular grant made to them, accordingly, of the said tract of land. Subsequent thereto, the said legislature has passed an act, whereby on the suggestion of unconstitutionality . . . and also of fraud and corruption in application to the legislative body, the first act, and the grants thereupon, are declared null and void.

On the foregoing case, the opinion of counsel is desired, whether the title of the grantees and their assigns, the latter being *bona fide* purchasers of them, for valuable considerations, be valid? Or, whether the last mentioned act be of force to annul the grant?

ANSWER

Never having examined the title of the state of Georgia to the lands in question, I have no knowledge whether that state was, itself, entitled to them, and in capacity to make a valid grant. I can, therefore, have no opinion on this point. But, assuming it, in the argument, as a fact, that the state of Georgia had, at the time of the grant, a good title to the land, I hold that the revocation of it is void, and that the grant is still in force.

Without pretending to judge of the original merits or demerits of the purchasers, it may be safely said to be a contravention of the first principles of natural justice and social policy, without any judicial decision of facts, by a positive act of the legislature, to revoke a grant of property regularly made for valuable consideration, under legislative authority, to the prejudice even of third persons on every supposition innocent of the alleged fraud or corruption; and it may be added that the precedent is new of revoking a grant on the suggestion of corruption of a legislative body. Nor do I perceive sufficient ground for the suggestion of unconstitutionality in the first act.

In addition to these general considerations, placing the revocation in a very unfavorable light, the constitution of the United States, article first, section tenth, declares that no state shall pass a law impairing the obligations of contract. This must be equivalent to saying no state shall pass a law revoking, invalidating, or altering a contract. Every grant from one to another, whether the grantor be a state or an individual, is virtually a contract that the grantee shall hold and enjoy the thing granted against the grantor, and his representatives. It, therefore, appears to me that taking the terms of the constitution in their large sense, and giving them effect according to the general spirit and policy of the provisions, the revocation of the grant by the act of the legislature of Georgia, may justly be considered as contrary to the constitution of the United States, and, therefore, null. And that the courts of the United States in cases within their jurisdiction will be likely to pronounce it so.

Fletcher v. Peck
10 U.S. (6 Cranch) 87 (Mar. 16, 1810)

In 1798 the federal government accepted Georgia's cession of its western territory and in return assumed the duty to settle the Yazoo claims. Over the next fifteen years, pro- and anti-Yazoo forces battled in the newspapers and Congress. By 1807, however, the effort to secure federal compensation for holders under the 1795 grants had failed four times in Congress, and the "Yazooists" turned to the federal courts. As Justice Johnson feared, *Fletcher v. Peck* was a contrived suit, brought solely in order to obtain a judgment from the Supreme Court that would further the Yazooists' claims in Congress. The Court's judgment in their favor did just that: in 1814 Congress appropriated money to settle the claims.

MARSHALL, *Ch. J.* . . . [After dismissing the suggestion that the state constitution had prohibited the sales, Marshall turned to the chief anti-Yazoo claim: that the sales were procured by corruption of the legislature.]

That corruption should find its way into the governments of our infant republics, and contaminate the very source of legislation, or that impure motives should contribute to the passage of a law, or the formation of a legislative contract, are circumstances most deeply to be deplored. How far a court of justice would, in any case, be competent, on proceedings instituted by the state itself, to vacate a contract thus formed, and to annul rights acquired, under that contract, by third persons having no notice of the improper means by which it was obtained, is a question which the court would approach with much circumspection. It may well be doubted, how far the validity of a law depends upon the motives of its framers, and how far the particular inducements, operating on members of the supreme sovereign power of a state, to the formation of a contract by that power, are examinable in a court of justice. If the principle be conceded, that an act of the supreme sovereign power might be declared null by a court, in consequence of the means which procured it, still would there be much difficulty in saying to what extent those means must be applied to produce this effect. Must it be direct corruption? or would interest or undue influence of any kind be sufficient? Must the vitiating cause operate on a majority or on what number of the members? Would the act be null, whatever might be the wish of the nation? or would its obligation or nullity depend upon the public sentiment? If the majority of the legislature be corrupted, it may well be doubted, whether it be within the province of the judiciary to control their conduct, and, if less than a majority act from impure motives, the principle by which judicial interference would be regulated, is not clearly discerned. Whatever difficulties this subject might present, when viewed under aspects of which it may be susceptible, this court can perceive none in the particular pleadings now under consideration.

This is not a bill brought by the state of Georgia, to annul the contract, nor does it appear to the court, by this count, that the state of Georgia is dissatisfied with the sale that has been made. [*Fletcher* was an action for breach of contract between private parties.] The case, as made out in the pleadings, is simply this: One individual who holds lands in the state of Georgia, under a deed covenanting that the title of Georgia was in the grantor, brings an action of covenant upon this deed, and assigns, as a breach, that some of the members of the legislature were induced to vote in favor of the law, which constituted the contract, by being promised an interest in it, and that, therefore, the act is a mere nullity. This solemn question cannot be brought thus collaterally and incidentally before the court. It would be indecent, in the extreme, upon a private contract, between two individuals, to enter into an inquiry respecting the corruption of the sovereign power of a state. If the title be plainly deduced from a legislative act, which the legislature might constitutionally pass, if the act be clothed with all the requisite forms of a law, a court, sitting as a court of law, cannot sustain a suit brought by one individual against another, founded on the allegation that the act is a nullity, in consequence of the impure motives which influenced certain members of the legislature which passed the law. The circuit court, therefore, did right in overruling this demurrer . . . The lands in controversy vested absolutely in James Gunn and others, the original grantees, by the conveyance of the governor, made in pursuance of an act of assembly, to which the legislature was fully competent. Being thus in full possession of the legal estate, they, for a valuable consideration, conveyed portions of the land to those who were willing to purchase. If the original transaction was infected with fraud, these purchasers did not participate in it, and had no notice of it. They were innocent. Yet the legislature of Georgia has involved them in the fate of the first parties to the transaction, and, if the act be valid, has annihilated their rights also. The legislature of Georgia was a party to this transaction; and for a party to pronounce its own deed invalid, whatever cause may be assigned for its invalidity, must be considered as a mere act of power, which must find its vindication in a train of reasoning not often heard in courts of justice.

But the real party, it is said, are the people, and when their agents are unfaithful, the acts of those agents cease to be obligatory. It is, however, to be recollected, that the people can act only by these agents, and that, while within the powers conferred on them, their acts must be considered as the acts of the people. If the agents be corrupt, others may be chosen, and if their contracts be examinable, the common sentiment, as well as common usage of mankind, points out a mode by which this examination may be made, and their validity determined.

If the legislature of Georgia was not bound to submit its pretensions to those tribunals which are established for the security of property, and to decide on human rights, if it might claim to itself the power of judging in its own case, yet there are certain great principles of justice, whose authority is universally acknowledged, that ought not to be entirely disregarded. If the legislature be its own judge in its own case, it would seem equitable, that its decision should be regulated by those rules which would have regulated the decision of a judicial tribunal. The question was, in its nature, a question of title, and the tribunal which decided it was either acting in the character of a court of justice, and performing a duty usually assigned to a court or it was exerting a mere act of power in which it was controlled only by its own will.

If a suit be brought to set aside a conveyance obtained by fraud, and the fraud be clearly proved, the conveyance will be set aside, as between the parties; but the rights of third persons, who are purchasers without notice, for a valuable consideration, cannot be disregarded. Titles which, according to every legal test, are perfect, are acquired with that confidence which is inspired by the opinion that the purchaser is safe. If there be any concealed defect, arising from the conduct of those who had held the property long before he acquired it, of which he had no notice, that concealed defect cannot be set up against him. He has paid his money for a title good at law, he is innocent, whatever may be the guilt of others, and equity will not subject him to the penalties attached to that guilt. All titles would be insecure, and the intercourse between man and man would be very seriously obstructed, if this principle be overturned. A court of chancery, therefore, had a bill been brought to set aside the conveyance made to James Gunn and others, as being obtained by improper practices with the legislature, whatever might have been its decision as respected the original grantees, would have been bound, by its own rules, and by the clearest principles of equity, to leave unmolested those who were purchasers, without notice, for a valuable consideration.

If the legislature felt itself absolved from those rules of property which are common to all the citizens of the United States and from those principles of equity which are acknowledged in all our courts, its act is to be supported by its power alone, and the same power may divest any other individual of his lands, if it shall be the will of the legislature so to exert it.

It is not intended to speak with disrespect of the legislature of Georgia, or of its acts. Far from it. The question is a general question, and is treated as one. For although such powerful objections to a legislative grant, as are alleged against this, may not again exist, yet the principle, on which alone this rescinding act is to be supported, may be applied to every case to which it shall be the will of any legislature to apply it. The principle is this: that a legislature may, by its own act, divest the vested estate of any man whatever, for reasons which shall, by itself, be deemed sufficient.

In this case, the legislature may have had ample proof that the original grant was obtained by practices which can never be too much reprobated, and which would have justified its abrogation, so far as respected those to whom crime was imputable. But the grant, when issued, conveyed an estate in fee-simple to the grantee, clothed with all the solemnities which law can bestow. This estate was transferrable; and those who purchased parts of it were not stained by that guilt which infected the original transaction. Their case is not distinguishable from the ordinary case of purchasers of a legal estate, without knowledge of any secret fraud which might have led to the emanation of the original grant. According to the well-known course of equity, their rights could not be affected by such fraud. Their situation was the same, their title was the same, with that of every other member of the community who holds land by regular conveyances from the original patentee.

Is the power of the legislature competent to the annihilation of such title, and to a resumption of the property thus held? The principle asserted is, that one legislature is competent to repeal any act which a former legislature was competent to pass; and that one legislature cannot abridge the powers of a succeeding legislature. The correctness of this principle, so far as respects general legislation, can never be controverted. But, if an act be done under a law, a succeeding legislature cannot undo it. The past cannot be recalled by the cost absolute power. Conveyances have been made, those conveyances have vested legal estates, and, if those estates may be seized by the sovereign authority still, that they originally vested is a fact, and cannot cease to be a fact. When, then, a law is in its nature a contract, when absolute rights have vested under that contract, a repeal of the law cannot divest those rights; and the act of annulling them, if legitimate, is rendered so by a power applicable to the case of every individual in the community.

It may well be doubted, whether the nature of society and of government does not prescribe some limits to the legislative power; and if any be prescribed, where are they to be found, if the property of an individual, fairly and honestly acquired, may be seized without compensation? To the legislature, all legislative power is granted; but the question, whether the act of transferring the property of an individual to the public, be in the nature of the legislative power, is well worthy of serious reflection. It is the peculiar province of the legislature, to prescribe general rules for the government of society; the application of those rules to individuals in society would seem to be the duty of other departments. How far the power of giving the law may involve every other power, in cases where the constitution is silent, never has been, and perhaps never can be, definitely stated.

The validity of this rescinding act, then, might well be doubted, were Georgia a single sovereign power. But Georgia cannot be viewed as a single, unconnected, sovereign power, on whose legislature no other restrictions are imposed than may be found in its own constitution. She is a part of a large empire; she is a member of the American union; and that union has a constitution, the supremacy of which all acknowledge, and which imposes limits to the legislatures of the several states, which none claim a right to pass. The constitution of the United States declares that no state shall pass any bill of attainder, *ex post facto* law, or law impairing the obligation of contracts.

Does the case now under consideration come within this prohibitory section of the constitution? In considering this very interesting question, we immediately ask ourselves, what is a contract? Is a grant a contract? A contract is a compact between two or more parties, and is either executory or executed. An executory contract is one in which a party binds himself to do, or not to do, a particular thing; such was the law under which the conveyance was made by the governor. A contract executed is one in which the object of contract is performed; and this, says Blackstone, differs in nothing from a grant. The contract between Georgia and the purchasers was executed by the grant. A contract executed, as well as one which is executory, contains obligations binding on the parties. A grant, in its own nature, amounts to an extinguishment of the right of the grantor, and implies a contract not to re-assert that right. A party is, therefore, always estopped by his own grant.

Since then, in fact, a grant is a contract executed, the obligation of which still continues, and since the constitution uses the general term contract, without distinguishing between those which are executory and those which are executed, it must be construed to comprehend the latter as well as the former. A law annulling conveyances between individuals, and declaring that the grantors should stand seised of their former estates, notwithstanding those grants, would be as repugnant to the constitution, as a law discharging the vendors of property from the obligation of executing their contracts by conveyances. It would be strange, if a contract to convey was secured by the constitution, while an absolute conveyance remained unprotected.

If, under a fair construction of the constitution, grants are comprehended under the term contracts, is a grant from the state excluded from the operation of the provision? Is the clause to be considered as inhibiting the state from impairing the obligation of contracts between two individuals, but as excluding from that inhibition contracts made with itself? The words themselves contain no such distinction. They are general, and are applicable to contracts of every description. If contracts made with the state are to be exempted from their operation, the exception must arise from the character of the contracting party, not from the words which are employed.

Whatever respect might have been felt for the state sovereignties, it is not to be disguised, that the framers of the constitution viewed, with some apprehension, the violent acts which might grow out of the feelings of the moment; and that the people of the United States, in adopting that instrument, have manifested a determination to shield themselves and their property from the effects of those sudden and strong passions to which men are exposed. The restrictions on the legislative power of the states are obviously founded in this sentiment; and the constitution of the United States contains what may be deemed a bill of rights for the people of each state.

No state shall pass any bill of attainder, *ex post facto* law, or law impairing the obligation of contracts. A bill of attainder may affect the life of an individual, or may confiscate his property, or may do both. In this form, the power of the legislature over the lives and fortunes of individuals is expressly restrained. What motive, then, for implying, in words which import a general prohibition to impair the obligation of contracts, an exception in favor of the right to impair the obligation of those contracts into which the state may enter?

The state legislatures can pass no *ex post facto* law. An *ex post facto* law is one which renders an act punishable in a manner in which it was not punishable when it was committed. Such a law may inflict penalties on the person, or may inflict pecuniary penalties which swell the public treasure. The legislature is then prohibited from passing a law by which a man's estate, or any part of it, shall be seized for a crime which was not declared, by some previous law, to render him liable to that punishment. Why, then, should violence be done to the natural meaning of words for the purpose of leaving to the legislature the power of seizing, for public use, the estate of an individual, in the form of a law annulling the title by which he holds that estate? The court can perceive no sufficient grounds for making this distinction. This rescinding act would have the effect of an *ex post facto* law. It forfeits the estate of Fletcher for a crime not committed by himself, but by those from whom he purchased. This cannot be effected in the form of an *ex post facto* law, or bill of attainder; why then, is it allowable in the form of a law annulling the original grant?

The argument in favor of presuming an intention to except a case, not excepted by the words of the constitution, is susceptible of some illustration from a principle originally ingrafted in that instrument, though no longer a part of it. The constitution, as passed, gave the courts of the United States jurisdiction in suits brought against individual states. A state, then, which violated its own contract was suable in the courts of the United States for that violation. Would it have been a defence in such a suit to say, that the state had passed a law absolving itself from the contract? It is scarcely to be conceived, that such a defence could be set up. And yet, if a state is neither restrained by the general principles of our political institutions, nor by the words of the constitution, from impairing the obligation of its own contracts, such a defence would be a valid one. This feature is no longer found in the constitution; but it aids in the construction of those clauses with which it was originally associated.

It is, then, the unanimous opinion of the court, that, in this case, the estate having passed into the hands of a purchaser for a valuable consideration, without notice, the state of Georgia was restrained, either by general principles which are common to our free institutions, or by the particular provisions of the constitution of the United States, from passing a law whereby the estate of the plaintiff in the premises so purchased could be constitutionally and legally impaired and rendered null and void . . .

JOHNSON, J.—In this case, I entertain, on two points, an opinion different from that which has been delivered by the court.

I do not hesitate to declare, that a state does not possess the power of revoking its own grants. But I do it, on a general principle, on the reason and nature of things; a principle which will impose laws even on the Deity. A contrary opinion can only be maintained upon the ground, that no existing legislature can abridge the powers of those which will succeed it. To a certain extent, this is certainly correct; but the distinction lies between power and interest, the right of jurisdiction and the right of soil.

The right of jurisdiction is essentially connected to, or rather identified with, the national sovereignty. To part with it, is to commit a species of political suicide. In fact, a power to produce its own annihilation, is an absurdity in terms. It is a power as utterly incommunicable to a political as to a natural person. But it is not so with the interests or property of a nation. Its possessions nationally are in no wise necessary to its political existence; they are entirely accidental, and may be parted with, in every respect, similarly to those of the individuals who compose the community. When the legislature have once conveyed their interest or property in any subject to the individual, they have lost all control over it; have nothing to act upon; it has passed from them; is vested in the individual; becomes intimately blended with his existence, as essentially so as the blood that circulates through his system. The government may indeed demand of him the one or the other, not because they are not his, but because whatever is his, is his country's.

As to the idea, that the grants of a legislature may be void, because the legislature are corrupt, it appears to me to be subject to insuperable difficulties. The acts of the supreme power of a country must be considered pure, for the same reason that all sovereign acts must be considered just; because there is no power that can declare them otherwise. The absurdity in this case would have been strikingly perceived, could the party who passed the act of cession have got again into power, and declared themselves pure, and the intermediate legislature corrupt. The security of a people against the misconduct of their rulers, must lie in the frequent recurrence to first principles, and the imposition of adequate constitutional restrictions. Nor would it be difficult, with the same view, for laws to be framed which would bring the conduct of individuals under the review of adequate tribunals, and make them suffer under the consequences of their own immoral conduct.

I have thrown out these ideas, that I may have it distinctly understood, that my opinion on this point is not founded on the provision in the constitution of the United States, relative to laws impairing the obligation of contracts. It is much to be regretted, that words of less equivocal signification had not been adopted in that article of the constitution. There is reason to believe, from the letters of Publius ["The Federalist"] which are well known to be entitled to the highest respect, that the object of the convention was to afford a general protection to individual rights against the acts of the state legislatures. Whether the words, "acts impairing the obligation of contracts," can be construed to have the same force as must have been given to the words "obligation and *effect* of contracts," is the difficulty in my mind.

There can be no solid objection to adopting the technical definition of the word "contract," given by Blackstone. The etymology, the classical signification, and the civil law idea of the word, will all support it. But the difficulty arises on the word "obligation," which certainly imports an existing moral or physical necessity. Now, a grant or conveyance by no means necessarily implies the continuance of an obligation, beyond the moment of executing it. It is most generally but the consummation of a contract, is *functus officio*, the moment it is executed, and continues afterwards to be nothing more than the evidence that a certain act was done.

I enter with great hesitation upon this question, because it involves a subject of the greatest delicacy and much difficulty. The states and the United States are continually legislating on the subject of contracts, prescribing the mode of authentication, the time within which suits shall be prosecuted for them, in many cases, affecting existing contracts by the laws which they pass, and declaring them to cease or lose their effect for want of compliance, in the parties, with such statutory provisions. All these acts appear to be within the most correct limits of legislative powers, and most beneficially exercised, and certainly could not have been intended to be affected by this constitutional provision; yet where to draw the line, or how to define or limit the words, "obligation of contracts," will be found a subject of extreme difficulty.

To give it the general effect of a restriction of the state powers in favor of private rights, is certainly going very far beyond the obvious and necessary import of the words, and would operate to restrict the states in the exercise of that right which every community must exercise, of possessing itself of the property of the individual, when necessary for public uses; a right which a magnanimous and just government will never exercise without amply indemnifying the individual, and which perhaps amounts to nothing more than a power to oblige him to sell and convey, when the public necessities require it . . .

I have been very unwilling to proceed to the decision of this cause at all. It appears to me to bear strong evidence, upon the face of it, of being a mere feigned case. It is our duty to decide on the rights, but not on the speculations of parties. My confidence, however, in the respectable gentlemen who have been engaged for the parties, has induced me to abandon my scruples, in the belief that they would never consent to impose a mere feigned case upon this court.

Jones v. Crittenden
4 N.C. (Car. L. Rep.) 55 (Jan. 1814)

The North Carolina legislature enacted a statute in 1812 providing debtors limited relief from legal execution of judgments against them. Upon providing two freeholders as sureties for the debt, the debtor was entitled to immunity from execution of a judgment until the first court term after February 1814. The act was challenged as a violation of the federal contracts clause.

TAYLOR, C. J. . . . In deciding the momentous question whether the will of the Legislature, as expressed in this act, be incompatible with the will of the people as expressed in their fundamental law, the Constitution of the United States, we disclaim all right or power to give judgment against the validity of the legislative act unless its collision with the Constitution appear to our understandings manifest and irreconcilable. On the contrary, if patient and dispassionate consideration of the subject produce anything short of entire conviction, we hold ourselves bound to support a law.

The constitutional will of the Legislature, inclination not less than duty prompts us to execute; for identified as its members are with the other citizens of the community, and faithfully representing their feelings and interests, we can never allow ourselves to think that the acts proceeding from them can be designed for any other purpose than the promotion of the general welfare, or can result from other than the purest and most patriotic motives.

We have deliberately viewed the question in every light in which the arguments of the learned counsel on both sides have presented it, and aided by such additional information as our own research or reflection could furnish, the result of our opinion is that the law in question is unconstitutional, and cannot be executed by the judicial department without violating the paramount duty of their oaths to maintain the Constitution of the United States.

This conclusion we derive (1) from the plain and natural import of the words of the Constitution of the United States; (2) from a consideration of the previously existing mischiefs which it was the design of that valuable instrument to suppress and remedy.

Amongst the important objects which the people of the United States designed to accomplish by adopting the Constitution, that of establishing justice, holds a conspicuous rank. This appears from the solemn declaration of the people themselves in the preamble to that instrument. The enlightened statesman by whom it was originally framed had reaped abundant instruction from history and experience. Long accustomed to contemplate the operation of those master principles and comprehensive truths which form at once the defenses and the ornament of human society, and which alone can justly form the basis of the social compact, they designed to give them practical effect for the benefit of the American people—to consecrate and make them perpetual. They well know that while the principle of justice is deeply rooted in the nature and interest of man and essential to the prosperity of states, it forms the strongest and brightest link in the chain by which the author of the Universe has united together the happiness and the duty of His creatures.

To give a proper direction to these general principles, the clause in the Constitution which presents the question before us, was inserted. Some of its provisions are transcribed from the articles of confederation; others are added because experience had demonstrated that without them the Union of the states would be imperfect. The words are, "No state shall enter into any treaty, alliance, or confederation; grant letters of marque and reprisal; coin money, emit bills of credit, make anything but gold and silver coin a tender in payment of debts; pass any bill of attainder, ex post facto law, or law impairing the obligation of contracts," etc.

The obligation of a contract may be impaired by various modes and in different degrees; and the restrictive clause in the Constitution does, according to our apprehension of its meaning, annul every act of a state legislature which shall thereafter produce that effect, plainly and directly, in any degree. When therefore, the validity of the law is maintained by the defendant's counsel because it does not allow a debtor, who promises to pay in one thing, to pay in another; because it does not absolutely restrain the debtor from paying according to his engagement; or, because it does not allow a third person to interfere between the contracting parties—the answer is that the examples cited furnish stronger instances of a violation of the Constitution; they may with stricter propriety be called cases of annulling a contract; but they certainly do not prove that the obligation of contracts is not impaired by the act under consideration.

Whatever law releases one party from any article of a stipulation voluntarily and legally entered into by him with another, without the direct assent of the latter, impairs its obligation; because the rights of the creditor are thereby destroyed, and these are ever correspondent to and coextensive with the duty of the debtor. The first principles of justice teach us that he to whom a promise is made under legal sanctions should signify his consent before any part of it can be rightfully canceled by a legislative act.

The binding force of a contract may likewise be impaired by compelling either party to do more than he has promised. If an act postponing the payment of debts be constitutional, what reasonable objection could be made to an act which should enforce the payment before the debt becomes due? If, notwithstanding the constitutional barrier, it is competent for the Legislature to hold out to all debtors that although they fail to pay their debts when they become due, and their creditors are in consequence compelled to sue them, they shall nevertheless be indulged with a certain time beyond the judgment, superadded to the ordinary delays for the law, may not the Legislature, with equal authority, announce to all creditors the right of suing for their debts and enforcing payment before the day? Yet the rights of both parties established by the contract are, in the eye of justice, equally sacred; and whether those of the creditor are sacrificed to the convenience of the debtor, or the subject be reversed, we are compelled to think that the Constitution is overlooked.

No unimportant part of the obligation of every contract arises from the inducement the debtor is under to preserve his faith. With many persons (and it may be hoped, the greater number), a sense of justice and respect for character form motives of sufficient strength; but how rarely does it happen that a man lending his money, or selling his property on credit, estimates such motives so highly as to deem them a safe and exclusive ground of reliance? In most cases he would reserve both money and property in his own possession, were he not assured that the law animates the industry and quickens the punctuality of his debtor, and that by its aid he can obtain payment in six or nine months. Hence the well considered ceremonies of bonds, mortgages, and deeds of trust, more useful as the instruments of coercive justice than as preserving the evidence of contract. The act under view destroys this assurance, and while it produces a state of things the existence of which at the time of contract would have restrained the creditor from parting with his property, it encourages the debtor to relax his efforts to be punctual. It weakens his inducements to fulfill his engagement, and thereby impairs its obligation.

The right to suspend the recovery of a debt for one period implies the right of suspending it for another; and as the state of things which called for the first delay may continue for a series of years, the consequence may be a total stagnation of the business of society by destroying confidence and credit amongst the citizens.

An argument urged and much relied on by the defendant's counsel is that the law in question bears only on the remedy, and is therefore within the sphere of legislative authority. But if in so doing it violates the Constitution, it is not less invalid than if it directly touched and annulled the right. Every one will agree that a law which should deny to all creditors the right of instituting the action of debt, covenant, assumpsit, or a bill in chancery, would invade the Constitution; that a law which should limit the recovery of all debts to so short a period after its passage that it would be impossible, according to the course of the courts, to obtain a judgment, would also be null and void. Though such laws, ostensibly, bear only on the remedy, yet they do in reality annihilate the right. The law before us, it is conceded, does not go to the extent of either instance, yet it certainly diminishes the importance and value of the right. It is difficult to conceive how a law could otherwise impair an existing right than by withholding the remedy, which is in effect to suspend the right.

The undoubted right of the Legislature to alter and reform the judicial system may, it is said, produce delay in the execution of a contract equal to that which results from the present law; and it is urged that all such acts must, upon the same principle, be declared unconstitutional.

We cannot acquiesce in the final conclusion drawn from these premises, which, without hesitation, we acknowledge to be correct.

All such laws the Legislature have an unquestionable right to enact, a right which the people have never surrendered, and the exercise of which is not forbidden by the Constitution of the United States. But it must be considered that the primary and essential object of all such laws is the promotion of the administration of justice, its advancement and improvement. If delay grow out of them, if anything that bears the semblance of a violation of contract follow in their train, it is merely the unintended incident and consequence of the exercise of a lawful authority. It is different with the law before us; its very design, as expressed in the title, is to do that against which the Constitution has opposed its veto.

Many analogous powers, it is argued, have long existed in the State under the authority of the law; that their exercise has been highly convenient to the citizens, and has been universally acquiesced in; that all these must cease to have effect if the suspension law is unconstitutional, to the manifest detriment of the community.

If such effects follow from our decision, there are not citizens in the State who will more sincerely deplore them than ourselves. But we feel too deeply what we owe to the responsibility of our stations, to the obligation of our oaths, and the rights of the people and their posterity, to be turned aside from what we believe to be the post of duty by any consideration of the consequences that may arise from continuing in it.

Let all these cases be patiently examined, and we think it will be seen that their analogy is not complete; that they may still exist, and the powers under them be rightfully exercised, notwithstanding the decision in the present case . . .

The right to pass this law is further derived from section 5 of the North Carolina Declaration of Rights, "That all power of suspending laws or the execution of laws by any authority without the consent of the representatives of the people is injurious to their rights, and ought not to be exercised."

[After denying that the quoted section of the state bill of rights affirmatively authorized the legislature to pass the stay law, Taylor concluded that the question was irrelevant.]

Every article in the Declaration of Rights, as well as the Constitution of the State, is subject to the paramount control of the Constitution of the United States, which, being the last solemn expression of the will of the people, annuls and destroys everything clearly irreconcilable with it . . .

The construction we give to the Constitution would have been adopted by us from a consideration of the instrument itself; but we think it fortified by the collateral illustrations furnished by the other ground of our opinion.

It is to be seen in the historical records of some of the states that, pressed and exhausted by their efforts in the great struggle for independence, they had recourse to various expedients to relieve their suffering citizens. In addition to the issue of bills of credit and paper money, some laws were passed wholly changing the nature of the contract; others postponed the payment of debts by authorizing it to be made in installments. The benefit resulting from these measures was partial and temporary, but the evil, as might have been expected, universal and permanent . . .

Terrett v. Taylor
13 U.S. (9 Cranch) 43 (Feb. 17, 1815)

The Virginia statute transferring vacant glebe lands from the Episcopal church to the country overseers of the poor, upheld by an equal vote of the Virginia Court of Appeals in 1804 (*Turpin v. Locket*), was challenged before the United States Supreme Court a decade later. By federal statute, the laws of Virginia were in force in Alexandria (then part of the District of Columbia), and the vestry of the Episcopal parish there sued the Fairfax County overseers in federal court to quiet title to the parish's glebe lands.

STORY, J., delivered the opinion of the court . . .

[He rehearsed the tortuous history of Virginia legislation concerning the Episcopal church.]

This summary view of so much of the Virginia statutes as bears directly on the subject in controversy, presents not only a most extraordinary diversity of opinion in the legislature as to the nature and propriety of aid in the temporal concerns of religion, but the more embarrassing considerations of the constitutional character and efficacy of those laws touching the rights and property of the Episcopal Church.

It is conceded on all sides that, at the revolution, the Episcopal Church no longer retained its character as an exclusive religious establishment. And there can be no doubt that it was competent to the people and to the legislature to deprive it of its superiority over other religious sects, and to withhold from it any support by public taxation. But, although it may be true that "religion can be directed only by reason and conviction, not by force or violence," and that "all men are entitled to the free exercise of religion according to the dictates of conscience," as the bill of rights of Virginia declares, yet it is difficult to perceive how it follows as a consequence that the legislature may not enact laws more effectually to enable all sects to accomplish the great objects of religion by giving them corporate rights for the management of their property, and the regulation of their temporal as well as spiritual concerns. Consistent with the constitution of Virginia the legislature could not create or continue a religious establishment which should have exclusive rights and prerogatives, or compel the citizens to worship under a stipulated form or discipline, or to pay taxes to those whose creed they could not conscientiously believe. But the free exercise of religion cannot be justly deemed to be restrained by aiding with equal attention the votaries of every sect to perform their own religious duties, or by establishing funds for the support of ministers, for public charities, for the endowment of churches, or for the sepulture of the dead. And that these purposes could be better secured and cherished by corporate powers, cannot be doubted by any person who has attended to the difficulties which surround all voluntary associations. While, therefore, the legislature might exempt the citizens from a compulsive attendance and payment of taxes in support of any particular sect, it is not perceived that either public or constitutional principles required the abolition of all religious corporations.

Be, however, the general authority of the legislature as to the subject of religion as it may, it will require other arguments to establish the position that, at the revolution, all the public property acquired by the Episcopal churches, under the sanction of the laws, became the property of the state. Had the property thus acquired been originally granted by the state or the king, there might have been some color (and it would have been but a color) for such an extraordinary pretension. But the property was, in fact and in law, generally purchased by the parishioners, or acquired by the benefactions of pious donors. The title thereto was indefeasibly vested in the churches, or rather in their legal agents. It was not in the power of the crown to seize or assume it; nor of the parliament itself to destroy the grants, unless by the exercise of a power the most arbitrary, oppressive and unjust, and endured only because it could not be resisted. It was not forfeited; for the churches had committed no offense. The dissolution of the regal government no more destroyed the right to possess or enjoy this property than it did the right of any other corporation or individual to his or its own property. The dissolution of the form of government did not involve in it a dissolution of civil rights, or an abolition of common law under which the inheritances of every man in the state were held. The state itself succeeded only to the rights of the crown; and, we may add, with many a flower of prerogative struck from its hands. It has been asserted as a principle of the common law, that the division of an empire creates no forfeiture of previously vested rights of property. And this principle is equally consonant with the common sense of mankind and the maxims of eternal justice. Nor are we able to perceive any sound reason why the church lands escheated or devolved upon the state by the revolution any more than the property of any other corporation created by the royal bounty or established by the legislature. The revolution might justly take away the public patronage, the exclusive cure of souls, and the compulsive taxation for the support of the church. Beyond these we are not prepared to admit the justice or the authority of the exercise of legislation.

It is not, however, necessary to rest this cause upon the general doctrines already asserted; for, admitting that by the revolution the church lands devolved on the state, the statute of 1776 [which confirmed the church's property rights] operated as a new grant and confirmation thereof to the use of the church.

If the legislature possessed the authority to make such a grant and confirmation, it is very clear to our minds that it vested an indefeasible and irrevocable title. We have no knowledge of any authority or principle which could support the doctrine that a legislative grant is revocable in its own nature, and held only durante bene placito [at the legislature's pleasure]. Such a doctrine would uproot the very foundations of almost all the land titles in Virginia, and is utterly inconsistent with a great and fundamental principle of a republican government, the right of the citizens to the free enjoyment of their property legally acquired.

It is asserted by the legislature of Virginia, in 1798 and 1801, that this statute was inconsistent with the bill of rights and constitution of that State, and therefore void. Whatever weight such a declaration might properly have as the opinion of wise and learned men, as a declaration of what the law has been or is, it can have no decisive authority. It is, however, encountered by the opinion successively given by former legislatures from the earliest existence of the constitution itself, which were composed of men of the very first rank for talents and learning. And this opinion, too, is not only a contemporaneous exposition of the constitution, but has the additional weight that it was promulgated or acquiesced in by a great majority, if not the whole, of the very framers of the constitution. Without adverting, however, to the opinions on the one side or the other, for the reasons which have been already stated, and others which we forbear to press, as they would lead to too prolix and elementary an examination, we are of opinion that the statute of 1776 is not inconsistent with the constitution or bill of rights of Virginia . . .

Upon a change of government, too, it may be admitted that such exclusive privileges attached to a private corporation as are inconsistent with the new government may be abolished. In respect, also to public corporations which exist only for public purposes, such as counties, towns, cities, &c., the legislature may, under proper limitations, have a right to change, modify, enlarge or restrain them, securing, however, the property for the uses of those for whom and at whose expense it was originally purchased. But that the legislature can repeal statutes creating private corporations, or confirming to them property already acquired under the faith of previous laws, and by such repeal can vest the property of such corporation exclusively in the state, or dispose of the same to such purposes as they may please, without the consent or default of the corporators, we are not prepared to admit; and we think ourselves standing upon the principles of natural justice, upon the fundamental laws of every free government, upon the spirit and the letter of the constitution of the United States, and upon the decisions of most respectable judicial tribunals in resisting such a doctrine. The statutes of 1798 and of 1801 are not, therefore, in our judgment, operative so far as to divest the Episcopal Church of the property acquired previous to the revolution, by purchase or by donation. In respect to the latter statute there is this farther objection, that it passed after the District of Columbia was taken under the exclusive jurisdiction of Congress . . .

Comment

The concept of "vested rights" was of central importance in early American constitutional discourse. Such a right—paradigmatically title in fee simple to real property—existed or did not exist as a matter of fact. Once a right to something "vested" (became complete or perfect), its holder was entitled to immunity from interference from the prior owner or the government; the right "becomes intimately blended with his existence" (Justice Johnson). The legislature, to be sure, could exercise jurisdiction over the object of the right, as it could over the person of the rightholder, but without compensation it could not "divest" the right. Some Americans disagreed over whether the original source of vested rights lay in nature (see Justice Johnson's reference to "a principle which will impose laws even on the Deity") or in the fundamental social compact creating human society, but this theoretical dispute was of little or no legal significance.

Vested rights came into being in several ways. An individual, or the state, could create a right by grant, either gratuitously or in return for payment. Executing agreements such as a contract to lend and borrow money created a right in each party to receive the performance the other had promised.

Throughout the late eighteenth and early nineteenth centuries, constitutionalists struggled to reconcile the apparent absoluteness of vested rights with the power of legislation. The pre-1787 history of state debtor relief laws, to which Hay in *Currie's Administrators* and Chief Justice Taylor in *Jones* referred, prompted the Philadelphia framers to include an ambiguous prohibition on laws "ex post facto" in character or "impairing the obligations of contract." The federal Supreme Court's 1798 decision in *Calder v. Bull* denied the relevance of the ex post facto clause to these issues, but left unresolved the meaning of the contracts clause or its relationship to the general principles of vested rights. At the same time, the slow growth in the use of charters of incorporation, then granted only by special legislative action, in private business raised the question of whether corporate privileges were immune from legislative alteration.

Chief Justice Taylor's opinion in *Jones v. Crittenden* offered a straightforward interpretation of the place of vested rights in American constitutionalism. He acknowledged that such rights stemmed from the transcendent "first principles of justice," but located judicial authority to protect them in the constitutional text, which included the contracts clause in order to "give a proper direction to these general principles." A state law that directly impaired the contractual right to receive repayment off debts at the time set by agreement therefore unconstitutionally "diminishes the importance and value of the right."

Curries's Administrators involved a claim that legislative alteration of a corporate charter divested the members' rights in the original charter and impaired the obligation of the contract between the state and the corporation. Spencer Roane, for the Virginia court, ignored the contracts-clause argument, and denied that corporate privileges could be vested rights. Unlike a grant of land, such privileges were legitimately granted, even to private entrepreneurs, only to secure public benefits. Like any other legislation, therefore, a charter could be modified or revoked whenever the legislature found the public good would be benefited by doing so.

Fletcher v. Peck involved the attempt of a state legislature to revoke its own land grants on the ground that they were obtained by corruption. Chief Justice Marshall's rejection of the attempt (in a case involving third-party purchasers of the land) rested on the premise that a grant of property, when completed, at that moment vested the right to the property in the grantee. The state legislature's authority to repeal earlier statutes could not change this fact about the past: "that [the rights] originally vested is a fact, and cannot cease to be a fact." Legislative revocation of the grants was a naked invasion of vested rights, and the legislature's attempt to justify the revocation was a claim to act as judge in a dispute to which it was itself a party.

Marshall found a second basis for the Court's decision in the contracts clause. Accepting the equation of a statutory charter or grant with a compact that Roane had rejected, Marshall reasoned that, even after execution, the grantor had the obligation not to impair its own action. Justice Johnson concurred separately to indicate his disapproval of Marshall's contracts-clause argument, which, Johnson feared, went "very far beyond the obvious and necessary import of the words" and was overly restrictive of legislative authority.

In *Terrett*, Story, for the Court, followed Johnson's preference for protecting vested rights on general rather than contracts-clause grounds. Story rejected the argument, accepted by Chancellor Wythe and Judges Tucker and Roane in *Turpin v. Locket,* that the Episcopal church's glebe lands were one of the privileges of its pre-Revolutionary character as an ecclesiastical establishment that the Revolution and the Virginia Declaration of Rights had taken from it. The Revolutionary change in government, Story wrote, worked no change in the rights of private parties, including churches, to their property. The state legislature's attempt to transfer the glebes to the county governments could only rest on the flat assertion that property rights were held at the legislature's pleasure. That claim, of course, was patently false.

The early vested-right cases left a great many issues unresolved. Different constitutionalists varied as to whether to base their arguments on extratextual principles of "justice and social policy" (Hamilton) or on the contracts clause. Roane's refusal to accord vested-right status to corporate privileges, the right/ remedy distinction that Taylor rejected, and Johnson's concern that Marshall's opinion justified interference with legitimate legislation foreshadowed later debates.

Eleven

Lessons of the War: The Search for a Republican Nationalism

The demands of the War of 1812 accelerated what conservative "Old Republicans" viewed as the erosion of the constitutional orthodoxy of 1798 and its replacement by a crypto-Federalist nationalism. In January 1815 Congress passed a bill to charter a second national bank; and though President Madison vetoed the bill, he did not do so on constitutional grounds. Many of his fellow Republicans saw the end of the war as the opportunity to reshape the federal government as an affirmative instrument of national policy.

Resolutions of the Hartford Convention (adopted on January 4, 1815)[108]

Public opinion in New England had long been unhappy with the Republican administrations in Washington when Congress declared war against Great Britain in 1812. The reasons were various: the perception that the "Virginia dynasty" had a lock on the presidency and that its members favored Virginia and the southern states generally in matters of policy and appointments; the fear that the Northeast's political power would steadily be diluted by the admission of western and southern states hostile to New England's economic interests and its increasingly firm opposition to the extension of slavery; and, perhaps most concretely, dissatisfaction with the willingness of Presidents Jefferson and Madison and the Republican majority in Congress to use economic sanctions such as the 1807 Embargo Act against the European belligerents—sanctions that had devastating effects on New England's economy. The War of 1812 exacerbated these complaints. Many New Englanders viewed the war as unnecessary and unjust, and the Madison administration's conduct of it seemed generally ineffective and particularly insensitive to the defense needs of the region. Northeastern congressional delegations clashed with the Republican majority over the wisdom and constitutionality of such measures as the Embargo Act of December 17, 1813, the Enlistment of Minors Act of December 10, 1814, and the unsuccessful conscription bill of the same year. The governors of Massachusetts, Connecticut, Rhode Island, and Vermont at various times defied federal requisitions on their state militias, or insisted on retaining state control over them when in service, on constitutional grounds.

Northeastern anger culminated in a call by the Massachusetts legislature in October 1814 for a regional convention to be held in Hartford in December of that year. Delegations from Massachusetts, Connecticut, and Rhode Island, and from certain counties in New Hampshire and Vermont met in secret session from December 15 to January 5, 1815, amidst widespread rumors that the convention would propose regional secession from the Union. The convention's final report, however, limited itself to proposing negotiations with the federal government over the militia question as well as a series of constitutional amendments. More ominously, the resolutions proposed a second convention if New England's demands were not met. The amendments were endorsed by the legislatures of Massachusetts and Connecticut, but were specifically rejected by nine other states; and the convention itself was discredited by the news that, even as it met, the national government had negotiated the Treaty of Ghent with Britain.

THEREFORE RESOLVED,

That it be and hereby is recommended to the Legislatures of the several States represented in this Convention, to adopt all such measures as may be necessary effectually to protect the citizens of said States from the operation and effects of all acts which have been or may be passed by the Congress of the United States, which shall contain provisions, subjecting the militia or other citizens to forcible drafts, conscriptions, or impressments, not authorized by the Constitution of the United States.

Resolved, That it be and hereby is recommended to the said Legislatures, to authorize an immediate and earnest application to be made to the Government of the United States, requesting their consent to some arrangement, whereby the said States may, separately or in concert, be empowered to assume upon themselves the defence of their territory against the enemy; and a reasonable portion of the taxes, collected within said States, may be paid into the respective treasuries thereof, and appropriated to the payment of the balance due said States, and to the future defence of the same. The amount so paid into the said treasuries to be credited, and the disbursements made as aforesaid to be charged to the United States.

Resolved, That it be, and it hereby is, recommended to the Legislatures of the aforesaid States, to pass laws (where it has not already been done) authorizing the Governours or Commanders in Chief of their militia to make detachments from the same, or to form voluntary corps, as shall be most convenient and conformable to their Constitutions, and to cause the same to be well armed, equipped and disciplined, and held in readiness for service; and upon the request of the Governour of either of the other States, to employ the whole of such detachment or corps, as well as the regular forces of the State, or such part thereof as may be required and can be spared consistently with the safety of the State, in assisting the State, making such request to repel any invasion thereof which shall be made or attempted by the publick enemy.

Resolved, That the following amendments of the Constitution of the United States, be recommended to the States represented as aforesaid, to be proposed by them for adoption by the State Legislatures, and in such cases as may be deemed expedient, by a Convention chosen by the people of each State.

And it is further recommended, that the said States shall persevere in their efforts to obtain such amendments, until the same shall be effected.

First. Representatives and direct taxes shall be apportioned among the several States which may be included within the union, according to their respective numbers of free persons, including those bound to serve for a term of years, and excluding Indians not taxed, and all other persons.

Second. No new State shall be admitted into the union by Congress in virtue of the power granted by the Constitution, without the concurrence of two thirds of both Houses.

Third. Congress shall not have power to lay any embargo on the ships or vessels of the citizens of the United States, in the ports of harbors thereof, for more than sixty days.

Fourth. Congress shall not have power, without the concurrence of two thirds of both Houses, to interdict the commercial intercourse between the United States and any foreign nation or the dependencies thereof.

Fifth. Congress shall not make or declare war, or authorize acts of hostility against any foreign nation without the concurrence of two thirds of both Houses, except such acts of hostility be in defence of the territories of the United States, when actually invaded.

Sixth. No person who shall hereafter be naturalized, shall be eligible as a member of the Senate or House of Representatives of the United States, nor capable of holding any civil office under the authority of the United States.

Seventh. The same person shall not be elected President of the United States a second time, nor shall the President be elected from the same State two terms in succession.

Resolved, That if the application of these States to the government of the United States, recommended in a foregoing Resolution, should be unsuccessful, and peace should not be concluded, and the defence of these States should be neglected, as it has been since the commencement of the war, it will in the opinion of this Convention be expedient for the Legislatures of other several States to appoint Delegates to another Convention, to meet at Boston, in the State of Massachusetts, on the third Thursday of June next, with such powers and instructions as the exigency of a crisis so momentous may require.

Comment

The Hartford Convention's proposed amendments were overwhelmingly regional and even partisan in nature. The proposal to reallocate congressional representation based on free persons only—thus eliminating the famous "three-fifth compromise" by which three-fifths of the number of a state's slaves were included in calculating its representatives—was directly aimed at reducing southern strength in the House of Representatives; and the amendment requiring a two-thirds congressional majority to admit new states was intended to give the Northeast a check on the increasing number of western and southern senators. The other amendments concerning congressional power and the presidency were similar in purpose, and the proposal to disable naturalized citizens from holding federal office reflected Federalist dislike for the Republican party's appeal to immigrants and its perceived political radicalism.

Joseph Story
Letter to Nathaniel Williams
(February 22, 1815)[109]

During the war, Story, as circuit justice, had been one of the most immediate symbols and direct wielders of federal power in New England. His letter to Williams illustrates the connections the experience of the war made between nationalism and Republicanism.

. . . Peace has come in a most welcome time to delight and astonish us. Never did a country occupy more lofty ground; we have stood the contest, single-handed, against the conqueror of Europe; and we are at peace, with all our blushing victories thick crowding on us. If I do not much mistake, we shall attain to a very high character abroad, as well as crush domestic faction. Never was there a more glorious opportunity for the Republican party to place themselves permanently in power. They have now a golden opportunity; I pray God that it may not be thrown away. Let us extend the national authority over the whole extent of power given by the Constitution. Let us have great military and naval schools; an adequate regular army; the broad foundations laid of a permanent navy; a national bank; a national system of bankruptcy; a great navigation act; a general survey of our ports, and appointments of portwardens and pilots; Judicial Courts which shall embrace the whole constitutional powers; national notaries; public and national justices of the peace, for the commercial and national concerns of the United States. By such enlarged and liberal institutions, the Government of the United States will be endeared to the people, and the factions of the great States will be rendered harmless. Let us prevent the possibility of a division, by creating great national interests which shall bind us in an indissoluble chain . . .

James Madison
Message to U.S. Congress
(December 5, 1815)[110]

Madison's first postwar address to the legislature was a programmatic reflection of the strongly nationalist feelings of most of the country.

. . . Although the embarrassments arising from the want of an uniform national currency have not been diminished since the adjournment of Congress, great satisfaction has been derived in contemplating the revival of the public credit and the efficiency of the public resources . . .

The national debt, as it was ascertained on the 1st of October last, amounted in the whole to the sum of $120,000,000, consisting of the unredeemed balance of the debt contracted before the late war ($39,000,000), the amount of the funded debt contracted in consequence of the war ($64,000,000), and the amount of the unfunded and floating debt, including the various issues of Treasury notes, $17,000,000, which is in a gradual course of payment. There will probably be some addition to the public debt upon the liquidation of various claims which are depending, and a conciliatory disposition on the part of Congress may lead honorably and advantageously to an equitable arrangement of the militia expenses incurred by the several States without the previous sanction or authority of the Government of the United States; but when it is considered that the new as well as the old portion of the debt has been contracted in the assertion of the national rights and independence, and when it is recollected that the public expenditures, not being exclusively bestowed upon subjects of a transient nature, will long be visible in the number and equipments of the American Navy, in the military works for the defense of our harbors and our frontiers, and in the supplies of our arsenals and magazines the amount will bear a gratifying comparison with the objects which have been attained, as well as with the resources of the country.

The arrangements of the finances with a view to the receipts and expenditures of a permanent peace establishment will necessarily enter into the deliberations of Congress during the present session. It is true that the improved condition of the public revenue will not only afford the means of maintaining the faith of the Government with its creditors inviolate, and of prosecuting successfully the measures of the most liberal policy, but will also justify an immediate alleviation of the burdens imposed by the necessities of the war. It is, however, essential to every modification of the finances that the benefits of an uniform national currency should be restored to the community. The absence of the precious metals will, it is believed, be a temporary evil, but until they can again be rendered the general medium of exchange it devolves on the wisdom of Congress to provide a substitute which shall equally engage the confidence and accommodate the wants of the citizens throughout the Union. If the operation of the State banks cannot produce this result, the probable operation of a national bank will merit consideration; and if neither of these expedients be deemed effectual it may become necessary to ascertain the terms upon which the notes of the Government (no longer required as an instrument of credit) shall be issued upon motives of general policy as a common medium of circulation.

Notwithstanding the security for future repose which the United States ought to find in their love of peace and their constant respect for the rights of other nations, the character of the times particularly inculcates the lesson that, whether to prevent or repel danger, we ought not to be unprepared for it. This consideration will sufficiently recommend to Congress a liberal provision for the immediate extension and gradual completion of the works of defense, both fixed and floating, on our maritime frontier, and an adequate provision for guarding our inland frontier against dangers to which certain portions of it may continue to be exposed.

As an improvement in our military establishment, it will deserve the consideration of Congress whether a corps of invalids might not be so organized and employed as at once to aid in the support of meritorious individuals excluded by age or infirmities from the existing establishment, and to procure to the public the benefit of their stationary services and of their exemplary discipline. I recommend also an enlargement of the Military Academy already established, and the establishment of others in other sections of the Union; and I can not press too much on the attention of Congress such a classification and organization of the militia as will most effectually render it the safeguard of a free state. If experience has shewn in the recent splendid achievements of militia the value of this resource for the public defense, it has shewn also the importance of that skill in the use of arms and that familiarity with the essential rules of discipline which can not be expected from the regulations now in force. With this subject is intimately connected the necessity of accommodating the laws in every respect to the great object of enabling the political authority of the Union to employ promptly and effectually the physical power of the Union in the cases designated by the Constitution.

The signal services which have been rendered by our Navy and the capacities it has developed for successful cooperation in the national defense will give to that portion of the public force its full value in the eyes of Congress, at an epoch which calls for the constant vigilance of all governments. To preserve the ships now in a sound state, to complete those already contemplated, to provide amply the imperishable materials for prompt augmentations, and to improve the existing arrangements into more advantageous establishments for the construction, the repairs, and the security of vessels of war is dictated by the soundest policy.

In adjusting the duties on imports to the object of revenue the influence of the tariff on manufactures will necessarily present itself for consideration. However wise the theory may be which leaves to the sagacity and interest of individuals the application of their industry and resources, there are in this as in other cases exceptions to the general rule. Besides the condition which the theory itself implies of a reciprocal adoption by other nations, experience teaches that so many circumstances must concur in introducing and maturing manufacturing establishments, especially of the more complicated kinds, that a country may remain long without them, although sufficiently advanced and in some respects even peculiarly fitted for carrying them on with success. Under circumstances giving a powerful impulse to manufacturing industry it has made among us a progress and exhibited an efficiency which justify the belief that with a protection not more than is due to the enterprising citizens whose interests are now at stake it will become at an early day not only safe against occasional competitions from abroad, but a source of domestic wealth and even of external commerce. In selecting the branches more especially entitled to the public patronage a preference is obviously claimed by such as will relieve the United States from a dependence on foreign supplies, ever subject to casual failures, for articles necessary for the public defense or connected with the primary wants of individuals. It will be an additional recommendation of particular manufactures where the materials for them are extensively drawn from our agriculture, and consequently impart and insure to that great fund of national prosperity and independence an encouragement which can not fail to be rewarded.

Among the means of advancing the public interest the occasion is a proper one for recalling the attention of Congress to the great importance of establishing throughout our country the roads and canals which can best be executed under the national authority. No objects within the circle of political economy so richly repay the expense bestowed on them; there are none the utility of which is more universally ascertained and acknowledged; none that do more honor to the governments whose wise and enlarged patriotism duly appreciates them. Nor is there any country which presents a field where nature invites more the art of man to complete her own work for his accommodation and benefit. These considerations are strengthened, moreover, by the political effect of these facilities for intercommunication in bringing and binding more closely together the various parts of our extended confederacy. Whilst the States individually, with a laudable enterprise and emulation, avail themselves of their local advantages by new roads, by navigable canals, and by improving the streams susceptible of navigation, the General Government is the more urged to similar undertakings, requiring a national jurisdiction and national means, by the prospect of thus systematically completing so inestimable a work; and it is a happy reflection that any defect of constitutional authority which may be encountered can be supplied in a mode which the Constitution itself has providently pointed out.

The present is a favorable season also for bringing again into view the establishment of a national seminary of learning within the District of Columbia, and with means drawn from the property therein, subject to the authority of the General Government. Such an institution claims the patronage of Congress as a monument of their solicitude for the advancement of knowledge, without which the blessings of liberty can not be fully enjoyed or long preserved; as a nursery of enlightened preceptors, and as a central resort of youth and genius from every part of their country, diffusing on their return examples of those national feelings, those liberal sentiments, and those congenial manners which contribute cement to our Union and strength to the great political fabric of which that is the foundation.

In closing this communication I ought not to repress a sensibility, in which you will unite, to the happy lot of our country and to the goodness of a superintending Providence, to which we are indebted for it. Whilst other portions of mankind are laboring under the distresses of war or struggling with adversity in other forms, the United States are in the tranquil enjoyment of prosperous and honorable peace. In reviewing the scenes through which it has been attained we can rejoice in the proofs given that our political institutions, founded in human rights and framed for their preservation, are equal to the severest trials of war, as well as adapted to the ordinary periods of repose. As fruits of this experience and of the reputation acquired by the American arms on the land and on the water, the nation finds itself possessed of a growing respect abroad and of a just confidence in itself, which are among the best pledges for its peaceful career. Under other aspects of our country the strongest features of its flourishing condition are seen in a population rapidly increasing on a territory as productive as it is extensive; in a general industry and fertile ingenuity which find their ample rewards, and in an affluent revenue which admits a reduction of the public burdens without withdrawing the means of sustaining the public credit, of gradually discharging the public debt, of providing for the necessary defensive and precautionary establishments, and of patronizing in every authorized mode undertakings conducive to the aggregate wealth and individual comfort of our citizens.

It remains for the guardians of the public welfare to persevere in that justice and good will toward other nations which invite a return of these sentiments toward the United States; to cherish institutions which guarantee their safety and their liberties, civil and religious; and to combine with a liberal system of foreign commerce an improvement of the national advantages and a protection and extension of the independent resources of our highly favored and happy country.

In all measures having such objects my faithful cooperation will be afforded.

Comment

In 1801 Jefferson inaugurated the era of the "Republican Ascendancy" with the maxim that "the sum of good government" was one that "shall restrain men from injuring one another" but "leave them otherwise free to regulate their own pursuits of industry and improvement." The "essential principles" of Republican constitutionalism that he identified were primarily negative, aimed at keeping the federal government limited and inexpensive. In 1815 Madison labeled the "theory" of small government and laissez-faire economics a "general rule" with many exceptions; and he urged Congress, as "the guardians of the public welfare," to take an active role in increasing "the aggregate wealth and individual comfort of our citizens." Madison endorsed protective tariffs to protect American industry, a national bank, the old Hamiltonian project of creating a national medium of exchange, a national university, a strong peacetime army and navy, and federally funded internal improvements. Madison and many other Republicans had moved a considerable distance from the old constitutionalism of suspicion toward a belief in the wisdom and legitimacy of a strong, activist federal government. Only Madison's brief references to the possibility of a "defect of constitutional authority" and to Congress acting "in every *authorized* mode" (emphasis supplied) hinted at the continuing importance of the "doctrines of '98" for Republicans of the late 1810s.

James Madison
Letter to Charles Jared Ingersoll
(June 25, 1831)[111]

The new Republican nationalism rapidly bore legislative fruit. In March 1816 Congress enacted a bill to create the Second Bank of the United States, which Madison signed. In April, Congress passed a tariff act continuing wartime import duties on cotton, wool, textiles, leather, paper, pig iron, and other goods over "Old Republican" objectives that such protective tariffs were not authorized by the Constitution. Many years later, Madison explained that he regarded the bank's constitutionality as established by precedent:

. . . The charge of inconsistency between my objection to the constitutionality of such a bank in 1791 and my assent in 1816, turns on the question how far legislative precedents, expounding the Constitution, ought to guide succeeding Legislatures and overrule individual opinions.

Can it be of less consequence that the meaning of a Constitution should be fixed and known, than that the meaning of a law should be so? Can, indeed, a law be fixed in its meaning and operation unless the Constitution be so? On the contrary, if a particular Legislature, differing in the construction of the Constitution from a series of preceding constructions, proceed to act on that difference, they not only introduce uncertainty and instability in the Constitution, but in the laws themselves; inasmuch as all laws preceding the new construction and inconsistent with it are not only annulled for the future, but virtually pronounced nullities from the beginning.

But it is said that the legislator having sworn to support the Constitution, must support it in his own construction of it, however different from that put on it by his predecessors, or whatever be the consequences of the construction. And is not the judge under the same oath to support the law? Yet, has it ever been supposed that he was required or at liberty to disregard all precedents, however solemnly repeated and regularly observed, and, by giving effect to his own abstract and individual opinions, to disturb the established course of practice in the business of the community? Has the wisest and most conscientious judge ever scrupled to acquiesce in decisions in which he has been overruled by the matured opinions of the majority of his colleagues, and subsequently to conform himself thereto, as to authoritative expositions of the law? And is it not reasonable that the same view of the official oath should be taken by a legislator, acting under the Constitution, which is his guide, as is taken by a judge, acting under the law, which is his?

There is, in fact and in common understanding, a necessity of regarding a course of practice, as above characterized, in the light of a legal rule of interpreting a law, and there is a like necessity of considering it a constitutional rule of interpreting a Constitution.

That there may be extraordinary and peculiar circumstances controlling the rule in both cases, may be admitted; but with such exceptions the rule will force itself on the practical judgment of the most ardent theorist. He will find it impossible to adhere, and act officially upon, his solitary opinions as to the meaning of the law or Constitution, in opposition to a construction reduced to practice during a reasonable period of time; more especially when no prospect existed of a change of construction by the public or its agents. And if a reasonable period of time, marked with the usual sanctions, would not bar the individual prerogative, there could be no limitation to its exercise, although the danger of error must increase with the increasing oblivion of explanatory circumstances, and with the continual changes in the import of words and phrases.

Let it, then, be left to the decision of every intelligent and candid judge, which, on the whole, is most to be relied on for the true and safe construction of a constitution; that which has the uniform sanction of successive legislative bodies, through a period of years and under the varied ascendency of parties; or that which depends upon the opinions of every new Legislature, heated as it may be by the spirit of party, eager in the pursuit of some favourite object, or led astray by the eloquence and address of popular statesmen, themselves, perhaps, under the influence of the same misleading causes.

It was in conformity with the view here taken, of the respect due to deliberate and reiterated precedents, that the Bank of the United States, though on the original question held to be unconstitutional, received the Executive signature in the year 181[6]. The act originally establishing a bank had undergone ample discussions in its passage through the several branches of the Government. It had been carried into execution throughout a period of twenty years with annual legislative recognitions; in one instance, indeed, with the entire acquiescence of all the local authorities, as well as of the nation at large; to all of which may be added, a decreasing prospect of any change in the public opinion adverse to the constitutionality of such an institution. A veto from the Executive, under these circumstances, with an admission of the expediency and almost necessity of the measure, would have been a defiance of all the obligations derived from a course of precedents amounting to the requisite evidence of the national judgment and intention.

It has been contended that the authority of precedents was in that case invalidated by the consideration that they proved only a respect for the stipulated duration of the bank, with a toleration of it until the law should expire; and by casting vote given in the Senate by the Vice President, in the year 1811, against a bill for establishing a National Bank, the vote being expressly given on the ground of unconstitutionality. But if the law itself was unconstitutional, the stipulation was void, and could not be constitutionally fulfilled or tolerated. And as to the negative of the Senate by the casting vote of the Presiding Officer, it is a fact, well understood at the time, that it resulted, not from an equality of opinions in that assembly on the power of Congress to establish a bank, but from a junction of those who admitted the power, but disapproved the plan with those who denied the power. On a simple question of constitutionality there was a decided majority in favour of it . . .

Comment

Madison agreed with Jefferson that there was no single official expositor of the Constitution and that public officials were entitled and obligated to exercise their own independent judgment on constitutional issues. Unlike Jefferson, Madison fully accepted the legitimacy of precedent in settling the proper interpretation of constitutional provisions.

Jackson v. Rose
2 Va. Cas. 34 (Gen. Ct. Nov. 1815)

Not all Republicans fully approved of Republican nationalism. The center of early opposition was in Madison's home state, Virginia, where states' rights Republicans maintained what they saw as a purer allegiance to the "doctrines of '98."

Jackson was a federal revenue collector who brought a suit in state court, pursuant to an act of Congress, to collect a penalty for selling foreign manufactured goods without a license. When the defendant challenged the state superior court's jurisdiction over this federal cause of action, the court certified the issue to the Virginia General Court.

WHITE, J., delivered the opinion of the Court:

This is an action of debt brought by the Plaintiff to recover a penalty inflicted by an Act of Congress to insure the collection of the Revenue of the United States: which penalty, the same Act says, may under circumstances, such as exist in this case, be recovered in a State Court; and the question submitted to the General Court is substantially this: Could Congress Constitutionally give to a State Court, jurisdiction over this case, or can such Court be authorized by an Act of Congress to take cognizance thereof?

The very statement of the question points out its extreme delicacy, and great importance. It involves the great Constitutional rights and powers of the General Government, as well as the rights, Sovereignty, and Independence of the respective State Governments. It calls upon this Court, to mark the limits which separate them from each other, and to make a decision, which may possibly put at issue, upon a great Constitutional point, the Legislature of the United States, and the Supreme Criminal Tribunal of one of the States.

Such a question, involving such consequences, ought to be approached with the utmost circumspection, with the most cool, dispassionate, and impartial investigation, and with a fixed determination, to render such judgment only, as shall be the result of solemn conviction. The Court has not been unmindful of these things: it has approached the subject with those feelings, and with that determination. It has bestowed its best consideration, its deepest reflection upon it: and after viewing it, in every point of light in which it has been placed by others, or in which the Court has been able to place it, has made up an opinion in which all the Judges present concur, and which it has directed me to pronounce.

But, before that is done, it will be necessary to lay down, and explain, certain principles upon which it is founded. First, it is believed that the Judicial power of any State, or Nation, forms an important part of its Sovereignty, and consists in a right to expound its Laws, to apply them to the various transactions of human affairs as they arise, and to superintend and enforce their execution. And that whosoever is authorized to perform these functions to any extent, has, of necessity, to the same extent, the Judicial power of that State or Nation which authorized him to do so. Secondly, that the Judiciary of one separate and distinct Sovereignty cannot of itself assume, nor can another separate and distinct Sovereignty either authorize, or coerce it to exercise the Judicial powers of such other separate and distinct Sovereignty...

Thirdly, that the Government of the United States, although it by no means possesses the entire Sovereignty of this vast Empire, (the great residuum thereof still remaining with the States respectively,) is nevertheless, as to all the purposes for which it was created, and as to all the powers vested therein, unless where it is otherwise provided by the

Constitution, completely Sovereign. And that its Sovereignty is as entirely separate and distinct from the Sovereignty of the respective States, as the Sovereignty of one of those States is separate and distinct from the other. So that, (unless as before excepted,) it cannot exercise the powers which belong to the State Governments, nor can any State Government exercise the powers which belong to it: and that there is no one thing to which this principle applies with more strength than to the Revenue of the United States, and things belonging thereto. It being notorious, that a desire to give Congress a complete and entire control over that subject, was the moving principle which called the present Government into existence.

It is admitted, however, that there are some exceptions in the Constitution to this last rule; they are such, however, as prove the rule itself. Thus by the second section of the third Article of the Constitution, among other things, it is declared that the Judicial power of the United States shall extend "to controversies between citizens of different States; between citizens of the same States, claiming lands under the grants of different States." These powers, in the nature of things, belonged to the State Sovereignties, and they were at the adoption of the Constitution, in complete possession of them. Nor could the Courts of the United States, merely as such, by any principle of construction, have claimed them, but there were reasons at that time deemed sufficient to justify the extension of the Judicial power of the United States, and it was extended to them, without, however, taking away the jurisdiction of the State Courts. So that, as respects those matters, the State Courts, and the Courts of the United States have concurrent jurisdiction *by compact* . . .

Upon the whole, however painful it may be, and actually it is to us all, to be brought by a sense of duty into conflict with the opinions and Acts of the Legislature of the United States, for which we entertain the highest respect, and the Constitutional Laws of which we feel ourselves bound to obey, and to execute with cheerfulness, when their execution devolves upon us, yet we cannot resist the conviction that this Law is, in this respect, Unconstitutional.

It is the unanimous opinion of this Court, that to assume jurisdiction over this case, would be to exercise a portion of the Judicial power of the United States, which by the Constitution is clearly and distinctly deposited in other hands, and that by doing so, we should prostrate that very instrument which we have taken a solemn oath to support . . .

The Virginia General Court's judgment in *Jackson* was delivered in November 1815. The following month, a far more important decision was announced by the state's highest court.

Hunter v. Martin
4 Munf. 1 (Va. Dec. 15, 1815)

For almost a quarter of a century, litigation over lands in Virginia once owned by Lord Fairfax went on in the Virginia courts. In 1813 the United States Supreme Court reversed a Virginia Court of Appeals decision in favor of one of the parties and issued a mandate to the Virginia court directing further proceedings in accordance with the Supreme Court's opinion. In April 1814 the Virginia court heard oral argument on the question of its obligation to obey the Supreme Court's order. Specifically, the court posed the question of whether section twenty-five of the Judiciary Act of 1789, which gave the Supreme Court jurisdiction to review state-court decisions rejecting federal-law claims, was constitutional. However, it was not until December 1815 that the court announced its decision, apparently because the Virginia judges, all Republicans, did not want to undermine the Republican federal government's ability to deal with Federalist states' rights sentiment in New England.

Judge CABELL. . . . The record having been carried by this writ of error into the Supreme Court of the United States, that Court reversed the judgment of this Court, and affirmed that of the District Court of Winchester, and ordered the cause to be remanded to this Court "with instructions to enter judgment for the appellant Phillip Martin." By the mandate directed to this Court, and reciting the judgment of the Supreme Court of the United States, the Judges of this Court are "commanded that such proceedings be had in the said cause, as according to right and justice and the laws of the United States and agreeably to said judgment and instructions of said Supreme Court, ought to be had." . . .

In such a case, has the Congress of the United States, a right, under the federal constitution, to confer on the Supreme Court of the United States, a power to *re-examine, by way of appeal or writ of error, the decision of the state Court; to affirm or reverse that decision; and in case of reversal, to command the state Court to enter and execute a judgment different from that which it had previously rendered?* I am deeply sensible of the extreme delicacy and importance of this question. I have diligently examined it according to my best ability, uninfluenced, I trust by any other feelings than an earnest desire to ascertain and give to the constitution, its just construction; being as little anxious for the abridgment of the federal, as for the extension of the state jurisdiction. My investigations have terminated in the conviction, that the constitution of the United States does not warrant the power which the act of congress purports to confer on the federal judiciary.

It was justly observed, in the argument, that our system of government is *sui generis*, unlike any other that now exists, or that has ever existed. Resting on certain great principles which we contend to be fundamental, immutable and of paramount obligation, it will not be found to want any of the powers of legitimate government; but, the distribution and modifications of those powers have no parallel. To the federal government are confided certain powers, specially enumerated and principally affecting our foreign relations, and the general interests of the nation. These powers are limited, not only by their special enumeration, but by the positive declaration that, all powers not enumerated, or not prohibited to the states, are reserved to the states, or to the people. This demarcation of power is not vain and ineffectual. The free exercise, by the states, of the powers reserved to them, is as much sanctioned and guarded by the constitution of the United States, as is the free exercise, by the federal government, of the powers delegated to that government. If either be impaired, the system is deranged. The two governments, therefore, possessing, each, its portion of the divided sovereignty, although embracing the same territory, and operating on the same persons and frequently on the same subjects, are nevertheless separate from, and independent of, each other. From this position, believed to be incontrovertible, it necessarily results that each government must act by its own organs: from no other can it expect, command, or enforce obedience, even as to objects coming within the range of its powers.

But whilst, on the one hand, neither government is left dependent upon the other, for the exercise of its proper powers, so on the other hand, neither government nor any of its departments, can act *compulsively*, on the other or any of its organs in their political or official capacities; with the single exception, perhaps, of the case where a state may be sued. In using the term *compulsive* action, I do not mean to restrain it to the idea of actual force, but to extend it to any action imposing an obligation to obey. The present government of the United States, grew out of the weakness and inefficacy of the confederation, and was intended to remedy its evils. Instead of a government of *requisition*, we have a government of power. But how does that power operate? On individuals, in their individual capacities. No one presumes to contend, that the state governments can operate compulsively on the general government or any of its departments, even in cases of unquestionable encroachment on state authority; as, for example, if the Federal Court should entertain jurisdiction, in personal actions, between citizens of the same state, not involving questions concerning the construction of the constitution of the United States, nor concerning the validity or construction of any statute, treaty, commission or authority of, or under, the general government, nor concerning the validity of any statute, commission or authority of, or under, any state government. Such encroachment of jurisdiction could neither be prevented nor redressed by the state government, or any of its departments, *by any procedure acting on the Federal Courts.* I can perceive nothing in the constitution which gives to the federal Courts any stronger claim to prevent or redress, *by any procedure acting on the state Courts,* an equally obvious encroachment on the federal jurisdiction. The constitution of the United States contemplates the independence of both governments, and regards the residuary sovereignty of the states, as not less inviolable, than the delegated sovereignty of the United States. It must have been foreseen that controversies would sometimes arise as to the boundaries of the two jurisdictions. Yet the constitution has provided no umpire, has erected no tribunal by which they shall be settled. The omission proceeded, probably, from the belief, that such a tribunal would produce evils greater than those of the occasional collisions which it would be designed to remedy. Be this as it may, to give to the general government or any of its departments, a direct and controlling operation upon the state departments, as such, would be to change at once, the whole character of our system. The independence of the state authorities would be extinguished, and a superiority, unknown to the constitution, would be created, which would, sooner or later terminate in an entire consolidation of the states into one complete national sovereignty . . .

I can perceive no force in the argument attempted to be drawn from the sixth article of the constitution of the United States, which declares that the constitution and the laws of the United States which shall be made in pursuance thereof, and all treaties made or which shall be made under the authority of the United States, shall be the supreme law of the land; and the Judges in every state shall be bound thereby. From this obligation no exemption will be claimed for the State Courts. But it imposes a subjection to the constitution and to the laws and treaties made under its authority; not a subjection to the Federal Courts. What that constitution is, what those laws and treaties are, must, in cases coming before the State Courts, be decided by the State Judges, *according to their own judgments, and upon their own responsibility.* To the opinions of the Federal Courts, they will always pay the respect which is due to the opinions of other learned and upright Judges; and more especially when it is considered that all the cases of Federal cognizance, may, as I shall hereafter endeavour to prove, be originally carried before the Federal Courts, and probably would always be carried there, unless there should be a conformity between the decisions of the State Courts, and of the Federal Courts. The Courts of this State have furnished repeated evidences of this respect for the decisions of the Federal Court—but it is *respect* only, and not the acknowledgment of *conclusive authority* . . .

If this Court should now proceed to enter a judgment in this case, according to the instructions of the Supreme Court, the Judges of this Court, in doing so, must act either as Federal or as State Judges. But we cannot be made Federal Judges without our consent, and without commissions. Both these requisites being wanting, the act could not, therefore, be done by us, constitutionally, as Federal Judges. We must, then, in obeying this mandate, be considered still as State Judges. We are required, as State Judges to enter up a judgment, not our own, but dictated and prescribed to us by another Court. This as to us would be either a judicial or a ministerial act—If it be the latter, I presume it will not be contended that the Federal Court has a right to make the Judges of this Court its ministerial agents—Let it then be a judicial act. But, before one Court can dictate to another, the judgment it shall pronounce, it must bear, to that other, the relation of a appellate Court. The term appellate, however, necessarily includes the idea of *superiority.* But one Court cannot be correctly said to be *superior* to another, unless both of them belong to the same sovereignty. It would be a misapplication of terms to say that a Court of Virginia is *superior* to a Court of Maryland, or *vice versa.* The Courts of the United States, therefore, belonging to one sovereignty, cannot be appellate Courts in relation to the State Courts, which belong to a different sovereignty—and of course, their commands or instruction impose no obligation.

The second section of the 3d article enumerates the cases to which the judicial power of the United States shall extend; and the 8th section of the first article declares that

Congress shall have power to make all laws which shall be necessary and proper for carrying into execution all the powers vested in the general government, or any department thereof. But this effectuating power, as it has been termed, must, of necessity, be limited to constitutional means. In relation to judicial powers, these means have been already shewn to be Federal Courts, and Judges duly commissioned . . .

All the purposes of the constitution of the United States will be answered by the erection of Federal Courts, into which any party, plaintiff or defendant, concerned in a case of Federal cognizance, *may* carry it for adjudication; for, it was never intended to force the parties into those courts against their will. The right of the *plaintiff*, to have his case tried before the federal courts, is unquestionable, as he may institute his suit in the State or Federal Courts, at his own option; and it will be sufficient for the *defendant* sued in a *State* Court, if the act of congress shall give him the power, to remove the case at any time before judgment into the Federal Courts. I cannot doubt that congress may give this power consistently with the constitution; for, otherwise, the judicial power of the United States might be eluded at the pleasure of any plaintiff. If then the plaintiff shall *elect* the state jurisdiction, by bringing his suit in the State Court, and the defendant shall also *elect* it by submitting to it, they must, from the nature of the judicial power reserved to the states, be *concluded* by the judgment, unless there be an appeal to some Superior Court, which I have endeavoured to shew is not the case with respect to the Federal Courts. If, after a judgment in a State Court, in any such case, there shall be a complaint of a want of uniformity of decision, of a defective execution of the laws of the union, of a violation of rights under the constitution, laws or treaties of the United States, or complaints of any other kind whatsoever, the answer to them all, both in relation to foreigners and others, is that the parties have elected their own tribunal; a tribunal, over which the general government has no controul, and for whose decisions, therefore, it owes no responsibility
. . .

Judge BROOKE. . . . The general question is, has the supreme court the power to issue its mandate to this court in any case?—the particular question will be, has it that power in the case before us?—Unless the general question shall be decided in its favour, it will be unnecessary to examine how far it has transcended its power in the case under consideration.

In deciding this first question, recurrence must be had to the Constitution itself;—for though I subscribe to the doctrine of one of the counsel, that, to the extent that the States have parted with their power, they ought to part with their pride, yet I cannot as implicitly assent to the position that, where state rights are violated, they can only be defended in the general government, in Congress, or by appealing to the people. The state authorities have been said, with great force, to be the guardians of the people's and their own rights. The right to resist infractions of the Federal Constitution, proceeding from the general government, or any department thereof, has been solemnly asserted in Virginia [in the Resolutions of 1798] and seems to result from the nature of the two governments.

[Brooke's opinion included the following footnote: "Note. The effect of the extension of the appellate power of the Supreme Court to the state courts, will be found, on a slight consideration, to be more repugnant to the federal character of the national government, than is the first supposed; it will give to it a strong feature of consolidated government, in the administration of the laws and acts of the Federal government. On the one hand, whilst the government of the United States will operate more feebly in the exercise of its constitutional powers, through organs not directly under its control—on the other, the state courts will be made the instruments of encroachment on state rights, in a way to give greater force to violations of the federal compact, than if the general government committed those violations through its own organs. The revision of the judgments of the state courts, by way of original jurisdiction, will be unaided by the additional weight of state adjudications founded on an implicit obedience to federal authority, and leave to the people, uninfluenced by state authority, an opportunity better adapted to the impartial investigation of the constitutionality of Federal adjudications."]

Judge ROANE. . . . The question which now arises, upon this mandate, is of the first impression in this court, and of the greatest moment. The court, consequently, invited the members of the bar to investigate it, for its information; several of whom, in addition to the appellee's counsel, discussed it, accordingly, in a very full and able manner; since which, it has received the long and deliberate consideration of the court. This course of the court, to say nothing of its general character, should have spared the appellee's counsel the trouble, of exhorting this High Tribunal, to divest itself of all improper prejudices, in deciding on this important question. Those counsel were also pleased to warn us of the consequences of a decision, one way, in reference, principally, to the anarchical principles prevalent at the time of the argument, in a particular section of the union [this reference is to the opposition to the federal government in New England that culminated in the Hartford Resolutions of 1815]. They ought to have remembered, that this court did not select the time for bringing this case to a decision, and that it is not for it, to regard political consequences, in rendering it's [sic] judgments. [Roane included a footnote stating that his "opinion was prepared, and ready to be delivered, shortly after the argument" in April 1814. "The crisis alluded to by the appellee's counsel has now, happily, passed away."] They should also have recollected, that there is a Charybdis to be avoided as well as a Scylla; that a centripetal, as well as a centrifugal principle, exists in the government; and that no calamity would be more to be deplored by the American people, than a vortex in the general government, which should ingulph and sweep away, every vestige of the state constitutions . . .

[Roane proceeded to criticize the reliance of appellee's counsel on "The Federalist," which Roane described as "a mere newspaper publication, written in the heat and hurry of the battle," by "a supposed favourer of a consolidated government" (Hamilton); and on the constitutional opinions of the First Congress, which, Roane pointed out, the federal Supreme Court had found erroneous in *Marbury v. Madison*.]

Throwing out of view, all these opinions, therefore, except so far as I may think them correct, and use them for the purpose of illustration, and taking for my guide the constitution, which cannot err, I will examine these important questions. I will also avail myself of such principles, as all the enlightened friends of liberty concur in, as essential to preserve the rights and promote the harmony of both governments. As a work containing a just exposition of these principles, I will, occasionally, refer to the celebrated report to the Virginia Legislature, in the year 1799. In addition to other claims to respect, it is to be remarked, that this document contains the *renewed* sense, of the people of Virginia, on the important subjects to which it relates . . . and that it had a principal influence in producing a new era in the American republic . . .

In order to understand the question correctly, it is proper to recollect, that the government of the United States is not a sole and consolidated government. The governments of the several states, in all their parts, remain in full force, except as they are impaired, by grants of power, to the general government . . . If after the [tenth] amendment [was ratified], any doubts could still exist, on this subject, they will be dissipated by the most unexceptionable authorities. In the report to the Virginia Legislature, before mentioned, for example, that body has resolved that "it views the powers of the Federal government, as resulting from the compact to which the co-states are parties; as limited by the plain sense and intention of the instrument, constituting that compact; and as no further valid than they are authorised by the grants enumerated in that compact."

So it was unanimously resolved, by the Supreme Court of the State of Pennsylvania, in the case of Commonwealth vs. Cobbet, that before the Constitution of the United States was adopted, the several states had absolute and unlimited sovereignty, within their respective boundaries, and all powers, legislative, executive, and judicial, except as they had been granted away, by the articles of confederation, and that they now enjoy all those powers, except such as have been granted to the government of the United States.

It results from this diversity in the two governments, that whereas, in a controversy respecting the constitutionality of a state law, it must be shewn to be unconstitutional, a law of the General Government must be proved to be constitutional; which can only be by shewing, that the power to pass it has been granted . . . [P]rinciples and authorities equally shew, that a power ought not to be considered as granted, because, in the opinions of the Judges expounding the Constitution, it ought to have been granted. This point, as to them, is entirely *coram non judice*. The people, alone are competent to decide it, and they have decided every power to be withholden, which has not been legitimately granted. Their will is supposed to be in accordance with their expressions: but if this were even otherwise, the answer to the Court would be, *"quod voluerunt, non dixerunt."* . . . [The climax of Roane's attack on section 25's constitutionality focused on the section's restriction of Supreme Court jurisdiction to state-court decisions rejecting a claim under federal law or overturning a federal statute.]

The novel spectacle of a judgment being final or not, as it may chance to be one side or the other, and of a court being of the last resort or otherwise, as its decision may happen to have been for one or other of the parties, is worthy of a system which only admits the judges to be impartial on one side of a given question! That, however, is a chimera, existing only in the imagination of a former congress. It was an after-thought, well calculated to aggrandize the general government, at the expence of those of the states; to work a consolidation of the confederacy; and can only be pretended to be justified by the broad principles of construction, which brought the alien and sedition laws into our code! I would consign it to a common tomb with them, as members of the same family, and originating in the same era of our government . . . It is not to be denied, that the jurisdiction now in question has been entertained by the Supreme Court in sundry instances. But that jurisdiction has gained ground by piece-meal, and has never received the solemn and deliberate discussion and decision of that tribunal. It has been adopted, also, under a latitude of construction and discretion in the Court, which is at war with the idea of limited and specified powers, in the general government. That decision was coeval, as I have already said, with sundry acts of the National Legislature, passed upon the same principle: but while those acts have been scouted, and repealed by general consent, under a more correct view of the constitution, the decision has been suffered to remain and to be acted on as a precedent! . . .

[The president of the court, Judge Fleming, read an opinion concurring with his colleagues, and the court joined in a brief statement of its holding.]

The following was entered as the court's opinion:

The court is unanimously of opinion, that the appellate power of the Supreme Court of the United States, does not extend to this court, under a sound construction of the constitution of the United States;—that so much of the 25th section of the act of congress, to establish the judicial courts of the United States, as extends the appellate jurisdiction of the Supreme Court to this court, is not in pursuance of the constitution of the United States; that the writ of error in this case was improvidently allowed under the authority of that act; that the proceedings thereon in the Supreme Court were *coram non judice* in relation to this court; and that obedience to its mandate be declined by this court.

Comment

The 1815 Virginia attack on Republican nationalism focused on the relationship between state courts and federal law. The judges of the general court, which declined to administer a federal revenue statute, and of the court of appeals, which refused to obey a mandate from the United States Supreme Court, showed a common constitutional vision of the states and the Union as "separate and independent" sovereignties (White). "Each government," Judge Cabell wrote, "must act by its own organs," rather than by conscripting or coercing the officials of the other. The mechanisms of the respective governments were to be kept completely distinct, just as federal and state powers were, with specific exceptions, mutually exclusive. Congress's attempt to give the federal Supreme Court appellate jurisdiction over state courts was an unconstitutional breach in the wall of separation between the Union and the states, justifiable only by "a latitude of construction and discretion" that contradicted the "limited and specified" character of the federal government (Roane). The judges were concerned to distinguish their opinions from "the anarchical principles" of the wartime New England Federalists. The inability of the federal government to compel state courts to obey *its* constitutional views, they insisted, did not diminish or affect their obligation "to obey, and to execute with cheerfulness" (White) the United States Constitution and constitutional federal statutes: the supremacy clause, after all, subjected state courts to federal law, not to federal officials. Nor did the decisions of the judges prevent Congress from ensuring that all questions of federal law could be decided by federal tribunals because the Virginia judges, unlike Chief Justice M'Kean in the famous *Cobbett* case, did not contest the constitutionality of Congress granting federal courts removal jurisdiction over all cases involving federal questions. The narrow reading of federal power in *Jackson* and *Hunter* was not directed to restricting the overall scope of federal power, but instead to protecting the institutional autonomy and intellectual integrity of the state courts. Neither decision, therefore, was a direct attack on Republican nationalism. Their importance lay at a different and deeper level, with their revitalization of the anti-centralizing rhetoric of 1798.

Martin v. Hunter's Lessee
14 U.S. (1 Wheat.) 304 (Mar. 20, 1816)

Martin returned to the federal Supreme Court to attempt to persuade the justices to enforce their earlier reversal of the Virginia decision. Chief Justice Marshall, who had a personal financial interest in the litigation, recused himself, as in the earlier decision, and Republican Justice Story once again spoke for the Court.

STORY, J., delivered the opinion of the court:
This is a writ of error from the Court of Appeals of Virginia, founded upon the refusal of that court to obey the mandate of this court, requiring the judgment rendered in this very cause, at February term, 1813, to be carried into due execution...

The questions involved in this judgment are of great importance and delicacy. Perhaps it is not too much to affirm that, upon their right decision, rest some of the most solid principles which have hitherto been supposed to sustain and protect the constitution itself. The great respectability, too, of the court whose decisions we are called upon to review, and the entire deference which we entertain for the learning and ability of that court, add much to the difficulty of the task which has so unwelcomely fallen upon us. It is, however, a source of consolation that we have had the assistance of most able and learned arguments to aid our inquiries: and that the opinion which is now to be pronounced has been weighed with every solicitude to come to a correct result, and matured after solemn deliberation.

Before proceeding to the principal questions, it may not be unfit to dispose of some preliminary considerations which have grown out of the arguments at the bar.

The constitution of the United States was ordained and established, not by the states in their sovereign capacities, but emphatically, as the preamble of the constitution declares, by "the people of the United States." There can be no doubt that it was competent to the people to invest the general government with all the powers which they might deem proper and necessary: to extend or restrain these powers according to their own good pleasure and to give them a paramount and supreme authority. As little doubt can there be that the people had a right to prohibit to the states the exercise of any powers which were, in their judgment, incompatible with the objects of the general compact; to make the powers of the state governments, in given cases, subordinate to those of the nation, or to reserve to themselves those sovereign authorities which they might not choose to delegate to either. The constitution was not, therefore, necessarily carved out of existing state sovereignties, nor a surrender of powers already existing in state institutions, for the powers of the states depend upon their own constitutions; and the people of every state had the right to modify and restrain them, according to their own views of policy or principle. On the other hand, it is perfectly clear that the sovereign powers vested in the state governments, by their respective constitutions, remained unaltered and unimpaired, except so far as they were granted to the government of the United States.

Those deductions do not rest upon general reasoning, plain and obvious as they seem to be. They have been positively recognized by one of the articles in amendment of the constitution, which declares, that "the powers not delegated to the United States by the constitution, nor prohibited by it to the states, are reserved to the states respectively, or to the people."

The government, then, of the United States, can claim no powers which are not granted to it by the constitution, and the powers actually granted, must be such as are expressly given, or given by necessary implication. On the other hand, this instrument, like every other grant, is to have a reasonable construction, according to the import of its terms, and where a power is expressly given in general terms, it is not to be restrained to particular cases, unless that construction grow out of the context expressly, or by necessary implication. The words are to be taken in their natural and obvious sense, and not in a sense unreasonably restricted or enlarged.

The constitution unavoidably deals in general language. It did not suit the purposes of the people, in framing this great charter of our liberties, to provide for minute specifications of its powers, or to declare the means by which those powers should be carried into execution. It was foreseen that this would be a perilous and difficult, if not an impracticable, task. The instrument was not intended to provide merely for the exigencies of a few years, but was to endure through a long lapse of ages, the events of which were locked up in the inscrutable purposes of Providence. It could not be foreseen what new changes and modifications of power might be indispensable to effectuate the general objects of the charter; and restrictions and specifications which, at the present, might seem salutary, might, in the end, prove the overthrow of the system itself. Hence its powers are expressed in general terms, leaving to the legislature, from time to time, to adopt its own means to effectuate legitimate objects, and to mold and model the exercise of its powers, as its own wisdom and the public interests should require.

With these principles in view—principles in respect to which no difference of opinion ought to be indulged—let us now proceed to the interpretation of the constitution, so far as regards the great points in controversy.

The third article of the constitution is that which must principally attract our attention. The first section declares, "the judicial power of the United States shall be vested in one Supreme Court, and in such other inferior courts as the Congress may, from time to time, ordain and establish." The second section declares, that "the judicial power shall extend to all cases in law or equity, arising under this constitution, the laws of the United States, and the treaties made, or which shall be made, under their authority; to all cases affecting ambassadors, other public ministers and consuls; to all cases of admiralty and maritime jurisdiction: to controversies to which the United States shall be a party; to controversies between two or more states; between a state and citizens of another state, between citizens of different states; between citizens of the same state, claiming lands under the grants of different states; and between a state or the citizens thereof, and foreign states citizens, or subjects." It then proceeds to declare, that "in all cases affecting ambassadors, other public ministers and consuls, and those in which a state shall be a party, the Supreme Court shall have original jurisdiction. In all the other cases before mentioned the Supreme Court shall have appellate jurisdiction, both as to law and fact, with such exceptions, and under such regulations, as the Congress shall make."

Such is the language of the article creating and defining the judicial power of the United States. It is the voice of the whole American people solemnly declared, in establishing one great department of that government which was, in many respects, national, and in all, supreme. It is a part of the very same instrument which was to act not merely upon individuals, but upon states; and to deprive them altogether of the exercise of some powers of sovereignty, and to restrain and regulate them in the exercise of others.

Let this article be carefully weighed and considered. The language of the article throughout is manifestly designed to be mandatory upon the legislature. Its obligatory force is so imperative that Congress could not, without a violation of its duty, have refused to carry it into operation. The judicial power of the United States shall be vested (not may be vested) in one supreme court, and in such inferior courts as Congress may, from time to time, ordain and establish. Could Congress have lawfully refused to create a supreme court, or to vest it with the constitutional jurisdiction? "The judges, both of the supreme and the inferior courts, shall hold their offices during good behavior, and shall, at stated times, receive, for their services, a compensation which shall not be diminished during their continuance in office." Could Congress create or limit any other tenure of the judicial office? Could they refuse to pay at stated times, the stipulated salary, or diminish it during the continuance in office? But one answer can be given to these questions; it must be in the negative. The object of the constitution was to establish three great departments of government; the legislative, the executive and the judicial departments. The first was to pass laws, the second to approve and execute them and the third to expound and enforce them. Without the latter it would be impossible to carry into effect some of the express provisions of the constitution. How, otherwise, could crimes against the United States be tried and punished? How could causes between two states be heard and determined? The judicial power must, therefore, be vested in some court, by Congress; and to suppose that it was not an obligation binding on them, but might, at their pleasure, be omitted or declined, is to suppose that, under the sanction of the constitution they might defeat the constitution itself: a construction which would lead to such a result cannot be sound . . .

If, then, it is the duty of Congress to vest the judicial power of the United States, it is the duty to vest the whole judicial power. The language if imperative as to one part, is imperative as to all. If it were otherwise, this anomaly would exist, that Congress might successively refuse to vest the jurisdiction in any one class of cases enumerated in the constitution, and thereby defeat the jurisdiction as to all; for the constitution has not singled out any class on which Congress are bound to act in preference to others . . .

But even admitting that the language of the constitution is not mandatory, and that Congress may constitutionally omit to vest the judicial power in courts of the United States, it cannot be denied that when it is vested it may be exercised to the utmost constitutional extent.

This leads us to the consideration of the great question as to the nature and extent of the appellate jurisdiction of the United States. We have already seen that appellate jurisdiction is given by the constitution to the Supreme Court in all cases where it has not original jurisdiction; subject, however, to such exceptions and regulations as Congress may prescribe. It is therefore, capable of embracing every case enumerated in the constitution, which is not exclusively to be decided by way of original jurisdiction. But the exercise of the appellate jurisdiction is far from being limited by the terms of the constitution to the Supreme Court. There can be no doubt that Congress may create a succession of inferior tribunals, in each of which it may vest appellate as well as original jurisdiction. The judicial power is delegated by the constitution in the most general terms, and may, therefore, be exercised by Congress under every variety of form, of appellate or original jurisdiction. And as there is nothing in the constitution which restrains or limits this power, it must, therefore, in all other cases, subsist in the utmost latitude of which, in its own nature, it is susceptible.

As, then, by the terms of the constitution, the appellate jurisdiction is not limited as to the Supreme Court, and as to this court it may be exercised in all other cases than those of which it has original cognizance, what is there to restrain its exercise over state tribunals in the enumerated cases? The appellate power is not limited by the terms of the third article to any particular courts. The words are, "the judicial power (which includes appellate power) shall extend to all cases," &c., and "in all other cases before mentioned the Supreme Court shall have appellate jurisdiction." It is the case, then, and not the court, that gives the jurisdiction. If the judicial power extends to the case, it will be in vain to search in the letter of the constitution for any qualification as to the tribunal where it depends. It is incumbent, then, upon those who assert such a qualification to show its existence by necessary implication. If the text be clear and distinct, no restriction upon its plain and obvious import ought to be admitted, unless the inference be irresistible.

If the constitution meant to limit the appellate jurisdiction to cases pending in the courts of the United States, it would necessarily follow that the jurisdiction of these courts would, in all the cases enumerated in the constitution, be exclusive of state tribunals. How otherwise could the jurisdiction extend to all cases arising under the constitution, laws and treaties of the United States, or to all cases of admiralty and maritime jurisdiction? If some of these cases might be entertained by state tribunals, and no appellate jurisdictions as to them should exist, then the appellate power would not extend to all, but to some cases. If state tribunals might exercise concurrent jurisdiction over all or some of the other classes of cases in the constitution without control, then the appellate jurisdiction of the United States might, as to such cases, have no real existence, contrary to the manifest intent of the constitution. Under such circumstances, to give effect to the judicial power, it must be construed to be exclusive; and this not only when the *casus foederis* should arise directly, but when it should arise incidentally, in cases pending in state courts. This construction would abridge the jurisdiction of such courts far more than has been ever contemplated in any act of Congress.

On the other hand, if, as has been contended, a discretion be vested in Congress to establish, or not to establish, inferior courts at their own pleasure and Congress should not establish such courts, the appellate jurisdiction of the Supreme Court would have nothing to act upon unless it could act upon cases pending in the state courts. Under such circumstances it must be held that the appellate power would extend to state courts; for the constitution is peremptory that it shall extend to certain enumerated cases, which cases could exist in no other courts. Any other construction, upon this supposition, would involve this strange contradiction, that a discretionary power vested in Congress, and which they might rightfully omit to exercise, would defeat the absolute injunctions of the constitution in relation to the whole appellate power.

But it is plain that the framers of the constitution did contemplate that cases within the judicial cognizance of the United States not only might but would arise in the state courts, in the exercise of their ordinary jurisdiction. With this view the sixth article declares, that "this constitution, and the laws of the United States which shall be made in pursuance thereof, and all treaties made, or which shall be made, under the authority of the United States, shall be the supreme law of the land, and the judges in every state shall be bound thereby, anything in the constitution or laws of any state to the contrary notwithstanding." It is obvious that this obligation is imperative upon the state judges in their official, and not merely in their private, capacities. From the very nature of their judicial duties they would be called upon to pronounce the law applicable to the case in judgment. They are not to decide merely according to the laws or constitution of the state, but according to the constitution, laws and treaties of the United States—"the supreme law of the land." ...

It has been argued that such an appellate jurisdiction over state courts is inconsistent with the genius of our government, and the spirit of the constitution. That the latter was never designed to act upon state sovereignties, but only upon the people, and that if the power exists, it will materially impair the sovereignty of the states, and the independence of their courts. We cannot yield to the force of this reasoning; it assumes principles which we cannot admit, and draws conclusions to which we do not yield our assent.

It is a mistake that the constitution was not designed to operate upon states in their corporate capacities. It is crowded with provisions which restrain or annul the sovereignty of the states in some of the highest branches of their prerogatives. The tenth section of the first article contains a long list of disabilities and prohibitions imposed upon the states. Surely, when such essential portions of state sovereignty are taken away, or prohibited to be exercised, it cannot be correctly asserted that the constitution does not act upon the states. The language of the constitution is also imperative upon the states as to the performance of many duties. It is imperative upon the state legislatures to make laws prescribing the time, places, and manner of holding elections for senators and representatives, and for electors of President and Vice-President. And in these, as well as some other cases, Congress have a right to revise, amend, or supersede the laws which may be passed by state legislatures. When, therefore, the states are stripped of some of the highest attributes of sovereignty, and the same are given to the United States; when the legislatures of the states are, in some respects, under the control of Congress, and in every case are under the constitution, bound by the paramount authority of the United States; it is certainly difficult to support the argument that the appellate power over the decisions of state courts is contrary to the genius of our institutions. The courts of the United States, can, without question, revise the proceedings of the executive and legislative authorities of the states, and if they are found to be contrary to the constitution, may declare them to be of no legal validity. Surely the exercise of the same right over judicial tribunals is not a higher or more dangerous act of sovereign power.

Nor can such a right be deemed to impair the independency of state judges. It is assuming the very ground in controversy to assert that they possess an absolute independence of the United States. In respect to the powers granted to the United States, they are not independent; they are expressly bound to obedience by the letter of the constitution and if they should unintentionally transcend their authority, or misconstrue the constitution, there is no more reason to giving their judgments an absolute and irresistible force than for giving it to the acts of the other coordinate departments of state sovereignty.

The argument urged from the possibility of the abuse of the revising power is equally unsatisfactory. It is always a doubtful course to argue against the use or existence of a power, from the possibility of its abuse. It is still more difficult, by such an argument, to ingraft upon a general power a restriction which is not to be found in the terms in which it is given. From the very nature of things, the absolute right of decision, in the last resort, must rest somewhere—wherever it may be vested it is susceptible of abuse. In all questions of jurisdiction the inferior, or appellate court, must pronounce the final judgment; and common sense, as well as legal reasoning, has conferred it upon the latter . . .

It is further argued that no great public mischief can result from a construction which shall limit the appellate power of the United States to cases in their own courts; first, because state judges are bound by an oath to support the constitution of the United States, and must be presumed to be men of learning and integrity; and secondly, because Congress must have an unquestionable right to remove all cases within the scope of the judicial power from the state courts to the courts of the United States, at any time before final judgment, though not after final judgment. As to the first reason—admitting that the judges of the state courts are, and always will be, of as much learning, integrity, and wisdom, as those of the courts of the United States (which we very cheerfully admit), it does not aid the argument. It is manifest that the constitution has proceeded upon a theory of its own, and given or withheld powers accordingly to the judgment of the American people, by whom it was adopted. We can only construe its powers, and cannot inquire into the policy or principles which induced the grant of them. The constitution has presumed (whether rightly or wrongly we do not inquire) that state attachments, state prejudices, state jealousies, and state interests, might sometimes obstruct, or control, or be supposed to obstruct or control, the regular administration of justice. Hence, in controversies between states; between citizens of different states; between citizens claiming grants under different states; between a state and its citizens, or foreigners, and between citizens and foreigners, it enables the parties, under the authority of Congress, to have the controversies heard, tried, and determined before the national tribunals. No other reason than that which has been stated can be assigned, why some at least, of those cases should not have been left to the cognizance of the state courts. In respect to the other enumerated cases—the cases arising under the constitution, laws, and treaties of the United States, cases affecting ambassadors and other public ministers, and cases of admiralty and maritime jurisdiction—reasons of a higher and more extensive nature, touching the safety, peace, and sovereignty of the nation, might well justify a grant of exclusive jurisdiction.

This is not all. A motive of another kind, perfectly compatible with the most sincere respect for state tribunals, might induce the grant of appellate power over their decisions. That motive is the importance, and even necessity of uniformity of decisions throughout the whole United States, upon all subjects within the purview of the constitution. Judges of equal learning and integrity, in different states, might differently interpret a statute, or a treaty of the United States, or even the constitution itself. If there were no revising authority to control these jarring and discordant judgments, and harmonize them into uniformity, the laws, the treaties, and the constitution of the United States would be different in different states, and might, perhaps, never have precisely the same construction, obligation, or efficacy, in any two states. The public mischiefs that would attend such a state of things would be truly deplorable; and it cannot be believed that they could have escaped the enlightened convention which formed the constitution. What, indeed, might then have been only prophecy, has now become fact; and the appellate jurisdiction must continue to be the only adequate remedy for such evils...

On the whole, the court are of opinion that the appellate power of the United States does extend to cases pending in the state courts; and that the 25th section of the judiciary act, which authorizes the exercise of this jurisdiction in the specified cases, by a writ of error, is supported by the letter and spirit of the constitution. We find no clause in that instrument which limits this power; and we dare not interpose a limitation where the people have not been disposed to create one.

Strong as this conclusion stands upon the general language of the constitution, it may still derive support from other sources. It is an historical fact that this exposition of the constitution, extending its appellate power to state courts, was, previous to its adoption, uniformly and publicly avowed by its friends, and admitted by its enemies, as the basis of their respective reasonings, both in and out of the state conventions. It is an historical fact that at the time when the judiciary act was submitted to the deliberations of the first Congress, composed, as it was, not only of men of great learning and ability, but of men who had acted a principal part in framing, supporting, or opposing that constitution, the same exposition was explicitly declared and admitted by the friends and by the opponents of that system. It is an historical fact that the Supreme Court of the United States have, from time to time, sustained this appellate jurisdiction in a great variety of cases, brought from the tribunals of many of the most important states in the Union, and that no state tribunal has ever breathed a judicial doubt on the subject, or declined to obey the mandate of the Supreme Court, until the present occasion. This weight of contemporaneous exposition by all parties, this acquiescence of enlightened state courts, and these judicial decisions of the Supreme Court through so long a period, do as we think, place the doctrine upon a foundation of authority which cannot be shaken, without delivering over the subject to perpetual and irremediable doubts...

We have not thought it incumbent on us to give any opinion upon the question, whether this court have authority to issue a writ of *mandamus* to the Court of Appeals to enforce the former judgments, as we do not think it necessarily involved in the decision of this case.

[The Court bypassed the state appellate court and directly affirmed the original trial court decision.]

JOHNSON, J. It will be observed in this case, that the court disavows all intention to decide on the right to issue compulsory process to the state courts; thus leaving us, in my opinion, where the constitution and laws place us—supreme over persons and cases as far as our judicial powers extend, but not asserting any compulsory control over the state tribunals.

In this view I acquiesce in their opinion, but not altogether in the reasoning, or opinion of my brother who delivered it. Few minds are accustomed to the same habit of thinking, and our conclusions are most satisfactory to ourselves when arrived at in our own way.

I have another reason for expressing my opinion on this occasion. I view this question as one of the most momentous importance; as one which may affect, in its consequences, the permanence of the American Union. It presents an instance of collision between the judicial powers of the Union, and one of the greatest states in the Union, on a point the most delicate and difficult to be adjusted. On the one hand, the general government must cease to exist whenever it loses the power of protecting itself in the exercise of its constitutional powers. Force, which acts upon the physical powers of man, or judicial process, which addresses itself to his moral principles or his fears, are the only means to which governments can resort in the exercise of their authority. The former is happily unknown to the genius of our constitution, except as far as it shall be sanctioned by the latter; but let the latter be obstructed in its progress by an opposition which it cannot overcome or put by, and the resort must be to the former, or government is no more.

On the other hand, so firmly am I persuaded that the American people can no longer enjoy the blessings of a free government, whenever the state sovereignties shall be prostrated at the feet of the general government, nor the proud consciousness of equality and security, any longer than the independence of judicial power shall be maintained consecrated and intangible, that I could borrow the language of a celebrated orator, and exclaim: "I rejoice that Virginia has resisted."

Yet here I must claim the privilege of expressing my regret that the opposition of the high and truly respected tribunal of that state had not been marked with a little more moderation. The only point necessary to be decided in the case then before them was "whether they were bound to obey the mandate emanating from this court." But in the judgment entered on their minutes, they have affirmed that the case was, in this court, *coram non judice*, or, in other words, that this court had not jurisdiction over it.

This is assuming a truly alarming latitude of judicial power. Where is it to end? It is an acknowledged principle of, I believe, every court in the world, that not only the decisions, but everything done under the judicial process of courts, not having jurisdiction, are, *ipso facto*, void. Are, then, the judgments of this court to be reviewed in every court of the Union? And is every recovery of money, every change of property, that has taken place under our process to be considered as null, void, and tortious? . . .

In this act [the Court's decision reaffirming its section 25 jurisdiction] I can see nothing which amounts to an assertion of the inferiority or independence of the state tribunals. The presiding judge of the State Court is himself authorized to issue the writ of error, if he will, and thus give jurisdiction to the Supreme Court; and if he thinks proper to decline it, no compulsory process is provided by law to oblige him. The party who imagines himself aggrieved is then at liberty to apply to a judge of the United States, who issues the writ of error, which (whatever the form) is, in substance, no more than a mode of compelling the opposite party to appear before this court, and maintain the legality of his judgment obtained before the state tribunal . . .

I flatter myself that the full extent of the constitutional revising power may be secured to the United States and the benefits of it to the individual, without ever resorting to compulsory or restrictive process upon the state tribunals; a right which, I repeat again,

Congress has not asserted; nor has this court asserted, nor does there appear any necessity for asserting . . .

Comment

Story's opinion was perhaps the most nationalist public document published since 1800, and was so offensive to states' rights Republicans that their leading journal, the Richmond *Enquirer*, reprinted Johnson's concurrence alone. Much of Story's argument was a direct assault on now traditional Republican pieties. The Constitution, he wrote, was the creation of the American people and *not* of "the States in their sovereign capacities." Federal powers were not necessarily "carved out" of a mass of state authority, and could act directly on state governments as well as on individuals. The Constitution "restrain[ed] or annull[ed]" much of the states' sovereignty; it was the "great charter of our liberties" in that it granted the federal government power, rather than because of its *limitations* on that government.

None of this was strictly necessary to the Court's judgment, as Johnson's concurrence suggested, and there can be little doubt that Story intended his opinion to be a public manifesto on behalf of Republican nationalism. Story, it bears repeating, saw his constitutionalism as Republican, despite his wholesale repudiation of much of the rhetoric of 1798. Unlike the nationalists of the 1790s, he did not reason primarily from the nature of national sovereignty or the necessities of government, but from the text, "the voice of the whole American people solemnly declared." Constitutionalism for Story the Republican was argument over the interpretation of a document rather than over the "policy or principles" of good government. His painstaking examination of the language of article three was authentically in the Republican tradition, as was his insistence that federal powers were either expressed in or given "by necessary implication" from the text. Even Story's argument that Congress was obligated to vest some federal court(s) with the entire jurisdiction authorized by article three was a typical Republican argument against the existence of congressional discretion.

The senior Republican justice, William Johnson, felt compelled to express disagreement on only one issue: the suggestion that the Court's process imposed on the state courts a legal obligation to act. Beyond that, he apparently regarded any disagreements he had with Story as minor variations in "habits of thinking," rather than fundamental differences in their understanding of the Constitution.

Joseph Story
Letter to William Pinkney
([?], 1816)[112]

Justice Story's opinion in *Martin*, despite his emphatic claim that Congress was obligated to "vest the whole judicial power" of the United States, apparently did not mean that he

thought the federal courts could assert jurisdiction in the absence of legislation. After *Martin* was decided, he drafted a bill to extend federal jurisdiction to its constitutional limits, and lobbied for its passage.

. . . The object of this section [of the proposed statute] is to give the Circuit court jurisdiction of all cases intended by the Constitution to be confided to the judicial power of the United States, where that jurisdiction has not been already delegated by law. If it was proper in the Constitution to provide for such a jurisdiction, it is wholly irreconcilable with the sound policy or interests of the Government to suffer it to slumber. Nothing can better tend to promote the harmony of the States, and cement the Union (already too feebly supported) than an exercise of all the powers legitimately confided to the General Government, and the judicial power is that which must always form a strong and stringent link. It is truly surprising and mortifying to know how little effective power now exists in this department. The most monstrous mischiefs and difficulties have already resulted from the narrow limits within which it is confined, and will be perpetually increasing. Indeed, little short of miracles can have prevented irreparable injuries. The only jurisdiction which has been completely delegated is that "of all cases of Admiralty and Maritime Jurisdiction;" and by turning to the third article of the Constitution you will readily perceive how very large a portion of the cases therein stated, are now utterly beyond our reach. I will barely illustrate my positions by a reference to a single class of cases.

No Court of the United States has any general delegation of authority "in all cases in law and equity arising under the Constitution, the laws of the United States, and the treaties made, or to be made, under its authority." The consequence is, that in thousands of instances arising under the laws of the United States, the parties are utterly without remedy, or with a very inadequate remedy. Even the United States themselves have no general power to vindicate their own rights in their own Courts; for the power to sue there is confined by the laws to particular cases . . .

I ought, indeed, to apologize for these suggestions, because I am perfectly aware, that you cannot but be possessed in a much higher degree than myself, of a knowledge of the great deficiencies in the jurisdiction, and the necessity and policy of an immediate remedy. If we are ever to be a great nation, it must be by giving vital operation to every power confided to the Government, and by strengthening that which mingles most easily and forcibly with the habits of the people. I hold it to be a maxim, which should never be lost sight of by a great statesman, that the Government of the United States is intrinsically too weak, and the powers of the State Governments too strong; that the danger always is much greater of anarchy in the parts, than of tyranny in the head. And if I were required to point the maxim by reference to the lessons of experience, I should, with the most mortifying and self-humiliating recollections, turn to my native state, as she stood and acted during the late war. May I add, that the present moment is every way favorable to the establishment of a great national policy, and of great national institutions, in respect to the army, the navy, the judicial, the commercial, and the internal interests, of the country. And I hope you will pardon me, when I assert, that I know not where a statesman might reap a harvest of more honorable laurels, or more permanent fame, than by fixing the judicial system of the United States upon its broadest constitutional basis; and I know not where the country can so properly look for such a personage, as to one who, while abroad, honored his country by an unequalled display of diplomatic science, and on his return illumined the halls of justice with an eloquence of argument, and depth of learned research, that have not been exceeded in our own age . . .

The printed bill was originally prepared by myself, and submitted to my brethren of the Supreme Court. It received a revision from several of them, particularly Judges Marshall and Washington, and was wholly approved by them, and indeed, except as to a single section, by all the other Judges. Judge Johnson expressed some doubt as to the eleventh section; but, as I understood him, rather as to its expediency than the competency of Congress to enact it. I think that I am at liberty to say, that it will be satisfactory to the Court, if it is passed. It will, indeed, give us more business, and we have now as much as we wish. But it will subserve great public interests, and we ought not to decline any thing which the constitution contemplates and the public policy requires . . .

Comment

Story was an active, if publicly unacknowledged, participant in the preparation and propagation of proposed federal legislation. His letter to Pinkney revealed the willingness of the other justices to condone and even assist these activities, as well as the Court's unanimous support for an extension of federal-court jurisdiction.

The Bonus Bill of 1817

The National Bank Act of March 1816 required the new bank to pay a $1.5 million bonus to the United States as consideration for its charter. In December 1816 Congressman John C. Calhoun, one of the leading Republican nationalists in the House, presented a bill that would designate the bonus payments as a fund to finance internal improvements such as roads and canals. The bill was opposed by some New England Federalists (on grounds of regional interest) and by the diminishing band of "Old Republicans."

John C. Calhoun
Speech in the U.S. House of Representatives
(February 4, 1817)[113]

. . . He [Calhoun] understood there were, with some members, Constitutional objections . . . It was mainly urged that the Congress can only apply the public money in execution of the enumerated powers. He was no advocate for refined arguments on the Constitution. The instrument was not intended as a thesis for the logician to exercise his ingenuity on. It ought to be construed with plain, good sense; and what can be more express than the constitution on this very point? The first power delegated to Congress is comprised in these words: "To lay and collect taxes, duties, imports, and excises: to pay the debts, and provide for the common defence and general welfare of the United States; but all duties, imports, and excises shall be uniform throughout the United States." First the power is given to lay taxes; next, the objects are enumerated to which the money accruing from the exercise of this power may be applied; to pay the debts, provide for the common defence, and promote the general welfare; and last, the rule for laying the taxes is prescribed—that all duties, imposts, and excises shall be uniform. If the framers had intended to limit the use of the money to the powers afterwards enumerated and defined, nothing could be more easy than to have expressed it plainly.

He knew it was the opinion of some that the words "to pay the debts, and provide for the common defence and general welfare," which he had just cited, were not intended to be referred to the power of laying taxes contained in the first part of the section, but that they are to be understood as distinct and independent powers, granted in general terms; and are gratified by a more detailed enumeration of powers in the subsequent part of the constitution. If such were in fact the meaning, surely nothing can be conceived more bungling and awkward than the manner in which the framers have communicated their intention. If it were their intention to make a summary of the powers of congress in general terms which were afterwards to be particularly defined and enumerated, they should have told us so plainly and distinctly; and if the words "to pay the debts, and provide for the common defence and general welfare," were intended for this summary, they should have headed the list of our powers, and it should have been stated that to effect these general objects, the following specific powers were granted. He asked the members to read the section with attention and it would, he conceived, plainly appear that such could not be the intention. The whole section seemed to him to be about taxes. It plainly commenced and ended with it, and nothing could be more strained than to suppose the intermediate words "to pay the debts, and provide for the common defence and general welfare," were to be taken as independent and distinct powers. Forced, however, as such a construction was, he might admit it and urge that the words do constitute a part of the enumerated powers. The Constitution, said he, gives to Congress the power to establish post offices and post roads. He knew the interpretation which was usually given to these words confined our power to that of designating only the post roads; but it seemed to him that the word "establish" comprehended something more.

But suppose the Constitution to be silent, said Mr. C., why should we be confined in the application of money to the enumerated powers? There is nothing in the reason of the thing that he could perceive why it should be so restricted; and the habitual and uniform practice of the Government coincided with his opinion. Our laws are full of instances of money appropriated without any reference to the enumerated powers. We granted, by an unanimous vote or nearly so, fifty thousand dollars to the distressed inhabitants of Caraccas, and a very large sum at two different times to the Saint Domingo refugees. If we are restricted in the use of our money to the enumerated powers, on what principle, said he, can the purchase of Louisiana be justified? To pass over many other instances, the identical power which is now the subject of discussion has, in several instances, been exercised. To look no further back, at the last session a considerable sum was granted to complete the Cumberland road.

In reply to this uniform course of legislation, Mr. C. expected it would be said that our Constitution was founded on positive and written principles, and not on precedents. He did not deny the position; but he introduced these instances to prove the uniform sense of Congress and the country (for they had not been objected to) as to our powers; and surely, said he, they furnished better evidence of the true interpretation of the Constitution than the most refined and subtle arguments.

Let it not be urged that the construction for which he contended gave a dangerous extent to the powers of Congress. In this point of view, he conceived it to be more safe than the opposite. By giving a reasonable extent to the money power, it exempted us from the necessity of giving a strained and forced construction to the other enumerated powers. For instance, he said, if the public money could be applied to the purchase of Louisiana, as he contended, then there was no Constitutional difficulty in that purchase; but if it could not, then were we compelled either to deny that we had the power to purchase or to strain some of the enumerated powers to prove our right. It had, for instance, been said that we had the right to purchase under the power to admit new States—a construction, he would venture to say, far more forced than the one for which he contended. Such are my views, said he, on our right to pass this bill . . .

Comment

One of the basic tenets of most Republican nationalists was the assertion (first made by Hamilton) that article one expressly delegated to Congress the power to spend federal money for the general welfare, constrained only by that body's discretion as to that welfare by the requirement of uniformity in the mode of raising the money. Like Story in *Martin*, Calhoun and other nationalist legislators discovered that a Republican allegiance to the text of the Constitution could vindicate an energetic federal government as well as limit it.

James Madison
Message to the U.S. House of Representatives
(March 3, 1817)[114]

Congress enacted the Bonus Bill. However, to the collective amazement of the congressional Republican leadership, which regarded the bill as the capstone in its efforts to carry out the nationalist program of President Madison's December 1815 message, he vetoed the bill on the last day of his presidency.

Having considered the bill this day presented to me entitled "An act to set apart and pledge certain funds for internal improvements," and which sets apart and pledges funds "for constructing roads and canals, and improving the navigation of water courses, in order to facilitate, promote, and give security to internal commerce among the several States, and to render more easy and less expensive the means and provisions for the common defense," I am constrained by the insuperable difficulty I feel in reconciling the bill with the Constitution of the United States to return it with that objection to the House of Representatives, in which it originated.

The legislative powers vested in Congress are specified and enumerated in the thirtieth section of the first article of the Constitution, and it does not appear that the power proposed to be exercised by the bill is among the enumerated powers, or that it falls by any just interpretation within the power to make laws necessary and proper for carrying into execution those or other powers vested by the Constitution in the Government of the United States.

"The power to regulate commerce among the several States" can not include a power to construct roads and canals, and to improve the navigation of water courses in order to facilitate, promote, and secure such a commerce without a latitude of construction departing from the ordinary import of the terms strengthened by the known inconveniences which doubtless led to the grant of this remedial power to Congress.

To refer the power in question to the clause "to provide for the common defense and general welfare" would be contrary to the established and consistent rules of interpretation, as rendering the special and careful enumeration of powers which follow the clause nugatory and improper. Such a view of the Constitution would have the effect of giving to Congress a general power of legislation instead of the defined and limited one hitherto understood to belong to them, the terms "common defense and general welfare" embracing every object and act within the purview of a legislative trust. It would have the effect of subjecting both the Constitution and laws of the several States in all cases not specifically exempted to be superseded by laws of Congress, it being expressly declared "that the Constitution of the United States and laws made in pursuance thereof shall be the supreme law of the land, and the judges of every State shall be bound thereby, anything in the constitution or laws of any State to the contrary notwithstanding." Such a view of the Constitution, finally, would have the effect of excluding the judicial authority of the United States from its participation in guarding the boundary between the legislative powers of the General and the State Governments, inasmuch as questions relating to the general welfare, being questions of policy and expediency, are unsusceptible of judicial cognizance and decision.

A restriction of the power "to provide for the common defense and general welfare" to cases which are to be provided for by the expenditure of money would still leave within the legislative power of Congress all the great and most important measures of Government, money being the ordinary and necessary means of carrying them into execution.

If a general power to construct roads and canals, and to improve the navigation of water courses, with the train of powers incident thereto, be not possessed by Congress, the assent of the States in the mode provided in the bill can not confer the power. The only cases in which the consent and cession of particular States can extend the power of Congress are those specified and provided for in the Constitution.

I am not unaware of the great importance of roads and canals and the improved navigation of water courses, and that a power in the National Legislature to provide for them might be exercised with signal advantage to the general prosperity. But seeing that such a power is not expressly given by the Constitution, and believing that it can not be deduced from any part of it without an inadmissible latitude of construction and a reliance on insufficient precedents; believing also that the permanent success of the Constitution depends on a definite partition of powers between the General and the State Governments, and that no adequate landmarks would be left by the constructive extension of the powers of Congress as proposed in the bill, I have no option but to withhold my signature from it, and to cherishing the hope that its beneficial objects may be attained by a resort for the necessary powers to the same wisdom and virtue in the nation which established the Constitution in its actual form and providently marked out in the instrument itself a safe and practicable mode of improving it as experience might suggest.

Thomas Jefferson
Letter to Albert Gallatin
(June 16, 1817)[115]

Writing to one of the most staunchly nationalist of his Republican friends, Madison's predecessor exemplified a constitutional viewpoint common among moderate Republicans.

. . . You will have learned that an act for internal improvement, after passing both Houses, was negatived by the President. The act was founded, avowedly, on the principle that the phrase in the constitution which authorizes Congress "to lay taxes, to pay the debts and provide for the general welfare," was an extension of the powers specifically enumerated to whatever would promote the general welfare; and this, you know, was the federal doctrine. Whereas, our tenet ever was, and, indeed it is almost the only landmark which now divides the federalists from the republicans, that Congress had not unlimited powers to provide for the general welfare, but were restrained to those specifically enumerated; and that, as it was never meant they should provide for that welfare but by the exercise of the enumerated powers, so it could not have been meant they should raise money for purposes which the enumeration did not place under their action; consequently, that the specification of powers is a limitation of the purposes for which they may raise money. I think the passage and rejection of this bill a fortunate incident. Every State will certainly concede the power; and this will be a national confirmation of the grounds of appeal to them, and will settle forever the meaning of this phrase, which, by a mere grammatical quibble, has countenanced the General Government in a claim of universal power. For in the phrase, "to lay taxes, to pay the debts and provide for the general welfare," it is a mere question of syntax, whether the two last infinitives are governed by the first or are distinct and co-ordinate powers; a question unequivocally decided by the exact definition of powers immediately following. It is fortunate for another reason, as the States, in conceding the power, will modify it, either by requiring the federal ratio of expense in each State, or otherwise, so as to secure us against its partial exercise. Without this caution, intrigue, negotiation, and the barter of votes might become as habitual in Congress, as they are in those legislatures which have the appointment of officers, and which, with us, is called "logging," the term of the farmers for their exchanges of aid in rolling together the logs of their newly-cleared grounds...

Comment

Both Madison and Jefferson supported internal improvements and, indeed, federal expenditures for them, *if* constitutionally authorized. Their objection to the Bonus Bill was that it would convert questions of the scope of congressional power into matters of pure legislative discretion. If Congress could legislate (or, which both regarded as equivalent, spend) for the general welfare at its discretion, then the Constitution would no longer be a rule of law marking the "definite partition between the General and State Governments," but a simple grant of all legitimate legislative authority. Both men regarded the amendment process as the proper solution to the "omitted case" of internal improvements requiring national attention. Madison's reference to "insufficient precedents" was an allusion to the argument that federal internal-improvement projects, like a national bank, were legitimized by earlier legislative precedents. The argument seemed particularly potent because the premier example, the Cumberland Road Act, was passed in 1806 and signed by Jefferson. Madison privately denied that act's precedential value on the ground that no one, including Jefferson, had carried out his duty to consider the constitutional question at the time; in his veto message, Madison found it more politic to be vague.

The 1818 Internal-Improvement Debate

In his first message to Congress on December 2, 1817, President James Monroe endorsed Madison's and Jefferson's belief that federal authority to fund internal improvements was desirable but required a constitutional amendment. The Republican leadership in Congress, however, rejected calls for an amendment, and attempted to enact an internal-improvement bill on the basis of a nationalist reading of congressional authority.

Henry St. George Tucker
Committee Report to the U.S. House of
Representatives
(December 15, 1817)[116]

Congressman Tucker was the son of the great Republican jurist, St. George Tucker.

... The laws of antecedent congressmen, approved by successive Executive Magistrates themselves, will be resorted to, as affording evidence of what may be regarded as conceded to be within the powers of the General Government. The commendable jealousy which they have manifested of all encroachments of State power, and their scrupulous adherence to the most rigid principles of construction, in the interpretation of the Constitution, affords a sure guarantee that more has not been admitted than may fairly be assumed within the provisions of that instrument. Taking, then, the acts of both the Executive and Legislative branches of the Government for our guide, we shall find it clearly admitted that there are some cases, at least, in which the General Government possesses the Constitutional privilege of constructing and improving roads through the several States.

Thus, by the act of the 29th of March, 1806, confirmed, amended, and enlarged by subsequent acts, a road was directed to be laid out and constructed from Cumberland, in the State of Maryland, to the State of Ohio, upon obtaining the consent of the States through which it should pass. The fund provided for this noble undertaking, was to consist of the proceeds of the sales of certain lands, the property of the United States, in the State of Ohio; so that this act furnishes the double admission, that "roads may be laid out by Congress through the several States, with their consent;" and that the expenses of constructing such roads may Constitutionally be defrayed out of the funds of the United States. The act was approved by the President [Jefferson], in office, in 1806, and other acts confirming, amending, and enlarging it, were passed by subsequent Legislatures, in the years 1810, 1811, and 1815, and approved by the President [Madison], in office, at those periods; nay, more, the three last acts contained appropriations to the amount of $210,000, payable out of any moneys in the treasury, but reimbursable out of the Ohio fund; a fund which might or might not prove adequate, and which, in point of fact, is believed hitherto to have been insufficient.

Similar to this act in some of its provisions, and analogous in principle, are the acts of April 21st, 1806 and of the 3d of March, 1817, authorizing roads to be opened from Nashville and Reynoldsburg, in the State of Tennessee, to different points in the Mississippi Territory. But these acts go still further than the former, in omitting to require the previous consent of the State of Tennessee, through whose territories a part of the roads was to pass, and in directing the expenses of making them to be defrayed out of the public Treasury of the United States, without providing for its reimbursement in any manner whatsoever . . .

And as the power is not denied in all cases, your committee will attempt to show that Congress has the power—

1. To lay out, improve, and construct, post roads through the several States, with the assent of the respective States. And,
2. To open, construct, and improve, military roads through the several States, with the assent of the respective States.
3. To cut canals through the several States, with their assent, for promoting and giving security to internal commerce, and for the more safe and economical transportation of military stores &c, in time of war; leaving, in all these cases, the jurisdictional right over the soil in the respective States.

In examining the soundness of these positions, your committee will not find it necessary to resort to what is called a liberal construction of the Constitution. They might, indeed, contend that as the powers here attributed to the United States are not in derogation of State rights, (since they can only be exercised by their assent) there is less reason for adhering to extreme rigor of construction. Where the authority claimed by the General Government is oppressive in its character, or dangerous in its tendencies; where it is asserted without deference to State assent, and in derogation of State power; where it is calculated to aggrandize the Union, and to depress its members, there may be some reason for holding the representatives of the nation to the "letter of their authority."

Nor is there any danger that such a power will be abused, while the vigor of representative responsibility remains unimpaired. It is on this principle that the framers of the Constitution mainly relied for the protection of the public purse. It was a safe reliance. It was manifest that there was no other subject on which representative responsibility would be so great. On the other hand, while this principle was calculated to prevent abuses in the appropriations of public money, it was equally necessary to give an extensive discretion to the legislative body in the disposition of the revenues; since no human foresight could discern, nor human industry enumerate, the infinite variety of purposes to which the public money might advantageously and legitimately be applied. The attempt would have been to *legislate*, not to frame a *Constitution*; to foresee and provide specifically for the wants of the future generations, not to frame a rule of conduct for the legislative body. Hence proceeds the use of the general phrase in the relation to the purpose to which the revenues may be applied, while the framers of the instrument, in the clause which concludes the enumeration of powers, scrupulously avoid the use of so comprehensive an expression, and confine themselves to the grant of such incidental power as might be both "necessary and proper" to the exercise of the specified powers.

Nor is it conceived that this construction of the Constitution is calculated to give that unlimited extent to the powers of the Federal government which by some seems to have been apprehended. There is a distinction between the power to appropriate money for a purpose, and the power to do the act for which it is appropriated; and if so, the power to appropriate money "for the general welfare" does not by fair construction extend the specified or incidental powers of Government. Thus, in the case under consideration, if the power to make a road or dig a canal is not given, the power of appropriating money cannot confer it, however generally it may be expressed. If there were no other limitation, the rights of the respective States over their soil and territory would operate as a restriction.

Whilst this appears to be a safe as well as fair construction of the Constitution, it is also that which has been practically given to it since the origin of the Government. Of this, the instances already mentioned furnish some evidence; and it is apprehended, that upon the rigid principles of construction asserted both in regard to the enumeration of powers and the appropriation of revenue, the acts of the Federal Government, including all its branches, will exhibit a continued series of violations of the Constitution, from the first session after its adoption, to the present day.

It would behoove us to turn over the statute book, and deliberately examine how, upon these principles, the laws giving bounties to fishermen; encouraging manufactures; establishing trading-houses with the Indians; erecting and constructing beacons, piers, and light-houses; purchasing libraries; adorning with paintings the Chamber of Congress; giving charity to suffering foreigners; constructing roads through the different States; and establishing banks—can be reconciled to the provisions of the Constitution...

Henry St. George Tucker
Speech in the U.S. House of Representatives
(March 6, 1818)[117]

...But why, it is asked, not amend the Constitution? The answer is easy. Those who do not believe we possess the power are right in wishing an amendment. Those who believe we have it would be wrong in referring it to the States; and as the Committee were of this opinion, they could not recommend an amendment. For, if an amendment be recommended and should not be obtained, we should have surrendered a power which we are bound to maintain if we think we possess it. In swearing to support this Constitution, we are not less solemnly bound to maintain all the just powers of the Federal Government than to preserve the States from its encroachments. We have no right, therefore, to put in jeopardy a power we believe to have been given us. We must decide according to our conscience, on the Constitutional question, and not refer the matter to State decision. There is no part of this Constitution which declares that doubtful questions shall be referred to the States. If there had been such a provision, it would doubtless not have rendered it necessary in such cases to obtain the acquiescence of three-fourths of the members of the Confederacy.

Suppose we think we possess the power, but refer it to the States for their decision. Six small States may deny it to us, against the general sentiment of the rest of the Union. But suppose we exercise the power, and the States deny its existence. They have, by the Constitution, the power of controlling us. They may provide that we shall not exercise it. It is true they must have a concurrence of fifteen out of twenty States to effect this negative amendment.

It seems indeed as if the struggle was to get the vantage ground which we occupy, if we believe ourselves invested with this power. Such indeed is the peculiar situation of things at the present moment, that it is pretty certain that three-fourths of the States would concur in neither opinion. A majority, it is believed, are in favor of the exercise of this power by the General Government. But, whilst it is evident that no negative amendment can be passed, it is equally certain that a proposition to amend the Constitution by giving this power to Congress would also fail because those States which believe we have the power would oppose an amendment. They would be right in doing so. For every unnecessary amendment only serves to narrow and circumscribe the construction of the instrument, and whilst it gives one power, furnishes a weapon by which ten more may be wrested from us. Thus, while it would seem to increase, it in fact diminishes the authority of the General Government, and we should soon find ourselves entangled in inextricable difficulties of construction arising from injudicious and unnecessary amendments . . .

Alexander Smyth
Speech in the U.S. House of Representatives
(March 7, 1818)[118]

It is contended by the select committee that, even if Congress have no power to construct roads and canals, they may notwithstanding give money to aid in the constructing of roads and canals by the States; that there is a distinction between a power to appropriate money for a purpose, and a power to do the act for which the money is appropriated. I deny to Congress the right to appropriate one shilling of the money of the people except for the purposes of executing their own powers or the powers of the Government or the powers of some department or officer of the Government; for no money can be drawn from the Treasury except in consequence of appropriations made by law; and no law can be passed except such as is necessary and proper to carry into execution the powers granted to Congress, those vested in the Government of the United States, or in some department or officer thereof.

When, therefore, a question arises whether Congress may appropriate money for a certain purpose or not, the answer must depend on that which shall first be given to another inquiry: whether it is necessary and proper for carrying into execution the powers of Congress, or of the Government of the United States, or of some department or officer thereof; and if it is not thus necessary and proper, Congress cannot pass the law to make the appropriation.

The appropriation of money which the select committee propose to make is not an appropriation of money for the general welfare, it is for the improvement of particular sections of country. In making war, maintaining armies and navies, regulating commerce, maintaining a judiciary, and so on, the whole people are concerned; but it is not so as to particular roads and canals. And as roads and canals are of local concern, they ought to be made by local impositions. Suppose that a law should pass according to the proposition of the select committee, and that in Maryland the fund should be applied to make a road from Annapolis to this city; that in Virginia the fund should be applied to make a road from Winchester to Richmond; should these roads be said to be of general concern, or to provide for the general welfare?

The power of levying money is expressly granted to Congress; and the object is declared to be, to pay the debts and provide for the common defence and general welfare of the United States. It is properly admitted by the select committee that the clause grants no power but to raise money. The common defence and general welfare are to be provided for by expending the money raised in the execution of the other powers expressly granted.

If Congress have greater latitude in making appropriations than in passing other laws, it is not given to them by the Constitution. It results from the circumstance that there exists no check on this power of the National Legislature except solemn promises of its members to support the Constitution. There is little probability of a question respecting the constitutionality of an appropriation law being brought before the judiciary. And as there is no efficient corrective of the power of the Legislature to pass acts of appropriation, we should be the more scrupulous and careful not to transcend the Constitutional authority granted to us by the people.

It does not remove the objection to this appropriation that all the States may share therein. Should that equal participation be considered as removing the objection, then we may make a like appropriation to defray the civil list of each state.

The "beneficent effects" of the proposed measure are urged as furnishing an argument in favor of a liberal construction, that is, a stretch of the Constitution. But who were they that ever seized upon power not granted to them, and did not offer the same argument in their justification? Caesar, Cromwell, and Napoleon overturned the liberties, and seized upon the whole power of their respective nations, with a view to produce "beneficial effects," according to them. The powers of Congress should not be extended by construction, in any case. Should that be done, all the advantages of a written constitution will be lost. Our Constitution will be no better than that of England where the rule of construction is, that whatever has been done may be done again. Although the select committee say that the power will only be felt in "the blessings it confers"; yet the Constitution does not grant Congress every power that may confer blessings. Every usurpation is dangerous in its tendency. Every additional power tends to the aggrandizement of the General Government. Every surrender of power that the States can be lured to make, tends to their degradation.

I dislike the aspect of this proposition. It will operate as an offer of money in exchange for power. If this power is to be asked for, let the State Legislatures decide upon the expediency of granting it before you place within their reach a sum of money upon condition that they will agree to give you up this power. A State will have no alternative but to grant the consent required, or submit to the greatest injustice.

Suppose that a State Legislature should refuse its consent, not choosing that the power of the General Government should be exerted in making roads within its territory; what will become of its share of the fund? It is to be withheld, and to remain suspended as a lure to induce the State Legislature to surrender their Constitutional powers. Meantime the fund will be in the name of the State, and daily augmenting; and sooner or later the largeness of the sum will overcome all scruples; the State Legislature will accept of the money for the benefit of the State, and surrender their rights. If such measures are adopted, you may purchase one power after another, from one State after another, until this Government, like the rod of Aaron, shall have swallowed up all the rest . . .

Henry Clay
Speech in the U.S. House of Representatives
(March 7, 1818)[119]

Mr. C. [Clay] begged leave, in the first place, to state, that he had imbibed his political principles from the same sources as the gentleman who had last addressed the [House;

Alexander Smyth]. From the celebrated production of Mr. Madison, when a member of the Virginia Legislature, of the period of 1799—which, if it had been the only paper which had ever emanated from his luminous pen, would have stamped his character as an eminent statesman—from that paper, and from others of analogous principles, he had imbibed those constitutional opinions which had influenced his political course. If he differed from those gentlemen who professed to acknowledge the same authority, the difference was not as to principles, but as to the application of them. At the period which gave birth to those papers, Mr. C. said, the State to which he belonged, and that from which he sprung, bore a conspicuous part in arresting the career of a mad administration. The attempt then was to destroy the Constitution by a plethora; but he begged the gentleman from Virginia [Smyth] to reflect, that that was not the only malady by which the Constitution could be afflicted; another complaint, equally dangerous to that Constitution, was an atrophy; and if, said he, I do not go along with them in the water-gruel regimen they would administer to the Constitution, in construing it to a dead letter, and reducing it to an inanimate skeleton, let me, not be charged with abandoning principle, but let them answer to the charge of thus attenuating the strength of that instrument.

He protested, he said, against construing this Constitution, as one would a bill of indictment, where any hole, through which a criminal might creep, was so much gained to the ingenious advocate. On looking at the political condition of this country we discover twenty local sovereignties having charge of their interior concerns, and of whatever regards the rights of property and municipal regulation, and one great sovereignty, for the purpose of general defence, for the preservation of the general peace, and for the regulation of commerce, internal and external. These objects, for which the General Government was established, ought to be constantly kept in view; and he would act contrary to the interest of his country who should deny to the Constitution—the sheet anchor of the national safety—that vigor which is necessary, in the exercise of its powers, to fulfil the purposes of its institution, and to carry this country to the high destination which it is one day to reach.

In expounding the instrument, he said, constructions unfavorable to personal freedom, or those which might lead to great abuse, ought to be carefully avoided. But if, on the contrary, the construction insisted upon was, in all its effects and consequences, beneficent; if it were free from the danger of abuse; if it promoted and advanced all the great objects which led to the confederacy; if it materially tended to effect the greatest of all those objects—the cementing of the Union, the construction was recommended by the most favorable considerations. He subscribed entirely to the doctrine, that power in the general government was deducible only from express grant, or as fairly incident to the express grant. But in interpreting the Constitution, we were not to shut our eyes against all those lights which common sense and experience had furnished in expounding all instruments. We were to look at the whole Constitution; at the history of the times when it was adopted; at contemporaneous expositions; and, above all, at the great aim and object of its framers. And he would say he hoped, without giving just cause for alarm, that he would give to the Constitution, in all that relates essentially to the preservation of this Union, a liberal construction. In cases where the power is admitted to reside somewhere in the General Government, but it was doubtful in which branch, he would contend that it belonged to Congress, as the safest repository. He would not yield his assent to what, he feared, was the too fashionable and prevailing sentiment, that of aggrandizing the Executive branch, and disparaging the Legislative . . .

Henry St. George Tucker
Speech in the U.S. House of Representatives
(March 12, 1818)[120]

Tucker vigorously disputed the accusation by the internal-improvement bill's opponents that he and his allies were "deserting the great principles of the Republicans in 1798."

...In the construction of this Constitution, there is not, there cannot be, a system of orthodoxy. Agreeing, as we do, in principle, there must always be a variety in the application. The instrument, conferring upon us incidental, as well as express powers, there must always be great difference of opinion, as to the "direct relationship," and "real necessity" of the accessory powers. Nothing can better illustrate it than the various shades of opinion on the question before us. Nor are the opponents of the resolution more consistent with each other than we are. Three gentlemen from Virginia, who have particularly distinguished themselves in opposition, all differ in essentials. The first gentleman who spoke (MR. SMYTH) admits, I conceive, all that I ask, in saying, that the revenues of the United States may be subscribed in stock to road and canal companies, "as a fiscal operation." But neither of the other gentlemen will yield their assent to this position. The same gentleman contends that, as accessary of military operations, the executive and military authority may make military roads in time of war, but the legislative body cannot authorize them. His colleagues disagree with him. On the other hand, another of these gentlemen (MR. BARBOUR) admits "the right of way," as accessary to the power to establish post roads, but his colleague (MR. NELSON) denies it. This last, in his turn, justifies the construction of the Cumberland road, which his friend (MR. BARBOUR) utterly disclaims. Sir, with these things before your eyes, who shall pretend to say what is orthodoxy— what is heterodoxy? It is impossible. It remains for us to act according to our consciences, without attempting a conformity to any particular sect or persuasion... Will gentlemen attempt to bring into the discussion of a question like this, the principles of mathematical science, or the attenuated logic of a metaphysics? The subject does not admit of it. You cannot lay down the powers of the Government with mathematical exactness. Plat down the boundaries of the two sovereignties, according to the principles of gentlemen, and a Kentucky land claim would not exhibit more embarrassing interferences. No, sir, it is not a mathematical, it is a moral certainty, that we are to expect on these great questions of political right. And how is this moral certainty to be better attained than by a practical construction, supported and fortified by the practice of the Government, and the uniform acquiescence of the nation, in analogous cases? This practice—this uniform acquiescence— these decisions of the nation, on Constitutional powers, which admit not of precise definition, but are rather to be referred to practical good sense and sound discretion—these, I say, serve as landmarks for subsequent legislatures. They are the buoys which the wisdom of the nation has fixed, to mark out the channel that divides the rival jurisdictions.

I do not contend, but have explicitly disavowed the idea, that we are bound by legislative precedents against the clear meaning of the Constitution. But I do contend, that when a principle has been long avowed and admitted, and acted upon, we ought not entirely to disregard it in deciding on a doubtful point. Do gentlemen suppose that if, which Heaven permit! this confederation of states shall last for a century, we shall, throughout that period, be continually mooting Constitutional points; holding nothing as decided; admitting no construction to have been agreed upon; and, instead of going on with the business of the nation, continually occupied with fighting, over and over again, battles a thousand times won?...

It is true that all sorts of precedents are not to be regarded. It would be absurd to speak of the alien and sedition laws as precedents. It would be absurd to attribute the sanctity of national acquiescence, to measures which were received with the deep-toned murmurs of national disapprobation...

Henry Clay
Speech in the U.S. House of Representatives
(March 13, 1818)[121]

... [I]n the period of 1798–9, what was the doctrine promulgated by Massachusetts? It was that the States, in their sovereign capacities, had no right to examine into the Constitutionality or expedience of the measures of the General Government... We see here an express disclaimer, on the part of Massachusetts, of any right to decide on the Constitutionality or expediency of the acts of the General Government. But what was the doctrine which the same State, in 1813, thought proper to proclaim to the world, and that too when the Union was menaced on all sides? She not only claimed, but exercised, the right which, in 1799 she had so solemnly disavowed. She claimed the right to judge of the propriety of the call made, by the General Government, for her militia, and she refused the militia called for.

There was so much plausibility in the reasoning employed by that State in support of her modern doctrine of "State rights," that, were it not for the unpopularity of the stand she took in the late war, or had it been in other times and under other circumstances, she would very probably have escaped a great portion of that odium which has most justly fallen to her lot. The Constitution gives to Congress power to provide for calling out the militia to execute the laws of the Union, to suppress insurrections and to repel invasions, and in no other cases. The militia is called out by the General Government, during the late war, to repel invasion. Massachusetts said, as you have no right to the militia but in certain contingencies, she was competent to decide whether those contingencies had or had not occurred. And, having examined the fact, what then? She said all was peace and quietness in Massachusetts, no non-execution of the laws, no insurrection at home, no invasion from abroad, nor any immediate danger of invasion. And, in truth, Mr. C. said, he believed there was no actual invasion for nearly two years after the requisition. Under these circumstances, had it not been for the supposed motive of her conduct, he asked if the case which Massachusetts made out would not be extremely plausible?

Mr. C. said he hoped it was not necessary for him to say that it was very far from his intention to convey anything like approbation of the conduct of Massachusetts. No! his doctrine was that the States as States, have no right to oppose the execution of the powers which the General Government asserts. Any State has undoubtedly the right to express its opinion, in the form of resolution or otherwise, and to proceed, by constitutional means to redress any real or even imaginary grievance; but it has no right to withhold its military aid, when called upon by the high authorities of the General Government, much less to obstruct the execution of a law regularly passed. To suppose the existence of such an alarming right, is to suppose, if not disunion itself, such a state of disorder and confusion as must inevitably lead to it.

Mr. C. said, that, greatly as he venerated the State [Virginia] which gave him birth and much as he respected the judges of its supreme court, several of whom were his personal friends, he was obliged to think that some of the doctrines which that State had recently held concerning State rights were fraught with much danger. Had those doctrines been asserted during the late war, and related to the means of carrying on that war, a large share of the public disapprobation which has been given to Massachusetts, might have fallen on Virginia. What were these doctrines? The Courts of Virginia have asserted that they have a right to determine on the Constitutionality of any law or treaty of the United States and to expound them according to their own views, even if they should vary from the decision of the Supreme Court of the United States. They have asserted more—that from their decision there could be no appeal to the Supreme Court of the United States, and that there exists in Congress no power to frame a law obliging the court of the State, in the last resort, to submit its decision to the supervision of the Supreme Court of the United States; or, if he did not misunderstand the doctrine, to withdraw from the State tribunals controversies involving the laws of the United States and to place them before the Federal Judiciary.

I am a friend, said Mr. C., a true friend to State rights; but not in all cases as they are asserted. The States have their appointed orbit; so has the Union; and each should be confined within its fair, legitimate, and constitutional sphere. We should equally avoid that subtle process of argument which dissipates into air the powers of this Government, and that spirit of encroachment which would snatch from the States powers not delegated to the General Government. We shall thus escape both the dangers I have noticed—that of relapsing into the alarming weakness of the Confederation, which was described as a mere rope of sand, and also that other, perhaps not the greatest danger, consolidation. No man depreciates more than I do the idea of consolidation; yet, between separation and consolidation, painful as would be the alternative, he should greatly prefer the latter . . .

Comment

The proponents of the 1818 internal-improvement bill presented a coherent and even brilliant defense of its constitutionality and of its adherence to the "doctrines of '98" (properly interpreted). They carefully distinguished two classes of federal legislation. Proposed legislation that was "in derogation of State rights" or "oppressive in its character" (Tucker) or "unfavorable to personal freedom" (Clay)—in other words, legislation like the Alien and Sedition acts—properly should undergo strict constitutional scrutiny. But congressional legislation that "promoted and advanced all the great objects" of the Constitution (Union, public safety, prosperity), as Henry Clay put it, could rely on an interpretation of the instrument "recommended by the most favorable considerations." Without questioning in any way the Republican commitment to constitutionalism as textual argument, the Republican nationalists insisted that the text was to be construed as a purposive document intended to accomplish affirmative national goals. To the charge that they were apostates from the "doctrines of '98," the nationalists responded that Republican constitutionalism was not a "system of orthodoxy" with a closed list of right answers, but consisted of a moral commitment to the principles of individual liberty, representative government, *and* national union. Republicanism, they insisted, required the preservation of the Constitution's "strength" and "vigor" as much as opposition to federal overreaching. (For this reason, the nationalists opposed Madison's and Monroe's call for an amendment as unworkable in practice and objectionable in principle.) Opposition to the efficacy of the federal government, such as that expressed by Massachusetts during the War of 1812 and by the Virginia Court of Appeals in *Hunter v. Martin*, was the contemporaneous constitutional problem.

The 1818 bill itself was a valid exercise of Congress's power to spend "for the general welfare." Unlike the other express powers, which were accompanied only by implied powers "both 'necessary and proper' " to their exercise, the spending power was explicitly granted in the most general terms, a textual distinction that recognized the need for broad legislative discretion in the expenditure of money. Congress's exercise of this discretion was disciplined primarily by its responsibility to the voters. The specific objects of the bill were, indeed, related to other enumerated powers (the war, commerce, and post road powers), and its general purpose—to increase American prosperity by improving the means of domestic travel and commerce—was entirely appropriate and consistent with the Republican commitment to the Union.

Perhaps the most interesting constitutional argument against the bill was made by states' rights Republican Alexander Smyth, of Virginia. He rehearsed the traditional Republican objections with great skill, and insisted that the unavoidability of congressional discretion in spending money required its members to take a stricter rather than a more liberal approach to construing their authority. Smyth also offered a powerful criticism of the provisions of the bill requiring a state's consent to improvements within its territory. Although the provisions were touted by nationalists as a concession to and safeguard for states' rights, Smyth argued that they were its most objectionable aspect because their effect would be a combination of bribe and blackmail that no state legislature could long resist.

*   *   *

Despite the efforts of Clay, Tucker, and others, the 1818 improvements bill was defeated in Congress.

William Johnson
Letter to James Monroe
(June 1822)[122]

A year after the Republican nationalists failed to enact an internal-improvement bill, their greatest legislative accomplishment came under constitutional attack before the federal Supreme Court. The second national bank act, even more than internal-improvement legislation, raised fundamental questions about the nationalists' constitutional views: in *M'Culloch v. Maryland* the Supreme Court—five of its seven members Republicans— unanimously upheld the constitutionality of the bank act. Chief Justice Marshall's opinion for the Court echoed the arguments of Republican nationalists such as Tucker and Clay, and in subsequent (anonymous) newspaper essays the Federalist Chief Justice defended the compatibility of *M'Culloch* with the Report of 1800 and strict Republican orthodoxy.

Even as Republican nationalism was acquiring the Supreme Court's endorsement, its political basis was eroding. Fierce debate over whether to admit Missouri as a slave state and a sharp economic downturn shattered the atmosphere of national consensus that characterized President James Monroe's first two years in office, and Monroe himself possessed in full measure Madison's reservations about extending congressional power too far from the letter of the Constitution. In May 1822, Monroe vetoed a bill to maintain and improve the Cumberland Road, a project originally funded under Jefferson's administration. The president explained his veto in a lengthy pamphlet which he sent to the justices of the Supreme Court as well as to the Congress. The pamphlet restated the central Republican theme of textual limitation on federal power and reiterated Madison's 1817 position that internal improvements bore too remote a relationship to Congress's enumerated powers to be constitutional. The justices designated William Johnson, the senior Republican member of the Court, to reply.

Judge Johnson has had the honour to submit the President's argument on the subject of internal improvements to his brother-judges and is instructed to make the following report.

The judges are deeply sensible of the mark of confidence bestowed on them in this instance and should be unworthy of that confidence did they attempt to conceal their real opinion. Indeed to conceal or disavow it would be now impossible as they are all of opinion that the decision on the bank question completely commits them on the subject of internal improvements as applied to post-roads and military roads. On the other points it is impossible to resist the lucid and conclusive reasoning contained in the argument.

The principle assumed in the case of the Bank is that the grant of the principal power carries with it the grant of all adequate and appropriate means of executing it. That the selection of those means must rest with the general government and as to that power and those means the Constitution makes the government of the U.S. supreme.

J. J. would take the liberty of suggesting to the President that it would not be unproductive of good, if the Sec'y of State were to have the opinion of this Court on the bank question printed and dispersed through the Union.

J. J. is strongly impressed with the President's views of the difficulty and delicacy attendant on any effort that might be made by the U.S. to carry into effect any scheme of internal improvement through the states, and as a question of policy or expediency sees plainly how prudent it would be to prepare them for it by the most conciliatory means.

Comment

The justices understood their decision in *M'Culloch* to be the Court's endorsement of Republican nationalism: a Constitution of textually limited federal power combined with congressional discretion to select whatever means Congress deemed appropriate to the exercise of those powers. In the late-twentieth century, most constitutional lawyers understand the Constitution (and *M'Culloch*) in similar fashion, but at the time *M'Culloch* and nationalist thought generally were overtaken by disagreement over slavery. The constitutionalists of 1791–1819 argued over questions of federalism, sovereignty, interpretation and discretion both on a theoretical level and in the context of many discrete issues. After 1819 those and other questions gradually became mere variations on an increasingly dominant theme—the place of human slavery in the American Republic. The Constitution's meaning, it turned out, could not be separated from the meaning of the nation itself.

Notes

1. Quoted in Mason, A., *The States Rights Debate* 107 (2d ed. 1972).

2. Currie, David P., *The Constitution in the Supreme Court: The First Hundred Years* (1985).

3. Madison, letter to William Eustis (May 22, 1823), 4 *Letters and Other Writings of James Madison* 317–318 (1865).

4. In his excellent lectures on *Constitutions and Constitutionalism in the Slave-holding South* (1989) at p. 1, Professor Don E. Fehrenbacher helpfully defines "constitutionalism" as "a complex of ideas, attitudes, and patterns of behaviour elaborating the principle that the authority of government derives from and is limited by a body of fundamental law."

5. Years later, Jefferson's vigorous call for a narrow reading of the federal Constitution's grants of power was to cause him some embarrassment when his administration and its congressional allies exercised power (most notably to purchase Louisiana) that arguably appeared to be neither textually delegated nor properly adjunct to some enumerated power. Jefferson's consistent justification of the purchase, which he privately viewed at the time as unconstitutional, was that he and the congressional majority had acted beyond the law in the best interests of the country, in a matter of the greatest urgency, and, being willing to "throw [themselves] on the justice of [their] country," (p. 160) were vindicated by popular approval.

6. The connection the opposition Republicans drew between the *federal* Constitution's textuality and its bias (as they saw it) against power logically might have influenced in a libertarian direction their treatment of state constitutions (which for the most part, were entirely instruments of restraint rather than specifications of authority). Although there were occasional hints of this (for example, Chancellor George Wythe's judgment in *Hudgins v. Wright*, p. 203, and Jefferson's reference in the 1798 Kentucky Resolutions to the Republicans' "attachment to limited government, whether general or particular [i.e., federal or state]," p. 133) there seem to be few systematic differences in this period between Republicans and Federalists on state constitutional issues (see, for example, the confusing lineup of opinion in *People v. Croswell*, p. 207).

7. See *M'Culloch v. Maryland*, 17 U.S. (4 Wheat.) 316, 421 (1819): "Let the end be legitimate, let it be within the scope of the constitution, and all means which are appropriate, which are plainly adapted to that end, which are not prohibited, but consistent with the letter and spirit of the constitution, are constitutional." Earlier in his opinion, Marshall acknowledged, as Clay had, that cases involving "the great principles of liberty" might require more searching interpretive scrutiny. *Id.* at 401.

8. The immediately relevant language of article three was: " . . . the judicial power shall extend . . . to controversies . . . between a state and citizens of another state."

9. The state constitution directed the legislature to appoint "judges of the supreme court of appeals, and general court, judges in chancery," etc. Nelson considered but rejected as too "critical a construction" of the text the argument that the repetition of the word "judges" "evinced an intention that the judges of the general court and those in chancery should be distinct persons" (p. 75).

10. Madison also expressed doubts about the value of the records of the state conventions, though those bodies were the legal creators of the Constitution-as-law. The state conventions' debates, he insisted, were not entirely to be trusted for accuracy: even Virginia's, the most trustworthy, "contained internal evidence in abundance of chasms and misconceptions of what was said" (p. 111). Even the conventions' formal acts—Madison had in view the various proposals for constitutional amendments—lacked "precision and system" and included "apparent inconsistencies" due to "[t]he agitations of the public mind on that occasion" and "the hurry and compromise" in which the amendments were drafted (pp. 111–12).

11. For two excellent, though by no means identical, treatments, see Goldstein, L., "Popular Sovereignty, the Origins of Judicial Review, and the Revival of Unwritten Law," 48 J. Politics 51 (1986); and Sherry, S., "The Founders' Unwritten Constitution," 54 U. Chicago L. Rev. 1127 (1987).

12. The first section of the 1776 Virginia Declaration of Rights ascribed to "all men" "certain inherent rights . . . namely, the enjoyment of life and liberty, with the means of acquiring and possessing property" (p. 192).

13. Marshall, of course, went on to hold that his *particular* federal court, the Supreme Court, lacked constitutional jurisdiction over Marbury's action because article three confined it to appellate review in such cases.

14. On occasion, somewhat similar themes can be found in legislative contexts. For example, Vice-President Aaron Burr privately expressed concerns in 1802 about the eventually successful attempt to abolish the circuit judgeships created by the 1801 "Midnight Judges Act." Although he believed it clear that Congress possessed the "Constitutional right & power" to do so, he questioned "whether it would be constitutionally Moral" (p. 163).

15. A reference to Hamilton's "Second Report on the Public Credit" (1790), in which he recommended the creation of a national bank.

16. The son of Judge St. George Tucker.

17. Madison dismissed the defeat of the first bank's renewal in 1811, which came about by Vice-President George Clinton's tie-breaking vote against the bill on constitutional grounds, as irrelevant. The Senate was evenly divided on the renewal bill "from a junction of those who admitted the power, but disapproved the plan, with those who denied the power. On a simple question of constitutionality, there was a decided majority in favor of it" (p. 294).

18. The importance of public acceptance in the maturation of legislative action into precedent encouraged the opponents of controversial statutes to

seek prominent means of memorializing their views. The Kentucky Resolutions of 1799, for example, announced the state's intention not to resist the Alien and Sedition acts, but immediately stated that, "in order that no pretext or arguments may be drawn from a supposed acquiescence on the part of this commonwealth in the constitutionality of these laws, and be thereby used as precedents for similar violations of the federal compact, this commonwealth does now enter against them its solemn protest" (p. 138). Years later, Henry St. George Tucker stated that "[i]t would be absurd to speak of the alien and sedition laws as precedents. It would be absurd to attribute the sanctity of national acquiescence, to measures that were received with the deep toned murmurs of national disapprobation" (p. 321).

19. *M'Culloch*, 17 U.S. (4 Wheat.) at 401.

20. Madison insisted, of course, that the judiciary's interpretations were *not* final as over against the views of "the parties to the constitutional compact" (p. 141). But the report as a whole made it clear that those "parties" were not the state governments but rather the "states" acting in their sovereign capacities as the loci of the popular will.

21. Quoted in Nenner, Howard, *By Colour of Law* 72 (1977).

22. 1 Annals of Congress 516 (1st Cong. 1789).

23. *Id.* at 500, 501.

24. 1 *Messages and Papers of the Presidents* 129 (1897) (message of Feb. 28, 1793).

25. *Id.* at 116 (message of Apr. 5, 1792).

26. Syrett, Harold C., ed. 17 *The Papers of Alexander Hamilton* 9, 12, n. 13 (minutes of conference, Aug. 2, 1794).

27. Madison staunchly denied that this was the case during the nullification crisis, which arose after Jefferson's death. See Koch, A., *Jefferson and Madison: The Great Collaboration* 287–288 (1950).

28. Draft of the Kentucky Resolutions, Ford, Paul L., ed. 7 *Writings of Thomas Jefferson* 301.

29. Addison, Analysis of the Report of the Committee of the Virginia Assembly (Philadelphia 1800), reprinted in Hyneman, C. S., and D. S. Lutz, eds. 2 *American Political Writing during the Founding Era, 1760–1805* 1055, 1057–1060 (1983). Addison's complaint at this point with the report was that the resolutions it purported to justify had asserted "a right of the Legislative of Virginia to judge of the violation of the compact," when by the report's own reasoning the resolutions were nothing more than the "opinion as individuals" of the state legislators. *Id.* at 1058, 1059.

30. The best discussion remains that of Charles Warren, who argued that the attack on judicial review was entirely opportunistic. *See* 1 *The Supreme Court in United States History* 215–222 (1922).

31. See *supra* text at note 23.

32. Johnson, S., *A Dictionary of the English Language* (1755), s.v. "sovereign."

33. Blackstone, William, 1 *Commentaries on the Laws of England* 234 (1765).

34. *Id.* at 236.

35. *Id.* at 49.

36. *Id.* at 51.

37. During the early 1700s, a school of political thought arose in England that was opposed to the politicians of "the Court," who dominated English political life for most of the century. This "Country" school or ideology seems to have influenced heavily the views of the late-colonial Whigs (or Patriots) in America who eventually led the Revolution. "Country" themes can also be traced in antifederalist rhetoric during the ratification period and in the thought of the Republicans in the 1790s. See Banning, Lance, *The Jeffersonian Persuasion* (1978).

38. Excerpted in Kurland, P., and R. Lerner, eds. 1 *The Founders' Constitution* 52–53 (1987).

39. Confusion and disagreement over the use of sovereignty language also pervaded the debates over the creation and ratification of the federal Constitution. See Powell, Jefferson, "The Modern Misunderstanding of Original Intent," 54 U. Chicago L. Rev. 1513, 1524–1529 (1987).

40. James Wilson referred to "the common-place rant of State sovereignties" in a speech to the Pennsylvania ratifying convention. McMaster, J., and F. Stone, eds. *Pennsylvania and the Federal Constitution* 384 (1888) (speech of Dec. 11, 1787).

41. Jay did refer to the states' "residuary sovereignty" (p. 66), but in a context suggesting that he was referring to "sovereignty" in the old sense of the term as "the right to govern."

42. I do not mean to imply that *M'Culloch* magically extirpated state-sovereignty thought from constitutional discussion. Marshall himself argued in defense of *M'Culloch*, whether out of conviction or expediency, that his opinion was compatible with the constitutional vision of the Report of 1800. *See* Gunther, G., ed. *John Marshall's Defense of McCulloch v. Maryland* 87–88 (1969) (newspaper essay of Apr. 24, 1819).

43. There are, of course, other interpretations of the "principles of '98" and their role in constitutional history. In his lectures on *Constitutions and Constitutionalism in the Slaveholding South* (1989), Professor Don E. Fehrenbacher, though agreeing with the states' rights interpretation put forward here, disputes their long-term importance. According to him, "[s]ubsequent use of the Resolutions in the sectional conflict has inflated and distorted their contemporary significance." *Id.* at 42. In a famous article, Adrienne Koch and Henry Amman accepted the historical importance of the Kentucky and Virginia resolutions while interpreting them as primarily concerned with the Federalist threat to individual constitutional rights and especially to freedom of speech and press. *See* "The Virginia and Kentucky Resolutions: An Episode in Jefferson's and Madison's Defense of Civil Liberties," 5 William & Mary Quarterly (3d ser.) 145 (1948).

44. The language of compact and strict construction were, in the 1791–1818 period, usually addressed to federalism issues. Occasionally, however, Republican constitutionalists used them to suggest a more general libertarian presumption against the existence of governmental power on any level. Jefferson, for example, wrote of "attachment to limited government, whether general or particular" (p. 133), but such references are rare.

45. Marshall, in contrast, attempted to reconcile *M'Culloch v. Maryland* with Madison's 1800 version of state-compact theory. *See supra*, n. 42.

46. For a modern reader, Johnson's example may obscure as much as it clarifies. To "stipulate" meant in Johnson's time "to bargain" or "to settle terms." Thus, where he wrote, "He surrenders at discretion," we might say something like, "He surrenders without negotiating any terms and is thus at the mercy of his enemy's will."

47. Professor G. Edward White's magisterial study of the later Marshall Court is the essential starting point for anyone interested in early nineteenth-century notions of "discretion." *See The Marshall Court and Cultural Change, 1815–35* (1989), especially at 195–200.

48. "The Congress shall have power to lay and collect taxes, duties, imposts and excises, to pay the debts and provide for the common defense and general welfare of the United States . . ."

49. "[The Congress shall have Power] to make all Laws which shall be necessary and proper for carrying into Execution the foregoing Powers, and all other Powers vested by this Constitution in the Government of the United States, or in any Department of Officer thereof."

50. Addison, *supra*, n. 26, at 1066.

51. See, e.g., Calhoun's 1817 speech (pp. 311–12).

52. *Osborn v. Bank of the United States*, 22 U.S. (9 Wheat.) 738, 866 (1824).

53. Translated from Coke's Latin, which Davis quoted in the original.

54. Reprinted from Hobson, Charles F., and Robert A. Rutland, eds. 13 *The Papers of James Madison* 372–382 (1981).

55. Reprinted from Allen, W. B., ed. 2 *Works of Fisher Ames* 850–862 (1983).

56. Reprinted from Peterson, Merrill D., ed. *Thomas Jefferson: Writings* 416–421 (1984).

57. Reprinted from Syrett, Harold C., ed. 8 *The Papers of Alexander Hamilton* 63–134 (1965).

58. Reprinted from Ames, Herman V., ed. *State Documents on Federal Relations* 8–9 (1970).

59. Reprinted from *id*. at 9–11.

60. Reprinted from Hyneman, Charles S., and Donald S. Lutz, eds. 2 *American Political Writing during the Founding Era* 937–94 (1983).

61. Reprinted from Rutland, Robert A., ed. 3 *The Papers of George Mason* 1254–1256 (1970).

62. Reprinted from 5 Annals of Congress 487 (4th Cong., 1st Sess. 1796).

63. Reprinted from Syrett, Harold C., ed. 19 *The Papers of Alexander Hamilton* 72–73 (1965).

64. Reprinted from 5 Annals of Congress 684 (4th Cong., 1st Sess. 1796).

65. Reprinted from Fitzpatrick, John C., ed. 35 *The Writings of George Washington* 2–5 (1940).

66. Reprinted from Hunt, Gaillard, ed. 6 *The Writings of James Madison* 263–295 (1906).

67. Reprinted from 8 Annals of Congress 1218 (5th Cong., 2d Sess. 1798).

68. Reprinted from Blackstone, William, 4 *Commentaries on the Laws of England* 150–153 (1769).

69. Reprinted from 8 Annals of Congress 2145 (5th Cong., 2d Sess. 1798).

70. Reprinted from Peterson, Merrill D., ed. *Thomas Jefferson: Writings* 449–456 (1984).

71. Reprinted from Hunt, Gaillard, ed. 6 *The Writings of James Madison* 326–331 (1906).

72. Reprinted from Ames, Herman V., ed. *State Documents on Federal Relations* 18–20 (1970).

73. Reprinted from Elliott, J., ed. 4 *The Debates in the Several Conventions on the Adoption of the Federal Constitution* 544–545 (Reprint 1968).

74. Reprinted from Hunt, Gaillard, ed. 6 *The Writings of James Madison* 341–406 (1906).

75. Reprinted from Mays, David John, ed. 2 *The Letters and Papers of Edmund Pendleton* 695–698 (1967).

76. Reprinted from Tucker, St. George, ed. 1 *Blackstone's Commentaries with Notes of Reference to the Constitution and Laws of the Federal Government of the United States and the Commonwealth of Virginia* Appendix 140–377 (1803).

77. Reprinted from Ford, Paul L., ed. 13 *The Writings of Thomas Jefferson* 58–60 (1897).

78. Reprinted from Peterson, Merrill D., ed. *Thomas Jefferson: Writings* 308–310, 310–312 (1984).

79. Reprinted from Ford, Paul L., ed. 9 *The Writings of Thomas Jefferson* 279–282 (1898).

80. Reprinted from 11 Annals of Congress 36 (7th Cong., 1st Sess. 1802).

81. Reprinted from Kline, Mary-Jo, and Joanne Wood Ryan, eds. 2 *Political Correspondence and Public Papers of Aaron Burr* 659–660 (1983).

82. Reprinted from *id.* at 675–676.

83. Reprinted from 11 Annals of Congress 644–648 (7th Cong., 1st Sess. 1802).

84. Reprinted from *id.* at 818–819, 822–823.

85. Reprinted from Allen, W. B., ed. 2 *The Works of Fisher Ames* 1334–1344 (1983).

86. Reprinted from Cullen, Charles T., and H. A. Johnson, eds. 4 *The Papers of John Marshall* 82–109 (1984).

87. Reprinted from King, Charles R., ed. 3 *The Life and Correspondence of Rufus King* 236–239 (1896).

88. Reprinted from Stewart, Jay, "Origins of Federal Common Law,": Part Two, 133 U. Pa. L. Rev. 1231, 1326–1328 (1985).

89. In the Thomas Jefferson Papers, Library of Congress.

90. Reprinted from Swindler, William F., ed. 10 *Sources and Documents of the United States Constitutions* 48–50 (1979).

91. Reprinted from Goebel, Julius, Jr., ed. 1 *The Law Practice of Alexander Hamilton* 808–833 (1964).

92. Reprinted from Ford, Paul L., ed. 9 *The Writings of Thomas Jefferson* 53–54 (1898).

93. Reprinted from *id.* at 59–60.

94. Reprinted from Goldsmith, William M., ed. 1 *The Growth of Presidential Power* 558–561 (1974).

95. Reprinted from *id.* at 563–574.

96. Reprinted from Ames, Herman V., ed. *State Documents on Federal Relations* 46–48 (1970).

97. Reprinted from Rutland, Robert A., and Thomas A. Mason, eds. 1 (Presidential Series) *The Papers of James Madison* 105 (1984).

98. Reprinted from *id.* at 114.

99. Reprinted from Hunt, Gaillard, ed. 8 *The Writings of James Madison* 132–133 (1908).

100. Reprinted from 22 Annals of Congress 984 (11th Cong., 3d Sess. 1811).

101. Reprinted from Ames, Herman V., ed. *State Documents on Federal Relations* 52–54 (1970).

102. Reprinted from 22 Annals of Congress 627 (11th Cong., 3d Sess. 1811).

103. Reprinted from *id.* at 134.

104. Reprinted from *id.* at 155.

105. Reprinted from Hopkins, James F., ed. 1 *The Papers of Henry Clay* 527–540 (1959).

106. Reprinted from 22 Annals of Congress 219 (11th Cong., 3d Sess. 1811).

107. Reprinted from Goebel, Julius, and Joseph Smith, 4 *The Law Practice of Alexander Hamilton* 430–431 (1980).

108. Reprinted from Ames, Herman V., ed. *State Documents on Federal Relations* 83–86 (1970).

109. Reprinted from Story, William W., ed. 1 *Life and Letters of Joseph Story* 253–254 (1851).

110. Reprinted from Hunt, Gaillard, ed. 8 *The Writings of James Madison* 335–344 (1908).

111. Reprinted from 4 *Letters and Other Writings of James Madison* 183–187, (1865).

112. Reprinted from Story, William W., ed. 1 *Life and Letters of Joseph Story* 293–296 (1851).

113. Reprinted from Meriwether, Robert L., ed. 1 *The Papers of John Calhoun* 398–409 (1959).

114. Reprinted from Hunt, Gaillard, ed. 8 *The Writings of James Madison* 386–388 (1908).

115. Reprinted from Ford, Paul L., ed. 10 *The Writings of Thomas Jefferson* 90–92 (1899).

116. Reprinted from 31 Annals of Congress 451 (15th Cong., 1st Sess. 1817).

117. Reprinted from *id.* at 1116.

118. Reprinted from *id.* at 1139.

119. Reprinted from Hopkins, James F., ed. 2 *The Papers of Henry Clay* 448–465 (1961).

120. Reprinted from 32 Annals of Congress 1318 (15th Cong., 1st Sess. 1818).

121. Reprinted from Hopkins, James F., ed. 2 *The Papers of Henry Clay* 467–491 (1961).

122. Reprinted from Morgan, Donald G., *Justice William Johnson: The First Dissenter* 123–124 (1954).

Additional Sources

A variety of other collections of original sources are available for constitutional-historical study. I intentionally have not included *M'Culloch v. Maryland* or the states' rights response to it on the assumption that anyone using this source book will also consult Gerald Gunther's *John Marshall's Defense of McCulloch v. Maryland* (1969), which includes the opinion of the Court as well as newspaper essays by John Marshall, Spencer Roane, and William Brockenbrough discussing the case.

Some other collections that a reader or student might wish to consult are listed below:

C. S. Hyneman & G. Carey, *A Second Federalist* (1967). Congressional speeches on constitutional subjects, arranged topically.

C. S. Hyneman & D. S. Lutz, *American Political Writing during the Founding Era, 1760–1805* (2 vols. 1983). Materials largely drawn from newspapers and pamphlets, arranged chronologically.

P. Kurland & R. Lerner, *The Founders' Constitution* (5 vols. 1987). Sources organized in the first volume according to major constitutional themes and in the succeeding volumes as commentaries on the clauses of the 1787 Constitution and the first twelve amendments.

S. Presser & J. Zainaldin, *Law and Jurisprudence in American History* (2d ed. 1989). Especially rich on "conceptions of national law" and the role of the federal courts in the early Republic.

M. I. Urofsky, *Documents of American Constitutional and Legal History* (1989). Major federal and state cases as well as a variety of extrajudicial documents.

Topical Index to the Introductory Essay and Comments